Language in Society 29

# Principles of Linguistic Change, Volume 2

# Language in Society



1 Language and Social Psychology
*Edited by Howard Giles and Robert N. St Clair*
2 Language and Social Networks (second edition)
*Lesley Milroy*
3 The Ethnography of Communication (second edition)
*Muriel Saville-Troike*
4 Discourse Analysis
*Michael Stubbs*
5 The Sociolinguistics of Society: Introduction to Sociolinguistics, Volume I
*Ralph Fasold*
6 The Sociolinguistics of Language: Introduction to Sociolinguistics, Volume II
*Ralph Fasold*
7 The Language of Children and Adolescents: The Acquisition of Communicative Competence
*Suzanne Romaine*
8 Language, the Sexes and Society
*Philip M. Smith*
9 The Language of Advertising
*Torben Vestergaard and Kim Schrøder*
10 Dialects in Contact
*Peter Trudgill*
11 Pidgin and Creole Linguistics
*Peter Mühlhäusler*
12 Observing and Analysing Natural Language: A Critical Account of Sociolinguistic Method
*Lesley Milroy*
13 Bilingualism (second edition)
*Suzanne Romaine*
14 Sociolinguistics and Second Language Acquisition
*Dennis R. Preston*
15 Pronouns and People: The Linguistic Construction of Social and Personal Identity
*Peter Mühlhäusler and Rom Harré*
16 Politically Speaking
*John Wilson*
17 The Language of the News Media
*Allan Bell*
18 Language, Society and the Elderly: Discourse, Identity and Ageing
*Nikolas Coupland, Justine Coupland and Howard Giles*
19 Linguistic Variation and Change
*James Milroy*
20 Principles of Linguistic Change, Volume 1: Internal Factors
*William Labov*
21 Intercultural Communication: A Discourse Approach
*Ron Scollon and Suzanne Wong Scollon*
22 Sociolinguistic Theory: Language Variation and Its Social Significance
*J. K. Chambers*
23 Text and Corpus Analysis: Computer-assisted Studies of Language and Culture
*Michael Stubbs*
24 Anthropological Linguistics
*William Foley*
25 American English: Dialects and Variation
*Walt Wolfram and Natalie Schilling-Estes*
26 African American Vernacular English: Features, Evolution, Educational Implications
*John R. Rickford*
27 Linguistic Variation as Social Practice: The Linguistic Construction of Identity in Belten High
*Penelope Eckert*
28 The English History of African American English
*Edited by Shana Poplack*
29 Principles of Linguistic Change, Volume 2: Social Factors
*William Labov*

# Principles of Linguistic Change

## Volume 2: Social Factors

WILLIAM LABOV
*University of Pennsylvania*

First published 2001

2 4 6 8 10 9 7 5 3 1

Blackwell Publishers Inc.
350 Main Street
Malden, Massachusetts 02148
USA

Blackwell Publishers Ltd
108 Cowley Road
Oxford OX4 1JF
UK



*Library of Congress Cataloging-in-Publication Data is available for this book.*

ISBN 0–631–17915–1 (hardback); ISBN 0–631–17916–X (paperback)

*British Library Cataloguing in Publication Data*
A CIP catalogue record for this book is available from the British Library.

Typeset in 10/12pt Plantin
by Graphicraft Limited, Hong Kong
Printed in Great Britain by T. J. International, Padstow, Cornwall

This book is printed on acid-free paper.

For Uriel Weinreich

# Contents

# *Foreword*

In 1966, Uriel Weinreich suggested to two of his recent graduates that we jointly prepare for an upcoming conference a general article on the principles that underlie the study of linguistic change and variation. The written version by Weinreich, myself, and Marvin Herzog appeared two years later as "Empirical foundations for a theory of language change" (Weinreich, Labov, and Herzog 1968). The strong influence that this paper had on later work in sociolinguistics stems from two principles that emerge from the draft completed before Weinreich's death in 1967. One is stated at the outset:

> The key to a rational conception of language change – indeed of language itself – is the possibility of describing orderly differentiation in a language serving a speech community. (p. 101)

The second is stated in the conclusion:

> The grammars in which linguistic change occurs are grammars of the speech community . . . idiolects do not provide the basis for self-contained or internally consistent grammars. (p. 188)

Evidence for orderly heterogeneity and the primacy of the speech community were drawn from two research projects: Herzog's study of Northern Poland (1965), based on the *Language and Culture Atlas of Ashkenazic Jewry*, and my own study of New York City, based primarily on a survey of the Lower East Side [LES] (Labov 1966a). The present volume also draws upon two major research projects, one the study of a single speech community, the other a dialect atlas. The speech community is Philadelphia, as studied by the Project on Linguistic Change and Variation [LCV] in the 1970s, a project designed to search for the social location of the leaders of linguistic change. The dialect atlas is the *Atlas of North American English: Phonology and Sound Change* [*ANAE*], which maps the current state of linguistic changes in progress in the United States and Canada. Both of these projects incorporate and exemplify two results of sociolinguistic research of the past three decades which are contrary to previous expectation, and difficult for previous theories of language change to account for:

1 Linguistic changes do not originate in the highest or lowest social classes, but in groups centrally located in the socioeconomic hierarchy.
2 In spite of the expansion and homogenization of the mass media, linguistic change is proceeding at a rapid rate in all of the major cities studied so far, so that the dialects of Boston, New York, Chicago, Birmingham, and Los Angeles are more different from each other than they were a century ago.

The two research projects are separated by a span of 20 years: LCV, the Philadelphia study, was the work of the 1970s, and the *Atlas of North American English* is the product of the late 1990s. Over a dozen papers and dissertations have reported LCV results.[1] Furthermore, a series of sociolinguistic studies have updated our knowledge of the Philadelphia speech community.[2] On the other hand, the *ANAE* results are still in the form of preliminary reports; the published *Atlas* will not appear until well after this volume. Yet this difference in age is not a difference in vitality, and the news from Philadelphia is far from stale. The comprehensive report that is provided here was not a real possibility in the 1970s. Since that time, there has been a steady advance in the techniques of sociolinguistic analysis and an accumulation of parallel results that allow us to construct a much clearer view of the process of change in Philadelphia.

The explicit goal of LCV was to test what was then the "curvilinear hypothesis," stated as (1) above. Though confirmation was first reported in Labov 1980, it can now be seen that the advanced position of the upper working class is only one component of the process of linguistic change in Philadelphia. This volume will define the leaders of linguistic change by juxtaposing stable sociolinguistic variables with new and vigorous changes in progress. A variety of multivariate analyses will yield a more detailed and accurate view of the speech community than earlier studies provided. Within each social class and neighborhood, we will be able to distinguish the leaders of linguistic change from those who simply follow behind, and draw detailed portraits of those leaders as they operate within their social networks in the give and take of everyday life. The mathematical tools to accomplish this – multiple regression, partial regression, principal

[1] Guy 1980; Guy and Boyd 1990; Hindle 1978, 1980; Labov 1980, 1981, 1984, 1989a, 1989b, 1990; Labov, Karan, and Miller 1991; Payne 1976, 1980.

[2] E.g., Ash 1982a, 1982b; Labov and Harris 1986; Labov and Auger 1998. In addition, a growing archive of recordings by students in Linguistics 560 at the University of Pennsylvania from 1973 to the present. While this is available only for student use, a series of yearly reports of neighborhood studies produces results that are generally available, and will be referred to occasionally throughout this volume.

component analysis – are not new. What has been added is a more sophisticated knowledge of the ways in which gender, social class, and age interact, so that we can use these methods with a better understanding of what to put together and what to take apart. The principles of linguistic change that emerge will be more highly constrained than the principles of the first volume, since they will be the product of interactions among the factors rather than simple, main effects of gender, age, or social class.

These results rest on the contributions of colleagues in these two major enterprises. In the study of Philadelphia, I was joined by Anne Bower, Elizabeth Dayton, Gregory Guy, Don Hindle, Matt Lennig, Arvilla Payne, Shana Poplack, and Deborah Schiffrin. Bower, Schiffrin, and Payne carried out the LCV fieldwork, through long-term neighborhood studies that drew upon ethnographic methods in combination with sociolinguistic interviews. They coded the sociolinguistic variables, constructed the socioeconomic and communication indices, and contributed at every stage to the search for the leaders of linguistic change. Dayton performed the acoustic analyses of the 112 speakers that is the major data base for the study of language change in Philadelphia. Hindle (1980) planned and carried out the telephone survey, and the analysis of Payne's recording of Carol Meyers throughout an entire day, which plays a major role in chapter 13.

In the Telsur survey and the *Atlas of North American English*, my chief collaborators are Sherry Ash and Charles Boberg, with contributions from Maciej Baranowski, David Bowie, Shawn Maeder, Thomas Macieski, Christine Moisset, Carol Orr, Tara Sanchez, and Hilary Waterman. Ash created the sampling design and sampling methods, and initiated the interviewing methods. Boberg is responsible for the good majority of the acoustic analyses and contributed many insights to the analysis of dialect distributions.

These are not my only colleagues in this enterprise. Throughout, I have drawn with pleasure and profit from the brilliant work of James and Lesley Milroy, Jack Chambers, Paul Kerswill, Peter Trudgill, and Penelope Eckert: my indebtedness to them appears at many stages of the work.

The book in its present form has been read with care by two of my colleagues at Penn: Gillian Sankoff and Ron Kim. They have corrected numerous inconsistencies and outright contradictions, and added to the clarity of this work in many ways. My copy-editor, Margaret Aherne, has contributed to the coherence and accuracy of this volume throughout.

## The overall plan of the work

This is the second volume in a series of investigations into the principles of language change. The three volumes planned are:

Volume 1: Internal factors (1994)
The study of apparent-time and real-time principles governing chain shifts; mergers, splits, and near-mergers; the regularity of sound change; functional effects on linguistic change.

Volume 2: Social factors (This volume)
The social location of the innovators of change; the role of socioeconomic class, neighborhood, ethnicity, and gender; the leaders of linguistic change; transmission, incrementation, and continuation of change.

Volume 3: Cognitive factors (forthcoming)
The effect of chain shifts on comprehension across and within dialects; the cognitive correlates of merger and near-merger; the acquisition and transmission of rules and constraints; the constant factor effect in phonology and syntax; the place of inherent variability and competing grammars.

## The nature of the principles involved

The principles of the first volume are intended to reduce a large number of phenomena to a small number of general statements. The three principles of chain shifting were tentatively reduced to one: that peripheral vowels become progressively less open on the peripheral track and more open on the nonperipheral track. The proposed resolution of the Neogrammarian Controversy was essentially that changes in phonetic realization of a category were regular, but that changes in category membership showed lexical diffusion. These generalizations and simplifications might well be called "explanations" in the sense that is sometimes given to this term. But that is not the use that is natural to this work. *Explanation* as used here is not a simplified description of events, but rather an account of their antecedent causes. In the historical and evolutionary approach followed here, explanations of linguistic change are not confined to internal linguistic principles, but relate linguistic behavior to facts and principles from other domains.

The three volumes of this work are differentiated not so much by their linguistic content but by the nonlinguistic material that is introduced. Though the first volume was largely concerned with the internal, linguistic factors that organize phonological change, an understanding of these factors was ultimately based on the physiological substratum of speech. This second volume, which deals with the impact of external or social factors upon language, will relate sociolinguistic principles to principles and findings of sociologists, social psychologists, and social historians.

Any focus on the causes of linguistic change requires some attention to the nature of the causes concerned. For many linguists who follow

Jakobson's teleological approach to language (1972), an understanding of linguistic structure and behavior requires a prior understanding of the intentions of the speaker. But this is a treacherous path to follow: we have no sure way of knowing what those intentions are. The causes of language change that are pursued in this volume are the antecedent conditions that govern and condition the change. These may involve or affect the speaker's state of mind, and that state of mind may very well bear upon the behavior that implements the change. It is clear that most speakers consciously want to convey to the listener the propositional content of what they are saying, and they are irritated and confused when that does not happen. The primary paradox of language change (chapter 1) is that it compounds such confusion.

Subjective reaction tests (chapter 6) yield some evidence of other states of mind that may influence linguistic change, but they mainly provide the motivation for irregular correction in the final stages. It is not uncommon to speak of linguistic changes as the result of speakers' desires to assume a certain social identity. But for most linguistic changes from below, operating well below the level of social awareness, the only evidence for such acts of identity is simply the fact that successive generations change their ways of speaking.

Efforts to explain language change in terms of the functions of language demand a similar insight into the speaker's state of mind, since "function" usually means what people are trying to accomplish as they speak (Hymes 1961). In this volume "function" has a more objective character. It refers to how a linguistic feature works or functions as seen in the consequences of its use. One linguistic pattern may function to produce another linguistic pattern, and a social condition such as sharp social stratification may function to produce a dichotomous distribution of a sociolinguistic variable.

The general approach of this volume is therefore to search for the material substratum of a language change. I will follow Meillet's position that the sporadic character of language change can only be explained by correlations with the social structure of the speech community in which it takes place (1926:17). This volume will draw upon the sociolinguistic studies of change in progress over the past thirty years by myself and others, with data from New York City, Detroit, Montreal, Panama City, Norwich, Chicago, Birmingham, Cairo, and Milton Keynes, but most of all from Philadelphia. The exploration will not be confined to summary statistics of social distributions. It will extend to a direct view of the speakers themselves, their positions in their local neighborhoods, their ways of expressing themselves, and their own views of the speakers who surround them. We will not dwell heavily upon what they have to say about language, which is very little, but we will pay attention to how they use the language as it changes.

This volume is a more or less continuous narrative that begins with the failure of efforts to explain change by universal principles in chapter 1, and ends in chapter 16 with general principles that are molded to the variable character of the societies in which change takes place. If these principles are at all successful in explaining the course of linguistic change, it is because they are the result of successful efforts to overcome the barriers between the university and the wider community. Indeed, the isolation of the university appears to be a major factor in determining the kind of explanations that are put forward. We will see that scholars who propose universal laws of linguistic change may fail to perceive the particular facts in their own neighborhood that contradict them. The problems that have baffled and confused scholars for centuries may not be the source of the difficulty: it is the structural position of the scholars themselves that may hide the explanation from view. The very strengths of the linguists may contribute to the problem: their gift for abstraction and generalization, their knowledge of the literature, their talent for expression, and their preeminence among their peers. From this paradoxical situation, we may be able to draw one finding of considerable importance: it is hard to understand the world by rising above it. We must deal with the world on an equal footing if we hope to resolve the paradoxes of linguistic evolution.

# *Notational Conventions*

The following notational conventions will be used throughout the three volumes of this work.

## Phonetics and phonology

*Italics* indicate words in their orthographic form.

**Bold** type indicates the abstract phonological elements that define historical word classes: short **a**, long **ē**, **ai**. A word class is the complete set of words that contain the phonological unit that the class is named for, and that share a common historical development. Word classes as intact unities are relevant to a particular period of time, as chapters 15–18 of volume 1 show. For these words, length is indicated by a macron: **ī**, **ē**, etc.

Brackets [ ] indicate IPA phonetic notation. The superscript notation for glides [aᴵ] is generally not used. Almost all the diphthongs discussed are falling diphthongs, so that the first element is the nucleus and the second element the glide: [aɪ], [ɛə], etc. The English upgliding diphthongs are usually shown as [aɪ], [aʊ], [eɪ], [oʊ], [ɪi], [ʊu], as these are the conventional forms most easily recognized. Where sources have used [ɩ] and [ω] I have retained those forms for the lower high vowels.

Slashes / / are used to indicate phonemes.

Parentheses ( ) indicate linguistic variables, which frequently cover the range of several phonemes: for example, (æh), (oh). The parenthesis notation indicates that attention will be given to the systematic dimensions of variation and the constraints upon it.

Acoustic plots used in this work show F2 on the horizontal dimension, with high values on the left and low values on the right, and F1 on the vertical dimension, with high values at the top and low values at the bottom. Both scales are linear.

## Research projects

Throughout this work, references are frequently made to the results of research projects conducted at the Linguistics Laboratory of the University of Pennsylvania under grants from the National Science Foundation. In many cases, the references are to publications in which those results were reported. In other cases, however, unpublished data and analyses are cited, and here it is often more appropriate to refer directly to the research projects themselves. The following abbreviations are used:

LES The study of the Lower East Side of New York City, the major component of the study of social stratification and change in the New York City dialect, as reported in Labov 1966a.

LYS A Quantitative Study of Sound Change in Progress, 1968–1972. The spectrographic study of patterns of chain shifting in a range of British and American dialects, together with a review of the historical record for such patterns, as reported in Labov, Yaeger, and Steiner 1972.

LCV Project on Linguistic Change and Variation, 1973–1977. The investigation of sound changes in progress in Philadelphia, based on the long-term study of 11 neighborhoods and a random survey of telephone users, as reported in Labov 1980, 1989a, 1990, Hindle 1980, Payne 1976, 1980, Guy 1980.

# Part A

## *The Speech Community*

# 1

# *The Darwinian Paradox*

It is only reasonable that a book about the principles of linguistic change should begin by asking how important these principles might prove to be – should we succeed in defining them – for the general understanding of language. For a sizeable part of the current linguistic enterprise, there can be very little interest in principles of this kind. The search for a universal, unchanging, and indeed unchangeable, grammar is oriented in an entirely different direction. As such, it lies outside the scope of this work, which is concerned with everything in language that changes or has changed. This seems to include much the larger part of linguistic categories, structures, and substance. It therefore seems natural to ask whether we understand the forces that are responsible for the extraordinary transformations that affect all but a bare skeleton of abstract relations.

The first volume of this work began by admitting that we do not. A long series of inquiries has left us with much detailed knowledge of constraints on and patterns of change, but no general explanation for the scope and persistence of this phenomenon. The continued renewal and far-ranging character of linguistic change is not consistent with our fundamental conception of language as an instrument of social communication. The situation is compounded by the unexpected finding that has emerged from recent sociolinguistic research: that linguistic change is continuing at a rapid rate in every city of North America that has been studied with any care.[1] This result clashes sharply with the common-sense expectation that constant exposure to the network standard on radio and television would lead to convergence and the gradual elimination of local dialects. Language change governs not only our history, but also our immediate present. The immanence of language change makes it easier for us to study, but it also heightens the urgency of the search for explanations. Much of the present volume is devoted to that search; but before we begin it may be helpful to look briefly at the effects of change.

[1] I limit this observation to North America, since it seems to hold for all of the English speaking cities of the USA and for both English and French speaking cities in Canada. Active changes from below have been traced in studies of the cities of South America, the United Kingdom, New Zealand, Egypt, Japan, and Korea, but in Europe and many other areas, community studies have placed more emphasis on changes from above, dialect leveling, and koine formation.

## 1.1 The social effects of language change

It may be useful to remind every reader of this work that all of us have suffered from the effects of language change in one way or another. These effects range from petty inconveniences to crushing disabilities that can consume years of our lives with unrewarding struggle against hopeless odds. First, we might notice the small family arguments that ebb and flow over the proper use of words. My generation called an ice box an *ice box*, since it used to hold a block of ice before it was electrified, but my children's generation insisted on calling it a *refrigerator*, and confined the use of "ice box" to the freezing compartment that makes ice cubes. My age group will also be ridiculed, perhaps more slyly, for calling something "swell" or "nifty," terms that are now marked as hopelessly old-fashioned unless they are used ironically.

On the other hand, many older citizens find themselves keenly irritated by new forms that have crept into the language, and expend a great deal of effort in demonstrating to their children the illogical character of *hopefully*, *aren't I*, or *like* as a conjunction. But even the most eloquent journalists and educators find that their rhetorical tools are not keen enough to cut the link that ties these forms to the younger speakers of the language. These defective forms return again and again until they are firmly fixed in the fabric of the language – when suddenly they appear as very natural and not at all defective, to all except a small group of traditionalists in professorial and editorial chairs.

The fact that traditionalists are usually fighting a losing battle is not enough to deter them from penalizing the students who take the winning side. Most of us have suffered by having our school papers downgraded by quixotic supporters of a dying tradition, who insist that infinitives cannot be split from their *to*s, that *data* require a plural verb, and that under certain subtle conditions we must spell and even pronounce the word *who* as *whom*.

The emotions aroused by grammatical forms are if anything more temperate than the feelings called up by sound changes, when they finally come to our attention. Middle class American parents in particular feel continually called on to correct the aberrant vowels used by their children, which seem to symbolize their association with the most vulgar elements of local society. These family disagreements over sounds rarely rise to the level of public disputes, because there is no vocabulary available to institutionalize them, but the dispute goes on at the local level with unremitting intensity.

When we observe such controversies in a foreign language, it is easy enough to see them as tempests in linguistic teapots. But in our own language, it is difficult to avoid being caught up in the storm of emotions generated by the contrast between newer and older ways of saying the same thing. It is not easy to step back far enough to ask the fundamental question: why does language change arouse such violent feelings?

Even as we are irritated and confused by linguistic change in progress around us, we suffer more serious disabilities from the results of changes that took place centuries ago. An enormous amount of time and effort is devoted to mastering English spellings such as *bight*, *drought*, *about*, *draft*, *draught*, *cough*, *trough*, and *enough*. The distinctions between *whale* and *wail*, *mourning* and *morning*, *colonel* and *kernel*, must now be mastered by brute memory, though they were quite transparent to earlier generations who had not suffered the effects of the sound changes that collapsed these categories. These spelling-demons are typical of a great many forms that were once a rational representation of the spoken language, but are now the fossilized evidence of language changes that are no longer part of the knowledge of the native speaker.[2] But even greater amounts of time are devoted to learning German, French, Spanish, or Russian, languages that were once mutually intelligible dialects of Proto-Indo-European. And even when a great investment in language learning is made, it may not be enough to overcome the elusive gap between the two language structures that has emerged as the result of language changes over centuries. We may find that no amount of practice allows us to master the native Russian production of palatalized and non-palatalized consonants, the native French rules for schwa deletion, or the use of aspect particular to either of these languages. Worse yet, most of us find that we are not very intelligent in a language other than our mother tongue. These are some of the disadvantages that follow from the fact of language change. What can we point to on the positive side? Some people say that they like to study foreign languages, and some invent secret languages to make it harder for others to understand them.[3] Linguists and language teachers get some employment from the results of linguistic divergence. But that seems to be about all the benefit there is to language change. It is hard to avoid the conclusion that language, as an instrument of communication, would work best if it did not change at all. Though we get some satisfaction from playing with language, and often find it useful to hide behind it, we do not profit in any obvious way from the results of systematic language change.[4]

[2] One might note here the argument advanced by Chomsky and Halle that English orthography can hardly be improved (Chomsky 1964, Chomsky and Halle 1968), based on the demonstration of cases where derivational alternations will support current spelling as a good representation of the underlying form. But the vast number of irregularities in English spelling are not supported by any alternations, but are the result of mergers that eliminate any basis for reconstructing the original forms. In general, morphophonemic alternations are irrelevant to the effects of mergers (see volume 1, chapter 13).

[3] One might point to the widespread use of playful secret languages and other word games as evidence for positive values associated with language learning.

[4] These informal remarks on the consequences of linguistic change will be amplified considerably by the observations and experiments reported in volume 3, which deals with the cognitive consequences of change.

It is not then so hard to understand why the general view of language change is a dismal one. We all seem to be suffering from a linguistic disease that has no cure, and language, like so much of the world around us, is seen as going from bad to worse. Though this "Golden Age" principle is quite general, it assumes an absolute form only in one area: the domain of language. In the course of studies of the speech community that began in the 1960s, I and my associates have interviewed many thousands of speakers in many English dialects and other languages. Whenever language becomes the overt topic of conversation, we find a uniformly negative reaction toward any changes in the sounds or the grammar that have come to conscious awareness. Communities differ in the extent to which they stigmatize the newer forms of language, but I have never yet met anyone who greeted them with applause. Some older citizens welcome the new music and dances, the new electronic devices and computers. But no one has ever been heard to say, "It's wonderful the way young people talk today. It's so much better than the way we talked when I was a kid."

## 1.2 The parallels between biological and linguistic evolution

The Golden Age principle does not necessarily apply to additions to vocabulary, or the borrowing of prestige features from another system. In all the discussion of language change to follow, I will be focusing on alterations in the mechanism of the language, its system of sounds and grammatical categories: the fundamental process that has led to the mutual unintelligibility of related dialects and languages over many centuries. Our view of this linguistic evolution is of course limited, and confined to those language families whose development has been reliably traced.[5] Indeed, most of the discussion of the causes of linguistic change is cast within the framework of the development of Indo-European. The reconstruction of this vast family tree offered to the scientific community a remarkable parallel to biological evolution that was widely observed and remarked upon. It is often said that the evolutionary transformation of species was demonstrated in linguistics before it had been clearly spelled out in botany and zoology (Lyell 1873:406; Christy 1983, ch. 1). Max Müller wrote: "in language, I was a Darwinian before Darwin" (1861). Though we might trace the origin of the evolutionary viewpoint in the works of many scholars, the problem set for this volume is best seen in Darwin's summary of the situation. *The Descent of Man* (1871) contains a very specific treatment of the parallels between linguistic and biological evolution as he saw them.

[5] For an evaluation of efforts to trace language families back further than this, see Ringe 1992.

(1) The formation of different languages and of distinct species, and the proofs that both have been developed through a gradual process, are curiously parallel.

Darwin finds fifteen similarities between the two processes, which he does not elaborate. The list below gives his phraseology in italics, and supplies current examples from the changes in progress that will be traced below.

1 *We find in distinct languages striking homologies due to community of descent*
The Northern Cities Shift (volume 1: pp. 177–201) emerges in the same form in the cities of Rochester, Buffalo, Syracuse, Cleveland, Gary, Detroit, and Chicago. All these cities were settled by the same westward movement from New York State.

2 *and analogies due to a similar process of formation*
The Pattern 3 chain shift developed independently in roughly the same form in Hauteville French, Sweden, Greece, and São Miguel in the Cape Verde Islands, without direct contact among them (Martinet 1955).

3 *The manner in which certain letters or sounds change when others change is very like correlated growth*
Parallel movements of front and back vowels appear in the Great Vowel Shift and in the raising of (æh) and (oh) in New York City, while parallel fronting of back vowels appears in the Southern Shift.

4 *We have in both cases the reduplication of parts*
The bilateral symmetry of phonological and grammatical systems is as marked as the bilateral symmetry of most organisms.

5 *The effects of long continued use*
The extreme reduction of high frequency function words often reaches the point where a morpheme is represented by a single phonetic feature, as in the reduction of the past tense morpheme *wen* in Hawaiian Creole English to a feature of length in [he wːɔk bai ðe we] 'He walked by the way' (Labov 1992).

6 *The frequent presence of rudiments, both in languages and in species, is still more remarkable*
Darwin gives the example of the elimination of schwa in the contraction of *I am* to *I'm*, removing "a superfluous and useless rudiment," as well as the retention of letters in spelling (where we might give the example of the *k* in *knee* and the *g* in *gnome*, which support no alternations).

7 *Languages, like organic beings, can be classified in groups under groups*
This is as true of the English dialects as of the Indo-European languages themselves. Thus the Boston dialect is plainly a member of the Eastern New England sub-group of the Northern dialect region.

8 *They can be classified either naturally, according to descent, or artificially by other characters*
While the Northern dialect area unites dialects with a common history of descent, the classification of the Southern Shift unites Southern England and the Southern United States, with no clear motivation in the history of settlement.

9 *Dominant languages and dialects spread widely*
The influence of dominant cultural centers on American dialects can be seen for many phonological features as a large (roughly) circular region surrounding Boston, Philadelphia, Richmond, and Savannah.

10 *and lead to the gradual extinction of other tongues*
Though many rural American dialects are stable or expanding, it is widely and reliably reported that others are in danger of disappearing (Schilling-Estes and Wolfram 1999) in the same manner as local French and German dialects (Hinskens 1992).

11 *A language, like a species, when once extinct, never . . . reappears*
Though this statement has been questioned in the case of Israeli Hebrew, it is widely accepted by linguists.

12 *The same language never has two birthplaces*
This certainly seems to be true for all of the English dialects we are studying, since a dialect is too specific and complex a configuration to arise independently in several places.

13 *Distinct languages may be crossed or blended together*
This is clearly the case for creole languages, which arise in one place from a mixture of language contributions. Most American English dialects are the result of regional koine formation from many intersecting English dialects.

14 *We see variability in every tongue, and new words are continually cropping up*
Variability is of course the main topic of our investigation. The renewal of regional vocabulary in the United States can be clearly documented in many semantic domains.

15 *Single words, like whole languages, gradually become extinct*
The rural vocabulary that was the principal defining characteristic of the regional dialects of the Atlantic states has to a large extent disappeared, as shown by the obsolescence of *singletree*, *stone boat*, and *darning needle*. This parallel is seen most clearly in the domains of slang and colloquial vocabulary.

Darwin uses the two last parallels to introduce the argument necessary to establish the similarity of biological and linguistic evolution: that linguistic evolution shows the same kind of natural selection that biological evolution does.

16 *The survival or preservation of certain favoured words in the struggle for existence is natural selection.*

Darwin then supports this view with a quotation from Max Müller:

(2) A struggle for life is constantly going on amongst the words and grammatical forms in each language. The better, the shorter, the easier forms are constantly gaining the upper hand, and they owe their success to their own inherent virtue.

The general consensus of 20th-century linguists gives no support to this contention, and finds no evidence for natural selection or progress in linguistic evolution. It is generally agreed that languages that have evolved in societies with subsistence economies based on hunting, gathering, or small-scale agriculture show a structural complexity that is equal to or greater than those spoken in technologically developed societies.[6] Darwin himself quotes Schlegel to this effect:[7]

(3) In those languages which appear to be at the lowest grade of intellectual culture, we frequently observe a very high and elaborate degree of art in their grammatical structure. This is especially the case with the Basque and the Lapponian, and many of the American languages. (cited by Darwin 1871:67)

[6] Hymes (1961) argues that we can recognize evolutionary advance in particular languages if we broaden our view to include writing as well as speech, formal and scientific discussion as well as conversation, international affairs as well as local ones. This "increase in range and variety of adjustments to environments" would include the development of scientific vocabulary, of a meta-language to discuss linguistic structure, and freedom in borrowing forms from other language systems. But Hymes finds it necessary to "bypass the question of evolutionary advance in grammatical features . . . and the question of increased efficiency and economy in language evolution."

[7] Though this quotation is in the paragraph immediately following the one comparing biological and linguistic evolution, it is not cited in reference to the question of natural selection in language but in connection with the argument against evolution from the perfection of language. Darwin's contention that the "perfection" of a language, like that of an organism, is often overestimated on the basis of superficial characteristics, is as sophisticated as one might expect from any 20th-century linguist. "A Crinoid sometimes consists of no less than 150,000 pieces of shell, all arranged with perfect symmetry in radiating lines; but a naturalist does not consider an animal of this kind as more perfect than a bilateral one with comparatively few parts, and with none of these parts alike, excepting on the opposite sides of the body. He justly considers the differentiation and specialisation of organs as the test of perfection. So with languages: the most symmetrical and complex ought not to be ranked above irregular, abbreviated, and bastardised languages, which have borrowed expressive words and useful forms of construction from various conquering, conquered, or immigrant races" (1871:71). Here Darwin's own argument might have been used against the proposition that language shows progressive evolutionary adaptation to its environment.

There is general agreement among 20th-century linguists that language does not show an evolutionary pattern in the sense of progressive adaptation to communicative needs.

(4) Taking linguistic change as a whole, there seems to be no discernible movement toward greater efficiency such as might be expected if in fact there were a continuous struggle in which superior linguistic innovations won out as a general rule. (Greenberg 1959:69)

But it is not merely the absence of evidence for evolutionary adaptation that runs counter to Darwin's argument for natural selection. The almost universal view of linguists is the reverse: that the major agent of linguistic change – sound change – is actually maladaptive, in that it leads to the loss of the information that the original forms were designed to carry. Though there is a wide range of divergent opinions on the nature of sound change, as we saw in Part D of volume 1, there is general agreement on the negative character of this fundamental process. Throughout the 19th century, the basic mechanism of change was seen as dysfunctional, and historical linguists aligned themselves firmly with the enemies of sound change.

## *Language change as a destructive force*

In 1816, Franz Bopp outlined principles for examining the history of language, including a recognition of the "gradual and graded destruction of the simple speech organism . . . and the striving to replace it by mechanical combinations . . ." (Lehmann 1967:43). Rasmus Rask recognized that the recovery from the effects of sound change is not a simple and immediate process: "grammatical inflections and endings are constantly lost with the formation of a new language . . . and it requires a very long time and intercourse with other people to develop and rearrange itself anew" (Lehmann 1967:32). In his first treatment of the Germanic sound shift, Jakob Grimm made it plain that such changes in the sounds of a language were destructive and unfavorable, and referred to them as "barbarous aberrations from which other quieter nations refrained" (Waterman 1963:20). Alexander von Humboldt treated phonetic constraints as a whole as unnatural, which must be subordinated to an intellectual factor, analogical reformation, which corrects them. "What has already been established to a certain extent in the phonetic pattern, violently seizes the new formation and does not permit it to pursue an essentially different path" (Von Humboldt 1836:56).

It is curious to find that Max Müller, Darwin's chief supporter for the idea that natural selection governed the evolution of words, himself characterized the major agent of language change as a process which destroyed the nature of language, and so caused "the life of language to become benumbed and extinct" (Müller 1861:54). August Schleicher was perhaps even more negative, and saw changes in both the sound and form of language as a decay or decline, with a consequent loss of meaning (Lehmann 1967:90). W. D. Whitney was an even stronger exponent of the destructive force of sound change:

(5) A language may become greatly altered by the excessive prevalence of the wearing out processes, abandoning much which in other languages is retained and valued. It is necessary that we take notice of the disorganizing and destructive workings of this tendency inasmuch as our English speech is . . . the one in which they have brought about the most radical and sweeping changes. (Whitney 1904:75)

In declaring that sound change was regular and exceptionless, and distinguishing it clearly from analogy, the Neogrammarians did not depart from the view that its effects were harmful to the major functioning of language. Hermann Paul did not see sound change as unnatural in itself; he attributed it to physiological factors that followed the laws of physics. At the same time, he expressed most eloquently the general consensus on the destructive character of the process:

(6) Thus the symmetry of any system of forms meets in sound change an incessant and aggressive foe. It is hard to realize how disconnected, confused, and unintelligible language would gradually become if it had patiently to endure all the devastations of sound change. (1891:202)

The negative evaluation of sound change continued in the 20th century, though it was not to be expressed so violently. Saussure summed up the situation in this way:

(7) That phonetic evolution is a disturbing force is now obvious. Wherever it does not create alternations, it helps to loosen the grammatical bonds between words; the total number of forms is uselessly increased, the linguistic mechanism is obscured and complicated to the extent that the irregularities born of phonetic changes win out over the forms grouped under general patterns . . . (1949:161)

## *The linguistic consequences of sound change*

Readings in the work of 19th- and early 20th-century linguists make it abundantly clear that they saw sound change as the primary, most systematic and omnipresent mechanism of linguistic change. It was evident to them that sound change interacted with morphological systems, disrupting paradigms, inserting asymmetries, and collapsing the fundamental distinctions that the system maintained; indeed, Saussure devoted an entire chapter to this topic. It was in terms of morphological systems that analogical change was seen most easily as the restorer of paradigmatic symmetry and efficiency. Since analogy is notoriously sporadic and difficult to systematize, sound change became almost by default synonymous with the notion of "linguistic change." Now that the study of syntax has emerged as a major part, perhaps the major part of linguistic structure, and studies of syntactic change have begun in earnest, it may seem that the study of sound change would become an ever smaller part of the study of linguistic change. Since the present work focuses on change in progress, and comparatively few examples of syntactic change in progress have been located, it might also seem that the study of present trends can give us very little access to linguistic history.[8] Nevertheless, it can be argued that change in the surface phonetics remains the driving force behind a very large number of linguistic changes, perhaps the majority. This includes the processes of cliticization, which triggers any number of syntactic consequences, vowel contraction and consonantal assimilations, shifts of syllabicity and reassignment of syllable boundaries, along with the vast body of segmental changes – lenition and fortition, deletion and epenthesis, monophthongization and diphthongization, change of place and fusion of features, and the development of tone and its intersection with intonation patterns. We receive with increasing frequency the suggestion of wholesale reorganizations of prosodic systems as a causal factor in linguistic change, but what phonetic changes trigger such prosodic revolutions are only dimly perceived. Some of the issues involved here will be developed more fully in volume 3. Here it will be sufficient to state the proposition that a study of the causes and effects of changes in the sound system remains the primary prerequisite for explanation and evaluation of linguistic change in general. Changes in the sound system here refer not only to low level phonetic change but to morphophonemic condensations specific to particular grammatical locations.

Given that understanding, we have little basis for quarreling with the 19th-century understanding of the effects of sound change upon language as a whole. The view of language change as pathological is not mere rhetoric. Volume 3 will report extensive studies of the cognitive consequences of sound change which document by observation and experiment that sound change has led to a considerable degree of mutual unintelligibility of the phonologies of North American dialects. Volume 1 brought forward quantitative linguistic evidence that the reduction of functional elements of high frequency, noted in parallel 5 in Darwin's list above, can hardly be seen as an improvement. As chapter 20 of volume 1 showed, the loss of final sounds in Spanish and Portuguese leads to a measurable loss of information. When tautosyllabic final /s/ disappeared in French, a number

[8] The most important being studies of the elaboration of syntactic structures in developing pidgins and creoles (Sankoff and Laberge 1973), which will play a prominent role in this volume and the following one.

of compensating processes preserved the plural meaning. But there remain many cases where the plural meaning can no longer be signaled in standard French by grammatical means. Thus De Gaulle once declared in a public speech, *Je m'addresse aux peuples . . .* As a result of French sound changes completed many centuries ago, the *x* of *aux* in pre-consonantal position and the *s* of *peuples* in final position exist only in writing: singular *au peuple* and plural *aux peuples* are homonymous. De Gaulle was forced to recognize the inability of spoken French to distinguish singular and plural at this point by adding the meta-comment *au pluriel.*

One of the most widely studied processes of consonant reduction in English is the simplification of clusters ending in /t/ or /d/. In my own Northern New Jersey speech, the high frequency of simplification of the consonant cluster *nt* in *can't* has made it difficult to distinguish positive *can* from negative *can't.*[9] It is not uncommon for a speaker of this dialect to ask, "Did you say C-A-N or C-A-N-T?"

Perhaps the most dramatic shortening of words has occurred in the history of northern Mandarin, with a consequent augmentation in the number of homonyms. In compensation for this, most Mandarin words are now two characters or morphemes instead of one. It would be difficult for Darwin to argue that the shorter form had triumphed due to its own inherent virtue, when in compensation it developed a form that is roughly twice as long.

What then are we to make of Darwin's final statement?

(8) The survival or preservation of certain favoured words in the struggle for existence is natural selection.

One can hardly argue with this conclusion: in this form, it is nothing but a restatement of the fact that some words survive and others do not. But its significance depends on the answers to two questions: (a) Are the factors that lead to the survival or preservation of individual words the same as those that operate to form the abstract sets of relations between sound and meaning? (b) Can the survival of particular forms or relations be shown to be the result of adaptation of language to its environment? So far, the answers to both questions are "probably not."

As far as words are concerned, the replacement of vocabulary seems to have many of the characteristics of random variability. It is not simply the existence of statistical regularity[10] which leads to this conclusion; it is the apparent impossibility of saying which words have a better chance of surviving and which do not, whether abbreviations will persist, and whether

[9] The New York City and Philadelphia rule that laxes the vowel of auxiliary *can* and distinguishes it from the tense vowel in *can't* does not operate here.

[10] That is, the lexicostatistic finding that roughly 19% of the basic vocabulary is replaced every 1000 years (Swadesh 1971).

at a given time the vocabulary will expand or contract.[11] The same situation does not prevail for linguistic structure, where a number of directional principles have emerged. The study of sound shifting has shown that vowels have a high probability of moving in a particular direction (volume 1: chs 5–9), that mergers expand at the expense of distinctions (volume 1: chs 11–14), that vowels before liquids are far more likely to merge than vowels before obstruents, that inflections in some positions in the paradigm are much more likely to disappear than others (Greenberg 1969), and that in general, heavily marked structures are less stable than unmarked ones.

As far as structural alterations are concerned, the consensus is reflected in quotations (5, 6, 7). Sound change, the most general and pervasive source of such changes, is not the result of any adaptation of language to its environment. Though analogy and dialect borrowing may compensate for some of the damage to linguistic structures caused by sound change, their operation is far too episodic and unpredictable to be compared to the systematic operation of natural selection.

Thus we cannot support Darwin's hope to complete the fifteen parallels between biological and linguistic evolution by including a sixteenth parallel: natural selection. We might sum up the situation as **Darwin's paradox**:

(9) **The evolution of species and the evolution of language are identical in form, although their fundamental causes are completely different.**

Throughout this volume, we will be alert to the possibility of responding to this paradox. It would be strange indeed if the detailed resemblances between linguistic and biological evolution were in no way dependent on the fundamental mechanism of change. It would be too ambitious to say that this paradox can be resolved; it can be interpreted and dealt with in ways that will suggest the shape of a resolution.[12]

One immediate way of reducing the force of this paradox was suggested by Darwin himself in the sentence immediately preceding his final conclusion (8).

(10) To these more important causes of the survival of certain words, mere novelty and fashion may be added; for there is in the mind of man a strong love for slight changes in all things.

[11] This is seen most clearly in the rapid replacement of the slang vocabulary, which affects many words but not others. While *super*, *swell*, *nifty*, and *keen* have shown signs of obsolescence in American English, *fantastic*, *great*, *terrific* have not, over a comparable period of time.

[12] Among recent writers on linguistic evolution from a sociolinguistic point of view, Chambers (1995) argues the most vigorously for the adaptive value of linguistic variation, and this seems consistent with Weinreich, Labov, and Herzog's (1968) argument that a thoroughly homogeneous language would be dysfunctional. Chambers does not, however, examine new linguistic changes in progress and their disruptive effect upon communication.

The desire for novelty is introduced by Darwin as a less important, minor factor. But if the major factor of natural selection is discounted, then we might conclude that the driving force behind linguistic evolution is random variation. Indeed, genetic variability is an important component of the evolutionary mechanism in biology. There are sufficient random variables in linguistic structure to account for the gradual isolation of languages separated by geographic barriers to communication, so that the diversification of Oceanic languages in Micronesia and Polynesia would be comparable to the development of distinct species on the Galapagos Islands. Yet variability is only a necessary condition for biological evolution: without natural selection, variability is not sufficient to account for the rapid evolution of distinct species and radiation of organisms with different adaptive structures into distinct evolutionary niches. Elevation of the novelty principle (10) to the major factor in linguistic evolution may reduce the force of the Darwinian paradox to (9′):

(9′) **The evolution of species and the evolution of language are identical in form, although the fundamental mechanism of the former is absent in the latter.**

Such a re-formulation would only sharpen the problem of understanding the causes of sound change. No amount of nondirectional variability or drive to exaggerate that variability can account for the directional chain shifts, mergers, and splits that were presented in volume 1.[13] If there is no adaptive radiation in language, and no natural selection, what then are the fundamental causes of sound change? There is no shortage of answers to this question. Before we attempt to apply current findings to the problem, it may be helpful to review the answers that have already been given.

## 1.3 Earlier proposals for the causes of sound change

From the beginning of the 19th century, linguists have made many efforts to identify the causes of sound change. Those who have considered the matter most deeply give a uniform report on the difficulty of the problem. In 1856, von Raumer summed up the state of current knowledge in this way:

(11) . . . we ascertain that the sounds of words have changed when we compare the older state of languages with the more recent. The process of the change itself however has not yet been investigated enough. If we penetrate deeper into the darkness which in many ways veils these questions, we find a huge multitude of highly different processes at work. (1856:72)

[13] For an effort to account for sound change as simply the random drift of the mean value around which tokens of a phoneme are dispersed, see Hockett 1958:441.

Some 60 years later, Saussure reviewed the situation in similar terms:

(12) The search for the causes of phonetic changes is one of the most difficult problems of linguistics. Many explanations have been proposed, but none of them thoroughly illuminates the problem. (1949 [1916]:147)

Finally, we may quote Bloomfield, writing in 1933:

(13) Although many sound-changes shorten linguistic forms, simplify the phonetic system, or in some other way lessen the labor of utterance, yet no student has succeeded in establishing a correlation between sound-change and any antecedent phenomenon: the causes of sound-change are unknown.

In spite of these cautions, many linguists have argued strongly for a particular explanation of sound change, and in the course of time a great many approaches to the topic have been exposed to argument and debate. Some will be of more value than others in our exploration here.

Beginning with the less valuable, we find that many explanations of linguistic change put forward in the 19th and early 20th centuries were materialist in spirit, but were supported by only the weakest kind of empirical evidence. As more data accumulated, explanations based on climate or topography are easily set aside as the counter-examples come to outnumber the examples. Furthermore, the mechanisms that were proposed for the link between the cause and the effect usually seem to us today naive in the extreme.[14] Of even less interest are the explanations based on physiological differences between speakers of various languages, which seem to be motivated more by convictions of racial superiority than scientific evidence.[15] The traditional arguments advanced for the causes of sound change that will most concern us here are basically three: the principle of least effort, the principle of density, and the principle of imitation.

### *The principle of least effort*

This principle seems to have been a part of linguistic thinking about change from the very beginning. It is cited today most often in the formulations of Saussure (1949:148–9), of Jespersen (1921), and of Bloomfield. Bloomfield's seems the most precise:

(14) It is safe to say that we speak as rapidly and with as little effort as possible, approaching always the limit where our interlocutors ask us to repeat our utterance, and that a great deal of sound-change is in some way connected with this factor. (1933:386)

[14] As for example that speakers in cold climates had to keep their mouths closed to prevent the cold air from entering their vocal cavity, and so had fewer open vowels.

[15] See Saussure's critical review of the arguments advanced for the causes of phonetic changes (1959:147).

In this formulation, the principle of least effort is a precise structural principle, bound between two limiting factors that determine exactly the extent of the reduction concerned. If the principle were made one step more explicit, it might state that the reduction of phonetic form stops at exactly before the point where information would be lost. Let us try to restate this accordingly:

(14′) Principle of least effort I. We speak with the least effort that is required to be understood by our addressees, but with sufficient effort to ensure that we are understood.

However, (14′) is not consistent with the view that sound change is destructive of meaning, as cited in (5, 6, 7). The very term *least effort* implies a limiting, asymptotic factor which can only be the preservation of meaning. Bloomfield did not disagree in the least with the traditional view that sound change destroys meaning.[16] If not, then the principle of least effort would require an alternative formulation of a very different character:

(14″) Principle of least effort II. We speak with less effort than is required to convey all of our meaning to our addressees.

But (14″) loses the characteristic Bloomfieldian precision. It says nothing of interest on how much or by what cause we fall short. (14′) defines how much reduction is possible, and implicitly attributes the reduction to a rational principle of efficiency, while (14″) says very little at all. To have any interest for a theory of language change, it would have to be reinforced as

(14‴) Principle of least effort III. Under the influence of factors $\mathbf{a}_1, \mathbf{a}_2 \ldots \mathbf{a}_n$, we reduce the phonetic information that we convey to our addressees, sometimes to the point that they do not understand us.

At this point, the principle of least effort would no longer lie at the focus of efforts to explain change. Rather, the task would be to identify the factors that lead to this behavior. *Laziness*, *carelessness*, and *ignorance* are perhaps the most frequent candidates for underlying causes, not only in popular treatments but in scholarly works of the 19th century. In his general treatment of the causes of linguistic change, Whitney refers to "linguistic degeneration," which is caused by:

(15) the wholly regrettable inaccuracies of heedless speakers, their confusion of things which ought to be carefully held apart, their obliteration of valuable distinctions. (1904:84–5)

[16] "In fact, sound-changes often obliterate features whose meaning is highly important . . . Homonymy and syncretism, the merging of inflectional categories, are normal results of sound-change" (1933:388).

Here Whitney focuses on the carelessness of these speakers, though elsewhere he deals equally with laziness and ignorance. At first glance, the three terms *laziness*, *carelessness*, and *ignorance* seem simply to express of the same moral disapprobation. Yet they can be differentiated in their implications for the mechanism of sound change when we introduce the dimension of rapidity of speech. In dealing with the principle of least effort, Whitney points out that

(16) we may call it laziness, or we may call it economy . . . it is laziness when it gives up more than it gains; economy, when it gains more than it abandons. (1904:70)

Syllable length is regularly associated with degree of approximation to target articulations, not only for the syllable nucleus, but for syllable margins as well.[17] The low level of effort associated with laziness would generally be correlated with slow speech, while the low level of effort attributed to carelessness would be associated with rapid speech. Thus for the careless speaker, a low level of attention or effort directed to the norms of correct speech would combine with the mechanical temporal effect of shorter time to reduce the phonetic information produced, while for the lazy speaker, the temporal effect would operate in the opposite direction.

On the other hand, ignorance has no direct relationship either to tempo or to the principle of least effort. If the speakers described by Whitney are indeed ignorant of classical and time-honored usages and of valuable distinctions, the changes in their language cannot be ascribed to the principle of least effort. Thus in the course of a merger, speakers who are aware of the distinction between *whale* and *wail* might neglect it through carelessness or laziness; it is their children who would then complete the sound change through ignorance of the distinction.[18]

## *Speech tempo*

The tempo of speech may be considered a distinct factor in sound change, since tempo may vary independently of effort. Bloomfield notes that Wundt attributed sound change to an increase in the rapidity of speech, and this in turn to the community's advance in culture and general intelligence. In contrast to the other treatments of the period, Wundt did not view such changes as a consequence of human failings, but rather as a product of

[17] This applies to changes in progress as well as stable variation. Volume 1, table 18.1 illustrates how following syllables, which shorten syllable duration, restrict the raising of (æh) for Carol Meyers in Philadelphia.

[18] In this case, since the distinction between voiced /w/ and voiceless /ʍ/ is still registered in spelling, and some schools continue to teach this usage, the younger generation could be said to exhibit carelessness, laziness, and ignorance in failing to acquire it in their formal speech.

intelligent behavior, associating greater speed of speech with higher intelligence. It is generally recognized that morphophonemic condensations that involve cliticization, syncope, degemination, consonant cluster simplification, and assimilation are associated with fast speech rules (Dressler and Grosu 1972, Gay 1977, Kaisse 1977, Beckman et al. 1992), and that over the course of time some of these contractions become institutionalized in the more formal structure of the language or as underlying forms.[19] Sankoff and Laberge 1973 report that one of the characteristic differences between native speakers of Tok Pisin and second language speakers is that native speakers talk much faster. Later, we will examine the linguistic changes that accompany this increase in tempo.

### *Discontinuities in communication*

A more general explanation of linguistic change was advanced by Bloomfield in his treatment of dialect geography, cited extensively in Part C of volume 1. In dealing with the high degree of differentiation in local European dialects, he wrote:

(17) The reason for this intense local differentiation is evidently to be sought in the principle of density. Every speaker is constantly adapting his speech-habits to those of his interlocutors; he gives up forms he has been using, adopts new ones, and perhaps oftenest of all, changes the frequency of speech-forms without entirely abandoning any old ones or accepting any that are really new to him. The inhabitants of a settlement, village, or town, however, talk much more to each other than to persons who live elsewhere. When any innovation in the way of speaking spreads over a district, the limit of this spread is sure to be along some lines of weakness in the network of oral communication, and these lines of weakness, in so far as they are topographical lines, are the boundaries between towns, villages, and settlements. (1933:476)

To the extent that this is true, a large part of the problem of explaining the diffusion of linguistic change is reduced to a simple calculation. Given the degree of variability indicated above, discontinuities in the networks of communication would inevitably lead to a random drift of neighboring dialects in different directions. Though Bloomfield thought that his own hypothesis was not within reach of empirical confirmation, it can be tested with figures on vehicular traffic and telephone communication. An examination of the dialect boundaries of the Eastern United States on the basis of average daily traffic flow show that Bloomfield's hypothesis holds for all

[19] Hock 1986:352–4 gives a characteristic example of the reduction of the relative marker *yo* in Old Irish, leading to a reinterpretation of the lenition of the following consonant as the relativizing signal.

boundaries but one (Labov 1974). Furthermore, the principle of density implicitly asserts that we do not have to search for a motivating force behind the diffusion of linguistic change. The effect is a mechanical and inevitable one; the implicit assumption is that social evaluation and attitudes play a minor role.

### *Language and dialect contact*

No treatment of the causes of linguistic change could be complete without a consideration of the effect of one system on another. Extensive treatments of the effects of dialect contact on language change are available in Trudgill 1986, Kerswill 1993, Chambers 1995, and Williams and Kerswill 1999. The present work is primarily concerned, however, with those changes that emerge from within a linguistic system, in which the problem of causation arises in its sharpest form.

### *Optimization of communicative function*

In more recent times, a number of theories of linguistic change have portrayed the process as part of a smoothly functioning mechanism that serves to maximize the communication of information. Far from interfering with communication, change is seen as maximizing the flow of information and the ease of obtaining it. The most prominent of these accounts is the functional approach of Martinet (1955). Martinet sees most sound changes as governed by the need to maximize the distinctiveness of phonemes. Phonemes shift their target positions and their fields of dispersion in order to preserve their margin of security. The instability of phonetic systems is due to the presence of two conflicting pressures: the psychological preference for symmetry, and the asymmetrical construction of the organs of articulation. Thus there is a tendency to preserve symmetry with the same number of distinctions of height in the front and the back, and a tendency to have fewer distinctions in the back since there is a smaller physiological space to differentiate back vowels.

Among the many empirical demonstrations of Martinet's position, two rank among the most substantial. Moulton (1962) demonstrated that the position of the allophones of /a:/ in Northern Switzerland was highly determined by the configuration of other low and mid long vowels in the front and the back. Haudricourt and Juilland (1949) showed that in a large range of languages, the fronting of the nucleus of /u/ and /o/ was associated with a reduction of the number of degrees of height among the back vowels from four to three. In volume 1, it was seen that the force of their argument is somewhat diminished by the extensive fronting of the long back vowels in American English dialects with a prior merger of long and short open /o/ and only three degrees of height in that region. Liljencrants and Lindblom

(1972) support the tendency to maximal dispersion of vowels with a review of reported vowel systems and a numerical simulation.

Chapter 20 of volume 1 argued that the chain shifting of vowels could be seen as conforming to Martinet's principles of maintaining margins of security in a way that maximized the efficiency of communication. The proposed mechanism of shift depended upon the consequences of misunderstanding: outlying vowel productions in the direction of smaller margins of security would have a greater tendency to be misunderstood than those in the direction of larger margins of security. As a result, the mean number of tokens in the data base available to a language learner would be shifted in the direction of the greater margin of security, and the field of dispersion of the phoneme would expand in that direction. In this mechanism, the teleological aspect of functional explanations disappears. However, two major problems remain unresolved under the functional explanation of chain shifting. First, it does not account for the massive mergers that are as common as or more common than chain shifts (volume 1, chs 10–12). Secondly, it does not include any account of the driving force that moves the vowel system in the first place.

More recent efforts to explain linguistic change depend upon more abstract characteristics of rule systems. King (1969) proposed to account for all linguistic changes as forms of rule simplification, though King (1975) retracted this argument in favor of a multivariate approach that takes social factors into account. Kiparsky (1971, 1982) argued that linguistic change tends to favor feeding relations of rules, maximizing their application, and that change also tends to minimize opacity and maximize transparency. Volume 1 argued that the most characteristic sound change is a change in the phonetic realization of a phoneme at a low level of abstraction, a postlexical output rule. The symmetrical generalization of such rules would represent rule simplification and maximization of application.[20] It was also argued in volume 1, chapter 8 that chain shifting could be treated as a unitary process no different in character from parallel shifting. Explanations from rule systematization could then compete with the functional explanations of Martinet.

To what extent can the various causes of sound change advanced be seen as adaptations of language to its environment and environmental needs? Here we must draw a fine line between the facilitation of communication and communication itself. Many factors involve shortening of the effort, mental or physical, required for the act of communication. The principle of least effort is such a form of facilitation, as is rule simplification (which may facilitate acquisition as well as production) and the maximization of

[20] Parallel arguments arise in the constraint-based mechanism of optimality theory; the generalization of a rule corresponds to an elevation in the ranking of a more general constraint.

transparency (which facilitates interpretation and acquisition). On the other hand, functional explanations proper are usually based on maximization of the information conveyed – either by increasing the total amount of information in the signal, or by calling the receiver's attention to a particular piece of information.

The pessimistic views (11, 12, 13) expressed by the major thinkers about linguistic change can now be understood more clearly. For each explanation brought forward, there is a competing explanation which can account for the same change. The Great Vowel Shift can be seen as the preservation of distinctions in the face of some unknown force that raised the long vowels, or as a generalization of that raising that simplifies the phonological system. Not only are there competing explanations for each phenomenon, but most of these explanations can predict the opposite of what occurred. Thus the maintenance of any given distinction, like that between /w/ and /ʍ/, conveys more information, but makes it harder to learn the language – not only because there is one more distinction to be maintained, but because one term of the opposition is a marked articulation. The generalization of a change from front to back vowels simplifies the structure of the system, but frequently leads to mergers in the back vowels.

There is a deeper problem that makes all of these explanations less than satisfactory. They all depend upon some permanent properties of the organism of the language structure; yet sound change is characteristically sporadic, accelerating at unpredictable rates and terminating at unpredictable times. Bloomfield was well aware of this aspect of the problem:

(18) Every conceivable cause has been alleged . . . No permanent factor, however, can account for specific changes which occur at one time and place and not at another.

Saussure is more elaborate on this point:

(19) . . . why did the phenomenon break through at one time rather than another? The same question applies to all the preceding causes of phonetic changes if they are accepted as real. Climatic influence, racial predisposition, and the tendency toward least effort are all permanent or lasting: why do they act sporadically, sometimes on one point of the phonological system and sometimes on another? (1959:15)

Meillet gave a precise answer to these questions:

(20) From the fact that language is a social institution, it follows that linguistics is a social science, and the only variable element that we can resort to in accounting for linguistic change is social change, of which linguistic variations are only consequences, sometimes immediate and direct, more often mediated

> and indirect. . . . We must determine which social structure corresponds to a given linguistic structure, and how in general changes in social structure are translated into changes in linguistic structure. (Meillet 1926:17–18; my translation)

This quotation is from Meillet's inaugural lecture of February 1906 as he assumed the professorial chair of the College de France formerly held by Bréal. The lectures that followed were explicitly devoted to this program. Meillet's social arguments draw upon well-established facts about the social relations of speech communities, and only occasionally refer to dialect differences or variation within the community. Nevertheless, his insight remains fundamental to the sociolinguistic approach to linguistic change developed in this volume. Curiously enough, the main proposal for the social correlates of language that was advanced in Meillet's time was that of Gabriel Tarde, who considered his own theory of society to be a major competitor to that of Durkheim.

## *Imitation*

In his *Laws of Imitation* (1873), Tarde developed a general theory of language based on an "inter-psychology" of individuals, diametrically opposed to the Saussurian concept of *langue* as a social fact. His argument included a theory of language change:

(21) It appears to me almost beyond dispute that language is a phenomenon of imitation: its propagation from high to low, from superior to inferior, whether it be without or within the nation, the acquisition of foreign words by fashion and their assimilation by custom, the contagion of accent, the tyranny of usage in itself, suffices to show at one glance its imitative character. (Tarde 1873: ch. 5)

Tarde discussed at length the nature of the creative act performed by these innovators. These are portrayed as superior individuals who are imitated by the "public" that admires them. Tarde also recognized the "law of least effort," but did not see it as the product of careless and heedless speech. Instead, he saw its operation as "inevitable" and "teleological," that is, tending toward an efficient form of simplification. At the same time, he insisted on a complementary force of "phonetic reinforcement," which "serves to introduce a new sense or emphasize the expression of an accepted sense." Far from regarding sound change as a blind, mechanical force, Tarde regarded it as a positive, creative process; he saw no clear separation between semantic and phonetic change.

Though Tarde's view of imitation is unidirectional in the social hierarchy, it is not necessary to limit the process to a transfer of features from higher to lower social groups. To explain the fact that speech forms stigmatized by the dominant social classes are maintained over long periods of time, and even expand in the face of that stigmatization, one is forced to consider the existence of an opposing set of values that do not readily emerge in formal situations (Labov 1972b:313), and some firm evidence has been produced for the existence of such covert prestige (Trudgill 1972, Labov et al. 1968). However, the force of Tarde's explanation may be considerably weakened if the term "prestige" is allowed to apply to any property of a linguistic trait that would lead people to imitate it. Thus the fact that a linguistic form has prestige would be shown by the fact that it was adopted by others.

### *Differentiation and alignment of social groups*

Bloomfield's principle of density, given as (17) above, dealt with geographic differentiation. He later generalized this principle to apply to social differentiation in a single community, in a description that applies closely to the results of recent sociolinguistic studies of urban communities:

(22) We believe that the differences in density of communication within a speech community are not only personal and individual, but that the community is divided into various systems of sub-groups such that the persons within a sub-group speak much more to each other than to persons outside their sub-group. The lines of weakness and, accordingly, the differences of speech within a speech community are local – due to mere geographic separation – and non-local, or as we usually say, social.

This account plainly gives a picture of the growth of social differentiation within the community, and in particular of the divergence of the dialects spoken by highly segregated racial groups in North American cities (Labov and Harris 1986, Bailey 1993). However, it does not account for the progressive diffusion of linguistic change across social groups, which is one of the main phenomena that we have to deal with in this volume, or the way in which the entire speech community advances in the course of linguistic change.

The orientation to the relations of language and society that is closest to my own point of view is that of Sturtevant (1947). He viewed the process of linguistic change as the association of particular forms of speaking with the social traits of opposing social groups. Those who adopt a particular group as a reference group,[21] and wish to acquire the social attributes of that group, adopt the form of speaking characteristic of that group. The opposition between the two forms of speaking continues as long as the social opposition endures, and terminates in one way or another when the social distinction is no longer relevant.

[21] In the technical sense developed by Merton 1957.

## 1.4 Different kinds of sound change

The various proposals for the causes of sound change cover physical, psychological, and social parameters of the speaker's situation. But very few of these discussions discriminate among the different kinds of sound change involved, in spite of the fact that many of the causes proposed apply to only a limited range of types. In the effort to bring empirical evidence to bear upon these proposals, it will be essential to make that discrimination.

### *Sound shifts*

For all of the discussions involving the principle of least effort, it is obvious that the writer was focusing, consciously or unconsciously, upon changes that reduce the amount of phonetic information provided by the articulation of speech.[22] Yet the principle of least effort applies primarily to changes of manner: consonant lenition, vowel reduction, and the deletion of segments. It does not apply at all to those sound changes that alter place of articulation, like the shift of Austronesian /t/ to /k/ in Hawaiian, the shift of apical obstruents to velars in Skikun discussed by Li (volume 1: 16–17), or any of the vowel shifts presented in volume 1:5–9. In both the Northern Cities Shift and the Southern Shift, a majority of the vowel changes involve an increase in the complexity and energy of articulation – lengthening, diphthongization, and movement to more extreme positions in phonetic space. Very few of these vowel shifts involve shortening, and even the laxing of diphthongal nuclei to the nonperipheral track frequently involve an increase in nucleus–glide differentiation within the syllable. Typically, the shift of New York /ay/ from [aɪ] to [ɒːi] and Philadelphia /aw/ from [æʊ] to [eːɔ] comprise a considerable increase in the length and complexity of the trajectory of the vowel. In general, changes in the place of articulation of segments cannot be explained by the principle of least effort, or by any of the factors that are used to motivate that principle: laziness, careless, or ignorance. Nor would rapidity of speech apply to such sound changes. Many efforts have been made to show that these changes represent an optimization of rule systems, though an overall assessment seems to show as much complication as simplification. The imitation of dominant social groups seems equally unlikely, since when such sound changes come to public attention, they are almost always stigmatized by the dominant social groups. Certainly sound shifts can carry social evaluation, as demonstrated by the subjective reaction tests carried out in New York City (Labov 1966a: ch. 12) and Philadelphia (chapter 6,

[22] Whitney is perhaps the most explicit on this point; lenition and deletion are the only types of phonetic change that are considered in his entire volume (1904).

this volume). It is an empirical question as to which sound shifts are the vehicles of which social values associated with which other groups in the social spectrum.

As opposed to sound shifts, there are many other types of changes that reduce phonetic information in the speech chain over time. Though lenition, merger, and deletion are all similar in this respect, they have different relations to the proposed causes of sound change presented above.

## *Lenition*

There is no shortage of sociolinguistic variables that are characterized by the lenition of phonetic forms. Studies of variation have focused on the aspiration of Spanish and Portuguese postvocalic (s), the vocalization of postvocalic (n) in Portuguese, Chinese, and African-American English, the loss of initial aspiration and vocalization of liquids in English, and so on. We can observe in Liverpool a modern counterpart of the lenition of voiceless stops to fricatives that marked Grimm's law, this time in postvocalic position. These are paradigmatic candidates to register the influence of the principle of least effort. In so far as these changes can be represented as a reassignment or spreading of features, rather than merger or loss of features, they are not easily interpreted as responding to the need for optimization of rule systems. On the other hand, they are usually not as heavily marked for social evaluation as other sociolinguistic variables and show more moderate stylistic shift with increase of audio-monitoring. Thus the role of imitation and reference group association may be not as prominent for changes involving lenition.

The data available for the empirical investigation of such changes in progress is limited. Most of the variables that have been studied are now quite stable, though they are undoubtedly the product of active sound changes at some time in the past. Chapter 3 of volume 1 gave real-time and apparent-time evidence for change in progress in Cedergren's study of the lenition of (ch) in the Spanish of Panama City (1973, 1984). The vocalization of (l) in American English appears to be a recent and vigorous change in progress from below (Ash 1982a,b), and we will draw heavily upon this phenomenon for an understanding of the social trajectory of a lenition rule later in this volume.

## *Mergers and splits*

In historical comparative linguistics, "sound change" is almost equivalent to merger, since mergers are the changes that are preserved most clearly in the historical record and in the comparison of languages. The innovations that identify nodes in family trees are therefore most heavily concentrated in this type of sound change. Whether the principle of least effort applies to such mergers is an interesting question; I do not know of any discussions of the topic. Clearly a merger represents a reduction in the amount of information provided by the speaker, though the mechanism of merger proposed by Herold represents merger as a gain of information (1990; see volume 1, ch. 12). One might argue that a merger is a conceptual type of least effort, just as the perseverance of variables or concord of number or gender may be argued to facilitate speech production.

When changes in place of articulation are accompanied with conditioned mergers, they may have strong effects upon the morpheme structure rules of a language and so are subject to arguments of rule simplification. Thus one stage of the reduction of final consonants in unstressed syllables of Greek, Italic and Romance, and Germanic led to a severe limitation on the features found in final position and in affixes – essentially to apicals. In many formulations, this would lead to a great simplification of the phonological representation of grammatical formatives.

In the area of social evaluation, mergers are distinctly opposed to sound shifts. It will become evident that mergers are almost invisible to social evaluation, and it is difficult to think of them as diffusing under the social pressures of social imitation and association. There are many mergers in progress in American English, and we have ample data on their social distribution. The discussion of the merger or near-merger of *ferry* and *furry* in Philadelphia in volume 1, chapter 14 provides a fine-grained view of variation at different levels of attention to linguistic categorization, and this will be related to a closer examination of stylistic effects on merger.

### *Deletions*

The lenition rules discussed above are often closely coupled with deletions, which may also be thought of as the last stage of lenition, but also as alternations with zero or merger with zero. Quantitative studies have been more closely involved with this type of variation than any other. The deletion of final (s) and (n) in Spanish and Portuguese, the deletion of final /t/ or /d/ in English and Dutch consonant clusters, and the alternation of /s/ morphemes with zero in African American English, are located squarely on the intersection of phonology and morphology, where we can study most closely the relation between sound change and the information available in the speech signal (volume 1, ch. 20). They are certainly open to interpretation as consequences of the principle of least effort, particularly when it is formulated as constrained by the need to convey information. All of these deletions also have profound effects on the distribution of syllable types, and ultimately on the canonical form of the syllable, as does the deletion of initial /l/ and medial schwa in French. Though they may represent complications of the grammar in their initial form, they are open to interpretation as simplifications in their final stages.

Unfortunately, none of these deletion variables have been shown to be involved with change in progress, so that our view of the initial and final stages is limited to what we can glean from the historical and comparative record.

Deletions resemble lenitions in their availability for social evaluation: a limited amount of social affect is displayed, considerably less than for sound shifts. We find, for example, that the social stratification of *-t/d* deletion is not by any means as sharp as that of (ing), and that stylistic differentiation is even smaller (Labov et al. 1968).

## 1.5 The narrow interface between language and society

At one point in the development of sociolinguistics, it was not uncommon for scholars to suggest that the social and linguistic aspects of language were coextensive in the sense that each linguistic element had a social aspect or evaluation. Yet the actual situation seems to be quite the reverse. For the most part, linguistic structure and social structure are isolated domains, which do not bear upon each other. As indicated above, those sound changes with clear structural consequences – mergers – are almost entirely without social evaluation. The force of social evaluation, positive or negative, is generally brought to bear only upon superficial aspects of language: the lexicon and phonetics. However, social affect is not in fact assigned to the very surface level: it is not the sounds of language which receive stigma or prestige, but rather the use of a particular allophone for a given phoneme. Thus the sound [iːə] is not stigmatized in general, since it is the prestige norm in *idea*, but it is stigmatized as an allophone of /æ/ in *man*. Similarly, social criticism is not directed at the word *finalize*, but rather at the stem /faynəlayz/, since it is equally shared by *finalizing*, *finalized*, and *finalizes*.

The evidence for the isolation of abstract linguistic structures from social evaluation and differentiation comes from many sources. In the quantitative analyses of variation, it is found that changes made by the addition or subtraction of internal, linguistic factors are reflected in changes in the values of other internal, linguistic factors, while values of the external, social factors remain identical; the same situation applies inversely when external, social factors are added to or subtracted from the analysis (Weiner and Labov 1983, Sankoff and Labov 1979). When analyses of linguistic factors are carried out independently for different social classes or for men and women, very few significant differences are found in the values for the two social groups (Braga 1982). Though the overall level for socially marked variables may vary widely across age groups or social classes, the internal constraints show remarkable constancy (Kroch 1989). In those parts of sociolinguistic interviews that deal overtly with language and its social evaluation, it is almost unknown for subjects to speak spontaneously of the existence or nonexistence of a contrast, or differences in conditions on rules. On the other hand, we will present in this volume evidence for strong social reactions to the phonetic realizations of particular phonemes, and for social evaluation of those realizations in particular words. Under some conditions, the presence or absence of particular grammatical formatives is remarked on, but primarily by those who have taken on the responsibility of enforcing a literary tradition.[23]

The relative segregation of social and structural elements in language is a major factor in distinguishing the possible causes of different types of sound change. Since this volume deals with the role of social factors in change, the primary focus will be on those elements of language that are most likely to be highly stratified in use and strongly evaluated in social perception.

## 1.6 The social location of the innovators

Sturtevant's views on the diffusion of sound change were based upon his own informal but penetrating observations of sociolinguistic patterns in the first half of the 20th century. His explanation of the path of linguistic change is essentially that it is a reflection of social change, responding most directly to the appeal of Meillet (1921). Yet it barely touches the question of the underlying causes of the continued renewal of change, and Sturtevant's brief comments do nothing to implement his views by showing how a particular change followed the course outlined. This volume will undertake that task, tracing the diffusion of linguistic change through the various layers of social structure. The goal is not only to describe the path of the change, but also to advance our understanding of its fundamental causes. The strategy to be followed here is to transform the traditional question "Why does language change?" into a different form: "Who are the leaders of linguistic change?"

Many of the earlier writers on sound change cited indicated that it would indeed be helpful to know which speakers were responsible for its initiation. If social factors are in fact connected with the onset and continuation of this process, it would be essential to know something about the social class, sex, ethnicity, or occupations of the innovators. For those

[23] There are exceptions to this generalization: negative concord in modern English is one. In one way or another the entire speech community shows sensitivity to this abstract structural pattern, which does not depend on the presence or absence of any one surface form. There is no change evident in this sociolinguistic pattern today, but chapter 3 will present some information on how this change in English structure came about.

who looked on sound change as an unmixed evil, the search was more or less a criminal investigation. Thus Whitney:

(23) Such phonetic changes . . . are inevitable and creep in of themselves; but that is only another way of saying that we do not know who in particular is to blame for them. Offenses needs must come, but there is always that man by whom they come, could we but find him out. (1904:43)

Whitney's description of the innovators cited above in (15) as "uncultivated and careless speakers . . . to whom the preferences of the moment are of more account than anything in the past or the future" is a classic description of the lowest social class in the eyes of the upper class. Such a prediction fits in with the negative character of the explanations that are usually advanced for sound change. But theoretical notions do not account altogether for Whitney's pursuit of these corrupters of the language. He plainly saw the opposition as one of social loyalties:

(24) New dialects are wont to grow up among the common people, while the speech of the educated and lettered class continues to be what it has been. (1904:44)

In condemning the effects of linguistic change, Whitney calls for social action to oppose them. The full quotation from which (15) was drawn is:

(25) The wholly regrettable inaccuracies of heedless speakers, their confusion of things which ought to be carefully held apart, their obliteration of valuable distinctions – all these are part and parcel of the ceaseless changes of language . . . they are only that part against which the best public sentiment, a healthy feeling for the conservation of linguistic integrity, arrays itself most strongly. (1868:84–5)[24]

In general, those linguists who pointed to the principle of least effort as the major factor in linguistic change would look for the most extreme examples of the change in progress among the lowest social classes. To the extent that discontinuities of communication within a speech community are the causes of change, with resulting ignorance of the normative standard, we would also expect to find the leaders of change in the lowest social class. However, the opposite prediction would be made by Tarde, who believed that linguistic change was always initiated by the highest group in the social

[24] The strongly moral overtones from these quotations, characteristic of 19th-century reflections on this subject, may be misleading. Whitney took a much more objective view of the effects of sound change than the moral overtones of these quotations convey. In fact, he saw "phonetic corruption" as the chief creative force in "the life and growth of language," as Lecture III from Whitney 1904 demonstrates throughout.

scale. Aligned with Tarde would be Wundt. Both believed that the condensations of rapid speech represented an increase in efficiency of speech, and were characteristic of the most intelligent and educated speakers.

Given this radical disagreement, it appears that there are significant theoretical consequences to the social location of the innovators of sound change. The Project on Linguistic Change and Variation in Philadelphia [LCV] accepted the challenge laid down by Whitney (23): to identify the social groups responsible for the continued course of sound change. Following Meillet's argument that the course of sound change must be accounted for by its interaction with social forces, we can identify those social forces by charting the position of the leading groups in the multidimensional fabric of the speech community.

## *The curvilinear pattern*

As noted above, early theories of the causes of linguistic change would predict that the innovators would be at either the top or the bottom of the social hierarchy. The first sociolinguistic studies of change in progress, in Martha's Vineyard (Labov 1963) and New York City (Labov 1966a), did not find either of these patterns. The first general sociolinguistic model of the mechanism of linguistic change (Labov 1965) proposed that change within the system could originate in any social group, and following Sturtevant's suggestion, would spread gradually through each neighboring social group until it reached in one form or another all members of the community.

Kroch (1978) pointed out that there were no examples of systematic linguistic change (as opposed to borrowing from outside, or change from above) initiated by an upper class. He proposed a dichotomous model in which natural linguistic change was initiated by working class speakers, while middle and upper class speakers reacted against such changes, correcting their speech in a direction opposed to natural change.

In an early discussion of the social location of the innovators of change from below (Labov 1972b:294–5), it was stipulated that the highest social class is not "as a rule" the innovating group, but it was also pointed out that "it seldom happens" that innovation spreads upward from the lowest social group.[25] Instead, it was observed that the innovating groups were always located in an upper working class, or lower middle class, and that

[25] This formulation presumes an analysis of the social hierarchy into more than two components. The actual basis for the division of social classes seems to be immaterial: some support for the pattern described below comes from studies with education as the class indicator; others with occupation; and still others with combined indices. But unless three, or preferably four, divisions of the social hierarchy are distinguished, the curvilinear pattern will be concealed. Thus from the point of view of the study of linguistic change in progress, descriptions of communities in terms of upper vs. lower class, or middle vs. working class, are not informative and may actually conceal whatever change is taking place.

in many cases, these two groups were almost identical in the advancement of the change in progress in vernacular speech. Thus the crucial division in the society from the point of view of language change was not middle class vs. working class, but rather centrally located groups as against peripherally located groups.

From these observations was formed the **curvilinear hypothesis**: while stable sociolinguistic variables showed a monotonic social class distribution, a monotonic distribution in age groups was associated with a curvilinear pattern in the socioeconomic hierarchy. The major evidence for this hypothesis was drawn from the raising of (oh), (ay), and (aw) in New York City (Labov 1966a), the backing of (el) in Norwich (Trudgill 1974b), and the lenition of (ch) in Panama City (Cedergren 1973). Figure 1.1 is drawn

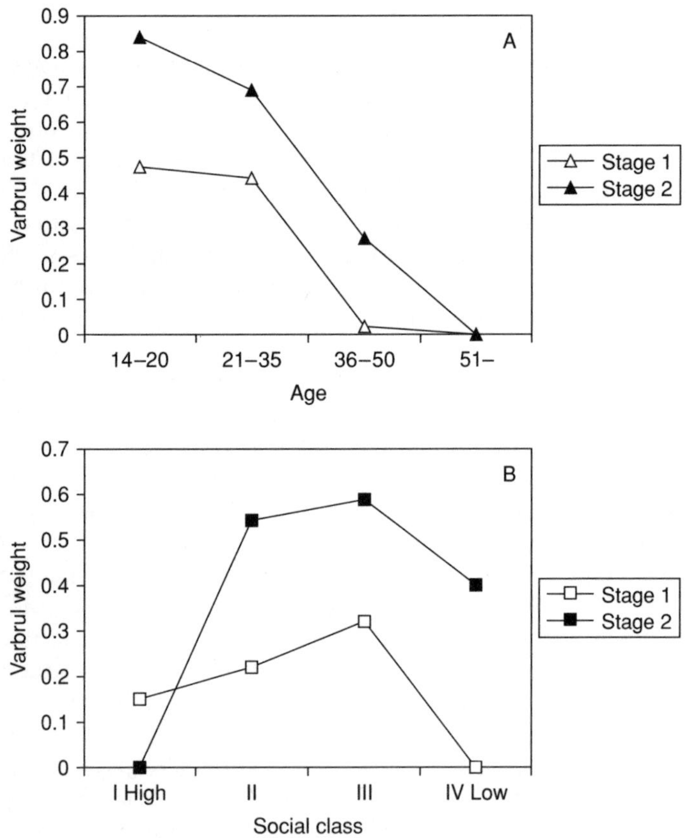


*Figure 1.1* Curvilinear pattern shown by Varbrul weights for social constraints on the lenition of (ch) in Panama City. Stage 1: weakened affricate. Stage 2: fricative. (A) Monotonic function of age. (B) Curvilinear function of social class (adapted from Cedergren 1973)

from Cedergren's Panama City data: it shows the characteristic coupling of a steady rise in the (ch) index with progressively younger speakers, and a curvilinear pattern in the social class domain.

The Project on Linguistic Change and Variation in Philadelphia [LCV] was proposed explicitly to test the curvilinear hypothesis in a community where about two-thirds of the vowels appeared to be involved in change in progress. Chapter 3 of volume 1 presented the results of the studies of change in apparent time, reinforced by observations in real time, that led to the establishment of five levels of change within the vowel system. Of the eleven changes in progress described there, the most important for the hypothesis are the new and vigorous changes: the fronting and raising of (aw) in *out*, *down*, etc.; the raising and fronting of (ey) in checked syllables in *made*, *pain*, etc.; and the centralization of (ay) before voiceless consonants in *right*, *fight*, etc. The social distribution of these and other changes will be described in chapter 5, which will provide ample evidence to confirm or disconfirm the curvilinear hypothesis. The social location of the leaders of linguistic change will then be examined further along many other social dimensions, and the results will be applied to illuminate and perhaps reduce the Darwinian paradox.

## 1.7 Individual, group, community

Many writers on sociolinguistic themes, including those whose work plays a major role in this volume, have argued that the major focus of sociolinguistic analysis should be placed on the individual speaker rather than the group (L. Milroy 1980:133–4, Douglas-Cowie 1978; see also Fillmore, Kempler, and Wang 1979). If the net result of such a policy is to plunge more deeply into the internal composition of the group, it is likely to be productive. This volume will begin with larger components of social structure, and proceed with finer and finer analysis until the leaders of linguistic change are located as specific individuals. The main data base will be the 112 speakers of the Philadelphia Neighborhood Study whose vowel systems were analyzed acoustically. The leaders of linguistic change will be located as outliers within a particular social class, a particular gender, in specific positions within local social networks. To understand the forces operating in linguistic change, we will necessarily be focusing upon a handful of individuals. We will study their personal statements, their social histories, and their philosophies of life. This focus on individuals is not inconsistent with the argument of my 1966 study of New York City that the behavior of the individual speaker cannot be understood until the sociolinguistic pattern of the community as a whole is delineated.

This investigation is not a search for individuals, but rather for social locations and social types. The leaders of linguistic change are not individual inventors of a certain form, but rather those who, by reason of their social histories and patterns of behavior, will advance the ongoing change most strongly. In tracing the forces that underlie linguistic change, I would follow Meillet in rejecting the reduction of social factors to the social psychology of individuals – the "inter-psychology" invented by Tarde. This approach continues the program advanced by Weinreich, Labov, and Herzog 1968, centered about the concept that the speech community and not the idiolect is the primary object of linguistic investigation. It is true enough that when we examine a community closely enough, it will inevitably appear that each individual's linguistic pattern differs in some respects from that of everyone else. Yet this unique object, the individual speaker, can only be understood as the product of a unique social history, and the intersection of the linguistic patterns of all the social groups and categories that define that individual. Linguistic analysis cannot recognize individual grammars or phonologies. Individual rules or constraints would have no interpretation and contribute nothing to acts of communication. In this sense, the individual does not exist as a linguistic object. However, each individual shows a personal profile of the comparative use of resources made available by the speech community.

Those who work outside of sociolinguistic principles of accountability must hope that the intuitions of several individuals will be sufficiently representative of the speech community to make the description of the language a valid one – a situation that is rarely realized. It is for this reason that all sociolinguists agree that the productions and interpretations of the individual speaker are the primary site for linguistic investigation. The position of this study is that these individuals are not the final units of linguistic analysis, but the components that are used to construct models of our primary object of interest, the speech community.

# 2

# *The Study of Linguistic Change and Variation in Philadelphia*

This volume pursues the causes of linguistic change through a search for the social location of the leaders of change. The usual route for a general inquiry of this kind is to assemble as many different studies as possible. Since each of these will have its own methodology, it is impractical to give detailed descriptions of them all, and the effects of any differences in method become an unexamined source of error. In this volume, one particular study will play a predominant role: the study of Linguistic Change and Variation in Philadelphia [LCV]. The original research, supported by the National Science Foundation, was carried out from 1973 to 1977, and followed by a wider study in Eastern Pennsylvania from 1977 to 1979. A number of the central subjects were re-interviewed in 1989–91 as part of a longitudinal study of normal aging (Labov and Auger 1998). From 1973 to the present, further information on Philadelphia neighborhoods has been gathered by students in the class on the Study of the Speech Community at the University of Pennsylvania though this data does not enter directly into the present report.

LCV was designed specifically to test the curvilinear hypothesis outlined in chapter 1. Results that support that hypothesis were first published in Labov 1980, and many other products of the LCV project dealing with synchronic and diachronic variation appeared in the following years.[1] In the succeeding decade and a half, these results formed the basis for three other inquiries into the course of linguistic changes in progress. In each

[1] LCV results covered a wide range of topics. Further information on the social location of the innovators of change (gender) was provided in Labov 1990. Guy 1980 and consequent publications dealt with consonant cluster simplification in the Philadelphia community and New York. Poplack 1979, 1980, 1981 dealt with the use of inflections in the Spanish of the Philadelphia community. Labov 1989b described in detail the split of Philadelphia *a* into tense and lax categories. Payne 1976, 1980 reported on the acquisition of the Philadelphia dialect by children from out-of-state families. Schiffrin 1981 and subsequent publications presented a discourse analysis of the Mallow St. section of the LCV Neighborhood Study as described below. Hindle 1980 described the telephone survey and the acoustic analysis of a single speaker recorded throughout a day. Volume 1 introduced a number of other LCV results.

of the chapters to follow, the LCV findings will be presented first; the results of other studies, in Philadelphia and elsewhere, will then be introduced to confirm, amplify, or question these results. The methods used by LCV are therefore of prime importance for evaluating the conclusions of this volume.

The field methods used by LCV were presented in some detail in Labov 1984. But it is still quite common for reviewers of sociolinguistic findings and for new researchers entering the field to base their conception of quantitative methodology on the New York City study of the Lower East Side done in 1963 (Labov 1966a, hereafter LES), though this work is over thirty years old at this writing. Many changes have taken place in sociolinguistic methods since LES that have drastically altered our approach in many ways. Four limitations of the 1963 methods are worth noting here:

- The survey of the Lower East Side that was the major component of LES was a random sample of individuals in individual households. The observations of generational differences and family and group interaction that were obtained were incidental rather than a part of the basic design.[2]
- The methods used by LES to solve the Observer's Paradox, and reduce attention paid to language, were only the first tentative steps taken in that direction. Much of the interview was still devoted to questions and answers drawn from the tradition of dialect geography, so that sections that could be labeled "casual speech" were relatively short, rarely more than 10 to 20 minutes of the interview.
- The measurements of sound change were based on a quantitative index created by aligning a number of categories of impressionistic phonetics along a monotonic and linear scale.
- The analyses of sociolinguistic patterns were done by cross-tabulations, which took at the most three dimensions of sociolinguistic structure into account, without the benefit of multivariate analysis or statistical treatment.

In other respects, the methods of LES went beyond the methods that were followed in many succeeding studies of urban speech communities, so that there have been losses as well as gains in the years that followed. LES included a wide range of methods for gathering data: the rapid and anonymous study of the New York City department stores; transcriptions of group interaction on the streets; a telephone survey of non-respondents.

[2] Of the 151 LES interviews, only 50 were with a single adult alone. In 15 cases, the spouse was present; in 51 there were children present (from 1 to 5); in 21 others, another adult relative or friend was present; and in 14, the interviews were with children alone.

The individual interviews of LES also included a wider array of field experiments than were usually found in succeeding studies: word lists, minimal pair tests, self-report tests, and subjective reaction tests.[3] The analyses of LES were not limited to the sociolinguistic distribution of individual variables, but examined the NYC vowel system as a whole, its development across time and across social groups. The graphic displays of LES cross-tabulations of social class, style, age, and ethnicity showed a regularity of sociolinguistic structure that does not appear when the effect of a given dimension is reduced to a single numerical value. These displays demonstrated the difference between fine grained and sharp stratification, and between independent and interactive effects, which were important components in the formation of sociolinguistic hypotheses on the diffusion of sound change.

LES brought individual members of the speech community to the forefront of the analysis, while succeeding studies were often confined to numerical statements of mean values. The view of sociolinguistic structure was illuminated by the skewed position of Nathan B., who did not adjust his speech to fit prevailing norms; of Mollie B., whose blindness led her to a special sensitivity to sociolinguistic variables in the speech of others but not in her own; and of Steve K., whose sociolinguistic trajectory involved him in a fruitless return to Brooklyn.[4]

The balance of this chapter will show how the limitations of the LES methods were overcome in LCV, while many of its virtues were preserved. The chapters that follow will show results obtained by these methods, using a range of quantitative analyses and descriptions of individual speakers to provide an accurate image of the innovators of linguistic change. The general description of methods will be embedded in an account of the Philadelphia speech community and how it was studied.

## 2.1 Sampling the community

### *The general sampling problem*

The initial problem that sociolinguistic research encounters is the size and complexity of the object to be studied. As volume 1, chapter 16 indicated, the Neogrammarians became somewhat discouraged by reports of variation

[3] The inquiry into African American Vernacular English (AAVE) in South Harlem conducted in the following years 1965–8 (Labov, Cohen, Robins, and Lewis 1968, or LCRL) enlarged these experimental methods to include imitation experiments, family background tests, classroom correction tests, and vernacular correction tests.

[4] In LES, individual speakers were often the exceptional cases. Portraits of archetypical individual speakers can also illuminate the general propositions; this was the practice of the Harlem study (Labov et al. 1968), and Rickford's work in Guyana (1979).

in urban dialects. The final section of the previous chapter developed the sense in which our primary object of investigation is not the individual, but the community; the problem of obtaining an accurate description of that community should not be underestimated. The first contribution of sociolinguistic research in the second half of the 20th century was to show that this variation was not chaotic, but well formed and rule-governed, that it was indeed an aspect of linguistic structure. The LES study demonstrated that the speech of New York City was not the chaotic flux that had discouraged earlier observers of the local dialect,[5] but was in fact quite regular and systematic. LES showed that each individual followed the same community-wide pattern of style shifting, and in a given stylistic context, society was well ordered into regular patterns. Furthermore, it appeared that popular belief in geographic variation within the city was not well founded. Like London and Paris, the New York City dialect region was a single geographic unit, and traditional geographic labels like "Bronx" or "Brooklyn" dialect turned out to be descriptions of social class patterns.[6]

These achievements in the study of the community required a systematic approach to the sampling problem. An accurate view of an urban community cannot be obtained by the study of a few individuals, or of small groups, nor even of extended social networks of 30 or 40 individuals. Most importantly, it cannot be obtained by any approach that begins with the personal connections of the investigators. A truly representative sample of the speech community must be based on a random sample in which each one of several million speakers has an equal chance of being selected. Such a sample requires an enumeration of those individuals, the selection by random numbers, and a vigorous pursuit of the individuals selected. This is a formidable task, but not outside of the capacity of a single investigator. One can modify the procedure by confining the enumeration to a sub-section of the city, or by constructing a stratified sample in which quotas are placed on various sub-groups, or by a schedule of substitution when the selected individuals cannot be located.[7] Furthermore, it appears that for linguistic purposes, a reliable sample of a very large city can be achieved with comparatively few speakers: in most cases, less

[5] For example, Hubbell's description of the use of /r/ by New Yorkers concludes with the statement: "The pronunciation of a very large number of New Yorkers exhibits a pattern in these words that might most accurately be described as the complete absence of any pattern" (Hubbell 1962:48).

[6] Chapter 7 will explore this issue in some detail. Though Philadelphians share the same structural patterns, some neighborhoods are in advance of others in the advancement of change.

[7] Much time and effort is expended in simply contacting the subjects selected. The Montreal study (Sankoff and Sankoff 1973) increased the efficiency of the sampling procedure with a minimal bias by a regular system of selecting alternate targets. If the person selected was not home, or did not satisfy the sampling criteria, the nearest neighbor was selected in a systematic pattern.

than a hundred.[8] But one cannot capture the regular structure of variation within a large community by any procedure that abandons the critical steps of enumeration and random selection. Unfortunately, a number of sociolinguistic studies of urban communities have retreated from this standard. In many studies, any individual who will agree to be interviewed was selected as long as he or she had the social characteristics desired to fill out an even distribution by sex, education, etc.[9] Other studies have been confined, sometimes with very good reason, to friends, relatives, and acquaintances of the investigators.[10] Studies of this kind will tell us a great deal about sociolinguistic variables that are sensitive to degrees of social distance, and illuminate the social mechanisms that lead to linguistic conformity and diversity; but unless they are accompanied by a wider random sample, they will not produce a clear view of the structure of the speech community as a whole and the regularity of the variation within it. Studies drawn from representative samples of the community have provided the basic and most reliable findings on sociolinguistic patterns: the independence of stylistic and social stratification, the hypercorrect pattern of the second highest status group, and the curvilinear pattern of change from below.

We must therefore recognize a fundamental conflict centered about the choice of field methods. The survey of isolated individuals carried out by LES gives a representative view of individual linguistic behavior, but fails to capture the way that speakers deal with family at home, with friends at

[8] The main sample used for the study of New York was 81 speakers; of Norwich 60 (Trudgill 1974b); Panama City 100 (Cedergren 1973); Montreal 120 (Sankoff and Sankoff 1973); Bahia Blanca 60 (Weinberg 1974); Ottawa 100 (Woods 1979); Paris 109 (Lennig 1978); Lille 101 (Lefebvre 1991); Belo Horizonte, Brazil 76 (de Oliveira 1983); Sao Paolo 40 (Tarallo 1983); Amman 154 (Abdel-Jawad 1981); Cairo 49 (Haeri 1996); Teheran 53 (Modaressi 1978); Anniston, Alabama 65 (Feagin 1979); Buenos Aires 87 (Lavandera 1975); Salt Lake City 65 (Cook 1969); San Juan 62 (Cameron 1991); Tokyo 88 (Hibiya 1988); Seoul 95 (Chae 1995); Glasgow 48 (Macaulay 1978). The sole exception was the study of Detroit by Shuy, Wolfram, and Riley (1967), where 795 speakers were interviewed; but the published analysis included only 25 speakers. Wolfram later studied 48 black speakers from this sample (1969).

[9] It should be recognized that we are often dealing with the politics of the possible, and that many excellent and important results have followed from a truncated methodology. To cite one example: Oliveira's study of Belo Horizonte (1983) was carried out at a time when political events had made recording a suspicious activity.

[10] Haeri's study of Cairo (1996), which plays a major role in this volume, is explicitly "not a random sample," but based on "introductions and friendship networks" (1996:23). Milroy's investigation of Belfast during the period of the troubles necessarily relied on this technique (Milroy and Milroy 1978). The studies of the African American English that have come closest to recording the vernacular have used this method (Labov et al. 1968, Baugh 1983, Labov and Harris 1986, Rickford et al. 1991, Cukor-Avila 1995, Dayton 1996), and these studies have provided us with the most reliable data on those aspects of AAVE that are most different from other dialects. Studies based on individual interviews of first acquaintances have been more useful for the study of those variables that AAVE shares with the larger speech community (adult series in Labov et al. 1968, Wolfram 1969).

their favorite hangout, or with superiors, colleagues, and underlings on the job. These individual surveys are the main source for sociolinguistic patterns, but they are missing the information that we need to understand how those patterns have come about. On the other hand, studies of groups and individuals in their networks can reduce the effects of observation and relate linguistic variation to the ebb and flow of social life, but unless they are coupled with a wider social survey, we will never know whether this is the main sociolinguistic story, or just a few chapters from the book.

The difficulties can be summed up as a Sampling Paradox: *the more confident we are that a sample represents a population, the less confident we are that the sample can explain the behavior of that population.* It is not hard to think of ways of resolving or reducing the force of this paradox, but they all involve new difficulties. One might take a *group* of speakers rather than individual speakers as the unit of sampling. Unfortunately, there is no known way of enumerating groups to give an exhaustive and comparable set of sampling units. Since residences are the usual unit of enumeration, one might interview the families who reside at each unit, thus systematizing the youth sample of LES. If an average family size was between three and four, then one would have to reduce the number of sampling units by one third; instead of 90 individuals, 30 families. This might give us a statistically significant view of sociolinguistic differentiation along one dimension, say social class, but not more than one such dimension, so that ethnicity or neighborhood might remain uncontrolled.

## *The LCV sampling strategy*

The solution to the sampling paradox developed by LCV followed the basic LES approach of having two separate surveys with complementary sources of error. For LES, the two samples were provided by a random sample of the Lower East Side, and a rapid and anonymous study of three large department stores. One gave a representative view of one area of the city with ample linguistic and demographic information on each individual interacting. The other gave a representative sample of the entire city with three times as many speakers, but very little linguistic and demographic information for each speaker. In Philadelphia, it was decided to obtain the representative view of the city through a telephone survey of individuals drawn from a random selection of telephone listings. These interviews would be relatively brief and formal. The main body of linguistic information would be drawn from studies of neighborhoods, selected as the same kind of judgment sample that is used in a small rural community like Martha's Vineyard (Labov 1963). In these neighborhoods, the investigator would carry out long-term studies of families, neighbors, and social networks, with both individual and group recordings. The neighborhood study would provide detailed demographic and linguistic information needed for analysis of phonetic and stylistic variation, and at the same time yield direct observations of social processes and communication patterns that are available to an investigator who is securely inserted into the local social networks.

The LCV project began with an extensive exploratory phase, involving almost a hundred interviews with individuals scattered throughout Philadelphia and its suburbs, along with six small communities located about the periphery of the Philadelphia region at a distance of about 50 miles from the city. Some of the interviews within the city were later integrated into the neighborhood study, but most were not. The information they provided was merged with a broader range of information about the city that was used to choose the sites of the neighborhood studies. To show the motivation for those choices, and provide the background for the many sociolinguistic studies of Philadelphia to follow, it will be helpful now to turn to a social portrait of that city.

## 2.2 The city of Philadelphia

Many sociolinguistic studies devote a full chapter to the history, geography, population, and culture of the city that is the site of their research. Though these facts and figures may have more or less intrinsic interest, they are seldom justified by their relevance to the language being described. The facts that seem most pertinent to the construction of a sociolinguistic sample are the total population and its pattern of dispersion, the economic and cultural relation of the city to its suburbs and the countryside, ethnic composition and settlement history, the major industries, other languages spoken, and geographic features within the city that would affect the patterns of interaction. The sampling plan also requires a detailed characterization of the various sections of the city: their social and ethnic composition, their reputations, and the residential architecture. In the USA, some of this data can be obtained from the census, and some from previous social histories of the city. Philadelphia is a well-studied city – among the best known in the country.[11] The most important sources for our work are the history of the city by Sam Bass Warner (1968), the history of the black community by W. E. B. DuBois (1967), the study of the upper class by Digby Baltzell (1958), collected essays on Philadelphia ethnic groups (Davis and Haller 1973), and the work of the Philadelphia Social History Project headed by Theodore Hershberg (1981). LCV drew upon these studies for the original design of the project, and we will refer to them frequently in our interpretation of the results. At the same time, much of the information needed on local neighborhoods was necessarily drawn from the exploratory studies of 1973–4 conducted by Arvilla Payne and Anne Bower.

[11] In studies of its social history and neighborhood formation, Philadelphia is second only to Chicago.

*Table 2.1* Six largest cities of the United States in 1980

| | *Population, 1980* | *Rank* | *Population growth rate, 1980–1992* |
|---|---|---|---|
| New York, NY | 7,071,639 | 1 | 3.4 |
| Chicago, IL | 3,005,072 | 2 | –7.9 |
| Los Angeles, CA | 2,968,528 | 3 | 17.6 |
| Philadelphia, PA | 1,688,210 | 4 | –8.0 |
| Houston, TX | 1,595,138 | 5 | 6.0 |
| Detroit, MI | 1,203,368 | 6 | –15.9 |

Source: US Census

## *Population and geography*

Table 2.1 shows the six largest cities of the United States in 1980 and their subsequent growth rates. Philadelphia was then the fourth largest city, but as the negative growth rate indicates, its status was declining, and it is now below Houston. It is the center of a Consolidated Metropolitan Statistical Area of 4,781,000 which has actually grown by 3% from 1980 to 1994, and the center of a larger Consolidated MSA of five and a half million.

Figure 2.1 is a map of the 18th National Transportation Analysis Region, showing Philadelphia at the center of this consolidated metropolitan configuration. The larger urbanized area extends into five surrounding counties in Pennsylvania and three in New Jersey, and is continuous with that of Wilmington in Northern Delaware.[12] Though we often speak of a Northeast conurbation extending from Boston to Washington, there is a clear separation between the New York urbanized area and Philadelphia on the northeast, and between Wilmington and Baltimore on the southwest. The size and relative isolation of Philadelphia as an urbanized area have important consequences for the sociolinguistic design. Studies of cities with populations of a million or more show that they influence the surrounding region much more than the surrounding region influences them. The linguistic character of a smaller city of 100,000 cannot be understood without knowledge of the surrounding regional dialects,[13]

[12] The *Atlas of North American English* [*ANAE*] shows that Wilmington shares most linguistic structures with Philadelphia.

[13] See for example Trudgill's (1974b) study of Norwich, England, Habick's (1980) exploration of Farmer City, or Wald's investigation of the Swahili of Mombasa (1973) where the city dialect is seen as the intersection of several regional components.

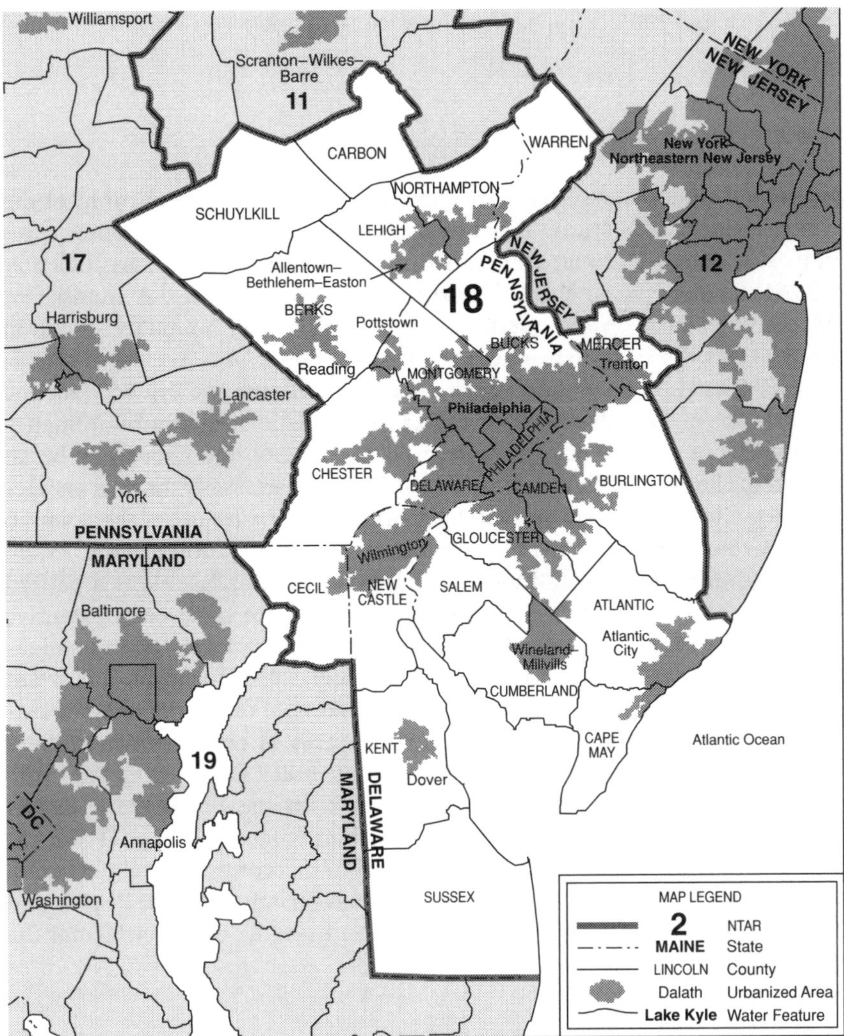


*Figure 2.1* The Philadelphia metropolitan area in the 18th National Transportation Region

but this is not the case for a metropolis like London, New York, Chicago, or Philadelphia. There are some features that are confined to the city limits of Philadelphia. The uniform Philadelphia distribution of tense and lax short **a** changes as we move outside of the city, but other traits are characteristic of the larger region. For some features, there is a smooth continuum that varies step by step along the axis from New York to Baltimore. For other linguistic features, there is a sharp break between

New York and Philadelphia,[14] but no such break between Philadelphia and Baltimore.

## *City limits*

Figure 2.2 offers a closer view of Philadelphia, showing the sections of the city relevant to this study. It is not large in area, compared to other cities of its size: only 135 square miles. There is a single downtown area, Center City, located between the Schuylkill and Delaware rivers. A number of LCV studies bear on the question of whether the city boundary shown in figure 2.2 is the important one, or whether a larger unit like the Philadelphia CMSA should be the basis of sampling. We will see evidence for the importance of Philadelphia as a center of linguistic and cultural influence for the entire region; but in other respects, the city line appears to be an important linguistic demarcation. In volume 1, chapter 14, the near-merger of *merry* and *Murray* was seen to be more characteristic of speakers within the city than speakers from the suburbs. Exploratory studies in the "Main Line" suburbs northwest of the city showed a more diffuse short **a** pattern than that shown for the city. In recent years, there have been extensive population movements from the working class areas of the city to contiguous areas of New Jersey, and research in Cherry Hill forms an important component of the LCV study. However, examination of the short **a** pattern in New Jersey shows significant differences in communities as close as Willingboro, shown on figure 2.2 some 5 miles north of Cherry Hill. Many other lexical and phonological features of the Philadelphia dialect are clustered more tightly within the city than without. The LCV sample was therefore a sample of the city, designed to be representative of the area within the city limits, except for two suburban regions (King of Prussia and Cherry Hill) that were created by emigration from the city shortly after the end of World War II.

## *Historical development*

The history of Philadelphia that is most relevant to its linguistic development falls into two components: the early settlement patterns of the 17th

[14] Kurath and McDavid 1961 and the *ANAE* assigns New York City to the Northern dialect region, and Philadelphia to the Midland. This is exemplified by the contrast between tense, peripheral long back vowels in New York as opposed to strong fronting of the same vowels in Philadelphia. Philadelphia consistently assigns the word *on* to the /oh/ class of *dawn* as opposed to /o/ in *Don*; this feature is perhaps the sharpest separation between Northern and North Midland dialects. *ANAE* places both New York City and Philadelphia in the Mid-Atlantic Region, on the basis of the similar short **a** split into tense and lax categories, and the raising of long open /oh/.

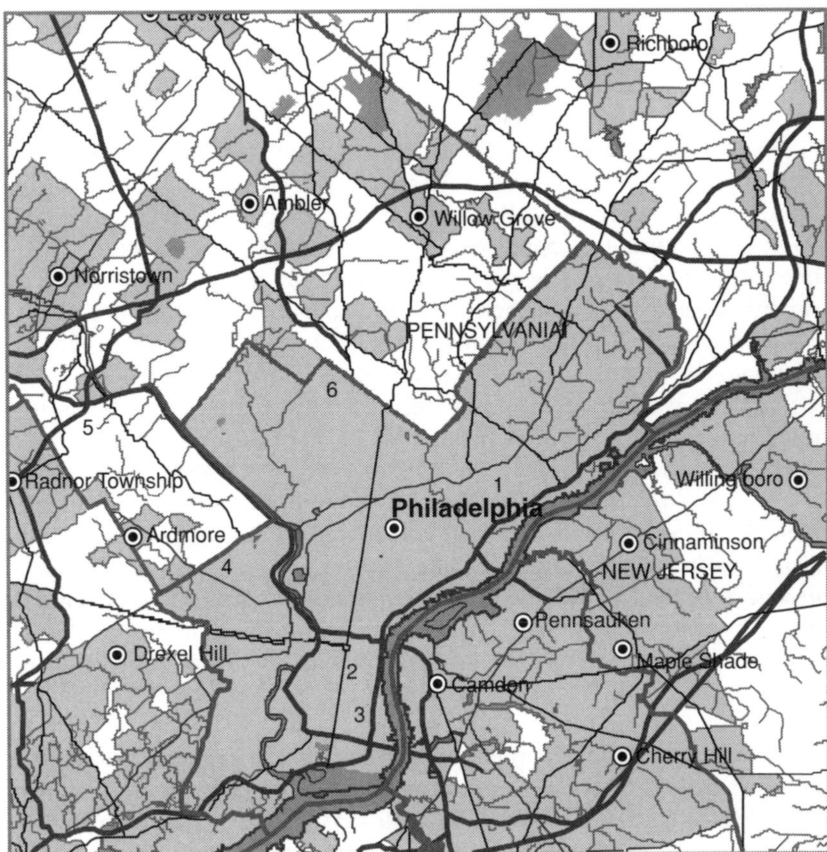


*Figure 2.2* The city of Philadelphia. Neighborhoods of the Philadelphia Neighborhood Study: 1 Wicket St. in Kensington; 2 Clark St. in South Philadelphia; 3 Pitt St. in Pennsport; 4 Mallow Street in Overbrook; 5 Nancy Drive in King of Prussia; 6 Chestnut Hill

and 18th centuries and the recent history of immigration in the 19th and 20th centuries. The first determines the basic linguistic system that dominates the history of the speech community, following the doctrine of First Effective Settlement (Zelinsky 1992:13).[15]

It seems clear that the relative importance of Philadelphia among American cities has suffered a long decline. In the earlier periods of American history, Philadelphia was always a major factor in politics, economics, and

[15] "Whenever an empty territory undergoes settlement, or an earlier population is dislodged by invaders, the specific characteristics of the first group able to effect a viable, self-perpetuating society are of crucial significance for the later social and cultural geography of the area, no matter how tiny the initial band of settlers may have been" (Zelinsky 1992:13).

ideology. It was founded by the Quakers, and their influence on attitudes and policies within the city has never been absent. It was the national capital until 1800, and was the leading city in manufacturing until the 1840s, when New York took the lead (Feldberg 1973).

Philadelphia has been said to be unique among 18th-century American cities in its policy of religious toleration, and its position as an anchor point in the "Underground Railroad" for escaping slaves reflected a long-established tradition of opposition to slavery among the Quakers. At the same time, the Quakers in the 1830s and 1840s generally supported the propertied electorate in the series of campaigns that opposed the wealthy to the unpropertied white artisans and mechanics (Alexander 1973).

Among the linguistic influences that determined the character of the local dialect, we can detect a number of features common to Scots-Irish immigrants from the north of Ireland. While all of the other major cities of the Eastern Seaboard adopted the London pattern of vocalized postvocalic /r/ – Boston, Providence, New York, Richmond, Charleston, Savannah – Philadelphia has retained a strongly constricted [r] in this position. The use of *anymore* in positive sentences like *Farmers are pretty scarce around here anymore* is general in Philadelphia, a grammatical pattern that is common throughout Northern Ireland. Another characteristic grammatical feature of Philadelphia, the use of the auxiliary *be* with *finish* and *done*, as in *I'm finished my breakfast*, is again widely reported in Northern Irish dialects.

The Philadelphia that we are studying now has added many components to the original population pattern. A comprehensive review of the development of social heterogeneity in Philadelphia is presented by the various chapters in Davis and Haller 1973 (particularly chs 6–12). During the 18th and early 19th centuries, immigration was primarily from English Protestants and Germans. Though the city was never a primary port of immigration like New York, the successive entrance of ethnic groups followed the same pattern as that of New York. The present composition of both cities is the result of three successive waves of immigration: the "Old" immigrants, Irish, Germans, and British, settled in the 1840s and 1850s; the "New" immigrants, Italians, Poles, and Russian Jews, arrived between 1885 and 1914; and the "newest" immigrants, African Americans and Hispanics, entered the northern cities in the years following World War II. The Philadelphia Social History Project (PSHP) has traced the history of this immigration through a detailed study of the census data in the latter half of the 19th century, with its consequences for the family, work, and residential patterns of the city.

Table 2.2, from Hershberg 1981, shows the ethnic composition of Philadelphia from 1850 to 1970. The totals on the bottom row register the successive waves of immigration as increases of roughly half a million. The 1850 population of 400,000 was more than doubled by the first wave of immigration of the Irish and Germans; by 1880, the Irish first and second

*Table 2.2* Percent black and foreign origin in Philadelphia: 1850–1970

| | *1850* | *1880* | *1900* | *1930* | *1970* |
|---|---|---|---|---|---|
| Black | 4.8 | 3.6 | 4.8 | 11.3 | 33.6 |
| Irish | | | | | |
| born | 17.6 | 11.9 | 7.6 | 2.7 | 0.4 |
| 2nd gen. | | 27.0 | 21.2 | 9.4 | 2.3 |
| German | | | | | |
| born | 5.6 | 6.6 | 5.5 | 1.9 | 0.6 |
| 2nd gen. | | 9.6 | 9.6 | 4.8 | 1.4 |
| Italian | | | | | |
| born | | 0.2 | 1.4 | 3.5 | 1.3 |
| 2nd gen. | | | 0.9 | 5.8 | 4.0 |
| Polish | | | | | |
| born | | 0.1 | 0.6 | 1.6 | 0.6 |
| 2nd gen. | | 0.3 | 0.3 | 5.8 | 1.8 |
| Russian (Jewish) | | | | | |
| born | | 0.03 | 2.2 | 4.5 | 1.3 |
| 2nd gen. | | | 1.3 | 5.3 | 3.2 |
| Total foreign | | | | | |
| born | 29.0 | 24.2 | 22.8 | 18.9 | 6.5 |
| 2nd gen. | | 30.4 | 32.1 | 31.7 | 16.6 |
| Total population | 408,081 | 840,584 | 1,293,697 | 1,950,961 | 1,950,098 |

Source: Hershberg et al. 1981, table 2, p. 468

generations represented 39% of the total population, and the Germans 16%; together with the 3.8% of British immigration, this comes to an almost 50% increase from immigration alone. The Italian population first makes a significant impact in 1900, and by 1930 the Italian first and second generations represented almost 10% of the population of two million. An equal number is received from Russia, largely Russian Jews; and if we add 150,000 immigrants from Poland, the total of this second wave of immigration is 26.6% of the 1970 population of 1,950,000, or 520,000.

The third wave of immigration, recorded in 1970, was the massive movement of blacks from the rural South to the northern cities. The population of blacks increased from 11% in 1930 to 33.6% in 1970. This was not accompanied by any further increase in the overall population; the replacement of the previous population by blacks was the result of several shifts to areas outside of the city limits: the upper middle class groups moved to the western and northwestern suburbs, the lower middle class and working class to southern New Jersey and southwest of the city. This trend has continued at a slower rate through the 1970s and 1980s: the 1990 census showed that the population declined to 1,700,000 and the percentage of blacks increased to 38% in 1980 and 40% in 1990.

All of these rapid waves of immigration produced problems of housing, and eventually led to the construction of the two- or three-story row houses that define the city of Philadelphia today.[16] Some of the residential patterns of early immigration have persisted; others have not. The German immigration of the 1850s was the first and most rapid, and heavily concentrated in the area northeast of Center City. But since that time, the German population has dispersed over most parts of the city, so that there is no heavy concentration of people of German stock today in any one area. The Irish were originally more dispersed, since there were simply not enough row houses in the central areas to hold them, and many wound up in "alley dwellings," improvised shacks in the back areas of regular houses. However, there was a heavy concentration in South Philadelphia and in Kensington.

The central problem of a neighborhood study was to construct a sample of residential areas that would represent the population that acquired and developed the Philadelphia vernacular in the course of the last hundred years.

## 2.3 The exploratory phase

In the first year of LCV operations, we engaged in a wide range of exploratory interviews. Almost 100 subjects were interviewed, and a number of vowel systems analyzed. It became clear to us that the study of the evolution of the Philadelphia vernacular would be concentrated in the white population, since the great majority of black speakers use a form of the African American Vernacular English that is almost identical to that used in New York, Detroit, Chicago, and Los Angeles. The range of socioeconomic classes to be covered would begin with the middle working class (since the lowest echelon of the working class was primarily black and Puerto Rican). Since the upper middle class had largely migrated to suburban areas, a representative sub-community would probably best be located outside of the city limits. No single area within the city itself could represent the working class or lower middle class groups, since various sections of the city showed concentrations of different ethnic groups with different rates of social mobility.

With the help of data from the 1970 Census and the many other studies of Philadelphia mentioned above, we picked five areas as sites for long-term neighborhood studies.

[16] I am drawing here upon Burstein 1981, one of the PSHP reports, for the most accurate and detailed view.

## 2.4 The Neighborhood Study

It was logical to include *Kensington* in North Philadelphia as one of the major sites. Kensington was historically a mill and factory section that attracted heavy Irish settlement in the middle of the 19th century (Warner 1968:178–83, Binzen 1970:85–99, Clark 1973, Hershberg 1981). The area figures in the folk tradition of Philadelphia as one of the toughest and most Irish sections of the city.[17]

Our second and third sites were located in *South Philadelphia.* This section of the city was populated in the mid-1800s by the overflow of Irish immigrants from Kensington, attracted by the cheap housing, railroads, and shipyards along the Delaware and Schuylkill Rivers (Clark 1973:135–54). The early 1900s brought waves of Italian immigrants, who settled in the areas below South Street, and by the 1930s, the area had become heavily Italian (Varbero 1973:264–72, Warner 1968:183–5). Though many of the more established and affluent Irish had by this time moved across the river into West Philadelphia, a remnant of the South Philadelphia Irish community can still be found along the Schuylkill River in the Gray's Ferry section,[18] and along the Delaware River in the "Two Street" or *Pennsport* section, that is, along Second Street (3 in figure 2.2). South Philadelphia is now identified primarily as an Italian area, the main source of support for Italians who are competing with the Irish for dominance in the public life of the city. "South Philadelphia" has become the accepted label for a stereotype of working class Philadelphia speech, as "Brooklynese" has for New York City (2 in figure 2.2).

A search for characteristic middle class neighborhoods must look away from the center of Philadelphia toward the city's boundaries,[19] and to the suburbs beyond. We selected one such area in *Overbrook,* at the periphery of West Philadelphia (4 in figure 2.2). In the middle-to-late 1800s, when Kensington mills and South Philadelphia shipyards were attracting immigrant labor, West Philadelphia consisted of small villages, farms, and private estates (Warner 1968). Through the first half of the 20th century, this district remained residential. In 1935, it contained only 6.8% of the city's factories, while the northeast areas that included Kensington contained 40%. At the same time, the northern half of West Philadelphia, which includes Overbrook Park, had taken on a distinctly lower middle class

[17] Among Philadelphia gangs, one of the best known is *K&A*, or *Kensington & Allegheny*. Like almost all Philadelphia street groups, it is named for the corner on which the group hung out most often.

[18] Gray's Ferry has been the site of the most recent racial conflicts to come to public attention, the product of an attack on black residents by white Irish youth.

[19] There is a sizeable upper middle class population in "Center City." But as we have found in other studies, these usually do not form integrated neighborhoods where we could study social interaction among the residents.

character: upwardly mobile Italians, Jews, and African Americans. (At the time of our study, Overbrook Park had a very high proportion of Jews.) Warner 1968 notes that compared to Kensington and South Philadelphia the intensity of neighborhood life in these areas was diminished – at least as far as adults were concerned.

The upper middle class area was selected with two purposes in mind. For the study of the acquisition of the Philadelphia dialect (Payne 1976, 1980), we needed an area where sizeable numbers of high-status families had moved into the Philadelphia region and large numbers of children of various ages were growing up with varying periods of exposure to the Philadelphia dialect. For our overall study of the social stratification of Philadelphia speech, we needed an upwardly mobile middle class population of people raised in the middle of Philadelphia, who had made the characteristic move to a new suburban community with detached houses. Such a move required that neighborhood ties be entirely recreated.

King of Prussia (5 in figure 2.2) is a suburb to the west of Philadelphia, connected to Center City by railroad or a 40-mile drive on the Schuylkill Expressway. Before World War II, it was farmland: since then, the area had been developed as a research and technical-industrial center. General Electric, Western Electric, IT&T, and General Motors situated administrative offices there, and these firms are largely responsible for the influx of white-collar and professional workers into this residential area.

A study of Philadelphia speech would be incomplete without a record of the speech used by the upper class of this area. No previous sociolinguistic study had included the upper class of that community. As we observed in chapter 1, some explanations of sound change are based on the idea that forms spread through borrowing by groups with lower prestige from groups with higher prestige; the upper class represents the upper limit of this process. The Philadelphia upper class is established in journalism and literature as an exclusive and privileged group at the highest level (Baltzell 1958). In 1978–9, Anthony Kroch carried out a study of the upper class through a series of chained introductions, using the interviewing methods of LCV (Kroch 1996), and these now form an integral part of the neighborhood study.

## *Selection of the blocks*

Each of the neighborhood studies was centered around a "block," defined as the set of houses that face each other across the length of a residential street from one intersection to another, along with the corner stores and other sites of social interaction. Two sets of criteria were used to choose a block to represent a particular neighborhood. First, the block should be representative of the neighborhood as a whole, as reflected in census tract figures for house values, occupation, percent foreign, and so on. We considered only blocks that were centrally located in the neighborhood selected, separated by some distance from regions with radically different population. This meant that none of the blocks we chose were close to areas with high percentages of African American residents.

A second consideration was that the kind of social interaction on the block should facilitate contact with social networks. This implied three characteristics of a favorable site:

(a) Residential stability with full occupation of dwelling units, and many adults who had grown up in the neighborhood.
(b) Relatively soft interfaces between public and private space,[20] with a resultant high level of social interaction among residents.
(c) A moderate number of shopping and recreation sites in the immediate vicinity, with a consequent high level of interaction.

Five blocks that satisfied these criteria were chosen to represent the five neighborhoods described above. They will be referred to in the chapters to follow as:

| | | | Census tract |
|---|---|---|---|
| Wicket Street | in | Kensington | 177 |
| Pitt Street | in | Pennsport | 42 |
| Clark Street | in | South Philadelphia | 40 |
| Mallow Street | in | Overbrook Park | 98 |
| Nancy Drive | in | King of Prussia | 2058 |

The upper class speakers interviewed by Kroch come from several different neighborhoods, but will be referred to by the best known of these, "Chestnut Hill" (6 in figure 2.2).

The most comprehensive analyses of the neighborhood studies will include several subsidiary neighborhoods with data from preliminary and exploratory work. The South Philadelphia neighborhoods will be supplemented by two additional networks: a series of interviews carried out in our exploratory work by W. Inverso among upper working class adult residents of central South Philadelphia, labeled simply "South Philadelphia;" and a final series of interviews carried out by Anne Bower of a corner group of adolescents at 6th and Wallace Sts. The North Philadelphia neighborhoods are represented by small samples from the working class areas of

[20] The concept of "hard" and "soft" interfaces was developed by the Danish architect Jan Gehl (1977), in his study of the effect of residential structure on social interaction. A *soft* interface is one that favors a high degree of interaction among residents; typical are row houses that enter directly on the street, or front yards with low fences that people talk across; a *hard* interface inhibits such interaction. Typical hard interfaces are high stone walls surrounding a property, or large lawns and setbacks that remove residents from contact with each other.

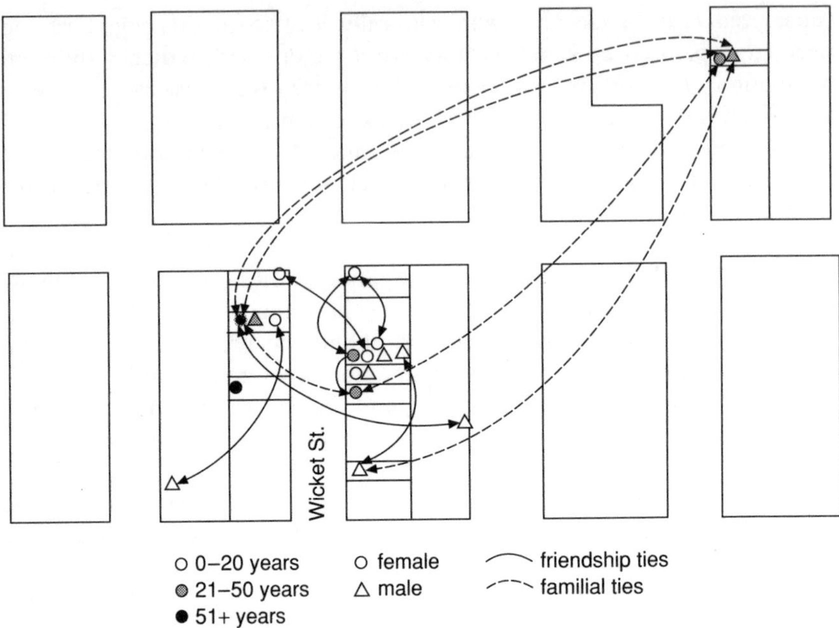


*Figure 2.3* Two family networks in the Wicket Street neighborhood

Fishtown and [Port] Richmond. The middle class groups are supplemented by several individuals from the northeast. But the most systematic and controlled data are derived from the five block studies. They represent the core of our analysis of the relation of social interaction to sociolinguistic stratification and change.

The block is a starting point for locating social networks, not a basic unit for the description of language. Inevitably, family and friendship ties within these networks carried our investigations outside the physical block as defined above. Nevertheless, the highly local character of interaction in the working class neighborhoods insured that a majority of the meaningful social contacts were on the block or very close to it. Figure 2.3 locates 20 speakers in the Wicket Street study: all but four are on the original "block."

The dashed lines on figure 2.3 show the family ties among the people interviewed; the solid lines show friendship ties. These relations are based on the participant observation of Anne Bower over a period of three years, rather than data derived from any one question. At first glance, it seems that all of these speakers are interconnected; but on closer examination, they can be seen to form two distinct social networks. At the northern end of the Wicket Street block, we find six persons from the Moran, Haley, Connelly, Donnelly, and Danehy families connected to four of the five members of the Corcoran family: this is the "Corcoran network," centered about the central member of the Corcoran family (Kate). Across the street is the Kendell family, the center of a more wide-ranging network that includes one individual on the next block and two relatives living several blocks away; altogether, three of the four members of the Kendell family are linked to five other persons. The sole point of contact is through the younger son of the Corcoran family who is a friend of a son of the Danehy family at the lower end of the block, who is related to an older couple who live several blocks away and who are in turn relatives of the Kendells.

The two networks are effectively disjunct, and to some extent hostile. Meg, the female head of the Kendell family, is a proper, upwardly mobile person, who became an office manager in the course of the study. Kate, the female head of the Corcoran family, does not consider herself a striver, and looks askance at people who think they are better than others. The linguistic behavior of these people will be related to their social behavior in a later chapter. The important point here is that a field worker who studied the block through a single contact would not have been able to enter both networks. Corcorans would not refer her to Kendells and Kendells would not refer her to Corcorans. The general pattern of LCV field work recognizes this problem, and requires that field work in any area begin with several unrelated entry points.

The Corcoran family will play a major role in our pursuit of the leaders of linguistic change in chapters 10–13. The approach to field methods used in the neighborhood studies and the techniques for gathering data are presented in Labov 1984.

## *Demographic characteristics of the blocks*

### CENSUS TRACT DATA

The neighborhoods described above include a number of census tracts; the blocks are selected in tracts that are representative of all the tracts in the neighborhoods. Census tract data has much more information than block data, and comparison of the blocks can best be made by using the tract information.

Table 2.3 lists a number of sets of indices that show how the five blocks are differentiated by education, house value, occupation, and ethnicity. Income and schooling set up four strata among the blocks:

Wicket Street

---

Pitt Street
Clark Street

---

Mallow Street

---

Nancy Drive

---

*Table 2.3* Census tract data for five neighborhoods

| | *Kensington: Wicket Street* | *Pennsport: Pitt Street* | *So. Phila: Clark Street* | *Overbrook: Mallow Street* | *King of Prussia: Nancy Drive* |
|---|---|---|---|---|---|
| Census tract | 177 | 42 | 40 | 98 | 2058 |
| Population | 11,215 | 12,759 | 13,074 | 9,325 | 6,943 |
| *Socioeconomic* | | | | | |
| Median family income ($) | 8,250 | 9,218 | 9,186 | 11,019 | 15,565 |
| Median school years | 9.5 | 9.7 | 9.6 | 12.2 | 12.9 |
| Median house value ($) | 6,500 | 7,800 | 11,000 | 14,300 | 28,000 |
| *Occupation* | | | | | |
| Total employed | 4,259 | 4,948 | 5,419 | 4,206 | 2,460 |
| Professional, technical (%) | 4.3 | 7.4 | 8.1 | 13.2 | 21.3 |
| Clerical (%) | 22.9 | 24.5 | 21.3 | 24.5 | 11.4 |
| Craftsmen, foremen etc. (%) | 15.9 | 15.9 | 18.1 | 11.8 | 6.3 |
| Service workers (%) | 10.6 | 13.9 | 12.4 | 6.5 | 4.2 |
| *Ethnicity (%)* | | | | | |
| Native-born | 80.4 | 76.6 | 50.7 | 46.7 | 83.2 |
| Native, foreign parents | 16.1 | 17.8 | 36.2 | 39.2 | 13.7 |
| Foreign-born | 3.5 | 5.6 | 13.1 | 14.1 | 3.0 |
| Origin: | | | | | |
| (UK), Eire | 5.2 | 2.0 | 0.9 | 0.4 | 0.6 |
| Italy | 1.4 | 2.5 | 43.6 | 7.5 | 3.1 |
| Eastern Europe | 7.5 | 12.3 | 0.9 | 34.5 | 3.6 |
| Percent black | 0.0 | 0.2 | 0.2 | 0.1 | 0.9 |

Source: US Census 1970

The value of houses (and rents) preserves this stratification, but separates Pitt Street clearly from Clark Street. Differences in the architectural development of the two blocks will play an important role in studying how cultural and ethnic patterns affect social interaction.

The occupational data in table 2.3 shows a broad range across all neighborhoods, which are differentiated quantitatively rather than qualitatively. The sharpest contrast is in the proportion of professional and technical workers, which is five times as great in Nancy Drive as in Wicket Street; again, Pitt Street and Clark Street are grouped together, with a small advantage for Clark Street. The percentage of clerical workers is almost the same for all blocks except for Nancy Drive, where it is about half. The highest percentage of skilled workers is to be found in Clark Street.

The figures on ethnicity in table 2.3 are somewhat obscured because the census definition of "Foreign stock" and figures on origins only include the first (non-native) and second generation. Since the Irish and German immigration occurred over a hundred years before 1970, the figures do not reflect the high percentage of Irish-Americans in Wicket Street. More recent immigration is indicated by the fact that almost half of the residents of the Clark Street tract are of Italian origin and over a third on Mallow Street are Jewish residents from Eastern Europe. Nancy Drive shows the smallest percentage of foreign stock. A good number of the Nancy Drive families are Irish-Americans, but further removed from their entrance into American society than the inner city populations, as one would expect from their social position.

None of the census tracts show a significant percentage of black residents; only at Nancy Drive does the figure approach 1%.

The combined view of socioeconomic indices might lead us to label Nancy Drive as an upper middle class neighborhood, Mallow Street as lower middle class, Clark Street and Pitt Street as upper working class, and Wicket Street as middle working class. But it will become clear that residence in a neighborhood does not define socioeconomic status, and the range within neighborhoods is considerable (see table 2.5 below).

The census also provides information on the particular blocks studied: table 2.4 shows percent black, percent under 18 years, over 62, and number of houses owned and rented. In terms of age distributions, Nancy Drive shows the expected high percentage of children and only 1% of the population is over 62: this is a new community recently settled by couples. The most striking difference among the blocks is the proportion of renters: the lowest socioeconomic block, Wicket Street, shows 16 of 58 houses rented, while everyone on Nancy Drive owns their own house. Yet the blocks are all similar – and characteristic of Philadelphia as a whole – in that they are stable communities of predominantly house owners.

*Table 2.4* Block statistics for five Philadelphia neighborhoods

| | *Kensington: Wicket Street* | *Pennsport: Pitt Street* | *So. Phila: Clark Street* | *Overbrook: Mallow Street* | *King of Prussia: Nancy Drive* |
|---|---|---|---|---|---|
| Percent black | 0.0 | 0.2 | 0.2 | 0.1 | 0.9 |
| Total population | 199 | 184 | 227 | 179 | 143 |
| Percent under 18 | 40 | 23 | 42 | 22 | 52 |
| Percent over 62 | 12 | 20 | 6 | 16 | 1 |
| Total housing units | 58 | 59 | 63 | 58 | 31 |
| Owner | 42 | 53 | 59 | 51 | 31 |
| Renter | 16 | 6 | 4 | 7 | 0 |

## *A direct view of the blocks*

It may be helpful here to provide a sketch of the physical and social layout of each block, as seen through the eyes of the field workers as they entered the block and made the initial contacts.

Wicket Street is a long, narrow assembly of fifty brick row houses, which differ only in the presence or absence of storm doors, aluminum sashes, and storm windows. It is a general characteristic of Irish-American row house neighborhoods that the outside structures are maintained without change. This Irish blue-collar neighborhood was evenly divided into families with teenage or married children, older retired couples, and single persons who have lived on the block 30 or 40 years. For the men, the modal occupation on Wicket Street was blue-collar: men's jobs are largely in the class of "operatives" – truck drivers, cab drivers, heavy construction equipment operators – but we also found mechanics, appliance repairmen, and skilled craftsmen. Several household heads had occupations associated with the lower middle class: salesmen or store managers. In spite of the relatively low economic status of Wicket Street, unemployment was minimal in the 1970s: only one family head was unemployed, and one was temporarily laid off. Working women were either clerical or service workers, but the majority stayed home. The median years of school completed for residents interviewed was 10.7, a year more of high school than the census tract as a whole.

The basically Irish Pitt Street neighborhood in Pennsport was similar to Wicket Street in many respects. The median years of school completed by those interviewed was also 10.7. A few more women worked than on Wicket Street, as clerical, service, or factory workers. Several heads of households owned small businesses, or managed sections of department stores or food stores. On the whole, Pitt Street residents showed slightly more upward mobility than those on Wicket Street. The outer appearance of the row houses indicated a high level of prosperity, with more new fronts and improvements. This is in part due to the presence of Italian norms for house upkeep (see below), and a weakening of the general Irish-American inhibition against such changes.

Clark Street shows a much greater variety of structural and functional changes in house fronts. Most of the 40 houses show alterations: windows widened, bow or bay windows installed, brick fronts replaced, stone facing applied, cornices straightened, or new steps with iron railings. Repeated renovations of this type are characteristic of the more prosperous Italian-dominated areas of the inner city. The older population of Clark Street included a number of retired people, whose former occupations indicated the same mixture of skilled blue-collar and white-collar jobs as the current working population: foremen, draftsmen, contractors, independent tailors, painters and paper hangers, insurance salesmen, car salesmen, and clerical workers. The median years of school completed by the people interviewed was 11.8, considerably above the census tract median and the other two working class neighborhoods.

The lower middle class area of Mallow Street also contains row houses, but the overall configuration is quite different. The streets are lined with trees, houses are set back from the street, and there is room for parking on both sides of the street. Most of the men interviewed were white-collar workers: salesmen, bookkeepers, civil service workers, department store section managers, small businessmen. Most women stayed home, though several worked part-time as elementary school aides or clerks. The median number of years of school completed by people interviewed was 11.3, less than the 12.2 of the census tract, and slightly lower than Clark Street. Nine of the 13 interviewed were Jewish.

Nancy Drive is on a cul-de-sac in a hilly area of King of Prussia. The street is lined with identical split level houses with red brick fronts and white aluminum siding, garages, front lawns, and landscaped grounds. The people interviewed had a median number of school years of 13.9, a year more of college than the tract as a whole. The men worked as accountants, salesmen, office and business managers, and supervisors for departments of the large corporations of King of Prussia. Half of the women worked at part- or full-time professional jobs or higher level white-collar jobs.

Though we first approached the neighborhoods as relatively homogeneous populations, distinct from each other, it became apparent that the range of socioeconomic status within the working class blocks was quite large, greater than the distinctions between the neighborhoods. The views just provided of the blocks indicate the material substrate from which the other parameters of the population will be drawn across neighborhoods: age, gender, social class, and ethnicity. Yet we will continue to test the effect of residence in one of these neighborhoods as one of the parameters to be used in tracing the path of linguistic change, and chapter 7 will focus upon neighborhood as a sociolinguistic parameter. The further analyses of chapters 10–12 will carry us into the patterns that govern interaction within each neighborhood.

## *Measures of social class and status*

Any discussion of social class must confront the difficulty that most American linguists have in dealing with this topic. Suspicion of the concept of social class is a long tradition in American academic and journalistic circles. On the one hand, this reflects a tendency to hear the term "social class" as a symptom of a left-wing ideology that evokes conflicts alien to our mobile society. Among sociolinguists, the reverse view is more common: the criticism that American sociology has somehow, in describing social class as a functioning and stable system, accepted the social inequities that are a part of that system and overlooked the conflicts within American society.

A third frequently expressed notion is that sociolinguists who use the techniques for describing social class developed in the United States have adopted a set of labels in an uncritical way, without examining their applicability to the particular community under study. The underlying assumption is that the indicators and constructs used to describe an American city are intended to apply to cities throughout the world. Studies of cities in Asia or South America often begin by refuting this presumed sociolinguistic imperialism.

In the course of rejecting socioeconomic categorization, some scholars have argued that social network data be substituted for social class analysis. It has been proposed more than once that the density or multiplexity of local networks can be used to account for linguistic behavior without taking into account the socioeconomic hierarchy and its assignment of symbolic capital. It seems unlikely that such local fine-tuning will account for the social stratification of the larger society. Chapter 10 of this volume will show that in fact, social network data forms an important addendum to socioeconomic analysis, not a substitute for it.

One or the other of these ideological positions has led some researchers to reject the use of social categories to subdivide their subjects. Instead, they advocate that speakers be grouped by frequencies of linguistic variables, and that the social characteristics of these linguistic groups be examined subsequently. This is equivalent to taking the linguistic variables as the independent variables, and social factors as dependent variables – a well recognized and useful procedure, which will be followed more than once in the course of this volume.[21] When the output clusters the data in ways that match recognized categories, the results can be gratifying, but these atheoretical approaches do not always extract clear answers to the questions posed. The interpretation of the dimensions of a factor analysis is a matter of persuasive insight rather than clear demonstration. Some groupings will show no common traits at all. This is almost inevitable where a curvilinear pattern is present: the fact that both lower and upper class Philadelphians show low values of (aw) does not mean that they share any positive features in contrast to others.

Since the principal aim of this investigation is to understand the evolution of language, and not the evolution of society, the analysis of this volume will begin with the more straightforward procedure of defining the linguistic variables as the dependent variables, and social factors as the independent variables. The primary task is to find out what factors determine the level of the linguistic variables, rather than to construct a new analysis of social life on the basis of linguistic behavior.

[21] Standard techniques for reducing variability within the data set include factor analysis (and principal component analysis), cluster analysis, and multi-dimensional scaling. See Poplack 1979, Horvath 1985, Horvath and Sankoff 1987, or the procedures of volume 1, chapter 18.

Many students of American society approach the measurement of social class from a subjective viewpoint, arguing that the fundamental basis of class is the prestige or status that people assign to various "crowds," "groups," or "classes" (Warner 1960, Hollingshead and Redlich 1958). At the same time, societies are stratified by differential access to socially valued resources, which can be measured objectively, and a great deal of effort has gone into correlating such objective indicators with measures of prestige. The objective "Index of Status Characteristics" developed by Warner was based on occupation (weight 4), income, house type, and dwelling area. Correlations of occupation with the subjective "Evaluated Participation" methods ranged from .91 to .78 (Kahl 1957:43). It is generally agreed that among objective indicators, occupation is the most highly correlated with other conceptions of social class, and much effort has gone into determining the prestige assigned to various occupations (Reiss 1965). However, many analysts feel that a multiple-item index is desirable. In 1961, Duncan matched the prestige assigned to occupations in NORC surveys with the 1950 census data on education and income levels of these occupations. Prestige was highly correlated with education (r = .84) and income (r = .85), somewhat more than education was correlated with income (r = .72). Multiple regression derived an expression which related education and income to prestige with an r of .91 (Duncan 1961). This approach to a combined index is updated by Nakao and Treas (1992).

Such combined indices are felt to be desirable for several reasons: a combined index will help explain more aspects of class-based behavior; it will tap different dimensions of socioeconomic status; and the consistency or inconsistency of various indicators will give us additional information about socioeconomic status patterns. A very large proportion of the useful and replicable results of sociolinguistic studies have been based on such indices; the curvilinear hypothesis that we are testing here was developed on the basis of objective quantitative measures of social class as employed by Trudgill (1974b), Cedergren (1973), and the original study of New York City (Labov 1966a).[22]

The first step in the construction of a socioeconomic index is to establish discrete categories for individual indicators. The LCV study created three six-category indices for occupation, education, and residence value, with categories close to those employed by the Census:

[22] For an early and comprehensive review of approaches to American class structure, see Kahl 1957, updated in Gilbert and Kahl 1993. The study of occupational indices, and methods of assigning prestige to them, is well developed by Reiss, Duncan, Hatt, and North (Reiss 1965) and worked out in detail in Duncan (1961) and Nakao and Treas (1990, 1992).

Education (E)

6 professional school
5 college graduate
4 some college
3 high school graduate
2 some high school
1 grade school

Occupation (O)

6 professional, owner-director of large firm
5 white-collar – proprietor, manager
4 white-collar – merchant, foreman, sales
3 blue-collar – skilled
2 blue-collar – unskilled
1 unemployed

Residence value (R)

6 $25,000+
5 $20,000–24,900
4 $15,000–19,900
3 $10,000–14,900
2 $5,000–9,900
1 $0–4,900

Let us now examine the distribution of these indices among the subjects interviewed in the five neighborhoods, to see how well we have succeeded in sampling the socioeconomic strata of Philadelphia through our neighborhood study. Figure 2.4 shows the percentage of each index value for each of the five neighborhoods. In figure 2.4(a), we can see that the two lowest ranking neighborhoods, Wicket Street and Pitt Street, have very similar occupational profiles, with the modal value in unskilled blue-collar jobs. Clark Street peaks at level 3, skilled blue-collar jobs. The small Mallow Street sample is concentrated in the lower level of white-collar occupations, and Nancy Drive shows the clear predominance of proprietors, owners, and professional people. Thus the occupational profiles of our neighborhood sample differs from the census tract data in a higher concentration of unskilled workers in Wicket and Pitt St. In this respect, Wicket and Pitt are more prototypical of the lower and middle working class than representative of the tract as a whole.

Figure 2.4(b) shows a rather different situation for the distribution of educational levels across neighborhoods. For all neighborhoods, the modal category is high school graduate. The only neighborhoods that show any number of persons with less than high school education are Wicket St. and

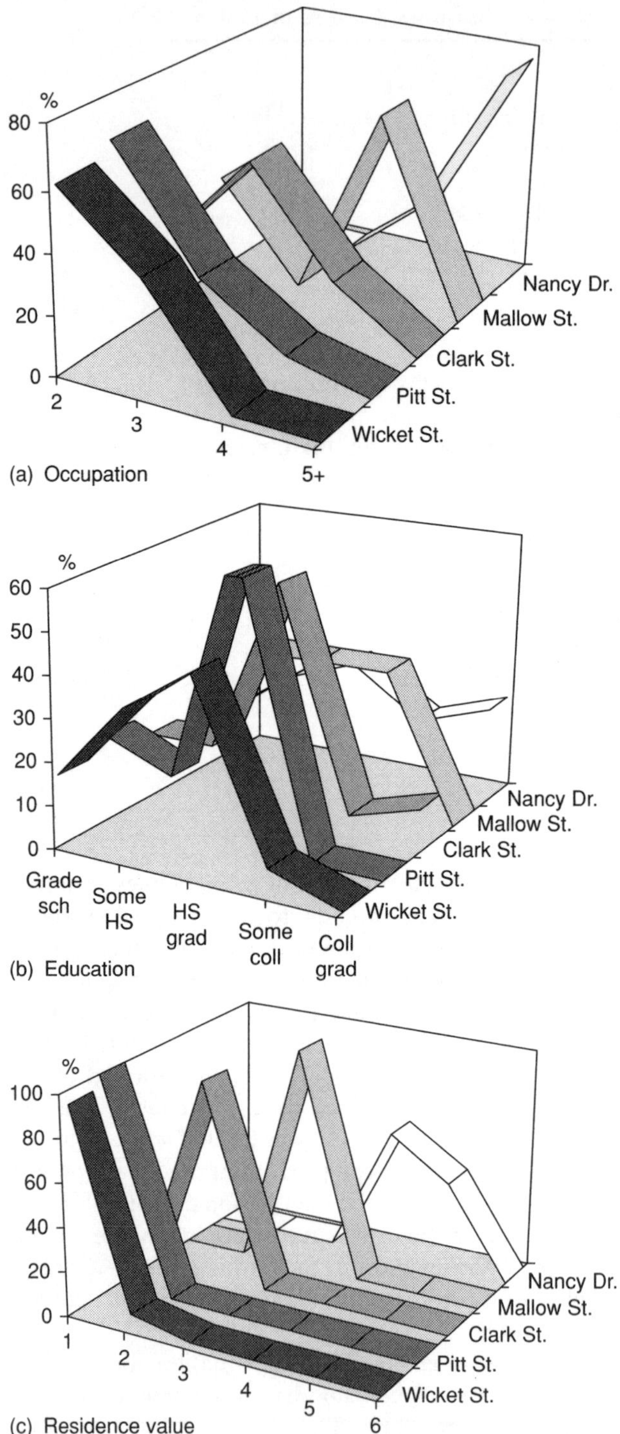


*Figure 2.4* Distribution of socioeconomic indices for five Philadelphia neighborhoods

Pitt St. The two South Philadelphia neighborhoods, Pitt St. and Clark St., have similar peaks for high school graduate, but Clark St. shows a small percentage with college training. It is evident that the block samples are less differentiated by education than by occupation.

It is only natural that house values would give us the sharpest stratification of the neighborhood blocks, since the houses on each block are very similar. Figure 2.4(c) shows the expected similarity of Wicket and Pitt St., with most house values at the lowest category 1; Clark St. next at 2; Mallow St. at 3; and Nancy Drive at 4 and 5. To sum up, the block samples were most clearly differentiated by house value, next by occupation, and least by education.

Since it is evident that the three indicators give only a partial view of the socioeconomic relations of the five blocks, a composite index of socioeconomic status (SES) is formed by summing the three scores to yield a single overall measure from 0 to 16. Table 2.5 shows the distribution of the SES index across all neighborhoods, including the data in individual and exploratory interviews. The five neighborhoods which have been most systematically studied are shown in rectangles. It is evident that there is considerable overlap in SES status across Wicket, Pitt, Clark, and Mallow Streets. On the other hand, all of our representatives of SES 11–14 are on Nancy Drive, and SES 15–16 is drawn from Kroch's interviews with upper class and upper middle class speakers. The modal values for the three working class groups (shown in bold) are shifted regularly upward, but there is no lack of contrast of the same SES rating in different neighborhoods. Multivariate analysis will then be able to isolate the separate contributions of neighborhood membership and SES index to the progress of change. Diagrams for the separate indicators: occupation, schooling, and house value, show similar patterns.

Two other measures of social position add to our view of social class and status: *House upkeep* deals with the most easily visible signs of social status; *Mobility* deals with family histories, which are not so visible.

### HOUSE UPKEEP

In preliminary studies, it appeared that the SES index correlated social classes and linguistic behavior across neighborhoods, but there were status differences within each neighborhood that were not being reflected by differences in the SES index. Block residents were critically conscious of differences in the way that others maintained their houses. Among several families on a block who received the same SES score of 6, there were differences in house upkeep that seemed to us significant. One person might have remodeled the kitchen and basement, another replaced the outdoor foyer, another not renovated at all. Since we were interested in the relation between linguistic change and local status, contrasts such as these might well be significant.

*Table 2.5* Distribution of SES index across neighborhoods

| | *Socioeconomic status index* | | | | | | | | | | | | | | |
|---|---|---|---|---|---|---|---|---|---|---|---|---|---|---|---|
| | *2* | *3* | *4* | *5* | *6* | *7* | *8* | *9* | *10* | *11* | *12* | *13* | *14* | *15* | *16* | *Total* |
| Wicket St. | 1 | 1 | 7 | 5 | 3 | 1 | | | | | | | | | | 18 |
| (Richmond) | | | 2 | | 3 | | | | | | | | | | | 5 |
| (Fishtown) | | | | 4 | | | | | | | | | | | | 4 |
| Pitt St. | | 2 | 2 | 7 | 3 | 1 | | | | | | | | | | 15 |
| Clark St. | 1 | | 1 | 2 | 4 | 5 | | 3 | 4 | | | | | | | 20 |
| (So. Phila.) | | | | 1 | 1 | | 2 | | | | | | | | | 4 |
| Mallow St. | | | | | | 1 | 1 | 1 | | | | | | | | 3 |
| (Northeast) | | | | 1 | 1 | | | 1 | | | | | | | | 3 |
| Nancy Drive | | | | | | | | | 2 | 7 | | 4 | 4 | | | 17 |
| Chestnut Hill | | | | | 1 | | | | | | | | | 7 | 15 | 23 |
| Total | 2 | 3 | 12 | 20 | 16 | 8 | 3 | 5 | 6 | 7 | 0 | 4 | 4 | 7 | 15 | 112 |

The following scale was designed to take neighborhood norms into account in registering differences in house upkeep. It does not apply to the King of Prussia neighborhood, Nancy Drive, or the upper class speakers, who are not differentiated in this respect.

4 Major renovations to exterior and interior. New modern fixtures in bathroom, newest furniture. New front facade, front door, cornice straightened with new brickwork and tiles, new windows and front steps. Pointed to with satisfaction and approval.

3 Internal improvements to kitchen and bathroom, enlarging of rooms, new additions to furniture. External: visible improvements in air conditioning, front steps, windows. When young house owners are making improvements of this kind, it is good evidence that they intend to make the neighborhood their permanent home.

2 Kept up: painted and clean. No recent modern decorating improvements or renovation. The house is *not* pointed to as being in bad shape. Often neighborhood residents give a reason for its less-than-modern appearance, i.e., "Oh, Old Mrs. Seriatta lives there – for 52 years," or "They're a young couple, just renting."

1 Dilapidated: not up to the "kept up" standards of the block, no evidence of an effort to maintain the house. Window sills need painting, the door is battered, front pavement is littered or dirty. The difference between "kept up" and "dilapidated" often depends on *who* is in the house, and how the neighborhood perceives the dwellers' ability to work on the house.

0 Rundown: not often found in the five neighborhoods. Again, it depends on how the neighbors perceive the ability of the residents as to whether it is termed "rundown" or "dilapidated."

Table 2.6 shows the distribution of these categories of house upkeep across the five neighborhood blocks. There are only a few houses labeled "rundown," and these are in the working class neighborhoods. The principal contrast is between "Kept up" and "Improved." The proportion of residences "Improved" to "Kept up" increases regularly from Wicket (5:11) to Pitt (9:4) to Clark (14:4) to Mallow St. (2:0). It follows that this dimension does register an additional aspect of social stratification within and across neighborhoods.

#### SOCIAL MOBILITY

A number of previous studies have indicated that social mobility can be as highly correlated with sociolinguistic stratification as socioeconomic class (Labov 1966b, Chambers 1995). For stable sociolinguistic variables and changes from above, upwardly mobile speakers tend to adopt the favored prestige forms more than others. So far, no one has examined the relation

*Table 2.6* Distribution of house upkeep across neighborhoods

| | House upkeep | | | | | | |
|---|---|---|---|---|---|---|---|
| | *0* | *1* | *2* | *3* | *4* | *No data* | *Total* |
| Wicket St. | 0 | 1 | **11** | 5 | 1 | 0 | 18 |
| (Richmond) | 0 | 0 | 0 | 5 | 0 | 0 | 5 |
| (Fishtown) | 3 | 0 | 0 | 0 | 0 | 1 | 4 |
| Pitt St. | 0 | 1 | 4 | **9** | 0 | 1 | 15 |
| Clark St. | 0 | 2 | 4 | **14** | 0 | 0 | 20 |
| (South Phila.) | 0 | 0 | 0 | 3 | 0 | 1 | 4 |
| Mallow St. | 0 | 0 | 0 | **2** | 1 | 0 | 3 |
| (Northeast) | 1 | 0 | 1 | 0 | 0 | 1 | 3 |
| Nancy Drive | 0 | 0 | 0 | 0 | 0 | **17** | 17 |
| Kroch series | | 0 | 0 | 1 | 0 | **22** | 23 |
| Total | 4 | 4 | 20 | 39 | 2 | 43 | 112 |

of social mobility to changes from below, or essayed the role of social mobility with multivariate analysis. The index of social mobility applies to the family as a whole: it is formed by comparing the head of the household's occupation with that of his or her parents, according to the following scale:

2 Higher (Upwardly mobile)
1 Equal (Stable)
0 Lower (Downwardly mobile)

Table 2.7 shows the distribution of social mobility across the five neighborhood blocks. There are only a few individuals who are downwardly mobile,[23] and in the upper class group, there are several who have not maintained their upper class position. On the whole, the population is upwardly mobile, with 56% in that category. The proportion of upwardly mobile to stable speakers rises in a pattern rather similar to house upkeep, from Wicket (8:10) to Pitt (8:7) to Clark (15:4). The small Mallow Street group shows only one upwardly mobile subject. But here Nancy Drive shows a very high proportion of upward mobility (15:2), registering the typical social histories of the upper middle class. In this respect, social mobility yields a wider range of stratification than we will find in house upkeep, and parallels the range of SES index, except for the upper class.

[23] In Philadelphia as in New York City (Labov 1966a), the majority of those who are downwardly mobile are found in the black population.

*Table 2.7* Distribution of mobility across neighborhoods

| | *Parents' occupation compared to head of household's* | | | | |
|---|---|---|---|---|---|
| | *Lower* *0* | *Equal* *1* | *Higher* *2* | *No data* | *Total* |
| Wicket St. | 0 | **10** | 8 | 0 | 18 |
| (Richmond) | 0 | 0 | 5 | 0 | 5 |
| (Fishtown) | 3 | 0 | 0 | 1 | 4 |
| Pitt St. | 0 | 7 | **8** | 0 | 15 |
| Clark St. | 1 | 4 | **15** | 0 | 20 |
| (South Phila.) | 0 | 0 | 4 | 0 | 4 |
| Mallow St. | 0 | 2 | 1 | 0 | 3 |
| (Northeast) | 1 | 1 | 1 | 0 | 3 |
| Nancy Drive | 0 | 2 | **15** | 0 | 17 |
| Kroch series | 2 | **18** | 3 | 0 | 23 |
| Total | 7 | 44 | 60 | 1 | 112 |

ETHNICITY

The review of the settlement and immigration patterns in Philadelphia, and the strategy for selecting neighborhoods, leads to the expectation that each of the five neighborhoods will represent a different spectrum of ethnicity. If the effect of neighborhood is to be distinguished from that of ethnicity, there must be some contrast of ethnicity within each block.[24] Table 2.8 shows that there is indeed a very sharp differentiation of ethnicity by neighborhood. Wicket Street is almost entirely Irish, as are the nearby subjects in Fishtown, though the Richmond subjects are of a variety of other backgrounds. Clark Street is predominantly Italian, but Pitt Street shows the mixture of Italian, Irish, and other that we originally expected in selecting this neighborhood. Mallow Street is Jewish. Nancy Drive is a mixture of White Anglo-Saxon Protestant (WASP), German, and Irish, while the upper class subjects are almost entirely WASP background.

In addition to the ethnic background, we will want to know how many generations intervened between the entrance of the speaker's family into American society and their present situation. Table 2.9 shows the

[24] We distinguished speakers' primary ethnicity from their secondary ethnicity (where parents differed from each other in their own primary ethnicity) and entered both variables into our multivariate analyses. Secondary ethnicity did not prove to be a detectable influence, and our discussion here and in what follows is in terms of a person's primary identification with ethnic background.

*Table 2.8* Distribution of ethnicity across neighborhoods

| | *Ethnicity* | | | | | | |
|---|---|---|---|---|---|---|---|
| | *Wasp* | *Irish* | *German* | *Jewish* | *Italian* | *Other* | *Total* |
| Wicket St. | 0 | **17** | 0 | 0 | 0 | 1 | 18 |
| (Richmond) | 1 | 1 | 0 | 0 | 0 | 3 | 5 |
| (Fishtown) | 0 | 3 | 0 | 0 | 0 | 1 | 4 |
| Pitt St. | 0 | **9** | 0 | 0 | 4 | 2 | 15 |
| Clark St. | 0 | 3 | 0 | 0 | **15** | 2 | 20 |
| (South Phila.) | 0 | 0 | 0 | 0 | 4 | 0 | 4 |
| Mallow St. | 0 | 0 | 0 | 3 | 0 | 0 | 3 |
| (Northeast) | 0 | 1 | 0 | 1 | 0 | 1 | 3 |
| Nancy Drive | **9** | 3 | 5 | 0 | 0 | 0 | 17 |
| Kroch series | **22** | 1 | 0 | 0 | 0 | 0 | 23 |
| Total | 32 | 38 | 5 | 4 | 23 | 10 | 112 |

*Table 2.9* Distribution of generational status across neighborhoods

| | *Generational status in the USA* | | | | |
|---|---|---|---|---|---|
| | *First* | *Second* | *Third* | *>Third* | *Total* |
| Wicket St. | 0 | 5 | **6** | 7 | 18 |
| (Richmond) | 0 | 0 | 5 | 0 | 5 |
| (Fishtown) | 0 | 0 | 1 | 3 | 4 |
| Pitt St. | 1 | 0 | 5 | **9** | 15 |
| Clark St. | 0 | **8** | **8** | 4 | 20 |
| (South Phila.) | 0 | 1 | 2 | 1 | 4 |
| Mallow St. | 0 | 1 | **2** | 0 | 3 |
| (Northeast) | 0 | 0 | 0 | 3 | 3 |
| Nancy Drive | 0 | 0 | **11** | 6 | 17 |
| Kroch series | 0 | 1 | 0 | **22** | 23 |
| Total | 1 | 16 | 40 | 55 | 112 |

generational status of the 112 speakers of the neighborhood study. There is only one speaker born outside of the USA, but 16 whose parents were, and 40 of the third generation. The distribution in the various neighborhoods is what we would expect from the account of immigration and settlement given at the beginning of this chapter.

## 2.5 The telephone survey

The basic strategy of the Philadelphia LCV project, as outlined in 2.1, required a second survey of the city that would complement the neighborhood study with a completely different profile of sources of error. The sample for the telephone survey was constructed by a random selection from telephone listings in the Philadelphia directory. The number was called, and the first person who responded was asked if he or she would like to help in a brief survey of Philadelphia English. A preliminary series of questions ascertained if the speaker was born in Philadelphia; if so, permission was asked to record. The telephone interview lasted from 15 to 30 minutes, as compared to 45 to 90 minutes for the neighborhood study. It was relatively formal; the section that obtained spontaneous speech was largely devoted to the person's schooling and residential history (which was often quite extended) and the character of the neighborhood. The subject was asked for his or her ethnicity, in terms of "family background." One section dealt with attitudes toward Philadelphia speech, and the elicitation of minimal pairs. On the whole, the telephone interview was considerably more formal than the neighborhood interviews, which often engaged the subjects, their spouses, and friends in intimate and excited interaction. They were also shorter, so that the total amount of data available for the study of vowel systems was more limited. A number of black subjects identified themselves as African American, or were plainly African American from their style of speech: they were not included in the main sample for analysis. The entire telephone survey was designed and conducted by Donald Hindle, and is reported in detail in Hindle 1980.

The telephone interview therefore contained a number of sources of error that interfered with the goal of obtaining a representative sample of the Philadelphia vernacular: limited quantity of data, formality of style, and the possibility that some speakers who were not identified as members of the black Philadelphia community were in fact members. A fourth and serious source of error was the selection from those Philadelphians whose telephones were listed, and those who were not (or did not have telephones). Fortunately, we have a good means of detecting and measuring any bias in the telephone survey that stems from the difference between people who list their phones and those who do not. For the 112 speakers of the neighborhood survey, we know exactly who lists telephones and who does not. Table 2.10 shows for the five blocks, the upper class, and auxiliary studies the numbers of subjects interviewed whose telephones are unlisted and listed. A total of 42 – 38% – are unlisted. Since one must pay to have the telephone service not be listed, most people we have asked assume intuitively that the number of unlisted telephones correlates with socioeconomic status, with the highest proportion of unlisted telephones for the upper and middle classes. Table 2.10 shows a striking reversal of

*Table 2.10* Telephone listings by SES index

| *SEC* | *Unlisted* | *Listed* | *Total* | *% Unlisted* |
|---|---|---|---|---|
| LWC | | | | |
| 2 | 1 | 1 | 2 | |
| 3 | 3 | 0 | 3 | 80 |
| UWC | | | | |
| 4 | 4 | 8 | 12 | |
| 5 | 11 | 9 | 20 | |
| 6 | 12 | 4 | 16 | 56 |
| LMC | | | | |
| 7 | 4 | 4 | 8 | |
| 8 | 0 | 3 | 3 | |
| 9 | 3 | 2 | 5 | 44 |
| MMC | | | | |
| 10 | 4 | 2 | 6 | |
| 11 | 0 | 7 | 7 | 31 |
| UMC | | | | |
| 13 | 0 | 4 | 4 | |
| 14 | 0 | 4 | 4 | |
| 15 | 0 | 7 | 7 | 0 |
| UC | | | | |
| 16 | 0 | 15 | 15 | 0 |
| Total | 42 | 70 | 112 | 38 |

this assumption. No upper and upper middle class subjects pay to have their telephones not listed. However, the 69 working class subjects in working class neighborhoods all had telephones, but 38 had paid for unlisting. This practice is uniform in the three intact blocks: Wicket St., Pitt St., and Clark St. The percentage of those with unlisted telephones is inversely related to social class, reaching a peak of 80% for the small lower working class group.

The field workers for the various neighborhoods can give a reasonable accounting for this remarkable distribution after the fact. In the working class neighborhoods, a telephone number is regarded as a valuable resource, a jealously guarded social asset. It is a mark of confidence to give someone one's telephone number. Indeed, a great deal of social friction can be created if someone gives out another person's phone number without authorization. Members of these closed social networks are not particularly interested in receiving phone calls from sales people, bill collectors, surveyors, or general members of the community outside their immediate social circle. The other side of the coin is that members of (relatively) closed working class networks do not need to make themselves available to a wide range of outsiders.

The situation of middle class people is the converse. They want to be available to community organizations, professional contacts, and acquaintances who live in distant places. They have many open network connections to people who may search them out from a distance or after long periods of time, and a telephone listing is an important route for such contacts. The inconvenience of always being available to the telephone is now countered by such devices as answering machines. This has never been a problem for upper class people who do not answer their own telephones.

The bias introduced into the telephone survey by the inaccessibility of central members of working class networks is a serious one. The telephone respondents may be on the whole secondary or even peripheral members of the social networks being studied. The basic patterns of social stratification and differentiation may well be diluted in the telephone survey. Fortunately, we can test the extent of this bias by entering into our multivariate analyses of the neighborhood studies an independent variable that shows whether or not the speaker's telephone is listed (chapter 5).

A further limitation of the telephone survey is the quality of the telephone signal itself. We cannot expect to obtain as accurate a view of the vowel qualities from a telephone signal that is essentially limited to a band width of 100 to 3000 Hz; chapter 5 will explore this problem.

Acknowledging these biases and limitations of the telephone survey, let us consider its advantages. Figure 2.5 shows the geographic dispersion of the respondents to the telephone survey. The pepper-and-salt distribution indicates that there is no geographic bias; the telephone survey includes areas of Philadelphia that are not at all represented in the neighborhood study (most of the Northeast; most of West Philadelphia; Manayunk; Roxborough; Germantown). At the same time, the telephone survey does draw subjects from the same areas within the city as the neighborhood studies, as indicated on the map. There are one or two areas that are poorly represented: the Southwest, and North Central Philadelphia (where there is a heavy concentration of black and Hispanic residents).

Table 2.11 compares the social distribution of the telephone survey with that of the neighborhood study on three dimensions: age, sex, and SES index groups (upper class subjects are not included). The 10-year age categories and the four socioeconomic groups are identical for the two samples. We can see that both cover a fairly wide range, with representatives of both sexes in most age and socioeconomic groups. The neighborhood study is fairly well balanced for gender (50 men to 47 women), but there is a strong bias toward women in the telephone survey (19 men to 41 women). This indicates a pattern that has been found in many other studies: in working class areas, many men do not make themselves available

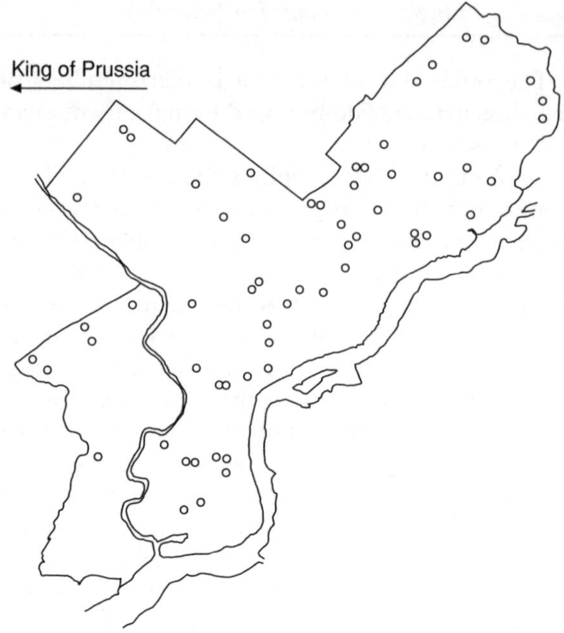


*Figure 2.5* Geographic distribution of Philadelphia subjects in the telephone survey

*Table 2.11* Distribution of subjects in the Philadelphia telephone survey and the neighborhood study by age, SEC, and gender. Upper class speakers not included.

| | *LWC, 0–3* | | *MWC, 4–6* | | *UWC, 7–9* | | *MC, 10–15* | | |
|---|---|---|---|---|---|---|---|---|---|
| *Age* | *F* | *M* | *F* | *M* | *F* | *M* | *F* | *M* | *TOTAL* |
| *The telephone survey* | | | | | | | | | |
| 5–14 | | | | | 1 | 2 | | | 3 |
| 15–24 | | 1 | 1 | | 3 | 2 | | | 7 |
| 25–34 | | | 2 | 1 | 3 | 3 | 3 | | 12 |
| 35–44 | | | 6 | 1 | 2 | 2 | 2 | 2 | 15 |
| 45–54 | | | 1 | | 2 | 1 | | | 4 |
| 55–64 | 3 | | 3 | 1 | 3 | 1 | 1 | 2 | 14 |
| 65–74 | 4 | | 1 | | | | | | 5 |
| TOTAL | 7 | 1 | 14 | 3 | 14 | 11 | 6 | 4 | 60 |
| *The neighborhood study* | | | | | | | | | |
| 5–14 | | | 3 | 4 | 2 | | 2 | 2 | 13 |
| 15–24 | | 2 | 5 | 9 | 1 | | 2 | 3 | 22 |
| 25–34 | 1 | | 7 | 4 | 2 | 3 | | | 17 |
| 35–44 | | | 3 | 2 | 1 | | 4 | 6 | 16 |
| 45–54 | | | 2 | | 1 | 1 | 2 | 3 | 9 |
| 55–64 | | | 1 | 1 | 1 | 2 | | 2 | 7 |
| 65–74 | 1 | 1 | 5 | 2 | 1 | 1 | | 2 | 13 |
| TOTAL | 2 | 3 | 26 | 22 | 9 | 7 | 10 | 18 | 97 |

on the telephone. We will want to keep these major differences in mind in interpreting any differences between the telephone survey and the neighborhood study. If the same social distribution of linguistic changes in progress should emerge in both, we can conclude that it is a very robust pattern indeed.

Because neither survey covers minority groups, the number of subjects in the lower working class, SES 0–3, is small. The main contrast of interest is between the middle working class, 4–6, the upper working class, 7–9, and the middle class groups. Because the telephone survey was not stratified by social class, the number of middle class subjects is relatively small: 10 out of 60 subjects. The largest proportion of telephone subjects is found in the upper working class. In spite of other limitations of the telephone study, this concentration may be helpful in searching for evidence of the curvilinear pattern according to the hypothesis developed in chapter 1.

# 3

# *Stable Sociolinguistic Variables*

## 3.1 The necessary background for the study of change in progress

This chapter will shift the focus of attention away from the problems of understanding linguistic change that have occupied the discussion so far in order to examine the opposite situation: stable linguistic variation. The first step in a considered study of linguistic change is not the examination of change, but rather an investigation of the sociolinguistic patterns in the particular speech community in question, in order to interpret the variable data of a suspected change in progress and differentiate it from stable sociolinguistic variables.

### *The relations of change and variation*

Early on, some students of variation thought that general principles would enable them to avoid a detailed examination of the sociolinguistic situation in each society (Bailey 1973). In this respect, they continued the traditional path toward an autonomous linguistics, in which explanations would come from within the field (Martinet 1955, Kurylowicz 1964). It was argued that linguistic change proceeded by purely linguistic principles, independent of any social effects. Accordingly, the analyst could interpret a report of linguistic variation as change in progress in a given direction without examining any further data on age distributions or real-time contrasts. Such inferences depended on the idea that "natural" changes were unidirectional.

> What is quantitatively less is slower and later; what is more is earlier and faster. (Bailey 1973:82)

#### THE NEED FOR EMPIRICAL INVESTIGATION OF EACH COMMUNITY

The program for autonomous linguistic principles that would abstract the investigation of change from the history of particular communities did not prove compatible with the data produced by sociolinguistic studies.

The recalcitrant nature of that data is displayed in three common features of change in progress:

1 Linguistic changes show a sporadic character, beginning and ending abruptly at times that are not predicted by any universal principles.
2 Stable, long-term variation that persists over many centuries in much the same form is perhaps even more common than changes which go to completion.
3 It is not uncommon to find retrograde movements, where the direction of change reverses, or opposing directions of movement in parallel communities.

All three of these features will appear in the changes in progress in Philadelphia which will be the major focus of this volume.

#### AN EMPIRICAL APPROACH TO GENERAL PRINCIPLES

This chapter will continue the search for the general principles that govern change by the modes of inference that were presented in volume 1, part A. As the final chapter of volume 1 pointed out, the broadest of these principles do not uniquely determine the output of a linguistic system. Yet if principles are of any use, they must rest on the foundation that similar forces produce similar results. The role of empirical research is to determine which configurations of social and linguistic factors are similar. While the same forces may operate persistently, they may be operating in a social context in which configurations of opposing forces reverse the normal result.[1] The LCV study of sound change in Philadelphia was formulated to test hypotheses that were formed in studies of New York City, Panama City, Norwich, and Detroit. To the extent that Philadelphia shares with these and other cities the general patterns of social and stylistic stratification of language, we can expect that changes in progress in the language will follow similar patterns, governed by similar principles.

We will therefore begin with an analysis of the stable sociolinguistic variables that have been studied most often in other English-speaking cities. To the extent that Philadelphia shows the same patterns for these variables as other cities, we can be confident that the principles of linguistic change drawn from the detailed analysis of Philadelphia will apply most generally.

### *Further exploration of the relations of apparent time to real time*

Volume 1, chapter 3 developed techniques for the analysis of age distributions viewed as "apparent time," and chapter 4 explored the relations of

[1] Though mergers are normally irreversible, some combination of social pressures may be strong enough to achieve such a reversal.

*Table 3.1* The relation of age-grading to change in progress

| | Socioeconomic class | | | |
|---|---|---|---|---|
| | *1 [Lowest]* | *2* | *3* | *4 [Highest]* |
| IA. Stigmatized feature: stable | | | | |
| Younger | high | higher | higher | low |
| Older | high | lower | lower | low |
| IB. Stigmatized feature: disappearing | | | | |
| Younger | [lower] | lower | lower | low |
| Older | [higher] | higher | higher | low |
| IIIA. Change from below: early stage | | | | |
| Youngest | high | high | high | medium |
| Young adults | medium | high | medium | low |
| Middle-aged | low | medium | low | low |
| Oldest | low | low | low | low |
| IIIB. Change from below: late stage with correction from above | | | | |
| Youngest | high | high | medium | medium |
| Young adults | high | high | low | medium |
| Middle-aged | medium | high | low | medium |
| Oldest | low | medium | low | low |

Source: adapted from Labov 1966a:325–31

this dimension to change in real time. Table 4.1 of that chapter set out four possible relations between the individual and the community: *stability*, where both remain constant; *age-grading*, where the individual changes but the community remains constant; *generational change*, where the individual preserves his or her earlier pattern, but the community as a whole changes; and *communal change*, where individuals and the community change together. A review of four real-time re-studies showed that an age-grading component was intimately mixed with the real-time changes that were taking place.

A more detailed model of the relations of real time and apparent time is seen in table 3.1, adapted from chapter 9 of Labov 1966a. Here it is apparent that stable variation cannot be distinguished from change in progress by the absence of significant differences in age distributions. On the contrary, in case IA when there is no change in the community as a whole, younger speakers use socially stigmatized features more than older speakers. Thus age-grading is a normal component of stable sociolinguistic variation.

The main problem then is to distinguish age-graded stable variation from generational change in progress. As we add the available sociolinguistic information to the picture, it begins to appear that stable age-grading is not independent of social class. In case IA, the highest and lowest social groups have the same values for both older and younger speakers: it is only the central groups that show age-grading. This situation is effectively reversed when the stigmatized feature begins to erode under social pressure. Younger speakers use it less than older speakers, but here again the significant differentiation is in the central groups, where the wave-like motion of change from below will begin.

This view of stable age-grading of a stigmatized feature can then be contrasted with one in which the stigmatized feature is being eliminated, as in the case of /ʌy/ in New York City or the elimination of rural Southern features in Anniston (Feagin 1979).[2] Here the age relationships are reversed, and younger speakers use stigmatized elements less rather than more.

Evidence for change in progress from below will be drawn from the more detailed profiles of type IIIA. Here change first appears in the middle-aged stratum of the second lowest status group, and spreads gradually to younger strata of neighboring social groups. This conforms to the curvilinear hypothesis, and not only permits change to begin in an interior social group, but precludes innovation in the extreme groups 1 and 4.

The advancement of the change from below leads to the complications of case IIIB. The change continues to progress in the two lowest social groups, but recedes in the higher groups, particularly in the second highest. As this correction continues, it gradually converges with type IA. As the 1966 discussion concluded, "The ensuing complications may become so great that we would be forced to give up the attempt to analyze apparent time, and rely instead upon whatever evidence we have from earlier studies in real time."[3]

The interpretation of apparent-time data therefore requires detailed information on social class distributions at all age levels.[4] In Philadelphia,

[2] Feagin's study allows us to contrast a number of cases of the elimination of older features of the rural pattern with the incoming increase in the use of the *get* passive, which follows the pattern of Type III in table 3.1.

[3] This type of correction is not inevitable, and is observed much more in Eastern and Southern cities than in the North Central and Inland North states.

[4] Much recent discussion of the problem has concentrated on the question of whether real-time data confirm apparent-time inferences. The most detailed exploration of this sort is the work of Bailey et al. 1991, who assemble strong bodies of evidence to contrast variables of type IB with those of type IIIB. Their initial approach to the problem does not reflect the considerations given above: "The basic assumption underlying apparent time, of course, is that unless there is evidence to the contrary, differences among generations of adults mirror

we were fortunate to obtain reasonable detailed real-time evidence for the fact that at least seven vowel phonemes are involved in real-time change. The converse side of the problem is to determine whether the sociolinguistic variables that we assume to be stable are in fact stable, and to see whether their age and social profiles match the patterns of table 3.1. The close comparison of stable and progressive variation in Philadelphia will then provide two distinct templates of age distributions. This can then be applied to help make inferences from apparent time when real-time data is not available, and ultimately illuminate the problem of transmission: how unidirectional change is transmitted across successive generations (chapter 13).

## 3.2 Variables to be examined in this chapter

Four sociolinguistic variables were selected by LCV to provide the stable base for the study of linguistic change.

(dh). The alternation of fricatives, affricates, and stops in the *initial* allophone of the interdental fricative /ð/. The dependent variable follows the usual coding conventions:

dh-0 fricative
dh-1 affricate or absence
dh-2 stop

The (dh) index is formed by the average value of the variants multiplied by 100.

*Neutralizations*: (dh) is neutralized when it follows apical stops, since it is then not possible to distinguish the affricate from the stop variant.

*Exclusions*: There are no lexical exclusions for this variable.

(dhv). The same set of variants as initial (dh) for the intervocalic allophone of /ð/. There are no neutralizations or exclusions.

(Neg). Negative concord: The incorporation of a negative element in indeterminates *any*, *or*, *ever* when they are C-commanded by a negative in deep structure. The dependent variable as recorded here is the percentage of negative concord applied in all possible occurrences. Non-application of the variable includes standard uses of the indeterminates

actual diachronic developments in a language when other factors, such as social class, are held constant" (p. 242). Table 3.1 projects the expectation that in stable sociolinguistic variation, when social class is held constant, there will be consistent age differences that do not reflect diachronic developments. Bailey et al.'s conclusion does converge with that given above: "apparent time differences must be interpreted in the light of other characteristics of a synchronic distribution that allow us to predict the direction of change" (p. 263).

as *any*, *or*, *ever*, or negative postposing (*He didn't do anything → He did nothing*).

The overall semantic context is usually sufficient to distinguish negative concord from logical double negation, but there is no absolute method of detecting ambiguity (Labov 1972a).

(ing). The alternation of /n/ and /ŋ/ in unstressed /ɪŋ/ syllables.

The dependent variable assigns 1 to apical articulation, and 0 to velar, so that the (ing) index is the percent apical articulation. In some areas, a tense vowel with an apical consonant is heard as equivalent to a velar articulation (Woods 1979). This is rare in Philadelphia speech, and is not a factor in the present study.

The overall envelope of variation includes words with the suffix *-ing*, monomorphemic nouns like *morning* and *ceiling*, and compounds with *-thing*: *nothing*, *something*. It therefore appears that it must be defined as a phonological alternation that affects all unstressed /ɪŋ/ syllables. However, almost all communities studied have shown strong grammatical conditioning: the closer the construction is to a verbal construction, the greater the use of the apical variant, and the closer to a nominal construction, the greater the percentage of the velar variant. The progressive construction normally shows the highest degree of apical use, followed by the participle in non-progressive constructions, adjectives, compound gerunds, simple gerunds, and lastly, simple nouns.

The Philadelphia data was originally coded with a full range of 12 grammatical environments, but this was reduced to three for the purposes of a sociolinguistic study: Progressive (including *going to*), Participle, and Noun (including the preposition *during*).

*Neutralizations*: There are no neutralizations for this variable; the apical/velar distinction is clear even when followed by a velar segment.

*Exclusions*: In Philadelphia, *anything* and *everything* always show velar articulation, presumably reflecting secondary or tertiary stress on the final syllable. *Something* and *nothing* are excluded from the nominal sub-group because they exhibit much higher levels of apical realization, and appear to form a different sociolinguistic variable.

Proper nouns with final *-ing* are also to be excluded in the Northern Cities. There is consistent velar articulation in place names like *Flushing* in New York and *Reading* in Pennsylvania, and in personal names like *Manning* and *Harding*. Non-final *-ing* can be apical in *Washington* but not in *Abingdon*, *Kensington*, or *Ellington*.

(ACor): The correction of tensed short /a/ in word lists. It has been demonstrated that the tensing of short **a** in the spontaneous speech of Philadelphians is almost invariant in the core pattern (Labov 1989b). In word lists, the correction of short **a** to a low front long vowel [æ:] is common, and forms a stable sociolinguistic variable. In the LCV interviews, word lists were read in only a third of the initial interviews, but there is sufficient data to measure the social distribution of this variable. Fifteen short **a** words were selected from the list, including all of the tensed allophones (before front nasals, before voiceless fricatives, and the three words before /d/ *mad*, *bad*, *glad*). The index is the number out of 15 that were corrected to a lax form.

### *Patterns of stable variation*

Before proceeding with the analysis of the stable Philadelphia variables, it will be helpful to examine more closely the joint pattern of social and stylistic variation characteristic of such variables found in LES. Figure 3.1 shows the social and stylistic stratification of (ing) in LES. The striking regularity of this display, reproduced in many sociolinguistic texts and surveys, demonstrates that variation in the urban speech community is not the chaotic result of dialect mixture, but a highly constrained pattern that closely determines the linguistic behavior of each speaker. This general impression can be made explicit in six specific features of a stable sociolinguistic variable:

1 Regular social stratification is maintained for each contextual style. (ing) is a monotonic function of social class: that is, each step upward in class status is associated with a decrease in the (ing) index.
2 Regular stylistic stratification is maintained for each social class. (ing) is a monotonic function of contextual style: that is, each increase in formality (or attention paid to speech) is accompanied by a decrease in (ing) values.
3 As a consequence of (1), all social groups are differentiated by their treatment of the variable, but as a consequence of (2), all social groups are similar in following the same pattern of style shifting. Thus figure 3.1 shows how the community is both unified and differentiated by the sociolinguistic variable.
4 The same variable, (ing), therefore serves as a marker of cultural levels and contextual styles.[5]
5 Though there is considerable individual variation within each group, it is not normally large enough to disturb the regularity of the pattern when 5 to 10 speakers are included in each group. Individuals whose deviation from the mean is large enough to disturb the pattern are marked by aberrant social histories.[6]

[5] Although the common-sense view of the matter, articulated in Kenyon 1948, is that the variables that define cultural levels are quite distinct from those that define contextual styles.

[6] As shown among others by the case of Nathan B. in Labov 1966a.

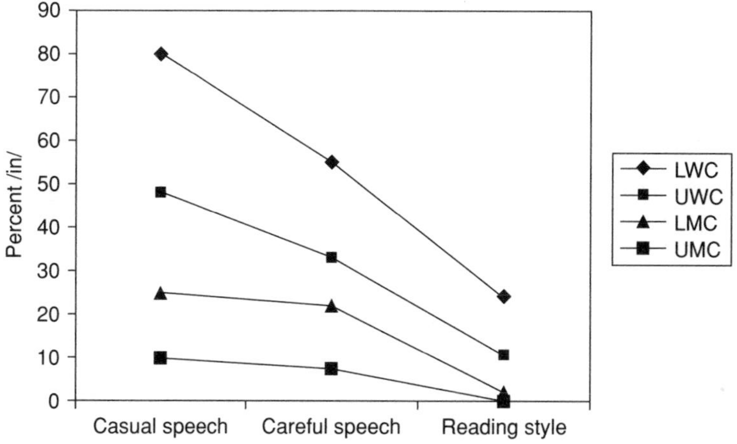


*Figure 3.1* Social and stylistic stratification of (ing) in New York City. LWC: lower working class; UWC: upper working class; LMC: lower middle class; UMC: upper middle class (from Labov 1966a).

6 Although the variable is highly constrained, it remains a random variable: that is, an event whose outcome cannot be predicted. The regularities of figure 3.1 rest upon a base of *inherent variation.*

In the thirty years that followed LES, many parallel studies of stigmatized variables were conducted, and the pattern of figure 3.1 has been replicated in a large number of communities, in many areas of the world.[7] Similar patterns are found in cross-tabulating prestige features, where the use of the variable increases with greater attention to speech, instead of decreasing. These cross-tabulations replicate the six features outlined above, but they do not show up with identical configurations in all speech communities. Patterns of stable sociolinguistic variation differ in three major ways:

1 *Sharp vs. gradient social stratification.* In place of the even spacing of social classes in figure 3.1, there may be sharp separation of opposing ends of the social spectrum. Thus the (ing) pattern in Norwich shows a sharp separation of the two middle class groups as against the three working class groups, a division of the speech community that reflects the sharper divisions among social classes in British society (Trudgill 1974b; see figure 3.3 below).

[7] Detroit (Shuy, Wolfram, and Riley 1967, Wolfram 1969), Norwich (Trudgill 1974b), South Harlem (Labov, Cohen, Robins, and Lewis 1968), Ottawa (Woods 1979), Bahia Blanca, Argentina (Weinberg 1974), Teheran (Modaressi 1978), Tokyo (Hibiya 1988).

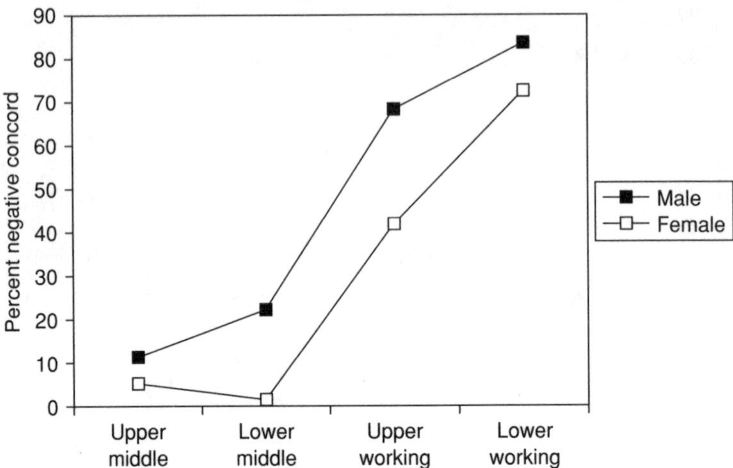


*Figure 3.2* Use of negative concord among African Americans in Detroit by class and gender (from Wolfram 1969)

2 *Sharp vs. gradient stylistic stratification.* The spacing of the styles in figure 3.1 is more arbitrary than the spacing of social classes. However, it is clear that there is no qualitative break between spontaneous speech – casual and careful – and controlled styles, where the subject is reading. In the Teheran dialect of Farsi, all of the sociolinguistic variables investigated showed an abrupt break when the subjects began to read: use of the colloquial urban variant dropped from the majority use in spontaneous speech to almost zero in reading (Modaressi 1978:104, figure 4-11). A similar situation appears in the raising of /o/ to /u/ in Seoul Korean (Chae 1995).

3 *The cross-over pattern*: Hypercorrect behavior of the second highest status group. It is a common feature of many sociolinguistic profiles that the second highest status group shows a steeper slope of style shifting than other groups. With increasing formality, this group shows a more rapid retreat from the use of a stigmatized form, or advance in the use of a prestige form. In extreme cases, this can lead to a cross-over of their values with that of the highest status group. Figure 3.2, from Wolfram's (1969) study of African American speakers in Detroit, shows that the lower middle class females have reduced the use of negative concord below that of the upper middle class.

### *The structural position of stable variables*

If the purpose of studying variation is to better understand the linguistic system as a whole, then we will be drawn to the study of variables that are most deeply implicated in that structure. Change within a vowel system typically has this character, where the movement or merger of one element almost always involves corresponding adjustments of the rest of the system. Studies of inflectional variables, like the aspiration and deletion of Spanish (s), involve considerations of concord within the noun phrase, subject–verb agreement, pro-drop, and more abstract syntactic issues. But when the aim is to understand better the way that social factors affect linguistic behavior, we are more likely to be drawn to the relatively isolated elements that are normally the focus of social affect.[8] Initial (dh) is intermediate in this respect. It is not intimately involved with the rest of the consonant system as a whole. Yet the New York City data shows a close parallel between (dh) and its voiceless partner (th), so that the variable may be defined as the whole class of segments with possible interdental articulation. On the other hand, it will appear that initial (dh) and (th) behave very differently from intervocalic and final allophones, so that it is only the initial allophones that are involved. In postlexical phonology, (dh) is linked structurally to the sub-system of stops. The lenis stop realization of /dh/ may be identical with the flap realization of /t/ and /d/ after stressed vowels and before an unstressed vowel so that *sew the top* and *soda top* can be homonymous in Philadelphia. The possibilities of homonymy are greatly expanded in *r*-less New York, where *Cedar Point* can coincide with *see the point*, *later brick* with *lay the brick*, *mow the yard* with *motor yard*, and so on. One might therefore project an inquiry into a functional relationship between (dh) and (r), to see if an increase in *r*-vocalization would in fact limit the use of stop variants of (dh) in the light of such a potential increase in homonymy.

If social variation were confined to the superficial realization of words and sounds, it would indeed be exterior to the grammar – a discrete set of choices from the grammar's output.[9] But stable sociolinguistic variables are located at an intermediate level of structure: they are not the surface sounds or words of the language, but are defined as the use of allophones or allomorphs in a particular structural context. Philadelphians have no social reaction to the lenis stop or flap as a sound, since the same sound is socially neutral in *latter*. Their social evaluations are directed at the

[8] Scherre and Naro 1992 demonstrate that an instance of subject–verb concord in Brazilian Portuguese is affected by social factors (education) only when it is isolated from discourse structure, that is, not preceded by other elements in a sequence of subject–verb marking. This is one of many indications that social affect bears upon the surface of language, and particularly those elements that are not involved in intricate structural relations.

[9] Some variables are defined at the most abstract level of grammatical organization, as an alternation between systems, as in the work of Kroch (1989), Santorini (1989), and Taylor (1994) on large-scale syntactic change. It would be surprising if such abstract syntactic phenomena as the decline of V-to-I movement were to exhibit the pattern of the socially evaluated sociolinguistic variables like (dh) and (ing).

absence of frication in the initial allophone of the interdental stops. The grammar therefore contains inherent variation, no matter how we might decide ultimately to describe that variation formally. Taking grammar in the largest sense to include phonology, these variables are in the grammar; they are constrained by the grammar; and they cannot be described apart from the grammar. But even so, they do not dominate any large portion of it, and the consequences of their alternation for the rest of the grammar are minimal.

### *Implications for multivariate analysis*

A serious effort to account for the social distribution of variation soon encounters the fact that there are more social dimensions that affect language behavior than we can display in a cross-tabulation. A complete account of sociolinguistic patterns must display the effects of speakers' gender, age, ethnicity, race, social class, urban/rural status, and position in social networks. The clarity and reliability of figure 3.1 therefore depends on one or both of two supporting conditions:

(a) that the effect of social class on (ing) is of a higher order of magnitude than the other social factors listed, and /or
(b) that the other social factors are independent of social class. That is, whatever the effect of gender, age, or ethnicity might be on (ing) levels, it is the same for all social classes.

A full assessment of the effects of intersecting social parameters, and a complete account of sociolinguistic structure, is only possible with multivariate analysis. A multivariate approach was first introduced into sociolinguistic studies in the form of the variable rule program (Rand and Sankoff 1991). It was motivated not by the need to analyze external, social factors, but rather to deal with the language-internal configuration of internal, linguistic constraints on variation (Cedergren and Sankoff 1974). The basic fact about internal factors that the variable rule program continually displays is that they operate independently of each other (Sankoff and Labov 1979). However, it was realized from the outset that social factors are typically not independent. Though it is convenient and useful to incorporate external and internal factors in the same analysis, a considerable amount of information can be lost in the typical variable rule analysis of speech communities.

Figure 3.1 shows graphically that style and social class influence (ing) independently through the parallel trajectories of the three lines – a feature that can be seen much more easily in a line diagram than a table. In either case, twelve measurements are required to display the information. In a variable rule analysis, this situation would typically be represented by seven numbers, in two independent factor groups, with probability weights for three factors in the style group and four factors in the social class group. The degree of independence of these groups is not displayed directly, though it is reflected in the overall fit of the model to the data.[10] The variable rule program can easily be adjusted to examine the effects of interaction by creating interactive factors, and whatever interaction is found can then be assessed more accurately than with cross-tabulations. However, there is nothing in the usual variable rule analysis that calls attention to the existence of interactions among the independent variables. It is therefore useful to alternate between cross-tabulations and multivariate analysis whenever we are dealing with social factors. While cross-tabulations display the existence of interaction, multivariate analysis can measure the size of the effect.

## 3.3 The stability of stable variables

This work focuses on linguistic change. Yet from the sociolinguistic point of view, the more striking phenomenon is the opposite of change – stability, and it can be said that the absence of change has the most important consequences for our understanding of linguistic structure. If variation is nothing but a transitional phenomenon, a way-station between two invariant stages of the language, it can have only a limited role in our view of the human language faculty. Inherent variation would then be only an accident of history, a product of the unsurprising finding that human beings cannot abandon one form and adopt another instantaneously. But the existence of long-term stable variation puts another face on the matter. If it is true that linguistic variables are transmitted in essentially the same form across twenty or thirty generations of speakers, then we must find a more important place for the expression of variable relations in the human linguistic ecology.

Evidence for the stability of sociolinguistic variables is of two kinds: negative and positive. Most often, variables have been considered stable because there was no strong, monotonic function of age of the type found for (el) in Norwich by Trudgill 1974b, (ch) in Panama City by Cedergren

[10] An exact fit of the variable rule model to the original data is only possible if all factors are independent of each other. Extreme deviations of the model from the data are reflected in high chi-square values for large cells, so that a rough measure of fit is provided by the average chi-square per cell: average values much higher than 1 per cell suggest the presence of interaction not accounted for. However, this measure also includes the unreliable chi-squares generated by small cells, and it is not easy to locate from the chi-square values the source of the interaction that is the cause of the lack of fit.

1973, or (eh) in New York City by Labov 1966a. The aspiration and deletion of Spanish (s), which has been found to show regular class stratification in a dozen different Spanish dialects, has never shown such an age distribution. But inferences of stability from negative evidence will always be faulty when the community as a whole changes its linguistic practices, a common situation in lexical change. Positive evidence that the same variation existed at an earlier period is more convincing. For example, the current lexically specific alternation between /æks/ and /æsk/, "ask," can easily be traced to its 8th-century origins in any dictionary of Anglo-Saxon, which list both *ascian* and *acsian*. We will want to bear in mind the possibilities of both types of evidence in examining the evidence for stable, long-term variation for the variables under consideration.

Table 3.1, category IA, reflects the relations found between the (ing) values of older and younger speakers in New York City, relations that were duplicated for (th) and (dh), the form of the voiceless and voiced interdental fricative. Except in the highest social group, the values were higher for the younger speakers. The same pattern will be found in Philadelphia. The major question that must be addressed in the balance of this chapter is whether this age differential reflects instability in time: are the stable sociolinguistic variables stable? The first approach to this issue is to examine the social history of these variables as far back in real time as the evidence will take us, beginning with (ing).

## *The history of (ing)*

The variable (ing) was the first sociolinguistic variable to be studied quantitatively, and has the widest range and most uniform pattern of all variables in English. The typical combination of social and stylistic stratification is shown in figure 3.3, adapted from Trudgill's 1974 study of Norwich, England.[11] Long-term stability appears more clearly in the case of (ing) than for any other sociolinguistic variable. The negative evidence is consistent: none of the many studies of (ing) have uncovered any evidence for change in progress. The motivation for examining it as a case of long-term historical continuity proceeded from the discovery of a previously unsuspected grammatical constraint. The /in/ form consistently shows higher frequencies for the progressive, lower for participles and adjectives, and lowest for gerunds and nouns.[12] The grammatical constraint forms a continuum from

[11] Sociolinguistic data consistent with this view of (ing) is found in Fischer's 1958 report on a New England village; Cofer 1972 for Philadelphia; Woods' 1979 study of Ottawa; Mock's 1979 study of a rural Missouri community; for Australian English, Wald and Shopen 1979 and Bradley and Bradley 1979.

[12] To the best of my knowledge, this grammatical constraint was discovered first by the 1976 (Elizabeth Dayton, et al.) class of Linguistics 560 at the University of Pennsylvania, and independently by Wald and Shopen in Australia (1979), and Peterson in 1985.

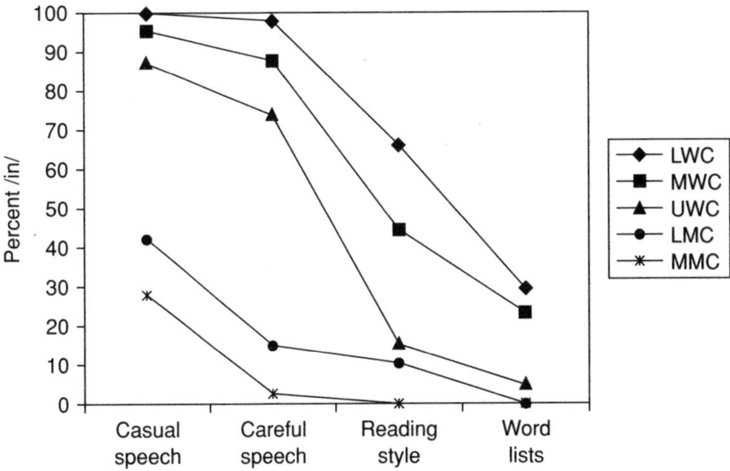


*Figure 3.3* Social and stylistic stratification of (ing) in Norwich (from Trudgill 1974b)

the most verbal types with the highest percentages of /in/, to the most nominal, with the lowest percentages.

There are relatively few other internal constraints on the (ing) variable. There seems to be no strong phonological conditioning before following velars or apicals, and as noted above, stress effects are categorical. Thus (ing) has all the hallmarks of a morphological alternation rather than a phonological reduction. It is not yet completely determined how detailed the noun-to-verb continuum is, since the number of syntactic subcategories is very large, and the frequency of many is quite low. Figure 3.4 shows the summed syntactic conditioning of (ing) for 33 adult speakers from the King of Prussia and Overbrook sections of the LCV Neighborhood Study. The highest use of /in/ is for the progressive future *going to*; this is clearly the result of the morphophonemic condensation of /gowiŋ+tuw/ → /gənə/. Otherwise, the highest /in/ value of 51% is shown for the progressive; this is a consistent and normal finding for the progressive, which is also the most frequent form (n = 541). There is a significant drop to 42% for the next category, the sizeable body of *-ing* forms that occur as participles modifying the verb phrase, as in *we go out there fishin'*. This again is significantly higher than the smaller group of miscellaneous complements at 37% that includes verb complements (*we used to go fishin'*), sentential complements (*I skipped lunch tryin' to lose weight*), and deletion of relative pronoun and auxiliary (*we caught one guy sneakin'*). This small group is not significantly different from the group of 94 gerunds at 34% (*just by guiding her hand*).

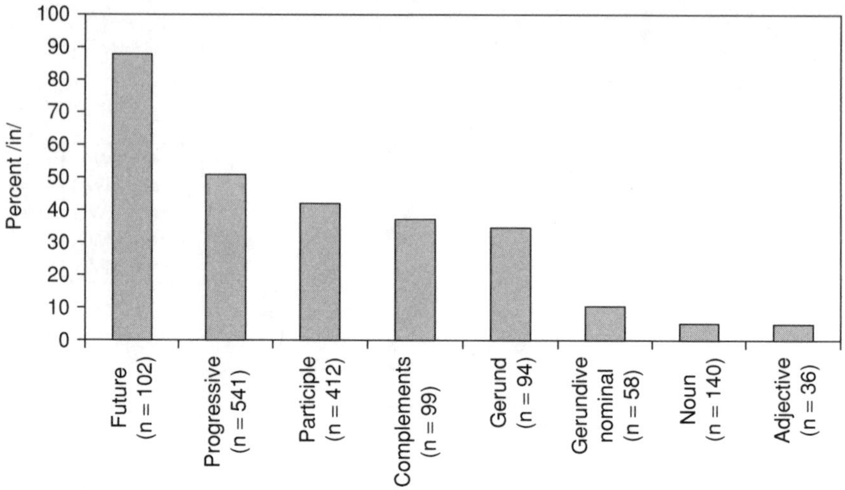


*Figure 3.4* Grammatical conditioning of (ing) for 33 adult speakers from the Nancy Drive and Mallow Street neighborhoods

All of these forms have verbal characteristics in the sense that they can assign theta-roles, including gerunds functioning as the head of a noun phrase as in the example above. There is a sharp drop to a set of nominal forms that have no such capacity: gerunds incorporated into noun phrases (*swimming pool*), nouns (*ceiling*, *morning*), and adjectives (*interesting*, *disgusting*). These are all at 10% /in/ and below, and are not significantly different from each other.

There are thus two ways of viewing the distribution of Philadelphia (ing). On the one hand there is a continuum of five distinct levels; on the other hand (setting aside the future), there are two distinct groups: a verbal and a nominal use of /ing/, which cluster at radically different levels.

The second striking fact about the grammatical conditioning of (ing) is that there is no plausible synchronic explanation for it. If for example there were detectable stress differences between the nominal and verbal forms (as in the contrast between *something* and *anything*), we would readily adopt stress as an explanation of figure 3.4. But in the absence of any such factor, one must consider the possibility that the syntactic conditioning of (ing) is simply a historical residue of some earlier variation. This possibility is strongly reinforced by the observation that /in/ is the direct and regular descendant of the Old English participial ending **-inde**, **-ende**,[13] just as /iŋ/ is the regular result of sound changes operating on the Old English verbal noun **-inge**, **-ynge**. This inference was first made explicit on the basis

[13] Through loss of final schwa, simplification of the final *-nd* cluster, and vowel reduction of /e/ in unstressed syllables.

of sociolinguistic data but had been anticipated on purely historical grounds by Dobson and others (1957:590–1).[14] The general scenario is that the specialization of the velar form for the nominal and the apical form for the verbal broke down in Early Middle English, and that the competition between these two has continued ever since as a sociolinguistic variable. The uniform adoption of the *-ing* spelling in orthography masked to a certain extent the continuing opposition of vernacular apical to formal velar pronunciation. The generalization of *-ing* was never complete, however, and as we have seen, the tendency for the velar form to appear in nominal uses and the apical form in verbal uses is quite strong, even today.[15]

Houston 1985 is a detailed investigation of the historical development of (ing). The synchronic part of her investigation begins with the quantitative analysis of (ing) in 20 British cities, using exploratory interviews that I conducted in the 1970s. All southern British cities show the grammatical conditioning similar to that shown for Philadelphia in figure 3.4. The areas that show a predominant use of the velar variant form an intact geographic region in the south of Britain that is outlined by the same isogloss that Moore, Meech, and Whitehall 1935 derive for the Early Middle English opposition of -**inde** and -**inge** in the participle. Thus there are geographic as well as syntactic indications of the historical continuity of the opposition,[16] transformations in the form and use of the gerund, and the late development of the progressive form. Her conclusion matches that of Dobson: that this is a genuine case of long-term historical transmission of a quantitative opposition.

The main concern here is not with the time-depth of the apical/velar opposition itself but with the time-depth of the historical variation. For how long has *-in'* functioned as the colloquial symbol of informal speech and *-ing* as the formal symbol of careful speech? There are two distinct points of view here. On the one hand, Wyld insists that "down to the thirties of the last century, *-in* and not *-ing* was the almost universal pronunciation among all classes of speakers – in fact, many thousands

[14] Dobson considers both possible origins of the /in/ form: an assimilation of /iŋ/ to the point of articulation of the high front vowel, or a continuation of the older participial ending, and concludes that the latter is more likely. He notes (p. 963) that *n* < *nd* is recorded by orthoepists from the 17th century in sources that reflect vulgar pronunciation.

[15] Though the choice of apical or velar forms has strong social evaluation, it is interesting to note that syntactic conditioning has none. We have not yet located any person who has clear intuitions, in advance of quantitative investigation, about the fact that *Good mornin'* is possible but far less likely than *I'm comin'*. (The detailed investigation of the Philadelphia situation will show, however, that there are subtle sociolinguistic consequences of the syntactic differentiation.)

[16] The historical aspect of Houston's investigation involves many discontinuities in the record, in particular the absence of direct evidence for the -**inde** form in the orthography of Early Middle English. She develops the hypothesis that the variation between *-ynge* and *-yng* spellings represents variation between /iŋ/ and /in/.

of excellent speakers never use any other form today" (1936:112). He argues further that the sociolinguistic variable was first formed as late as the 1830s as a middle class hypercorrect spelling pronunciation, but was not accepted by the upper classes until much later. Wyld's view seems strongly influenced by the history of his own family. From other evidence, the origins of the modern sociolinguistic opposition are much earlier: Danielsson (1948) notes that "Clement 1587 is the first authority known to me who formulates a special warning to the teacher not to let the pupil pronounce [-in] for [iŋ], e.g., *speakin'* for *speaking*." Kökeritz (1953) believes that Shakespeare pronounced the ending *-ing* as [in] or syllabic [in̩], and that the *-g* was added as a silent letter. If this were the case, it hardly seems possible that spelling pronunciations would not have developed for the upwardly mobile merchant classes. In any case, we find the sociolinguistic variable well developed in the novels of Dickens. Gerson 1967 lists 1216 instances of spellings reflecting the /in/ form, heavily concentrated among working class and lower class speakers. Sam Weller and his father T. Weller, who are often cited as a major effort of Dickens to represent colloquial working class speech in *Pickwick Papers*, account for 43% of the entire corpus. Only one speaker reflects the aristocratic tradition claimed by Wyld: a Marchioness who uses two examples of *-in-* in *The Old Curiosity Shop* (p. 481).

We have every reason to believe, then, that the present-day social opposition of the formal, standard velar pronunciation and the informal, nonstandard apical pronunciation, has a stable history dating back to at least the beginning of the 19th century and probably to the beginning of the 17th. Among present-day English speech communities, Southern States English, northern English, and Scots stand out as exceptions: there the /in/ form is used almost exclusively in speech, even of the most formal kind.

### *The history of (th) and (dh)*

The first step backward in the historical record is a small one. In 1962, Hubbell's study of pronunciation in New York City finds traces of (th) stops in the speech of only 2 of his 16 upper middle class informants, none for (dh). For the lower middle class informants, 4 of 9 showed no stops, and 2 showed moderate to heavy use of stops for both (th) and (dh). All lower class informants used some stops, and two showed heavy use.

In the late 1940s, Yakira Frank's dissertation on New York City speech (1948) reported the voiceless affricate (th-2) in the speech of young uneducated informants in all positions. She adds that the dental [t] occurs in free variation with the affricate (p. 80). Frank writes that "two instances of the voiced stop /d/ for /ð/ occur in the speech of two young uneducated informants as in *without* and *the both of us*" (p. 81).

The records of the *Linguistic Atlas*, dating from about this time, are in disagreement (Kurath and McDavid 1961). The general frequency of stops and affricates is much lower than in the LES study of the other sources. This might throw considerable doubt on the stability of (th) and (dh), were it not for the fact that the *Atlas* transcriptions are conservative in all other respects, contradicting both earlier and later records.[17]

The most incisive and definitive observations come from Babbitt (1896), a native of upper New York State who described the speech of New York in the last decade of the 19th century:

> The most striking and important peculiarity in consonants is the substitution of *t* and *d* for /θ/ and /ð/. This does not take place in all words, nor in the speech of all persons, even of the lower classes; but the tendency exists beyond doubt . . . I observed very few cases of natives who could not, and did not in some words, pronounce the interdentals correctly, and the substitution of *d* and *t* for them is not heard in the speech of the better classes . . . [For most people], The definite article, the pronouns *this* and *that*, the ordinal numerals in *th*, and such everyday words, are almost uniformly pronounced with the *d* or *t*, while anything in the nature of a "book-word" keeps the orthodox interdental . . .

Babbitt also notes that newspapers ridicule working class speech by writing *De Ate* for *The Eighth* [Assembly District], just as they ridicule the use of /ʌy/ as "*goil*" and "*woild.*" The social distribution of (th) and (dh) has not, however, undergone the rapid evolution of /ʌy/, but remains as it was at the turn of the century.

A second excellent observer of the New York City scene was O. Henry. Like Babbitt, he was an outsider, born in North Carolina, and first came to New York in 1902. A very large part of his prodigious output was devoted to observations of New York City speakers.[18] He made careful efforts to distinguish the social level of New Yorkers in both grammar and pronunciation:

> There was a smart kind of a kid in the gang – I guess he was a newsboy. "I got in twent-fi' mister," he says, looking hopeful at Buck's silk hat and clothes. "Dey paid me two-fifty a mont' on it. Say, a man tells me dey can't do dat and be on the square? Is dat straight? Do you guess I can get out my twent-fi'?" (from "The Tempered Wind," O. Henry 1945, p. 259)

In celebrating the inherent kindliness of citizens toward strangers in "The Making of a New Yorker," O. Henry introduces a good Samaritan who offers a glass of beer to an accident victim: "Drink dis, sport" (O. Henry 1945:287).

[17] As, for example, in showing no vowel for tensed short **a** higher than raised [æ˔], though Babbitt 1896 testifies that this vowel reached the level of *where*.

[18] His last words are reported as, "Pull up the shades so I can see New York; I don't want to go home in the dark" (Henry 1945).

We can conclude that from a qualitative viewpoint, the (dh) variable functioned in pretty much the same way in 1900 as it did in 1966 and as it does today.

### *Negative concord*

Negative concord is defined as the incorporation of negative morphemes into indeterminates and auxiliaries that are commanded by a negative without the addition of any further semantic negation (Labov 1972a). The history of negative concord is not so well known as that of (ing), and one would hope for a detailed study of its origins in Early Middle English. It is well known that negative concord was an established feature of Old English; and in Early Modern English there was a strong tendency to limit negation in the surface structure to a single representation, without spreading to following indeterminates. The first discussions of this as a prescriptive rule, based on either logical or grammatical considerations, are to be found in 17th-century grammarians.

Leonard 1929 reviews the prescription of double negation by 18th-century grammarians, who agree as a group on the prohibition of negative concord and an insistence that each negative is a fresh negation of the predication. Van Ostade (1982) presents data from 30 other 18th-century grammarians, and shows a gradual increase in the amount of attention given to negative concord across the century. While the examples they criticize are drawn from 17th-century literature, it seems that by the end of the 18th century they were reacting to the persistent use of negative concord in informal speech. At the beginning of the century, some novelists used negative concord freely (Richardson) while others used it only in informal quoted speech (Defoe). By the end of the century, double negation was no longer used in formal speech or writing and we can infer the existence of the social stratification that has continued to the present.

The use of negative concord seems to be coextensive in time with the use of (ing) and *ain't* as sociolinguistic markers. O. Henry's view of the speech of working class Irish New Yorkers strongly features the double negative, spreading to both *any* and *either*, as in this speech from "A Harlem Tragedy":

> Everybody can't have a husband like Jack. Marriage wouldn't be no failure if they was all like him. . . . What I want is a masterful man that slugs you when he's jagged and hugs you when he ain't jagged. Preserve me from the man that ain't got the sand to do neither. (O. Henry 1945:297)

The evidence for the stability of the three variables we are considering can therefore be considered very strong for this past century, and quite strong for the century preceding. Though there is some dispute, there is also a good case for extending them backward to the 18th and 17th centuries.

## 3.4 The sociolinguistic sample of Philadelphia

The set of speakers to be used for the exploration of the three stable sociolinguistic variables in Philadelphia is the *sociolinguistic sample*, totaling 183 speakers. The sociolinguistic sample includes the 89 speakers from the neighborhoods described in chapter 2, along with several subsidiary networks, but not the 23 upper middle class and upper class speakers in the Chestnut Hill series. To this core sample is added a much larger number of associated friends and family members of the basic sound change sample. The sample includes many complete families, and in most neighborhoods has a greatly enlarged representation of pre-adolescent speakers from ages 8 to 12 and adolescents from 13 to 17. The contrast between their behavior and that of adults will play a major role in the interpretation of apparent-time data.

Table 3.2 shows the characteristics of the sociolinguistic sample organized by neighborhood, tabulating a subset of the scales and ratings given for the basic sample in chapter 2. Generation is given as a mean of individual scores on distance from the immigrant generation, and the foreign language knowledge rating is a mean of individual scores according to the following scale: 0 no foreign language background; 1 passive understanding of grandparents; 2 passive understanding of parents; 3 spoke only foreign language up to school age, never much since; 4 occasional use of foreign language with older people; 5 regular use of foreign language with older people; 6 dominant in foreign language. At the top of the table are three neighborhoods in North Philadelphia: Wicket Street in Kensington, the chief focus of the Neighborhood Study discussed in chapter 2; and 10 speakers drawn from nearby areas of Fishtown and Richmond. The entire area has the lowest socioeconomic ranking; the Fishtown sub-group consists of six young men of low occupational status. Wicket is predominantly Irish, but as a whole, this group is more than two generations removed from the immigrant period, with little foreign language background.

The next group of four, from South Philadelphia, show the two focal neighborhoods, Pitt and Clark. The South sub-group is a network of ten lower middle class men and women interviewed by a graduate student from the area who knew them personally, primarily upwardly mobile white-collar workers. At the opposite extreme is Wallace: a corner group of 13 young men and women (average age 18) who were attached to an area we will refer to as 6th and Wallace. They were interviewed by Bower to provide a social network at the less respectable end of the social scale in South Philadelphia, to balance the prosperous Clark Street and the middle of the road Pitt St. The percent Italian in South Philadelphia ranges from 41% at Pitt St. to 90% at "South." Clark is the only neighborhood that is at all close to the immigrant period, and also shows a number of speakers with a knowledge of Italian.

*Table 3.2* Characteristics of the sociolinguistic sample by neighborhood

| *Name* | *N* | *% female* | *Mean age* | *Occupation* | *Res. value* | *Mean SEC* | *% Italian* | *% Irish* | *% Jewish* | *Generation* | *Foreign language* |
|---|---|---|---|---|---|---|---|---|---|---|---|
| North Philadelphia | | | | | | | | | | | |
| Wicket | 25 | 52 | 34 | 2.05 | 1.05 | 4.84 | 0 | 84 | 0 | 2.06 | 0.00 |
| Fishtown | 6 | 0 | 17 | 1.40 | 1.00 | 5.00 | 0 | 50 | 0 | 2.75 | 0.25 |
| Richmond | 4 | 50 | 26 | 2.25 | 1.50 | 4.50 | 0 | 0 | 0 | 2.00 | 1.00 |
| South Philadelphia | | | | | | | | | | | |
| Pitt | 22 | 64 | 25 | 2.27 | 1.18 | 5.05 | 41 | 41 | 5 | 2.32 | 0.43 |
| Clark | 28 | 61 | 43 | 2.79 | 1.93 | 6.93 | 82 | 11 | 0 | 1.75 | 2.43 |
| South | 10 | 70 | 40 | 2.60 | 1.70 | 7.20 | 90 | 0 | 10 | 2.00 | 2.10 |
| Wallace | 13 | 62 | 18 | 1.62 | 1.00 | 4.31 | 54 | 23 | 8 | 2.31 | 0.62 |
| NE | 5 | 60 | 21 | 2.50 | 1.75 | 7.00 | 0 | 20 | 20 | 2.50 | 0.00 |
| West Philadelphia | | | | | | | | | | | |
| Mallow | 24 | 54 | 29 | 3.67 | 3.00 | 8.25 | 8 | 4 | 88 | 2.11 | 0.00 |
| King of Prussia | | | | | | | | | | | |
| Nancy Drive | 46 | 41 | 26 | 4.02 | 6.24 | 11.63 | 24 | 13 | 0 | 2.27 | 0.00 |
| Total | 183 | | | | | | | | | | |

One important area of Philadelphia that is not well represented in either the basic LCV sample or this expanded sociolinguistic sample is the Northeast, a vast area of people who have migrated out of the more central neighborhoods.[19] The sociolinguistic sample has 5 speakers as a token representation.

The Mallow Street neighborhood in Overbrook, in West Philadelphia, appears here as a group with higher occupational status, higher house values, and a higher average socioeconomic status [SES] than the groups considered so far. It is also a predominantly Jewish neighborhood. The 24 speakers represented here are a much larger group than those of the basic sample of chapter 2, so that the Jewish group is much better represented than in that sample.

Finally, the middle class Nancy Drive neighborhood in King of Prussia is expanded to 46 speakers. This includes the children of the Philadelphia families studied by Payne in her investigation of the acquisition of the Philadelphia dialect (1976). Since this subset of the sample was designed to obtain as many children as possible, it is not accidental that many of these middle and upper middle class speakers had large families. The small Italian and Irish proportions among them do not represent a strong ethnic influence, since they are all many generations away from the immigrant period and show no foreign language background.

## 3.5 Cross-tabulation of (dh) by class and style

Figure 3.5a is a cross-tabulation of (dh) by class and style which will allow us to compare the Philadelphia sociolinguistic pattern with the well-known configurations of the same variable in New York City and Detroit. Five divisions of the socioeconomic scale are used: 0–2, lower working class; 3–6, middle working class; 7–9, upper working class; 10–12, lower middle class; 13–15, upper middle class. Though only two styles of speech are shown, it is immediately evident that the Philadelphia pattern reproduces the regular pattern of social and stylistic stratification of figure 3.1. For both styles, there is a monotonic distribution, and each class shows a clear stylistic difference. In casual speech, the style pattern is almost linear. Figure 3.5b is a direct comparison of the New York and Philadelphia (dh) patterns. Though Philadelphia (dh) values are higher, the pattern is the same.

A more accurate view of this variable will require a multivariate analysis, in which all the other significant influences on (dh) will be taken into account at the same time, including the crucial dimension of age of the speaker. Multiple regression will be used for this purpose.

[19] The Northeast is well represented in the telephone sample, results of which are analyzed and compared with the LCV sample in ch. 5.

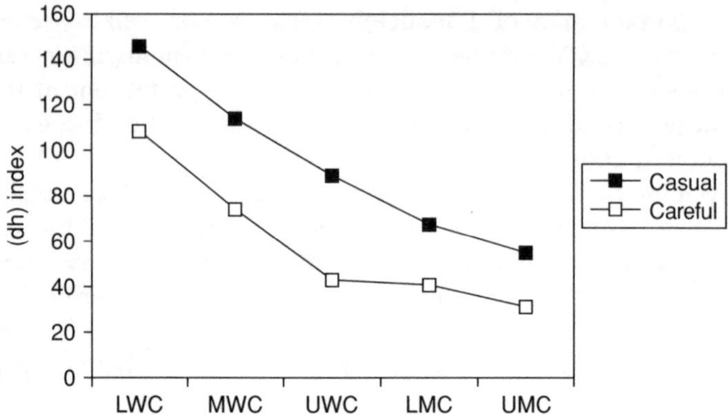


*Figure 3.5a* Cross-tabulation of (dh) by socioeconomic class and style for the Philadelphia Neighborhood Study

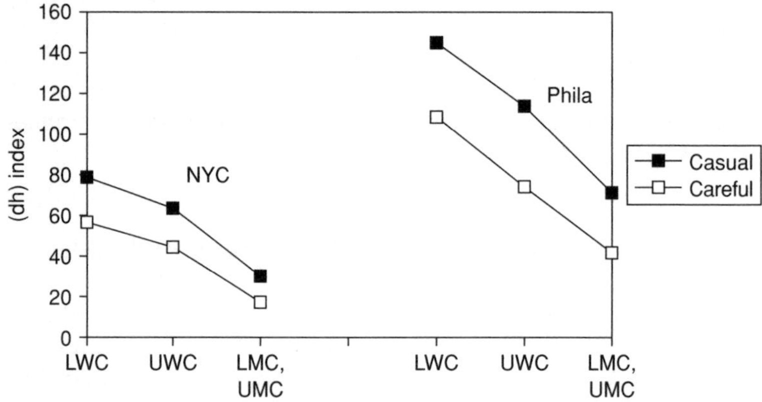


*Figure 3.5b* Comparison of New York City and Philadelphia (dh) patterns

Many sociolinguistic variables, like *-t,d* deletion, are best represented as binary choices, and analyzed as binary dependent variables using the variable rule program. Others, like measurements of vowel raising, are inherently continuous quantitative variables, and are best treated by multiple regression, or the general linear model. For the stable sociolinguistic variables (dh), (ing), and (neg), we have a choice of either strategy. If the focus is on internal constraints, and a large proportion of the combinations of factors are empty cells, the variable rule program is appropriate, since it operates on tokens rather than percentages and weights the heavily filled cells more strongly. When the focus is on social factors, there will be a high percentage of filled cells and we can operate most efficiently with a quantitative dependent variable and multivariate programs like multiple regression, ANOVA, or the general linear model. A quantitative dependent variable is most appropriate for (dh), since it allows us to form a continuous index that registers the intermediate status of the affricate.[20] It is less attractive with negative concord, where the data is sparser. The main motivation for using regression in the analysis of the sociolinguistic variables is to form a baseline for comparison with the multiple regression analysis of Philadelphia vowels involved in change in progress.

Either variable rule or regression analysis provides several distinct strategies for examining interaction among the social variables: the creation of interactive independent variables (e.g., "lower middle class women") or, if the quantity of data is sufficient, running separate analyses for the independent variables in question. The work to follow uses the second method.

The analyses to be reported here include all of the independent variables described in chapter 2. If a given independent variable is not listed in a particular analysis, it was found to be not significant. The tables and figures to follow will present analyses in which all and only all the significant effects are retained, except in cases where the nonsignificance of a given variable is crucial. Some of these variables are nominal, like ethnicity, and others are ordinal, but discrete, like age or education. The first step in the examination of the stable sociolinguistic variables is to carry out the simplest multiple regression where the quantitative variables – age, socioeconomic class, house upkeep, mobility, generational status, and foreign language knowledge – are retained in their full quantitative form. In the tables, the regression coefficients for quantitative independent variables will be supplemented by a column labeled *Effect*, where the coefficient is multiplied by the full range of the variable, and normalized on 100% (divided by 2).

The first variable to be considered is initial (dh). Table 3.3 is the first regression of initial (dh) by style. Five social variables determine the (dh) level; all are highly significant except for the effect of mobility. We note first in casual speech, four social factors whose effects can be ordered from strongest to weakest:

(a) The most powerful effect on (dh) is social class: the lower the SEC index, the higher the (dh) index.
(b) There is also a strong age effect, about half the size of social class: younger speakers have higher (dh) values.
(c) The third effect is female gender: women show lower (dh) values than men, but this only accounts for 13% of the range.
(d) Social mobility is a fourth effect, of about the same magnitude, but much less significant ($p < .05$ level while $p < .0001$ for gender).

[20] A problem in constructing a quantitative index is the zero variant, as in *Look at 'at*, which is quite important in some dialects, and is often assigned the same value as an affricate. In Philadelphia, the zero variant plays a less important role, and did not affect our calculations significantly.

*Table 3.3* First regression of initial (dh) by style

| *Variable* | *Coefficient* | *Effect* | *t-ratio* | *Probability* |
|---|---|---|---|---|
| *Casual speech* | | | | |
| SEC | –5.77 | 37.47 | –5.00 | ≤0.0001 |
| Age | –0.75 | 28.34 | –4.56 | ≤0.0001 |
| Female | –26.91 | –13.45 | –4.26 | ≤0.0001 |
| Mobility | –8.05 | –12.06 | –2.11 | 0.0370 |
| So. Phila | 34.56 | 17.28 | 4.90 | ≤0.0001 |
| Constant 174.04 | $r^2 = 47.8\%$ | | n = 153 | d.f. = 145 |
| *Careful speech* | | | | |
| SEC | –4.62 | 35.10 | –4.12 | ≤0.0001 |
| Age | –0.72 | 27.27 | –4.58 | ≤0.0001 |
| Female | –26.75 | –13.38 | –4.01 | ≤0.0001 |
| Mobility | –6.47 | –9.70 | –1.77 | 0.0785 |
| So. Phila | 26.44 | 13.32 | 3.69 | ≤0.0001 |
| Constant 130.59 | $r^2 = 41.5\%$ | | n = 151 | d.f. = 145 |

In addition to these general social factors, there is a particular differentiation of neighborhood. Taking SEC, age, gender, and mobility into account, residence in South Philadelphia still favors higher (dh) values by a sizeable and significant effect of 17%.

The table shows a closely parallel situation for (dh) in careful speech. All social factors except mobility operate at the same level of significance, though the overall level is lower, with a constant of 130 as against 174 for casual speech, and correspondingly lower values for the coefficients.

The question arises as to whether the pattern of regular social and stylistic variation of figure 3.5 will be preserved when all other factors are taken into account. Figure 3.6 shows the results of a regression analysis where membership in each social class is taken as a separate variable, and includes all the other variables of table 3.3. For each style and social class, the expected value of (dh) is calculated by multiplying the coefficient by the value of the variable (which is always 1 for such dummy variables) and adding the result to the constant. The display of figure 3.6 shows an even more regular pattern of social and stylistic stratification than figure 3.5.

Table 3.3 leaves no room for doubt that (dh) is a sociolinguistic variable in Philadelphia, but the large and significant age coefficient, two-thirds as large as the social class coefficient, puts into question whether it is a stable variable. Recalling the prediction of the model in table 3.1, that younger speakers will use a stigmatized variable more than older speakers, this effect is not unexpected. The question remains as to how to differentiate this variable from a change in progress, given a strong and significant age-grading.

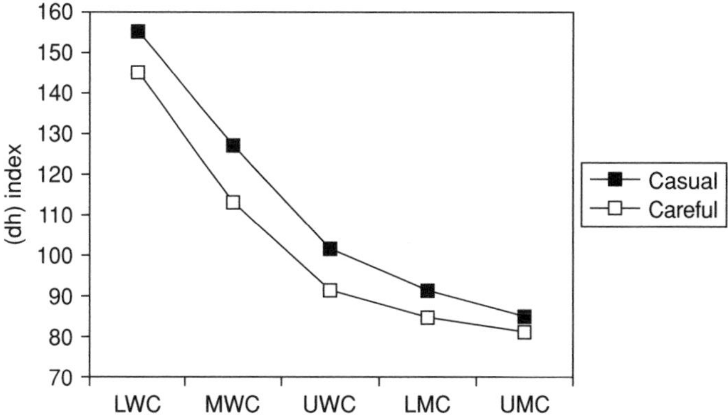


*Figure 3.6* Expected values of (dh) for socioeconomic class and style, from regression analysis including all other significant social variables

*Table 3.4* First regression of negative concord (neg) by style

| *Variable* | *Coefficient* | *Effect* | *t-ratio* | *Probability* |
|---|---|---|---|---|
| *Casual speech* | | | | |
| SEC | −5.36 | 69.68 | −5.85 | ≤0.0001 |
| Age | −0.32 | 24.25 | −2.40 | ≤0.0001 |
| Female | −13.91 | −26.91 | −2.75 | ≤0.0067 |
| So. Phila | 11.96 | 11.96 | −2.30 | ≤0.0228 |
| Jewish | −17.00 | −17.00 | −2.11 | 0.0370 |
| Constant 88.54 | $r^2$ = 32.3% | | n = 155 | d.f. = 149 |
| *Careful speech* | | | | |
| SEC | −3.20 | 41.60 | −4.52 | ≤0.0001 |
| Age | −0.28 | 21.28 | −2.61 | ≤0.0099 |
| Female | −14.71 | −14.71 | −43.64 | ≤0.0004 |
| So. Phila | 21.00 | 21.00 | 4.50 | ≤0.0001 |
| Jewish | −10.80 | −10.80 | −1.69 | 0.0935 |
| Constant 56.14 | $r^2$ = 35.0% | | n = 163 | d.f. = 157 |

Table 3.4 shows the comparable figures for (neg). Here the SEC effect is considerably greater than for (dh), rising to 70% of the range in casual speech. The effect of age is about the same as for (dh), but the effect of being female is twice as high: that is, females are much less likely than males to use negative concord. The positive South Philadelphia effect is also present, but upward mobility is not. Instead, there is a moderate negative bias of Jewish ethnicity, at the .03 level in casual speech. Again,

*Table 3.5* First regression of (ing) by style

| *Variable* | *Coefficient* | *Effect* | *t-ratio* | *Probability* |
|---|---|---|---|---|
| *Casual speech* | | | | |
| SEC | −2.92 | 37.96 | −4.78 | ≤0.0001 |
| Age | −0.34 | 25.84 | −3.40 | ≤0.0008 |
| Female | −11.50 | −11.50 | −3.12 | ≤0.0021 |
| Jewish | −20.48 | −20.48 | −3.88 | 0.0001 |
| Constant 120.71 | $r^2$ = 24.4% | | n = 178 | d.f. = 173 |
| *Careful speech* | | | | |
| SEC | −4.57 | 59.41 | −5.33 | ≤0.0001 |
| Age | −0.56 | 42.90 | −4.75 | ≤0.0001 |
| Female | −11.46 | −11.46 | −2.68 | ≤0.0081 |
| Jewish | −27.62 | −27.62 | −3.61 | ≤0.0001 |
| Constant 124.65 | $r^2$ = 35.9% | | n = 176 | d.f. = 171 |

the same effects recur for careful speech, but (except for South Philadelphia) at a more moderate level. There is no doubt that the use of (neg) is heavily controlled by socioeconomic position. But again the question arises to plague us: how can we distinguish (neg) from a change in progress?

A comparable regression on (ing) is given in table 3.5. The three major social factors appear in the same form, with SEC as the strongest effect. But in contrast to the other two variables, the SEC and age effect for (ing) are stronger in careful speech than in casual speech. The effect of gender is the same as with (dh), and it is identical in both styles. The South Philadelphia neighborhood influence is not strong enough to appear as a significant effect, but again the Jewish factor appears as a sizeable inhibitor of the use of the colloquial form.

The sociolinguistic patterns displayed by (dh), (neg), and (ing) are remarkably consistent. They are strongly affected by socioeconomic class, moderately by age, and weakly by gender. Lower class, younger, and male speakers use more of the stigmatized features than higher class, older, and female speakers. Three weakly correlated features play an occasional role in this picture: residence in South Philadelphia favors the use of stigmatized features, while Jewish ethnicity and upward mobility disfavor them. The total amount of variance explained by these factors is sizeable, as shown by adjusted $r^2$. It is greatest for (dh) in casual speech, almost 50%, and least for (ing) in casual speech, only one quarter.

Table 3.6 shows that the use of stops and affricates in intervocalic position – (dhv) – is a very different kind of variable. It is influenced only by socioeconomic class, and that at a very moderate rate, and only in casual speech.

*Table 3.6* First regression of intervocalic (dhv): casual speech

| *Variable* | *Coefficient* | *Effect* | *t-ratio* | *Probability* |
|---|---|---|---|---|
| SEC | –4.91 | 31.95 | –4.18 | ≤0.0001 |
| Constant 39.38 | $r^2$ = 12.6% | | n = 115 | d.f. = 113 |

## 3.6 Cross-tabulation by age

The use of a single quantitative age dimension in figures 3.3–3.6 is only a first approximation to the actual distribution of the stable sociolinguistic variables in apparent time. It portrays the effect of age on (dh), (neg), etc., as linear. If there were a direct causal relationship between age and these variables, a linear relationship would not be implausible, but there is no reason to think that increasing age causes a person to use fewer stops for (dh), in the way that it leads to a crystallization of the cornea. An understanding of age effects on language – the principles that govern distributions in apparent time – requires an understanding of the changes in social relations across speakers' life histories that bear upon their acquisition and use of linguistic norms and their ability to put them into practice. These include their changing affiliations with successive reference groups, their acquisition and employment of symbolic capital, and relaxation of the norms of the dominant society in old age. Divisions of the age continuum into groups must be roughly consonant with life stages. In modern American society, these events are alignment to the pre-adolescent peer group (8–9), membership in the pre-adolescent peer group (10–12), involvement in heterosexual relations and the adolescent group (13–16), completion of secondary schooling and orientation to the wider world of work and/or college (17–19), the beginning of regular employment and family life (20–29), full engagement in the work force and family responsibilities (30–59), retirement (60s). Any divisions in the age continuum will cut across certain social class differences in the characteristic location of the transitions, especially in the post-adolescent years; it is the early groupings that are most informed by sociological work. For the main extent of adult life, sociolinguistic behavior will be traced by decades.

Figure 3.7 shows the age distribution of the three Philadelphia variables that were introduced in this chapter as candidates for stable sociolinguistic variables. In all three, casual and careful speech appear as parallel curves, rising and falling together: style is effectively independent of age.

The three figures show remarkably similar patterns, which are neither flat nor linear. The highest values are found among speakers under 18; adults generally decline with age to a minimum in the 40–49 year range;

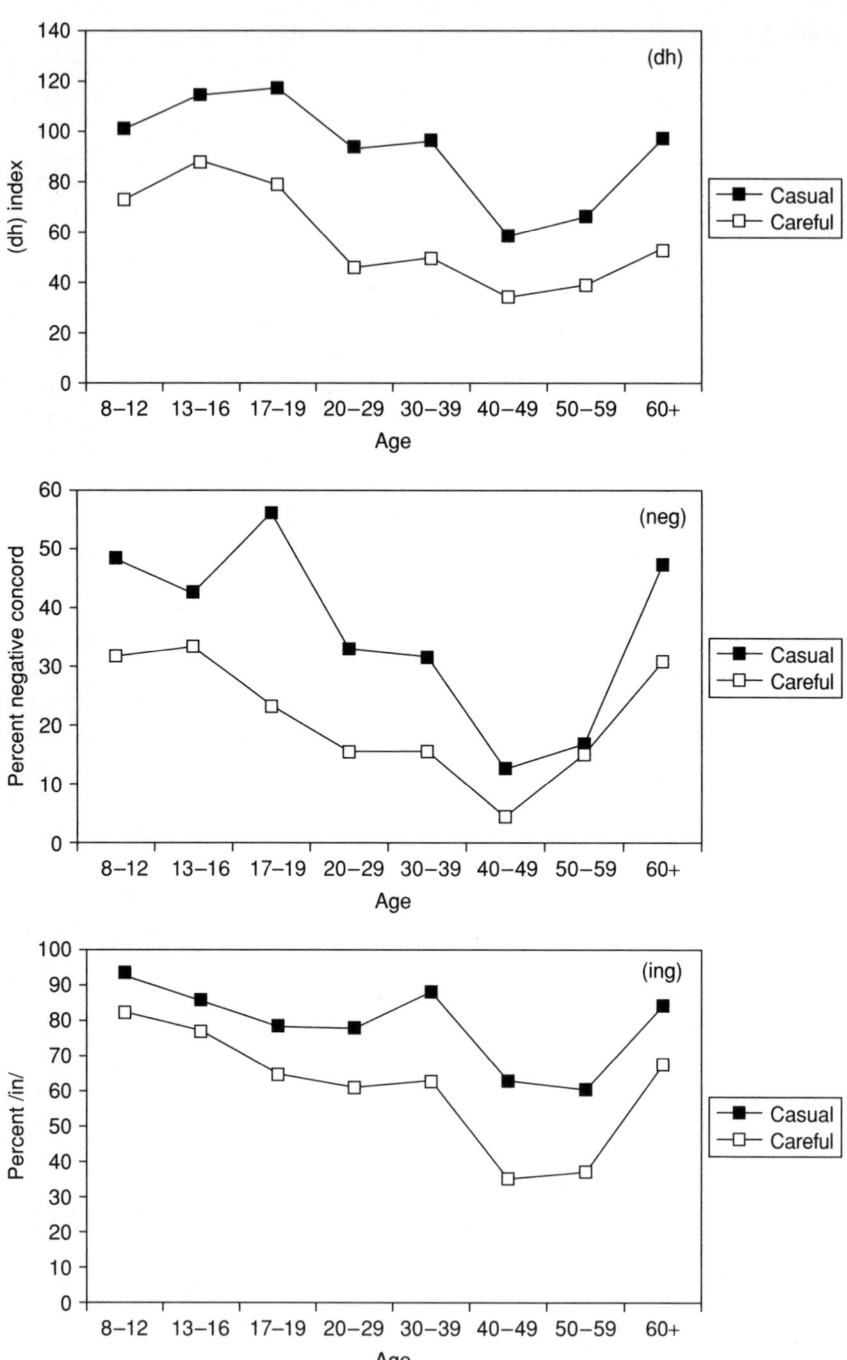


*Figure 3.7* Three sociolinguistic variables in the Philadelphia Neighborhood Study, by age and style

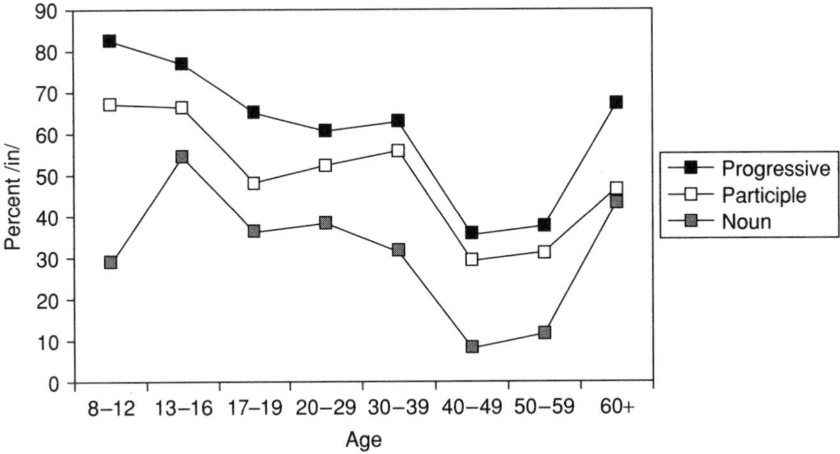


*Figure 3.8* Distribution of (ing) by grammatical category and age in the Philadelphia Neighborhood Study

and speakers over 60 show a decided increase. The most remarkable rise for this oldest group is shown for (neg). In the general pattern the three diagrams are effectively the same.

In figure 3.7, the progressive sub-category is used to represent (ing); it represents 78% of the data in casual speech and 68% in careful speech. Since the grammatical constraints are in general independent of social constraints, one would expect the other two sub-categories to show parallel trajectories. Figure 3.8 demonstrates that this is the case for careful speech.[21]

Figure 3.9 presents the corresponding age and style distribution for (dhv), confirming the conclusion drawn from the first regression analyses that this is a different type of variable. Most age groups depart only minimally from the standard fricative level at (dhv-00). There is a very sharp peak in the 17–19 year range whose significance must be explored further, and a smaller peak for the speakers over 60, parallel to the patterns shown in the other figures.

## *The social significance of casual and careful speech*

The next step in the analysis will be to examine these age distributions across social class. So far, the patterns of casual and careful speech have appeared as parallel curves, independent of age distributions; small

[21] The data for casual speech does not show the same parallelism, but considerably more irregularity. This is not the result of low numbers: there are 6608 tokens in careful speech, and 8493 in casual speech.

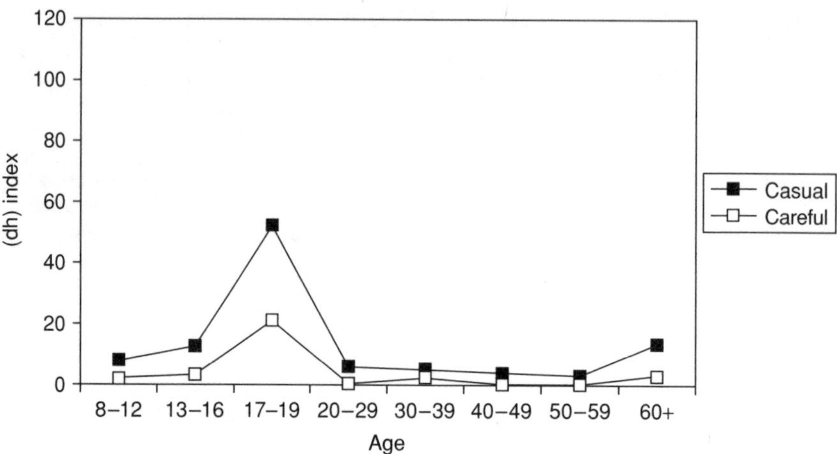


*Figure 3.9* Distribution of intervocalic (dhv) by age and style in the Philadelphia Neighborhood Study

differences will begin to appear in the intersection of social class and age with style. We will first look at careful speech, since patterns of social stratification are somewhat clearer and more regular here than in casual speech. This might seem to be reversing the normal direction of sociolinguistic methodology, which puts a great deal of emphasis on the techniques for removing or side-stepping the constraints of the interview situation that produce "careful" speech. The sections that we label "casual speech" are highly prized, representing our closest approach to the vernacular in the interview situation.

Yet an approach to the vernacular is not the whole story. A view of casual speech is essential in assessing whether a certain linguistic feature is variable or categorical; in eliciting the most advanced forms of change in progress; and in getting the most accurate information on the distribution of word classes, which is always clearest in the vernacular. On the other hand, the speakers' reactions to the interview situation give us a clearer view of overt sociolinguistic norms. The patterns of social stratification that constitute the stable sociolinguistic variables are essentially the result of the patterns of interaction across the community, that is, interaction among acquaintances and strangers rather than among close friends. That is why rapid and anonymous surveys, like the New York City Department Store study, can quickly and accurately show the social and stylistic pattern of the entire community. In most early sociolinguistic work, the sections we called "casual speech" were only brief excursions in the direction of the vernacular. However, the Philadelphia Neighborhood Study used sampling and interview methods that were more successful in capturing the kinds of speech observed in long-term participant observation. As chapter 2 pointed out, our analyses are based on first interviews of the neighborhood study in order to obtain comparable results, rather than the four or five recordings that often followed. But the technique of community study meant that the first interviews were "first" in this sense only for the first persons contacted in the social network. Bower, Schiffrin, and Payne were very often well known to the speaker by the time of the interview. They had already sat in the kitchen where the recording took place, been vouched for by good mutual friends (who were often present), and been introduced to the main dimensions of local society and gossip.[22]

To put it another way, "casual" and "careful" speech are relative terms. They refer to the sections of the interview that are more or less affected by the effects of recording and observation. The advance in sociolinguistic techniques leads to a shift of both stylistic levels toward the vernacular, and this makes comparison across studies more difficult. If we juxtapose the Philadelphia (dh) data to the New York City (dh) data as in figure 3.5b, it is evident that careful speech in Philadelphia is roughly equivalent to, perhaps a little more advanced than, casual speech in New York City. If Philadelphia casual speech is therefore a better approximation to the vernacular than we achieved in New York City, we can expect Philadelphia careful speech to reproduce more accurately the regular social stratification that appeared in the casual speech of New York City. We will find comparable shifts when we compare Philadelphia (ing) to Norwich (ing) or Philadelphia (neg) to Detroit (neg).

This discussion of style is not simply a technical matter of how to locate the vernacular or how to compare speakers across social levels. It relates to the substantive question of the nature of social stratification, and the forces that maintain the stable differentials between classes. If control of the standard language is viewed as a basic form of symbolic capital (Bourdieu 1980), then sociolinguistic stratification is the result of the differential ability of speakers to produce the standard forms or inhibit the nonstandard forms. Working class speakers then appear as limited by lack of exposure to standard forms and inadequate practice with their use, and the stable patterns we have been examining are maintained by continuing differential access to these linguistic resources. On the other hand, the sociolinguistic pattern can be seen as a stable balance of competing norms. In this view, the nonstandard forms represent an alternate form of symbolic capital that carries full value in working class social networks, and serves the needs of members of that society. The first view reflects a general consensus as to how people should speak; this is the dominant form of expression whenever an interview or a conversation turns to a

[22] The evidence cited in note 21 on the relative proportions of (ing) tokens in careful and casual speech confirm the fact that an unusually high percentage of the neighborhood interviews satisfy the criteria of casual speech, as opposed to a minority in earlier work.

discussion of language differences. The second view is expressed much less often, and evidence for it is more indirect: it implies a general disagreement on linguistic norms and a conflict between competing norms. I will refer to these two opposing views hereafter as the *consensual* and *competitive* models of sociolinguistic structure.

In the detailed examination of the Philadelphia community, the social distribution of patterns of careful speech will provide the clearest view of the consensual model. To the extent that casual speech patterns are different, their evidence will bear on the validity of the competitive model.

## 3.7 Cross-tabulations by age and social class

Figures 3.8–3.9 displayed two features of age distribution that show promise of refining our view of the relationship of apparent time to real time and the transmission of linguistic features across generations: the adolescent peak and the middle-aged trough. But this pattern may be an artifact of other distributions. Table 3.2 shows that the various neighborhoods and social classes do not share the same age distribution. The more middle class, socially mobile neighborhoods, Nancy Drive and Mallow Street, are missing the oldest generation of speakers over 60, and their mean age is in the mid 20s. More detailed cross-tabulations of age and social class in the figures to follow will show whether the adolescent peak and the middle-aged trough are general features of age levels, or the product of socioeconomic skewing of those age levels in the sample.

A certain amount of condensation of both scales is needed to be sure that there is a reasonable amount of data in each cell. Our interest in the adolescent peak precludes any collapsing of age categories among younger speakers, but the adults can be presented in groups of 20 rather than 10 years. The SEC scale is presented in four groups: 2–6, "Lower Working Class;" 7–9, "Upper Working Class;" 10–12, "Lower Middle Class;" 13–14, "Upper Middle Class." The data for the upper middle class is limited to two age groups: 13 to 16 and 40 to 59.[23]

Figure 3.10 shows considerable interaction of age and social class for (dh), (neg), and (ing): different social class groups show different patterns in apparent time. In the lower working class data, the adolescent peak and middle-aged trough are identifiable, but there is no sharp upward turn for speakers over 60. Upper working class speakers are not far from the lower working class for the youngest age groups, but there is a sharp downward shift beginning with 17- to 19-year-olds. Except for (ing), the lower

[23] This is because it is heavily based on the new community of King of Prussia, where our interest in the acquisition of the Philadelphia dialect led us to focus on families with parents in their 40s and children in their teens.

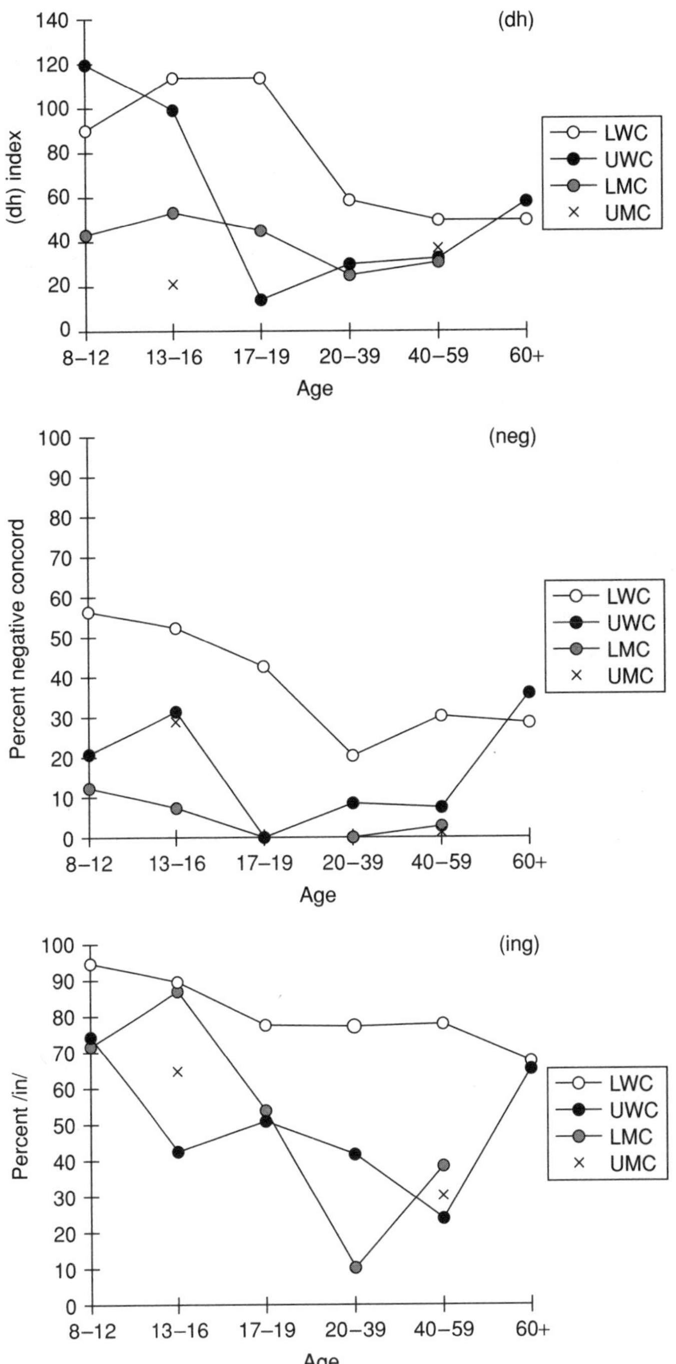


*Figure 3.10* Distribution of three sociolinguistic variables by SEC in careful speech in the Philadelphia Neighborhood Study

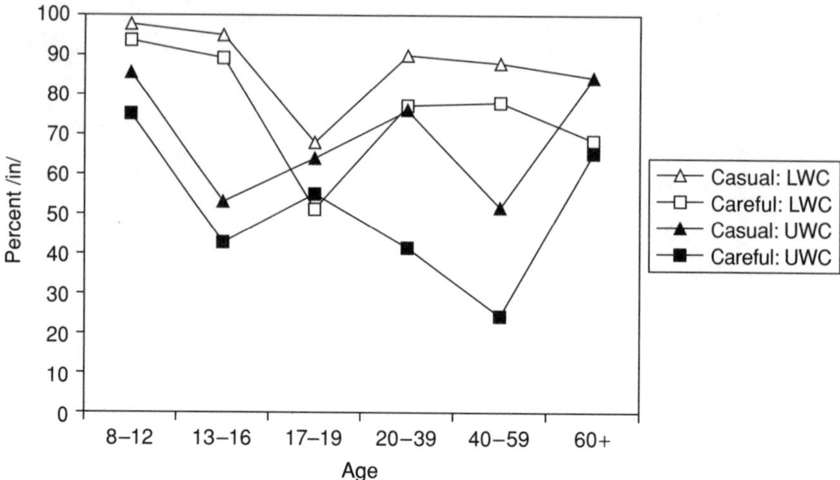


*Figure 3.11* Comparison of (ing) values in casual and careful speech for working class subjects in the Philadelphia Neighborhood Study

middle class keeps a low profile throughout. It is evident that negative concord is the most sharply stratified of these three; the difference between lower working class and others is greatest here.

A striking deviation from regular class stratification is shown by the upper middle class youth 13–16 years old, who show a (neg) value of 31. The actual figures for the three speakers involved – all male – are 0 out of 1, 1 out of 3, and 3 out of 5 instances of negative concord.[24] These are small numbers, and heavily influenced by the third speaker, Keith D. It is interesting to observe that no speakers with strong negative concord like Keith were found among the lower middle class youth. The lack of consistency in the use of negative concord by middle class speakers supports the competitive model: that some middle class youth are sensitive to the competing working class norm and adopt it. The same group of upper middle class youth show high values for (ing), higher than the upper working class. It appears that upper middle class youth form part of the adolescent peak of figure 3.5 – the two male parents of these three adolescents show only 31% /in/.[25]

The (ing) patterns for casual speech are quite similar to those for careful speech. Figure 3.11 compares the two styles for the two working class

[24] The speaker – Keith D. – who used 3 out of 5 also used negative concord 2 out of 3 times in casual speech.

[25] The data for negative concord on the parents suggests that the behavior of Keith D. was part of a family pattern. His father, Alfred D., was the only upper middle class person to use negative concord in careful speech: 1 out of 14 tokens in careful speech, and 6 out of 16 in casual speech.

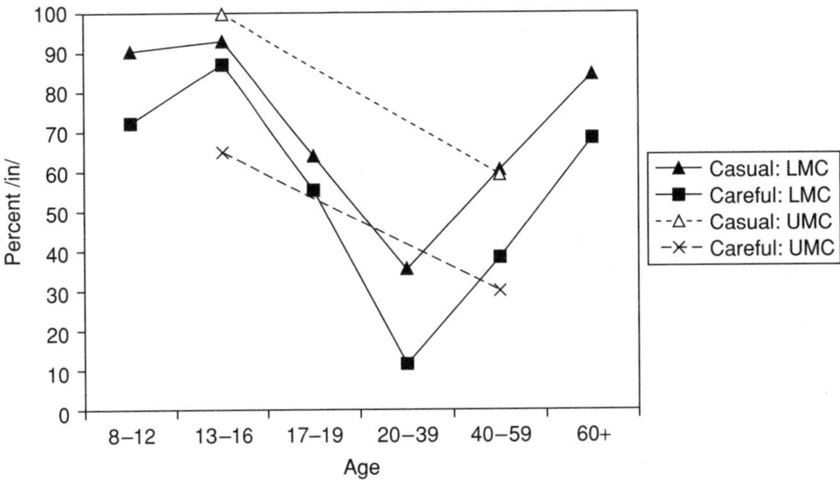


*Figure 3.12* Comparison of (ing) values in casual and careful speech by age for middle class subjects in the Philadelphia Neighborhood Study

groups, and 3.12 for the middle class groups. In general, the style shifts are moderate, except for working class adults, and upper middle class youth. In casual speech the middle class youth come close to 100% /in/, while in careful speech their parents' generation approaches 100% /iŋ/. Much of what has been said about the history of (ing) is consistent with the idea of competing norms available to the entire population. The extreme behavior of the upper middle class youth can then be interpreted as an early socialization into the art of style shifting. On the other hand, one can also argue that the working class speakers lack the ability to use the /iŋ/ norm consistently in spontaneous speech. It remains a moot question whether working class speakers have no desire or motivation to depart from the /in/ model or lack the ability to do so.

At this point, we have almost exhausted the possibilities of cross-tabulation. It seems likely that many of the issues just raised would be clarified by distinguishing male from female speakers. It would be essential to divide each group into male and female, and sub-divide the South Philadelphia or Jewish speakers. But even with this sizeable data base of 183 speakers and 16,000 tokens for (ing), further sub-division would leave only individual, idiosyncratic variation to examine. At least five dimensions are operating on the stable sociolinguistic variables, and only a multivariate analysis can show their joint influence. But as this section has demonstrated, it is not feasible to mount a multivariate analysis that posits that the effects of age and social class are linear. A second regression analysis will use what has been learned from cross-tabulations to produce a more accurate view of the social pattern of stable sociolinguistic variables.

## 3.8 Second regression analysis

Instead of using a single quantitative dimension for age and social class, the second regression analysis will use grouped age and social class categories. These will replicate the categories of the cross-tabulations with one addition. The location of the adolescent peak will be explored more closely by separating the 13- to 16-year-old group into 13 to 15 and 16. This will take advantage of the fact that the sociolinguistic sample has 16-year-olds with SEC ratings ranging from 4 to 11. For the age groups, the residual category, against which all others will be compared, is the oldest group of speakers, those over 60. The residual category for social class will be the lowest group, the lower working class, SEC 2–3. For each of the groups, the speaker will be assigned a value of 1 if he or she is a member of that age or SEC group, otherwise 0.

Figure 3.13 gives the results of this second regression analysis for (dh) in careful speech. On the left the nine age groups show positive values, but there is a clear separation of adults from youth. None of the adult groups are significantly different from the reference group of 60+ at zero, while all of those under 20 are. There is a strong peak at the age of 16. The differences are not only significant, but they are sizeable: the 16-year-olds have values close to 90, that is, almost half of the possible range, while all other groups show values close to 40, one fifth of the possible range. The

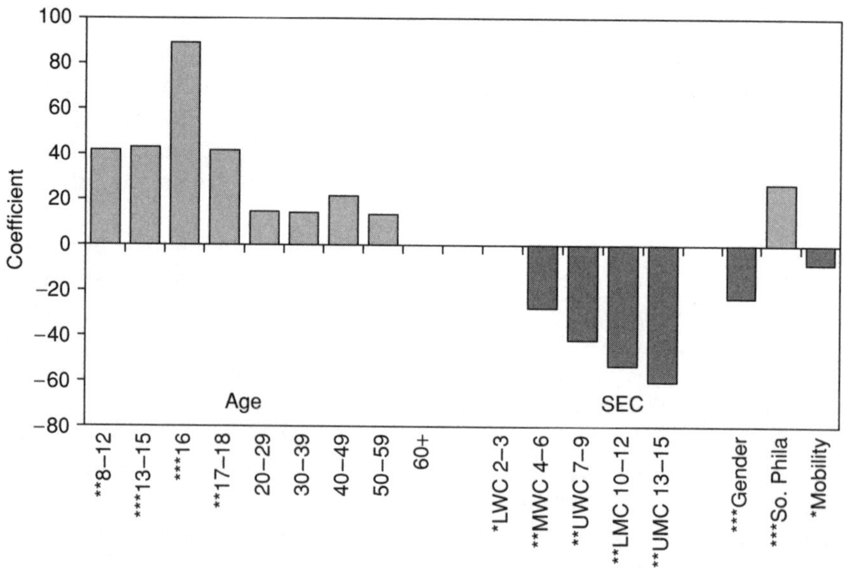


*Figure 3.13* Regression coefficients for (dh) in careful speech with 9 age groups and 5 social classes (p * < .05, ** < .01, *** < .001). For gender, female = 1.

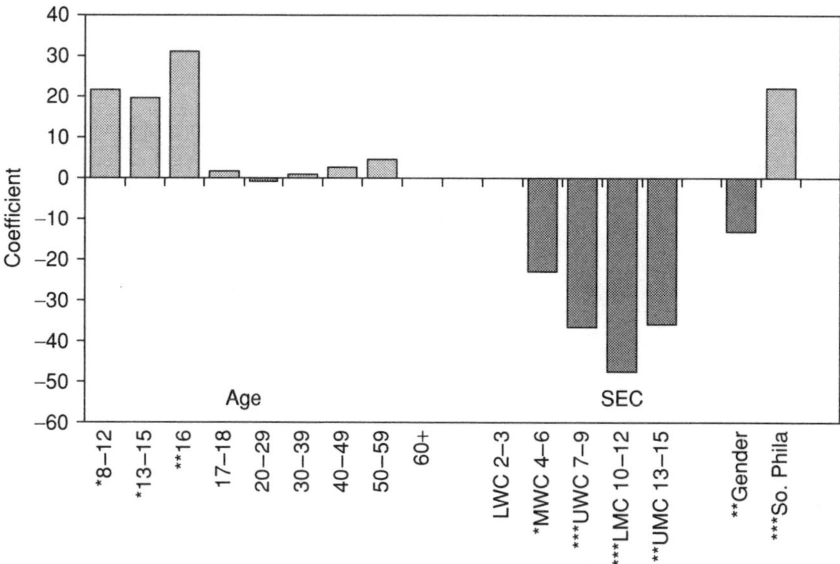


*Figure 3.14* Regression coefficients for (neg) in careful speech with 9 age groups and 5 social classes (p * < .05, ** < .01, *** < .001). For gender, female = 1.

difference between the 16-year-olds and the 13–15 group is significant at the .001 level.

To the right, the social class groups show a clear monotonic function differentiating each from the lower working class, with steadily decreasing coefficients of –33, –46, –57, and –64. The gender effect is preserved at the same level as the first regression, along with the positive effect of South Philadelphia and the negative effect of upward mobility. The same pattern is preserved in detail in the analysis of (dh) in casual speech.

Figure 3.14 shows a remarkably similar pattern for (neg) in careful speech. Again the adult age groups are undifferentiated, departing only minimally from the zero reference, while younger speakers show a significant and sizeable effect in the use of (neg), with a significant peak for the 16-year-olds. The social class groups are similar, though there is no significant difference between lower working and middle working class. Again, the effects of sex and South Philadelphia residence that we saw in the cross-tabulations are preserved.

Finally, figure 3.15 repeats the pattern for (ing) in careful speech. Again we see the adolescent peak at 16, and the absence of significant departure from zero for the adults. The social class pattern is, however, not monotonic, but differentiates middle class from working class. The other constraints again repeat the pattern we have seen in the first regression, but at a lower level of significance.

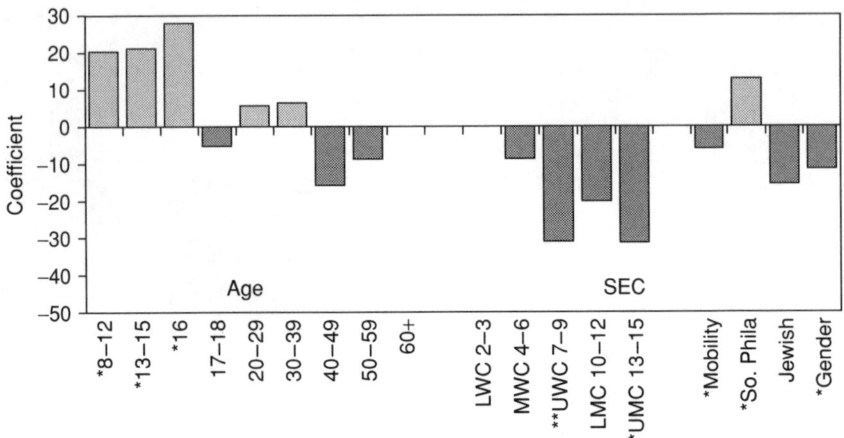


*Figure 3.15* Regression coefficients for (ing) in careful speech with 9 age groups and 5 social classes (p * < .05, ** < .01, *** < .001)

The picture that emerges from the second regression is clear and consistent. Taking all effects together, it appears that most of the fluctuations of the cross-tabulations are the result of intersecting influences and the fact that the neighborhood study could not, in principle, be perfectly balanced for gender, ethnicity, neighborhood, age, and social class. The regular effect of gender – that women use fewer nonstandard forms than men – is preserved throughout as a substantial and significant effect. Residence in South Philadelphia has an equal and opposite effect on all three variables. Two minor effects are not as consistent: upward mobility and Jewish ethnicity act to inhibit the use of nonstandard forms. No other independent variables besides age and social class have any significant influence on the three variables. Except for the one case of Jewish ethnicity, there is no ethnic influence on these variables: being Irish, German, Italian, or Wasp made no difference. Nor did having a foreign language background, nor being first, second, or third generation from the time of immigration. There was no detectable influence of differences in house upkeep. And aside from South Philadelphia, neighborhood or area made no difference.

For adults, age made no difference. The higher use of the nonstandard forms by youth that was predicted in the original 1966 model of table 3.1 was strongly confirmed, with the additional fact – which may or may not be specific to this city or this sample – that in mid-adolescence there is a very high peak, which falls off rapidly in late adolescence.

The primary determinant of the stable sociolinguistic variables is of course social class: the higher the position of a speaker in the social scale, the smaller is the frequency of nonstandard forms.

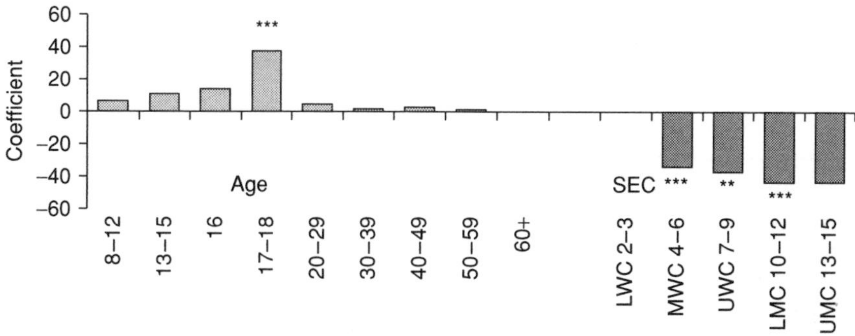


*Figure 3.16* Regression coefficients for intervocalic (dhv) in careful speech with 9 age groups and 5 social classes (p * < .05, ** < .01, *** < .001)

The similarities among the three sociolinguistic variables are the most striking result of this investigation. They differ in small respects. The late adolescent youth form part of the peak for (dh); and (ing) shows a bimodal rather than a monotonic function of social class. (ing) is the only variable to show an ethnic effect, and negative concord is not influenced by social mobility.

On the other hand, there is little resemblance at all between these three stable sociolinguistic variables and the intervocalic variable (dhv). Figure 3.16 shows that there is only one age group that favors the non-standard form: the 17- to 18-year-old group. Moreover, all social classes agree in opposing themselves to the lower working class in not using it. In other words, intervocalic stops are a clear lower working class marker, primarily used in late adolescence.

## 3.9 An exploration of social class indicators

So far, the analysis has made use of the LCV combined index of socio-economic class (SEC) as described in chapter 2. The community studies that developed and used such indices examined their components in minute detail. The Mobilization for Youth Survey, which developed the combined index used by LES, constructed and tested alternate indices, and the indicators of occupation, education, and income were examined individually (Cloward and Ohlin 1960). The LES study presents data on individual indicators and several alternative ways of combining them. Similar considerations went into the construction of social class indicators in the studies of Detroit, Norwich, Panama City, and Montreal, with different results for different communities.

The basic concept involved is that of a socioeconomic hierarchy, not a discrete set of identifiable classes. In order to test the hypothesis of the

LCV study – the existence of a curvilinear social class pattern in change from below – it is necessary to divide that hierarchy into at least four sections. The independent variables of occupation, education, and house value adopted by the LCV study of Philadelphia are different measures of the relative positions of a speaker in that hierarchy which allow us to make such provisional divisions. They are not themselves determinants of social class, a concept that involves the more subjective component of status, and the more elusive fact of power. In the final interpretation, there may be evidence for discontinuities in that hierarchy, but so far, the tables of chapter 2 show a continuous range of SEC values.

The three types of indicators have three different relations to a speaker's life trajectory and life chances. The New York City study showed that they had different relations to linguistic variables that reflected these differences. Occupation is most closely linked to family background, and tends to be the strongest determinant of linguistic patterns established early in life, like (dh). On the other hand, educational status changes continuously throughout the early years, and education is linked more closely with superposed variables that are acquired later in life, like NYC (r). Income changes the most and reflects the most recent socioeconomic position of a speaker; it therefore tends to have the weakest relation to linguistic patterns. Thus individuals who do not fit into the typical range of their social class are frequently those who show status incongruence among the indicators: for example, a plumber whose income and residence reflect a recently acquired prosperity may display linguistic features more typical of his earlier career.[26]

This section will compare the different components of the LCV index in their correlations with the three stable sociolinguistic variables. The results of the second regression will form the base for comparing the view of the community given by each indicator for each variable in each style, eliminating all nonsignificant independent variables. The entire adult age range will form the residual reference group against which the various divisions of age groups under 20 will be compared. Analyses will then differ as to whether the 8–12 group or the 17–18 group will be retained; in all cases, the 13–15 and 16-year-old group will be maintained. The familiar variables of gender, South Philadelphia residence, mobility, and Jewish ethnicity will be retained in their usual place, unless the new analysis reduces their significance below the .10 level.

The SEC variable will then be removed, and the three separate indicators inserted: the 6-level index of occupations, based on the census categories; the number of years of schooling completed; and house values. Each of these will be examined for its significance, and removed if it fails to reach the .05 level.

[26] See the case of Emilio D. in Labov 1966a:478–9.

### *Two forms of the educational indicator*

The presence of large numbers of young speakers in the sociolinguistic sample raises a question about the educational ratings. Consider an 8-year-old member of a King of Prussia family in the third grade. The father may have an educational level of 18, the mother 14. If we assign the rating of 3, this speaker will have the same rating as an 84-year-old lower working class Irishman who quit school at the age of 9 to go to work. Yet everything about the family situation leads us to expect that this child will reach an educational level equal to or higher than the parents'.

The issue is a substantive one, not merely a question of method. If the effect of educational level on language is a general cultural pattern, a set of attitudes toward language and language learning, the child should be assigned the same rating as the parents. If, on the other hand, education influences language according to what is actually learned in school, year by year, then we should use the third grade as the educational level, and stick to the basic definition: years of schooling completed.

Two separate indices were constructed: one of the child's actual grade level (Ed1), the other assigning to him or her the parents' educational level (Ed2). Educational level was not significant in many analyses; but significant or not, there was no single case in which the Ed2 index was more highly correlated with the linguistic variable than the Ed1 index, and none in which the Ed2 index was itself significant. The conclusion is clear. In this community, and perhaps elsewhere as well, the effect of education is cumulative. Children's use of linguistic variables is determined by how much schooling they have received, not the general educational milieu of the family.

Table 3.7 presents two analyses of (dh) in careful speech. The relevant lines for comparison are shown in bold. Among the three indicators, occupation was the only one selected. The coefficient of –8.44 may be multiplied by 5 (the range of the index, which runs from 0 to 5) to show an effect of –42.2: one fifth of the possible range of 200. The standard error is 2.74, and the t-ratio, the number of standard errors in the coefficient, is therefore –3.08. With an n of 151, and eight significant factors, this has 143 degrees of freedom, and the probability of this being due to chance is 1 out of 400. The F-ratio of this analysis is 17.8, and the adjusted $r^2$ is 47.3, indicating that it accounts for 47.3% of the variation.

The bottom half of the table compares this result with one in which the combined SEC index is entered instead of the three separate indicators. We can compare the bold line with the first analysis; all the other figures vary only slightly. The regression coefficient for SEC is –4.00. This is much less than that for occupation, but the effect is somewhat greater, since the maximum range for SEC is 13 (15 – 2), and 13 × (–4.00) is –52. The standard error is slightly less, so that the t-ratio is larger, and the resulting

*Table 3.7* Comparison of socioeconomic indicators for (dh) in careful speech

| *Variable* | *Coefficient* | *Effect* | *Std Err.* | *t-ratio* | *Probability* |
|---|---|---|---|---|---|
| *Analysis A: using occupation, education, house value* | | | | | |
| 8–12 | 24.80 | | 8.68 | 2.85 | 0.0050 |
| 13–15 | 23.75 | | 8.12 | 2.92 | 0.0040 |
| 16 | 77.44 | | 12.46 | 6.21 | ≤0.0001 |
| 17–18 | 32.11 | | 12.43 | 2.58 | 0.0108 |
| **Occupation** | **–8.44** | **–42.2** | **2.74** | **–3.08** | **0.0025** |
| Female | –22.18 | | 5.82 | –3.81 | 0.0002 |
| Mobility | –8.34 | | 3.43 | –2.43 | 0.0162 |
| So. Phila | 29.75 | | 6.08 | 4.90 | ≤0.0001 |
| **$r^2$ = 47.3** | n = 151 | | F-ratio = 17.8 | | |
| *Analysis B: using SEC* | | | | | |
| 8–12 | 27.98 | | 8.57 | 3.26 | 0.0014 |
| 13–15 | 28.80 | | 8.17 | 3.53 | 0.0006 |
| 16 | 75.40 | | 12.30 | 6.13 | ≤0.0001 |
| 17–18 | 38.06 | | 11.85 | 3.21 | 0.0016 |
| **SEC** | **–4.00** | **–52** | **1.052** | **–3.80** | **0.0002** |
| Female | –23.56 | | 5.70 | –4.13 | ≤0.0001 |
| Mobility | –7.438 | | 3.39 | –2.19 | 0.0299 |
| So. Phila | 25.46 | | 6.28 | 4.05 | ≤0.0001 |
| **$r^2$ = 48.9** | n = 151 | | F-ratio = 19 | | |

probability is 1 out of 5000 instead of 1 out of 400. The F-ratio is slightly larger (19 as against 17.8), and the amount of variation explained is a bit higher (48.9% as against 47.3%).

Both analyses are excellent in terms of the amount of variation explained; SEC and occupation are almost equivalent. This implies that the other two indicators, education and house value, are contributing very little. In spite of the fact that the SEC analysis has a slight edge, the simpler indicator of occupation would be preferable – if this were a consistent pattern across variables and styles.

In general, occupation accounts for more of the variance than the other two indicators, and it is a significant contributor in five of the six comparisons. But examining the six cases carefully, a variety of configurations appears. Table 3.8 compares the socioeconomic indicators for the three stable variables in both casual and careful speech, extracted from analyses that follow the procedures of table 3.7.

The first two lines repeat the results of table 3.7. For (dh) in casual speech, a different situation appears. Instead of occupation, the only indicator selected is house value. The coefficient is large, –12. This is multiplied

*Table 3.8* Comparison of SEC and individual indicators in regression analyses of three stable sociolinguistic variables

| *Variable* | *Coeff.* | *Effect* | *Std Err.* | *t-ratio* | *Prob.* | *F* | $r^2$ |
|---|---|---|---|---|---|---|---|
| (dh) careful | | | | | | | |
| Occ | −8.44 | −51 | 2.74 | −3.08 | 0.0025 | 17.8 | 47.3 |
| SEC | −4.00 | −52 | 1.05 | −3.80 | 0.0002 | 19.0 | 48.9 |
| (dh) casual | | | | | | | |
| House | −12.00 | −48 | 2.72 | −4.40 | 0.0001 | 16.5 | 44.9 |
| SEC | −5.42 | −70 | 1.20 | −4.53 | 0.0001 | 16.7 | 45.3 |
| (neg) careful | | | | | | | |
| Occ | 7.19 | −36 | 1.92 | −3.74 | 0.0003 | 14.4 | 34.7 |
| SEC | −3.35 | −43 | 0.70 | −4.81 | 0.0001 | 17.3 | 37.6 |
| (neg) casual | | | | | | | |
| Occ | −10.37 | −52 | 2.26 | −4.03 | 0.0001 | 9.27 | 29.1 |
| Ed | −2.81 | −48 | 1.35 | −2.08 | 0.0393 | | |
| SEC | −5.58 | −73 | 0.94 | −5.96 | 0.0001 | 13.1 | 32.0 |
| (ing) careful | | | | | | | |
| Occ | −10.26 | −51 | 1.96 | −5.24 | 0.0001 | 16.3 | 39.4 |
| Ed | −3.24 | −55 | 0.71 | −4.56 | 0.0001 | | |
| SEC | −4.53 | −59 | 0.73 | −6.23 | 0.0001 | 16.8 | 31.1 |
| (ing) casual | | | | | | | |
| Occ | −8.95 | −44 | 1.64 | −5.47 | 0.0001 | 10.4 | 22.1 |
| SEC | −3.52 | −46 | 0.65 | −4.83 | 0.0001 | 8.77 | 18.0 |

by 4 to show the effect, since house values range from 1 to 5. The resulting effect is about the same level as for occupation in careful speech, though considerably lower in effect than SEC. The standard error is slightly more than a fifth of the coefficient, so the probability is quite low. On the whole, house value does an excellent job of constraining the variable – but this is the only case where it turns out to be significant. In all other analyses, house value is small and uncorrelated with the linguistic variable. This is surprising, since as table 2.3 shows, the neighborhoods are more clearly stratified by house values than any other feature. However, it does correlate with the reasoning advanced above: that the value of the house a person is living in is in general adjusted more recently than the other indicators, and not likely to reflect a linguistic pattern that was established early in life.

The situation with (neg) in careful speech is about the same as for (dh) in careful speech. Occupation is the only significant indicator, and it operates at the .03 level. On the other hand, the effect of SEC is larger, and the standard error is proportionately smaller, so that the probability is three times smaller, and the F-ratio higher. For (neg) in casual speech, occupation has a strong effect, and educational level is also significant at the .05 level. The combined F-ratio is, however, not large, only 9.27, and the percentage of variation explained is only 29.1. SEC alone does not amount to as large an effect, but the probability is low and the F-ratio is higher.

For the third variable, (ing), two indicators are selected in careful speech: occupation and education, both significant at the .0001 level. The SEC index does not have as great an effect as these two combined, and $r^2$ – the amount of variance explained – is less. Finally, the configuration for (ing) in casual speech repeats the most common situation of this table. Occupation is the only indicator selected, and the effect is almost as great as for the combined SEC index.

Among the socioeconomic indicators, occupation is clearly the most influential factor, followed by educational level, while house value has the least influence. Throughout, we see that the stratification of the socio-economic hierarchy is clearest in careful speech; as we approach the vernacular, the differences between the strata are reduced. In table 3.8, occupation is the strongest indicator in the three analyses of careful speech; in casual speech, each variable shows a different pattern.

Given the strength of occupation in the analysis of stable sociolinguistic variables in careful speech, it would be unreasonable not to examine its value as an analytical tool in the study of change in progress in the chapters to follow. Where occupation is a strong determinant, it can be linked to social processes more easily than the combined index. But it is clear that the combined index is more regular and reliable than any one indicator. For each variable, and each style, SEC is a strong and reliable effect, from 40 to 70% of the range of the variable, well below the .001 level of significance. In all cases but one, the SEC index also yields higher F-ratios and higher $r^2$. If we were to adopt occupation as the sole measure of social class, no stratification of (dh) in casual speech would appear at all. When all three indicators are entered into each analysis, the result is a varied and miscellaneous configuration. Beyond the general predominance of occupation, there is no pattern visible yet that would allow us to predict when house value or education is a significant influence.

The stability of SEC as a measure of social class goes beyond the data of table 3.7. In carrying out the various regressions, one can observe the stability of an independent variable by the amount it changes when other variables are added or removed. A robust variable like SEC remains significant as the array of other variables changes. But the weight and significance of education and house value change radically as we enter or remove other variables.

It may seem mysterious at first that a combined index is superior to occupation even when the two other indicators are not significant. But even when the overall effect of house value and education does not determine the behavior of a linguistic variable, these indicators serve to correct and compensate for idiosyncratic effects and uncertainties in the socioeconomic classifications. A person's occupation may be wrongly rated or it may not have the usual influence on speech. The assignment of the occupation of the breadwinner to wives who are not working, or children, is bound to introduce uncertainties. The assignment of the same house value to everyone living in that house is not subject to the same uncertainty, even if it has less effect on speech. The combined index therefore achieves a stability that makes it superior to any single socioeconomic indicator.

## 3.10 Conclusion

The results of this examination of stable sociolinguistic variables have provided a base line against which we can measure the evidence for change in progress. The first step in testing the curvilinear hypothesis is to see if it is true that stable variables show a monotonic distribution along the socioeconomic hierarchy, and a flat distribution across age levels. Despite the appearance of a significant age factor in the first regression, it is now established that the age distribution is flat in the adult range for stable sociolinguistic variables, and that the higher levels of nonstandard forms predicted for younger speakers are concentrated in late adolescence.

The alignment with the socioeconomic hierarchy has been demonstrated in a number of tables and diagrams. Once age is taken into account, there is a marked tendency towards a binary division of social class for the stable sociolinguistic variables (figure 3.10, figure 3.15). Figure 3.10 indicates that the intermediate position of the upper working class for (dh) in figure 3.6 is largely a product of interaction with age: young speakers under 17 are aligned with the lower working class, while those over 17 are at the middle class level. This shifting allegiance of the upper working class shows up in a number of other sociolinguistic studies, as in the (ing) pattern in Norwich (figure 3.3) or the subjective reaction pattern in South Harlem (figure 8.5 in Labov 1972b). The monotonic function of social class is largely a product of the sensitivity of the upper working class to the norms maintained by the lower middle class. For the adult population, stratification is monotonic, if not evenly spaced across the socioeconomic hierarchy. The original formulation of this half of the curvilinear hypothesis should then be modified to read:

Stable linguistic variables are not a function of age among adults, but are a monotonic function of social class.

Later chapters will explore more deeply the relation of gender to these patterns, since it is not to be expected that the single regression factor used in this chapter does justice to the interaction of gender with age and social class. We will also look more deeply at the significance of the adolescent peak for the problem of transmission of linguistic change across generations. The next step, however, is to carry out a comparable analysis for those linguistic variables that show evidence of change in progress. These elements of the Philadelphia vowel system are involved in a complex series of mutual systematic relationships. That system will be considered as a whole in the following chapter, before carrying out the analysis of change in progress in chapter 5.

# 4

# *The Philadelphia Vowel System*

The present inquiry into the location of the innovators of linguistic change makes extensive use of a series of ongoing changes in the Philadelphia vowel system. Volume 1, chapter 3 presented an overview of that vowel system and the changes in progress, and volume 1, chapter 4 showed how real-time data could be used to consolidate the inferences drawn from apparent time. This chapter will place the Philadelphia dialect within the larger matrix of American English, and then present a more detailed and concrete view of the vowel system in which the changes in progress are occurring.

## 4.1 The Philadelphia dialect area

The main finding of the *Linguistic Atlas* of the Atlantic states (Kurath 1949, Kurath and McDavid 1961) was that American dialects did not fall into two major groups but into three. In addition to the North and the South, Kurath recognized a third region called the *Midland.* The Midland territory, as later research shows, covers most of Pennsylvania, most of Ohio, Indiana, and Illinois, the Southern Mountain area, and a vast region extending further to the west (Carver 1987; *Atlas of North American English*). The only Midland area on the Atlantic seaboard is the port of Philadelphia.

The settlement of the Midland involved a long and continuous pattern of westward migration, and much of it passed through Philadelphia. In addition to those who were tabulated as Philadelphia immigrants in the last chapter, large numbers of Scots-Irish, Palatine Germans, and other settlers passed through the city on their route to the west. They were oriented toward Philadelphia not only as their port of entry, but as the principal metropolis of the 18th century, "second only to London in the English-speaking world" (Kurath 1949). There is no doubt that the city's way of speaking English had a formative influence on the Midland dialect, since the first settlers in any area determine to a large extent the cultural patterns that follow, long after they have ceased to be a majority (Zelinsky 1992).

The study of the social location of the leaders of change in Philadelphia will profit most from linguistic changes in progress that are specific to the city. These will enable us to track linguistic developments across the social

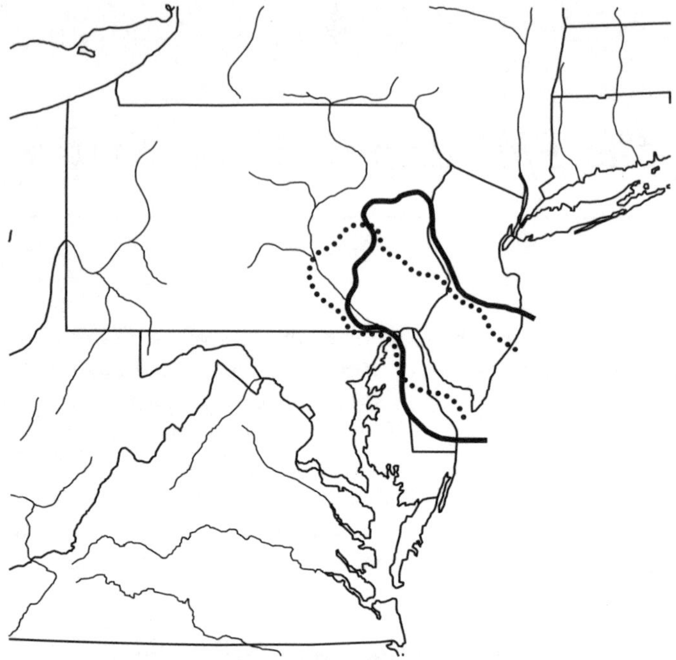

*Figure 4.1* The Philadelphia area defined by lexical isoglosses. Solid line: outer limit of *hot cakes* "griddle cakes;" dashed line: *bagged school* "played truant." (Source: Kurath 1949, map 22)

configurations described in the last chapter. It may be helpful then to review the features of Philadelphia English to see which are most suitable for this purpose.

Within the Midland, there is a region of eastern Pennsylvania delineated by the distribution of words such as *pavement* "sidewalk" and *baby coach* "baby carriage", which is most accurately designated as the "Philadelphia dialect area." Figure 4.1 shows the *Linguistic Atlas* isoglosses for *bagged school* "played truant" and *hot cakes* "griddle cakes" which define a Philadelphia lexical area.[1] My own study of the use of *hoagie* "submarine sandwich" again shows a global region of Philadelphia influence expanding to a radius of about 50 miles.[2]

Within the city, the LCV exploratory interviews show a wide variety of children's lore, games, words, and pronunciations that are found only in Philadelphia. In the street game of *half-ball*, the rubber ball that is pitched

[1] For other Philadelphia markers, see Lebofsky 1970.

[2] The influence of Philadelphia is better shown by the distribution of the cultural practice that combines hoagies (or submarine sandwiches) with the Philadelphia steak sandwich, a thin-sliced steak grilled with onions and cheese and served on the same long roll.

to the batter is split in half; this is as specific to Philadelphia as *sliding pond* or *selugi* is to New York. Yet like most of the words used to define the regional dialects of American English, the majority of these Philadelphia markers are falling into disuse. Payne's study of the acquisition of the Philadelphia dialect found that the knowledge of traditional Philadelphia markers ranged from a low of 5.6% (*tellypole* for *telegraph pole*) to 58% (*lunch kettle* for *lunch pail*) or 86% (*pavement* for *sidewalk*). On the other hand, there are a certain number of current Philadelphia markers, like the use of *hoagie* for "submarine sandwich", or *yo* as a call for attention, which rest on a vigorous and widespread adult culture. Payne found that these are acquired quickly and automatically by adults as well as children as they move into the Philadelphia area. It is therefore not likely that a study of lexical change could profit from the use of apparent time distributions.

There are several striking grammatical features of the Philadelphia dialect, but they do not form an interrelated system in the way that vowels do, and none of them appears to be involved in ongoing change. Tucker 1944 reports the use of positive *anymore* as a feature of the Philadelphia dialect, and LCV studies indicate that it is available to any Philadelphian in spontaneous speech, despite erratic responses to direct inquiry (Labov 1972d, Hindle 1974, Hindle and Sag 1973). But positive *anymore* turns out to be a general characteristic of the Midland dialect as a whole. The Philadelphia dialect is also marked by the use of auxiliary *be* with the verbs *finished* and *done*, as in *I'm done biology*, *When can you be finished five shirts?* But this also turns out to be a feature of much wider distribution, and shows no tendency to evolve in parallel with the phonological system. What grammatical changes in progress we do observe in Philadelphia are quite general in the English language, like the shift to the use of the *get* auxiliary with the passive (Weiner and Labov 1983, Feagin 1979).

In all the Euro-American dialects that we have studied, the major area of active linguistic change is phonology, and within phonology, the major arena of change is in the vowels and the liquids.[3] Ash has traced the progress of the vocalization of /l/ in Philadelphia (1982a, 1982b), but this is not at all specific to the city; it appears to be part of a widespread trend in American English, somewhat more advanced in western Pennsylvania than eastern Pennsylvania. Philadelphia shows a systematic advance in the use of hushing sibilants in initial /str/ clusters: again, this appears to be general to many areas of the Midland dialect.

Philadelphia is no exception to the generalization that linguistic change in North America is most active in the vowel system. Part B of volume 1 showed that vowel shifts follow general principles, and that vowel changes

[3] On the other hand, change in the tense and aspect system seems to be the major area of change in African American Vernacular English.

are organized into general patterns like the Northern Cities Shift or the Southern Shift. The question then arises as to whether vowel shifts can serve our purpose of tracking changes specific to Philadelphia. Fortunately, it appears that the particular pattern of vowel shifting found in Philadelphia is indeed characteristic of that city. Though it shares some features with the major regional patterns in the USA, the Philadelphia pattern is a unique combination that readily distinguishes local speakers from outsiders. Several chapters of volume 1 dealt with the specific Philadelphia distribution of short **a** words into tense and lax classes; the combination of lower level phonetic movements is no less unique to the city. It is all the more important, then, that the various vowel changes in progress be studied not in isolation, but as components of an interrelated structure. Part B of volume 1 was devoted to the general principles that govern change within such structures. Whatever general insights were gained there should be applied to the Philadelphia vowel system as the setting for the search for the leaders of linguistic change.

## 4.2 A general framework for the description of the Philadelphia vowel system

A general framework for the description of vowel systems was first presented in the discussion of chain shifts in progress in volume 1, chapter 6:159–64. The motivation for that framework became more evident when the general principles governing vowel shifts were more fully developed in chapters 5–9. English dialects do not then appear as a miscellaneous collection of varieties, but can be assembled into a few major types spread across vast geographic areas, driven in opposite directions by the forces of systematic sound change. A local system, like that of Philadelphia, can best be understood when it is placed within this larger framework.

The Philadelphia system as we approach it here is a combination of relatively stable elements and elements undergoing change in progress. A systematic description of these sound changes will require a point of departure or *initial position*. Such an initial position must satisfy two criteria: (1) each of the current sound changes must be represented at an earlier, relatively stable stage, and (2) the representation must be the same for Philadelphia and all neighboring dialects.

Within the evolutionary and historical perspective of this study, we are free to take up any point in the history of the language as an initial position from which to trace the evolution of a given set of dialects. The degree of abstraction of these initial forms depends upon the nature and extent of the sound changes in question. If mergers are involved, the initial position will show the maximum number of distinct forms; if splits are involved, the minimum. For conditioned sound changes, like the vocalization of postvocalic /r/, the initial position will show the undifferentiated forms, e.g., /r/ in all positions; it may also include the state of differentiation of a number of allophones at this earlier stage. Since chain shifts by definition preserve the original number of distinctions, the initial representations will be identical in this respect but if the chain shift has crossed sub-systems, it may involve a radically different set of phonetic features.

An initial position is an abstraction that may not correspond to any actual uniform prior state of the set of dialects in question, since other intersecting sound changes, including retrograde movements, may have been operating at an earlier period. Its major function is to relate the Philadelphia changes to the larger patterns of change taking place in English dialects.

The initial position for the Philadelphia system contains considerably more detail than that presented in volume 1, chapter 6 for American English dialects in general. A number of allophones are included: xxC indicates a checked vowel, xxF a free vowel, xx0 a vowel before voiceless consonants, and xxV a vowel before voiced consonants and word-final position. In addition, a central position is recognized for the nuclei of upgliding vowels, although a more economical representation is possible with only two degrees of fronting and backing. The mid-central vowel in *bird* is not included here as a vowel (Bloomfield 1933:164) but will be represented in figures 4.2ff. as (r).

Table 4.1 displays a set of 21 elements which are each

(a) attached to historical *word classes*;
(b) located by a set of hierarchically organized phonetic features;
(c) identified by a broad phonetic notation;
(d) assigned a contrastive status relative to each other.

Each of these properties can be further clarified.

*Table 4.1* Initial position of Philadelphia vowels

| | Short | | Long | | | | | | | |
|---|---|---|---|---|---|---|---|---|---|---|
| | | | Upgliding | | | | | | Ingliding | |
| | | | Front glide | | | Back glide | | | | |
| | V | | Vy | | | Vw | | | Vh | |
| | Front | Back | Front | Center | Back | Front | Center | Back | Front | Back |
| High | i | u | iyC<br>iyF | | | | | uwC<br>uwF | | |
| Mid | e | ʌ | eyC<br>eyF | | oy | | | owC<br>owF | | oh |
| Low | æ | o | | ay0<br>ayV | | | aw | | æh | ah |

(a) The concept of a *word class* in synchronic description is discussed in volume 1, chapter 6:164. It is the synchronic reflex of a historical construct. A word class is a set of words in which the defining segment occurs under the same relevant phonetic conditions and preserves its identity throughout the process of sound change. Each of the elements in table 4.1 represents such a class.

Word classes can be further divided into sub-classes, as the relevance of various phonetic conditions is established. By *relevance*, I mean that the effect of that phonetic environment on the realization of the vowel is significantly greater than the perturbations caused by the residual set of random influences. The checked and free sub-classes of /ey/ and /ow/ maintain their distinct phonetic targets for most of the dialects related to Philadelphia, and this distinction can become greatly expanded in the course of sound change.

We need not attend to every relevant condition, but greater accuracy in the tracing of sound change in progress will be achieved by specifying word sub-classes quite narrowly. In some cases, this will appear in the specifications for the measurement of the vowels in the classes. Thus in the sub-class of /æh/ with initial obstruent/liquid clusters (in *grand*, *black*, etc.), we find that the F1 and F2 values of the nucleus are significantly depressed (volume 1: pp. 182–3, 457–69, 506–7), so much so that in a set of ten tokens of /æh/, several such tokens would seriously distort the mean values in relation to other vowels that did not include them. In the 16th-century *meat/mate* near-merger, a small sub-class of words with initial obstruent/liquid clusters – *great*, *break*, *drain* – did not follow the raising of the main class of **ea** words (volume 1, pp. 295–8). The course of sound change in progress often creates new sub-classes when the effects of phonetic environments are exaggerated and tokens are dispersed over a wider phonetic range. These sub-classes may lose their identification with the larger class, but normally the widely divergent sub-classes are re-united as the change goes to completion. In the case of *great*, *break*, and *drain*, they joined instead the lower word class of long **ā** in *brake*, *grate*, etc.

It is sometimes thought that the process of phonetically motivated subdivision would continue indefinitely, until every word forms its own subclass, but this is not the case. The smaller phonetic influences, such as the difference between the effect of initial /d/ and /t/ in *Dan* and *tan*, are lost in the random variations of other minor factors, segmental and prosodic. If this were not so, our analysis of changes in mean values in spontaneous speech would depend upon the accident of which words were spoken.

(b) The phonetic dimensions indicated or implicit in this initial position are in part defined by the changes in progress being studied. It is almost inevitable that a vowel system will show a front/back distinction and a high/low distinction. But whether there are two, three, or four distinctive levels in each dimension depends upon the common phonetic inputs of the dialects involved in changes in progress. For the upgliding vowels in table 4.1, a central position is assigned because in the surrounding dialects, /aw/ and /ay/ share the nucleus [a] at the most open area of the acoustic vowel triangle; the [æ] nucleus of Philadelphia /aw/ is the further development of the nucleus–glide differentiation of the reflex of M.E. **ū**: [u: → ɷu: → əu → ɐu → au → æu].

In table 4.1, the dimensions of front/back and high/low are ternary, rather than binary. For phonological rules or constraints that operate at a more abstract level, a binary representation of [±back] or [±high, ±low] may be advantageous; to make contact with the more concrete level of instrumental measurements, an n-ary notation of five or six levels is appropriate.

The phonetic dimensions or features indicated in table 4.1 are not all at the same level of abstraction. The hierarchical nature of the feature geometry is an essential part of the theory of sound change involved. The highest level of abstraction is the opposition of short and long vowels, reflected in the invariant distributional fact that short vowels occur only in checked syllables. Chain shifts typically operate within the short or long subsystems. Thus the Northern Cities Shift affects short vowels (volume 1: 177–95). Pattern 4 includes an extended chain shift in the front upgliding vowels (volume 1:209–18). Parallel shifts show a front–back symmetry, as in the London lowering of the nuclei of /ey/ and /ow/ (volume 1:169). Here the Vy and Vw classes are grouped under UPGLIDING, reflecting an earlier identification as the set of long monophthongs. Most parallel shifts operate upon the same levels of height, affecting HIGH, MID, or LOW vowels in both front and back: the most striking example in New York and Philadelphia is the parallel tensing and raising of /æh/ and /oh/ in the Vh system (volume 1:168). There is also a parallel shift of all back vowels in the Southern Shift, where /uw/, /ow/, and /aw/ are fronted in parallel (volume 1:551–2).

The feature [±tense] does not appear in this classification. It reflects a more concrete level of phonetic accountability, since movements of some (tense) vowels on the peripheral path and other (lax) vowels on the nonperipheral track can be traced with the help of instrumental measurements.

(c) The binary notation used here is consistent with the fact that the classification into short, upgliding, and ingliding vowels dictates the directions of sound change predicted within the system. A unary notation like /i, ɪ, e, ɛ, æ/ incorporates some of the phonetic facts of the initial position, but the low level of abstraction conveys none of the hierarchical structure discussed under (b), and it requires an elaborate feature notation to supplement its deficiencies. More importantly, this unary notation fails to reflect the fundamental phonological principle of English vowels that prohibits VV sequences without intervening glides, and motivates many of the sound change developments to be considered here.

The set of ingliding vowels is less developed in the *r*-ful Philadelphia dialect than in the *r*-less dialects, which develop a complete set of six ingliding vowels.[4] The typographically convenient use of /h/ for an inglide goes back to Bloch and Trager (1942), and appears somewhat too abstract for many analysts today.[5] On the other hand, standard English orthography uses the same notation to represent a long or ingliding vowel in *oh*, *bah*, *eh*, *yeah*, preserving the insight that English words do not end with a vowel. Most importantly, the use of /h/ captures the abstract character of this semivowel, which oscillates between a centering glide and a lengthening of the nucleus, depending primarily on where the nucleus is located.[6] In modern English dialects, the lengthening of short vowels almost always leads to the development of this inglide. When the low vowels are first lengthened, no inglide appears at first, but on later raising it becomes increasingly evident. The split of short **a** and short **o** into short and long categories is best shown then as a split between /æ/ and /æh/, /o/ and /oh/.

(d) The phonemic status notation to be used here is reflected in the cell structure of table 4.1. Each distinct cell represents a phoneme of the initial position, and entries within cells are allophones.[7] The discussion to follow will largely concern linguistic variables, indicated by parentheses: this notation applies equally well to phonemes and allophones. The unconditioned raising of /oh/ and the conditioned raising of /eyC/ will be referred to as the variables (oh) and (eyC), since such linguistic variables frequently cross phonemic boundaries. When the phonemic status of the element becomes important to the discussion, notation like /oh/ and [eyC] will be used.

## 4.3 Earlier records of the Philadelphia vowel system

In volume 1, the sound changes that affected the initial position of the Philadelphia vowel system were presented in five categories: completed changes, changes nearing completion, mid-range changes, new and vigorous changes, and incipient changes (volume 1:79–82). This classification was supported by citations from three sources of real-time evidence from the 1930s and 1940s, thirty to forty years before the LCV study. L. Sprague De

[4] In Philadelphia, the tensed low vowels develop very distinct inglides, but the classes /ih/, /eh/, /uh/ are represented only sparsely with such words as *idea* and *yeah*. However, there is a sizeable section of the population that shows vocalization of /r/, concentrated among the Italians of South Philadelphia.

[5] For a history of this notational development from Bloomfield to Bloch and Trager, see Gleason 1961.

[6] See the Mid-Exit Principle (volume 1:284).

[7] Since the sound changes we are concerned with do not include developments before intervocalic /r/, the near-merger of *ferry*/*furry* in Philadelphia is not represented, and there are no cases that blur the distinction between phoneme and allophone.

Camp published a transcription of the speech of a 16-year-old Philadelphia schoolgirl reading "The North Wind and the Sun" in *Le Maître Phonétique* in 1933. The phonetic transcriptions of the Philadelphia informants for the *Linguistic Atlas* were published in Kurath and McDavid 1961 [PEAS], based on eight transcriptions made in the field by Guy Loman in the 1940s. R. Whitney Tucker published a discussion of the Philadelphia dialect in *American Speech* in 1944. This section will re-organize the evidence as it supports the portrait of the initial position of table 4.1, and fill in phonetic detail.

In all of these records, Philadelphia appears to be moving within the orbit of the Southern Shift. Patterns 3 and 4 are both well represented. The three transcripts can be rated in terms of the degree of advancement of these processes:

| | |
|---|---|
| PEAS | most conservative |
| De Camp | intermediate |
| Tucker | most advanced |

Though the PEAS records were taken after De Camp's, they are from older, more conservative informants; De Camp's 16-year-old schoolgirl would be one of the most advanced speakers of her time. Her resemblance to highly expressive young female speakers of New York and Philadelphia, the leaders in the LES and LCV records, is shown in the affrication of initial /d/ and /t/.[8]

## *The short vowels*

There is no evidence of any shift from the expected positions of the short vowels as phonemically /i, e, æ, a, ʌ, u/ realized phonetically as [ɪ, ɛ, æ, ɑ, ʌ, ɷ]. Tucker makes no mention of any notable peculiarity of the short vowels, and De Camp uses only the phonetic symbols just given. PEAS shows some use of ɪ̶ and some backing of /æ/ and /a/ for the cultivated speaker.[9]

## *The front upgliding vowels*

For /iy/, De Camp shows only [i]; PEAS indicates only moderate diphthongization. Tucker, however, observed traces of a Southern Shift: "the first element is often close *e* [e] or a sound approximating the Slavic *jery*." Since impressionistic transcriptions are not sensitive to degree of backing,

[8] Tucker does not identify his speakers, but he seems to be recording an extreme form of the then current dialect; so extreme, in some cases, that one would be tempted to doubt his transcription if it were not for his perceptive structural insights and acute comparisons with other dialects.

[9] PEAS gives [æ˃] in *ashes*, [æ:˃] in *bag*, for /æ/, and for /a/, several cases of [ɑ˃].

we must infer that this was neither as front as [e] nor as back as [ʌ], but an upper mid nucleus on the nonperipheral track.

For /ey/, De Camp records only [εi] for both checked and free positions. PEAS uses a comparable notation [εɨ] for most vowels. For both checked and free, one token of a mid high nucleus [e] appears. However, some indication of a differentiation appears in the notation for (eyF) in the syllabus of the cultivated speaker: [ε˃vɨ]. This suggestion of the Southern Shift at work is strongly reinforced by Tucker who states that "In 'long *a*,' as in *day*, the first element ranges from [æ] to [a]," and compares it to Cockney in this respect.[10]

For /ay/, PEAS does not differentiate (ay0) from (ayV), and uses a back nucleus [ɑɨ] for both; nor does De Camp who uses both [ai] and [ɑi] (but with one backed [ɒɪ] for (ayF) in *nearby*). Tucker states specifically that both /ay/ and /aw/ have identical nuclei before voiced and voiceless finals, though they are quite different in his own speech and "in most American dialects."

All records of early 20th-century Philadelphia /oy/ agree in using a close nucleus [o].

The overall picture of the front upgliding vowels is the least consistent in these sources. There are slight hints of lowered open vowels in De Camp and PEAS, but Tucker shows a full-fledged Southern Shift. He sums up the situation with a portrait of a complete Southern Shift: "the first element is shifted toward the back from [ɪi] to [ʌi], from [eɪ] to [aɪ], from [ɔɪ] to [oɪ]." Though Tucker's view may be exaggerated, it is consistent with his characterization of Philadelphia as "intermediate, linguistically as well as geographically, between New York and the South."

## *The back upgliding vowels*

Fronting of the nuclei of all three back upgliding vowels was noted by the three sources, but not the differentiation of checked and free. De Camp registers for /uw/ a central nucleus [ʉ] for both checked and free, with one example of a front unrounded nucleus in *soon* [sɪʉn]; for /ow/, [ɜʊ] and [öʊ]; and for /aw/, an oscillation between [æʊ] and [aʊ]. PEAS is more conservative, reporting for /uw/ only a slightly fronted [ʊ˂u˂] or [u:˂]; for /ow/, about the same numbers of central and back nuclei for both checked and free; the central nuclei alternate between rounded and unrounded. Before nasal consonants, where we usually find strong fronting, only 2 of 8 tokens show fronted [æu], and before /t/ (Map 29), 3 of 6; /aw/ shows only central nuclei.

[10] Though Tucker is a keen observer in many ways, he is surely exaggerating here. He adds that Cockney has gone farther, to [ɑɪ], but my own studies of the London vowel system have never shown a nucleus back of center for /ey/.

As expected, Tucker gives a more advanced picture of the Philadelphia changes. For /uw/, he reports a fully fronted and unrounded [ɪːʊ], and for /ow/, a fully fronted [ɛːʊ] or [œːʊ].[11] For /aw/, he again identifies Southern influence, noting accurately that the [æːu] pronunciation that Philadelphia shares with the South is found only in rural areas in the North.

It seems clear, then, that the Philadelphia participation in the Southern Shift was stronger for the Vw class than for Vy, since all three observers noted it, and that the tendency toward an unrounded nucleus had already appeared at this earlier stage.

## *Ingliding vowels*

The split between /æ/ and /æh/ was clearly characteristic of Philadelphia for this period. Ferguson (1975, but writing in 1945) not only outlines the word classes involved in the split, but identifies the nucleus of /æh/ with the mid position of /ehr/ in *care*. De Camp shows no trace of the split, though the text of "The North Wind" included *having*, *traveler* (lax today) and *after*, *last* (tense today). It is possible that his middle class speaker, though only 16 years old, was already showing correction. PEAS is extremely conservative here, even more so than in New York City. Signs of the tensing process appear in the syllabus of the cultivated speaker, who shows an ingliding [æːə] in *half* and *glass*, though not in *aunt*. Curiously enough, Tucker makes no mention at all of the short **a** tensing, but remarks only that "'broad *a*', where it occurs, is noticeably rounded, as is often the case in New York speech."

One might conclude that the tensing of short **a** began only after World War II; but as noted in volume 1, this is hardly possible. As we will see below, all of the older LCV speakers, born as early as 1890, show this lexical rule in a strong and consistent way.

The back chain shift of /ahr/ → /ohr/ → /uhr/ was not noted by De Camp, since he has no words with /ahr/. PEAS records a conservative [ɑː] for /ahr/, but there are a few examples of a back unrounded vowel and one [ɒː]. /oh/ shows only the conservative [ɔ], with or without an inglide. Again it is Tucker who gives a clear picture of the chain shift in progress. He notes the tensing of short open **o** in *on*, and remarks that along with the vowel of *awful*, *talk*, *thought* it is "prolonged, tense and rounded, and has become much closer (though still not approaching a genuine close *o* as in German)." He finds that the sound is similar to that of New York City, though close to the South in the distribution of words affected. Tucker

[11] Tucker's accuracy as an observer must be questioned here, since he includes *old* along with *go* as a type word for this change; in Philadelphia, this is hardly possible; /ow/ is never fronted before /l/.

then notes that these tendencies are even stronger before /r/: "*a* is distinctly rounded, i.e., pronounced as open *o* [ɔ]." He then adds that "*-ar-* is never confused with *-or-*, for in the latter combination the *o* is rather long and very close [o]. Contrast therefore *far* [fɔːrː] *four* [foːr]."

Tucker also observes the special behavior of Philadelphia vowels before liquids: the lack of fronting before /r/; monophthongization of diphthongs before /r/ and /l/, including /oy/, /ay/, and /ey/.[12] He also noted the homonymy of *owl* and *Al*, *Powell* and *pal*, which results from monophthongization of /aw/ before /l/ and vocalization of the liquid.

It is clear from the systematic character of Tucker's observations that he is by far the most reliable and linguistically informed of the three sources. The only points that are hard to interpret in his view of the Philadelphia dialect in the 1940s are the extreme opening of /eyF/ and the absence of tensed /æh/. Tucker's notes seem to have been drawn from his informal observations of spontaneous speech, rather than from direct elicitation or readings.

Let us sum up the bearing of these three sources on the status of the five levels of sound change in progress as they might have been observed in the 1930s:

1 Completed changes: none.
2 Nearly completed changes: the fronting of the nucleus of /aw/, and the raising and backing of /ahr/ to mid position.
3 Mid-range changes: the lowering of the nucleus of (eyF); the raising of /oh/ and /ohr/ to lower mid position.
4 New and vigorous changes: the fronting and unrounding of /uw/ and /ow/.
5 Incipient changes: the lowering of the nucleus of free (iyF).

It is difficult to place the tensing and raising of (æh) in this list. Otherwise, the picture is quite clear: in the 1940s, Philadelphia functioned as the northernmost of the southern cities, with a moderate implementation of all aspects of the Southern Shift.

Both De Camp and Tucker describe a Philadelphia accent that is identical with that of the surrounding area of Eastern Pennsylvania and Southern New Jersey. In the *Atlas* records, Philadelphia is consistently more conservative than the surrounding dialects (for the diphthongization of /iy/ and /ey/, and fronting of /uw/ and /ow/). Ferguson makes clear distinctions between New York, Baltimore, and Philadelphia in the short **a** split, but does not compare the city with its immediate surroundings.

[12] This makes his slip on the word *old*, noted in note 11, all the more exceptional.

## 4.4 The Philadelphia vowel system in the 1970s

This section will examine the Philadelphia vowel system in the recorded speech of some characteristic members of the community, drawn from the LCV neighborhood studies in the 1970s. The view of the Philadelphia vowel system to be provided here is based on the internal relations among the vowel systems of five speakers, ranging in age from 84 to 13. The speakers will be drawn from the Wicket St. neighborhood in Kensington, the oldest settled working class area (chapter 2), where one can observe the full range of vowel systems from the most conservative to the most advanced.

As in the chapters to follow, the data will be presented primarily as formant means (F1 and F2) for each speaker. The methods of measurement used will be presented in the next chapter. These techniques were slower than the methods used today by the *ANAE* (though not less accurate). In sampling the stressed vowels, LCV set target quotas of 3 to 10 vowels; 3 for vowels like (ahr) or (e), which did not seem to be involved in change in progress; 5 for vowels involved in nearly completed or mid-range changes, like (æhN) or (owC); and 10 for vowels engaged in new and vigorous changes, like (ay0) or (aw). Since many of the phonemes have two or three allophones of interest, a given phoneme may be represented by 10, 15, or 20 tokens. But for several of the less frequent vowels, like /oy/, there may be only 1 or 2 tokens to represent the mean.

In the chapters to follow, the three allophones of tensed /æh/ will be presented separately; here they have been combined into a single overall mean.

### *Joe Donegan, 84: the earliest stratum*

Figure 4.2 shows the mean values of the vowel system of the oldest male speaker on Wicket St., Joe Donegan, who was 84 years old when he was interviewed in 1974. His parents came from Ireland in the late 19th century, and he was of the first native-born Irish generation. He had an eighth grade education, and worked as an unskilled laborer, at a lower level than his father. His house value was rated at the lowest level, less than $5000, but received an upkeep rating of 3, "improved." Donegan gives us the most conservative view of the Philadelphia vowel system, in some ways more conservative than that of the middle-aged *Atlas* informants who represent his age cohort.

Like the other diagrams to be presented in this chapter, figure 4.2 is based on unnormalized data. It shows the typical male concentration of formant positions in the lower sections of the physical vowel space occupied by the community as a whole. The highest F1 mean is about 800 Hz, and the highest F2 mean at 2200 Hz. The following discussion of Donegan's system will of course refer to the relative positions of the vowels

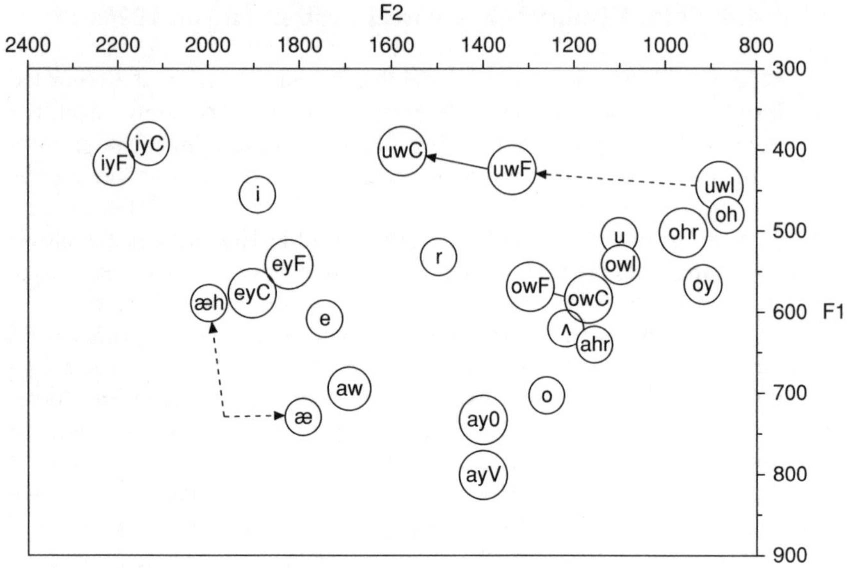


*Figure 4.2* Vowel system of Joe Donegan, 84, Wicket St.

within that system. Their positions relative to vowels used by others cannot be established until normalization is achieved.

In these diagrams, arrows with dotted lines represent the trajectories of the phonemes from initial position; arrows with solid lines connect allophones that move together but at a different rate.

### COMPLETED CHANGES

The early changes described as completed in chapter 3 are completed here. /ahr/ is raised to a mid back peripheral position at 641,1155. This will be true of all later systems, and needs no further comment, since this vowel does not move beyond this position in younger speakers. Secondly, the nucleus of /aw/ is fronted to the position of /æ/; the slight difference between the positions of /aw/ and /æ/ is not significant. This can be added to the list of completed changes that differentiate Philadelphia from more northerly dialects. It is not a terminus, however, but a staging position for further advance.

Both of these are consistent with earlier reports in real time.

### NEARLY COMPLETED CHANGES

The list of Philadelphia sound changes ranks the raising of /æh/ as nearly completed. Donegan's system shows an earlier stage where this raising is in mid-career. It is fronted and raised to lower mid position at 590,1995. This confirms the report of Ferguson from 1945 (1975), and leads us to believe that De Camp, PEAS, and Tucker were simply deficient in this respect.

The Pattern 3 chain shift of /ahr/ → /ohr/ → /uhr/ is also at an early stage. /ohr/ is raised only slightly to a lower high position, no higher than /u/, and is actually lower than /oh/. Again, this matches earlier reports.

MID-RANGE CHANGES

The second aspect of the Pattern 3 chain shift, the fronting of /uw/ and /ow/, was well established in Philadelphia according to earlier reports in real time. Donegan's system is more conservative than those accounts. It is true that both (uwC) and (uwF) are fronter than the reference level of unfronted /uwl/. But (uwC) has advanced only to high central position; (uwF) – which is normally well front of center – is actually less fronted than (uwC). (owF) is only slightly fronted, and (owC) is very close to back /owl/.

NEW AND VIGOROUS CHANGES

There is no sign of the raising of /aw/ to mid position. The retrograde upward movement of (eyC) has not begun: in fact, there is little differentiation of (eyC) and (eyF). This does not match the open position of (eyF) reported by Tucker, which may have been a female feature. Finally, the difference between (ay0) and (ayV) is quite small, and the nucleus of (ay0) is far from /ʌ/. The slight difference is probably not perceptible enough to contradict Tucker's observation that the two allophones are identical.

INCIPIENT CHANGES

There is of course no indication of the incipient lowering of the short front vowels, which are stable in earlier reports.

In general, Donegan represents a stage before any of the new and vigorous changes had begun, consistent with earlier observations in real time.

### *Helen Ryan, 65: an early stage of female speech*

Figure 4.3 is the vowel system of Helen Ryan, who was 65 years old when she was interviewed on Wicket Street in 1974. She is again second-generation Irish, and a central member of the Kendell network (figure 2.3). Mrs Ryan had no more education than Joe Donegan, leaving school in the 7th grade. Her house was basically the same as Donegan's, valued at less than $5000, but she received the highest rating on upkeep. She received an SES rating of 3 as compared to Donegan's 2. Since she is 20 years younger we would expect to find her system somewhat more advanced than his; eventually we will see that her sex and her higher social position also contribute to this effect.

In the Pattern 3 back chain shift, there is no further advance of /ohr/, which is still lower than /oh/. But there is a remarkable difference in the fronting of (uw) and (ow). (uwC) has advanced to a nonperipheral front position (and the nucleus is lowered to a mid position), while (uwF) is

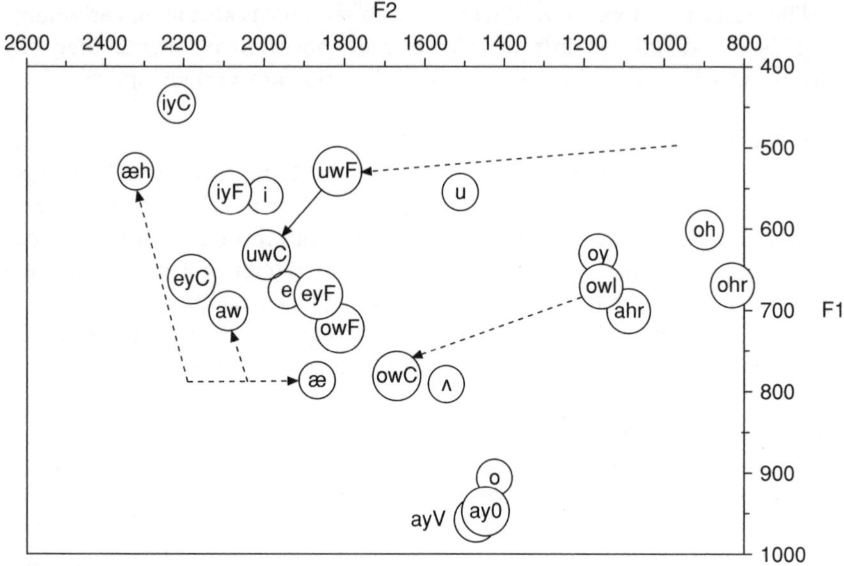


*Figure 4.3* Vowel system of Helen Ryan, 65, Wicket St.

distinctly front of center. Both (owF) and (owC) are in front nonperipheral position; again, the checked allophone is lower, not far from the nucleus of (eyF).

Among the front vowels, (æh) has moved beyond mid position to lower high, just below /iyC/. Behind it, the nucleus of (aw) has risen to mid position; it is the only one of the new and vigorous changes to show movement. There is no perceptible shift of (ay0) from the conservative position of Donegan's system, though (eyC) is now fronter than (eyF).

In short, Helen Ryan's vowel system is differentiated from Donegan's in bringing to life three of the characteristic sound changes of the Philadelphia community: the raising of (æh), nearly completed; the fronting of (uw) and (ow), in mid range; and the raising of (aw), a new and vigorous change in progress.

### *Kate Corcoran, 45: the modern Philadelphia system*

The central figure of the Corcoran network on Wicket Street (figure 2.3) is Kate Corcoran, who was 45 when interviewed in 1973. She is third-generation Irish. She finished the 10th grade, and her husband held a skilled job, but not as good a position as his father. The house is identical in its basic value with those of Donegan and Ryan. But it is almost an ideological point for Kate that she is not a striver, seeking for elevated status, and her house is accordingly rated as "kept up" rather than improved.

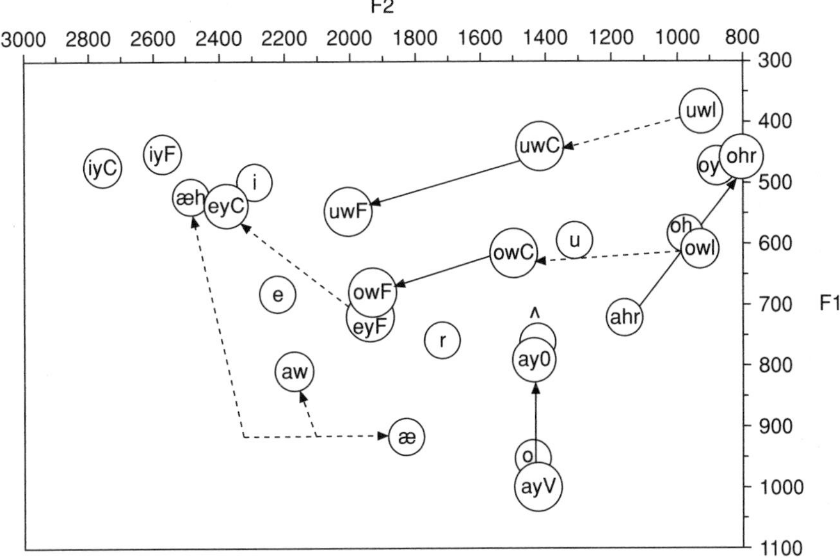


*Figure 4.4* Vowel system of Kate Corcoran, 45, Wicket St.

The vowel system shown in figure 4.4 shows a much more complete development of the Philadelphia sound changes than figures 4.2–4.3. The nearly completed changes are nearly complete. The back chain shift is complete, with (ohr) in high position almost at a level with (uwC). The nucleus of (oy) has followed, while (oh) remains behind in upper mid position. The raising of (æh) has carried it to high position, close to (iyC) and (iyF).

The mid-range fronting of (uw) and (ow) has now developed fully the dichotomy between checked and free. (uwF) and (owF) are both front non-peripheral vowels. The nucleus of (owF) is again in close proximity to that of (eyF). (uwC) and (owC) are back of center, though still considerably advanced beyond the bench marks of /uwl/ and /owl/.

All three of the new and vigorous changes are clearly activated. The nucleus of (aw) is well above lax /æ/ (though no more advanced than Helen Ryan's). The retrograde movement of (eyC) is now clearly in evidence; it has reached a height equal to /i/, though more peripheral. A considerable gap has opened up between (eyC) and /e/. Thirdly, the nucleus of (ay0) is well centralized, almost identical to that of /ʌ/.

Regression analyses of the short front vowels indicate a nonsignificant lowering which may be an incipient change in progress (see chapter 15). But since there is no clear evidence at this stage, the notation /i/, /e/, /æ/ is preserved to indicate relative points of stability. Within a single system, it is difficult to distinguish between the relative raising of (æh), (eyC), and (aw) and a relative lowering of /i/, /e/, /æ/.

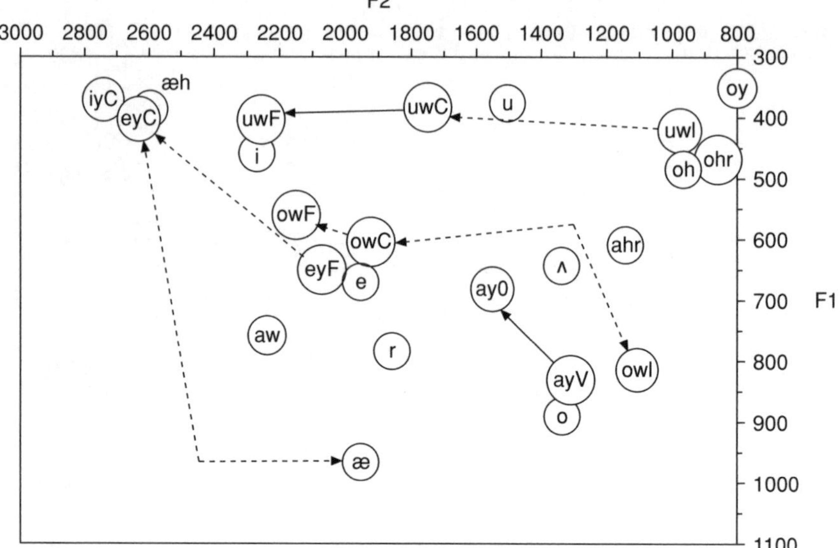


*Figure 4.5* Vowel system of Barbara Corcoran, 16, Wicket St.

## *Barbara Corcoran, 16: an advanced Philadelphia system*

A controlled view of the development of the Philadelphia system can be had by looking across generations within the same family. Barbara is the daughter of Kate, and figure 4.5 shows the mean values of a vowel system that is considerably more advanced than that of her mother.

### NEARLY COMPLETED CHANGES

At this point, both (ohr) and (oh) have reached high position, next to (uwl), while /oy/ is even higher. In the front, (æh) has achieved upper high position, next to /iyC/.

### MID-RANGE CHANGES

The free back vowels are fully fronted; (uwF) is next to /i/, and (owF) is in front position, above /eyF/. For the corresponding checked vowels, it appears that (owC) has advanced further than (uwC), and is only slightly behind its free counterpart. The back allophone of /ow/ before /l/ has not shifted forward, but it has shifted downward to a remarkable extent.

### NEW AND VIGOROUS CHANGES

These show the full extent of movement. (aw) has risen to upper high position, and (eyC) overlaps with (iyC). The distinction between /ayV/ and (ay0) is sizeable though it can be noted that (ay0) is shifted slightly to the front, fronter than /ʌ/.

Figure 4.6 is a vowel chart produced by Plotnik with individual tokens for Barbara's vowel system. The key to the vowel chart is shown at right; the main words of interest are labeled directly, and their word class membership will be evident. The back vowel categories of the initial position are shown as solid symbols, while those that are central or front are open symbols.

In the high back corner one can observe considerable overlapping of four vowel classes: (ohr) in *corner*, *more*, *whore*; (oy) in *boy*; /uwl/ in *school*; and (oh) in *ball*, *talk*. Directly below them can be observed (ahr) in mid back position: *party*, *part*, and *dark*. Despite small differences in the means, it is evident that these are all high back vowels. Since they all have different off-glides, no mergers are involved, though there is reflected here the general Philadelphia merger of /ohr/ and /uhr/ in *more* and *moor*.

Another equally compact cluster is found in high front position. Tense /æh/ is shown with downward-pointing triangles; lax /æ/ with open squares. (The dimension of raising is here measured by progress along the front diagonal, from low center to upper left.) One finds the complete separation of these two classes typical of all Philadelphians in spontaneous speech (Labov 1989b). Between the lowest of the tense vowels (*bad* at 620,2481) and the highest of the lax vowels (*cavity* at 905,2110), there is a great gap. The raising of (æh) is about as complete as one might expect: *bath*, *camp*, *bad*, *mad* are in upper high position along with the /iy/ vowels (shown by open circles with arrows pointing to upper left).

It is interesting to observe that some (æh) words before oral consonants are even higher and fronter than those before nasals. The cluster of seven (æh) words before nasals is usually fronter and/or higher than others; it is only when the change has reached completion that the oral and nasal allophones overlap to this extent.

The (aw) tokens are marked by triangles with arrows pointing to upper right, suggested by the direction of the glide in initial position. Raising of /aw/ produces the greatest fronting in *pounds* and *counselor*. As a whole, these tokens are in lower high and upper mid position, and are marked by their peripheral character. The glides in almost all cases descend to lower right, that is, towards [ɔ]. The second new and vigorous change has brought (eyC) also into upper high position: cf. the word *gained*, which is as advanced along the front diagonal as any other vowel. *Gates* is concealed directly below this. On the other hand, *ate* is in upper mid position. Nevertheless, *ate* is considerably higher and fronter than the (eyF) tokens *okay*, *may*, *say*, which are sharply segregated in lower mid or upper low position.

The moderate mean position of (ay0) in Barbara Corcoran's speech conceals considerable variation. The nucleus of *night* is quite high, well above the mid-point, but *sight* is not far from *side* and *mind*. Most importantly, one can observe that these nuclei have shifted forward, a tendency that differentiates women from men.

Figure 4.6 also labels some (uw) and (ow) vowels. One can see that in free position, the vowels are well fronted; *zoo*, *go*, *no*, are in a front,

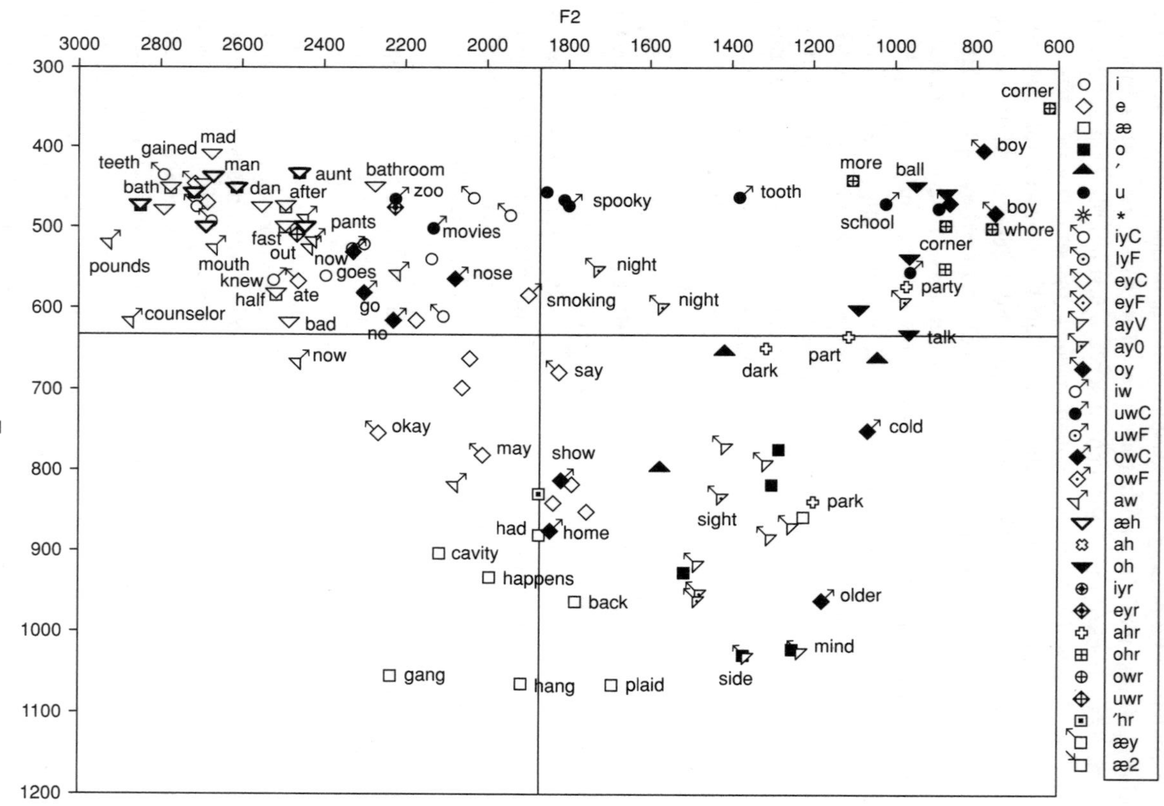


*Figure 4.6* Individual vowel tokens in the vowel system of Barbara Corcoran

nonperipheral track. On the other hand, the checked vowels *spooky* and *tooth*, *nose* and *smoking* are distinctly less fronted.

To sum up, this highly differentiated, advanced vowel system shows a great concentration of vowels in high peripheral position, with only a few tokens from less completed changes occupying the more central areas of the vowel space.

### *Rick Corcoran, 13: the male counterpart*

The last diagram in this series shows the vowel system of Barbara's younger brother Rick. As later chapters will show, male speakers are expected to be considerably behind females of the same age and social background for most of the sound changes in the system. This is true for the nearly completed raising of (æh), where Rick's mean value is in lower high position, distinctly lower and backer than /iyC/. It is also true for the raising of (eyC), which does not overlap very much with /iyC/; it is much fronter than /eyF/, but not much higher. The fronting of (uwF) and (owF) is much more moderate than in his sister's vowel system: they are squarely in central, not front position.

#### THE MALE ADVANTAGE

There are two Philadelphia sound changes for which males are ahead of females, and they are well exemplified in Rick's vowel system. The first is the raising of (ohr) and (oh) to a high back position. Figure 4.7 shows a

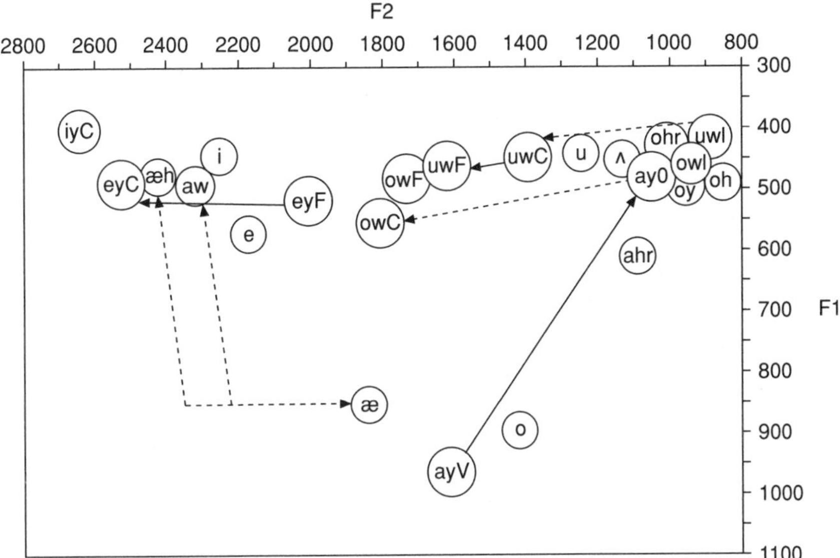


*Figure 4.7* Vowel system of Rick Corcoran, 13, Wicket St.

tight cluster of mean values in that area, where (ohr) is just barely below /uwl/. The most remarkable advance is the raising and backing of (ay0). For Rick Corcoran, this is a high back vowel. Since it is unrounded, it is not as back as (ohr) and /uwl/, but it is not much lower. /ʌ/ has followed the same trajectory.

These individual vowels provide dramatic evidence of rapid sound change across three generations, where vowel nuclei move from one extreme of the vowel space to the other. The chapters to follow will assemble the mean values of 112 speakers in a normalized vowel space. Multiple regression on those means will help to unravel the ways in which social class, gender, age, and social network position are correlated with this advancement of change. Before proceeding, it may be helpful to add a dynamic component to this brief overview of the Philadelphia vowel system by simply charting their mean values against age.

## 4.5 Development of sound changes in apparent time

The diagrams to follow trace the development in apparent time of ten Philadelphia sound changes as reflected in mean values of ten-year age groups in the Philadelphia Neighborhood Study. We cannot of course average the unnormalized physical values of the combined sample of men, women, and children, since differences in vocal tract length lead to radical differences in physical realization of the "same" sound. The mean values to be shown below are normalized, using methods to be developed in detail in the next chapter.

In chapter 3 of volume 1, an overview of the Philadelphia sound changes in progress was provided by figure 3.6, reproduced here as figure 4.8. The mean values for 112 subjects of the Philadelphia Neighborhood Study are shown, and the age coefficients measuring movement in apparent time are indicated by arrows whose length is proportional to the age coefficient. The head of the arrow indicates the expected value of F1 and F2 for speakers 25 years younger than the mean, and the tail indicates the corresponding position for speakers 25 years older than the mean.

Five of the vowel changes involve raising along the front diagonal of the vowel system. It will appear throughout that the physical index of these changes that is most sensitive to social variables is F2, rather than F1. Accordingly, figure 4.9 compares the mean values of the second formants, decade by decade, for the three allophones of /æh/: (æhN), (æhS), and (æhD), along with the two new and vigorous changes, (aw) and (eyC).

Figure 4.9 shows a monotonic increase in values with decreasing age, with somewhat less regular progression for the variable with the least data, (æhD). As the individual vowel charts made clear, the most advanced of the three /æh/ allophones is (æhN) in *man*, *understand*, etc. The other two

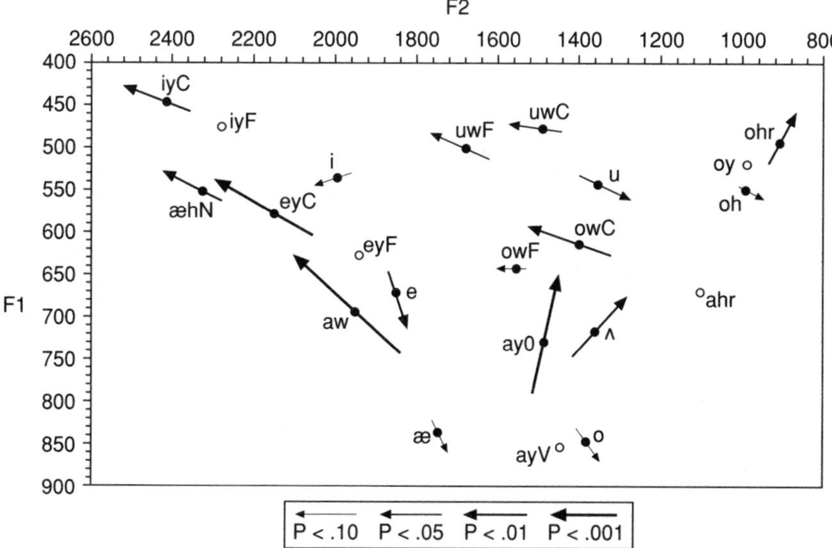


*Figure 4.8* Mean values of all Philadelphia vowels with age coefficients for the Neighborhood Study. Circles: mean F1 and F2 values. Heads of arrows: expected values for speakers 25 years younger than the mean. Tails of arrows: expected values for speakers 25 years older than the mean

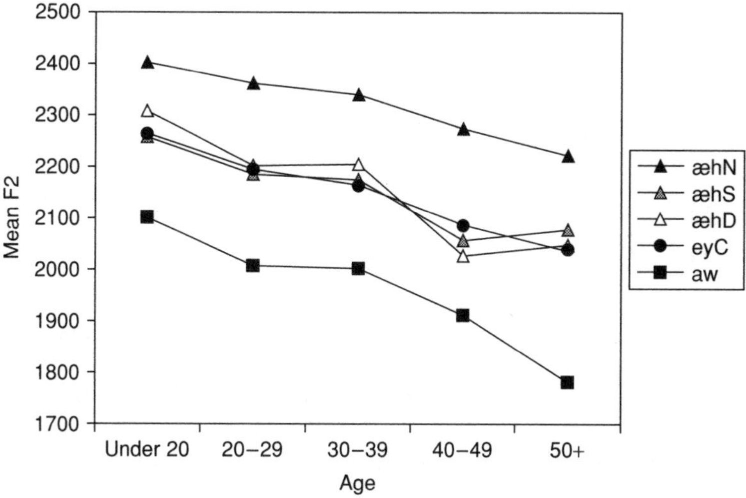


*Figure 4.9* Mean second formants by 10-year age groups of five Philadelphia sound changes involving raising and fronting

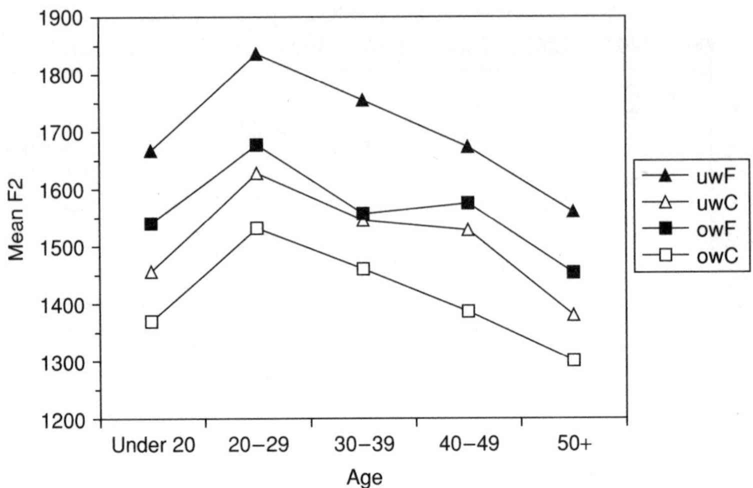


*Figure 4.10* Mean second formants by 10-year age groups of four Philadelphia sound changes involving fronting of back vowels

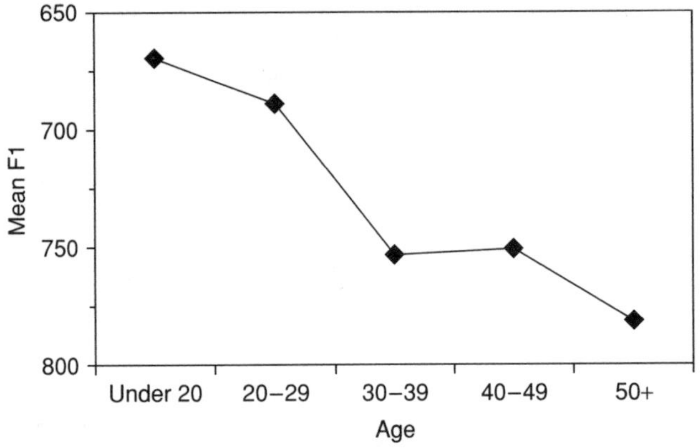


*Figure 4.11* Mean first formant for (ay0) by 10-year age groups

allophones follow some 150 Hz behind, and (eyC) shows the same range of F2 values. At a lower level, the figure shows a regular increase in the fronting of the nucleus of (aw).

Figure 4.10 displays the change in apparent time for the back vowels involved in fronting: free and checked (uw) and (ow). Here F2 is the only relevant dimension. The pattern is strikingly different from the front sound changes. There is a general increase from older to younger speakers, but it is not as regular; for (owF), the 40–49 group is more advanced than the 30–39 group. The peak is located not in the youngest group, but in the 20–29 decade. The most advanced change is free (uwF), and the least advanced, (owC). For both vowels, the free allophone is well in advance of the checked allophone.

One of the ten variables involves changes in F1: (ay0), the raising of the nucleus of /ay/ before voiceless consonants. Figure 4.11 shows the mean F1 values for the five ten-year age groups. Again, there appears to be a simple monotonic relationship between age and the variable.

The documentation of change in apparent time is clear enough. This chapter has also presented the evidence for change in real time which supports the view that these age distributions reflect a diachronic development in the Philadelphia speech community. Chapter 5 will undertake the next step, locating the leaders of linguistic change within that community. For this purpose, simple mean distributions and cross-tabulations will not be sufficient, and the tools of multivariate analysis will be employed.

# Part B

## *Social Class, Gender, Neighborhood, and Ethnicity*

# 5

# *Location of the Leaders in the Socioeconomic Hierarchy*

The first four chapters of this book have laid the groundwork for an inquiry into the causes of linguistic change through the search for the social location of the leaders. If the concept of "social location" is to be meaningful, it must be relevant to the structure of the community concerned. Chapter 2 provided a view of Philadelphia and its history which showed how various ethnic groups arrived, situated themselves in the industrial economy, and located themselves in the neighborhoods that LCV used as the main base for sampling. Chapter 3 then yielded a profile of stable sociolinguistic variables across age, gender, social class, and neighborhood that will serve as the template against which change in progress can be measured. Chapter 4 gave a historical portrait of the vowel system in which the linguistic changes in progress are embedded, mapped the current state of this evolving system as a series of portraits of individuals, and gave a first portrait of distributions in apparent time.

## 5.1 The data set

This chapter will apply the methods of chapter 3 to correlate the linguistic variables of chapter 4 with the independent variables described in chapters 2 and 3. The input data for this analysis is a set of measurements of the vowel systems of 112 speakers. For each speaker, the data base contains ratings on the following independent variables: gender, age, education, occupation, house value, SEC index, house upkeep, social mobility, neighborhood, communication indices (to be discussed in chapter 10), primary ethnicity, secondary ethnicity, generational status, foreign language background, and telephone listing. Many of these independent variables have been used in the analyses of chapter 3, and others will be considered in this chapter.

The vowel measurements that comprise the dependent variables of these analyses are derived from the linear predictive coding of allophones of 16 phonemes. For some phonemes, the variable involved in change in progress

*Table 5.1* Vowel variables in the LCV analysis of the Philadelphia vowel system

| | |
|---|---|
| Short vowels | |
| /i/ | (i) |
| /e/ | (e) |
| /æ/ | (æ) |
| /o/ | (o) |
| /ʌ/ | (ʌ) |
| /u/ | (u) |
| Upgliding diphthongs | |
| /iy/ | (iyC) checked |
| | (iyF) free |
| /ey/ | (eyC) checked |
| | (eyF) free |
| /ay/ | (ay0) before voiceless consonants |
| | (ayV) elsewhere |
| /oy/ | (oy) |
| /aw/ | (aw) |
| /ow/ | (owl) before /l/ |
| | (owC) other checked |
| | (owF) free |
| /uw/ | (uwl) before /l/ |
| | (uwC) other checked |
| | (uwF) free |
| Ingliding diphthongs | |
| /æh/ | (æhS) before front voiceless fricatives |
| | (æhN) before front nasal consonants |
| | (æhD) before voiced stops |
| /ah/ | (ahr) before /r/ |
| /oh/ | (ohr) before /r/ |
| | (oh) elsewhere |

is defined as the entire phoneme; for others, there are distinct variables corresponding to separate allophones. The 26 variables are shown in parentheses notation in table 5.1. For each variable, the data base contains 12 statistics: the mean value, number of measurements, and standard deviation for F1, F2, F3, and F0. This array of 112 × 26 × 4 × 3 is the data set that will be used to locate the innovators of Philadelphia change in progress.

## 5.2 Accuracy and sources of error

The first quantitative studies of vowel changes in the speech community used impressionistic phonetics (Labov 1963, Labov 1966a, Trudgill 1974b,

Cook 1969), and set up quantitative scales across what appeared to be a linear series of possible sound types. This is the fastest and simplest method, and would permit the expansion of data bases considerably if there were some way of limiting sources of error and achieving intersubjective agreement.[1] But that is still an elusive goal for impressionistic phonetics, which is subject to many well-known subjective biases. Since the most skilled transcribers of impressionistic data are already informed by the theoretical issues they are studying and influenced by the phonemic categories of their own dialects, it is inevitable that this knowledge will affect their subjective judgements of the locations of vowels (Ladefoged 1957).[2] Considerable evidence has been given to show that the transcriptions of researchers trained in the *Linguistic Atlas* tradition seriously under-report the level of linguistic change in progress, or miss the new phenomena altogether.[3] It is true enough that some of the most important sociolinguistic studies of the 1990s have used impressionistic transcription of vowel changes with extremely reliable results (Eckert 1999, Kerswill and Williams 1994). Yet whenever possible it is desirable to replace or supplement impressionistic transcriptions with instrumental measures.

In general, instrumental methods have a great advantage over impressionistic transcriptions in accuracy and reliability – and most importantly, in objectivity. Volume 1 made considerable use of vowel charts based on these methods, but for the most part, it was not necessary to discuss the confidence limits of each measurement. The major phenomena presented – the Northern Cities Shift and the Southern Shift – are constituted by vowel movements that are so sizeable that even if the range of error were 100 Hz, the picture would not be radically different.[4] But in this volume,

[1] This method could be checked and calibrated by acoustic measurements, as in Labov 1963.

[2] Objective record of such biases appears in "personal boundaries" in dialect atlases, where what appears to be an isogloss is actually a difference in transcribing practices (and beliefs) among linguists (Kurath 1939). One such bias was encountered in the impressionistic transcriptions of the reflexes of /ay/ and /oy/ in Essex by field workers for the *Survey of English Dialects* (volume 1, chapter 17).

[3] Such understatement appeared in the report on New York City raising of short **a**, which Babbitt recorded in 1896 as at the level of *where*, but was shown in the 1940s *Atlas* records as raised [æ˔]. Chapter 6 of volume 1 showed that the Southern Shift raised and fronted short vowels to the peripheral position of the long vowels in other dialects, but all *Atlas* transcriptions show lax nuclei for these ingliding vowels. The transcriptions of adolescent Chicago speakers in Pederson 1965 show none of the movements of the Northern Cities Shift that are reported in volume 1, chapter 6. There is no reason to believe that any research group would be free of the effect of such preconceptions if they did not have the additional insight afforded by acoustic measurements.

[4] Greater accuracy was of course required in the measurement of near-mergers in part C. For the most part, volume 1 presented the analysis of individual systems. The summing of speakers to show the shift of the community as a whole was foreshadowed primarily in chapter 3, in the discussion of apparent time studies, where the Philadelphia mean values and age coefficients were first presented.

the problem of locating the leaders of linguistic change demands a higher degree of precision and a greater concern for measurement errors. Individual vowel measurements will be the basis for a more extended and refined analysis involving the superposition of many speakers on a normalized grid, and a regression analysis with 20 to 30 independent variables. The effect of measurement errors in these procedures must be examined carefully.

## *Formant measurement*

The major operations of most vowel measurements is to extract the central tendencies of the first two formants at a point in time that represents the acoustic impression of the location of the nucleus. Delattre, Liberman, Cooper, and Gerstman (1952) used the pattern playback technique to demonstrate that the location of these two formants could be used to produce vowels whose timbre corresponded quite well to the expected positions of cardinal vowels in the traditional vowel quadrangle. Though there are many reasons to believe that information from F3 and F0 enters into judgments of vowel timbre, plots of F2 and F1 have proved to give a satisfactory framework for tracing a wide range of vowel shifts in progress.

The first instrumental studies of sound change in progress used the Kay Sonograph, an electro-mechanical device that displayed the energy distribution of the sound patterns by frequency and time. To select the center of the formants, Labov, Yaeger, and Steiner 1972 [LYS] used a digital decision tree based on narrow-band spectrograms, which reduced the range of error to one quarter of a pitch period (ch. 2).[5] These techniques have long since been replaced by computational methods, of which linear predictive coding [LPC] is the most widely used. The measurements in the LCV data base were derived by a two-step procedure: a hard-wired spectrum analyzer (Spectral Dynamics 301C) produced a spectrum, and an LPC routine (Makhoul 1975) extracted the peaks of the supra-glottal spectrum from the frequency domain.

An initial and obvious advantage of modern methods of vowel measurement is speed: analysis with an LPC algorithm can be from ten to a hundred times faster than the spectrograph. Using LPC-based software available today, a highly skilled operator for the *Atlas of North American English* can complete a study of some 300–500 vowels of a single speaker in a single day, an operation that required a week using the LCV method,

[5] This is not unsatisfactory for men's voices, where a quarter of a pitch period is about 25 Hz, but less so for women's voices, where measurements are then ±50–75 Hz. The conventional method of drawing a line through the center of formants on wide-band spectrograms may actually be more accurate in some cases, but it offers no way of estimating the range of error, and given the asymmetrical character of many formants, this error may be considerable.

and about 90 hours for an experienced worker measuring spectrograms. We can examine many more tokens of a given phoneme, and study many more speakers than we could in the past. This gain in quantity provides a more reliable view of the vowel systems and of sound changes in the speech community.

There also appears to be a gain in reliability. The same person measuring a spectrograph repeatedly does not often arrive at the same number. Given a section of the digitized speech wave that begins and ends at fixed values, repeated application of the same pitch-synchronous LPC algorithm will always give the same results.[6]

At first glance, the LPC algorithms appear to increase objectivity and reduce the operations that call for the judgment of the individual investigator. The LPC analysis isolates the supra-glottal spectrum from the harmonic spectrum of the glottis, and combined with a peak-picking procedure directly produces two numbers representing formant centers, along with further information on band widths and amplitudes. It would seem that all the analyst has to do is to pick the point in time that will represent the vowel.

As far as accuracy of measurement is concerned, there is no doubt that LPC routines are sensitive tools for locating the peaks or central tendencies of vowel formants. One way of assessing this internal accuracy is to take measurements along the length of a vowel token that was produced by continually varying the timbre from the most closed front vowel to the most open: [i i˕ e˔ e e˕ ɛ˔ ɛ ɛ˕ æ˔ æ æ˕]. A series of measurements were made every 16.7 msec on such a token by the LPC algorithm described above, and the results superimposed upon a comparable series of measurements made at the UCLA Phonetics Laboratory. Since it is not likely that the jaw is moving in two directions at once, the degree of monotonic ordering of points serves as a rough measure of the internal accuracy of the LPC algorithm. If the probable error for any given point is greater than the difference between points, a see-saw pattern will appear; if a monotonic function appears, one can assume that the probable error is less than the difference between points. The results indicated that LPC measurements can be accepted as having an internal accuracy of 5 to 10 Hz, considerably better than the quarter pitch period that is the limit of error to be derived from narrow-band spectrographs.[7]

[6] For this reason alone, pitch-synchronous LPC analysis is to be preferred over methods which use windows that may begin at any point in the pitch period.

[7] This internal accuracy must not be taken to mean that LPC measurements carry us to within 10 Hz of the actual formant means and the vowel timbre actually produced by the speaker. There are many open questions as to whether the measurements taken correspond to the phonetic elements that are linguistically significant in the production and decipherment of words by members of the speech community.

Given these advantages, the shift to an LPC or equivalent algorithm is inevitable. But there are many pitfalls and uncertainties in the use of LPC measurements that can and do produce gross errors, greater than the errors one would make on a spectrograph. Considerable care must be taken if such gross errors do not wipe out all the advantages that have been gained.

Different LPC measurements will not only vary in values for the formant locations, but frequently vary in the number of formants shown. An F2 in one measurement will re-appear as an F3 in another, while the old F3 now appears as F4, and it is not a simple matter to decide if the new F2 represents an artifact or the phonetic signal. If one were making repeated measures of stable vowels, all in an expected position, these gross errors will appear as outliers. But they are not so easily detectable when rapid change in progress is involved. Figure 4.6 showed, for example, that tokens of the same phoneme may be located many hundreds Hz apart. In some situations, the same speaker may actually have two distinct norms. To detect errors of this kind requires repeated checking of measurements against auditory impressions. This can be done only after several hundred tokens are assembled into a single two-dimensional plot: until then, outliers and aberrant measurements will not be easily detected.

In the light of this situation, it is important to institute a general process of comparison of phonetic impressions and instrumental measurements. Absolute phonetic accuracy is not the issue here: rather, the goal is to be sure that when one token is heard as distinctly higher than another, it will show a lower F1 in the two-formant plot, and that when a second token is heard as distinctly backer than another, it will show a lower F2 measurement. In practice, the policy is to check outliers against auditory impressions. This is becoming easier as current technology develops. There remains an underlying problem that cannot easily be resolved. Errors that produce outliers may be detected more easily than errors that lie close to the mean. As a result, error correction reduces within-group variance and increases between-group variance. This kind of normalization may not always be justified, and may give the illusion that phonemes are more tightly clustered around their central tendency than they actually are. The best solution would be to check a sample of measurements within the main distribution in the same proportion as one checks measurements clearly outside it. In practice, the need to produce measurements in a reasonable time makes this difficult to do.

### *Selection of vowel tokens*

The general analysis of vowels to be presented here is confined to stressed final syllables in spontaneous speech. The Philadelphia telephone survey made use of a wider range of tokens, including polysyllables and less stressed nuclei, as well as word list pronunciations, but the main view of vowel systems presented here is through the central tendencies of the fully stressed nuclei. The general procedure was to begin with the second tape of a sociolinguistic interview, and select each stressed vowel in a given allophonic category until a quota was reached. As the last chapter specified, this quota was 5 tokens for the main vowels of interest (and in some cases, 10). For most of the vowels studied, two or three relevant allophones were identified, so a given phoneme involved in change was represented by 10 to 20 tokens.

The selection of relevant allophonic environments drew upon the findings of LYS as well as certain allophonic distinctions particular to Philadelphia. Syllables with liquid finals are always treated separately, and never merged with a word class ending in obstruents. Syllables with initial glides /y/ and /w/ are not selected, since these have a profound effect on formant positions and the glide is not easily isolated from the position of the nucleus. Initial consonant clusters of obstruent plus liquid (as in *block*, *pride*, *clean*) are also segregated, since in this environment the liquid forms part of the nucleus and formants are regularly depressed outside the normal distribution (see LYS:66–8, and figures 6.5, 6.8, and 6.10 in volume 1).

### *Identification of the nucleus*

One area where the judgment of the individual analyst remains a factor is in the selection of the point in time in the wave form where the LPC measurements will be taken to represent the syllable nucleus. A detailed study of the behavior of any given vowel will begin by tracing the entire trajectory of many tokens from start to finish, beginning and ending with the consonantal transitions. But one cannot study the relative position of hundreds of full trajectories: it is necessary to select one, or possibly two points in time for any given token in order to assign to it a position relative to other tokens of the same phoneme and to neighboring phonemes. For this purpose, it is essential to avoid measurements within the consonantal transitions, or within onglides or offglides. Ideally, the point of measurement will be the central tendency of the nucleus as both the target the speaker is aiming at, and the central acoustic impression that the listener obtains. The location of such a point is straightforward when the formants show a steady state of 50 to 100 msec, or a parabolic trajectory with a clear maximum or minimum. But many vowels follow more complex trajectories, sometimes moving from one steady state to another, or combine steady states with trajectories that show points of inflection at a very different location. Decision procedures for many of these situations remain to be verified experimentally.

LCV used the following procedure to select the point of measurement of the vowel nucleus:

(a) If an F1 maximum appeared outside of a transition, it was selected.
(b) Within an F1 steady state, an F2 minimum or maximum was used to specify the nucleus more closely.
(c) For short syllables with no F1 maximum (like *pick*), a pitch period close to the center of the resonant portion was taken; always with the consideration that the nucleus must be approximately 40 msec from the beginning of consonantal transitions. In such cases, the second resonant pitch period was generally selected for voiceless initials; with voiced initials, the third.
(d) For the raising and fronting of tensed short **a** in *man*, *bad*, etc., the F2 maximum is preferred to the F1 maximum since it corresponds better to the impression of the maximum height of the vowel (see volume 1:252–3). This also applies to the nucleus of /aw/ as it becomes tensed in Philadelphia.[8]

### *Instrumental measurement of telephone signals*

The question naturally arises as to whether telephone signals permit accurate instrumental measurements of vowels. The telephone band is limited to a range of 100–3000 Hz, and there is considerable distortion within that range. A test was therefore made of the same signal recorded directly and after telephone transmission. Figure 5.1 compares the measurements made for the trajectories of 7 vowels in closed syllables: /biyt, beyt, bæhd, bæt, bat, bowt, buwt/. The dashed lines show the signals recorded over the telephone, the solid lines those recorded directly. In general, the direct measurements show smoother trajectories. The points where the nuclei would be measured for most vowels show no consistent differences between direct and telephone signals. On figure 5.1, the high vowel /iy/ shows a sizeable difference in the expected direction, that is, the telephone measurements show higher F1. This is understandable since low frequency information is lost in telephone transmission. The other notable difference occurs with /æ/, which is not accounted for as easily. Here the percentage difference in F1 is much less than with /iy/.

This comparison indicates that telephone recordings can be used with some confidence, as long as F1 measurements of high vowels are not crucial to the issues being examined. At the same time, it is clear that

[8] For the nuclei of both (aw) and (æh), there is a discontinuity of structure as the vowel rises to mid and high position. The lax, low syllables have only one point of inflection, an F1 maximum. The tense, mid, or high syllables show an F1 maximum followed by an F2 maximum (the furthest front excursion) and then an F1 minimum (the highest excursion, often with lowest energy); in this case, the F2 maximum is selected. If these different strategies for identifying syllable nuclei correspond to the way that the vowels are perceived by members of the community, the result may be a discontinuity between the tense and lax forms of /aw/.

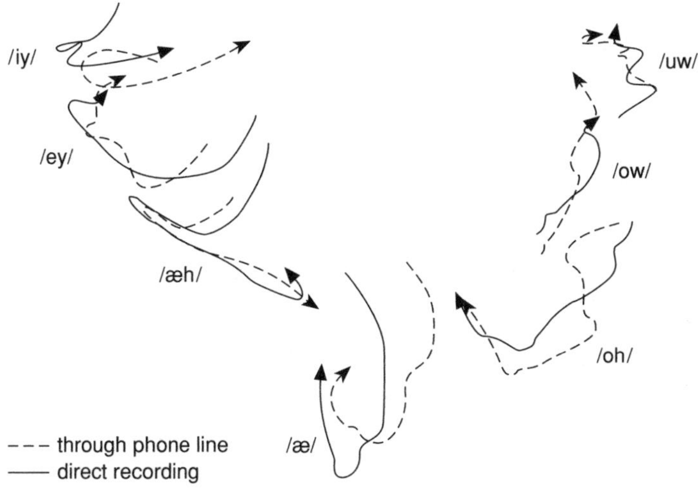


*Figure 5.1* Comparison of trajectories of seven vowels based on LPC measurements of signals recorded directly and transmitted over a telephone line

measurements of telephone recordings are bound to contain more error and be less reliable than direct recordings.

## *Normalization*

Let us concede for the moment that the measurements of vowel formants are reliable and closely correlated with acoustic impressions, that gross errors are eliminated, and we have gained a high degree of confidence that the measurements are within 25 Hz of what they are aiming at. This increase in accuracy may actually be a step backward for the comparison of speakers across the community.

The relative accuracy of LPC measurements provides a satisfactory basis for the investigation of the internal relations of the vowels of any one speaker: the relative positions of the nuclei, the directions and trajectories of glides, and dispersions within phonetic categories. The problem arises when we try to capitalize on these advantages of instrumental measurement in the study of sound change across the community – a problem which does not exist for the impressionistic measures used in earlier sociolinguistic studies. This problem proceeds from the well-known fact that vowels produced by different speakers may be heard as the same though they are quite different in formant position and other physical properties; and vowels with similar formant values may be heard as quite different in timbre. The acoustic differences are greatest for speakers with very different vocal tract lengths, so that vowels of the same timbre produced by men, women, and children show a wide range of physical realization.

The problem is classically realized in the data set provided by Peterson and Barney (1952) for ten vowels pronounced by 76 speakers in the frame /h_d/, and then identified in random order by 70 judges. On the whole, the judges did remarkably well in identifying these vowels, despite the great range of variation in physical realizations. The *normalization* problem for phoneticians is to duplicate mathematically the transformation carried out by such listeners.

In order to trace the path of sound change across populations of Philadelphia speakers, including men, women, and children from 12 to 74 years of age, it was necessary for LCV to solve the normalization problem in a reliable and realistic way. But there is no consensus on what a good solution to the normalization problem would be. If all members of the population shared the same phonetic targets for each phoneme, the problem would be relatively straightforward. The fundamental definition for a successful method of normalization would be that after transformation, all of the sounds that are heard as "the same" will have the same acoustic measurement – this is, that they will show a normal distribution around the same target F1 and F2 frequencies. The task of speaker-independent speech recognition, broadly conceived, is to recognize in the speech signal produced by speakers the phonemic category that they intend, no matter what the phonetic realization of those categories may be.

One of the classic tests for a system of normalization is to reduce the distance between the mean values for the "same" vowels spoken by men, women, and children in the Peterson–Barney data (Gerstman 1967, Wakita 1975). However, the Peterson–Barney categories are defined phonemically, not phonetically.[9] If speakers of different ages, social classes, or ethnic groups differ in their target means for the variable (aw), and the normalization method reduces all (aw) to a single target, it will have lost the data that the research project was designed to gather. It will be necessary to normalize phonetic differences within categories, so that a very high (æh) for speaker A will appear as higher than a moderately raised (æh) for speaker B, and an extremely fronted (uw) token spoken by a woman A will have the same general relation to the community dispersion of (uw) as an extremely fronted (uw) spoken by a male B.[10]

[9] The F1/F2 plots of the Peterson–Barney data indicate that the principal differences within the vowel categories are those between men, women, and children, but no test has been made for other significant differences. The expansion of the confusion matrix among the low back vowels suggests that the judges were heterogeneous in regard to whether the word class of long open **o** (/oh/) was distinguished from that of short open **o** (/o/).

[10] Such "phonetic normalization" is not necessarily finer than a phonemic normalization, since the phonetic realizations of a category in process of change may range over an acoustic distance equivalent to two or three stable phonemes. The finer discriminations within a phonetic category are no finer than the distances that may separate tokens of two distinct phonemes in close proximity in the optimum normalization: a high /e/ may be discriminated from low /i/ by a distance no greater than the just noticeable differences of the formants involved.

LCV therefore needed a normalization algorithm that eliminates only those differences that are due to physical differences among speakers, but not social differences. Three methods were tested: the method of Nordström and Lindblom (1975) that used the mean value of F3 of low vowels to estimate vocal tract length as a single scaling parameter; the method of Nearey (1977) which used the logmean of all formants of all vowels to develop a uniform scaling parameter; a 6-parameter regression designed for us by D. Sankoff to produce maximum clustering. Instead of a single parameter for each speaker, six parameters are used to convert each old F1 and F2 to a new F1 and F2 that will minimize the deviations of tokens about each mean for that speaker. For the new F1, one coefficient is assigned as a constant, a second as a multiplier of the old F1 values, and the third as a multiplier of the old F2 values. Another set of three parameters determines the form of the new F2.

The basic strategy adopted by LCV was to rate the three normalization methods by their degree of clustering of the Peterson–Barney data and the Philadelphia neighborhood data, and then determine where in this range of clustering social information is preserved and where it is lost. In other words, LCV searched for the maximum clustering of phonemic targets that preserves social differences that we know are present in the population.

Figure 5.2 shows the clustering characteristic of each method of normalization. The F-ratios indicate the degree of separation of the ten Peterson–Barney means for the unnormalized data, the Nordström–Lindblom method based on the third formants of low vowels (1975), a critical-band normalization, the logmean normalization (Nearey 1977), and the 6-parameter regression of Sankoff. The 6-parameter regression was by far the most powerful in clustering the Peterson–Barney and other data sets, producing tight, widely separated means for each phoneme. The Lindblom–Nordström, critical band, and Nearey normalizations were intermediate in this respect. This did not resolve the question as to which was the best normalization. To answer this question, it would be necessary to find a variable that was not correlated with vocal tract length. Gender is a powerful social variable in this data; impressionistic measures show that women are well in advance of men for the new and vigorous changes (eyC) and (aw), according to impressionistic measures. In instrumental terms, this appears as higher F2 for women in these new and vigorous changes. But in unnormalized data, women also have higher F2 as a result of their shorter vocal tracts. The biological effect is then confounded with the social effect.

Hindle (1978) attacked this problem by using the variable (ay0), where impressionistic evidence shows a raising of the nucleus among younger speakers. Here the instrumental correlate of the change is the lowering of F1. Since younger speakers have shorter vocal tract lengths, unnormalized data will show them with higher rather than lower F1 values. To the extent that the normalized data shows a significant age coefficient for (ay0), this

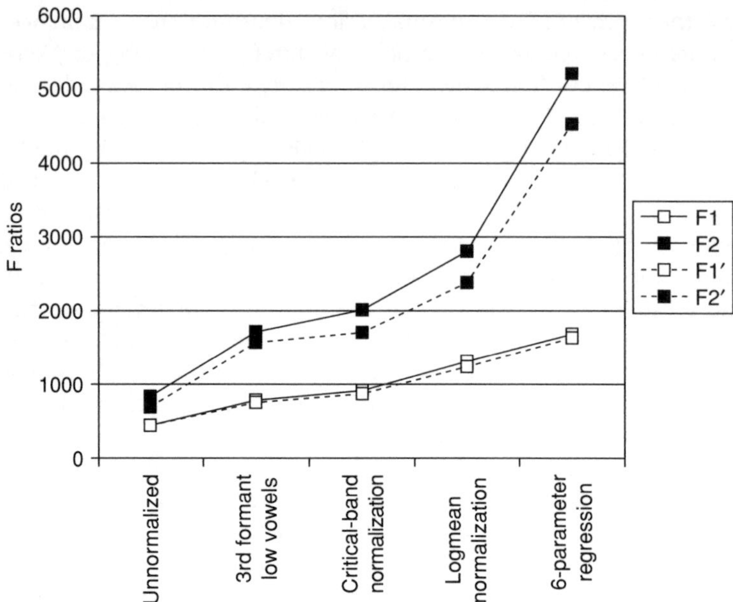


*Figure 5.2* Degree of clustering of seven vowel tokens by F-ratios for unnormalized Peterson–Barney data and the same data transformed by four normalization methods. Solid lines: all P–B data. Dashed lines: P–B tokens identified correctly by judges

contrary effect of vocal tract length would have been removed. Hindle's results showed that the unnormalized data and regression methods showed no significant age coefficients, but the logmean and F3 scaling methods showed sizeable effects, indicating that they were in the range of an appropriate normalization.

One weakness of the Hindle demonstration is that males are in advance of females in the centralization of (ay0). This means that although the effect of age in the unnormalized data runs counter to the direction of the change, the tendency for males to have lower F1 than women for physical reasons runs parallel to it. The most effective test of the normalization methods requires a variable that is independent of vocal tract length. Such a test is provided by the sociolinguistic stratification of the variable (æh). Impressionistic measures show that there is a strong social stratification of the degree of phonetic raising and fronting of tensed /æh/. While there are only small differences among working class speakers, middle class speakers show decidedly less raising and fronting than working class speakers, and the higher the social position of the speaker, the lower the nucleus of (æh). In other words, this almost completed change behaves like the stable sociolinguistic variable (dh) studied in chapter 3.

Figure 5.3 shows the results for this study of the normalization of (æh) under four conditions – unnormalized, mean F3 normalization, logmean

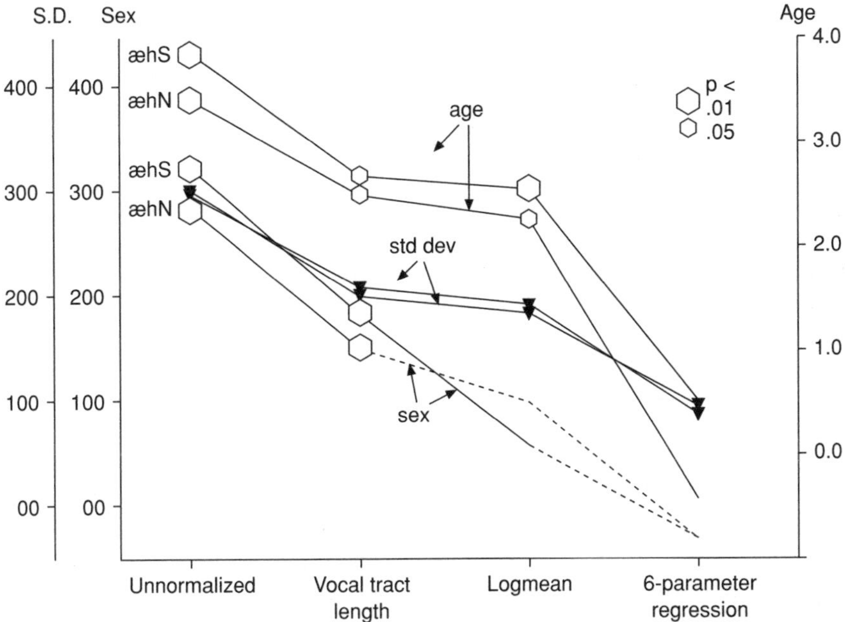


*Figure 5.3a* The effect of three methods of normalization on gender coefficients and the degree of clustering shown by F-ratios and standard deviations for second formant of /æh/ before voiceless fricatives and nasals in the Philadelphia Neighborhood Study

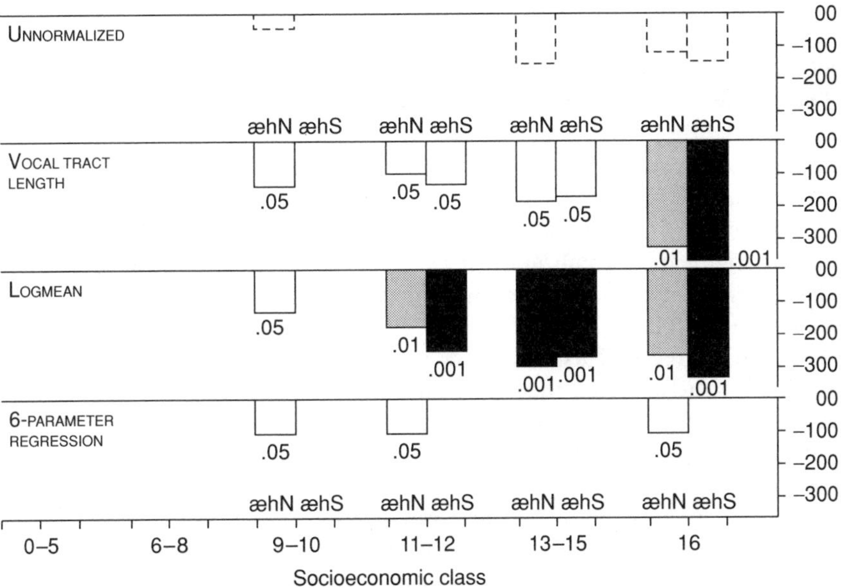


*Figure 5.3b* The effect of three methods of normalization on the regression coefficients for social classes for the second formant of /æh/ before voiceless fricatives and nasals

normalization, and the 6-parameter regression. Figure 5.3a shows the effects of clustering on two (æh) variables: (æhN) and (æhS), with three types of data: age coefficients, sex coefficients, and standard deviations (with three distinct vertical axes as indicated). The size of the symbols indicates the degree of significance of the two sets of coefficients. All three of these follow the same pattern, with highest values for the unnormalized data and lowest values for the 6-parameter regression. Figure 5.3b shows the effects of normalization on the social class data. No significant effects are found for the unnormalized data and very few for the 6-parameter regression. Clear social stratification emerges for the two intermediate normalizations. The stratification is most significant and clearest for the logmean normalization.

As a result, we selected the logmean method for normalizing the LCV vowel files. There is a slight advantage of the logmean normalization over the F3 method in preserving social stratification, though the differences between the two methods are not great. The main reason for selecting the logmean normalization is that the F3 method could not be used for normalizing the telephone survey, since the cutoff of the telephone frequency range at 3000 Hz interferes with F3 readings for many vowels. Since the logmean normalization was equal or superior to the F3 normalization in all tests, and could be used for both the neighborhood study and the telephone survey, it was the logical choice for reducing the 183 speakers studied to a single frame of reference.

### EFFECT OF NORMALIZATION ON AGE COEFFICIENTS

The multiple regression analysis of the Philadelphia vowels will begin with the study of the effect of age of the speaker on the phonetic position of each vowel. This is the central classificatory mechanism for the entire analysis, and the effect of normalization on age coefficients is a crucial matter. Table 5.2 compares age coefficients for the data and for the logmean normalization for eight vowels: three almost completed changes, two mid-range, and three new and vigorous changes. The age coefficient is followed by the t-ratio, and then the standard deviation to show the degree of clustering. For each vowel, the standard deviation is smaller for the logmean than the unnormalized data. The effects of normalization on the size and significance of the correlations follows the logic outlined above in the discussion of the motivation for a choice of normalization method.

Figure 5.4 shows the effect of normalization on age coefficients, separating the pattern for the five F1 measurements involved from the six F2 measurements. Each of the changes involving F1 measurements implies raising of the vowel. If this change is in fact taking place in apparent time, older people should have higher F1, relative to their vowel systems as a whole, and younger people should have lower F1 relative to their systems.

*Table 5.2* Effect of age coefficients on normalization

| *Variable* | *Normalization* | *Formant* | *Coeff.* | *t-ratio* | *Std dev.* |
|---|---|---|---|---|---|
| *Almost completed changes* | | | | | |
| æhS | None | F1 | −9.9 | 1.7 | 75 |
| | | F2 | −5.8 | 5.0 | 304 |
| | Logmean | F1 | 0.9 | 2.7 | 59 |
| | | F2 | −3.1 | 3.8 | 185 |
| æhN | None | F1 | — | — | 85 |
| | | F2 | −4.8 | 4.7 | 300 |
| | Logmean | F1 | 0.9 | 2.7 | 58 |
| | | F2 | −2.5 | 2.7 | 193 |
| *Mid-range* | | | | | |
| owC | None | F2 | −3.9 | 3.2 | 250 |
| | Logmean | F2 | −3 | 3.2 | 194 |
| uwC | None | F2 | −4.7 | 2.9 | 336 |
| | Logmean | F2 | −2.3 | 1.6 | 273 |
| *New and vigorous* | | | | | |
| ay0 | None | F1 | 1.56 | 3.2 | 113 |
| | Logmean | F1 | 2.31 | 6.9 | 78 |
| aw | None | F1 | 1.62 | 3.6 | 95 |
| | Logmean | F1 | 2.36 | 6.9 | 90 |
| | None | F2 | −7.5 | 7.16 | 336 |
| | Logmean | F2 | −5.7 | 6.9 | 230 |
| eyC | None | F1 | — | — | 79 |
| | Logmean | F1 | 1.18 | 4.7 | 52 |
| | None | F2 | −6.9 | 7 | 304 |
| | Logmean | F2 | −3.5 | 4.3 | 190 |
| Probability of t-ratios at d.f. 73: | | | | | |
| | | *0.10* | *0.05* | *0.01* | *0.001* |
| | | 1.67 | 2.00 | 2.39 | 2.66 |

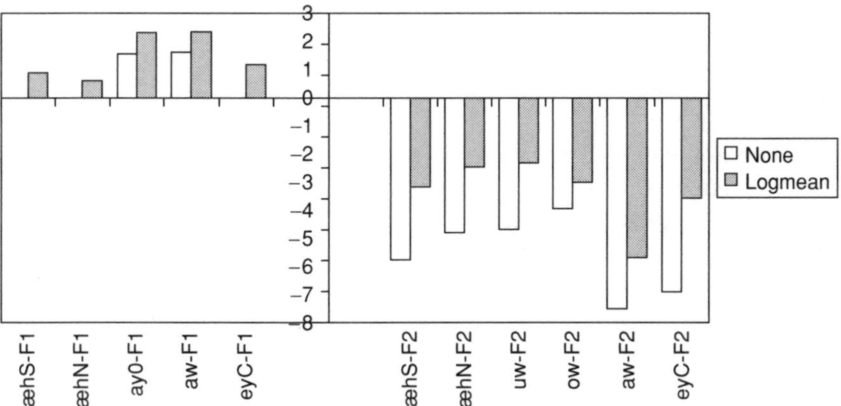


*Figure 5.4* The effect of the logmean normalization on age coefficients for F1 of five vowels and F2 of six vowels in the Philadelphia Neighborhood Study

The left-hand side of figure 5.4 shows that for each F1 measurement, the logmean normalization increases in magnitude and significance. In other words, increasing age is significantly correlated with lower F1 and decreasing age is correlated with higher F1. In this case, the fact that younger speakers used higher vowels, produced by their relatively lower F1, had been masked in the unnormalized data because their shorter vocal tract lengths produced higher F1 values in terms of absolute physical measurements, since centralization is equivalent to lowering of F1. The normalization removes this physiologically motivated difference and allows the true age differentials to emerge.

On the right half of the figure, all of the unnormalized values for F2 are greater (negative) values than the normalized values. These changes involve fronting, or raising of F2. If such changes are in fact taking place in apparent time, then there should be a negative correlation of age with F2, and this is true for both the normalized and the unnormalized data. Given the evidence cited above concerning the social stratification of (æh), and the effect seen on F1, the conclusion is clear that the unnormalized data exaggerates the F2 effect. The unnormalized columns represent the joint effects of the shorter vocal tract lengths of younger people, leading to higher F2, and the fact that they pronounce these vowels in fronter positions with higher F2. The legitimate inference is that the normalized figures are more accurate reflections of the changes taking place in the vowel system than unnormalized data.

## 5.3 First regression: age correlations

The last chapter summarized the distributions of the Philadelphia vowels in apparent time by the use of simple means, the simplest form of univariate analysis. This section will begin with a more accurate view of the situation, using the technique of multiple regression analysis that was applied to stable sociolinguistic variables in chapter 3. The first step is to discover which vowels have significant age correlations in the normalized form, and which do not. The multiple regression analysis that developed this information examined all of the independent variables listed at the beginning of this chapter. Figure 3.6 of chapter 3, volume 1, reproduced in chapter 4 of this volume, shows the relative movements in apparent time of all vowels of the Philadelphia system, including stable vowels that show no correlation with age. The present study of social influences on linguistic change will examine ten vowels that are most characteristic of the Philadelphia system. They fall into three groups from a phonetic perspective:

*Table 5.3* First regression: age coefficients of ten Philadelphia vowels

| | *F2* | *p* | $r^2$ | *F1* | *p* | $r^2$ | $r^2$ *comb.* |
|---|---|---|---|---|---|---|---|
| (uwF) | –2.58 | n.s. | 0.01 | 0.34 | n.s. | 0.01 | 0.01 |
| (uwC) | –2.7 | 0.0300 | 0.03 | 0.365 | 0.09 | 0.017 | 0.03 |
| (owF) | –4.3 | 0.0100 | 0.051 | 0.6 | 0.03 | 0.031 | 0.05 |
| (owC) | –2.64 | 0.0040 | 0.064 | 0.74 | 0.006 | 0.057 | 0.06 |
| (æhS) | –2.97 | 0.0025 | 0.072 | 0.98 | 0.005 | 0.062 | 0.07 |
| (æhN) | –3.18 | 0.0005 | 0.096 | 0.81 | 0.011 | 0.049 | 0.10 |
| (æhD) | –4.41 | <0.0001 | 0.138 | 0.64 | 0.06 | 0.026 | 0.14 |
| (eyC) | –3.81 | <0.0001 | 0.142 | 1.04 | 0.0001 | 0.137 | 0.14 |
| (aw) | –5.75 | <0.0001 | 0.287 | 2.9 | 0.0001 | 0.31 | 0.31 |
| (ay0) | 1.54 | 0.0030 | 0.068 | 2.25 | 0.0001 | 0.32 | 0.33 |

Front vowels undergoing raising and fronting: (æhN), (æhS), (æhD), (aw), (eyC)
Back vowels undergoing fronting: (owC), (owF), (uwC), (uwF)
Low vowel undergoing raising: (ay0)

Table 5.3 shows the results of a simple regression analysis for F1 and F2 of each of these vowels against age as a quantitative variable. For each formant, the age coefficient is shown and its probability level, followed by the adjusted $r^2$ that registers the amount of variation explained by age. The ten items are ordered by the increasing values of the last column, which is the maximum of the variation explained by the two dimensions.

The list can be divided into three groups on the basis of the degree of involvement in change, somewhat different from the classification used in volume 1.

Uncertain movements in apparent time: (uwF), (uwC)
 Age coefficients moderate, very low significance, and very little variation accounted for by age.
Moderate shifts in apparent time: (owC), (owF), (æhS), (æhN)
 Moderate age coefficients, at a level of significance greater than .05 but less than .001, with 5 to 10% of the variation accounted for by age.
Strong movement in apparent time: (æhD), (aw), (eyC), (ay0)
 Strong age coefficients, below the .0001 level of significance, accounting for up to 30% of the variation.

The first two variables can be set aside for the moment as not significantly involved in change now in progress. Not only is there little age differentiation among the 112 speakers, but this chapter will also show there is no socioeconomic differentiation of the fronting of /uw/.

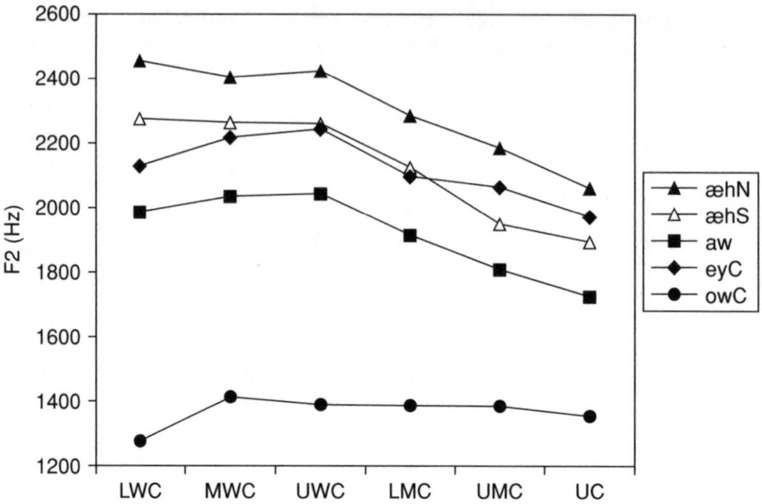


*Figure 5.5* Expected mean values for social classes for five Philadelphia vowels (regression coefficients for each social class are added to the regression constant)

## 5.4 First tabulation of social class

A first view of the leaders in Philadelphia vowel changes can be derived from the distribution of vowel measurements across the same group of SEC categories used in chapter 3: lower working class [SEC 2–3], middle working class [SEC 4–6], upper working class [SEC 7–9], lower middle class [SEC 10–12], upper middle class [SEC 13–15], upper class [SEC 16]. Setting aside the two /uw/ vowels as not fully engaged in change, five cases of change in progress involve the fronting of F2 as a major dimension of change.[11] Figure 5.5 compares the social class pattern for these five vowels by aligning the distributions of the mean second formants. The top line is the most advanced on the F2 axis: (æhN); below this is the less advanced allophone, (æhS). For the (æh) variables, there is little differentiation of the first three social classes, and a regular fall-off for the three middle and upper class groups. At the same level as (æhS) is the new and vigorous change (eyC) and below this, (aw). Both show a slight rise from the lower working class to the middle working class, and a further rise to the level of the upper working class, with a less precipitous decline for the higher status groups that follow. At the bottom of the figure is the middle-range change, the fronting of (owC). It is not clear here if there is a local maximum or not, nor is there clear evidence of a decline of the middle class groups.

[11] For the (æh) variables, (eyC), and (aw), which move up along the front diagonal, F1 is also involved: but there is much weaker and less consistent social differentiation along this axis.

The first glimpse of social distributions for the Philadelphia vowel system shows three distinct patterns. For the oldest changes, the raising of the (æh) allophones, there is no differentiation of the lower half of the social spectrum, and a negative correlation with higher social class similar to what we observed for the stable sociolinguistic variables. For the middle-range changes, the fronting of (ow), there is a suggestion of a leading position for the central social classes, but it is not a clear one. For the two new and vigorous changes, the curvilinear pattern is well established. It remains to be seen if these differences are significant and stable, or the product of other factors that differentiate speakers.

The one variable that is primarily associated with a movement of F1, the centralization of (ay0), does not show a social pattern of this type at all. If any social group is ahead, it is the upper class speakers who are in the lead.

### *The social pre-eminence of the second formant*

Table 5.3 showed significant age coefficients for both F1 and F2 for the vowels that are raising along the front periphery: (aw), (eyC), and the (æh) allophones. There is no doubt that the Philadelphia system is following the general principles developed in chapters 5–9 of volume 1: tense nuclei have moved and are moving up along the front and back peripheries. The study of internal constraints on the raising of (æh) in volume 1 (pp. 505–15) used a definition of *height* as the Cartesian distance along the front diagonal. Approaching the analysis of social constraints, we encounter the surprising finding that social correlations for these vowels are almost entirely concentrated in the second formant. The only independent variable where F1 equals F2 in strength and significance is age. Table 5.3 shows that whenever sound changes involve both F1 and F2 – (aW), (eyC), (æh) – the age coefficient for F2 is more than twice as large, and there is little additional variance explained by combining F1 and F2. Furthermore, when F1 and F2 are combined so that the dependent variable is upward movement along the front diagonal, the result is intermediate in all respects. The conclusion is that nothing is to be gained by introducing F1 into the analysis of sociolinguistic constraints on the sound changes along the front diagonal. As far as the (uw) and (ow) variables are concerned, we do find occasional F1 effects, indicating that more open vowels are associated with lower class speakers, but the patterns are not consistent or significant enough to carry us further in the pursuit of general principles.

This predominance of F2 in the social correlations of the front peripheral vowels is all the more striking since chapters 12 and 14 of volume 1 established that F1 is predominant on the cognitive dimension. The phenomenon of near-merger was almost entirely based on cases where F1 differences had been minimized, and productive differences in F2 of

100–300 Hz distinguished the vowels. It therefore seems that there is a complementary distribution between the sociolinguistic functions of these two dimensions. English speech communities appear to use differences in F1 for cognitive or categorical differentiation, and differences in F2 for establishing social identity. How this correlates with individual psycho-acoustic mechanisms remains to be seen. In any case, our study of the Philadelphia sound changes will now proceed on the basis of F2 differences for all variables but (ay0).[12]

## 5.5 Second regression: age and social class

Table 5.4 presents results of multiple regression analyses with three independent variables: age as a quantitative factor, gender, and socioeconomic class, with the lower working class serving as the residual, zero level. The dependent variables are all those Philadelphia vowels with significant age coefficients. Since gender is almost always a powerful factor in the sociolinguistic array, it is included in the second regression, but it will not be explored in detail until chapters 8 and 9.

The adjusted $r^2$ in the right-most column of table 5.4 indicates that a considerable amount of the variance is explained by these three factors for the (æh) variables and (aw), a moderate amount for (eyC), and much less for (uw) and (ow).

*Table 5.4* Second regression of Philadelphia vowels with age, gender, and social class. Significance: *italics*, $p < .10$; plain, $p < .05$; underlined, $p < .01$; **bold**, $p < .001$

| | *Age* | *Fem.* | *LWC* | *MWC* | *UWC* | *LMC* | *UMC* | *UC* | $r^2$ |
|---|---|---|---|---|---|---|---|---|---|
| (æhN) | −1.61 | 70 | | | | | **−174** | **−293** | 0.42 |
| (æhS) | *−1.14* | | | | | −138 | **−314** | **−368** | 0.48 |
| (æhD) | −2.79 | **120** | | | | −184 | **−229** | **−232** | 0.41 |
| (uwC) | −2.53 | | | | | 198 | | | 0.08 |
| (owF) | −2.49 | 71 | | | | | | | 0.08 |
| (owC) | −2.68 | 79 | | | | | | | 0.10 |
| (aw) | **−5.19** | 128 | | | 86 | | | −129 | 0.44 |
| (eyC) | **−3.93** | 100 | | | 109 | | | | 0.23 |

[12] Significant F1 differences are also observed for the raising of (ohr), with male speakers in the lead. For this nearly completed change there are inherent problems in measurement, and the frequency of tokens in spontaneous speech is limited, so (ohr) has not been used for this study.

In table 5.4, the social distribution of the almost-completed fronting of the (æh) allophones is a monotonic function of social class, but differs from the stable sociolinguistic variables in figures 3.13–3.15 in that the differentiation is confined to the middle and upper classes. There is no significant difference among the three working class groups LWC, MWC, and UWC, where the values of the variable are at a flat, high level (figure 5.5). The middle and upper class groups retreat steadily from this plateau.

Table 5.4 clearly displays the curvilinear pattern of the new and vigorous variables (aw) and (eyC). The social differentiation of (aw) is somewhat stronger than that of (eyC), indicated by the greater age coefficient, the significant negative figure for the upper class, and the higher degree of variance explained. But in both cases the upper working class is the most advanced group.

## 5.6 Third regression: re-analyzing the age dimension

Chapter 3 showed that stable sociolinguistic variables in Philadelphia are not entirely undifferentiated in the age dimension. The initial finding that younger speakers favored these variables was resolved by a finer analysis of the age spectrum to appear as a sharp adolescent peak in an otherwise flat distribution. A comparable analysis for the vowel variables is called for. Since the sample of 112 subjects in this chapter does not include as many youth as the 183 subjects in chapter 3, it may not be possible to trace the behavior of the adolescent group in as fine detail. Data on the 17–19 year old group is missing, and the profile of youth will depend on pre-adolescents 8–12 years old, and the adolescents 13–16.

The third regression takes the youngest group, 8–12, as the residual unit in the age group. This is numerically equivalent to the view obtained by taking the oldest group as residual, but it has the advantage of displaying the significance of the initial steps in the change as against the earliest stage. The age breakdown of six Philadelphia vowels is accordingly shown in figure 5.6, by separately plotting age coefficients for each of the age groups.

The general pattern for five of the variables is quite similar, and far from linear. A peak among adolescents 13–16 is followed by a decline to a plateau for adults that extends from 20 to 49 years, and then a drop to a lower level for those over 50. The mid-range variable (owC) follows a different trajectory from the others with a peak among young adults, 20 to 39 years old, and a marked decline for adolescents.[13]

[13] This is only one of many indications to come that the fronting of (uw) and (ow) follows a different social pattern from the raising and fronting of the front vowels.

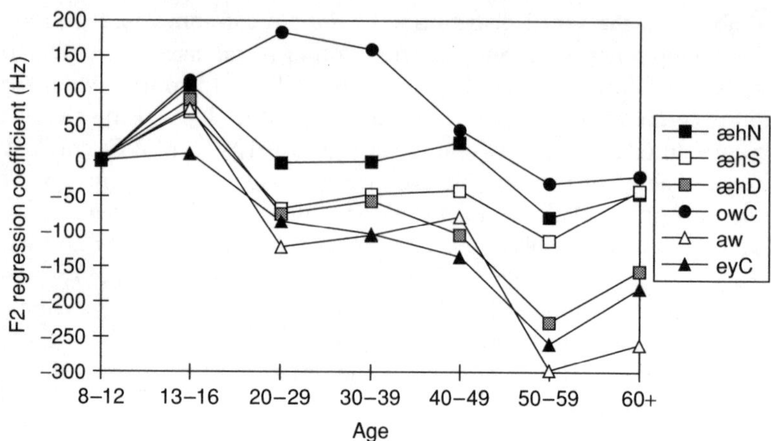


*Figure 5.6* Third regression of Philadelphia vowels: analysis of age groups for six vowel variables

The common feature, shared by all but one vowel, is that the adolescent group 13–16 shows higher values than the pre-adolescents, 8–12. The size of the difference is not radically different for (owC), (æhN), (æhS), (æhD), and (aw), though it is significant in itself only for (æhN). The exception is the most recent change, the retrograde raising of /eyC/, where no difference is found between these two age groups. We will return to this feature in our efforts to understand the transmission problem: how these changes are transmitted across generations (chapter 13). It is worth noting at this point that a lower level for the youngest group should not be misinterpreted as evidence that the sound changes are being reversed or coming to a halt.

Proceeding downward from (owC), it can be seen that the nearly completed change, (æhN), has a relatively flat trajectory for the rest of the age groups, with no significant differences among adults. The small overall age coefficient in table 5.4 is largely the result of the adolescent peak, a point to be noted below. Slightly below this is the path of (æhS), which runs parallel and somewhat lower for the main group of adults 20–59 years old, but joins (æhN) for the oldest age group. Since the mean of (æhS) is well behind (æhN) in figure 5.4, there is every reason to believe that this difference is a real one, though none of these values are significantly different from the zero base for the youngest speakers.

As noted above, (eyC) shows a lower value for the adolescents 13–16 than the other variables. For the adults, it joins (æhD) and (aw) in a downward path, where the older adults 40–59 are significantly differentiated from the others. The differentiation of (æhD) from the other two (æh) allophones follows naturally from the simple age coefficients in table 5.3:

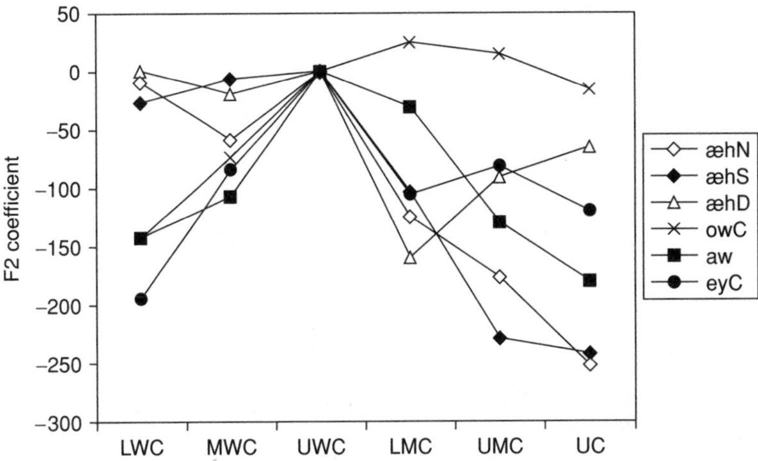


*Figure 5.7* Third regression of Philadelphia vowels: analysis of social class for six vowel variables

(æhN) 3.18, (æhS) 2.97, (æhD) 4.41. It can be identified as a vigorous change, if not a new one.

Apart from the lower level for pre-adolescents, (aw), (eyC), and (æhD) show the monotonic functions of age expected from changes in progress.

The final step in this analysis is then to examine the trajectories of the six vowels across social space. Figure 5.7 superimposes the social class coefficients for each vowel from the third regression in which age groups are distinguished as well as class. To emphasize the extent to which the curvilinear pattern fits this data, the upper working class is taken as the reference point for comparison, fixed at 0. It then appears that the two new and vigorous changes, (eyC) and (aw), rise and fall in a symmetrical way around this reference point. On the other hand, the almost completed changes (æhN) and (æhS) are asymmetrical: they show no significant differentiation for the working class groups, but decline more steeply for the middle class groups than (eyC) and (aw). (æhD) is essentially the same. The fact that it does not appear to fall as steeply as the other two (æh) allophones for the highest two groups is not determinate, since the values of these coefficients are not significant.[14] The case of (owC) is again a mixed one: it follows the path of the new changes for the working class groups, declining along with them, but is essentially flat for the middle class groups.

[14] The (æhD) variable, which rests on only the three words *mad*, *bad*, *glad*, suffers from a scarcity of data. Of the 112 speakers, 13 have no (æhD) values, and many of the values are based on fewer than 5 vowels. The only other missing cases are one each for (æhN) and (æhS).

The third regression has demonstrated that the new and vigorous changes show monotonic age functions, while the other vowel changes do not. Furthermore, this analysis has confirmed the curvilinear hypothesis that associates such monotonic age functions with the leading position of an interior social group.

## 5.7 The centralization of (ay) before voiceless consonants

Though there are three new and vigorous changes in Philadelphia, the discussion of social correlates has so far focused only on two. In the first regression, it appeared that F1 of (ay0) has a strong age coefficient, but no significant distribution across social class groups. Figure 5.8 shows the age distribution by plotting the age coefficients by decade. The residual group, set at the zero level, is the speakers over 50. The coefficients become increasingly negative with younger speakers, since F1 falls as (ay0) is centralized. The over-50 group is a full 50 Hz behind the 40–49 group, but the difference is not significant. There is once again an adolescent peak in the 13–16 group, which is distinctly higher than for those under 13.

Figure 3.6 of volume 1, reproduced in the last chapter, shows that the centralization of (ay0) is not a simple F1 movement, but is accompanied by a shift toward the back of the vowel system. We not only hear [fəɪt] but frequently [fʌ˖ɪt], especially after labial consonants.

Figure 5.9 traces the mean age values for this backing tendency. The values are flat for those over 30, but there is a sharp lowering of F2 for the young adults 20–29 and a steep increase in this shift for those under 20. However, a regression analysis shows only one significant coefficient: –75 for speakers 13–16 years old, and this accounts for only 5% of the variance. The existence of this adolescent peak suggests a parallel with the stable

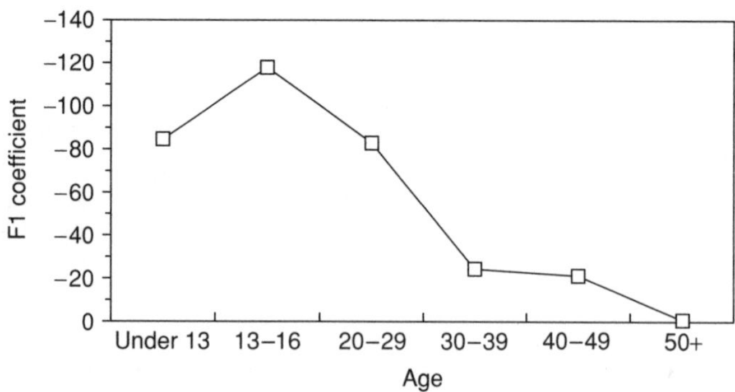


*Figure 5.8* Age group coefficients for F1 of (ay0)

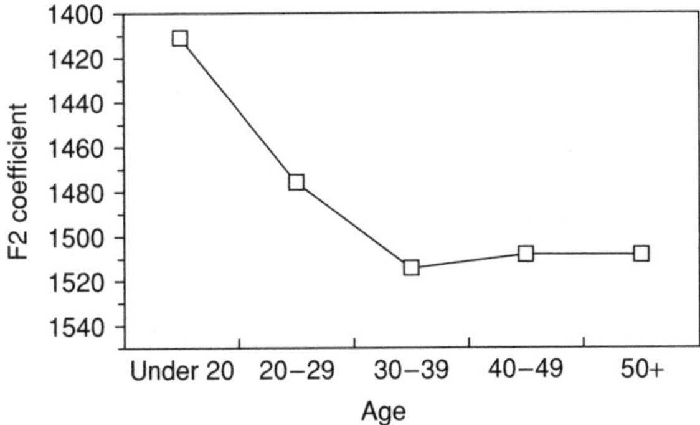


*Figure 5.9* Mean age values for F2 of (ay0)

sociolinguistic variables of chapter 3, but there are no significant social class correlations. The backing of (ay0), therefore, is at present a marginal phenomenon in the social ecology of the Philadelphia vowel system, and falls into the class of incipient sound changes.

The centralization of /ay/ before voiceless consonants is of course a very general phenomenon in American English, and does not mark Philadelphia in particular. It is strong throughout Pennsylvania, and much of the upper Midwest. As "Canadian raising," it is a well-known and frequently discussed pattern that not only defines Canadian English, Canada, but is firmly entrenched in such diverse areas as upper New York State (Kurath and McDavid 1961, Maps 26–9), northern Virginia, and Martha's Vineyard (Labov 1963). Chapter 8 will examine data on (ay0) from the *Atlas of North American English* in the Inland North. In its generality, (ay0) is also differentiated from (aw) and (eyC), which are specific to Philadelphia.

## 5.8 The telephone survey

This chapter began with a consideration of the many sources of error that are present in the data that we have been considering so far. These may be summarized as follows:

1 The neighborhoods chosen may not provide a representative sample of the Philadelphia speech community because of incomplete listing of types of neighborhoods or errors in selecting neighborhoods as representative of these types.
2 Errors may occur in the selection of speakers as representative of neighborhoods.
3 The effects of observation may not be reduced enough to guarantee that the recordings truly represent the speech of everyday life.

4 Errors may occur in selecting tokens as representative of phonemes or allophones: for example, the vowels of *downtown* may not show the development of /aw/ as clearly as a single stressed syllable *town*.
5 Errors may be made in selection of the point in time taken to represent the nucleus of the vowel, so that the values may reflect the articulation of an onset or glide rather than the nucleus.
6 Errors are found in linear predictive coding, the result of interference from ambient noise, too rapid fall-off of the signal amplitude with increasing frequency, failure to resolve two neighboring formants, and other causes which may lead to substituting nasal formants for oral formants, or other types of gross error.
7 Normalization may be incomplete so that differences in age and gender in the advancement of change are confounded with physiological differences, or over-normalization may remove data that is essential to the sociolinguistic analysis.
8 Errors may be introduced in multiple regression due to too much overlap of independent variables, or lack of sufficient contrast between them in the data base.

Given so many sources of error, there is no way to be certain that they do not accumulate to hide the phenomena we are looking for, or introduce spurious ones. If we are fortunate, the accumulated errors will have no particular direction, and do no more than diffuse or reduce the size of the relationships between a linguistic variable and its social correlates. If the relationship is then robust enough, it will emerge in a significant form no matter what form the analysis takes.

The strategy introduced in chapter 2 was to approach the Philadelphia vowel system from two directions, using two procedures with complementary sources of error. The telephone survey was relatively free of error sources 1 and 2. As a random sample of telephone listings, it yielded a geographic distribution much broader than that of the neighborhood studies. Whatever bias was present in the selection of neighborhoods and speakers in the neighborhoods was a different bias from the selective bias of the telephone survey. This geographically random sample was also socially random – within the limits of telephone listing.[15] On the other hand, error source 3 is considerably magnified for telephone samples, since the interviews are short, relatively formal, and without support from other members of the social network. Considering the noise and frequency limits of the telephone signal, error source 6 is also magnified, particularly for F1, and with it, error source 5 also.

[15] The bias created by the choice of telephone listings, which drops unlisted telephones and speakers without telephones from the population, will be discussed below. The problem of accessibility – speakers who answer or do not answer the telephone – has a correlate in the neighborhood study, since there are always persons who are difficult to interview.

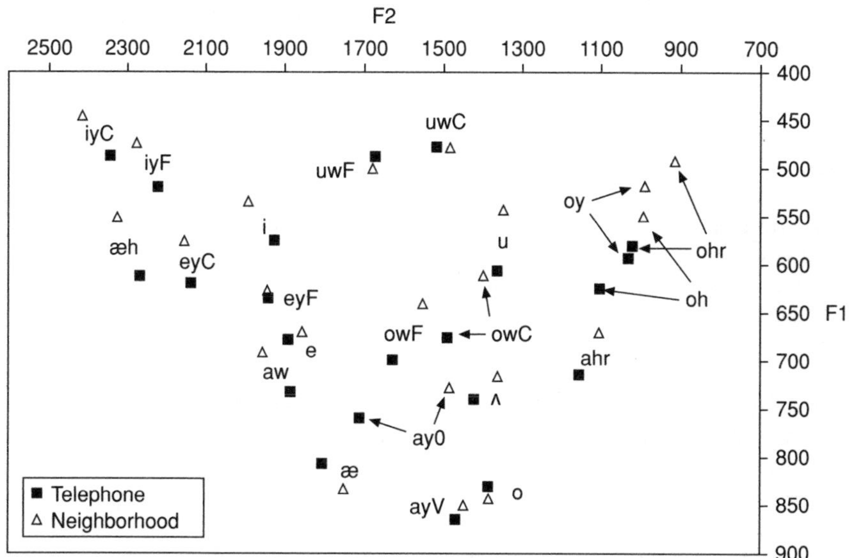


*Figure 5.10* Superposition of mean values for the neighborhood study and the telephone survey; logmean normalization applied to both data sets separately

Given these differences in error sources, it will be encouraging indeed if the results of the telephone survey should mirror, to some degree, the results of the neighborhood study. Let us first examine the degree of agreement in the portrait of the vowel system as shown in the mean values of the 26 phonemes and allophones.

Figure 5.10 superimposes the Philadelphia vowel system measured in the telephone survey on the F1/F2 plot derived from the neighborhood study, figure 5.4. The triangles represent the mean values from the neighborhood study, and the squares the telephone mean values.

The two sets of measurements are normalized independently, so that any degree of agreement seen here is a substantive agreement in the representation of the vowels themselves. The overall location of the vowel space is almost identical along the mid-central line; in mid-central high position, the /uw/ vowels are quite close for both sets; in low position, the /o/ and /ayV/ vowels are in almost identical positions. The major difference between the telephone and neighborhood surveys is in the high back vowels. As figure 5.1 indicated, the telephone survey is least reliable for the F1 positions of these high vowels, and figure 5.10 shows a systematic downward shift of the high vowels in front and back. Table 5.5 shows the average values of these differences for high and mid vowels. It is clear that the high vowels are less peripheral in the telephone study; the same tendency prevails in the mid vowels but to a smaller extent. These differences may be due to mechanical differences in recording and measurement

*Table 5.5* Average differences between telephone and neighborhood means for high and mid vowels

| | *All* | *Front* | *Back* |
|---|---|---|---|
| High vowels | | | |
| F1 difference | 61 | | |
| F2 difference | | −65 | 89 |
| Mid vowels | | | |
| F1 difference | 38 | | |
| F2 difference | | −14 | 42 |

procedures. Some of the high vowel differences can certainly be accounted for in this way. On the other hand, much of the difference in the mid vowels is the result of the linguistic effects of formality. The telephone interviews are shorter and more formal than those of the neighborhood studies, without the same long-term personal contacts that modified the effects of observation. Chapter 9 will show that such differences in social context can modify the realization of Philadelphia vowels in ways that are very similar to the differences shown in figure 5.10. That is, the telephone vowels are less advanced along the path that sound change is following.

The largest single difference in the realization of a phoneme is the position of (ay0), which is much further front in the telephone survey. The previous section showed that the raising of (ay0) is a pattern common to the community as a whole, while backing is a special characteristic of younger working class males. It is this group that is least represented in the telephone survey.

In spite of these differences, an almost identical pattern of sound change in progress emerges from the two studies. Table 5.6 gives the age coefficients for the two studies for the ten vowels analyzed so far. The results are remarkably consistent. The two surveys agree in finding that the largest movements in apparent time are the fronting and raising of (aw) and (eyC) and the centralization of (ay0). In both data sets, the three new and vigorous changes (eyC), (aw), and (ay0) have the highest and the most significant age coefficients in the same direction. With the exception of (owF), the telephone survey shows a lower level of significance than the neighborhood survey. Since there are only half as many subjects, and the noise and error factors in measurement are larger, this is to be expected. But the pattern is identical. The major effects for both surveys are F2 of (eyC) and (aw), and F1 of (ay0). The telephone survey coefficients for F1 of (eyC) and (aw) are about half the size of those in the neighborhood study, and below the .05 level of significance. While the neighborhood study finds a low, nonsignificant backing of (ay0), no effect appears in the telephone study.

*Table 5.6* Comparison of age coefficients of telephone and neighborhood studies. Bold: primary sociolinguistic parameters

| | | *F1* | | *F2* | |
|---|---|---|---|---|---|
| | | *Coeff.* | *t-ratio* | *Coeff.* | *t-ratio* |
| *New and vigorous* | | | | | |
| (eyC) | Tel | 0.72 | 1.4 | **–4.6** | **2.9*****|
| | Nbr | 1.28 | 4.2*** | **–3.82** | **4.2***** |
| (aw) | Tel | 0.77 | 1.3 | **–3.70** | **2.1*** |
| | Nbr | 1.83 | 4.8*** | **–3.99** | **4.8***** |
| (ay0) | Tel | **2.1** | **4.9***** | | |
| | Nbr | **2.33** | **6.2***** | 1.1 | 1.7 |
| *Mid-range changes* | | | | | |
| (owC) | Tel | 0.49 | 0.9 | **–4.5** | **3***** |
| | Nbr | 0.74 | 2.2* | **–3.2** | **3.2***** |
| (owF) | Tel | | | –1.8 | 2.1* |
| | Nbr | 0.23 | 0.7 | –1.55 | 1.7 |
| (uwF) | Tel | | | | |
| | Nbr | –4.1 | 1.5 | –2.44 | 2.1* |
| *Almost completed changes* | | | | | |
| (æhS) | Tel | 2.30* | 1.3 | **–5.3** | **1.1** |
| | Nbr | 0.58 | 1.5 | **–1.48** | **1.9** |
| (æhN) | Tel | | | | |
| | Nbr | 0.63 | 1.6 | **–2.06** | **2.4**** |
| (æhD) | Tel | | | | |
| | Nbr | 0.22 | 0.6 | **–2.5** | **2.5**** |

* $p < 0.05$, ** $p < 0.01$, *** $p < 0.001$

For the mid-range fronting, there is almost as high a level of agreement. For both studies, the strongest age effect is found for F2 of the vowel which is furthest behind: (owC). A small but nonsignificant tendency to lower (owC) appears in both. The telephone study does not find any significant age coefficients for (uwF). As noted before, the two low formants of this vowel show considerable difficulty in measurement, and it is not surprising that the telephone survey is less reliable here.

For the three allophones of (æh), there is agreement only in the degree of fronting before fricatives. For the other two, only the neighborhood study shows a significant effect. Again, this corresponds to the relative difficulties of measurement, since the nasal resonances found in the /æ/ variants often interfere with accurate readings of LPC output.

It can be concluded that the telephone survey is a consistent subset of the neighborhood study findings on age distributions. None of the vowels which failed to show movement in apparent time in the neighborhood study did so in the telephone survey. The two surveys give us the same view of Philadelphia changes in progress, a result that reinforces considerably our confidence in the validity and reliability of the data.

## *Gender*

Though gender coefficients will not be examined in detail until chapter 8, they offer another index of the extent of the confirmation yielded by the comparison of the two studies. Table 5.7 shows the degree of agreement between the telephone survey and the neighborhood study for gender coefficients. Female gender has the value of 1, male of 0. Therefore positive values for F2 indicate the value (in Hz) of the advance of women over men in the fronting of the vowels involved. Negative values for F1

*Table 5.7* Comparison of gender coefficients in telephone and neighborhood studies

| | | *F1* | | *F2* | |
|---|---|---|---|---|---|
| | | *Coeff.* | *t-ratio* | *Coeff.* | *t-ratio* |
| New and vigorous | | | | | |
| (eyC) | Tel | –49 | 2.5** | 82 | |
| | Nbr | | | 85 | 2.81*** |
| (aw) | Tel | | | 104 | 2.4** |
| | Nbr | | | 113 | 4.4*** |
| (ay0) | Tel | 68 | 5.6*** | | |
| | Nbr | 41 | 3.68*** | | |
| Mid-range changes | | | | | |
| (owC) | Tel | | | 210 | 3.8*** |
| | Nbr | | | 92 | 2.84*** |
| (owF) | Tel | | | 166 | 4.7*** |
| | Nbr | | | 130 | 1.93* |
| (uwF) | Tel | | | | |
| | Nbr | | | | 1.87 |
| Nearly completed | | | | | |
| (æhS) | Tel | | | | |
| | Nbr | –21 | 1.77 | 32 | 1.14 |
| (æhN) | Tel | –50 | 3.2*** | 126 | 1.7 |
| | Nbr | –20 | 1.64 | 64 | 2.35* |
| (æhD) | Tel | –46 | 2.2* | 117 | 2.9*** |
| | Nbr | –34 | 2.89*** | 112 | 3.57*** |

* $p < 0.05$, ** $p < 0.01$, *** $p < 0.001$

indicate the extent to which women are using higher vowels than men. There is consensus for the new and vigorous changes. For (aw) and (eyC), women are ahead of men; for (ay0), men are ahead of women. The only notable difference in the pattern is that for (eyC); this advance is registered in F1 rather than F2. As expected, the level of significance shown for the neighborhood study is one level higher than for the telephone survey.

For the mid-range changes, the F2 values show general agreement; women are 100 to 200 Hz in advance of men. The only disagreement is found for (uwF), which is, as before, less reliable.

In the rows for the three (æh) variables, there is striking agreement, with women leading men consistently. For (æhS), the telephone survey fails to show a significant difference, but otherwise we find congruence. In one case, F1 for (æhN), the telephone survey actually shows a stronger effect than the neighborhood study.

The same pattern of gender differences in the Philadelphia sound changes emerges from the two surveys, with only small differences between them.

### *Socioeconomic class*

The findings on the curvilinear pattern in socioeconomic class were consistent and significant, but they were not as robust as the age or gender effects. Given the fact that the telephone survey shows lower levels of significance for the strong age and gender effects, it might seem doubtful that the curvilinear pattern would emerge. Yet it does.

Table 5.8 presents an analysis of the social class coefficients for the new and vigorous changes in the telephone survey. The values for (aw) show a significant peak emerging for F2 in SEC group 8–9. A less significant peak of –55 appears for F1, and for F2 of class 7. The figures for (eyC) show a nonsignificant peak in the same place. The pattern for (ay0) is quite different, as in the neighborhood study: instead of a curvilinear pattern, there is broad distribution without any well-defined peak. Table 5.8 establishes the fact that the leading position of the upper working class in Philadelphia is a general phenomenon, not at all confined to the particular neighborhoods we were engaged in.

### *The bias of telephone listings*

Subjects were located for the telephone survey by a random selection from telephone listings. Chapter 2 reviewed the bias introduced by the extraordinary class differences in telephone listing. The effect of this bias can be controlled through information available in the neighborhood studies. For all subjects in the neighborhood study, there is complete information

*Table 5.8* Socioeconomic class coefficients of the telephone survey (Superscripts are t-ratios; bold figures are significant at the .05 level or beyond)

| | | Socioeconomic class | | | | | |
|---|---|---|---|---|---|---|---|
| | | *1–4* | *5–6* | *7* | *8–9* | *10–12* | *13–15* |
| (aw) | | | | | | | |
| | F1 | | | | $-55^{1.7}$ | | |
| | F2 | | | $77^{1.4}$ | **$149^{2.3}$** | | |
| (eyC) | | | | | | | |
| | F1 | | $42^{1.8}$ | | $39^{1.5}$ | | |
| | F2 | | | | $121^{1.5}$ | | |
| (ay0) | | | | | | | |
| | F1 | **$-42^{2.1}$** | | **$-48^{2.7}$** | $-38^{1.7}$ | | |
| | F2 | | $-64^{1.6}$ | | | | |

on whether telephone numbers were listed or not. This information was then entered into the regression analyses of the neighborhood studies as 1 if listed, 0 if not. If the omission of speakers with unlisted phones interfered with the comparable use of the telephone and neighborhood studies, this would show up as a significant effect of the telephone listing variable for one vowel or another in the neighborhood study.

This effect was examined for both formants for all vowels and all social sub-groups in the system. No regression analysis was found in which telephone listing had a significant effect on the realization of a vowel. Nor did the inclusion or exclusion of telephone listing in the analysis result in significantly different values for other variables.

## 5.9 Components of the socioeconomic index

Chapter 3 reviewed the utility of composite socioeconomic indices as opposed to individual indicators of social position like education or occupation. This will be particularly important for the study of change in progress. Any differences in the effects of different indicators may yield further information on the location of the leaders of change, and beyond this, may yield a clue as to the mechanism that leads to the advance of the change itself.

First it may be helpful to examine the internal relations of the three indicators. Table 5.9 shows the Pearson product-moment correlations among them. It is evident that house value and occupation are closely correlated, but that education is less closely correlated with either.

*Table 5.9* Pearson product-moment correlation of the individual socioeconomic indicators

| | *Occupation* | *Education* | *House value* |
|---|---|---|---|
| Occupation | 1.000 | | |
| Education | 0.533 | 1.000 | |
| House value | 0.854 | 0.593 | 1.000 |

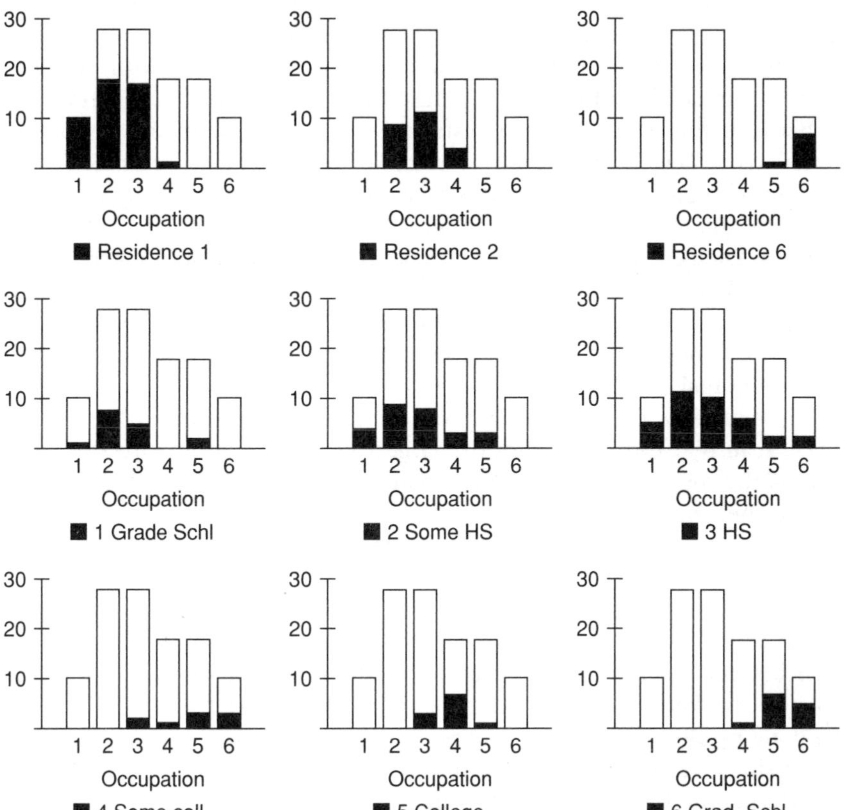


*Figure 5.11* Cross-distributions of occupation by residence and education

Figure 5.11 is a series of histograms that show the relations of residence value and education to occupation. The first three show the distribution of three levels of residence value across the six occupational levels. The black bars in the first histogram show the percent distribution of speakers whose house value is in the lowest category. If occupation and residence were perfectly correlated, only the first left-hand bar would be black. In fact, the majority of those with occupational levels 2 and 3 (unskilled and skilled workers) have house values in that lowest category. This reflects the typical situation with Philadelphia row houses, where housing in many areas is uniform and values are relatively low – especially true in North Philadelphia. The second diagram shows that the second level of house values is spread through occupational categories 2–4, and the third shows that there is a close connection between highest occupational level and highest house value. These distributions conform to the high correlation of .854 in table 5.9.

The weaker connection of occupation with education is reflected in the second and third rows of figure 5.11. The third histogram in the second row shows the very broad range of occupations held by people with no more than a high school education, covering the entire span of occupations.

Because the stable sociolinguistic variables are essentially monotonic functions of position in the socioeconomic hierarchy, it was possible to do a direct comparison of the effects of various indicators by inserting them as single quantitative dimensions into the regression analysis. Tables 3.7 and 3.8 showed that, in general, occupation was correlated more closely with the linguistic factors than education or house value, but this was not always true. In every case, the combined index of socioeconomic position yielded a stronger and more consistent pattern of social stratification than any individual indicator.

The situation with changes in progress is more complex. It is not necessarily true that the index with the largest coefficient in a regression analysis is the most revealing. If the curvilinear pattern of change in progress holds, then the single dimension along which the variable rises and falls might show no relationship at all as a single quantitative variable. On the other hand, when the residence, occupational, and educational groups are all added to a single analysis, the end result is confusion – nothing is significant. In order to compare the effect of each individual dimension, it is necessary to graph the pattern of coefficients in a single, comparable framework, from analyses in which all other factors are the same. This will be done by alternatively substituting for the 6-point SEC scale in the third regression, the 6-point occupation, education, and residence scales. In each case, the residual group will be the highest one.

There are four ways in which the resultant patterns might be evaluated: (1) the smoothness or regularity of the curvilinear or monotonic function; (2) the levels of significance of the points that define the trajectory; (3) the total variation explained as shown by the adjusted $r^2$; (4) the F-ratios of the entire analysis. The first of these is not particularly useful: by the simple process of averaging, the combined index will always show a smoother curve than the individual indicators. The fourth is an exact reflection of the third, and adds no additional information. The indices will therefore be compared to the combined index by measures (2) and (3).

Figures 5.12–5.15 superimpose the social class trajectories derived from regression analyses in which the social dimension is alternately education, house value, occupation, and the combined SEC index. Significance levels are shown as: (*) < .10; * < .5; ** < .01; *** < .001; **** < .0001. The first case for us to examine is the change that is most advanced and has the strongest social significance, (æhN). The next chapter will show that this raised and tensed vowel of *man, Camden, dance* is the element of the Philadelphia system that is most often remarked on and corrected. In figure 5.12 all the indicators agree in showing no significant difference among the three lowest categories: they are all close to the zero level of the upper working class. The sharp decline in the three highest social groups is shown by occupation, house value, and the combined index, but education is a less precise indicator of this process. For education, there is only one point that approaches significance, just below the .05 level. The close association between occupation and house value is illustrated by the parallel movement of the two curves here, as we would expect from the correlation of .85.

Figure 5.13 gives the parallel picture for (æhS). There is very little difference between the trajectories of occupation and house value, and again education fails to show a clear differentiation. Occupation and the combined index show higher levels of significance than residence, but the differences are only slight.

The differentiation of the indicators is much more marked for the new and vigorous changes. Figure 5.14 shows that for (aw), the combined index is superior to any individual indicator in terms of consistent and significant points defining the curvilinear pattern. The highest level for education is

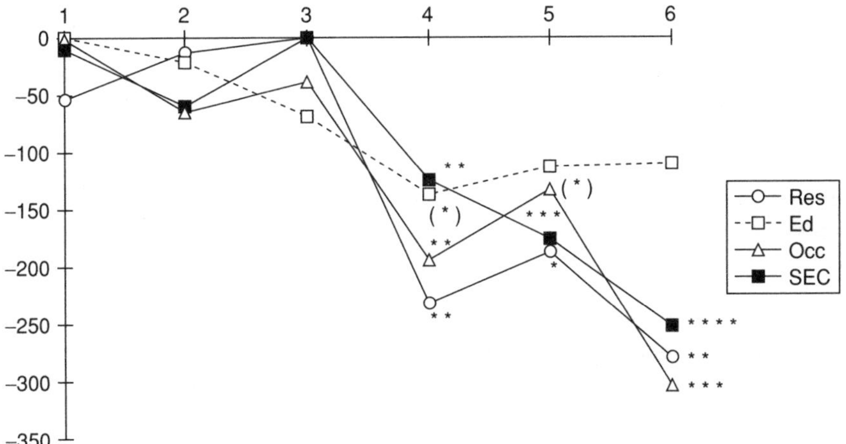


*Figure 5.12* Components of the monotonic social class pattern for (æhN). Significance of coefficients: **** p < .0001, *** p < .001, ** p < .01, * p < .05

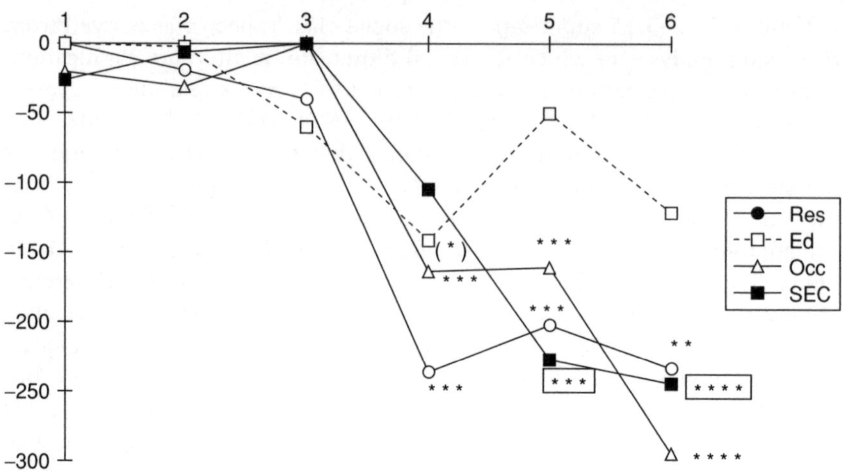


*Figure 5.13* Components of the monotonic social class pattern for (æhS) (significance as in figure 5.12)

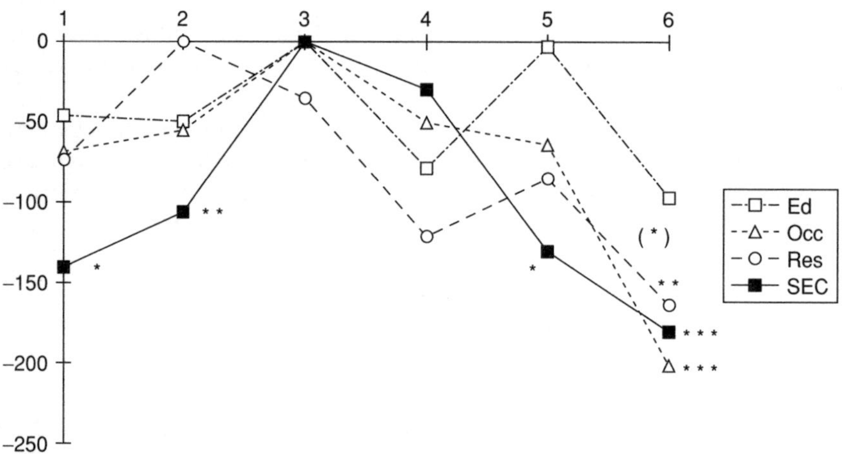


*Figure 5.14* Components of the curvilinear social class pattern for (aw) (significance as in figure 5.12)

the fifth category; for residence, the second; while occupation and the combined index concur at the third category. The combined index shows four significant points, but occupation and education only one.

Figure 5.15 shows the corresponding pattern for the newest change, the retrograde movement of (eyC). Here education seems almost irrelevant. The middle class decline from the peak in the third group is shown most clearly through occupation, while the pattern of progressively lower values

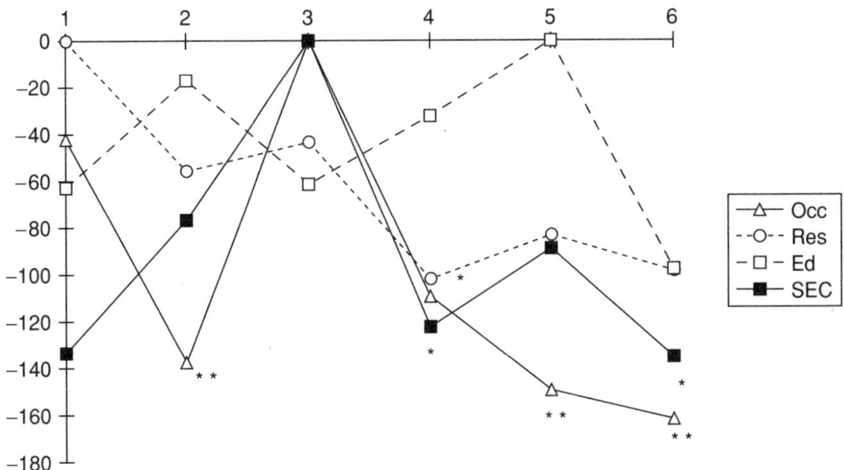


*Figure 5.15* Components of the curvilinear social class pattern for (eyC) (significance as in figure 5.12)

in the working class groups is clearest in the combined index. On the whole, occupation gives us the greatest degree of significance: four significant points as against two for the combined index.

The predominance of occupation for the most recent change suggests that the combined index is preferable only for those changes that have become engaged in the processes of sociolinguistic differentiation which extend over large portions of the speaker's life span. For young people growing up, the occupation of the breadwinner(s) of the family is the strongest determinant of their linguistic behavior – the linguistic matrix from which the speaker emerges. Though house value is closely correlated, movements to better (or worse) locations are events that influence linguistic behavior at a later stage. Education is a cumulative, socializing effect whose influence becomes stronger later in life. The development of the very newest changes, like (eyC), is therefore less influenced by later socialization, and will be tied most closely to the linguistic pattern of the family and most closely correlated with occupation.

Figure 5.16 shows the relative explanatory value of the three indicators in terms of their contributions to the total variance explained – the adjusted $r^2$ of the analysis. The effect of education is the least, especially for the older changes in progress. For (æhN), there is little difference among the other three. For (æhS) and (aw), the combined index is best, followed closely by occupation and house value. But for (eyC), there is a distinct superiority of occupation. If the reasoning which accounts for this is correct, the predominance of occupation for (eyC) should be maximal among the youth, while the use of adults should be controlled by a larger complex of factors. The last set of points on figure 5.16 shows the results of an analysis where

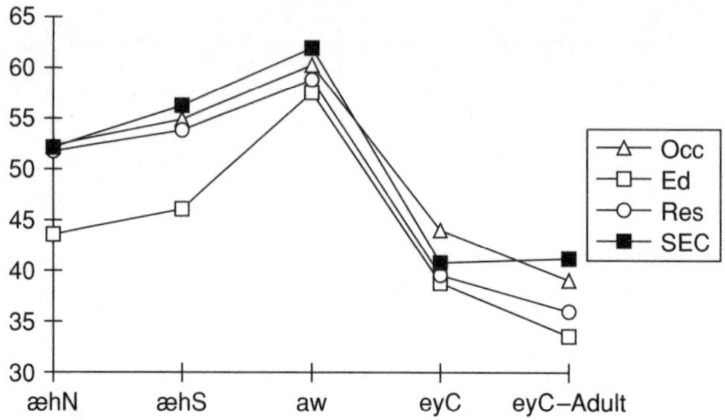


*Figure 5.16* Variation explained by regression analyses utilizing individual indicators and the combined index

all speakers below 20 years old are eliminated. The usual ordering of indices is restored: the combined index with the highest $r^2$, followed by occupation, house value, and education.

## 5.10 An overview

The relationship of linguistic change from below to the socioeconomic hierarchy does not correspond to any of the early discussions of the causes of sound change reviewed in chapter 1. New and vigorous changes are not inhibited or promoted by higher or lower occupation or education or social status. Instead, these analyses of change in progress have shown a series of social properties associated with successive stages of development.

Incipient changes. There is little to say about the earliest changes. Incipient changes like the lowering of (e) and (æ) or the backing of (ʌ) do not have strong enough correlations with age or social factors to be informative. A clear view of the social location of a change in progress appears only when its age coefficient becomes significant, reflecting the fact that it is approaching the middle section of its S-shaped curve.

Nearly completed changes. The linguistic changes that are the easiest to locate and recognize are those that are the most advanced, and our view of the progress of sound change is best constructed by working backward, from almost completed to mid-range to new and vigorous. The most advanced changes resemble the stable sociolinguistic variables in many ways. Their values are an almost monotonic function of the socioeconomic hierarchy, and they display the same late adolescent peak that was found for (dh), (neg), and (ing). None of the advanced vowel changes are as sharply stratified as the stable sociolinguistic variable (neg); social stratification is concentrated in the middle classes, as with (ing). The allophone (æhD) is intermediate in this respect. It still shows a strong age correlation, indicating that the raising and fronting of *mad, bad, glad* is an ongoing process, but the social distribution is similar to that of the other two allophones.

MID-RANGE CHANGES. The changes that were originally labeled "mid-range" turn out to be largely completed, or at least stabilized. They seemed to be in the middle of their range, with means that are half-fronted. But the Philadelphia fronting of (uw), checked and free, and (owF), are not currently attached to any vigorous movement in apparent time or anchored in any social process.[16] Later chapters will show that the progress of these changes in Philadelphia is part of a broad, continental development. Only the most retarded in this process, (owC), shows a strong social correlate, and this seems to reflect a different history from that of the new and vigorous changes taking place at present. Like them, it seems to be strongest in the lower middle class, but it is the other middle classes who are now following closely behind, rather than the working classes. By one means or another, this characteristic feature of the Southern Shift has escaped stigmatization and become associated with middle class norms.

NEW AND VIGOROUS CHANGES. The *Atlas of North American English* shows that the fronting of the (aw) nucleus is a widespread phenomenon, affecting all but Northern dialects. It is a continuation of the nucleus–glide differentiation that led from [u:] to [əu] to [aʊ] to [æʊ], and as such, might not be considered a new event. But the concomitant raising of the nucleus to [e] and the falling of the glide target to [ɔ] are new developments in Philadelphia, and not found in the surrounding areas of Pennsylvania and the Upper South.[17] This chapter has made it clear that the raising and fronting of (aw) is most advanced in a centrally located social milieu which in our terminology forms part of the upper working class. Though (aw) is not at a high level of conscious social awareness, and is rarely a subject of social comment, there are signs that the middle class speakers are beginning to inhibit its advance, differentiating themselves more and more from the leaders. In chapters to follow, we will look more deeply into the social mechanism involved here.

There are close parallels between (eyC) and (aw), but in many ways (eyC) shows evidence of being a more recent change, and carries us closer to the detectable beginnings of change from below. The leaders in the raising of (aw) are the leaders for (eyC): the r-correlation between them is .729. But unlike (aw), (eyC) represents a departure from the previous direction of the Southern Shift toward a Northern pattern. It also differs from (aw) in

[16] These are the sole Philadelphia vowels to be strongly influenced by ethnicity; see chapter 7.

[17] An exact parallel is found in our instrumental measures of New Zealand dialects (Christchurch). Guy Bailey has reported such phonetic developments in some Southern dialects, but the vowel charts of the *Atlas of North American English* have not yet located many examples parallel to Philadelphia.

that the curvilinear pattern is symmetrical (figures 5.7, 5.14–5.15). For (eyC), the upper middle class is no further behind the leading groups than the lower working class. We may see here the original pyramidal structure in which a sound change gradually spreads from one neighboring group to another, undistorted by the attribution of stigma or prestige.

The Philadelphia study was designed to test the curvilinear hypothesis with which this work began. Given that evidence, it can now be restated as *Principle 1* or the *Curvilinear Principle*:

*Linguistic change from below originates in a central social group, located in the interior of the socioeconomic hierarchy.*

If linguistic change were governed by a binary opposition between middle class and working class (Kroch 1978), the task of sampling the speech community could be greatly simplified. In fact, many sociolinguistic studies have attempted to assess the relation between social class and language by a binary division of the socioeconomic hierarchy: middle class vs. working class, or upper class vs. lower class. Though two-part sampling will capture the basic opposition reflected in the stable sociolinguistic hierarchies of chapter 3, even in that case it will fail to capture important aspects of sociolinguistic structure, as in the special behavior of the second highest status group. A binary division is likely to miss entirely any changes from below that are concentrated in an interior social group. In the cases studied here, the leaders of linguistic change span the division between working class and middle class (see (aw) and (owC) in figure 5.7). Figure 2.4 showed the intimate admixture of working class and lower middle class in Clark St. There is nothing about white-collar or blue-collar occupation that distinguishes the leaders of linguistic change from below. Rather, it is their central location in the community: as later chapters will show, not merely central in terms of the abstract socioeconomic hierarchy, but central in terms of local activity, local interaction, and local prestige.

## 5.11 Further observations of class distributions

In recent years, two important studies of change in progress have incorporated a fine enough sample of social strata to bear upon the curvilinear hypothesis.

Guy et al. 1986 drew upon Horvath's (1985) study of Sydney to trace the age and social class distribution of high rising intonation in Australian English. As table 5.10 shows, there is a monotonic relation between age and the use of this Australian rising intonation pattern. Three divisions of the social class spectrum were established: middle class, upper working, and lower working. As the table shows, the highest use was found in the

*Table 5.10* Use of high rising intonation in Sydney, by age and social class

| *Age* | $p_i$ | *Social class* | $p_i$ |
|---|---|---|---|
| 11–14 yrs | 0.64 | Middle | 0.40 |
| 15–19 yrs | 0.67 | Upper working | 0.51 |
| 20–39 yrs | 0.51 | Lower working | 0.59 |
| 40+ yrs | 0.21 | | |

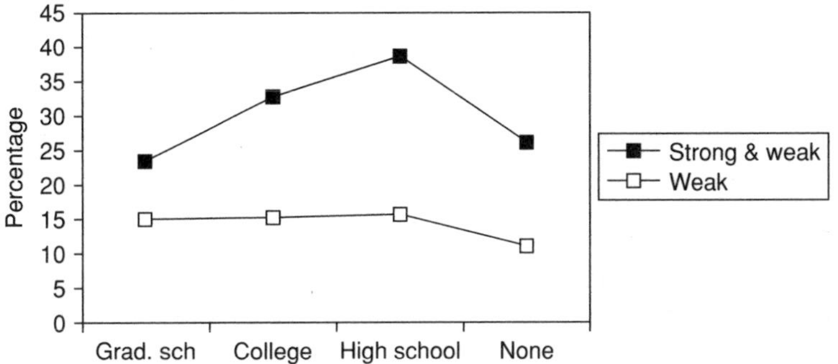


*Figure 5.17* Strong and weak palatalization of /t,d/ in Cairo Arabic by educational classes (from Haeri 1996, graphs 11–12)

lowest social class. This appears to be a counter-example to the curvilinear hypothesis. However, the Australian situation looks somewhat different when men and women are separated, and we will return to these data in chapter 8.

In Haeri's study of Cairo Arabic (1996), a new and vigorous change was located: the palatalization of /t/ and /d/ before front vowels. A total of 49 speakers were analyzed, evenly divided by gender. Palatalization took two forms: weak and strong, where the strong form had longer releases, with higher frequency bursts of noise. Figure 5.17 is constructed from Haeri's data to show the distribution of strong and weak palatalization by education.[18] The curvilinear character of the data appears in this cumulative view, in which the upper line represents total palatalization. It is evident that the high school group shows the greatest degree of palatalization as a whole. We will return to Haeri's data in the examination of gender effects, since this pattern is in fact characteristic of the women who are the leaders of change.

[18] Haeri actually uses a more sophisticated index of social class, which will be examined in chapter 8 when palatalization is traced separately by gender. Data for the entire population is provided only for education.

## 5.12 The curvilinear pattern and the causes of change

The basic strategy of this pursuit of the causes of change is to identify the leaders of change in progress; in place of the question "why?" I have substituted the question "who?" Convergent evidence has been presented that the innovators of change, in so far as we have identified them in New York City, Norwich, Panama City, Philadelphia, and Cairo, are located in the central sections of the socioeconomic hierarchy. There is no evidence to support the views of 19th-century linguists that change originates in the highest sections of society, or in the lowest. On the contrary, these peripheral groups follow behind the innovative central groups. To our astonishment, members of the upper class, who send their children to private schools and keep their distance from the rest of the community, turn out to be good Philadelphians. They speak a conservative but distinctively Philadelphian variety of English, and like members of the upper middle class or lower class, follow trends that are set by the upper working class and lower middle class.

The immediate result is to rule out a number of the competing theories of the causes of linguistic change, at least as far as rotations of the vowel system are concerned. The first of these is that change is the result of relative isolation, that is, the breakdown of communication between the originating group and the rest of the community. Change in Philadelphia does not originate in isolated groups who drift away from the main trends of Philadelphia speech because they have limited communication with it. Change is not connected with lack of contact with the dominant norms of society. Change in Philadelphia does not come from lower class speakers with minimal education and minimal exposure to the conservative norms of university-dominated English. Change as we witness it here is not motivated by the principle of least effort, which does not apply to the tensing and raising of short vowels, the diphthongization and fronting of back vowels, or the development of other complex articulations, all characteristic features of the newer Philadelphia urban dialect.[19]

## 5.13 Are sound changes part of an adaptive process?

What light does the curvilinear pattern shed on the initial question of this volume: can linguistic diversification be accounted for by any process of environmental adaptation? If there is no immediate cognitive advantage to the Philadelphia sound changes, there may be social advantages. While

[19] That is not to say that many sound changes are not characterized by lenition and governed by the principle of least effort. In Philadelphia, the vocalization of /l/ is an ongoing process of this type, active in final, intervocalic, and postconsonantal positions.

the most common accounts of the causes of change in the 19th century pointed to the negative or destructive aspects of sound change, the most common accounts in the second half of the 20th century look to positive explanations.[20] I have cited Sturtevant's 1947 suggestion that linguistic change is brought about by the association of two competing linguistic forms with competing social groups. This view is not distinct from the position of Le Page and Tabouret-Keller (1985), who see the adoption of new linguistic forms as "acts of identity," by which speakers maximize their social advantage. Both attribute linguistic change to: (1) the association of positively regarded traits and social privileges with membership in a given social group, and (2) the association of a linguistic form with membership in that social group. If such attitudes are to be used to account for linguistic diffusion, it is necessary to posit a covert belief structure: that speakers feel that their adoption of the linguistic form will lead others to attribute to them the positive traits of the given group and allow them to share in the privileges of that group.

While such covert attitudes and beliefs may actually be involved in linguistic change, they are not usually supported by material evidence. Most such arguments assume rather than demonstrate that linguistic variation is adaptive. The fact that speakers talk in a certain way is taken as evidence for their desire to be identified with or be differentiated from a particular group. A solution to the Darwinian paradox is assumed in advance, and the problem is not to find out if there is an adaptive value to linguistic evolution, but rather to find out which form of adaptation is operating.

The Martha's Vineyard study (Labov 1963) is frequently cited as a demonstration of the importance of the concept of local identity in the motivation of linguistic change. However, we do not often find correlations between degrees of local identification and the progress of sound change. Hazen 2000 is an impressive advance toward providing empirical support for the concept of local identity. He shows how the concept of expanded vs. local identity can be used to explain differential linguistic development among African American speakers in Warren County, North Carolina. The question remains as to whether the same conclusions could be drawn from frequencies of interaction with speakers with different systems, following Bloomfield's principle of density. In other words, language change may simply reflect changes in interlocutor frequencies which are in turn the result of changes in social preferences and attitudes.

The strategy of this inquiry is to draw as much as possible on concrete evidence of actual behavior as evidence for such questions. To the extent that social differences in language behavior can be mapped onto the matrix

[20] Chambers 1995 argues strongly for the adaptive value of linguistic variation, but does not consider explicitly the problem of the adaptive value of change, which is the topic here.

of communicative interaction, we must give priority to this pattern of interaction in accounting for the linguistic facts. The curvilinear pattern of a sound change from an originating group to neighboring groups may then be the simple product of frequencies of interaction. The account based on covert attitudes is redundant to the extent that the network of daily interaction brings people into contact with the new form in proportion to their distance from the originating group.

One might ask why the linguistic changes we have been reviewing take place in one direction and not in the other. The answers to this question are fairly well established in volume 1. In the fronting and raising of (aw), the nucleus of the vowel is following the front peripheral track in a unidirectional manner. If two Philadelphians exchange mutual linguistic influence over a series of interactions, this unidirectional bias will ensure (for reasons that we still grasp only dimly) that the result will be a shift in a predictable direction. The speaker with the less advanced raising of (aw) will be influenced more than the speaker with the more advanced raising.

Even if the direction of the change can be accounted for in this way, we are still left with its location. Why should the innovating speakers be located in the upper working class rather than the upper middle class or the lower working class? Nothing in the principles of volume 1 could account for this. Is there any property of the social interaction matrix that would allow us to predict a central location for the leaders of change? This is a problem that will be explored in chapters to come. But in the light of the preceding discussion, the first task must be to investigate the subjective dimension of changes in progress, and see what evidence can be advanced that would be consistent with the curvilinear origins of these social changes and would motivate speakers of other social groups to adopt them.

# 6

# *Subjective Dimensions of Change in Progress*

The investigation of changes in progress in this volume has focused entirely upon the objective evidence of speech production. The study of changes in perception was given considerable attention in volume 1, particularly in the presentation of general principles governing splits and mergers in Part C. This was essentially a study of the cognitive aspects of change: alterations in the perception of category boundaries and the suspension of the semantic function of a distinction that preceded the final collapse of two phonemic categories into one. In Part B, the study of the general principles of chain shifts was entirely focused on speech production. The central cognitive aspect of chain shifting is the absence of change, that is, the preservation of distinctions, a constant feature that can be noted rather than studied.[1] Unlike splits and mergers, these sound shifts develop social evaluations of considerable strength, and their subjective correlates are an important aspect of the study of the social dimension of change that is the focus of this volume.

## 6.1 Field methods for the study of subjective reactions to language change

The research projects that produced the data on speech production reviewed in chapter 5 also included a variety of field experiments to register the speakers' perceptual reactions and subjective evaluations of the changes in progress. None of the results are easy to interpret in isolation, no matter how the data were gathered. Subjective responses take on meaning only against the background of the spontaneous speech of the same individuals and the community as a whole.

The simplest of the subjective methods tap the subjects' cognitive perceptions of "same" and "different" across phonological categories: *minimal*

[1] The cognitive consequences of chain shifting were the principal focus of the project on cross-dialectal comprehension, which will be reported in volume 3 of this work.

*pair* and *commutation tests*. A second type registers the subjects' abilities to perceive their own speech patterns: the *self-report test* (Labov 1966a, ch. 12, Trudgill 1974b). Subjects are given a range of linguistic variants and are asked to say which one comes closest to their own use. Though the task is overtly one of simple perception and categorization, the results turn out to reflect adherence to the social norms of how speech should be pronounced rather than a report of actual use. In general, people report themselves using forms closer to the overtly recognized prestige norm of the community than their actual use.

A variety of *family background tests* have been used to test subjects' ability to identify ethnic background or regional dialect from samples of speech (Labov et al. 1968: II:266–85). In general, these experiments have shown that listeners have less ability than they think they do to identify speakers in this way. In part, this may be due to a relative insensitivity of Americans to dialect differences,[2] but it is also due to the difficulty of defining the dimensions that would be the basis of linguistically controlled experiments.

The most fruitful experimental measures of subjective reactions to linguistic variation have been through *matched guise* tests, which tap subjects' unconscious attitudes toward languages and dialects. The technique originated by Lambert and his colleagues at McGill generates stimuli with the help of speakers who are judged to be balanced bilinguals or bidialectal speakers (Anisfeld and Lambert 1964, Lambert 1967). Listeners are exposed to short passages of speech from the same person in two different guises: French and English, Quebecois and continental French, Arabic and Hebrew, African American English and standard English. The two guises must be separated by alternations of other speakers in different guises; if the subjects realize that they are judging the same speaker in two linguistic guises, a much weaker and more diffuse set of attitudes are evoked.

In the original matched guise experiments, subjects rated the speech passages on an extended series of personality scales: intelligence, reliability, honesty, friendliness, etc. The results showed an extraordinary degree of consensus in the population: speakers of both French and English, for example, agreed in judging the same person when speaking English as more intelligent, reliable, honest, etc., than when speaking French. In these studies, no information is available on the linguistic features that carried the social information: the speech productions were identified globally as characteristic of the dialect. A limited number of matched guise experiments have been devised to detect attitudes toward particular linguistic

[2] See Labov and Harris 1994 for a report of a legal case that was initiated by the inability of Americans on the west coast to distinguish an Eastern New England accent from a New York accent, or Preston 1996 for the limited perceptions of regional dialects by Americans.

variables. The study of the Lower East Side of New York City (Labov 1966a, ch. 11, Labov 1972b, ch. 6) included a matched guise experiment that concentrated many examples of the same variable in a single passage, contrasting this with a "zero passage" which contained no variable of interest. Subjects were asked to judge what was the highest rated occupation that speakers could hold, speaking as they did. These experiments showed that change from above, the importation of constricted (r) as a prestige feature, was accompanied by a categorical shift to the positive evaluation of this feature on the part of all subjects born after 1945. Reactions to change from below, the raising of (æh) and (oh), showed that those who used the most advanced forms of a variable in their vernacular were the most likely to stigmatize these forms in the speech of others.

The 1966–8 study of adult African American speakers in South Harlem (Labov et al. 1968) also used a subjective reaction test that concentrated linguistic variables: in this case, stable sociolinguistic variables like (dh). In response to the question on job suitability, subjective reactions showed the same monotonic correlation with the socioeconomic hierarchy as we found in the study of (dh) in production: the higher the (dh) index, the lower the job rating. A question on how likely the speaker was to come out on top in a street fight showed the complementary pattern. However, the class distribution of these responses showed that the impression that vernacular forms were associated with toughness was much stronger among middle class speakers than upper working class subjects, and was barely observable among lower working class speakers. A third question was introduced to elicit the subjects' affective response to the speaker: *how likely was this person to become a friend of yours if you got to know him?* (the speakers were all male in this test). Responses to this question matched responses to the job suitability question for the middle class and upper working class born in the North; for others, they were the inverse of the job suitability responses.

Frazer 1987 studied subjective evaluations of five phonological variables across the North/Midland line in Ohio.[3] Subjects from Northern cities (principally Chicago) and small Midland cities (principally Colchester) agreed in stigmatizing several Midland features: the use of [æ] in (aw), raised and fronted variants of (e), and the use of palatal glides or retroflexion in *wash*. The most striking result was that subjects agreed in the negative view of the fronting of (aw) even though Frazer 1983 showed that this feature was on the increase in urban speech in that area.

[3] The matched guise technique was not used here. Stimuli were readings of four different speakers from "Arthur the Rat" which concentrated the variables in question. The question posed was "Would you be proud if a friend or a member of your family spoke this way?" with a five-point scale ranging from "certainly" to "certainly not." The main results were significant below the .01 level.

In these subjective reaction tests, some progress seems to have been made in eliciting the social evaluations that correspond to the social stratification of speech. The attitudes that reflect overt norms of prestigious or proper behavior are of course the easiest to elicit, both for stable sociolinguistic variables and for changes from above. Given a stable system of sociolinguistic stratification, it seems reasonable to propose that these overt norms are balanced by a set of covert norms, which give positive value to the nonstandard forms that people use in everyday life. One might put forward a principle that every overtly stigmatized feature has prestige in the social contexts where it is normally used, and that every prestige feature will be awarded an equal and opposite stigma in those opposing contexts. But this is adding little more than what we observe from actual speech production: different social groups continue to speak in different ways. Unless we have actual evidence that people are consistently rewarded or penalized for speaking in specific ways, the attitudes that we elicit in such tests might well be considered a mere reflection of speech behavior, rather than effective forces in social life. In fact, the judgments that people make in such test situations are often wildly exaggerated beyond any reasonable measure. Some New Yorkers say, for example, that "they would never hire" someone who used high values of (oh), very similar in fact to their own. Others say that a person who speaks in such and such a style could not hold any job at all. Yet there is little solid evidence to date that the way a person speaks has a serious influence on their life chances.[4]

I would therefore hesitate to put forward subjective reaction tests as a way of isolating the causes of linguistic change. Rather they must be considered as sensitive measures of the place of a given variable on a scale of social awareness. As a rule, social awareness of a given variable corresponds to the slope of style shifting. Changes from above are normally high on this scale. Some stable sociolinguistic variables, like (dh), (ing), and (neg), are quite high; others, like *-t,d* deletion, elicit only moderate style shifting and subjective reactions. Changes from below begin as *indicators*, stratified by age group, region, and social class. At this stage, they show zero degrees of social awareness, and are difficult to detect for both linguists and naive speakers. As they proceed to completion, such changes usually acquire social recognition as linguistic *markers*, usually in the form of social stigma, which is reflected in sharp social stratification of speech production, a steep slope of style shifting, and negative responses on subjective reaction tests. Ultimately, they may become *stereotypes*, the subject of overt comment, with a descriptive tag that may be distinct enough from

[4] There are of course extreme cases, such as that of Nathan B. discussed in Labov 1966a:250. This is a far cry from arguing that the (dh) index presented in chapter 3 is a factor in hiring and firing, promoting and demoting a person on the job.

actual production that speakers do not realize that they use the form themselves.[5]

Subjective reaction tests and self-report tests can therefore serve as sensitive indicators of the relative development of a change from below. They will allow us to compare one variable with another in degree of social awareness, and solidify our knowledge of the stages of linguistic change in progress in a community. They also generate important data on gender differences, which will be important in our consideration of this crucial aspect of linguistic change in progress in the chapters to follow.

In the third year of the Philadelphia Neighborhood Study, a second set of interviews was carried out across the neighborhoods to acquire systematic data on social networks and social interaction within each neighborhood (to be reported in chapter 10). These interviews also included a number of field experiments on cognitive and social perception. The data from the self-report tests and subjective reaction test will allow us to pursue the subjective dimension of the linguistic changes in progress in Philadelphia.

## 6.2 The Philadelphia Self-Report Test

Five Philadelphia variables were selected for the self-report test. These included four from the Philadelphia vowel changes in progress: the nearly completed change (æh), the middle-range change (ow), and the new and vigorous changes (aw) and (ay0). The stimulus tape consisted of four variants of each variable, pronounced by myself:

| | 1 | 2 | 3 | 4 |
|---|---|---|---|---|
| *man* | mæːn | mæ˔ːn | mɛːn | meᵊn |
| *go* | goω | go<ω | gəω | gɛ>ω |
| *now* | naω | næo | nɛo | neːɔ |
| *fight* | faɪt | fa˔ɪt | fəɪt | fə>ɪt |
| *moved* | muωvd | mʉ>ωvd | mʉ<ωvd | mɪωvd |

The four choices in each case ranged over the full range of variants heard in the community; they might be labeled in order as *corrected*, *conservative*, *advanced*, and *extreme*. Subjects were told that they would hear for each word four different pronunciations that are used in Philadelphia, and would be asked to say which one was closest to their own usual way of saying it. They then listened to a recording in which, for each variable and each variant, the number of the variant was given followed by two pronunciations of that variant. After each set of four, they gave their response.

[5] Thus high values of (dh) are referred to as *deses*, *dem*, and *doses*, with a fully voiced initial [d], though the actual use is a lenis stop or flap.

*Table 6.1* Means and standard deviations of responses to self-report test for 91 subjects

| | *man* | *now* | *fight* | *go* | *moved* |
|---|---|---|---|---|---|
| Mean | 2.26 | 2.27 | 1.48 | 1.78 | 2.28 |
| Std deviation | 0.66 | 1.02 | 0.58 | 0.85 | 0.81 |

Table 6.1 shows the mean responses and standard deviations for the five variables. Three of the vowels show almost identical means, with 2.26, 2.27, and 2.28 for (æhN), (aw), and (uwC). Responses to (ay0) averaged considerably lower, and (owF) was intermediate. Though these figures are of course a product of the choice of the stimuli for the four variants, they do reveal a general consistency in subjects' perception of the pattern.

Let us begin the analysis of the self-report test by assuming that it is a faithful reflection of the phonetic and phonological system of Philadelphia – in other words, that we can describe that system by asking native speakers what they say, as we so often do in other areas of linguistics. To the extent that self-report reflects the speech production patterns of chapter 5, we should get similar regression coefficients for the two modes of behavior.

The data on speech production in the neighborhood study is shown in the upper half of table 6.2, which extracts from table 5.4 the regression coefficients for age, sex, and SEC for the five variables that were used in the self-report test. The age figures capture the rate of change in apparent time for the nearly completed change (æhN), the middle-range (owF) and (uwC), and the new and vigorous changes (aw) and (ay0).[6] A significant female advantage is shown for (æhN), (aw), and (owF), while (ay0) shows the reverse effect. On the social class dimension, (æhN) shows a regular decline of the middle classes characteristic of a marked sociolinguistic variable, while (aw) shows the curvilinear pattern with a peak in the upper working class and a decline for the upper class. These social factors explain about 40% of the variance for (æhN), (aw), and (ay0). The lower middle class peak for (uwC) may also reflect a curvilinear pattern, but the percentage of variance explained for (owF) and (uwC) is so small (8%) that it is not to be weighed heavily.

The lower half of the table shows a parallel analysis for the 91 speakers of the self-report study. It is almost blank. Only one small age coefficient appears, for (ay0) in *fight*. Only one gender coefficient appears, for (uwC)

[6] The (ay0) age coefficient is positive, since older speakers have higher F1 values. As in all comparisons and combinations of F1 and F2, it is multiplied times two to match the graphing conventions and general perceptual patterns.

*Table 6.2* Regression coefficients for age, sex, and SEC for five Philadelphia vowels in speech production and the self-report test. Significance: **bold,** p < .001; <u>underlined</u>, p < .01; plain, p < .05

| | *Age* | *Sex* | *LWC* | *UWC* | *LMC* | *UMC* | *UC* | *Upward mobility* | $r^2$ |
|---|---|---|---|---|---|---|---|---|---|
| *Speech* | | | | | | | | | |
| æhN2 | –1.61 | 70 | | | | **–174** | **–293** | | 0.42 |
| aw2 | **–5.19** | 128 | | 86 | | | <u>–129</u> | | 0.44 |
| owF2 | <u>–2.49</u> | 71 | | | | | | | 0.08 |
| ay0(x2) | **4.44** | –72 | | | | | | | 0.38 |
| uwC2 | –2.53 | | | | 198 | | | | 0.08 |
| *Self-report* | | | | | | | | | |
| man | | | | | –0.40 | | | 0.45 | 0.11 |
| now | | | | | | | | | 0 |
| go | | | | | | | | | 0 |
| fight | –0.009 | | | | | | | | 0.05 |
| moved | | –0.40 | 0.55 | | | | | | 0.06 |

in *moved*, and this is for the one variable that did not show a gender coefficient in speech. The two social class coefficients that do appear do not form any clear pattern. It is interesting to note that upward mobility, which did not play a role in any of the speech analyses, here adds .4 to the expected level of reporting.[7] None of these effects are beyond the .05 level. Since there are 40 cells in the table, at least 2 of the 5 numbers are expected to be the results of chance fluctuation.

To sum up, any thought that we might gain insight into the Philadelphia vowel system by asking speakers how they talk must be set aside. Such data show no change in progress, gender differentiation, or social stratification. The only variable that shows any hint of social effects is (æhN), and there the figures are not easy to interpret. Given the sizeable quantity of data, and the detailed information on the social characteristics of the subjects, how can one explain the nearly uniform distribution of self-report across the 91 subjects? It is possible that the lack of significant social effects is merely the result of noisy data – that people are answering randomly. Another possibility is that the same social norms dictate appropriate answers to each individual, regardless of their actual speech patterns.

[7] Since upward mobility often duplicates the effect of higher social class position (Labov 1966b), one would expect this figure to be negative. Yet it shows speakers who are upwardly mobile reporting themselves as using higher values of (æhN) than others do. This finding must be filed away for interpretation when we have assembled more information on the innovators of sound change.

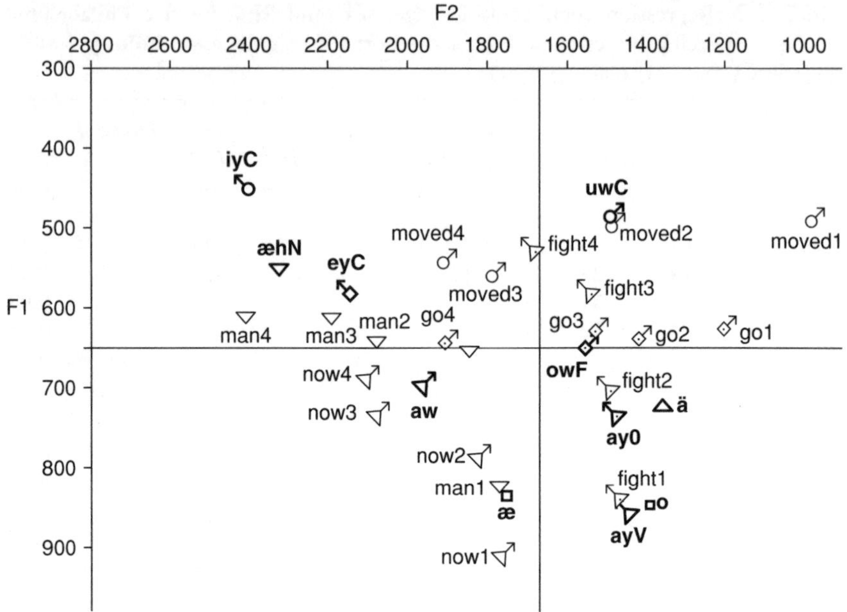


*Figure 6.1* Formant measurements for the stimuli used in the self-report test (spoken by WL) and mean normalized values from the 112 speakers of the Philadelphia Neighborhood Study (bold). Self-report vowels were normalized by scaling factors *w1/m1* and *w2/m2*, where *w1*, *w2* are the F1 and F2 values for WL's pronunciation of [æ] in *bad*, and *m1*, *m2* are the F1 and F2 of the community mean for lax /æ/

So far, we have been comparing heterogeneous groups of speakers, since the self-report tests were carried out in second interviews that did not reach all subjects of the neighborhood study. There are in fact only 38 subjects for whom we have both speech analyses and self-reports. To better interpret the self-reports obtained, it will be necessary to compare them more precisely with the facts of speech production for each individual. The first step is to relate the stimuli of the self-report test tape to the acoustic plot of the means of Philadelphia vowels. Figure 6.1 plots the nuclei of the four versions of the five vowel variables of the self-report test: *man* (æhN), *now* (aw), *fight* (ay0), *go* (ow), and *moved* (uw). On the same diagram, in bold, are shown the mean values for the 112 speakers of the Neighborhood Study. These are the normalized values transformed into a single reference grid by the logmean method discussed in chapter 5. To fit the measurements of the WL pronunciations of the self-report test as closely as possible to this grid, a two-parameter normalization was used, based on the location of low front [æ]. For both F1 and F2, the ratio of the normalized community value to the WL value was determined, and then the F1 and F2 of each WL measurement was multiplied by the F1 or F2 ratio.[8] Figure 6.1 shows that this normalization was reasonably successful. The low vowels show a close approximation of WL *man1* to the Philadelphia mean for /æ/, and WL *fight1* to the Philadelphia mean for /ayV/. These are the intended phonetic targets. Among the high vowels, the close approximation of WL *moved2* to the community /uwC/ shows that the height of the self-report measurements was appropriately adjusted.

Following the path of the five variables across figure 6.1, it appears that the procedure achieved the goal of an even spacing across the relevant phonetic dimension. The four *now* values follow the path of the front diagonal, *fight* shows a monotonic F1 sequence,[9] and *go* and *moved* show a regular forward progression of F2. The only exception to this even spacing is the (æhN) variable registered by *man1–4*. *Man1* is placed in the low front position characteristic of lax /æ/. *Man2–4* are all in mid position, and show a series of steps along F2 rather than along the front diagonal. They are not quite as high as the community mean for (æhN).[10] This jump between the three tense and the one lax values is characteristic of the shift that some members of the community show in reading, though spontaneous speech shows almost no correction of this sort (Labov 1989b).

Since the self-report test and measurements of speech production are successfully superimposed, the correct response for any given subject would be the one of the four variants that is closest to the person's own (normalized) mean value in speech production. For each of the 38 subjects with acoustic and self-report data the Cartesian distances were determined between the mean speech production value for each vowel variable to each of the four variants. The variant with the minimum distance would then be the "correct" response. Accuracy of response was then measured by subtracting the mean of speech production from the correct response. Thus if a subject chose *man2* and his or her mean value for (æhN) was closest to *man3*, the *reporting score* would be −1.

Figure 6.2 is a set of five histograms showing the distribution of reporting scores from −3 to 3. It is immediately apparent that values are clustered on the negative side for all five: there is a strong tendency to under-report the degree of advancement of sound change in one's own speech.[11] The

[8] The F1 ratio was 1.1813 and the F2 ratio was 1.0870.

[9] (ay0–3) and (ay0–4) shift slightly to the front; we later found that it is more characteristic of male speakers in Philadelphia to shift toward the back.

[10] As chapter 5 shows, F2 is the dimension most sensitive to social differentiation. Nevertheless, it would have been better if *man2–4* had followed the front diagonal, combining changes in both F1 and F2.

[11] Here, "under-reporting" corresponds to "over-reporting" in the original self-report tests of Labov 1966a and Trudgill 1972. The New York City experiment tested subjects' reaction to the new prestige norm of consonantal [r] in postvocalic position, and subjects tended to report more [r] than they used. The Philadelphia test examined subjects' reactions to changes from below. In under-reporting their use of the new variants, they over-reported their use of the conservative, older forms. See below for their degree of awareness of these features.

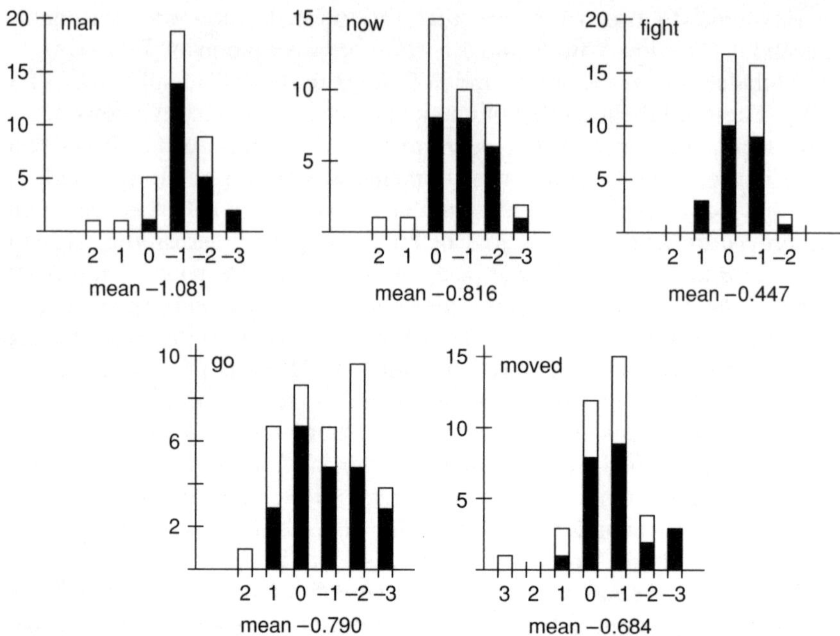


*Figure 6.2* Distribution of self-report scores for 38 subjects with both vowel analyses and test scores available. Scores are the differences between the test response and the "correct" response, determined as the test variant closest to the subject's mean speech production. Black area: female subjects; white area: male subjects

mean scores for all variables are significantly lower than 0, with a t-test showing $p < .0001$.

Two possible interpretations of this consistent under-reporting are apparent. On the one hand, under-reporting may reflect the fact that subjects are not aware of the degree of advancement of these changes from below, and are not able to perceive their own use. On the other hand, under-reporting may register the formation of community norms in reaction to the advanced forms of the change, and subjects may be reporting their normative impressions of what they should say rather than what they do say. This would then be parallel to the self-reporting of the use of (r) in New York City, which reflected the extent to which speakers thought that postvocalic /r/ should be pronounced as a consonant rather than what they actually said.

One way of deciding between these opposing alternatives is to note what Philadelphians say about the advanced forms of the sound changes. Anne Bower kept meticulous records of every remark made by the 33 subjects of the self-report test in Wicket St., Pitt St., and Clark St. The greatest number of overt comments were made about (æhN) and (ay0), the variables that showed the highest and lowest degree of under-reporting in figure 6.2. These comments were of a radically different character.

In response to *man3*, members of the Clark St. networks ruefully acknowledged their own use. Angela B. asked, "Would you believe it? that I say it that way?" Eddie R. said, "Unfortunately, it's South Philly slang, not the best pronunciation," and Aileen L. added, "I guess I'm picking it up from the kids." Meg K., the leading member of the K. network on Wicket St. (chapter 2), conceded the same point. "I guess #3. I don't like it, it doesn't sound too good." When Celeste S., the central figure of the Clark St. network, heard *man4*, she said, "Bill musta been listening to my vowels!" And when another member of the group selected *man1* as typical of her own speech, Celeste admonished her, "Mary, you do not say it that way!"

On the contrary, responses to *fight3,4* quite regularly showed a lack of recognition. Neddie R. of Clark St. said, "I can understand #2, but I never even heard #3 or #4." Matt R., an older member of the Clark St. network, said, "I never heard anybody say 'FEET'," Others assigned these forms to some foreign source: "English people," "Boston," "New Yorkers from Brooklyn."[12] Agnes D. from Clark St., an Italian neighborhood, assigned *fight3,4* to "Two-streets! sounds like the Irish on 2nd St." A few people detected something characteristic of younger speakers. Barbara C., the center of the C. network on Wicket St., remarked that "#3 and #4 sound strange, like tough kids."

While responses to (æhN) showed recognition, most response to (ay0) showed the reverse. Since under-reporting was maximal for (æhN) and minimal for (ay0), it stands to reason that extreme under-reporting accompanies a high degree of social recognition – the second alternative presented above. When subjects report lower (æhN) than they actually use, they are responding to the norm that they should not say *man3* or *man4*. But because all vowels show significant under-reporting, including (ay0), it follows that the first alternative is also a factor in producing this result – that Philadelphians have limited awareness of the changes in progress.

There were only three or four comments on each of the other variables in the self-report test. Most of these were to the effect that the *now*, *go*, and *moved* variants sounded alike, with the occasional exception of the first or the last. In each case, there was one revealing and perceptive comment. In response to *now4*, Meg K. from Wicket St. said, "Oh wow!

[12] One might wonder if some feature of my pronunciation of *fight3,4* strayed so far from the Philadelphia pronunciation that people did not recognize it. This does not seem likely. In 1986, a television crew from the local Channel 10 interviewed me in connection with the finding that black and white dialects were diverging. In the evening show, I appeared saying that "Young white kids from Philadelphia say [fə>ɪt]." The camera cut to a shot of an interviewer putting a microphone in front of an adolescent boy in Kensington: "Say [faɪt]." The boy said, "[fə>ɪt]." The two pronunciations of [fə>ɪt] heard within 10 seconds of each other were plainly identical.

That's awful! But who hangs out the window and says #1?" In Clark St., a remarkably precise analysis of *go* was made by May D., a close friend of Celeste S., who was also secretary of the local church. "You can tell Upper Darby of the Northeast, by the way they say *go*, like in #2. Those little suburban sections, for some reason, sound that way, like #2 or #3. Not #4, that sounds like Kensington or Two-Street." Three people singled out *moved4* for comment, as younger, or different. Sally F. of Clark St. responded, "Oh God! That's how we say it, but it ain't too cool!"

The self-report test therefore gives further support to the inferences presented in chapter 3 of volume 1 on the sequencing of the Philadelphia vowel changes. (æhN) is a nearly completed change, with a high degree of social recognition and considerable social stigma, with maximal social stratification in speech; (ay0) is a new and vigorous change with little social recognition as well as little social differentiation in speech. So far, the others show intermediate behavior.

How can this view of general under-reporting be used to illuminate the earlier finding of this section, that the distribution of self-report was socially uniform? If there is a general under-reporting, constant throughout the population, this would not obscure the social stratification of a variable like (æhN), but simply displace it downward. At the same time, the degree of under-reporting is the inverse of the degree of advancement of the change. Figure 6.3 is a scattergram of the 37 subjects who show

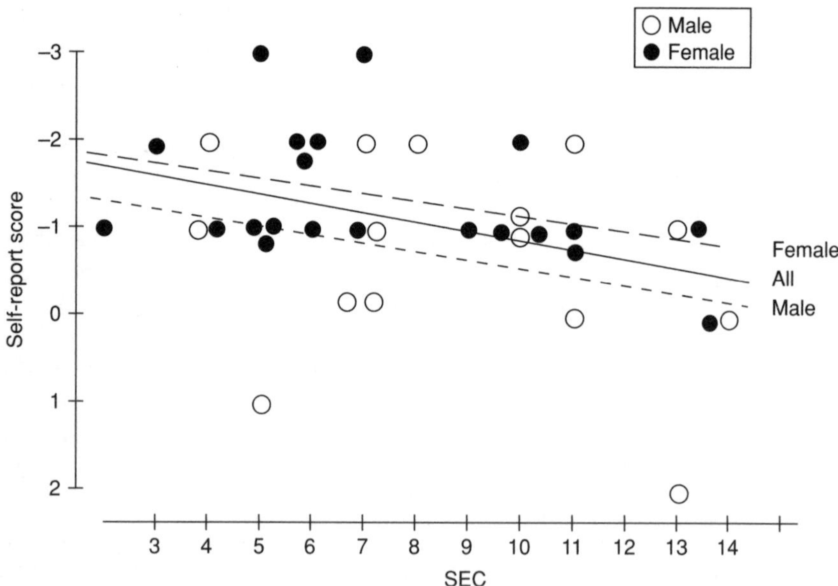


*Figure 6.3* Distribution of self-report scores for *man* by SEC and gender

(æhN) values in speech production and self-reports on *man*. The vertical axis is the self-report score, ranging from an under-reporting of –3 to an over-reporting of 2. The horizontal axis shows SEC index for each speaker. The regression line shows that the lower the SEC value, the greater the tendency to under-report. The expected value for the upper middle class subjects is close to 0; in other words, they are reasonably accurate in their reports.[13] On the other hand, all five subjects in SEC 3–4 under-reported their use of *man*. Only two subjects over-report this variable, both male. The gender differences in self-report are in the expected direction: the partial regression lines for male and female indicate that females have a greater tendency to under-report. This is significant at the .05 level. On the other hand, males and females are alike in both following the same tendency for greater under-reporting with lower social class, which is also independently significant at the .05 level.

These two independent effects, of social class and gender, are the inverse of the distributions that we find in speech. They therefore explain how it is that self-report scores themselves are uniformly distributed, or at least show little significant social differentiation. The two sets of independent inverse effects more or less cancel each other. This explains why in general the results of formal elicitation, word lists, or direct questioning have so little value in the study of the speech community. The effect of social norms operates to erase much of the social differentiation that forms the backbone of the sociolinguistic structure.

None of the other self-report variables show this extreme degree of inverse social differentiation found for (æhN). As shown by the overt reactions cited above, (æhN) is the only one that has reached the level of a stereotype – a strongly stratified and recognized sociolinguistic variable. To the extent that the changes in progress are hidden from social awareness, self-report is less influenced by linguistic norms. Thus we might expect the most accurate reports on (ay0). Unfortunately, the obverse problem of social recognition then becomes proportionately stronger: since early stages of changes in progress are hidden from social awareness, speakers cannot recognize the forms that they actually use. For (ay0), the regression line relating self-report to SEC is flat, but the amount of noise is proportionately increased.

The self-report results echo the general principle first found in the New York City study, that those who use the highest degree of stigmatized forms are the strongest in stigmatizing the use of those forms in others (Labov 1966a, chapter 9). It remains to be seen if this principle emerges in the subjective reaction tests in Philadelphia. But the main conclusion to

[13] With the exception of one man who shows an over-reporting of 2. He was one of the few people who selected *man4*; a way of bending over backwards to avoid social norms that is not common.

be drawn from the self-report tests is a methodological one: that one cannot expect to trace the sociolinguistic pattern of a community by self-report. To the extent that social processes raise the recognition rate of a socially stratified form, the tendency to under-report levels the social distinctions.

## 6.3 The Philadelphia Subjective Reaction Test

At an early stage of the project on linguistic change and variation in Philadelphia [LCV], a reading text was prepared comparable to the text used in New York City, a narrative about a camping trip told by an adolescent male in which five linguistic variables were concentrated in successive paragraphs. This text was the basis for a construction of a matched guise subjective reaction test [SRT], which elicited from subjects their unconscious evaluations of individual linguistic variables.[14]

One paragraph was written to have no marked sociolinguistic variables, with sentences like, "It was a lot different from what we expected." Other paragraphs concentrated instances of (æh), (ow), (ay0), and (aw). A fifth paragraph showed concentrations of a consonantal change in progress that has not yet been discussed: (str). Many American speakers show variation in the hissing or hushing quality of /s/. In Philadelphia, a shift toward a hushing quality occurs when /s/ precedes /tr/ as in *street, straight*. It is triggered by the palatal quality of the aspirated [r]; in the Philadelphia vernacular, /tr/ is quite close to /č/, so that *trolley* and *Charlie* can be mistaken. The variable ranges from a hissing [s], used only by cultivated speakers, to a normal sibilant with considerable hushing quality, to a fully hushing sibilant equivalent to the [š] in *sheet*, and an even more extreme form with distinct rounding of the fricative. The hissing quality is associated with a higher range of energy in the noise spectrum, with a minimum of about 4000 Hz, while the hushing quality shows progressively lower noise frequencies, ranging down to 1200 Hz.

The text was read by a number of the 70 Philadelphia speakers who were interviewed in the exploratory stage of the project, and from these readings, four speakers were selected to represent a range of pronunciations characteristic of Philadelphia (table 6.3). Speaker CF was an upper class woman from Chestnut Hill whose husband owned a chemical plant; she was active in many charities and private school programs. RD was a lower middle class woman from Nancy Drive in King of Prussia; both she and her husband held clerical jobs. Speaker MK is Meg K., the head of the Kendell network on Wicket St., who was cited several times in the discussion of self-report; she represents the upwardly mobile upper working

[14] The subjective reaction test described below was designed by Steve Herman for the LCV Project.

*Table 6.3* Representative Philadelphia speakers

| | *Age* | *Neighborhood* | *SEC* |
|---|---|---|---|
| CF | 40 | Chestnut Hill | 16 |
| RD | 40 | King of Prussia | 11 |
| MK | 31 | Wicket St. | 6 |
| CS | 32 | Richmond | 4 |

class. Her husband was a bartender; she was working then as a receptionist but several years later had become the office manager. Speaker CS is from Port Richmond, an area of Kensington even less prosperous than Wicket St. Her husband was a welder and truck driver; she was working as a waitress at the New Jersey shore.

For each speaker, a sentence from the reading was selected that concentrated each of the five variables, and the zero sentence with no marked variable. The stimulus tape thus comprised the 24 sentences of table 6.4, presented to subjects with the variables and speakers in random order. The numbers in parenthesis are the 4-step categories of the self-report test. Reactions were obtained on a 7-point scale of *job suitability* and *friendliness*. The job suitability scale was presented to subjects as a series of horizontal lines, each divided into seven sections, with the heading, "What is the highest job this person could hold, speaking as she does?" The highest rating, #7, was marked "Television personality," and the lowest, #1, "No job at all." Data was obtained from 99 subjects in the course of the second interviews.

Sentences were selected from the reading passage on the basis of their fluency and approximation to the value of the vowels used by that speaker in spontaneous speech.[15] Table 6.4 shows that the same sentence was used in many cases to represent the same variable, but not in every case. Variation of sentences was also needed to avoid the focus of attention on the variables in question.

Figure 6.4 shows two of the stressed vowels of the SRT on an F1/F2 plot, with each speaker identified by the typography of the labels. The distribution of these forms can be compared to the impressionistic ratings, always bearing in mind that there are other phonetic features involved besides the F1/F2 position of the nucleus. Figure 6.4 shows the same phonetic range for the Philadelphia variables that appeared in figure 6.1

[15] An exception to this rule is the reading of (æh) by CF, which showed regular correction to lax /æ/. As shown in Labov 1989b, Philadelphians (as opposed to New Yorkers) show a vanishingly small percentage of such correction in spontaneous speech, including the upper class.

*Table 6.4* Sentences used in the Philadelphia subjective reaction test, with ratings (in parentheses) according to the four levels of the self-report test

Zero

CF: It was a lot different from what we expected.

RD: It was a lot different from what we expected.

MK: We studied up and bought some equipment a couple of weeks before we left.

CS: It was a lot different from what we expected.

(æh)

CF: We began casting (1) at half (1) past (1) one.

RD: We never managed to land (3) a damn (4) thing, and really got mad (4) because of our bad (3) luck.

MK: We really got mad (4) because of our bad (3) luck.

CS: We began casting (2) at half (2) past (2) one.

(aw)

CF: We took down (1) the tent and set out (2) toward a mountain (1) about two hours (2) south (2) of us.

RD: We took down (3) the tent and set out (3) toward a mountain (3) about (2) two hours (3) south (3) of us.

MK: We scouted (2) around (2) for wood, and found (2) some without (3) much trouble.

CS: We took down (3) the tent, and set out (3) toward a mountain (3) about (2) two hours (1) south (3) of us.

(ow)

CF: Toting (2) a heavy load (2) over a stony (2) road (1) got to us though.

RD: Jerry came over (2) to show (2) me which way to go (3).

MK: So Jerry came over (2) to show (3) me which way to go (4); the trail opened (2) up over (2) to the left.

CS: It was tough to know (3) which trail to go (3) on though (3).

(str)

CF: City streets (1) are all straight (1), but country trails are just rocky strips (1), and walking got to be a real strain (1).

RD: City streets (2) are all straight (2), but country trails are just rocky strips (2), and walking got to be a real strain (2).

MK: City streets (2) are all straight (2), but country trails are just rocky strips (2).

CS: City streets (3) are all straight (3), but country trails are just rocky strips (3), and walking got to be a real strain (3).

(ay0)

CF: It was quite a fight (1), trying to put in the two big pipes (1), but we finally did it.

RD: It was quite a fight (2), trying to put in the two big pipes (2), but we finally did it.

MK: It was a fine sight (3); we got a bite (3) to eat and got to sleep by nine.

CS: It was a fine sight (2).

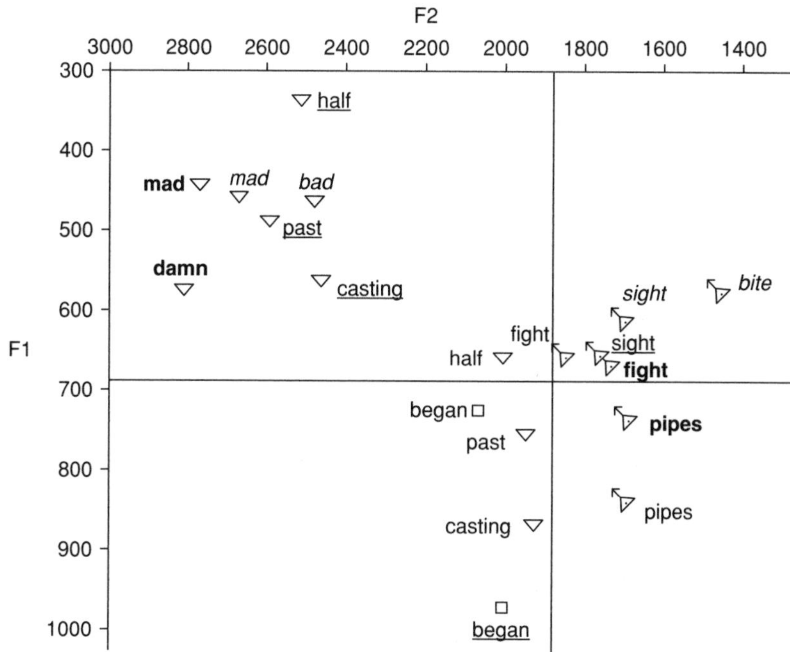


*Figure 6.4* F1/F2 positions of (æh) and (ay0) in the Philadelphia subjective reaction test. Plain labels: upper class speaker CF; bold labels: lower middle class speaker RD; italic labels: upper working class speaker MK; underlined labels, lower working class speaker CS

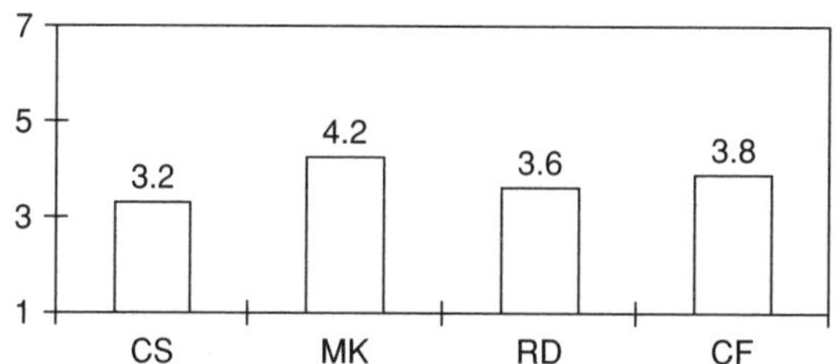


*Figure 6.5* Mean ratings of the four speakers of the Philadelphia subjective reaction test in the zero passage on the job suitability scale (7 = television personality, 1 = no job at all)

for the self-report test. The special phonetic characteristics of each distribution will be discussed along with the results for each.

The zero passage was used as the basis for calibrating reactions to individual variables. Figure 6.5 shows the mean responses to the zero passage on the job suitability scale, with the actual values shown above each bar. The zero ratings were concentrated slightly above the middle of the range

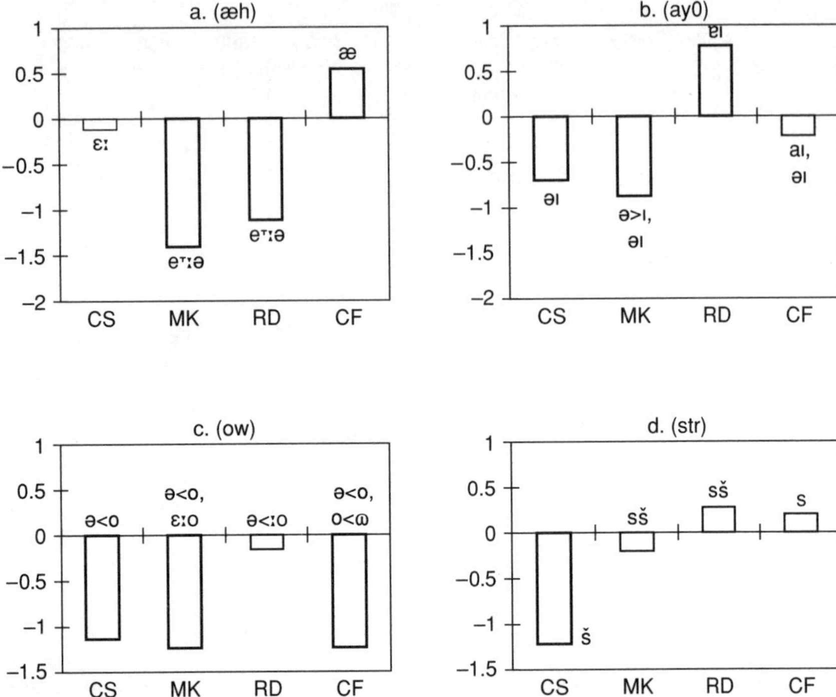


*Figure 6.6* Mean differences between zero passage and subjective reactions to linguistic variables on the job suitability scale. Columns that are significantly different from 0 at the level $p < .001$ are bold; others are not significantly different from 0

(3.5), extending from 3.2 to 4.2. It is clear that the evaluation of voices and reading styles of the four speakers does not exactly match ranking by socioeconomic class; in fact, the highest rated speaker was Meg K. from Wicket Street.

For each of the five variables, the relevant data are the difference between the rating given by the subject to that speaker in the zero passage, and the rating given to the same speaker for the given variable. Figure 6.6a–d shows the overall mean results for four variables, beginning with(æh). The locations of the (æh) tokens on figure 6.4 can be oriented by their relation to lax /æ/, which is exemplified by the two tokens of the word *began1*. All fully stressed tokens of (æh) spoken by CF are in this area, categorized as (1). These corrected forms are heard favorably by Philadelphians, who raise the job suitability rating of CF by a mean of .55 in figure 6.6a. Correspondingly, they lower the ratings of both MK and RD, who use advanced values of (æh) (shown in figure 6.4 as *mad* and *damn* for RD, and *mad* for MK). In figure 6.6a, these are viewed negatively by the subjects, who lower these two speakers by a sizeable amount: −1.41 and −1.1 (MK, who was rated higher at the outset, has more to lose). The more moderate pronunciation of the lower class speaker, transcribed as [ɛː], is treated neutrally. The critical dimension in these comparisons is F2, rather than F1: it is the fronting of the nuclei of RD and MK that appears to trigger the reaction. If the vowels were compared by their F1 values, the subjective reactions would be much harder to interpret. This is in accord with the finding of chapter 5, that F2 values display much stronger social correlations than F1 values.

The self-report tests opposed (ay0) to (æhN) in the degree of social recognition received. But figure 6.6b shows that SRT judges are almost as sensitive to (ay0) as to (æhN). Examination of figure 6.4 shows that the most extreme form of (ay0) is the backed raised vowel of *bite* pronounced by MK. MK is also lowered more than any other speaker in figure 6.6b. RD, who was downgraded for her use of (æh) in figure 6.6a, is here considerably elevated because both of her vowels are heard as basically low, with an [ɐ] nucleus. CF shows both [ɔɪ] and [aɪ], and her rating is effectively neutral. Thus the inspection of the (ay0) productions shows that although Philadelphians cannot consciously recognize the advanced forms in self-report tests, they do react unconsciously in the SRT test to downgrade the use of advanced forms.

The case of (ow) in figure 6.6c is much less clear. The instrumental measurements of the nuclei of the (ow) tokens produced by the four speakers form a globular distribution around mid center (not shown in figure 6.4). All speakers produce at least one nucleus well front of center. The degree of rounding or unrounding is critical here, and this is not well reflected in F1/F2 plots. The most extreme unrounded *go* is that of MK. Though there is little differentiation in speakers' productions, only three of the four speakers are downgraded in figure 6.6c; for reasons that are unclear to me, RD is not. In general, Philadelphians react to a fronted nucleus in (ow) as local and not suitable for public formal speech, but the details of their reactions are not easily mapped on impressionistic or acoustic dimensions.

The fourth variable to consider here is (str), the consonantal change in progress. Figure 6.6d shows that the Philadelphia subjects do not sharply differentiate the hissing [s] from the partial hushing sibilant labeled (str-2). However, the full hushing quality that is used by CS is downgraded sharply, with a mean decline from the zero passage of 1.2.

So far, the results all illustrate a categorical quality in the subjective reactions of Philadelphians. The 20 sets of 99 responses fall into two classes: they are either significantly different from zero at less than the .001 level, or they are not significantly different from zero. The case of (æh) was unique in that there were two reactions: an upgrading of the correction of /æh/ to /æ/, and a downgrading of the use of advanced forms of local

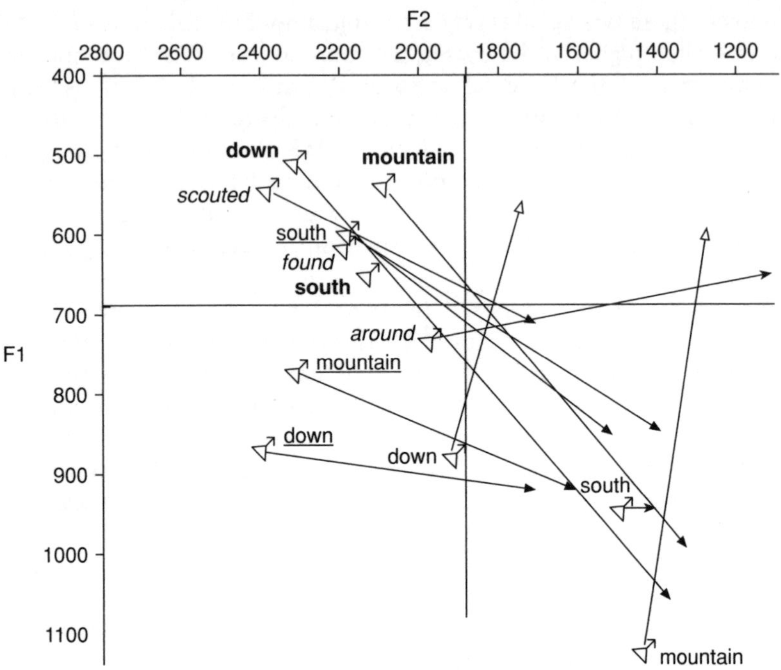


*Figure 6.7* F1/F2 positions of (aw) in the Philadelphia subjective reaction test. Plain labels: upper class speaker CF; bold labels: lower middle class speaker RD; italic labels: upper working class speaker MK; underlined labels, lower working class speaker CS. Arrows indicate trajectories of the glides

/æh/. Otherwise, the responses show that in the framework of the job suitability question, Philadelphians reject the advanced forms of change in progress, drawing a sharp line between moderate and advanced forms of change in progress. The matched guise format elicits reactions to new and vigorous changes like (ay0) that are not available for overt recognition in self-report tests.

The last variable to be considered is (aw), which is more complex than the others in that both the position of the nucleus and the direction of the glide are involved. Figure 6.7 maps the pronunciations of (aw) in the subjective reaction test for the four speakers. The trajectories of the glides are differentiated by the arrowheads: hollow triangular heads designate the glides that move toward the conservative target [ɷ], open line heads show the moderate or transitional direction, and solid arrowheads indicate the direction of the glide for the advanced change. It can be seen that the upper class speaker CF uses low central nuclei for (aw), which glide generally towards [ɷ]. The other speakers use mid or high, well fronted nuclei which generally glide towards [ɔ]. However, MK shows more variation in her pattern than the others. While her *scouted* is well raised and fronted, *found*

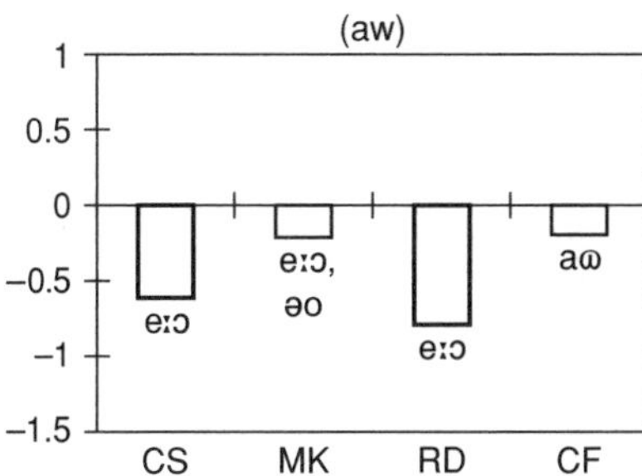


*Figure 6.8* Mean differences between zero passage and subjective reactions to (aw) on the job suitability scale (significance is as shown in figure 6.6)

is lower, and *around* is in a central position with a glide heading back toward [o]. The vowels used by the lower class speaker CS show lower F1 values than the others, but F2 is fully advanced. As noted above, F2 is the socially sensitive dimension, and this is consistent with the impressionistic judgments that CS's values are at level 3, as indicated in table 6.4.

Figure 6.8 shows the responses of the Philadelphia subjects to the (aw) sentences of the subjective reaction test. The results are clear: RD and CS are downgraded heavily, but for CF and MK there is no significant difference from the zero passage. This indicates that the consistent use of advanced forms by RD and CS, and particularly the reversal of glide direction, leads to a negative reaction on the job suitability scale.

All of these results show that Philadelphia subjects are able to detect the use of advanced forms of local changes in progress in the matched guise test, and will consistently downgrade these local forms on the job suitability scale.

So far, the results for the subjective reaction test have been presented in a global manner, for the entire set of 99 subjects. The question naturally arises as to whether this sample population evaluates the linguistic variables in the same way. Are there differences in the way that men and women, young and old, higher class and lower class, react to the Philadelphia phonological variables? The answer generally is no. There is an extraordinary uniformity to this data set which is even more striking than the uniform distribution of self-report. In speech production, we find that age, gender, and social class are major factors in the distribution of changes in progress, yet multiple regression analyses show no significant effects of age, gender, or social class for the five responses to the job suitability scale. This replicates the major finding of the New York City and Norwich studies – that speech communities show a uniform set of evaluative norms.[16]

[16] The more subtle aspect of the New York City study, that shows stronger negative reactions among those who use the highest degree of stigmatized forms, is not replicated here.

*Table 6.5* Regression coefficients for effect of age < 19 years on differences from zero passage in responses to job suitability scale for speaker RD in the Philadelphia subjective reaction test

| *Variable* | *n* | *Coefficient* | *t* | *p* < | *Adj* $r^2$ *(%)* |
|---|---|---|---|---|---|
| (æh) | 99 | 1.42 | 3.49 | 0.0007 | 10.2 |
| (aw) | 99 | 1.53 | 3.47 | 0.0008 | 10.1 |
| (ay0) | 99 | 0.75 | 1.94 | 0.0556 | 2.7 |
| (ow) | 99 | 0.85 | 2.16 | 0.0332 | 3.6 |
| (str) | 99 | 0.52 | 1.35 | 0.0799 | 0.8 |
| Zero | 99 | 0.75 | 2.47 | 0.0154 | 4.9 |

Indeed, this leads us to a well-founded sociolinguistic principle, which may be labeled the Principle of Uniform Evaluation, or Principle 3:

*A regularly stratified linguistic variable is evaluated in a uniform manner by the speech community.*

However, one unexpected and surprisingly consistent age effect did emerge. Table 6.5 shows that subjects under 19 years old (24 of 99) rated the use of the vowel variables by one particular speaker considerably higher than older speakers did. The effect is a large one, particularly for (æh) and (aw), where the figures are almost identical. Comparison with figures 6.6 and 6.8 shows that the effect is about half as large for (ay0) and (ow), but still significant at the .05 level, and quite small for (str). Nothing similar is found for any other speaker.

It is always a difficult problem to account for such a speaker-specific effect. Nevertheless, the special characteristics of RD emerge quite readily when we examine figures 6.4 and 6.7. She is a lower middle class woman from Nancy Drive who uses advanced forms of (æh) and (aw) that are most characteristic of the upper working class, and the nuclei of those vowels (bold) are close to or even more extreme than those of the upper working class speaker MK (italics). Adults downgrade her for these productions on the job suitability scale, but the 24 youthful subjects do not do so. Table 6.6 shows the mean values of the differences between each variable and the zero passage for the two age groups. For the (æh) passage, younger subjects do not downgrade RD at all; for (aw), her scores go up, not down; and for the other variables, there is a lesser degree of elevation. There is some characteristic of RD's middle class verbal style that neutralizes or cancels the effects of raised and fronted (æh) and (aw) for the youthful judges, even though for other speakers they are as sensitive to these variables as are the older judges.

*Table 6.6* Mean differences from zero passage for judges below 19 years and others for five linguistic variables of speaker RD in the Philadelphia subjective reaction test

| | *<19 years* | *19+ years* |
|---|---|---|
| (æh) | −0.04 | −1.46 |
| (aw) | 0.36 | −1.16 |
| (ay0) | 1.33 | 0.58 |
| (ow) | 0.50 | −0.35 |
| (str) | 0.67 | 0.15 |
| Zero | 4.33 | 3.58 |

The figures for the zero passage in tables 6.5 and 6.6 show that in addition, younger speakers like RD's basic voice or delivery significantly better than older speakers do. The details of this voice quality are not easily conveyed in print; but RD, as compared to CF and MK, has a lower, slightly hoarser, more forceful, less feminine and less cultivated articulation.

On the whole, this one social differentiation of the subjective reaction test is consistent with the general finding that the sociolinguistic norms of the speech community are not fully acquired by most members of the community until they are fully adult (Labov 1964).[17]

We have seen that the Philadelphia speech community has a surprisingly well-established, uniform set of normative reactions to linguistic changes in progress even when these variables are not recognized consciously. If the norms reflected in the job suitability scale were effective in regulating the speech of everyday life, then the diffusion of linguistic change from one social group to the other would certainly be checked. The results of this chapter so far may be considered to deepen this puzzle rather than illuminate it. In fact, they may be taken as an extended exposition of the fundamental sociolinguistic question posed to me in 1967 by a woman from New York: "Why do I say [wɒi] when I don't *want* to?"

Chapter 5 reviewed the inference made by many sociolinguists that these overt norms are opposed by a set of covert norms, equally or more effective in daily life, which assign "covert prestige" to changes in progress. It has been suggested that speakers who use and develop these sound changes hear the advanced forms as representing adherence and loyalty

[17] This age stratification of sociolinguistic norms appears only when a wide range of sociolinguistic behaviors are concerned, including the results of self-report and subjective reaction tests. Though speakers as young as 4 years old acquire adult patterns of style shifting (Roberts 1993), this does not mean they have acquired the full complement of adult norms. If the dominant prestige norms are concerned, one can expect to find the rate of acquisition to be socially stratified (Labov 1964).

to local norms and values; or as symbolic of masculinity or toughness; or as expressing a warmer, more personal, more human, or more friendly approach to life. It would follow that the social diffusion of (æh) and (aw) from the innovating center in the upper working class is a response to these covert attitudes on the part of speakers in the middle working class and lower middle class who are also motivated by these covert norms, who take the upper working class as a reference group and hope to participate in this local identification. The sound changes studied here have spread throughout the entire Philadelphia speech community in the past and show no signs of being arrested at any geographic or social frontier within the city.[18] To the extent that social attitudes are involved in this process, it must follow that upper middle class and upper class speakers share in the assignment of local prestige to changes in progress.

Thus far, no firm evidence has been advanced to show that this is so for linguistic changes from below. The SRT *friendliness* question was designed to detect – as far as one can in a field experiment – indications of such covert prestige. Previous experiments in the black community with stable sociolinguistic variables did show some evidence of such opposing norms (Labov et al. 1968). We therefore asked subjects: "If you got to know this speaker well, how likely is it that she would become a good friend of yours?" Responses were given on a 7-point scale with the two extremes labeled "Very likely" and "Not very likely."

Evidence for covert norms would have appeared in a pattern of responses to the friendship scale that reversed the direction of responses to the job suitability scale. No such tendency emerged. In general, the friendship question replicated the results of the job suitability question. For 15 of the 20 sets of responses, paired t-tests showed no significant difference between answers to the job suitability question and answers to the friendship question. Like the job suitability scale, friendship scale responses were determined by their difference from the zero passage. The five significant differences between the job suitability and friendship scores were as follows:

1 (æh) The friendship differences from the zero passage were significantly lower than the job suitability differences for the corrected forms of the upper class speaker CF. Instead of being elevated by .55, they were lowered by .15, a difference of .7 with a significance of $p = .00003$.
2 (str) In the job suitability scale, CS was downgraded by −1.2 for the hushing quality of her fricative; on the friendship scale, this was significantly reduced to −.55 (for the difference, $p = .004$); this was still significantly lower than the zero passage ($p = .005$).

[18] Always with the proviso that the limits of the speech community here defined are confined to the white majority, excluding African Americans and most Hispanic speakers.

3, 4 (ay0) The negative effect for CS and the positive effect for RD (figure 6.6b) were both removed, with no significant differences from the zero passage on the friendship scale.

5 (ow) The negative rating for MK of −1.23 compared to the zero passage was reduced to −.83, an effect at the p = .05 level.

Reviewing the small number of significant differences between the two scales, one would have to conclude that evidence for covert norms failed to appear. The first and most significant of these differences bears upon the evaluation of the correction of (æh), rather than the advance of the change: though people admired CF for correcting to [æ], they did not like her for it. Effects 2 and 5 showed a moderate or small reduction of the negative effect of the advanced forms, rather than a reversal. Effects 3 and 4 show that two reactions to the job suitability scale in opposite directions were cancelled.

One might think that the reversal of the overt norms was masked because it appears only in one segment of the population. Indeed, this was the case in the South Harlem study, where friendship was aligned with job suitability for the middle class and Northern working class groups, but with the fight question for lower class and working class speakers from the South. But in the Philadelphia reaction to changes in progress, there are almost no significant social differences in the alignment of friendship with the job suitability scale. The only social difference of interest to emerge is once again the remarkable differentiation of the youth and adults in their reactions to speaker RD. Table 6.7 is a very close match to table 6.5. The more favorable responses of younger speakers to RD follow the same pattern, at a somewhat weaker level. The favorable response to the zero passage is even stronger. Whatever the explanation for this adult/youth split, it confirms the finding that the friendship and job suitability scale tap the same set of responses in this experimental setting.

*Table 6.7* Regression coefficients for effect of age < 19 years on differences from zero passage in responses to friendship scale for speaker RD in the Philadelphia subjective reaction test

| *Variable* | *n* | *Coefficient* | *t* | *p* < | *Adj* $r^2$ *(%)* |
|---|---|---|---|---|---|
| (æh) | 92 | 0.91 | 2.07 | 0.0416 | 3.5 |
| (aw) | 92 | 0.87 | 2.57 | 0.0119 | 5.8 |
| (ay0) | 92 | 0.68 | 1.82 | 0.0721 | 2.5 |
| (ow) | 92 | 1.05 | 2.81 | 0.0061 | 7.0 |
| (str) | 92 | 0.62 | 1.355 | 0.1251 | 1.5 |
| Zero | 92 | 1.00 | 3.17 | 0.0021 | 9.0 |

*Table 6.8* Correlation matrix of subjective reaction judgments for speaker RD. Cells with last letter "J" = job suitability scale; cells with last letter "F" = friendship scale

| | *æhRDJ* | *awRDJ* | *strRDJ* | *ay0RDJ* | *owRDJ* | *æRDF* | *awRDF* | *strRDF* | *ay0RDF* | *owRDF* |
|---|---|---|---|---|---|---|---|---|---|---|
| æhRDJ | 1 | | | | | | | | | |
| awRDJ | 0.576 | 1 | | | | | | | | |
| strRDJ | 0.458 | 0.340 | 1 | | | | | | | |
| ay0RDJ | 0.231 | 0.407 | 0.500 | 1 | | | | | | |
| owRDJ | 0.469 | 0.536 | 0.499 | 0.526 | 1 | | | | | |
| æRDF | 0.097 | 0.015 | –0.11 | –0.070 | –0.061 | 1 | | | | |
| awRDF | 0.113 | 0.247 | 0.081 | 0.125 | –0.022 | 0.460 | 1 | | | |
| strRDF | –0.03 | –0.04 | 0.187 | –0.01 | –0.135 | 0.403 | 0.370 | 1 | | |
| ay0RDF | –0.01 | 0.086 | 0.083 | 0.071 | –0.146 | 0.267 | 0.308 | 0.473 | 1 | |
| owRDF | 0.087 | 0.085 | 0.203 | 0.113 | –0.025 | 0.319 | 0.283 | 0.555 | 0.370 | 1 |

The similarity in overall pattern between job suitability and friendship judgments suggests that subjects may have simply misunderstood or ignored the instructions. Perhaps they were doing the same task twice! The judges may have been reacting to a single scale of judgments: good speech vs. bad speech. If this were so, then the friendship scale will simply duplicate the job suitability scale for each judgment, and no new information is involved. One way of checking this is to examine the correlations for each scale internally against the correlations across scales. Table 6.8 shows the correlation matrix for speaker RD. The ten cells outlined in the triangular box at upper left are the correlations of the five job suitability judgments with each other (that is, their differences from the zero passage). The ten cells outlined at lower left are the corresponding correlations within the friendship scale judgments. The cells not outlined are the 25 mixed cases.

Table 6.8 confirms the results so far that (æh) and (aw) are closely connected, in both their phonetic movements and their social evaluation, as the correlation of .576 at upper left shows. On the other hand, (ay0) follows a rather different path, in its social distribution, phonetic character, and social evaluation, as shown by the lower correlation of .231 with (æh). A similar set of relations appears at lower right, in the correlations among the friendship scale variables. What is most striking, however, is the fact that all of the numbers in the outlined cells are much higher than those at lower left that are not outlined. This means that the job suitability judgments and the friendship judgments for RD are not the same. Although they form the same overall patterns, responses to the two scales are distinct and separate decisions.

We can review this situation for all speakers by taking the mean of all internal correlations for each scale, and comparing these to the means that correlate judgments across scales. Figure 6.9 shows the result. The upper set of four lines with solid symbols displays the mean correlations for the four speakers; the bottom set of four lines, with open symbols, shows the corresponding standard deviations. The mean correlations for judgments for job suitability show a remarkable consistency for the four speakers, concentrated at .46, with standard deviations below .1. Mean correlations for the friendship scale in the center are even higher for all but RD, and equally concentrated as shown by the standard deviations. At the right side are the mean correlations across job and friendship scales, all at a low level below .2. For all speakers, judgments on job suitability and friendship are effectively uncorrelated.

It follows that the absence of any reversal of evaluation on the friendship scale does not indicate that the subjects failed to grasp the nature of a friendship scale or were simply echoing their judgments on the job scale. Friendship judgments did not reveal any positive evaluation of the linguistic variables at any point in the social spectrum, or any desire for

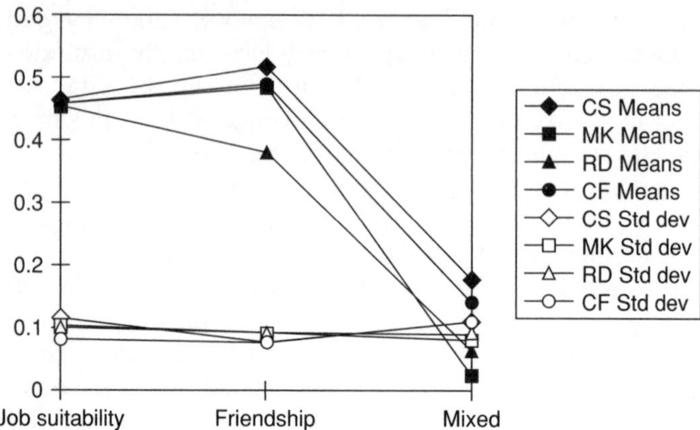


*Figure 6.9* Mean correlations among differential judgments of linguistic variables for four speakers within the job scale, within the friendship scale, and across job and friendship scales

the subjects to align themselves with the advanced forms of linguistic change in progress.

In the data reported here, Philadelphians have shown a strong pattern of negative evaluation of changes in progress, and no clear evidence of covert, positive evaluation of their own behavior. One might think that this was due to a global negative evaluation of the Philadelphia dialect equal to or even stronger than that found in New York City. In general, the working class speech patterns of the great cities are negatively evaluated: this holds true for Paris, London, Glasgow, New York, and Boston as well as Philadelphia. It may be that evidence for positive attitudes toward the evolving urban dialect is masked by this effect. The comments from subjects in the self-report test showed that advanced forms of (æh) are consciously stigmatized.

However, these comments fall far short of the corresponding quotations from New Yorkers given in chapter 13 of Labov 1966a, and the stigmatization of the Philadelphia dialect is mild by comparison with New York. There is almost no correction of the short **a** pattern in the spontaneous speech of Philadelphians, while in New York, there are very few who do *not* correct the corresponding pattern. Moreover, the LCV explorations of overt attitudes toward Philadelphia show that attitudes toward one's own speech reverse the self-deprecation of New Yorkers.

The following four general questions on Philadelphia speech were included in our second interviews:

Question #1: What do you think of Philadelphia speech?
Question #2: Would you take it as a compliment if somebody told you you sounded like a Philadelphian?

*Table 6.9* Responses to LCV questions on general attitudes toward language, by sex and SEC, from 50 members of the Philadelphia working class (%)

| | | *SEC* | | | *Sex* | |
|---|---|---|---|---|---|---|
| | *All* | *1–3* | *4–6* | *7–9* | *M* | *F* |
| Q. 1, 2: Attitude toward Philadelphia speech | | | | | | |
| Positive | 62 | 67 | 72 | 58 | 68 | 59 |
| Negative | 32 | 33 | 28 | 42 | 25 | 34 |
| Neutral | 6 | 0 | 0 | 0 | 7 | 6 |
| Total | 100 | 100 | 100 | 100 | 100 | 99 |
| Q. 3 Can you tell if someone comes from So. Phila? | | | | | | |
| Yes | 60 | 33 | 55 | 83 | 50 | 73 |
| No | 20 | 50 | 22 | 8 | 33 | 16 |
| Not sure | 20 | 16 | 22 | 8 | 17 | 10 |
| Total | 100 | 99 | 99 | 99 | 100 | 99 |
| Q. 4 Efforts to change one's own speech | | | | | | |
| Yes | 20 | 16 | 11 | 50 | 11 | 26 |
| No | 74 | 83 | 83 | 42 | 83 | 71 |
| Neutral | 6 | 0 | 6 | 8 | 6 | 2 |
| Total | 100 | 99 | 100 | 100 | 100 | 99 |

Question #3: Could you tell if someone came from South Philadelphia by the way they talked?
Question #4: Have you ever tried to change the way you talk?

Table 6.9 gives the distribution of responses to these questions from 50 working class speakers from South Philadelphia, Kensington, and Overbrook.[19] Answers to the first two questions were combined to yield a positive, negative, or neutral attitude toward Philadelphia speech. The third question tests the subjects' recognition of the most prominent stereotype of Philadelphia speech. The fourth has proved to be the most sensitive indicator of the strength of negative attitudes toward a local dialect.

In the light of everything that has been said so far, it should be clear that direct questions are the weakest way of determining underlying attitudes toward a language or dialect. But since the same questions were put to the subjects of the Lower East Side survey in New York City, they offer one means of comparing the strength of overt negative attitudes toward the local vernacular in Philadelphia and New York.

[19] The number of middle class speakers from King of Prussia considerably outweighed the 9 upper middle class subjects in the Lower East Side study, so the closest comparison can be made in this way.

The differences are quite striking. In responses to the first two questions, the majority thought badly of New York City speech, while the majority of Philadelphians said that they felt good about the way people in their city talked. More than two-thirds of the New Yorkers reported that they had tried to change their speech, but only 20% of the Philadelphians. In both cities, there was a pronounced tendency for women to answer positively to this question more than men. This confirms our other indications that the stigmatization of Philadelphia speech is much weaker than the extreme form we find in New York City.

The limited data available on general attitudes toward Philadelphia speech offers some opportunity to look at the crucial distinction between middle working class and upper working class. Chapter 5 showed that the SEC 7–9 group, labeled "upper working class," is the leading group in the raising and fronting of (aw) and (eyC). One might expect here some indication that the leading group was less negative in this global view of Philadelphia speech. Table 6.9 suggests the reverse. While only 1 of 6 members of the lower working class group 1–3 reported efforts to change her speech, half of the upper working class group did so. A similar trend appears in answer to the question, "Could you tell if someone comes from South Philadelphia?" (*South Philadelphia* being the stereotype for working class Philadelphia speech). Ten of 12 members of the upper working class thought so.

## *Conclusion*

Let us now sum up how the study of subjective reactions contributes to an understanding of the social factors in linguistic change. As noted above, the uniform character of sociolinguistic evaluation is one of the three bases for the central dogma of sociolinguistics: that the linguistic behavior of individuals can only be understood through a knowledge of the communities of which they are members. The findings of this chapter can only strengthen our appreciation of the uniformity of the social evaluation of speech in the community. At the same time, they must deepen our appreciation of the fundamental paradox that is confronted by this volume: the more we discover of the consistency and uniformity of linguistic and sociolinguistic structure, the more difficult it is to account for linguistic change. The general, conscious consensus is that language should not change, and that any changes that have occurred are bad. The fact that change continues implies the existence of hidden weaknesses in that normative structure. We infer that there must be hidden or covert values that motivate change. But so far, it must be admitted that the evidence for those underlying values is weak.

It is reasonable to argue that covert values do not easily emerge in sociolinguistic interviews and field experiments in which the overt prestige of the standard language is a dominant presence. This is a general characteristic of the experimental situation, and affects those who follow the laboratory methodology of social psychology. Thus Ryan (1979) addresses the question, "Why do low-prestige language varieties persist?" with the firm conviction that they are maintained by covert values. But her experiments failed to show them:

> The expected group differences, indicating stronger solidarity preferences for the nonstandard speech by Mexican Americans than Anglo Americans, were not observed. It may be that the formal setting (a group study conducted in a high school classroom) inhibited the Mexican Americans from revealing their true feelings of solidarity and identification with their ethnic speech.

The chapters to follow will attempt to bypass this limitation by drawing on the extended character of the Philadelphia Neighborhood Study, which combined extensive and repeated interviews with long-term participant observation, as well as other studies of face-to-face interaction among peers. In what follows, we will be alert for evidence of conflicts of values that have eluded us so far. It may be that the further search for the social location of the leaders of linguistic change will throw light on this question.

Chapter 5 established the scope of the problem of linguistic change by the larger perspective gained from surveys of New York, Norwich, Panama City, Montreal, Sydney, and Philadelphia. The leaders have been located in this larger scene as members of the skilled working class or lower middle class within the framework provided by those studies. The chapters to follow will move steadily toward a more precise characterization of the social location of the leaders in Philadelphia, beginning with the differentiation by neighborhood and ethnicity.

# 7

# *Neighborhood and Ethnicity*

The main data base for chapters 5 and 6 was drawn from the Philadelphia Neighborhood Study, and it might seem only natural that the concept of *neighborhood* would play a central role in the analysis. But neighborhood has more often been used as a methodological unit than a substantive element in sociolinguistic studies. It will be helpful to review this methodological history before attacking the question as to what role neighborhoods can play in the development and diffusion of linguistic change.

Neighborhood studies can be taken as one instance of the more general class of site studies. Such site studies can be opposed to random samples of communities. The latter is the basic tool of survey methodology; the former is the preferred method of urban ethnographers. The advantages and disadvantages of the two approaches are clear. A random sample of individuals, constructed by enumerating the population and giving every individual an equal opportunity of entering the sample, is the only reliable way of finding out what are the behaviors, opinions, and practices characteristic of a large urban community or nation. Most of the findings of quantitative sociolinguistics that support the principles put forward in this and the previous volume have been discovered and replicated by this method. The chief limitation of sampling through individuals is that it does not yield a direct view of the social processes that have created the patterns discovered, and the analysts are forced to infer them by indirect means. The site study gives up the aim of representing the larger community for the sake of gaining a deeper understanding of how the speakers relate to each other. Through recordings of individuals, pairs, and groups, notes taken through passive observation, and long-term participant observation at the site, the investigator can compare the behaviors of parents and children, friends and enemies, leaders and followers. In the best of all possible worlds, the investigator can actually observe the social processes that create language change.

It is obvious that random sampling is not needed in the study of rural communities with population in the hundreds, as in the investigation of sound change in the village of Chilmark on Martha's Vineyard, in Charmey, or in Ocracoke on the Outer Banks. There the site and the community coincide. The first quantitative studies of large cities were based on random samples, or stratified random samples: New York (Labov 1966a), Norwich (Trudgill 1974b), Panama City (Cedergren 1973). The most rigorous application of this methodology is the study that created the Montreal corpus (Sankoff and Sankoff 1973), which enumerated all 165 census tracts with a proportion of French speakers equal to or greater than the proportion in the city, and randomly selected residences within those tracts to fill a tightly constructed pattern of age, sex, and social class. Many other urban studies have relaxed those requirements, and located their subjects through friends, recommendations, or other convenient ways until their quotas were filled (e.g., Amman, Abdel-Jawad 1981; Belo Horizonte, de Oliveira 1983; Sydney, Horvath 1985; Tokyo, Hibiya 1988). Since less rigorous methods were often found to be sufficient to display regular patterns of class stratification, gender differentiation, and ethnic diversity, it may be that smaller numbers and less carefully constructed samples are adequate for sociolinguistic analysis. However, the more difficult questions of the mechanism of linguistic change that are posed in these volumes may require data sets even more carefully constructed than the first random samples.

A neighborhood study begins with the selection of a residential neighborhood as a site, usually beginning with a "block" as defined in chapter 2. Though a neighborhood study may not represent an entire city, it can be constructed in such a way that it gives an accurate view of a fairly sizeable section. The New York City random sample was actually a study of one large group of neighborhoods, the Lower East Side. It was only through its convergence with the department store study that it could be interpreted to represent all of New York City. The studies of African American English in South Harlem were based primarily on neighborhood studies of adolescent males in local neighborhoods, focusing on three selected blocks (Labov, Cohen, Robins, and Lewis 1968). Their representative character was determined by the fact that they included all of the named groups in the area; by an enumeration of all the youth in a 15-story high rise with the help of pre-adolescent members of the community; by correlation with school records; by comparison with a random sample of adults; and ultimately by their convergence with studies in many other cities throughout the country.

In designing the investigation of sound change in Philadelphia, it was decided to split the methodological tasks in two. Since the focus was on the social location and diffusion of linguistic change, the main body of data consisted of interviews from long-term neighborhood studies, where the social relations could be directly observed, and the field workers – Anne Bower, Deborah Schiffrin, and Arvilla Payne – became personal acquaintances, in some cases good friends, with the speakers who were recorded. As described in chapter 2, the neighborhood was first defined as a residential block (and named after it), then expanded to include members of the social networks who lived off the block but in the immediate vicinity. The neighborhood was then never equivalent to the block: in one sense larger, in another sense smaller, since we never interviewed every one of the 100 or so residents on any given block.[1] The ten residential neighborhoods selected formed a judgment sample of the white Philadelphia community; their representative character was confirmed by the random sample of telephone users, as described in chapter 5.

As discussed in chapter 2, the ten neighborhoods varied considerably in their degree of coherence and intactness. The four that will be the focus of this chapter comprise 70 of the 112 speakers of the neighborhood study. The number of speakers analyzed instrumentally for each neighborhood and their general locations are:

| | | |
|---|---|---|
| Wicket St. | 18 | Kensington, north Philadelphia |
| Clark St. | 20 | south central Philadelphia |
| Pitt St. | 15 | southeast Philadelphia |
| Nancy Drive | 17 | King of Prussia |

So far, the search for the social location of the leaders of linguistic change has used general indicators of position in the socioeconomic hierarchy that are independent of the neighborhoods that the speakers live in. The chapters to follow, particularly 10 and 11, will draw on many kinds of data from research into the social relations among the speakers, data that depends crucially on their neighborhood locus. This chapter asks whether residence in a particular neighborhood will affect the relative advancement of sound change for a given speaker.

## 7.1 The relation of local differentiation to linguistic change

First, it may be helpful to review the position of *neighborhood* in the earlier results of sociolinguistic investigations. Most local neighborhoods appear to be characterized by their class composition rather than their geographic location within the city. Yet there is a popular and universal belief in the existence of local dialects within the large cities. Though the term *Brooklynese* is well entrenched in American culture, no empirical studies have been carried out in and across the borough of Brooklyn to determine whether there is a *Brooklynese* distinct from the speech of other boroughs. Every feature attributed to this local dialect corresponds to the features of

[1] In one case, we were able to enumerate in a recording the social history of every resident on a block (Clark St.), through the help of our principal subject, Celeste S.

working class New York City speech as described in the literature with no reference to Brooklyn (e.g., Babbitt 1896, Hubbell 1962, Labov 1966a). The available evidence indicates that a major metropolis of over a million inhabitants is reasonably uniform within its geographic limits, but highly differentiated by social class, ethnicity, gender, and race. This does not mean to say that there are no geographic dialects, or that those who distinguish an East London accent from a West London accent are incorrect, but simply that no evidence has yet been advanced to support such constructs.[2] It seems likely that there would be lexical differentiation of local neighborhoods, and even neighborhood differences in the incidence of phonemes. The crucial question for this volume is not whether there are discrete and identifiable forms of language in local neighborhoods, but whether there are neighborhood differentials in the systematic advance of changes in progress.

It may be helpful to ask what general principles, if any, might govern the effect of neighborhood residence on the advance of linguistic change. A precondition for this discussion is to distinguish *small-scale* from *large-scale* changes. Within a large metropolis, there may be an indefinite number of small-scale changes which diffuse in local neighborhoods and are arrested at their natural boundaries. Large-scale changes expand to the limits of the speech community.

If there were no neighborhood patterns in large-scale change, this would mean that the leaders of change, whoever they might be, advance the new forms independently and in lock-step throughout the metropolis. If the change in question was triggered by an earlier change in the same community, such a uniformity is not hard to conceive, since the causal factors are already diffused. If the initiating factor was an external influence, in the form of increased contact with speakers of other dialects, geographically uniform change would depend upon geographically uniform contact. Such a widespread increase in contact occurs during major wars, and for this reason, World War II has been a watershed of linguistic behavior in many countries and for many linguistic variables. The best-known case is that of the reversal of the prestige norm of *r*-less pronunciation in New York City in favor of an *r*-ful form, which occurred directly after World War II (Labov 1966a: chs 9, 11), and not long afterwards, in other *r*-less cities of the Eastern seaboard.

Can such an external mechanism be responsible for change from below? In New York City, the shift to a positive evaluation of consonantal /r/ affected all those under 40 in 1963 – those born after 1923. The oldest of these would have joined the armed forces at an age very close to the end of the period when linguistic change from below can affect the basic

[2] This is of course another case where social class differences are reinterpreted as geographic ones, where "East-enders" becomes the current label for "working-class."

system. Given the evidence of chapter 3 of volume 1, and the third regression of chapter 5, it seems possible that the present Philadelphia changes did begin shortly after World War II. Figure 5.6 shows that (eyC) and (aw) are active only for people under 50. These people were born after 1925. During World War II, the youngest of them would have been in the 18–28 age group, and many of them would have been in the services. This involves many difficult aspects of the *transmission* problem (chapters 13–14), but the possibility that this major punctuating event is involved in the mechanism of change cannot be discarded.

A uniform increase in contact with other dialects may also be an effect of the mass media. But all of the evidence generated in this volume and elsewhere points to the conclusion that language is not systematically affected by the mass media, and is influenced primarily in face-to-face interaction with peers: that is, the principle of interaction of chapter 1.

If, on the other hand, evidence for local differentiation of these changes should emerge, with one neighborhood consistently ahead of the others in the same social class range, our reasoning must lead in a different direction. In recent years, a great deal of attention has been given to the association of linguistic variables with local identity or "territoriality" (Le Page and Tabouret-Keller 1985, L. Milroy 1980:16, 80). As with the covert values discussed in the last chapter, the evidence for the association of such values is largely the linguistic distributions themselves. If speakers on a local corner, local neighborhood, or small town share some linguistic feature in common, it may be inferred that this difference carries out the function of distinguishing them from outsiders. This seems very likely. On the other hand, there is always the possibility that the effect is due to Bloomfield's principle of density: that the more often people talk to each other, the more similar their speech will be. Thus a neighborhood effect may be no more than a mechanical result of communication patterns.

The study of local identity as a factor in linguistic change has been advanced most recently by Hazen's work in Warren County, North Carolina (2000). His examination of attitudes, aspirations, and patterns of interaction led him to distinguish speakers with local identity from those with expanded (nonlocal) identity, a distinction that predicts linguistic behavior as well as or better than the distinction of positive, neutral, or negative orientation toward the local community on Martha's Vineyard. At the same time, it has not been shown what part of this effect may be due to differences in frequency of interaction with speakers of other dialects.

Granted an assignment of social value to a linguistic form, it will be crucial to know whether a feedback loop exists. If the use of a linguistic form acts to effectively decrease social distance and increase solidarity, this will lead to an increase in the amount of interaction among the speakers concerned, and consequently raise the quantitative level of the variable with an increasing local maximum.

A further condition is required before such local maxima can be tied to a large-scale linguistic change across a community of several million people. The local maximum must expand to those outside of the local group in steadily widening circles. This is not inevitable. If the linguistic feature acts to increase the frequency of interaction within the group, then conversely, a lower level or absence of use by others may be assigned a negative value, and this would correspondingly decrease frequency of communication across group boundaries. In this case, the local pattern may maximize internally but shrink in area.

Sturtevant's suggestion for the social motivation of linguistic change (1947) is that the new forms become associated arbitrarily with social traits of the originating group. Thus any reluctance of the originators to increase their communication with outsiders might be countered by the desire of these outsiders to communicate more with them. A different possibility is that linguistic change proceeds through the passive observation of linguistic features by outsiders, who adopt them without the benefit of intimate interaction with the originators. This returns us to the problems we had in assigning influence to the mass media, and runs counter to the interactive principle, which is implicit in the principle of density. If we accept the evidence that systematic linguistic change must be the result of face-to-face interaction (and the main evidence for this will not be introduced until much later in this volume), then large-scale linguistic change implies that interaction of the originating group with outsiders does not decrease but increases over time.

The focus of this chapter will be on the existence of the local maxima, rather than their role in the mechanism of large-scale change. If there are significant geographic differentials in Philadelphia, independent of age, gender, social class, or ethnicity, we can return to the question as to whether these local maxima could be the results of mechanical patterns of local interaction, of differential contact with other dialects, or of patterns of social evaluation specific to local neighborhoods.

## 7.2 The Belfast neighborhoods

The most careful and detailed study of local neighborhoods is that of L. Milroy in Belfast (1980). The three neighborhoods, Ballymacarett, Clonard, and Hammer, were selected to be comparable in their socio-economic status: all were working class concentrations officially described as "blighted," and would fall into the category of "lower working class." They are most comparable to the North Philadelphia neighborhoods of Kensington (including Wicket), Fishtown, and Richmond, where unemployment is high and workers are as a whole semi-skilled.[3] They are differentiated primarily as Protestant (Hammer, Ballymacarett) vs. Catholic (Clonard) and West Belfast (Hammer, Clonard) vs. East Belfast (Ballymacarett). Whereas East Belfast has heavy industry and a stable shipyard, the linen industry that once supported West Belfast has declined drastically, and those who have jobs have to travel some distance to work. In this respect, West Belfast resembles North Philadelphia and East Belfast, South Philadelphia.

The Belfast report (L. Milroy 1980) shows only one unqualified neighborhood effect: (i), the centralization of short /i/, which is most strongly developed in the Hammer. Otherwise, Milroy stresses the complexity of the interaction between neighborhood and other dimensions. Her figure 5.4 shows that for (a), the backing and raising of short **a** in *man, hat, grass*, etc., Ballymacarett has higher values for men and lower values for younger women than in the other two neighborhoods. Her figure 5.6 displays a similar situation for (th), the deletion of /ð/ in *mother, brother*, etc. Figure 5.5 shows that for ($\Lambda^2$), the unrounding of short **u** in *pull, took, shook*, etc., the Clonard neighborhood has higher values for older women and younger men. These complexities suggest that the changes to be found in Belfast are typical of those often found in established European speech communities: a shift away from the older, stigmatized vernacular forms (often rural in character) towards the regional or national standard, a change from above led by women and resisted by men (L. Milroy 1980:186ff; see also Holmquist 1988, Gal 1980, Hinskens 1992). Ballymacarett, the Protestant community with more economic resources, leads the way in this process. There is also the gradual shift of lexical items across phonemic categories, usually a reduction of the members of a stigmatized category, with a subtle and complex shift of social evaluations (1980:190).[4] The Belfast study does not report new and vigorous sound changes parallel to (eyC) and (aw) in Philadelphia, or the many others found in New York, or the inland North, where the entire community generates new phonetic relations that have never been observed in those regions before. Yet a closer look at the Belfast data shows that the situation is not so different after all, underlining those aspects of Milroy's important findings that exhibit changes from below and confirm the importance of geographic neighborhood.

[3] In the Philadelphia study, most of the residents are classed as "middle working class," since they contrast with a lower working class that is largely black and Hispanic. Given Milroy's (1980:75) description of the Belfast subjects as marginals, or an external proletariat, they would be aligned more with the non-whites in Philadelphia in terms of social status.

[4] One such change in Belfast is the transfer of members of the marked class of short /u/ words that can be unrounded: *pull, took, foot*, etc. (L. Milroy 1980:189). This may be contrasted with the Philadelphia situation, where the class of tensed short /a/ words is steadily growing (Labov 1989b).

*Table 7.1* Regression coefficients for nine Belfast variables by gender, age, and neighborhood. Significance: **bold** figures, p < .001; underlined, p < .01; plain, p < .05; *italic* p < .10

| | *(th)* | *(a)* | *(e*$^1$*)* | *(e*$^2$*)* | *(ʌ*$^1$*)* | *(ʌ*$^2$*)* | *(ai)* | *(i)* | *(o)* |
|---|---|---|---|---|---|---|---|---|---|
| Means | 56.16 | 2.53 | 81.6 | 64.5 | 42.7 | 29.32 | 2.28 | 2.02 | 90.3 |
| Std dev. | 30.01 | 0.53 | 23.7 | 21.7 | 20.7 | 23.92 | 0.35 | 0.34 | 16.4 |
| Male | **34** | **0.59** | **27** | **21.5** | | | | | |
| Younger | | | | | | | | 0.27 | 13.8 |
| Younger men | | | | | | 20.74 | | | |
| Older men | | | | | 15.1 | −16.1 | | | |
| Younger women | | | | | | *−14.2* | | | |
| Hammer | | | | | | | *0.19* | 0.28 | 12.3 |

L. Milroy 1980 includes an appendix with mean values of eight variables for the 46 speakers of the Belfast study, characterized by gender, age (grouped into two categories, 40–55 and 18–25), and neighborhood.[5] Table 7.1 gives the results of my own regression analyses of this data which show the comparative size and significance of each effect. The means and standard deviations in the first two rows give the basis for judging the relative size of each effect registered by the regression coefficients. Interactions were checked with an ANOVA analysis; whenever significant interactive categories are found, they are then entered into the regression analysis as combined categories, such as younger men, older men, younger women, and older women, with the last being used as a residual category. The results of the regression analysis will then be identical with the ANOVA results.

The multivariate analysis of table 7.1 agrees closely with the effects reported in the original study, with only a few minor differences. But the results can be compared more closely in this format with the third regression of chapter 5 and the neighborhood analyses to follow in this chapter.[6]

The first four variables show a main effect of male domination, with no significant age or neighborhood effect. This agrees with Milroy's table 5.1 (p. 123) in both direction and significance of the effects. (The size of the

[5] The appendix also provides network scores, which will be added to the analysis in chapter 10.

[6] (e$^1$) is the percentage of low vowels for short /e/ in monosyllables closed either by a voiceless stop, or by a voiceless obstruent preceded by a liquid or a nasal (*bet*, *peck*, *rent*, *else*, etc.). (e$^2$) is the same variable in polysyllables. (ʌ$^1$) is the percentage of rounded vowels in /ʌ/ words; here the male effect is confined to older men, showing a further erosion of the vernacular form. (ʌ$^2$) is the reverse variable for a smaller lexical set (*pull*, *took*, *shook*, *foot*), where unrounded forms alternate with rounded forms.

(th) coefficient is particularly striking: 60% of the mean value.) For ($\Lambda^1$) and ($\Lambda^2$) there is a complex age and gender effect. Younger men strongly favor ($\Lambda^2$) and older men disfavor it, suggesting a change in progress, at least among men. Neighborhood effects are confined to the last three columns.

The last two columns show significant neighborhood and age effects. (i) is the centralization of short /i/; (o) is not discussed elsewhere in the volume. Both show a strong general advantage of younger speakers, about 15% of the mean, and a strong neighborhood effect. If this shift in apparent time corresponds to shifts in real time, then these last two variables would represent continuing change from below in Belfast. In any case, they are clearly and strongly associated with the Hammer, a Protestant neighborhood in the midst of the predominantly Catholic West Belfast.

The Milroys' Belfast work does not distinguish neighborhood from religion (or ethnicity), since in Belfast neighborhoods are solidly Protestant or Catholic. The fact that the Hammer is in the lead coincides with the results of McCafferty's (1998) study of the second largest city of Northern Ireland, Derry/Londonderry. His main focus is on the Protestant/Catholic opposition, which he considers to be an ethnic one. Linguistic changes spreading from Belfast to Derry/Londonderry are adopted primarily by the younger Protestant speakers, and spread only slowly to the Catholic population later.

There will be more to learn from the Belfast study when we turn to the role of social networks in linguistic change (chapter 10). So far, the main finding is a negative one: the absence of sharp geographic differentiation in Belfast. The three neighborhoods use the same variables in approximately the same way: they show no qualitative differences that would mark them as discretely different dialects of Belfast English. There is also indication that change in Belfast spreads across neighborhood boundaries, despite the high degree of segregation of Protestants and Catholics, and the absence of any direct contact during the time of the troubles. In that sense, the Belfast data must ultimately bear on the mysterious question as to how the great cities achieve relative geographic uniformity.

## 7.3 The relation of neighborhood to social class in Philadelphia

Chapter 2 compared the four neighborhoods for their economic and social characteristics. In contrast to the Belfast study, these neighborhoods were chosen for the socioeconomic diversity between them rather than their similarity, and they are clearly stratified in this respect. Table 7.2 shows the distribution of socioeconomic class for the four neighborhoods to be studied here, with the rest combined into an "Other" category.

*Table 7.2* Distribution of socioeconomic class across neighborhoods (bold figures = modal value)

| | *LWC* | *MWC* | *UWC* | *LMC* | *UMC* | *UC* | *Total* |
|---|---|---|---|---|---|---|---|
| Wicket St. | **9** | 8 | 1 | 0 | 0 | 0 | 18 |
| Pitt St. | 4 | **10** | 1 | 0 | 0 | 0 | 15 |
| Clark St. | 2 | 6 | **8** | 4 | 0 | 0 | 20 |
| Nancy Drive | 0 | 0 | 0 | **9** | 8 | 0 | 17 |
| Others | 2 | 12 | 6 | 0 | 12 | 10 | 42 |
| Total | 17 | 36 | 16 | 13 | 20 | 10 | 112 |

The bold figures show the modal value for each neighborhood: Wicket is the lowest, with a slight predominance of lower working class (SEC 0–4) speakers; Pitt is next, with a clear concentration of middle working class (SEC 5–6); Clark is centered in the upper working class (SEC 7–9), and Nancy Drive in the lower middle class (10–12). At the same time, the range within each neighborhood is considerable. Clark Street shows four of the six social categories among its residents, and Wicket and Pitt both show three. The middle working class speakers are spread across three neighborhoods rather evenly. Given this dispersion, the regression analysis has sufficient information to determine which is more influential in the advancement of linguistic change, social class or neighborhood.

Chapter 5 found three types of social class distribution for the various linguistic changes in the Philadelphia vowel system. Socially stigmatized, nearly completed variables like (æhN) and (æhS) displayed a linear, monotonic function of class, at various levels of significance. The female-dominated new and vigorous changes (aw) and (eyC), and middle-range (owC) and (uwC), showed curvilinear patterns. The male-dominated (ay0) showed no social distribution at all. Given the relative independence of neighborhood and social class in table 7.2, it is possible that these patterns would be seriously modified by the addition of neighborhoods to the regression analysis effects. The curvilinear principle might turn out to be the product of the concentration of upper working class speakers in the most advanced neighborhoods, typified by Clark Street, since "South Philadelphia" is after all the stereotype of the Philadelphia dialect.

## 7.4 Results of the fourth regression analysis: adding neighborhoods

The fourth regression of the Philadelphia variables is built on the configuration of the third regression, with one simplification: all speakers under 20 are combined into a single group. Each neighborhood is represented by a dummy category that assigns a value of 1 if the speaker lives in that neighborhood, and 0 if he or she does not. All neighborhood variables are then added to the regression, including those in the "Others" category in table 7.2. The nonsignificant neighborhood variables are then removed beginning with the least significant, until only significant neighborhood effects remain. Any age categories that are not significant in either the third or the fourth regression are then removed.

## *Nearly completed changes*

Table 7.3 presents the results for nearly completed changes. The third regression, with the change in the age range mentioned above, is compared to the fourth regression, with neighborhood variables added. Where

*Table 7.3* Effect of adding neighborhood factors (fourth regression) to gender, age, and social class (third regression) analyses of the second formant of nearly completed changes (æhN) and (æhS). Underlined figures are 10% differences, bold figures differences of 20% or more

| | *Third regression* | | *Fourth regression* | |
|---|---|---|---|---|
| | *Coefficient* | *Prob.* | *Coefficient* | *Prob.* |
| *(æhN)* | | | | |
| Constant | 2347 | ≤0.0001 | 2244 | ≤0.0001 |
| Female | 70 | 0.0161 | 63 | 0.0265 |
| LMC | **–125** | **0.0114** | –81 | 0.1003 |
| UMC | **–212** | **≤0.0001** | –134 | 0.0092 |
| UC | **–304** | **≤0.0001** | –214 | ≤0.0001 |
| Under 20 | 84 | 0.0674 | 107 | 0.0188 |
| Wicket St. | | | **122** | **0.0086** |
| Pitt St. | | | **128** | **0.01** |
| Clark St. | | | **115** | **0.0088** |
| $r^2$ (adj) | | 46 | | 51 |
| *(æhS)* | | | | |
| LMC | **–131** | **0.0089** | –91.748 | 0.0621 |
| UMC | **–317.5** | **≤0.0001** | –230.13 | ≤0.0001 |
| UC | **–337.5** | **≤0.0001** | –239.53 | ≤0.0001 |
| Under 20 | 58.3456 | 0.2066 | **83.614** | **0.064** |
| Wicket St. | | | **98** | **0.0334** |
| Pitt St. | | | **137.8** | **0.0044** |
| Clark St. | | | **151.03** | **0.0007** |
| $r^2$ (adj) | | 51 | | 57 |

a given coefficient effect is about 10% larger in one analysis, it is underlined; when it is 20% or more larger, it is shown in bold figures.

Table 7.3 shows strong neighborhood effects for both (æhN) and (æhS). For (æhN), Wicket, Pitt, and Clark each contribute over 100 Hz to F2, at a high level of significance; for (æhS), Wicket St. has slightly less effect. This means that the residual groups, Nancy Drive and the upper class neighborhoods, have a contrary effect, reducing the fronting of (æh). However, the monotonic social class cline in the third regression is not replaced by this neighborhood effect. It remains at a high level of significance (except for the LMC), at about two-thirds of its value. The sex effect for (æhN), favoring women, is slightly reduced. On the other hand, the main age effect is considerably strengthened. In the third regression, age was not significant for these nearly completed changes, even though the first and second regressions had shown small but significant correlation with age. Here age is restored, with a sizeable advantage for those under 20 for (æhN), and a smaller result for (æhS).

The last line of each section shows adjusted $r^2$, indicating the percentage of variation explained.[7] Here the addition of the neighborhood factors increases the amount of the variance accounted for by 10%. This is only a moderate increase, indicating that some of the sizeable neighborhood effects were previously attributed to social class. In other words, the absence of neighborhood factors in the third regression led to an increase of 50% in the effect attributed to social class.

Is this a local effect? Probably not. It is more reasonable to say that this is another way of looking at the general feature of social stratification of stigmatized variables. The working class neighborhoods together share some linguistic practices and attitudes: in this case, these speakers are freer to use [eːə] or [ɛː] for *man* and *pass*, in spite of the consensus in subjective reactions that [eːə] is to be avoided.

## *New and vigorous changes*

The crucial test of the curvilinear principle involves the new and vigorous changes (aw) and (eyC), which showed a significant advantage for upper working class speakers in the third regression. Table 7.4 examines the effect of adding neighborhood factors to the original social constraints. The general advantage of all three working class neighborhoods in table 7.3 gives way to a strong predominance of Wicket St.: 222 Hz for (aw) and 188 Hz for (eyC), both at the $p < .0001$ level. A smaller contribution from

[7] The adjusted $r^2$ differs from ordinary $r^2$ in that it compensates for the fact that any addition of any factor group, no matter how insignificant or irrelevant, will have an effect in increasing $r^2$. This is done by dividing the residual sum of squares by the residual degrees of freedom, and the total sum of squares by the total degrees of freedom.

*Table 7.4* Fourth regression of the second formant of new and vigorous changes (aw) and (eyC): addition of neighborhood effects. Underlined figures show a 10% increase in the effect, bold figures an increase of 20% or more

| | *Third regression* | | *Fourth regression* | |
|---|---|---|---|---|
| | *Coefficient* | *Prob.* | *Coefficient* | *Prob.* |
| *(aw)* | | | | |
| Female | 125 | ≤0.0001 | 117 | ≤0.0001 |
| UWC | 93 | 0.0353 | **147** | **0.0002** |
| UC | **–118** | **0.021** | –50 | 0.279 |
| Under 20 | 260 | ≤0.0001 | 303 | ≤0.0001 |
| 20–29 | 171 | 0.0019 | 152 | 0.0017 |
| 30–39 | 144 | 0.0091 | 169 | 0.0008 |
| 40–49 | 68 | 0.2078 | **144** | **0.0028** |
| Wicket St. | | | **222** | **≤0.0001** |
| Pitt St. | | | **140** | **0.0013** |
| $r^2$ (adj) | | 46 | | **58** |
| *(eyC)* | | | | |
| Female | 103 | 0.0017 | 95 | 0.0016 |
| UWC | 114 | 0.0136 | 94 | 0.0344 |
| Under 20 | 172 | 0.0007 | **205** | **≤0.0001** |
| 20–29 | 103 | 0.0674 | 119 | 0.0248 |
| 30–39 | 50 | 0.3735 | **105** | **0.0474** |
| Wicket St. | | | **188** | **≤0.0001** |
| Clark St. | | | **106** | **0.0136** |
| $r^2$ (adj) | | 29 | | **41** |

Pitt St. is found for (aw) and from Clark St. for (eyC). These neighborhood effects do not weaken the curvilinear pattern; on the contrary, the leading position of the upper working class is quite secure. In the case of (aw), this prominence moves from 93 Hz at the .03 level to 147 Hz at the .0002 level, and is slightly weaker, but almost the same, for (eyC). The age effects are strengthened even more than in table 7.3. A small negative contribution of the upper class disappears for (aw). The total result of this addition of neighborhood factors is seen in sizeable increases of the adjusted $r^2$: from 46 to 58 (aw), and from 29 to 41 (eyC).

For the new and vigorous changes, then, the local advantage of the working class neighborhoods is additive. Unlike the nearly completed changes, it does not compete with or interfere with the effects of age, gender, or social class. This neighborhood effect is highly concentrated in Wicket St., the lowest of the intact neighborhoods in socioeconomic terms. This is a striking result. The popular stereotype of Philadelphia working

*Table 7.5* Fourth regression of the second formant of (aw), with Pitt St. divided into those over and under 20 years of age

| | *Fourth regression* | |
|---|---|---|
| | *Coefficient* | *Prob.* |
| *(aw)* | | |
| Female | 139 | ≤0.0001 |
| UWC | 141 | 0.0003 |
| Under 20 | 294 | ≤0.0001 |
| 20–29 | 193 | ≤0.0001 |
| 30–39 | 214 | ≤0.0001 |
| 40–49 | 149 | 0.0005 |
| Wicket St. | 210 | ≤0.0001 |
| Pitt St. <20 | 230 | 0.0012 |
| $r^2$ (adj) | | 58 |

class speech is "South Philadelphia," not "North Philadelphia" or "Kensington;" more specifically, "South Philadelphia Italian," not "Kensington Irish." In chapter 2 it was pointed out that Kensington is the oldest established working class area in Philadelphia. The rest of this chapter will yield further evidence that Philadelphia changes from below are most advanced in Wicket St.

How much interaction exists among the social factors of table 7.4? An ANOVA analysis of all possible interactions was run for (aw). The Pitt St. neighborhood showed interaction with adults 20–29 and with adults 30–39 at the .01 level, and at the .05 level with adults 40–49. Pitt St. has only one speaker older than 49: Rose J., who is 66 years old, but five speakers under 20. Pitt St. was therefore split into two groups, those under 20 and those 20 and over, and the regression analysis re-run. Table 7.5 shows the results. While the female and upper working class advantage remains constant, there is a step upward in size and significance of all the age coefficients. The Pitt St. youth now appear with a 230 Hz advantage, a coefficient a little higher than Wicket St. as a whole, which of course remains at the same level.

A more detailed view of what is happening is provided by figure 7.1, a scatterplot of the second formant of (aw) for the 70 speakers of the four intact neighborhoods. The four partial regression lines are equivalent to the regression analyses of table 7.4. It is clear that the Wicket residents led in the fronting of (aw) at the outset. However, the slope of the regression line for Pitt St. is steeper, reflecting the more rapid advance of younger Pitt St. speakers seen in table 7.5. Clark St. also shows a steeper slope

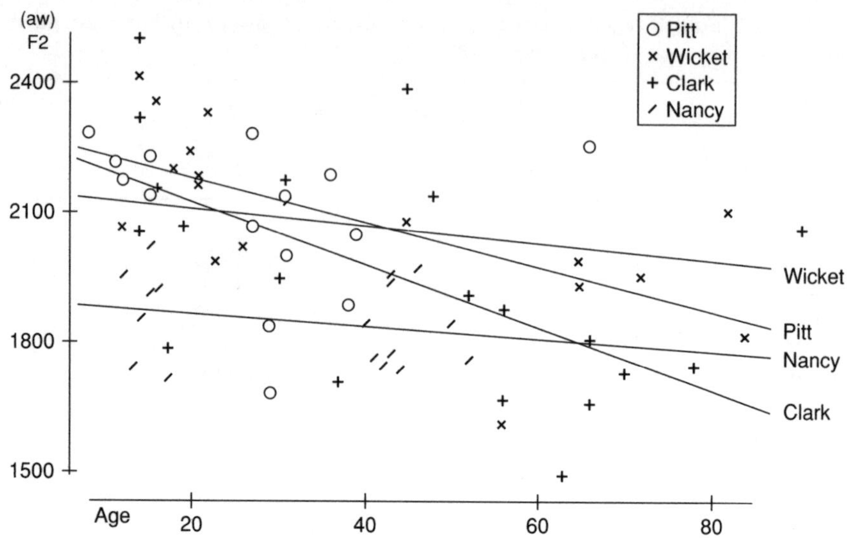


*Figure 7.1* Scatterplot of F2 of (aw) by age for 70 members of four intact Philadelphia neighborhoods

than Wicket. According to these linear projections, the South Philadelphia neighborhoods have passed Kensington in the youngest generation. On the other hand, the middle class Nancy Drive follows at a slower pace.

An examination of the tokens plotted clarifies the situation further. Wicket St., shown with x's, is generally quite advanced, and has not actually lost momentum. There is only one Wicket St. speaker among the lowest figures, below 1800 Hz, and there are quite a few older speakers, above 60, who are located above the general mean of 1950 Hz. The younger generation has not fallen behind: three x's are among the most advanced speakers under 20. The Clark St. residents, shown by + symbols, are not as high on the scale in general, but there are a few outliers who are far ahead of expectation for their neighborhood; these are leaders of linguistic change who will occupy more and more of our attention in the chapters to follow. The Pitt St. residents are shown by circles, which fall into two groups. Those between 20 and 40 are in the mid range; those under 20 are in a tight group above 2100 Hz. This relative discontinuity is what is expressed numerically by the interaction between Pitt St. and age.

Figure 7.1 confirms in detail the conclusion of the regression analysis that Wicket St. is indeed the leading area in the fronting of (aw) in the first half of the apparent time period. The relatively sudden increase in the Pitt St. speakers below 20 and the outliers on Clark St. indicates an outward spread of (aw)-fronting from Kensington (the larger district represented by Wicket St.) into South Philadelphia in the 1950s and 1960s.

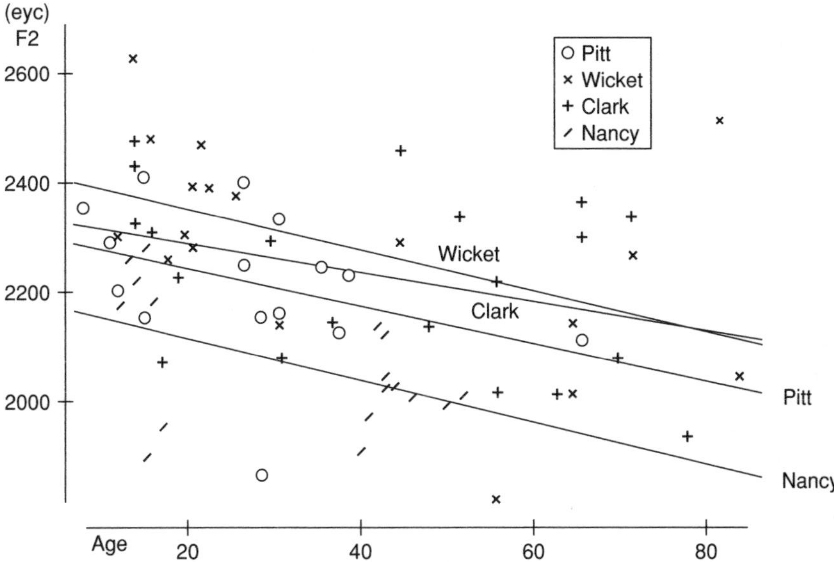


*Figure 7.2* Scatterplot of F2 of (eyC) by age for 70 members of four intact Philadelphia neighborhoods

The situation with (eyC) is less complex. No significant interactions appeared in the ANOVA analysis, and figure 7.2 shows that the regression lines are almost all parallel, though the Clark St. slope is somewhat less steep than the others.

## *Middle-range changes*

So far, the middle-range changes that involve the fronting of the back vowels have not played a prominent part in the analysis. Table 7.6 shows that these changes in progress strengthen considerably the findings from the new and vigorous changes in table 7.4. The checked vowel (owC) in *boat*, *road*, etc. does not show any significant class effects. The age pattern also differs from that of (aw) and (eyC): the leading group is not the youngest, but the young adults 20–29 years old. The effect of neighborhood is almost entirely additive, and the amount of variance explained is almost doubled. Again we see a strong and significant contribution of Wicket St., alone among the working class neighborhoods. For the first time, there is a prominent positive contribution from a middle class neighborhood, Nancy Drive, almost equal to that of Wicket St. The significance of this finding will appear more clearly in what follows.

The picture is even clearer for the free vowel (owF) in *go*, *know*, etc. Adding neighborhood factors more than doubles the total variance explained, from 12% to 30%. A social class factor which was absent in the

*Table 7.6* Third and fourth regressions of the middle-range changes (owC), (owF), and (uwC): addition of neighborhood effects. Underlined figures show a 10% greater effect, bold figures an effect greater by 20% or more

| | *Third regression* | | *Fourth regression* | |
|---|---|---|---|---|
| | *Coefficient* | *Prob.* | *Coefficient* | *Prob.* |
| *(owC)* | | | | |
| Female | 70 | 0.0473 | 70 | 0.0314 |
| Under 20 | 72 | 0.1877 | 57 | 0.2752 |
| 20–29 | 230 | 0.0003 | 214 | 0.0002 |
| 30–39 | 150 | 0.0161 | **186** | **0.0015** |
| Wicket St. | | | **178** | **0.0002** |
| Nancy Drive | | | **147** | **0.0046** |
| $r^2$ (adj) | | 15 | | **28** |
| *(owF)* | | | | |
| Female | 63 | 0.0732 | 77 | 0.0161 |
| LMC | | | **114** | **0.0293** |
| 20–29 | **239** | **0.0002** | 172 | 0.0029 |
| 30–39 | 114 | 0.064 | 114 | 0.0417 |
| 40–49 | 140 | 0.0226 | 106 | 0.0656 |
| Wicket St. | | | **126** | **0.006** |
| Clark St. | | | **–162** | **0.0002** |
| $r^2$ (adj) | | 12 | | **30** |
| *(uwC)* | | | | |
| Female | 62 | 0.2089 | **82** | **0.07** |
| LMC | 269 | 0.0012 | **316** | **≤0.0001** |
| Under 20 | 45 | 0.5557 | 43 | 0.5512 |
| 20–29 | **266** | **0.0023** | 200 | 0.0159 |
| 30–39 | 185 | 0.0344 | 214 | 0.0118 |
| Wicket St. | | | **185** | **0.0076** |
| Clark St. | | | **–155** | **0.0144** |
| $r^2$ (adj) | | 14 | | **25** |

third regression now appears as a lower middle class advantage of 114 Hz, at the .03 level. This is comparable to the curvilinear peak at the upper working class for (aw) and (eyC). The female advantage is strengthened, and the age effect of the young adults somewhat weakened. The expected strong contribution of Wicket St. is now accompanied by a large *negative* coefficient for Clark St. (The significance of the reversal of the position of Clark St. will not be evident until the end of this chapter.)

All of these findings for (owF) are reinforced by the results in table 7.6 for checked (uwC) in *suit, boot, mood,* etc. Again the female advantage is strengthened and the curvilinear peak for the lower middle class is considerably strengthened to 316 Hz. The age effect is again weakened in the 20–29 year age group and strengthened for 30–39 year olds. And again there appears a strong advantage for Wicket St. and a large negative figure for Clark St. The total variance explained is almost doubled, from 14% to 25%.

Finally, this inquiry confirms the indications of chapter 5 that the free vowel (uwF) is not to be included in these studies of changes in progress. It does not show age coefficients or social constraints at any significant level, and therefore might well be ranked among completed changes for Philadelphia. Chapter 14 will examine the relative progress of the fronting of /uw/ and /ow/ for all the dialects of North America, and bring forward a richer body of evidence to confirm this suggestion about (uwF).

Reviewing the three middle-range changes (owC), (owF), and (uwC), it appears that they are all variations on the same theme. At first glance, (owC) looks very different, with no lower middle class effect, and a neighborhood effect of Nancy Drive. But a glance at table 7.2 shows that Nancy Drive has even more lower middle class speakers than upper middle class. For reasons that are not entirely clear, the program found more explanation in locality than in class for (owC), though the two are closely linked. In general, all of these middle-range changes show a common pattern which differentiates them from the new and vigorous changes (aw) and (eyC). They show a peak among young adults rather than among speakers under 20, which indicates that they may be slowing down or even reversing. Secondly, the curvilinear pattern peaks in the lower middle class, not the upper working class.

The analysis of neighborhood effects in the new and vigorous changes, (aw) and (eyC), clarified the situation considerably, without lessening our appreciation for the leading position of Wicket St. The ANOVA analysis of interaction in the fourth regression revealed several significant interactions, involving Wicket St. and the younger age groups, as well as gender and Wicket. If we distinguish three groups of Wicket St. speakers: those under 20, those between 20 and 29, and the rest, all other interactions disappear.

Table 7.7 shows the results with this subdivision of Wicket St. The leading position of Wicket St. does not disappear; on the contrary, the numbers have risen to the 300 Hz level. But the pre-eminence of Wicket is now concentrated in the younger age ranges. In general, the middle-range changes peak in the 20–29 year age group; those under 20 are not as advanced. This is not the case for Wicket St., however. It is the youth under 20 who have the most advanced forms (and, for (owC) alone, the young adults 20 to 29). Otherwise, table 7.7 resembles table 7.6. The lower middle class peak remains the same, but the age effects are somewhat attenuated. This is a natural consequence of introducing the sub-category of Wicket youth, absorbing part of the age effect. What is striking here is

*Table 7.7* Re-analysis of (ow) variables to register interaction of Wicket St. and age

| | *(owC)* | | *(owF)* | |
|---|---|---|---|---|
| | *Coefficient* | *Prob.* | *Coefficient* | *Prob.* |
| Gender | 73 | 0.0189 | 88 | 0.0049 |
| 20–29 | 130 | 0.0169 | 143 | 0.0018 |
| 30–39 | 155 | 0.0008 | | |
| LMC | | | 115 | 0.0184 |
| Wicket St. <20 | 290 | 0.0008 | 275 | 0.0012 |
| Wicket St. 20–29 | 307 | 0.0003 | | |
| Nancy Drive | 158 | 0.0006 | | |
| Clark St. | | | −183 | ≤0.0001 |
| $r^2$ (adj) | | 34 | | 32 |

that the advantage of Wicket St. in the process is not a property of older speakers, and it seems therefore unlikely that the explanation for the leading position of Wicket St. is simply that Kensington is the oldest established working class neighborhood. Linguistic change in Wicket is advancing at a more rapid rate now, or to put it more accurately, any tendency for the Philadelphia community to pull back from the fronting of the mid vowels is not found in Wicket St.

The third vowel change of table 7.6, (uwC), does not show any interactions among the factors involved. The lower middle class peak and the leading position of Wicket remain intact.

### *The case of (ay0)*

From every indication, the centralization of (ay0) will follow a completely different pattern from that of the other variables. First, it is the only one of the variables that involves F1 rather than F2. Secondly, it is the only one that is male-dominated. Table 7.8 presents the fourth regression for (ay0), with neighborhood factors added.[8] Comparable effects will also show opposite signs, since the change is in the direction of lowering the value of F1 for the nucleus.

Table 7.8 shows a distinct reinforcement of the male advantage with the addition of neighborhood factors. The full range of significant age effects – the most complete array in the third regression – is unchanged. The

[8] In reading table 7.8, one must bear in mind that F1 is given twice the space of F2 in the acoustic displays, and that to compare the effect of these social constraints in a way that is consistent with them, the numbers should be doubled.

*Table 7.8* Fourth regression of (ay0): addition of neighborhood effects. Underlined figures show a 10% increase in the effect, bold figures an increase of 20% or more

| | *Third regression* | | *Fourth regression* | |
|---|---|---|---|---|
| | *Coefficient* | *Prob.* | *Coefficient* | *Prob.* |
| Male | 36 | 0.0027 | 42 | 0.0003 |
| Under 20 | −131 | ≤0.0001 | −133 | ≤0.0001 |
| 20–29 | −112 | ≤0.0001 | −109 | ≤0.0001 |
| 30–39 | −53 | 0.0116 | −62 | 0.002 |
| 40–49 | −50 | 0.0152 | −49 | 0.0145 |
| 50–59 | −46 | 0.0352 | −49 | 0.0209 |
| Wicket St. | | | **−42** | **0.0079** |
| $r^2$ (adj) | | 39 | | **45** |

addition of a moderate Wicket St. component is then a simple addition, and the variance explained rises from 39% to 45%.

An examination of all possible interactions among the factors of table 7.8 shows no interactions. The leading position of Wicket St. is independent of all other factors.

## 7.5 An overview of neighborhood effects

At the outset, this chapter raised the possibility that there might be no neighborhood effects: that Philadelphia would turn out to be geographically uniform. This is plainly not the case: the leading position of Wicket St. in Kensington is fully established in all cases, including the male-dominated centralization of (ay0). Furthermore, the effect is large and significant except in the one case of the nearly completed change (æhS). Other neighborhoods appear occasionally in this scenario. For the nearly completed changes, the two working class South Philadelphia neighborhoods are as strong as Wicket St., and therefore the effect may be considered one of class rather than geography. But for the middle-range changes and the new and vigorous changes, Wicket St. is the only constant. Pitt St. shows up for (aw), at least for the younger speakers; Clark St. for (eyC); and Nancy Drive for (owC). In addition, there is the negative effect of Clark St. for (owF) and (uwC), which will be re-examined below.

Given the leading position of Wicket St., it seems appropriate to ask how this finding is related to what was found in chapter 5. There it appeared that the lower and middle working class are never leading elements in linguistic change while the upper working class or lower middle class are

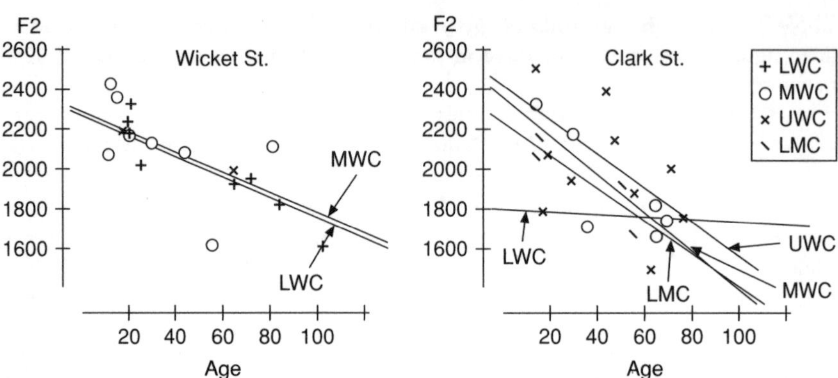


*Figure 7.3* Scatterplots of fronting of (aw) by age for two Philadelphia neighborhoods, with partial regression lines for social class groups

consistently in the lead. It followed that the innovators of change from below are drawn from the more prestigious, centrally located members of local society. The geographic effect seems to point in the other direction. Table 2.3 showed that Kensington has the lowest mean income, the lowest mean years of schooling, and the lowest house values of the five areas. It is the lowest ranking neighborhood that leads.

There is nothing inherently paradoxical about this situation. Wicket St. was not selected for its social characteristics, but as a geographical area, and it is the settlement history of that geographical area that is relevant. However, it would be good to know if the curvilinear pattern is maintained within neighborhood. Figure 7.3 shows separate scatterplots for the 18 speakers living on Wicket St. and the 20 speakers living on Clark St. Partial regression lines are shown for the relation between age and fronting for each socioeconomic group. All lines are more or less parallel, with the exception of the lower working class group on Clark St. On Wicket St., there is no difference at all between lower working class and middle working class, but since there is only one "x" symbol for an upper working class speaker, the curvilinear pattern is simply not in evidence. On Clark St., the upper working class symbols ("x") predominate and occupy the upper region of the diagram.

Table 7.9 provides separate regression analyses of (aw) in the two neighborhoods. Given the reduced numbers, age groups are also reduced to three categories: youth under 20 years, adults 20–49, and the older residual group above 50. The two sets of figures are remarkably similar. The chief differences are that in Clark St. the female advantage is twice as high, and that the main adult group shows higher values.

The last column shows the projected differences between the two neighborhoods for each age group, derived by adding the age coefficients to the constants. It is clear that Wicket St. is well ahead of Clark St. for each age

*Table 7.9* Regression analyses of fronting of (aw) for Wicket St. and Clark St., showing projected differences for each age group

| | *Wicket St.* | | *Clark St.* | | |
|---|---|---|---|---|---|
| | *Coefficient* | *Prob.* | *Coefficient* | *Prob.* | *Projected difference* |
| Constant | 1828 | ≤0.0001 | 1558 | ≤0.0001 | |
| Female | 143 | 0.0515 | 264 | 0.0024 | |
| Under 20 years | 396 | 0.0006 | 379 | 0.0003 | 287 |
| 20–49 years | 225 | 0.0111 | 345 | 0.0017 | 150 |
| 50+ years | 0 | | 0 | | 270 |
| Upper working class | 164 | 0.2803 | 108 | 0.1579 | |
| n | | 18 | | 20 | |
| $r^2$ (adj) | | 56 | | 67 | |

level, indicating that it has probably been leading in the fronting of (aw) at least as far back as the turn of the century. The upper working class peak appears in both. But it is not to be taken seriously in Wicket St., since it represents a value for only one speaker, and even in Clark St. it falls short of significance. Given the fact that the curvilinear pattern predominates in Clark St. and similar neighborhoods, it remains to be seen how we can relate the advanced position of Wicket St. to the absence of the social class that leads the change in other neighborhoods.

## 7.6 Ethnicity

Ethnicity is a social identity that is attributed to people by virtue of their descent, an acquired rather than an achieved characteristic. It represents the answer to the question "What are you?" What makes one ethnic group different from another will differ from one society to another. In many cases, communal groups are centered about religious affiliation, not as a matter of personal choice, but as a matter of family descent. Milroy 1980 and McCafferty 1998 assign the Ulster distinction of Protestant and Catholic to ethnicity rather than religion. A youth born in the Clonard is Catholic by virtue of family membership, and belief structures are not involved. In the United States, Jewish identity is even more clearly a matter of descent rather than religious affiliation. On the other hand, "Protestant" and "Catholic" are not treated as ethnic identities in the United States. The Irish, Polish, Italian, and Puerto Rican ethnic groups are generally Catholic, but the division between Protestant and Irish Catholic is not a fundamental distinction of ethnic identity in the United States, any more than the distinction between Catholic and Protestant African Americans.

A certain amount of personal latitude is recognized in the assignment of primary and secondary ethnicity. Each person was assigned both a primary and a secondary ethnicity; if their parents shared the same ethnicity, these were the same. When a person's parents differed in ethnicity, the "primary" ethnicity was assigned on the basis of their personal life history, associations, marriage, and self-identification. Thirty-three of the 112 speakers in the neighborhood study had mixed ethnic identity; this of course reflects the degree of marriage across ethnic lines. Since ethnic groups do not actively recruit members, they are preserved in the long run only by barriers against intermarriage, and this 28% represents the limits or weaknesses in ethnic identification. At the same time, marriage with a member of another ethnic group does not imply an individual choice unrelated to social structure: as is well known, marriage partners are closely tied to frequency of contact, and the degree of contact between ethnic groups within the city is the product of social forces outside the control of an individual.

Considering the five social factors that are the focus of the last several chapters – social class, age, gender, neighborhood, and ethnicity – it seems only logical that ethnicity would have the strongest effect on linguistic change. Like language, ethnicity is transmitted and acquired directly from one's parents. There is usually a close relationship between language and ethnicity. Even in the United States, where foreign languages are usually abandoned after two generations, speakers of the first native generation will have some active knowledge of the mother tongue of their parents, and almost always a reasonably strong passive knowledge. It stands to reason that the language of a community will be influenced when it acquires large numbers of speakers with such a foreign language background, and that the ethnicity of the speakers will be a major factor in differentiating speakers involved in language change. But this expectation has been consistently defeated.

The studies of ethnic groups that are most relevant to the present inquiry into language change will concern minority groups who have abandoned the immigrant language in favor of English, but still differentiate themselves from other speakers of English by effects traceable to the parents' or grandparents' mother tongue. Mother tongue influences of immigrant minority groups on the mainstream language can be referred to as *adstratum* effects. Of particular interest to the present study will be any adstratum effects that appear to motivate or accelerate language change in progress.

We should exercise considerable caution in formulating any general principles on the relation of ethnicity to language change. The generality of the curvilinear principle rests on the fact that all large cities show socioeconomic stratification. The chapters to follow will demonstrate that gender differentiation follows principles of extraordinary generality, based on certain constancies in the relation of men and women across societies.

But though the population of most complex societies is differentiated by ethnicity, the relations among those ethnic groups, and their use of language, shows little uniformity throughout the world. The findings on adstratum effects will therefore be confined to the types of societies on which they were founded: the large developed countries with strong linguistic assimilation.

The populations of all of the large North American cities, except for the Southern states, include large numbers of immigrant ethnic groups who are one or two generations away from the use of the immigrant language. In the Lower East Side of New York City, only a very small percentage of the residents had the ethnic affiliation of the original Dutch or English settlers. The population of most large Eastern cities was formed by successive waves of European immigrants, which changed radically in character over 50-year periods in a pattern similar to that described for Philadelphia in chapter 2. In the mid-19th century, Irish and German migrants dominated the immigration pattern. Towards the end of the century, and for the first quarter of the 20th century, the largest groups were Italians, Jews from Russia and Eastern Europe, Poles, Greeks, and Ukrainians. In the second half of the 20th century, the greatest immigrant population of foreign language speakers has been from speakers of Spanish, and more recently, from various East Asian groups.

Given the fact that the ethnicity of speakers is the trait most closely related to language, it is quite surprising to find very little differentiation of the English of the population by ethnicity. Of all the social factors examined in sociolinguistic studies of New York, Philadelphia, Boston, and the Northern Cities, the ethnic group of the speaker's family and knowledge of the immigrant language has the least effect. Moreover, most of these effects were in a direction quite different from what would have been predicted from the structure of that immigrant language. In New York City, all ethnic groups except African Americans participated in the raising of /æh/ and /oh/ from low to mid to high. Italians showed distinctly higher values of (æh) and Jews favored the raising of (oh) (Labov 1966a). This is not what one would have predicted if the second generation (that is, first native generation) had carried the vowel system of Italian or Yiddish into their English. None of the Yiddish dialects of Eastern Europe have a high back ingliding vowel [oə]; a first-generation Yiddish accent in English shows a low back [ɒ] for both /o/ and /oh/ and [ɛ] for /æ/. The Italian dialects of southern Italy do not show a high ingliding vowel [eə] or [iə], and a first-generation Italian accent shows [a] for [æ]. This suggested that ethnic influences might generally be the obverse of direct influence, triggered by the general desire to avoid the stigmatized features of the foreign accent of the speaker's parents.

If such a hypercorrect pattern exists, it is not the immediate result of language contact, but a more general factor that persists over time as the

*Table 7.10* Phonological variables for subjects with foreign- and native-born parents in New York City

| | *Upper middle class Jewish younger men [21–39 yrs]* | | | | *Working class Jewish older women [40–65 yrs]* | | | |
|---|---|---|---|---|---|---|---|---|
| | *(æh) scores* | | *(oh) scores* | | *(æh) scores* | | *(oh) scores* | |
| | *2nd gen.* | *3rd gen.* | *2nd gen.* | *3rd gen.* | *2nd gen.* | *3rd gen.* | *2nd gen.* | *3rd gen.* |
| n | 3 | 6 | 3 | 6 | 6 | 3 | 6 | 3 |
| Mean | 31.0 | 30.3 | 27.0 | 24.5 | 28.6 | 28.6 | 19.9 | 20.6 |
| Std dev. | 7.8 | 5.8 | 1.6 | 4.8 | 3.9 | 10.0 | 3.5 | 1.1 |
| t | 0.15 | | 0.86 | | 0.47 | | 0.33 | |

knowledge of the foreign language diminishes. If it were a result of language contact, one would predict that the advantage would be stronger in the second (first native) generation, and weaker in the third. Table 7.10 shows such a comparison for two closely matched sets in New York City: upper middle class Jewish younger men, and working class Jewish older women. The scores for the second and third generation do not differ significantly at any point, and for the most part are very close indeed (Labov 1976).

This suggestion of ethnic hypercorrection as the basic mechanism is reinforced by the findings of Laferriere (1979) in Boston, a study that focuses primarily on the sociolinguistic patterns of ethnicity. The main linguistic variable in question is the low back vowel [ɒ] of *for, morning, short, fork, or,* which represents the phoneme /ohr/ in dialects that distinguish it from /owr/ in *four, mourning, port, ore,* etc., pronounced with an upper mid ingliding vowel. Because the low back vowel is stigmatized as stereotypical of the Boston dialect, many speakers show discrete oscillation between the use of /ohr/ and /owr/. Figure 7.4 shows the percent use of the low back vowel by three ethnic groups. Just as in New York, the Italian speakers are here opposed to the Jewish group. One interpretation is that Jews are here more sensitive to the social impression conveyed by Boston /ɔhr/, or perhaps less inclined to identify themselves as Bostonians. But there is also a linguistically motivated generalization: just as in New York, Jews of the second and third generation favor higher back ingliding vowels.

Another study of the Jewish community was the report on Grand Rapids by Knack (1991). She interviewed 33 middle-aged, upper middle class local residents with an eye to tracing linguistic differences between Jews and non-Jews. Her sample was evenly divided into Jewish men, Jewish women, non-Jewish men, and non-Jewish women. The main variable Knack

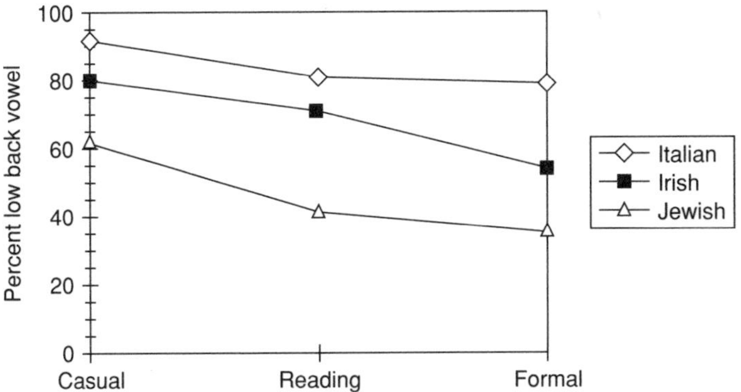


*Figure 7.4* Percent use of low back [ɒ] for /ohr/ words by three ethnic groups in Boston in three stylistic contexts (from Laferriere 1979)

studied was the same as the one in which Jews were more advanced in New York City: (oh) in *talk*, *law*, *cost*, *off*, etc., and closely related to the feature studied by Laferriere. Grand Rapids is one of the Inland North cities involved in the Northern Cities Shift, and as chapter 5 of volume 1 showed, (oh) becomes progressively lower and fronter, but always maintains a distance from (o), which moves to an even fronter position. In Knack's data, one can see that both Jews and non-Jews are involved in the Northern Cities Shift, but that the Jews are much slower to follow the trend.

Knack used an impressionistic index of the height of the vowel similar to that in the New York City study: 1 [o], 2 [ɔ˔], 3 [ɔ], 4 [ɒ], 5 [ɑ]. The difference between Jews and non-Jews on this scale was small but consistent. Analysis of the data (her table 9.1) shows that the mean value for non-Jews is 4.12, with a standard deviation of .14, while the Jews show a mean of 3.75 with a standard deviation of .25. The overlap between the two groups is therefore not very great. Knack finds a gender difference, but only among Jews. Table 7.11 is a regression analysis comparable to those earlier in this chapter, which shows how gender and ethnicity interact.

These results seem to confirm the idea that there is a relation between a Yiddish language background and the raising, backing, and rounding of (oh), which might best be explained by a reaction against the linguistic model of the first generation. This suggests a principle of *counter-reaction*: that the main effect of a foreign language background on an ethnic group is to provoke a language development in a direction opposite to that of the immigrant language. However, the Grand Rapids community has a history that suggests explanations of a different type. The community was first founded in the mid-19th century by German Jews who did not use Yiddish, and the Reform congregation that stems from this group is still an important part of the sample. Direct contact with New York, even for

*Table 7.11* Regression analysis of (oh) in Grand Rapids for 33 speakers by gender and ethnicity

| | *Coefficient* | *Prob.* |
|---|---|---|
| Constant | 4.12 | ≤0.0001 |
| Jewish women | –0.47 | ≤0.0001 |
| Jewish men | –0.27 | 0.0044 |
| $r^2$ (adj) | | 49 |

Source: table 9.1 of Knack 1991

the native-born Grand Rapids Jews, turns out to be an important predictor of the degree of raising of (oh), data to be developed further in the next chapter.

There are many other mysterious and puzzling ethnic effects that do not correspond to this principle or any other known principle, to be considered in the following sections of this chapter.

## 7.7 (r) in Philadelphia

Philadelphia is an *r*-pronouncing dialect. Except for certain dissimilating words like *quarter*, *ordinary*, *forward*, and *corner*, white Philadelphians consistently pronounce postvocalic /r/ as a constricted central consonant. However, on any day in the year, one may hear a very general pattern of vocalized /r/ from the men who run the stalls and shops at the 9th Street Market, an open-air produce market spread across several blocks in the Italian area of South Philadelphia. The first impression is that *r*-lessness is concentrated in the South Philadelphia Italian community.[9] To get a more precise view, an analysis of this variable was carried out for 60 speakers from three areas of South Philadelphia – Clark St. (27), Pitt St. (20), and the Fox network (13).[10] The variable (r) is here defined as the occurrence of vocalic or nonvocalic realizations of underlying /r/ in postvocalic tautosyllabic position, that is, when a following consonant or pause prevents any reassignment to a next syllable. The analysis distinguishes careful speech from casual speech, using the criteria given in chapter 2, and within each style, distinguishes three linguistic contexts: stressed syllables ending with a simple /r/ coda; stressed syllables with a complex /rC/ coda; and unstressed syllables (almost always /ər/).

[9] In so far as the white community is concerned. For the entire black community, comprising 38% of Philadelphia, (r) is a variable, with a much higher degree of vocalization.

[10] The transcription of South Philadelphia (r) was carried out in its entirety by Anne Bower. More South Philadelphia subjects are included than those in the main sample of 112.

*Table 7.12* Effect of Italian ethnicity on (r) vocalization in South Philadelphia

| | *Ethnicity* | | | | |
|---|---|---|---|---|---|
| | *Primary* | | *Primary and secondary* | | |
| | *Italian* | *Others* | *Italian* | *Others* | *Total* |
| Some (r-0) | 25 | 9 | 23 | 11 | 34 |
| No (r-0) | 12 | 14 | 8 | 18 | 26 |
| Total | 37 | 23 | 31 | 29 | 60 |
| Fischer's exact test | 0.0336 | | 0.0086 | | |

The first step is to distinguish among the Philadelphians who clearly vocalize some tokens of (r) and those who do not. The 60 speakers split almost evenly into 26 who never vocalize (r) and 34 who sometimes do. Only one speaker, Matt R. of Clark St., 66 years old, is a consistent vocalizer with a score of 100% in all contexts and both styles (31 out of 31). The other 33 show an (r) range from near 0 to 75, with a mean of 39 and a standard deviation of 20.

## *Is (r) vocalization an Italian feature?*

Table 7.12 displays (r) scores for the 60 South Philadelphians. The Italian/non-Italian distinction is not absolute but is quite strong. On the left-hand side appears the tabulation for the 37 speakers whose primary ethnicity is Italian; on the right-hand side, the tabulation for the 31 who are assigned both primary and secondary ethnicity as Italian.

This result is a strong one. When we take both ethnic assignments into account, 23 Italian speakers show some vocalization of (r) and only 8 do not. About two-thirds of the others show consistent *r*-pronunciation.

Is there any linguistic connection between Italian language background and the vocalization of (r)? There is no direct correlation: the southern Italian and Sicilian dialects spoken by the immigrants to South Philadelphia have a strong, apico-alveolar trilled /r/ which does not show the variability in question.[11] Italian /r/ is clearly a consonantal liquid, with a [+consonantal] feature of apical tongue contact that is absent in English /r/. It is possible that the vocalization of /r/ originated in the Italian community when new

[11] In the vast majority of cases, Italian /r/ occurs in intervocalic position, but there are a few words like *per* where it occurs finally.

*Table 7.13* Vocalization of (r) by knowledge of Italian for South Philadelphians with Italian ethnicity

| | *Foreign language knowledge* | | | | | | | | |
|---|---|---|---|---|---|---|---|---|---|
| | *0* | *1* | *2* | *3* | *4* | *5* | *6* | *n.d.* | *Total* |
| No (r-0) | 5 | 2 | 1 | 2 | 2 | 0 | 0 | 1 | 13 |
| Some (r-0) | 9 | 4 | 2 | 3 | 3 | 1 | 1 | 1 | 24 |
| Total | 14 | 6 | 3 | 5 | 5 | 1 | 1 | 2 | 37 |

speakers of English with an Italian phonological system identified English postvocalic /r/ as a glide rather than a consonant, and produced a vocalic glide as their nearest phonological equivalent. If this is indeed the origin of (r) vocalization, there should be some relationship between this variable and knowledge of Italian. As originally presented in chapter 3, the foreign language knowledge variable has 6 levels: 0 no foreign language background; 1 passive understanding of grandparents; 2 passive understanding of parents; 3 spoke only foreign language up to school age, never much since; 4 occasional use of foreign language with older people; 5 regular use of foreign language with older people; 6 dominant in foreign language. Table 7.13 shows the distribution of (r) vocalization and knowledge of Italian for the 35 speakers whose primary ethnicity was Italian. Despite the small numbers, it is apparent that there is no correlation. This becomes even more apparent when we remove those whose secondary ethnicity is not Italian. All six of these speakers are located in the first column: they have no knowledge of Italian at all. Four show no vocalization and 2 show some. For those in the first column whose primary and secondary ethnicity is Italian, we find 7 with vocalization and only 1 without. It is clear that (r) vocalization is not decreasing with decreasing knowledge of Italian.

A sizeable gender effect appears as well. Table 7.14 shows the effect of gender on the distribution of (r) vocalization for Italians vs. others. Among the men, 15 out of 17 with Italian ethnicity showed some vocalization, but only 8 out of 14 women. No gender effect appeared for other ethnicities. There is no reason to think that women are less exposed to the influence of Italian than men. We can conclude that (r) vocalization is a sociolinguistic variable, not a linguistic reflex of an Italian adstratum.

Although this distribution appears at first to be strong evidence for a gender difference, multivariate analysis shows that it is actually a social class factor. Table 7.15 gives the results of a regression analysis with the degree of vocalization as the dependent variable. Italian ethnicity (Italian-1 = primary and secondary) is the first and most significant factor, contributing 47 out of a possible 100. The second factor is SEC, the

*Table 7.14* Effect of Italian ethnicity (primary and secondary) on vocalization of (r) in South Philadelphia, by gender

| | *Male* | | | *Female* | | |
|---|---|---|---|---|---|---|
| | *Italian* | *Others* | *Total* | *Italian* | *Others* | *Total* |
| Some (r-0) | 15 | 2 | 17 | 8 | 9 | 17 |
| No (r-0) | 2 | 4 | 6 | 6 | 14 | 20 |
| Total | 17 | 6 | 23 | 14 | 23 | 37 |
| Fischer's exact test | | | 0.0336 | | | 0.0086 |

*Table 7.15* Significant regression coefficients for some vocalization vs. no vocalization for 60 South Philadelphia residents

| | *Coefficient* | *Prob.* |
|---|---|---|
| Italian-1 | 47 | 0.0001 |
| Upward mobility/upkeep | –16 | 0.0170 |
| SEC | –7 | 0.0200 |
| $r^2$ (adj) | | 33% |

combined socioeconomic index.[12] This yields a coefficient of –7. Since the total range in this neighborhood is SEC 2 to SEC 10, the range of the SEC effect is 56 points. SEC appears here as a monotonic factor: the higher the SEC, the less tendency to use vocalization. The third factor is one that so far has not played a role. It combines two closely correlated indicators of upward mobility discussed in chapter 2: house upkeep (with a range of 0–2) and social mobility, with a range of 0–2. The combined index is twice the value of social mobility plus house upkeep.[13] This contributes a negative factor of 16 points.

The overall picture that emerges is that vocalization is concentrated among South Philadelphians of Italian extraction, and is socially recessive:

[12] Here the combined SEC index is more useful than any individual indicator. None of the individual indicators: occupation, education, or house value, are significantly correlated with vocalization.

[13] House upkeep is particularly important in South Philadelphia, where residents show their relative social status by radical changes to the facades, stoops, doors, and windows of their houses, as opposed to North Philadelphia neighborhoods, where the compelling social norm is to maintain the same appearance as one's neighbors. For some of the 60 speakers of the (r) analysis, we do not have one or the other rating. If there is one value, it is expanded to the range of the whole index; if there is neither, the mean for the entire index is substituted.

*Table 7.16* Regression coefficients for (r) vocalization for 34 South Philadelphia speakers who show some vocalization

| | *Coefficient* | *Prob.* |
|---|---|---|
| Italian male | 38 | ≤0.0001 |
| House upkeep | −7 | 0.0709 |
| Upward mobility | −10 | 0.0827 |
| Age | 0.28 | 0.0467 |
| $r^2$ (adj) | | 56% |

*Table 7.17* Effect of style on percent (r) vocalization in South Philadelphia, by ethnicity and gender

| | *Italian* | *Others* | *Male* | *Female* |
|---|---|---|---|---|
| Careful | 23 | 7 | 27 | 7 |
| Casual | 40 | 15 | 42 | 19 |

that is, its use is inhibited by upward social status and mobility. So far, no change in apparent time is indicated.

## *Analysis of the (r) vocalizers*

To get a clearer picture of what is happening to (r) in South Philadelphia, let us examine its distribution among the 34 speakers who show some degree of vocalization. Table 7.16 shows four significant coefficients in decreasing order of importance. Italian ethnicity is a strong factor, but here combined with gender: there is no significant contribution from women or males of other ethnicity. House upkeep and social mobility, important features of South Philadelphia society, here appear with only moderate effects and significance, but both contribute to the high level of total explanation: an $r^2$ of 56. Finally, there is some indication of change in apparent time. The moderate positive age coefficient indicates that the older a speaker is, the greater the degree of vocalization; an age difference of 50 years would then lead to an expected difference, all other things being equal, of 15%.

There is also a strong and general differentiation of casual and careful style in the vocalization of (r). Table 7.17 shows the style shift for speakers of Italian ethnicity vs. others and for males vs. females. In a regression analysis of style shift as the dependent variable, the shift emerges as stronger (by 17 points) for younger Italian speakers even though age favors vocalization in general.

*Table 7.18* Regression coefficients for (r) of all South Philadelphia speakers who show some vocalization

| | *Stressed* | | *Unstressed* | |
|---|---|---|---|---|
| | *Coefficient* | *Prob.* | *Coefficient* | *Prob.* |
| Age | 0.7 | 0.0042 | | |
| Italian-2 male | 29 | 0.0030 | 21 | 0.0535 |
| $r^2$ (adj) | | 45% | | 12% |

## *Internal differentiation of (r) by stress*

The sociolinguistic character of South Philadelphia (r) emerges more clearly when we distinguish allophones that differ sharply in their distributions and development. The unstressed syllables in *neighborhood, father, her dog,* behave quite differently from stressed syllables. Table 7.18 shows the two strong effects on stressed (r). Age is a strong contributor: with a coefficient of .7, an age differential of 50 years would correspond to a 35% difference in vocalization rates. An equally strong factor is the effect of being a male of Italian ethnicity. In other words, the predominance of vocalization for Italian males is accompanied by a general decline across all age groups. This in itself does not add very much to our knowledge of the principles of language change from below. Whether or not (r) vocalization is the result of an adstratum effect, it appears here as a lower status feature of a stigmatized vernacular that is being abandoned by those who are upwardly mobile (tables 7.15–7.16), and reduced by younger speakers. This is not particularly different from the dialect-leveling effects that were observed in Belfast and other European cities, as well as rural American dialects. As this type of convergence is part of a general trend to abandon stigmatized forms, coinciding with the general norms of proper speech, it needs little further explanation.

The situation is radically different with unstressed (r). Regression analysis shows only one barely significant factor affecting this variable: a coefficient of 21 for Italian males, with a probability value of .055, which explains only 12% of the variance. In contrast to stressed (r), unstressed (r) remains stable. The change is therefore one from general vocalization as a marked feature of Italian males, to a less prominent vocalization of unstressed (r) which is shared by a large part of the South Philadelphia community. We have in fact observed some vocalization of unstressed (r) among younger speakers in North Philadelphia, but never any vocalization of stressed (r).

The development of (r) in Philadelphia therefore represents a decline in the effect of ethnicity together with a generalization of the less marked form of the variable.

## 7.8 Other unexplained adstratum effects

Our failure to give a linguistic accounting of the vocalization of (r) in South Philadelphia is not a unique event. A number of other linguistic variables have appeared that are strongly correlated with ethnicity and are logically based on adstratum effects, yet resist any linguistic explanation. I will briefly sketch three examples that have been well documented.

### *The Slavic effect on the merger of /o~oh/*

Perhaps the most striking example of ethnic influence appears in the sudden expansion of the merger of /oh/ and /o/ in Eastern Pennsylvania, documented by Herold (1990; see volume 1:321–7). Herold demonstrated that this sound change was tightly focused in coal-mining towns, where the population had undergone a sudden reversal of ethnic composition with the immigration of large numbers of Slavic-speaking miners from Eastern Europe. However, she was unable to find any mechanism that would connect the languages spoken by the immigrants with this merger. Pittsburgh exhibited the same merger at an earlier period, again in close conjunction with a sizeable immigration of a Polish-speaking population, but Polish has a contrast of a lower mid back rounded and low back unrounded vowel. No convincing connection has yet been found between a Polish substratum and the merger of /o/ and /oh/ or monophthongization of /aw/.

### *Confusion of* let *and* make

Members of a Linguistics 560 class working in South Philadelphia observed a series of utterances that reflected a reversal or neutralization of the distinction between *make* and *let*. After a woman's husband was observed making over-friendly approaches to a number of other women at a local dance, a friend asked her, "How could you make your husband dance with all those women?" In the course of a narrative, a South Philadelphia woman said, "It would let Jesus cry." A story about a baby who was almost scalded included the sentence, "She made her baby get burned."

These were only a small number of sentences, all spoken by Italian-Americans. In order to find out if there was any general basis for it, Hoekje (1978) constructed a field experiment in which 25 members of the neighborhood they were studying were asked to give grammaticality judgments for eight sentences containing *make* and *let* in English. The non-Italians agreed in 149 out of 152 judgments, while the subjects of Italian background agreed in only 75 out of 102 judgments on whether to use *make* or *let.*

This is an extraordinary difference. We do not at present know of any semantic differences in Italian *lasciare* and *fare* and English *make* and *let* that would account for this ethnic effect.

### *The Puerto Rican use of* later

During the mid-1980s, the research project on the relation of urban minorities to linguistic change [UMLC] examined the contrast of linguistic forms across the Euro-American, Hispanic, and African American communities in North Philadelphia. In the course of this work, Wendell Harris as a participant observer noted a number of utterances in the English of Puerto Ricans who had intimate connection with blacks, which reversed the usual use of *later* and *earlier*. He recorded many examples of people saying, "I was over your house later, but you weren't there," where the intended meaning was clearly "earlier." Since that time he has continued to note examples of this phenomenon, which is widely current in the English of this section of the Puerto Rican community, but has never been noted from any other speakers. I have consulted with many linguists with an extensive knowledge of this dialect of Spanish and others, but we have been unable to find any contrast between Spanish *tarde* and English *later* that would account for this adstratum effect.

The conclusion must be that our understanding of the mechanism of language contact, particularly in semantics, is simply not sufficient to account for the phenomena.

## 7.9 Ethnic effects on Philadelphia vowel changes

Let us now return to the series of Philadelphia vowel changes that are the main focus of this discussion of neighborhood and ethnicity. The story is in general a simple one: ethnicity differs from age, gender, social class, and neighborhood in that it has little systematic effect on linguistic change in progress. For most of the sound changes, there are no ethnic effects. When ethnic effects do appear, they do not interact with the relations that have already been established and they are usually unique to a particular vowel. With one possible exception, ethnic effects contribute nothing to our understanding of the mechanism of the Philadelphia vowel shifts.[14]

[14] In all of the discussions to follow, subjects will be classed as having a given ethnicity only if both parents have that ethnicity.

*Table 7.19* Effects of Italian ethnicity on the fronting of (uw) and (ow) in the Philadelphia Neighborhood Study

| | *Coefficient* | *Prob.* | *Increase in $r^2$* |
|---|---|---|---|
| (owC) | −103 | 0.0296 | 2.1 |
| (owF) | −139 | 0.0108 | 3.7 |
| (uwC) | −226 | 0.0005 | 2.4 |
| (uwF) | −103 | 0.0597 | −0.7 |

For the nearly completed changes (æhN) and (æhS), no significant effects appear. For the new and vigorous change (eyC), the same can be said. In the fronting of (aw), there is one odd effect: a coefficient of −205 for the speakers of German extraction. It is unlikely that there is anything systematic in this development. The four speakers of primary and secondary German extraction all live in King of Prussia, and apparently share the quality of using a conservative form of (aw).

The one clear effect of ethnicity that does appear is in the fronting of (uw) and (ow). Table 7.19 displays a consistent negative effect of Italian ethnicity on all four variables. Whereas neighborhood effects were entirely additive, three of the four ethnic effects replace the neighborhood effect. The coefficients for Clark Street in (owF) and (uwC) in table 7.6 are now replaced by the regular effect of Italian ethnicity. Clark St., as chapter 2 showed, is the most Italian of the neighborhoods: 14 of the 20 subjects of vowel analysis on Clark St. are Italian (and one case of mixed ethnicity). Though there is a great deal of overlap between Italian ethnicity and residence in Clark St., there is enough contrast for the regression program to decide – at least in three of the four cases – that Italian ethnicity was the decisive factor in fronting. The increase in variation explained is therefore only moderate: as the last column of Table 7.19 shows, there is only about 2.5% increase in adjusted $r^2$, and a slight loss for the fourth variable (uwF).

### *Why do Italians lag in the fronting of back vowels?*

Given this clear demonstration that Italians are from 100 to 200 Hz behind other ethnic groups in the fronting of (uw) and (ow), the question must be raised as to whether the use or knowledge of Italian is responsible. It is perfectly true that Italian has a simple back /u/ with no diphthongizing or fronting tendency, and there is no evidence that the local Italian dialects spoken by immigrants to Philadelphia were any different. If the absence of a phonetic [ɪu] or [ü] is responsible for the data of table 7.19, it should have produced the same result in Philadelphians with Irish or Polish backgrounds, but it did not. There is nothing unique, as far as I can see, in the linguistic history of Italian-Americans that would lead them to inhibit the fronting of back nuclei. No clear linguistic explanation for this fact has yet appeared. The lack of a linguistic motivation for this ethnic effect is parallel to the three other cases reviewed above.

## 7.10 The role of neighborhood and ethnicity in linguistic change

The examination of neighborhood and ethnicity has further illuminated the changes in progress in the city of Philadelphia. It is now clear that Wicket, in the oldest settled working class area, is the most advanced neighborhood for almost all of the changes being studied. It is almost as clear that the ethnicity of the speakers has very little effect on the course of change in progress. It remains to ask whether these findings bring us closer to the location of the leaders of linguistic change, or help to formulate the general principles that govern change.

If there is a general principle to be extracted from the study of ethnicity in New York, Boston, Grand Rapids, and Philadelphia, it is a negative one. Despite the fact that ethnicity is logically linked to the differentiation of language behavior through use and knowledge of the immigrant language, it has proved to be weaker and less general in its effects than gender, age, and social class, which have no inherent connection with linguistic differentiation. Whatever ethnic effects are found involve only one or two elements of the linguistic system in process of change. This might follow naturally from the fact that the two linguistic systems are not likely to differ in general, but only at particular structural points. Unfortunately for this argument, and for our sense of achievement as linguists, the ethnic effects are rarely predicted or explained by the direct comparison of the two systems.

The study of neighborhoods does not easily lead to general principles of language change. Unlike gender or social class, neighborhoods are particular products of particular historical events. Can we find some property of Wicket St. that is likely to recur in London or Shanghai? It was mentioned several times that it is the oldest settled of the intact working class areas. It is a general principle of dialect geography that changes in progress reach their most advanced level in the areas where they originated, and less advanced levels in the outlying areas to which they diffuse.[15] It was also shown that Wicket St. is the poorest of the white areas. Even if the chief exponents of the change are drawn from more upwardly mobile

[15] This is the usual way of accounting for the level of the Great Vowel Shift changes in Southern England, displayed in the maps of chapter 17 of volume 1.

segments of the population, they will not themselves be able to reverse the local advantage of the area where the change originated. As yet, the number of studies that have shown geographic differentiation of change within large cities is quite small. The fact that change in progress in Philadelphia is still led by the oldest and poorest neighborhood is not enough to allow us to predict that this will hold true in any large city.

The most general question that the neighborhood data bear upon is whether the present structural uniformity of the Euro-American Philadelphia speech community is the result of city-wide diffusion from an originating center or of some general factor that affects all Philadelphians equally. Chapter 4 examined the extent to which the Philadelphia sound changes are driven by general structural principles or by general regional trends. It was found that the defining Philadelphia features are optional fork-points among structural possibilities that are particular to the city: the configuration of tense and lax short **a**, the retrograde movements of (eyC) and (ay0), the reversal of the glide direction of (aw), and the near-merger of /e/ and /ʌ/ before /r/.

The neighborhood effects found in this chapter point toward diffusion of these features from a local center. It is clear that Philadelphians are differentiated by their residential location in the course of change in progress, even when many other factors are taken into account. It now seems likely that the relative uniformity of the metropolis is the product of diffusion from an originating center rather than a universal influence that simultaneously affected the entire city. The apparent-time pattern indicates diffusion outward from Kensington of the mid-range changes (owC), (owF), (uwC), and the three new and vigorous changes (aw), (eyC), (ay0). The raising and fronting of (æh) is now common to all working class areas, and it is not possible to say if Kensington was the originating center of this variable at an earlier time.

The vocalization of (r) represents a minor current within the Philadelphia system that indicates a similar pattern. A change centered in a particular ethnic group – South Philadelphia Italians – is diffusing throughout the population in its least obtrusive form.

A diffusion of the new and vigorous changes from Kensington creates a problem for the search for the leaders of linguistic change that did not exist before. What is the relationship between the upper working class leaders of sound change located in South Philadelphia and the middle and lower working class speakers in Kensington neighborhoods where the sound changes seem to have originated? This problem will be reconsidered in chapters 10 to 12, which follow the flow of influence in social networks. But before we can consider these issues, we must confront even more puzzling issues of linguistic differentiation by gender.

# 8

# *The Gender Paradox*

The review of the possible and probable causes of linguistic change in chapter 1 highlighted Bloomfield's conclusion that "the causes of sound change are unknown," against the background of his acknowledgment that "every conceivable cause has been alleged." Twentieth-century discussion of the causes of change has been polarized into arguments for autonomous factors, limited to language structure and the act of speaking, or for the pre-eminence of external, social factors.[1] The subdivision into five components by Weinreich, Labov, and Herzog 1968 recognizes the predominance of internal factors in two (the constraints and transition problems), external factors in two (evaluation, actuation), and one which looks both ways (embedding). Yet it is only natural that the majority of linguistic arguments will focus on internal factors, since linguists are well equipped to deal with the structural and articulatory factors of volume 1, and social factors have not shown the same degree of systematicity. Even the objective factors that organize the socioeconomic hierarchy, treated in chapter 5, are looked on with suspicion by many sociolinguists (cf. chapter 2).

When external factors are considered, several strategies minimize the need for a detailed examination. One is to account for the diversification of linguistic behavior through purely mechanical factors like the principle of density, which abstracts from the complexities of social life and requires no study of the social positioning or attitudes of the speakers involved.

If diversification is the product of differential frequencies of acts of communication,[2] then conversely speakers involved in intimate, day-to-day communication will show a corresponding homogeneity. Any case of change in the face of intimate contact would be a counter-example, and lead toward other explanations. One might propose that the stratified variables within a large urban community constitute such a counter-example. Yet the vertical stratification of large speech communities may be the product of differential communication patterns, though no precise data is available

[1] For the autonomous position, one may consider Kurylowicz (1964) and Martinet (1955). For the social position, see Thomason and Kaufman (1988).

[2] See "Linguistic change as a form of communication" (Labov 1974).

to prove it. It is not inconceivable that the spread of (aw), (eyC) through the population is predictable by frequencies of interaction.

The second strategy for reducing the need to examine social factors is the catastrophic view, endorsed by Martinet (1955).[3] The course of sound change is viewed as governed by the internal, structural consequences of a few widely separated disruptions of the social fabric. In recent years, quantitative studies of past and present changes have indeed focused our attention on the importance of external factors: migrations, invasions, and other massive disruptions of the structure of the speech community.[4] One might accept these findings, and yet retain the view that normal linguistic change is entirely determined by internal factors: the principle of least effort; the effects of frequency and analogy; pressures to fill gaps and to maintain symmetry and margins of security; tendencies to maximize simplicity, transparency, and rule application; "natural" re-orderings of constraints. This restriction greatly simplifies the study of language change. A few characteristic speakers at any stage of the language will then provide all the evidence necessary, and there is no need to sample populations or engage in the analysis of social structure.

Gender plays a crucial role in the argument of this volume against such efforts to limit the role of social factors in the explanation of linguistic change. No one can deny that husbands and wives, brothers and sisters, are involved in intimate communication in everyday life. Yet gender is a powerful differentiating factor in almost every case of stable social stratification and change in progress that has been studied.[5]

While the relations of the sexes are often affected by catastrophic changes in the speech community, they are not created and determined by them in the same way that social classes and ethnic groups are. As far as we know, the present relations of the sexes are not the result of any qualitative revolution, nor have we witnessed genocidal programs designed to eliminate one sex or the other. Despite radical changes in the economic position of women in the societies that we will be considering, they remain the major caretakers of children[6] and they remain a secondary status group. The differentiation of the sexes appears to be the result of pervasive social

[3] It is apparently the view held by writers in the generative tradition as well. Chomsky and Halle 1968, for example, take into account the effects of the Norman invasion and the massive influx of Romance vocabulary in changing the basic stress patterns of English.

[4] In the history of English, recent work has documented extraordinary linguistic consequences of such social movements as the Mercian supremacy (Toon 1983), World War II (Labov 1966a), and the migration of Southern blacks to northern cities (Bailey and Maynor 1987).

[5] The chief exceptions have appeared recently in studies of Far Eastern cities: Seoul (Hong 1991, Chae 1995) and Tokyo (Hibiya 1988).

[6] The US Census shows that for the 6,274,000 fathers whose wives were employed, 1,164,000 or 18.5% provided primary care for children under 5. This represents a slight increase over the 1988 figure of 16.9% (Casper 1997).

factors that alter more slowly than other social relations (Brouwer 1989). It follows that sexual differentiation as a social factor must enter into the explanation of ongoing linguistic change as a continuous process.

Everyone agrees that gender is a social factor – language is not differentiated by the biological aspects of sex differences.[7] Yet the attribution of gender is quite simple and straightforward in field work. Although it is agreed that the causal factors involved are the social instantiation of gender roles, and not biological sex, all analyses of gender differentiation begin by dividing the population into males and females, rather than a measure of socially defined degree of masculinity or femininity. Unless there is specific information to the contrary, field workers record gender assignment as a given and obvious social factor, without explicit inquiry into the person's sexuality, and this assignment is presumed to rest upon the subject's biological sex.[8] Given the very general interaction of gender with social class, there can be no doubt that the route by which this categorization affects language is mediated through social factors. Gender effects also take different forms for different types of changes: stable sociolinguistic variables, change from above, or change from below. If gender as a social factor is intimately involved with linguistic change, it is difficult to limit social factors to the mechanical effects of communicative patterns or remote catastrophes, and one is inevitably led to the exploration of other social factors.

This chapter will first present gender differentiation in the Philadelphia speech community as an instantiation of the principles now generally recognized. The following chapter will use the Philadelphia data to resolve the puzzling questions that center about the role of gender in linguistic change. After a consideration of social networks in chapter 10, chapter 11 will resolve these questions.

## 8.1 Gender differentiation of stable sociolinguistic variables in Philadelphia

The stable sociolinguistic variables that were examined in chapter 3 all showed a significant effect of gender. Since the focus of that chapter was on socioeconomic class, the size, significance, and uniformity of the gender effect was not examined directly. Table 8.1 shows that differentiation by gender is a stable and sizeable feature of the sociolinguistic structure of the Philadelphia speech community. *Female* is coded as 1 in the regression

[7] See, however, the arguments advanced by Chambers and by Gordon and Heath below.

[8] Despite the interest shown in recent years in searching for specific features of homosexual speech, reports on gender differences in language continue to report numbers of males and females, rather than "straight males," "gay males," etc.

*Table 8.1* Gender coefficients for stable sociolinguistic variables in the Philadelphia Neighborhood Study, by contextual style

| | *Casual* | *Careful* |
|---|---|---|
| (dh) | −27**** | −27**** |
| (neg) | −14** | −15*** |
| (ing) | −11** | −11** |

**** $p < 0.0001$, *** $p < 0.001$, ** $p < 0.01$

analyses and male, 0. The negative figures therefore indicate that female speakers use nonstandard forms less than male speakers by a factor of 10 to 15 per cent (the (dh) range is 0–200). The coefficients for casual and careful speech are remarkably similar, indicating that it is not merely a special sensitivity of women to the interview situation.

A closer view of gender differentiation of stable variables can be obtained by displaying the mean values for men and women in different social classes and styles in figure 8.1. The first diagram displays the differences in mean (dh) values for men and women for the five social classes for careful speech (solid lines) and casual speech (dashed lines). For all social classes and both sexes, (dh) operates the same way as a stylistic variable: higher values are shown in casual speech than in careful speech. For all but the lowest social class, men use higher values than women.[9] The effect of gender is consistent, but moderate: in general, style is a more powerful factor than gender. The two dotted lines are higher than the two solid lines in all cases but one. The strongest difference between men and women is found in the middle working class; this is the only case where a t-test shows significance for a comparison of gender for a given class and style, at the .05 level for both styles.[10]

The view of (ing) in figure 8.1 is quite different. Gender differences are small but consistent for the two lower groups, who use high values of (ing) throughout. A significant drop is found in the upper working class, where sex differences disappear. Then for the two middle class groups, extreme gender differentiation appears: men use very high values in casual speech, and women use low values of (ing) in both styles. The general picture

[9] The reversal of the pattern in the lowest social class holds for two of the three variables, but it is not significant. This may be due to the fact that the numbers are small: there are only three females in the lower working class group. It is also possible that this displays a general trend for gender differences to be reversed in the lowest social class where women do not have access to generally accepted norms (Nichols 1976).

[10] However, if we set aside the lack of gender differentiation for the lowest class as normal for that class, the combined significance of the class differences for the other four classes is below the .01 level (= twice the sum of the negative logs of the individual probabilities).

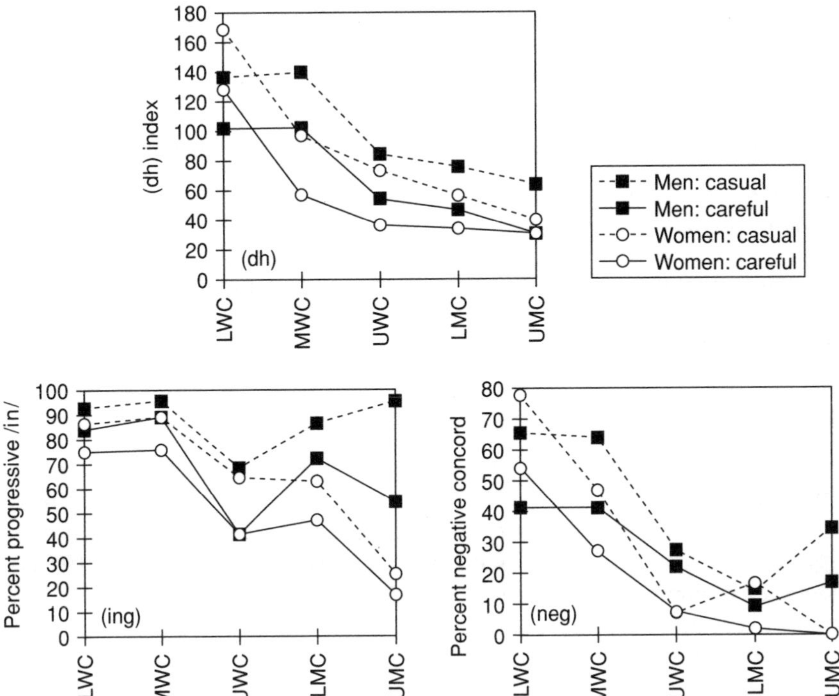


*Figure 8.1* Gender differentiation of three stable sociolinguistic variables by socio-economic class and style in the Philadelphia Neighborhood Study

then is that (ing) is a strong gender marker for the middle class, where the effects are sizeable and significant at the .01 level in casual speech.

Figure 8.1 also shows the expected sharp differentiation in the use of negative concord of the two lower classes from the three higher classes. Again, women use less than men for all but the lower working class. The most extreme differentiation of the sexes is again in the upper middle class, where the effect is at the .01 level in casual speech.[11]

These results show that the behavior of women is far from uniform across the Philadelphia speech community; there is an intimate and complex interaction between style, gender, and social class. At the same time, the great majority of observations fit in with the overall conclusion of table 8.1: that women use a lower level of stigmatized variables than men.

[11] A departure from the sharp social stratification that we expect from (neg) is the relatively high value for upper middle class men in casual speech (35). This may be due to the unusually high degree of rapport established by the interviewer, Arvilla Payne, with the middle class sample in King of Prussia.

## 8.2 The general linguistic conformity of women

Perhaps the broadest and most widely instantiated sociolinguistic generalization concerns the careful behavior of women with stable sociolinguistic variables. It can be stated as *Principle* 2, *the linguistic conformity of women*:

*For stable sociolinguistic variables, women show a lower rate of stigmatized variants and a higher rate of prestige variants than men.*

Evidence for this principle is drawn from a wide range of studies of common variables and a wide range of speech communities, rural and urban, western and non-western.

### *Stable sociolinguistic variables*

One of the most widely studied English variables is (ing), the alternation of [n] and [ŋ] in unstressed /ing/ that we have just examined in Philadelphia. Female speakers were found to use the prestige form [ŋ] more than male speakers in New England (Fischer 1958), New York City (Labov 1966a), Detroit (Wolfram 1969), Norwich (Trudgill 1974b) and many other cities in the British Isles (Houston 1985), Australia (Shopen and Wald 1982, D. and M. Bradley 1979), Ottawa (Woods 1979), Philadelphia (Cofer 1972), and many other areas. In a study of a single Ozark family, Mock 1979 shows teenage children assuming the sexual opposition of their parents for (ing).

The English interdentals /θ, ð/ provide a wide range of evidence for the tendency of female speakers to avoid the nonstandard affricate and stop forms: in New York City (Labov 1966a), Detroit (Shuy, Wolfram, and Riley 1967, Wolfram 1969), North Carolina (Anshen 1969), and Belfast (Milroy and Milroy 1978). Negative concord shows a strong male/female difference, with women using the stigmatized form less than men in New York City (Labov 1966a), Detroit (Shuy, Wolfram, and Riley 1967), Anniston, Alabama (Feagin 1979), and Philadelphia.

In a single study, Wolfram 1969 documented the relatively conservative behavior of African American women in Detroit for nine nonstandard variants: negative concord, (ing), stop forms of *th*, simplification of final *-t,d* clusters, deletion of final apical stops, vocalization of (r), absence of third singular /s/, absence of possessive /s/, and deletion of the copula. The only nonstandard variant where there were insignificant differences between men and women was the use of invariant *be*.[12]

[12] This is an element of AAVE that does not correspond to any particular feature of standard English. The Detroit interviews were comparable to the interviews of the New York City Lower East Side study, carried out by whites in a relatively formal setting, rather than the Harlem or Philadelphia studies in the African American community, and therefore offer the maximum opportunity to observe the differential response of black men and women to a formal situation.

The Montreal study showed the conservative behavior of Québécois women in regard to a number of variables (Thibault 1983). Mougeon and Beniak (1987) on Ontario French speakers showed that women were much less likely than men to borrow core terms such as English *so* (.41 vs. .59) and to use such colloquial conjunctions as *ça fait que* instead of *alors* (.32 vs. .68). Mougeon et al. (1988) found women much less likely to use the nonstandard Québécois auxiliary *je vas* (.26 vs. .39). In all these cases, women reflect the preferred pattern of the highest social class and of formal speech.

In Glasgow, Macaulay found that male school children used the stigmatized vowels of the local dialect more than females (1978). In Spain, Silva-Corvalán 1986 studied the alternation of conditional and imperfect subjunctive in *si*-clauses – the same variable that was the focus of Lavandera in Buenos Aires (1975). Men showed more than twice as high a use of the nonstandard conditional in the sociolinguistically sensitive focus of the variable: the apodosis of counter-factual sentences. Silva-Corvalán 1986 studied pleonastic clitics in Chilean Spanish, and found that men had a higher tendency to use this nonstandard form.

The quantitative study of Copenhagen by Gregersen, Pedersen, and their associates focused on a set of allophones of short /a/ which show a wide phonetic range from [ɛ] to [ɑ˃] (Gregersen and Pedersen 1991). Before apical consonants and finally, the vowel is front for all social classes, but working class speakers are differentiated by their use of back phones before labials, velars, and /j/. For the socially diagnostic allophones there is a sizeable gender difference, with women using forms that are significantly fronter than men's – that is, shifted toward the middle class norms.

Perhaps the most striking differentiation of the sexes was found by Eisikovits (1981), who studied the use of 12 English variables in interviews with high school students in Sydney. Boys had the expected higher use of the nonstandard forms than girls, especially as they grew older. When Eisikovits divided all utterances into those that followed the comment of a peer and those that followed a question of the interviewer, boys showed diametrically opposite patterns of response from girls in six of the seven variables (figure 8.2).

The conservative tendency of women is not limited to urban, industrial, or western societies. Throughout Latin America this pattern appears, in large cities and in isolated rural areas as well: in the Caribbean (Alba 1990, López 1983), and in various countries and languages of South America (Albo 1970). Silva-Corvalán studied the use of pleonastic clitics in the Spanish of Santiago, Chile. This is plainly a lower class phenomenon, since among those with 12 or more years of schooling, there were only 2 uses by 2 individuals. She presents the gender data of table 8.2 for 32 subjects with 3 or fewer years of schooling. The adolescent peak appears only for males. In Philadelphia (dh), the adolescent peak is shared by both males

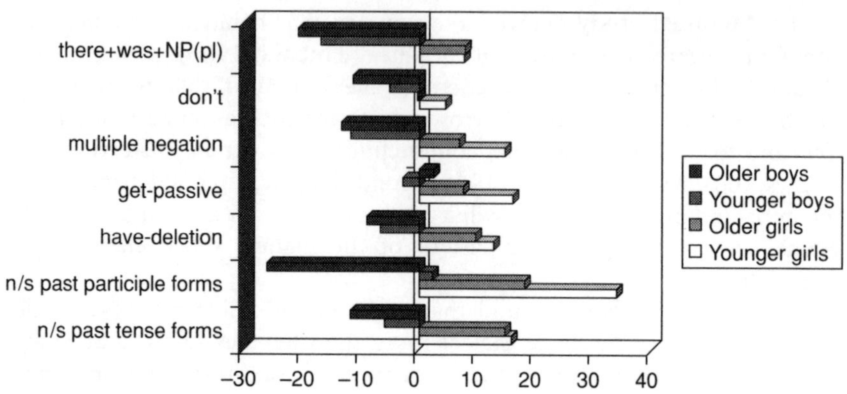


*Figure 8.2* Percent difference between use of the nonstandard variable when previous speaker was a peer or the interviewer, for Sydney high school students by age and gender (adapted from Eisikovits 1981, table 6)

*Table 8.2* Percent pleonastic clitics by age and sex in Santiago, Chile

| | *Age* | | | |
|---|---|---|---|---|
| | *4–6* | *15–17* | *30–45* | *50+* |
| Female | 3 | 4 | 8 | 10 |
| Male | 4 | 32 | 10 | 16 |

Source: Silva-Corvalán 1981

and females, though it is considerably stronger among males, as shown in figure 8.3.

In Bahia Blanca, Argentina, Weinberg (1974) traced the retention and deletion of postvocalic /s/, the subject of the many studies reported in chapters 19 and 20 of volume 1. Figure 8.4 displays the gender differentiation of the retention of /s/, by three styles and three social classes. Gender and style operate in parallel, with about the same weight, but they are not entirely independent. Females in the intermediate status group, Class 3, show a sharper slope of style shifting in reading and careful speech than males do, reaching 88% retention in careful speech and 100% in reading.

In Taiwanese Mandarin, Lin (1988) found that the largest single factor constraining the use of retroflex consonants in careful speech was the sex of the speaker: women moved away from the categorical apical forms of colloquial speech to a preponderant use of retroflexion in formal styles, but men showed a much more moderate style shift. Hong's study of Seoul

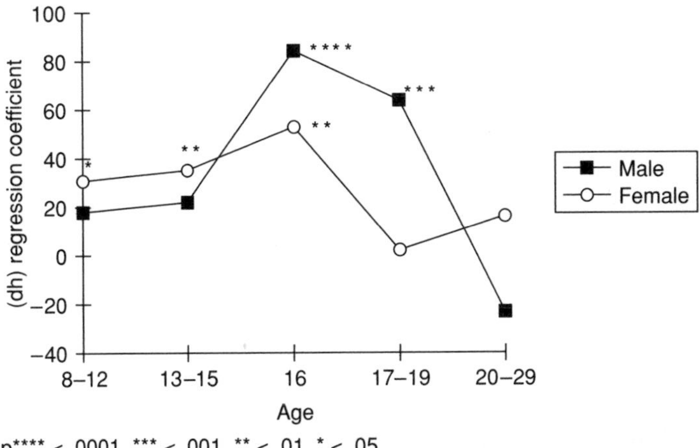


*Figure 8.3* Gender differentiation of adolescent peak in regression coefficients for (dh) in careful speech in the Philadelphia Neighborhood Study

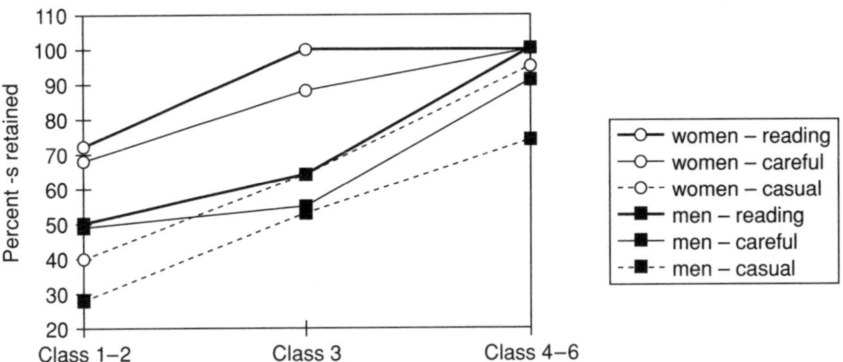


*Figure 8.4* Gender stratification of (s) in Bahia Blanca by social class and style (from Weinberg 1974)

Korean (1991) found that women lagged behind men in the tensing to [l] of initial liquids in English loan words *radio*, *racket*, etc. for all but the lowest social class.

Not all sociolinguistic variables show a sex effect. Morales (1986) found no significant difference in the velarization of /n/ in Puerto Rican Spanish. Gryner and Macedo (1981) did not find a significant sex effect in their study of the palatalization, aspiration, and deletion of non-plural /s/ in Brazilian Portuguese. Hibiya found no significant sex differences for the several Tokyo variables that she studied (1988). But the great majority of the variables studied do show this effect; and until recently there were no cases reported where men appeared to favor the prestige form more than women. A number of such cases appeared in a contiguous area in the Near East and South Asia. Jain 1973 and Gambhir 1981 showed that men are more conservative in their reports of their own speech in India. In Amman, for all social classes, men favored the use of the *qaf* prestige form more than women (Abdel-Jawad 1981); this pattern was replicated in Nablus (Abdel-Jawad 1987). Again, Modaressi 1978 found that in Teheran, women used the local colloquial forms of the variables (an) and (æš) more than men in all social classes. On the other hand, Jahangiri's 1980 study of the same city showed the characteristic female avoidance of stigmatized forms in 12 of the 14 variables studied.[13] Yet in one case, the deletion of glottal stop, women were well ahead of men.[14] Bakir 1986 studied three sociolinguistic variables among speakers of Iraqi Arabic, and found that men used more standard forms in all cases. Figure 8.5a (adapted from Haeri 1996) juxtaposes data from studies by Abdel-Jawad 1981, Schmidt 1986, and Sallam 1980 to indicate the uniformity of this pattern.

There is therefore a widespread reversal of the positions of men and women predicted by Principle 2 in two Muslim-dominated societies. A first guess at explanation is that women may play less of a role in public life in those societies (Labov 1982). But figure 8.5b shows that this reversal is general across educational groups. Furthermore, it is even greater in the highest educational group, where women have more access to public norms. Haeri 1987 and Abdel-Jawad have challenged the existence of a reversal in gender behavior in the Near East, arguing that it is based on an erroneous interpretation of the role of Classical Arabic as comparable to the standard languages of the West. Haeri points out that the closest parallel to such standards is not Classical Arabic but the modern urban forms of Arabic that women do in fact prefer – the glottal stop in place of /q/ in Amman, and the colloquial but prestigious Teheran forms – and that women in those societies actually were behaving like women in other societies. The vast majority of non-/q/ tokens that women use in the studies of figure 8.5 are not the Bedouin form /g/ or the fellahin-favored form /g/, but rather the urban hamza /ʔ/.

For Principle 2 to operate, women must have access to the prestigious norms that it describes. Nichols 1976 reports that African American women on the South Carolina mainland show less tendency to switch from Gullah to English than do their counterparts on a sea island with tourist development.

[13] For the stereotypical raising of /an/ to [un], as in *Teher[un]*, Jahangiri found almost the same values for men and women.

[14] But as Hudson (1995, p.c.) points out, this is the only variable that did not show a clear effect of education, and is therefore not a clear case of a stable sociolinguistic variable.

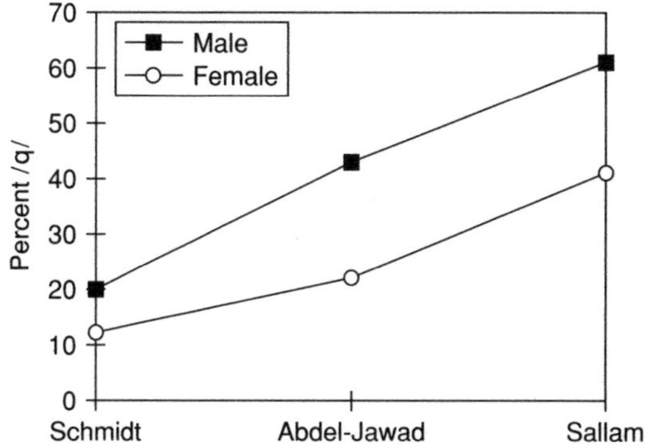


*Figure 8.5a* Use of /q/ by gender in three Arabic studies

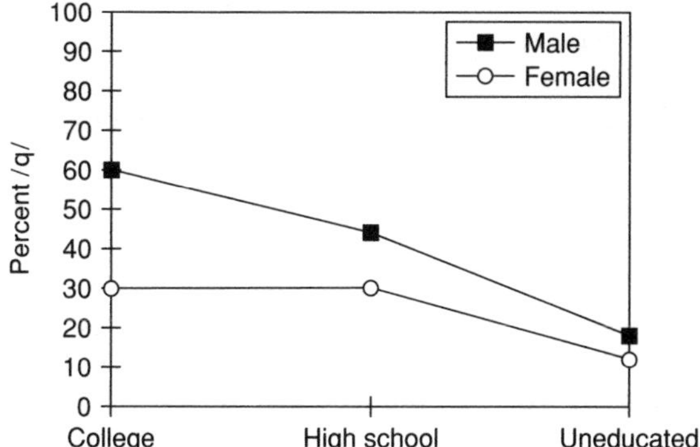


*Figure 8.5b* Use of /q/ by gender and education in Muslim areas

The Philadelphia data of figure 8.1 shows a tendency for women of the lowest social group to use stigmatized variables as much as men. Many studies of speech communities find lower class women who do not participate in the wider system of sociolinguistic norms.[15] It stands to reason that the principle only applies to those who have access to those norms.

Principle 2 is a strong and broad generalization that must be explained by women's social role in the speech community. The cases that depart from the general pattern are from two well-defined cultural areas: the Far East (Tokyo and Seoul) and the Near East.

[15] Silva 1988 suggests that this is the case for the reversal of the traditional backing of /a/ in Sao Miguel Portuguese, although the male predominance for his 12 informants was not statistically significant.

### *The interaction of sex and social class*

Cross-tabulations of stable sociolinguistic variables by sex and social class consistently show strong interactions between these factors, comparable to those that appeared in figures 8.1–8.3 (Labov 1966a, Shuy, Wolfram, and Riley 1967, Wolfram 1969, Anshen 1969, Levine and Crockett 1966).[16] In general, the second highest status group shows the greatest gender differential, along with the highest degree of linguistic insecurity (Labov 1966a) and the sharpest slope of style shifting. The tendency to avoid stigmatized forms and prefer prestige forms is greatest for the women of the lower middle class, and is often minimal for the lower class and upper middle class. Figure 8.6 shows the characteristic pattern of stigmatized forms in the use of negative concord for African American speakers in Detroit (Wolfram 1969). The left-hand side displays the percentage of negative concord used. Here the absolute sex differences between the two intermediate groups are greater than the differences for the two extreme groups. The lower middle class pattern is diagnostic: lower middle class men show higher use of negative concord than their upper middle class counterparts, but lower middle class women use less than upper middle class women. The right-hand side of figure 8.6 charts the ratios of male to female use, where the lower middle class shows a spectacular increment.

Such extreme interaction of sex and social class is characteristic of well-established variables that are widely recognized in the community, and have risen to the level of *stereotypes* that are the subject of public discussion. They show extreme style shifting as well as class stratification. This appears clearly in figure 8.7, drawn from Trudgill's study of (ing) in Norwich. The bold black line for lower middle class women stands out from all the others, with a much sharper slope of style shifting from casual to careful speech.

### *Change from above*

Many reports of linguistic change deal with alterations in the social distribution of well-known linguistic variables. These fall into the general category of *change from above*: they may take the form of the importation of a new

[16] Interactions of this type are rarely shown in the multivariate logistic regression analyses first introduced into sociolinguistic studies in 1974 (Cedergren and Sankoff 1974). As shown above, the assumption of independence which holds quite well for internal factors is not a useful one for external factors, and the custom of adding external factors to a variable rule analysis has probably concealed more than it has revealed. It is not uncommon to find a factor group including *male* and *female* applied to an entire community, as if gender were independent of social class, age, and ethnicity. This practice is in fact an appropriate target of the criticism of earlier sociolinguistic treatments of gender (Eckert and McConnell-Ginet 1992), as opposed to many earlier studies which located in their cross-tabulations the interactions that reflect the social character of gender effects.

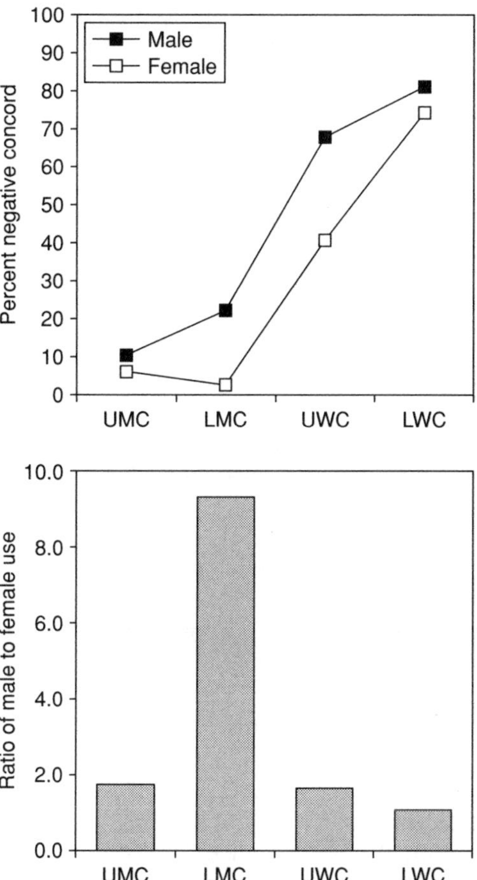


*Figure 8.6* Sexual differentiation of negative concord for African American speakers in Detroit (from Wolfram 1969:162)

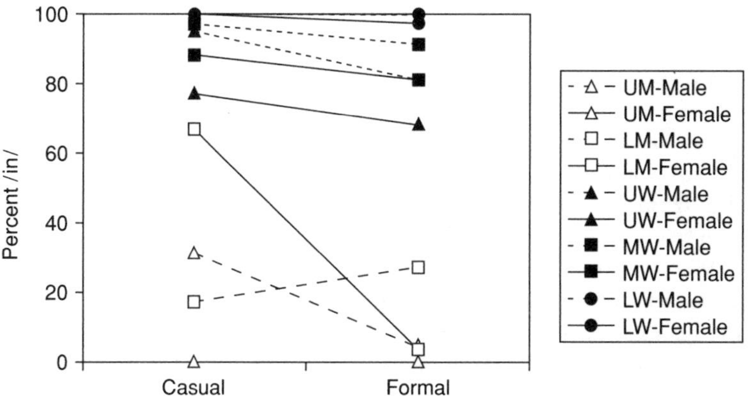


*Figure 8.7* Shifts of style in spontaneous speech by sex and class for (ing) in Norwich (from Trudgill 1974b)

prestige feature from outside the speech community, or the re-distribution of forms with known prestige values within the community. Changes from above take place at a relatively high level of social consciousness, show a higher rate of occurrence in formal styles, are often subject to hypercorrection, and sometimes form overt stereotypes similar to stable sociolinguistic variables. Since changes from above share many of the properties of stable sociolinguistic variables, it is not surprising that the role of the sexes is similar, and women lead in both the acquisition of new prestige patterns and the elimination of stigmatized forms. This is another aspect of the hypercorrect behavior of the second highest status group which may be stated as *Principle 3*.

*In linguistic change from above, women adopt prestige forms at a higher rate than men.*

The adoption of the (r)-pronouncing norm in New York City is led by women (Labov 1966a), and the reversal of the Parisian chain shift is equally a female-dominated change (Lennig 1978). In Belfast, Milroy and Milroy (1978) show that the raising of /ɛ/ from [a] toward [e] in *neck*, *desk*, etc. is strongly favored by women. Urban Belfast women follow behind the more prestigious suburbs in this reversal of the traditional lowering process (p. 352). That it is a change from above is shown by the fact that the more advanced forms are favored in careful speech (p. 357).[17]

Kemp and Yaeger-Dror (1991) show that French-speaking women in Montreal abandon the traditional back pronunciation of [ɑ] in *-ation* more rapidly than men in favor of the continental standard [a]. The abandonment of traditional rural dialects is normally led by women, as in the case of the Spanish village of Ucieda, documented by Holmquist (1987, 1988) for the reversal of the raising of final /o/ to [u]. Clarke reports dialect shifts in Montagnais, an Algonkian language spoken in the village of Sheshatsiu, Labrador (1987). Most of these represented the adoption of the prestigious Southwestern dialect, and where gender differences did appear (5 out of 10 cases), women were in the lead. It can be seen that sensitivity of women to prestige forms extends to societies that are not overtly stratified.

Shifts from one language to another are conscious shifts and are always changes from above, as in the shift from Hungarian to German studied by Gal (1978, 1980). Language shifts, like dialect re-distributions, are often tightly tied to economic factors. The predominance of women therefore cannot be expected to hold when the language is associated with work situations open only to males, as in the case of Papua New Guinea: here

[17] While in contrast, the backing of /a/, a new vernacular tendency, is led by men, and favored in the least monitored styles (see below).

census reports show that twice as many males as females acquire the use of the national languages English, Tok Pisin, and Hiri Motu (Sankoff 1980:123, table 5–2).

The interaction of sex and social class that was found for stable sociolinguistic variables is even more characteristic of changes from above. In such cases, we frequently find that members of the second highest status group surpass the level set by the highest status group, producing the "cross-over pattern" first seen in the importation of constricted (r) in New York City. Though both men and women of the second highest group display this pattern, it is more extreme for women than for their male counterparts.

### *Interpreting the careful behavior of women*

If the purpose of studying gender differentiation is to apply this knowledge to understanding the causes of linguistic change, it seems only natural to ask why women follow Principles 2, 3, and 4. Here we enter a difficult area. We have advanced so far on the basis of observation and experiment, seeking to build a linguistic science on the most solid foundations. The findings form a clear and detailed quantitative pattern that is replicated throughout the world in a way that cannot be accidental. However, the social interpretation of gender differentiation inevitably engages speculation on attitudes and motivations, cultures and ideologies, where a linguist is no better able to resolve the alternatives than anyone else. We cannot refuse the invitation to respond to the question, "why do women behave as they do?" Yet it is important to distinguish the uncertain character of the answers from the high degree of confidence in the knowledge generated so far. Below I will sketch the several competing explanations, and indicate what sociolinguistic data is relevant to each. The important result to follow is that none of these explanations bear on the behavior of women in the main topic of concern of this volume, linguistic change from below.

One of the first interpretations advanced for the greater linguistic conformity of women was based upon the power and status differential between the sexes. In their review of male–female language differences, Wolfram and Schilling-Estes (1998) emphasize the concept that women have less economic power than men and therefore rely more on symbolic capital (pp. 194–6). If this hypothesis could be clearly demonstrated in quantitative terms – the less economic power, the more conformity – it could form part of the cumulative knowledge structure that we are trying to build in the study of language change and variation. This interpretation finds support in the many findings that show women's adherence to prestige norms outpacing their actual control of speech production. Women show higher scores in tests of Linguistic Insecurity (Labov 1966a, Owens and Baker

1984), and in Self-Report, over-reporting their use of the prestige norm (Labov 1966a, Trudgill 1972). The careful sociolinguistic behavior of women is therefore seen as a reflection of socioeconomic weakness, and of a psychological as well as sociological insecurity.[18]

If sociolinguistic conformity is the result of the power differential of the sexes, the greatest gender differentiation of language should be in that social group that shows the greatest differentiation of economic power. Principle 3 points to the second highest status group, the lower middle class, as the group in question. Yet in our Philadelphia study at least, this is the group in which power differences between men and women are minimal. Many lower middle class women have advanced more rapidly in white-collar positions than their husbands who hold skilled blue-collar jobs.

Chambers (1995) has developed an opposing argument which takes a positive view of the linguistic conformity of women, interpreting their wider range of style shifting as the product of their superior linguistic skills.

> It is plausible to speculate that . . . the neuropsychological verbal advantage of females results in sociolinguistic discrepancies such that women use a larger repertoire of variants and command a wider range of styles than men of the same social groups even though gender roles are similar or identical. (pp. 136–7)

Chambers reviews the data in the psychological literature to show that in a wide variety of tests of linguistic abilities, women have a small but significant advantage over men, and argues that this is the source of their ability to use higher rates of prestige features and lower rates of stigmatized features. In other words, women are more able to do what all people say they should do.

Chambers is clear on the fact that this is a very small but significant effect. He contends that it is of biological rather than social origin, and couples it with reports that men show greater incidence of verbal disorders (Kimura 1983). Yet a closer examination of the literature indicates that these effects are of social origin, rather than biological. His principal source, Maccoby and Jacklin 1974, gives few details on linguistic behavior, but their summary contains three overall conclusions: (1) the female advantage

[18] A very different view is advanced by Gordon (1997): that women's avoidance of stigmatized speech patterns is the result of social conventions associating those patterns with sexual looseness. Her subjective reaction tests, administered to private school students and trainee teachers, measured middle class evaluations of three constructed personalities, associating cultivated, general, and broad New Zealand speech with photographs of the same person wearing clothes judged appropriate to "upper middle class, middle class, and lower class" young women. The "lower class" construct was almost unanimously judged as the most likely person to sleep around.

reported in early studies of first language learning (1 to 3 years) has become less evident with time; (2) there is no evidence of a female advantage from 3 to 11 years;[19] and (3) clear evidence of female superiority begins with school test scores at the age of 11.

Sherman 1978 devotes an entire volume to the thesis that sex-related differences in verbal skill are culture-bound. Hoyenga and Hoyenga 1993 point out the cultural malleability of the phenomenon in that the size of the sex differences has been decreasing over the years, and when the verbal portion of the Scholastic Aptitude Test was changed in 1972, males began to achieve higher scores than females.

The very small size of the female advantage in test scores (accounting for less than 1% of the variance in large-scale tests: Sherman 1978:43) makes it difficult to see how it could produce the very large differences between men and women cited above. It might be effective if we were dealing with a slowly incrementing, evolutionary change, where each generation passes on its advantage to the next. But if the Chambers argument is to explain the synchronic patterns of gender differentiation, the biological advantage would have to produce these large effects independently in each generation.

A further difficulty for attributing female conformity to greater verbal abilities is that it predicts that women would be more accurate observers and reporters of their own speech than men. If sensitivity to linguistic symbols and the ability to manipulate them is responsible for higher linguistic conformity among women, this would require a more accurate perception of the behavior to be modified as well as the target to be reached. But this is not the case. As noted above, women over-report their use of the prestige norm much more than men, and in most cases, men are more accurate self-reporters than women.[20] It seems hard to avoid the conclusion that women's linguistic conformity is primarily a social, not a biological, phenomenon.

In returning to the social aspect of linguistic conformity, we might put into question the concepts of weakness, uncertainty, and embarrassment that are associated with insecurity and hypercorrection. In re-thinking the concept of "linguistic insecurity," I would suggest that it may be regarded as an aspect of social mobility rather than social insecurity. The "Index of Linguistic Insecurity" is actually a measure of the subject's recognition of an exterior standard of correctness. In the history of English, the creation of such a standard was in part a product of the upward social mobility of

[19] ". . . let us simply note that for large unselected populations the situation seems to be one of very little sex difference in verbal skills from about 3 to 11."

[20] But as exceptions to this statement, note that men over-reported their use of the local norm in Trudgill's studies of Norwich (1972) and that men over-reported their use of the prestige norm in Jain's work in India (1973).

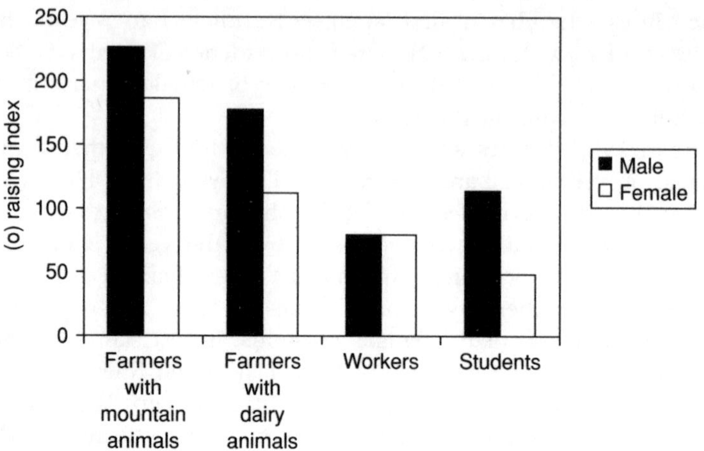


*Figure 8.8* Replacement of local norm of /o/ raising in Ucieda by sex and occupational type (from Holmquist 1985)

the merchant class (Leonard 1929).[21] It is possible to interpret the linguistic conformity of women as a reflection of their greater assumption of responsibility for the upward mobility of their children – or at least of preparing the symbolic capital necessary for that mobility.

A striking example of women's response to economic motivation appears in the ethnographically sophisticated study of change from above by Holmquist in the Spanish village of Ucieda (1988). The recessive rural dialect of Ucieda is marked by a raising of final /o/ to [u]. The younger the speaker, the less the use of [u], and women lead in this retreat by a sizeable margin. Holmquist also shows that women have a strong preference for factory jobs in the town, while many men would rather work economically marginal farms in the mountains. The more extreme form of this rural agricultural pattern uses a specially adapted type of mountain animal, while more modern farmers have shifted to dairy farming. Figure 8.8 shows that the incoming [o] form is highly correlated with gender and with the shift from farm to factory work. It also appears that the gender effect disappears among factory workers. This finding suggests

[21] In reviewing the motivations for the 18th-century development of the doctrine of correctness, Leonard makes it plain that the main emphasis was on improving the standards of speech used by gentlemen, and only a few (Buchanan, Ash, Coote, Withers) wrote for the edification of people engaged in trade (Leonard 1929:169). But it was also true that the linguistic "battle of élites" was fought most hotly by persons who had had to earn and prove their gentility. This type of upward mobility is exemplified by Robert Baker, author of the much discussed *Reflections on the English Language . . .* (1770), who admits that "he had had only six years of schooling, no greek, and only Latin enough to forget" (Leonard 1929:174).

that the linguistic conformity of women can represent a direct adaptation to economic and social conditions, as in Gal's study of language shift, and is not necessarily mediated through the search for advantages for one's children.

One might therefore think that gender differentiation as we see it here will begin to disappear as women enter the work force. However, the normal difference between men and women appeared in a study of the New York Lower East Side that focused only on people active in the work force. For the stable sociolinguistic variable (th), 13 working women showed a mean value of 19.4 and 28 working men showed a mean value of 42 (Labov 1966a: figure 15, chapter 8). A study of men and women in Amsterdam by Brouwer (1989) was designed to test this issue directly, contrasting the use of broad Dutch vowels by women who were working as compared to those who remained as housewives. It was expected that working women would shift toward the vernacular norm which was more heavily used by men. No such effect appeared: there was no significant difference between the two groups of women. This implies that changes in the occupations and lifestyles of women may not result in immediate changes in linguistic behavior. We are then dealing with a long-standing cultural pattern, an objective social fact, that is not the result of the response of each individual to the current situation.

## 8.3 Gender differentiation of changes from below

The discussion so far has provided only the preliminary background to the investigation of the role of gender in linguistic change. The main focus of this volume is on *changes from below*, that is, the primary form of linguistic change that operates within the system, below the level of social awareness. These include the systematic sound changes that make up the major mechanism of linguistic change.

### *The major tendency: women in advance*

The earliest accountable report of linguistic change in progress was that of Gauchat (1905), who showed that in the Swiss French village of Charmey, women were at least one generation ahead of men in the diphthongization of (a:) and (e:) and the monophthongization of (a$^{o}$). Hermann revisited Charmey in 1929 and found that these changes had gone to completion except for diphthongization before /r/. Table 8.3 shows that for those variables that continued to show progress, women were in the lead. On the other hand, the aspiration of /θ/ in pronouns proved to be a stable sociolinguistic marker at the same level as at the turn of the century, and here the differences were slight.

*Table 8.3* Gender differentiation of three variables in Charmey in 1929 (Source: Hermann 1929)

| | *Men (n = 21)* | *Women (n = 19)* |
|---|---|---|
| Changes in progress | (%) | (%) |
| /o/ → a° before /r/ | 58 | 70 |
| /e/ → $e^i$ before /r/ | 33 | 69 |
| No change in progress | | |
| /θ/ → h in -tu | 80 | 86 |

Women have been found to be in advance of men in most of the linguistic changes in progress studied by quantitative means in the past several decades: in New York City, the raising of (æh) and (oh) (Labov 1966a), as well as the backing of (ah) and the fronting of (aw); the backing of (el) in Norwich (Trudgill 1974b); and the lenition of (č) in Panama City (Cedergren 1973). The earliest report of the Northern Cities Shift was Fasold 1969, who examined the fronting of (æh), (o), and (oh) by 12 men and 12 women in the Detroit survey. He found that women were leading in all three cases. Eckert's study of the Northern Cities Shift among high school students in Livonia, a suburb of Detroit, found girls leading boys for the same three variables (1986).[22] Luthin 1987 shows that women lead men by a considerable margin in the new fronting of /ow/ in the Berkeley area; similar observations have been made throughout the West Coast.

There are fewer data available on the progression of the Southern Shift than the Northern Cities Shift, but the evidence we have indicates that women are leading. In a study of nine members of an Ozark family, Mock (1979) shows the clear advance of the younger females in the lowering and backing of the nucleus of /ey/.[23]

In the Southern and Western United States, some of the most active sound changes involve the laxing of vowels before /l/, yielding homonymy of *steel* and *still*, *sail* and *sell*, *fool* and *full*. Nicholas (n.d.) traced the laxing of /ey/ in the Appalachian dialect of Jackson County, North Carolina, and found that women were clearly in the lead. Di Paolo (1988) found similar results for all three vowels in her Intermountain Survey of Salt Lake City, Utah. Adolescents were the chief exponents of the change in pronunciation, and girls led boys: 53% to 0% for (iyl), 60% to 7% for (eyl), 47% to 20% for (uw). The research group headed by Guy Bailey at Texas A&M

[22] The female advantage does not extend to two other elements of the Northern Cities shift, however: the backing of (e) and (U).

[23] The same family that registered the conservative behavior of females in respect to (ing) (Mock 1979).

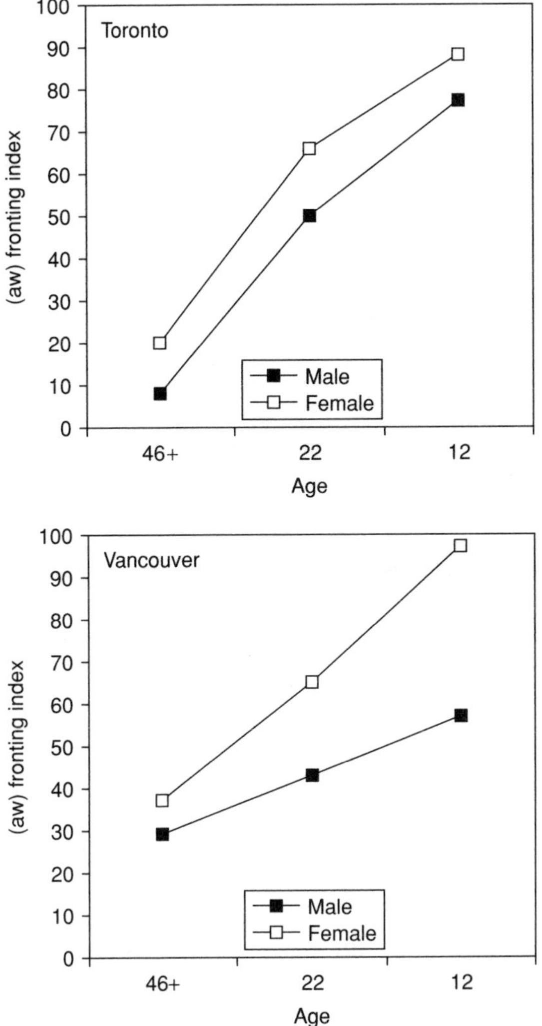


*Figure 8.9* Fronting of (aw) by age and sex in two Canadian cities (from Chambers and Hardwick 1985)

has found similar predominance of females for the laxing of (iyl) (Bailey et al. 1991).

In Canada, Chambers and Hardwick (1985) traced the development of a new norm for (aw), a fronting that is first added to and then substituted for the traditional centralization before voiceless finals. Women are the leaders in both Toronto and Vancouver, as figure 8.9 shows. On the other hand, young men in Toronto show a tendency in the opposite direction, to use a back rounded nucleus for this diphthong.

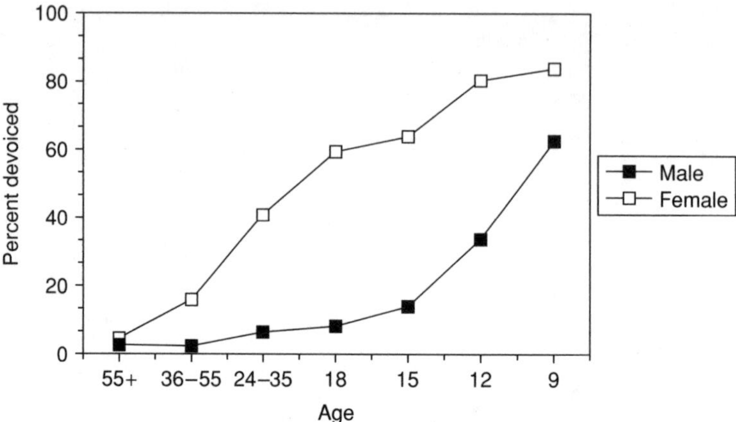


*Figure 8.10* Devoicing of /ž/ in Buenos Aires by sex and age (from Wolf and Jiménez 1979, table 5; n = 12,898)

Of the many studies of social variation in Latin American Spanish, only a few have found sound change in progress. Cedergren's research in Panama City (1973) found a regular increase in the lenition of (č) in younger age groups, and women favoring the change more than men. One of the most extensive studies of change in Spanish is the investigation of the devoicing of /ž/ in Buenos Aires by Wolf and Jiménez (1979). Through studies of adults and high school students across social classes, they found a strong shift toward the devoiced variable in younger age groups; figure 8.10 shows some of the evidence that led them to the conclusion that "females are the leaders in the spreading of the change and they are almost a whole generation farther along" (p. 16).[24] This is indeed a change from below: there is no overt social reaction to the change in Buenos Aires and there was no stylistic shift when the most formal styles were compared with interview style, casual style, and candid recording.

In Hong Kong, Bauer 1982 traced the development of syllabic /m/ for syllabic /ŋ/ in the local dialect of Cantonese: the change was initiated by women in the 30–40 age range. In the next generation, most teenage males adopted the change categorically, and surpassed the level of most women.

Chae 1995 is a study of the raising of /o/ in Seoul Korean from [o] to [u], a long-standing historical process that has gone to completion in stressed syllables, but is now affecting non-initial unstressed syllables,

[24] These conclusions were based on studies across five or six years of 36 college-educated adults, 12 lower class adults, and 240 high school students from 9 to 18 years old. They were verified by a separate analysis of 90 speakers from the sample of Lavandera 1975.

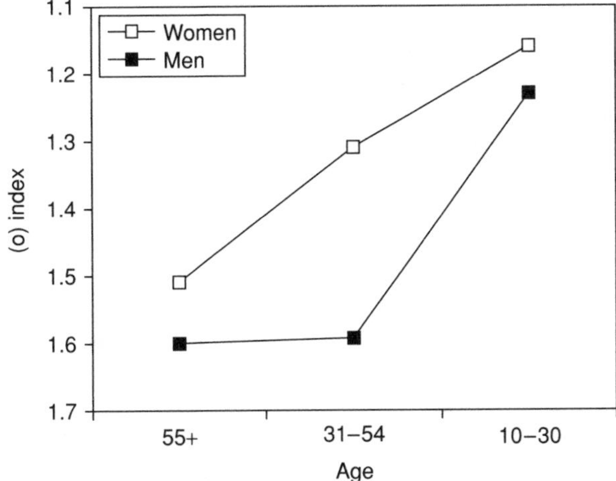


*Figure 8.11* The raising of (o) in Seoul Korean, by gender and age (from Chae 1995)

concentrated in a number of grammatical morphemes. Figure 8.11 shows that women are a full generation ahead of men in the raising process, which was accelerated in the age group 31 to 54 years. This gender difference is constant in five contextual styles, from narrative to the reading of individual sentences, and holds for four social classes.[25]

Chapter 5 presented Haeri's data on the social distribution of the new and vigorous change in progress in Cairo Arabic, the palatalization of /t/ and /d/ (figure 5.17). We can now add the fact that women are well ahead of men in this process in both strong and weak palatalization. Figure 8.12 shows the progress of strong palatalization in Cairo by gender for three age groups. Men are far behind women, and have not yet begun to accelerate in this process.

The various changes in progress reviewed here show a consistent majority pattern of women leading men. Depending on the stage of the change within the purview of the investigators, we see females diverging from males, as in Vancouver; females advancing ahead and in parallel with males, as in Toronto; or males converging with the advanced position of females, as in Buenos Aires and Hong Kong. In none of these cases do we see the creation of stable sex differentiation. Rather, the mechanism of the change crucially involves the initiating role of women at the outset, and the later adoption of the change by men.

[25] Though here the slope of style shifting is least for the "lower middle class," suggesting a different class configuration from the western communities. The leading social class in this change is the lowest of the four studied by Chae.

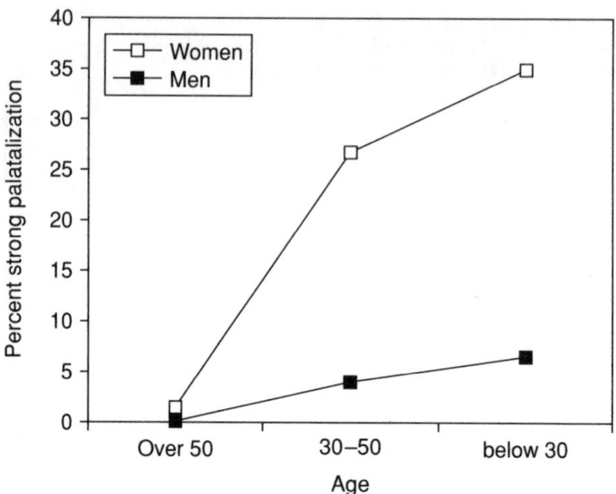


*Figure 8.12* Distribution of strong palatalization in Cairo Arabic, by age and gender (from Haeri 1996, graph 1)

### *The minor tendency: men in advance*

For a smaller number of changes in progress, men have been found to be in advance of women. On Martha's Vineyard, the centralization of (ay) and (aw) was led by men (Labov 1963). As we will see below, a similar shift of (ay) before voiceless finals in Philadelphia is also dominated by men. In Norwich, Trudgill found that the unrounding of (o) was a male-dominated change. In Belfast, Milroy and Milroy 1978 found the reverse process: the backing and rounding of /a/ is strongly dominated by men.

The mechanism of change is therefore not linked to sex differences in any clear and simple way. Either sex can be the dominant factor. But the cases where men are in the lead form a small minority. Furthermore, the male-dominated changes are all relatively isolated shifts. They do not include chain shifts that rotate the sound system as a whole: all such chain shifts examined so far are dominated by women.

### *Gender differentiation of the Northern Cities Shift*

So far, the view of the behavior of men and women has been based on a sizeable number of cases, but scattered across the few communities that have been selected for a sociolinguistic study, for one reason or another. The *Atlas of North American English* offers a more systematic basis for such an assessment, since it is designed to show the current state of all of the active sound changes in the United States and Canada. The data is the product of a telephone survey [Telsur] that samples the urbanized areas of

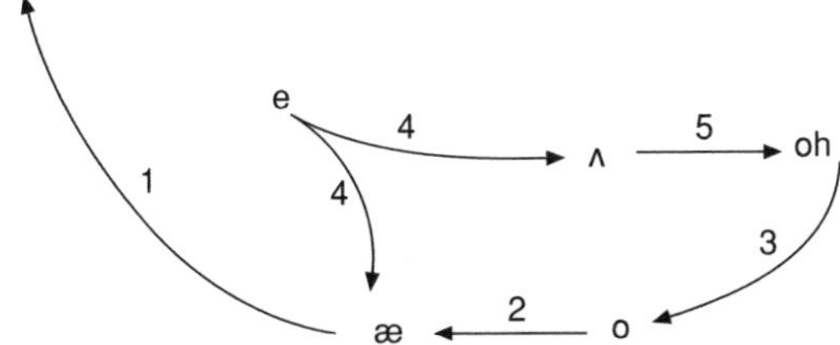


*Figure 8.13* The Northern Cities Shift

the continent on the basis of both population and geography. On the basis of this data, Labov, Ash, and Boberg (in press) define the dialect areas of the United States, and draw the boundaries of the Inland North, the region that contains and is defined by the Northern Cities Shift (NCS; see chapter 6 of volume 1). The southern limit of this region is determined by an isogloss extending the lexical division between the North and the North Midland in Pennsylvania, reflected in the distribution of North and North Midland words in data from the dictionary of *American Regional Dialects* (Carver 1987). The eastern boundary is the Hudson Valley, the northern boundary is Canada, and the western boundary extends westward to southeastern Wisconsin. It should be noted that the NCS is an urban phenomenon, following the cascade model of diffusion which proceeds from the largest cities to the next largest city and so on downwards (Trudgill 1974a, Callary 1975). The Inland North contains many of the largest cities of the United States: Chicago, Detroit, Cleveland, Buffalo, and Rochester.

The NCS is a revolutionary shift of the short vowels of English, which have been otherwise relatively stable for over a thousand years. It is a set of five new and vigorous changes that are intimately linked in the functional economy of a chain shift, and it offers a good opportunity to examine the gender differentiation of change from below. Its main course may be sketched as five steps affecting the positions of five short vowels.

### *Social differentiation of the NCS in Detroit*

The early stages of the NCS were first noted by Fasold, in an unpublished paper analyzing results of the Shuy, Wolfram, and Riley study of Detroit (1967). Impressionistic ratings were used to divide all tokens into cases of (æ) which were raised, and cases of (o) which were fronted. The results show (1) that women are very much in the lead, and (2) that women display a curvilinear pattern in the social class dimension, but men do not.

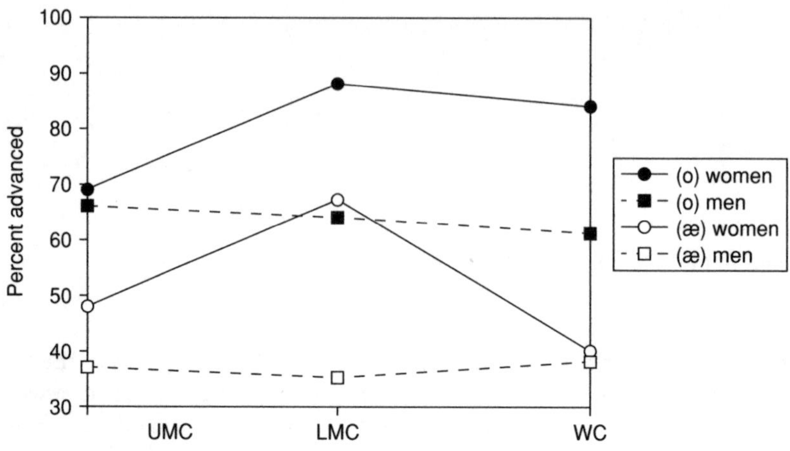


*Figure 8.14* Two stages in the Northern Cities Shift in Detroit, by class and gender (adapted from Fasold 1969)

## *Gender data in the* Atlas of North American English

Although the *Atlas of North American English* [*ANAE*] is designed to study spatial diffusion rather than social variation, it provides ample contrast of male and female subjects. At least two local subjects are drawn from each speech community, including one woman between the ages of 20 and 40. Acoustic analysis was carried out on the vowel systems of 56 speakers in the Inland North. These measured vowel systems are normalized with a set of 180 other speakers, using the logmean method discussed in chapter 5.

Table 8.4 shows the gender differentiation of the NCS in the coefficients of a regression analysis where the independent variables were gender, population size, and percent African American in the urbanized areas. In almost all cases, gender was the strongest factor or the only significant factor in the advance of the sound change.

In Detroit, Eckert (1988, 1999) found significant advantage for high school girls in the three oldest stages of the shift (1, 2, 3), but not for the most recent stages (4, 5), where membership in the Jock/Burnout social categories was a significant factor. The broader results in table 8.4 are generally consistent with her findings, with two exceptions: there is no significant gender influence on the fronting of /o/, and there is a female advantage in both the backing and the lowering of /e/.

An overall view of the progress of the NCS can be obtained by principal components analysis, which will organize the individual formant shifts in a smaller set of dimensions. Figure 8.15 shows the results of such an

*Table 8.4* Gender coefficients in the regression analysis of 56 speakers in the Inland North for elements of the Northern Cities Shift

| Step | | Sex coefficient favors | | |
|---|---|---|---|---|
| | | *Female* | *Male* | *p* < |
| 1 | Raising of /æ/ | **–48** | | 0.01 |
| 1 | Fronting of /æ/ | **48** | | 0.05 |
| 2 | Fronting of /o/ | | | |
| 3 | Lowering of /oh/ | | | |
| 4 | Backing of /e/ | **–84** | | 0.01 |
| 4 | Lowering of /e/ | **40** | | 0.0001 |
| 5 | Backing of /ʌ/ | | | |

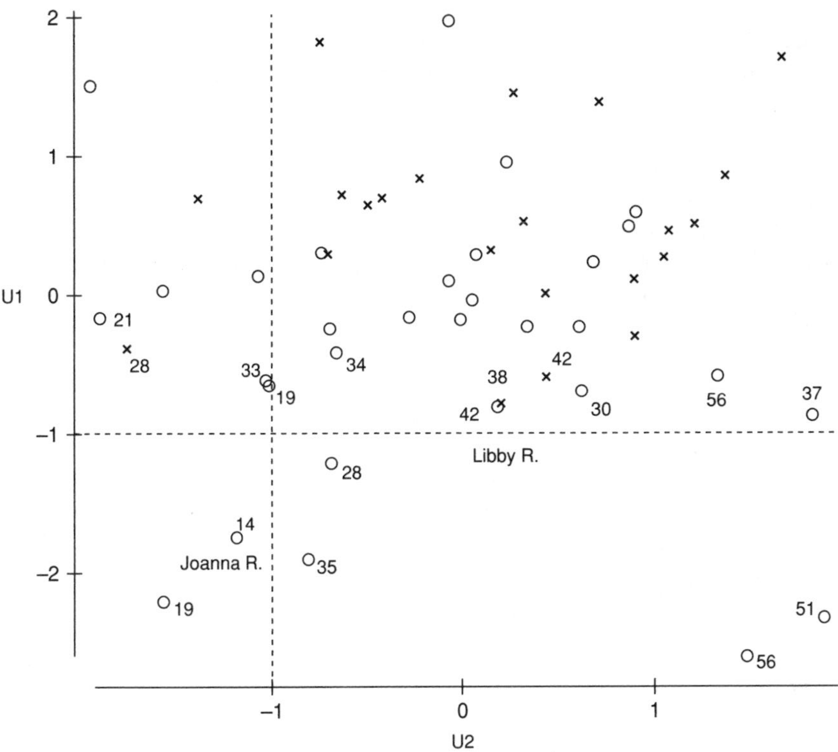


*Figure 8.15* Scatterplot of the two first principal components in an analysis of 56 speakers in the Inland North, using F1 and F2 of /e/, F1 and F2 of /æ/, F2 of /o/, F2 of /ʌ/, F1 and F2 of /oh/. Crosses represent male speakers; circles, female. Numbers are speakers' ages

analysis utilizing F1 and F2 of /e/, F1 and F2 of /æ/, F2 of /o/, F2 of /ʌ/, F1 and F2 of /oh/. The two dimensions, U1 and U2, are the first two components, which account for 33% and 22% of the variance respectively. Each symbol indicates the U1 and U2 values of a given speaker from the Inland North: women are shown by circles, men by x's. The numbers in the lower third of the diagram represent the ages of the speakers.

Principal components can be difficult to interpret, but displays like figure 8.15 are transparent. The U1 dimension is plainly correlated with progress of the NCS. The four circles at the bottom left of the diagram are the leading exponents of the NCS in the Telsur data, and are often used to exemplify the most advanced vowel systems. It is no accident that U1 is also correlated with gender: circles are heavily concentrated in the upper third, and x's in the lower third. At lower right is the youngest and most brilliant exponent of the NCS, 14-year-old Joanna R. of Detroit. The age sequence of these advanced speakers strongly suggests that the U2 dimension reflects increasing age of the speaker. Libby R., 42, is Joanna R.'s mother: she is located just where this interpretation of U1 and U2 would place her.

The relations of U1 and U2 to age are shown in figure 8.16. The left-hand side plots U1 against age of the speaker. Our primary concern here is with gender; partial regression lines are accordingly shown for men and women. The line for women is practically flat, and the line for men shows a small upward slope. U1 is plainly correlated with gender. The six speakers with U1 values lower than –1 are all women. The right-hand side of figure 8.16 shows a very strong inverse correlation of U2 with age of women, but a weak direct effect for men. It is clear that women are the leaders of linguistic change in the Inland North. For the NCS as a whole, women are in advance of men.

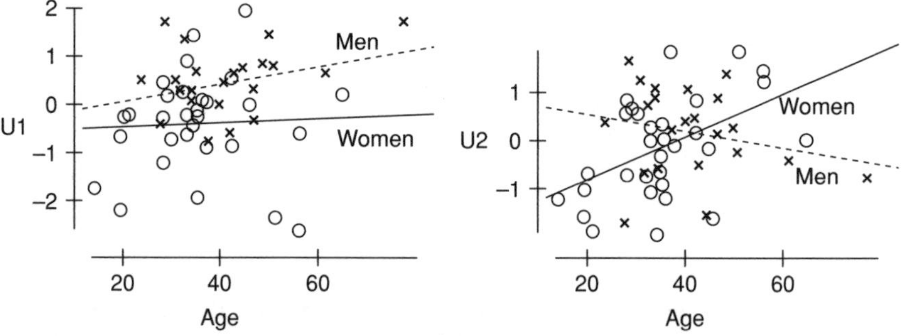


*Figure 8.16* Scatterplots of U1 and U2 against age from the principal components analysis of figure 8.15. Crosses represent male speakers; circles, female

*Table 8.5* Sex coefficients for Philadelphia sound changes

| *Variable* | *Female-dominated* | *Male-dominated* |
|---|---|---|
| COMPLETED | | |
| Backing of (ahr) | 43* | |
| ALMOST COMPLETED | | |
| Fronting of (æhN) | 50* | |
| Fronting of (æhS) | 31 | |
| Fronting of (æhD) | 97** | |
| Raising of (ohr) | | 17* |
| MID-RANGE | | |
| Fronting of (uwF) | | |
| Fronting of (uwC) | 76 | |
| Fronting of (owF) | 46 | |
| Fronting of (owC) | 60* | |
| NEW AND VIGOROUS | | |
| Fronting of (aw) | 89** | |
| Fronting of (eyC) | 49* | |
| Raising of (ay0) | | 36** |
| INCIPIENT | | |
| Lowering of (i) | | |
| Lowering of (e) | 16 | |
| Lowering of (æ) | 35* | |
| Raising of (ʌ) | | 29* |

xx = $p < 0.10$, xx* = $p < 0.05$, xx** = $p < 0.01$

## *Gender differentiation in Philadelphia*

With this background, let us now examine the situation in Philadelphia, where a much richer body of social information is available to examine the social location of the leaders of linguistic change.

Table 8.5 shows the gender coefficients for the Philadelphia variables involved in change in progress, which were first introduced in chapter 3 of volume 1. The sign of the numbers is adjusted so that for each gender, positive values indicate a shift in the direction of the change. Since female vs. male is always 1 vs. 0, the gender coefficient corresponds to the actual size of the differential in Hz.

The figures shown without asterisks are of questionable significance, where p is greater than .05 but less than .10. They conform to the overall pattern of the table, where the coefficient indicates that, all other things being equal, females show more advanced forms of the changes for all but the raising of /ohr/ and the centralization of /ay0/. The centralization of /ʌ/ appears to be linked to the latter, as they represent parallel shifts of the same nucleus.

The completed change of /ahr/ shows a residual female advantage in backing. We might expect this to be replicated in the backing of /ohr/ as it advances slowly in a merger with /uhr/, since this process is linked with /ahr/ in a chain shift. But the only sexual differentiation of /ohr/ is found in the F1 dimension.

Among the nearly completed changes, all three allophones of /æh/ are listed, and all three show a female advantage, significant in two of the three cases. The gender differentiation here is the inverse of social correction of an established sociolinguistic variable. Though the raising of /æh/ is corrected far less in Philadelphia than in New York City, some Philadelphians follow the same steep slope of correction in formal styles. Women then display the most advanced forms of a stigmatized variable in their casual speech, and the least advanced forms in their pronunciation of word lists and minimal pairs.

The mid-range changes – the fronting of /uw/ and /ow/ – show a consistent female advantage, except for the most advanced form which was also apparently the earliest: (uwF).[26] The most significant female advantage is found for the least advanced and latest of these changes, (uwC). This suggests that the female advantage in the fronting of these vowels will disappear as the changes reach completion with fully fronted, nonperipheral nuclei.

The strongest female advantage appears in one of the new and vigorous changes, (aw), and it appears quite strongly in another, (eyC). But the third of these, (ay0), shows a significant effect of male domination. There is also a certain amount of parallelism with the development of /aw/ in Canada shown in figure 8.9 (Chambers and Hardwick 1985). Women in Vancouver and Toronto favor the fronting of the nucleus, and the reversal of traditional centralization, which is accordingly stronger among men. Chambers and Hardwick also found a new phonetic development among younger Toronto males: a phonetic backing and rounding of the nucleus to [ɔʊ]. Backing is also the dominant direction for Philadelphia (ay0), though the only gender differentiation is found in the F1 dimension.

### *General explanations for the leadership of women*

Once it is recognized that women are generally in advance of men in the development of linguistic change, we are impelled again to search for some accounting – this time, for a unified explanation of gender differentiation in both stable and unstable situations.

[26] The absence of a significant age coefficient in chapter 5 and other social constraints in chapter 7 are consistent with the absence of a significant gender coefficient here. (uwF) has most of the attributes of a completed change, though chapter 9 will show that some age and gender differentiation remains.

One way of presenting a unified account is to argue that both conservative and innovative behaviors reflect women's superior sensitivity to the social evaluation of language. In stable situations, women perceive and react to prestige or stigma more strongly than men do, and when change begins, women are quicker and more forceful in employing the new social symbolism, whatever it might be. Unfortunately, such an explanation is little more than a restatement of the observed facts. Furthermore, it assigns social sensitivity to early stages of change that are remote from levels of social awareness.

In the preceding section, we considered the more substantive argument of Chambers 1995 that the conformity of women is the result of women's superiority to men in all aspects of verbal behavior. The available evidence does point to a small but significant advantage of women in verbal test scores. Though such an advantage might be too small to explain the large differences in response to prestige and stigmatized markers, it might apply to linguistic change in progress. If the female advantage has a biological basis, no matter how small, it is not impossible that its cumulative effects over time would result in the gender patterning of linguistic change that we observe. While Chambers' argument cannot be disregarded, it seems best to pursue the social basis of the female predominance in linguistic change, pending more convincing demonstrations of a biologically based cognitive superiority.

Gordon and Heath (1998) have called for a re-consideration of the phonetic basis for the distribution of female and male advantage in linguistic change in progress. They pursue a tendency noted in Labov 1990 for females to lead in the upward movement of peripheral tense vowels that increased the dispersion of the vowel system, and males to lead in centralizing movements. This notion was not taken further at that time, since it could not account for consonantal changes like that of figure 8.10, or the female predominance in the mergers of vowels before /l/, which proceed by laxing and centralization of the tense member of the opposition (see in particular Di Paolo 1988 cited above). Nor would it account for Gauchat's observations on the female lead in the diphthongization of (a:) and (e:) and the monophthongization of (a°) in Charmey (1905). Gordon and Heath concede these limitations, but argue that if we eliminate consonantal changes, interactions with consonants (like the laxing before /l/), and upgliding diphthongs, we can explain the female predominance in the remaining set of vowel changes, which would include the main Philadelphia changes and the Northern Cities Shift. They also include in their scope the female/male opposition in the development of the nucleus of /aw/ by Chambers and Hardwick (figure 8.9 above) and consonantal Arabic data on the male predominance in /q/ and other pharyngeals.

One should not quickly set aside the evidence for a physical basis for sound symbolism advanced by Gordon and Heath. The opposition of dark/pharyngeal to bright/palatal seems to be dominant in both Arabic

(Haeri 1996) and French, with the former favored by males, the latter by females. The raising and fronting of /aw/ is associated with an expressive gesture with extreme lip spreading that has strong female connotations in our culture. It is diametrically opposed to the centralizing, close-mouthed gestures associated with the raising of (ay0) in Martha's Vineyard and Philadelphia. Nevertheless, the evidence that points in the opposite direction is too strong to allow us to explain the female lead in linguistic change in progress by universal phonetic factors.

While the centralization of /ay0/ is a male-dominated feature in Philadelphia and Martha's Vineyard, data from the *Atlas of North American English* shows that men have no such advantage for the country as a whole. A regression analysis was carried out on (ay0D): a dependent variable formed by the difference between the F1 of /ay/ before voiced consonants and finally, and /ay0/ before voiceless consonants. For the 99 subjects in the Inland North and North Central States, a strong advantage of 50 Hz appears for women, with $p < .0001$.

There are other cases where the same variable differs in gender advantage from one area to another. The raising of (oh) in New York is led by women; the raising of (ohr) in Philadelphia is led by men. Gordon and Heath cite Eckert's finding that the backing of /e/ is led by men in Detroit; but as we have seen, women have a strong advantage in the backing of this vowel in the Inland North as a whole.

It would be quite satisfying if we could arrive at a straightforward grouping of male- and female-dominated changes by their phonetic character. However, none of the suggestions put forward so far seem convincing. As in the argument for the verbal superiority of women, biological explanations fail to account for the diversity and sporadic nature of sound change. Such biological tendencies may be part of the quantitative formulation that will ultimately account for the direction of change, but it is not yet possible to measure their specific linguistic effect. We return to the observation of Meillet, that no universal principle can explain the irregular course of sound change.

### *Juxtaposing the principles*

We must then conclude that there is a pattern of gender differentiation that is not based on any phonetic or physiological difference between men and women. It can be stated as an independent *Principle 4*:

*In linguistic change from below, women use higher frequencies of innovative forms than men do.*

It is not easy to reconcile this nonconformist behavior of women with their conformist behavior in other cases. Juxtaposing Principles 2, 3, and 4, we can recognize a **Gender Paradox**.

**Women conform more closely than men to sociolinguistic norms that are overtly prescribed, but conform less than men when they are not.**

The following chapter will look more closely at this situation by studying the development of male–female differences across generations and social classes in the course of linguistic change in the Philadelphia speech community.

# 9

# *The Intersection of Gender, Age, and Social Class*

The apparent contradiction in the principles of gender differentiation was phrased in terms of two opposing tendencies of women. One might just as well see the pattern as a contradiction in the behavior of men: they are less conforming than women with stable sociolinguistic variables, and more conforming when change is in progress within the linguistic system. But because the subject of this volume is linguistic change, the focus will be more on women than men, since as we have seen, women are the principal innovators in the process of change. Since it offers the most detailed and accurate view of the course of linguistic change, the Philadelphia Neighborhood Study will be used to investigate more deeply the linguistic behavior of women. In this chapter, an examination of the interaction of social class, gender, and age will distinguish the linguistic conformity of women from their leading role in changes in progress.

First, let us consider the relative size of gender differentiation in the various stages of linguistic change. Figure 9.1a shows the mean differences for the various changes that primarily affect F1, beginning with the most recent, incipient changes – the lowering of /i/ and /e/ – and proceeding to more active changes, the raising of /ʌ/, the new and vigorous raising of /ay0/, and then the nearly completed raising of /ohr/ and the completed raising of /ahr/. The size of the age coefficient is indicated by the line with black squares; it is multiplied by 20 to show the effect for one generation, and the absolute value is plotted against the size of the gender coefficient in Hz. The coincidence of these two values shows that the gender differential is tightly correlated with the rate of change in apparent time, and confirms once again that the size of this effect is about one generation. Figure 9.1b examines the same situation for the seven variables that involve F2, again proceeding from newest to oldest. The incipient fronting of /iyC/ may not actually be a change in progress. As we have seen, the fronting of /eyC/ and /aw/ are new and vigorous changes. Next is the fronting of /æhD/ before stops, the least advanced of the three allophones of /æh/, and then the nearly completed fronting of /æhS/ before fricatives and /æhN/ before nasals. At the extreme right is the one change that is in fact completed, the

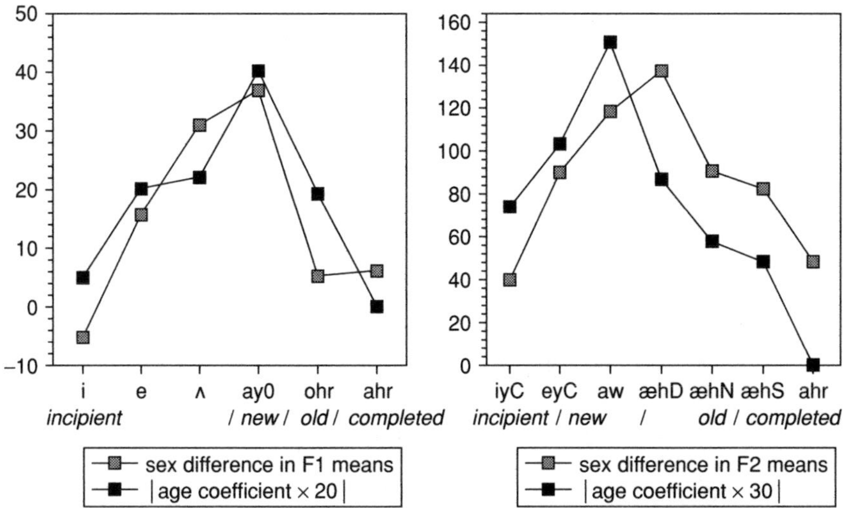


*Figure 9.1* *a* Mean gender differences in F1 and age coefficients for six Philadelphia sound changes. *b* Mean gender differences in F2 and age coefficients for six Philadelphia sound changes

backing of /ahr/. The absolute values of the age coefficients, here multiplied by 30, follow the same curvilinear pattern as the gender differences. Here, however, the coincidence is not as great as with the F1 changes. The gender differences show a lag, peaking later than the age coefficients. This difference between F1 and F2 may be related to the general finding, presented in chapter 5, that all social correlations are stronger with F2 than F1.

In many cases, sound changes involve a simultaneous movement along both axes, as in the raising and fronting of /æh/ along the front diagonal. When F1 and F2 are combined into a measure of raising along the front diagonal, as in chapter 19 of volume 1, the result is a satisfactory picture of the linguistic processes and internal constraints. However, the view of social correlations is much clearer for F2 alone.

In figure 9.1b, the greater gender differences with older changes reflect the greater tendency of women to react negatively to the stigmatization of sound changes as they near completion, a tendency that will be displayed much more prominently in what follows. This situation is consistent with Eckert's finding in the Detroit area: that gender differences are characteristic of the three older changes of the Northern Cities Shift but not the two newer ones (1986, 1989b).

The curvilinear patterns of figures 9.1 are not unrelated to the curvilinear principle that governs linguistic changes in progress. This principle can be stated as a pair of correlations: monotonic socioeconomic patterns are correlated with stable patterns in apparent time, and curvilinear

*Table 9.1* Regression coefficients for occupation, age, and neighborhood by gender for six Philadelphia changes in progress in the Neighborhood Study. Significance: **bold**, $p < .001$; <u>underlined</u>, $p < .01$; *italic*, $p < .05$

| | (*æhN*) | | (*æhS*) | | (*owF*) | | (*owC*) | | (*aw*) | | (*eyC*) | |
|---|---|---|---|---|---|---|---|---|---|---|---|---|
| | *M* | *F* | *M* | *F* | *M* | *F* | *M* | *F* | *M* | *F* | *M* | *F* |
| Constant | 2311 | 2468 | 2147 | 2282 | 1606 | 1712 | 1374 | 1611 | 2031 | 2170 | 2204 | 2201 |
| Unskilled | 0 | 0 | 0 | 0 | 0 | 0 | 0 | 0 | 0 | 0 | 0 | 0 |
| Skilled | 94 | −15 | 64 | 21 | <u>232</u> | 216 | <u>223</u> | 81 | *140* | 33 | *135* | <u>140</u> |
| Clerical | 18 | <u>−218</u> | −54 | <u>−166</u> | 26 | 17 | 42 | 56 | 70 | −45 | *−3* | *48* |
| Managerial | 76 | <u>−222</u> | −23 | <u>−257</u> | 43 | 42 | 140 | −147 | 24 | −104 | −29 | 0 |
| Professional | −54 | **−379** | −100 | **−380** | *−13* | *−3* | 98 | −26 | −74 | −223 | −68 | −22 |
| Age | **−3.73** | −1.24 | *−2.63* | −1.50 | *−2.77* | −5.01 | *−2.47* | <u>−3.87</u> | **−5.72** | **−5.18** | <u>−3.13</u> | <u>−3.13</u> |
| Wicket St. | **213** | 65 | <u>169</u> | 66 | <u>47</u> | 104 | 118 | <u>218</u> | <u>195</u> | *159* | <u>203</u> | *151* |
| Pitt St. | **240** | 42 | <u>256</u> | 70 | <u>−44</u> | 294 | −77 | −25 | <u>164</u> | 82 | 64 | 71 |
| Clark St. | 101 | *120* | <u>192</u> | *141* | **−304** | −190 | *−146* | −105 | −58 | 89 | 87 | 115 |
| $r^2$ | 52.8 | 52.9 | 47.4 | 58.2 | 27.3 | 8.9 | 19.4 | 37.3 | 53.8 | 51.8 | 38.8 | 32.5 |

patterns in the socioeconomic hierarchy are correlated with monotonic functions in apparent time. One can trace the transition between the two types in table 5.4 and figure 5.7. The oldest changes, reaching stability, show the monotonic social correlation, while the newest changes are curvilinear.

Chapter 5 reviewed Kroch's suggestion that this result was not incompatible with his 1978 position that all changes begin in the undifferentiated working class. If the curvilinear pattern is a by-product of the retreat of lower working class males from a female-dominated change, then the earliest stages of change should show a flat pattern for all working class groups, and the curvilinear pattern will appear only for men, but not for women. This chapter will examine the interaction of gender with the curvilinear pattern by carrying out separate analyses for men and women. Table 9.1 shows the results for the two nearly completed changes (æhN) and (æhS), the middle-range changes (owF) and (owC), and two new and vigorous changes, (aw) and (eyC), in regression analyses comparable to table 5.4.

Up to this point, measures of the socioeconomic hierarchy have been based on the combined SEC index of occupation, education, and house value. The final section of chapter 5 showed that occupation was correlated more closely with the new and vigorous changes in progress than the other two, and at some points occupation gave even more significant correlations than the combined index. As we pursue the identification of the innovators of change in the chapters to follow, occupation will reveal more than the other indices about the particular person's daily pattern and way of life, and also be linked more directly to the linguistic market places in which linguistic capital is exchanged. This exploration of gender differences will therefore begin with occupation as the index of socioeconomic position, rather than the combined SEC scale.

Five divisions of the occupational hierarchy are displayed, along with the coefficients for age and for the three working class neighborhoods that showed significant results in table 7.4. To make the analyses of all six sound changes comparable, the same independent variables are retained across table 9.1, whether or not they produce significant coefficients.

Figure 9.2 is a graphic projection of the occupational profiles for the separated sexes from table 9.1. The coefficient for each occupational group is added to the constant for each sex for the six sound changes in progress, and the coefficient for the advantage of female gender from table 8.5.[1] Where two allophones of the same phoneme are involved, the same vertical scale is preserved to facilitate comparison.

For the two nearly completed changes (æhN) and (æhS), both genders show a more or less linear pattern: higher values are associated with lower

[1] Since the separate analyses for male and female in table 9.1 do not take the difference between male and female into account, they project values around the same means.

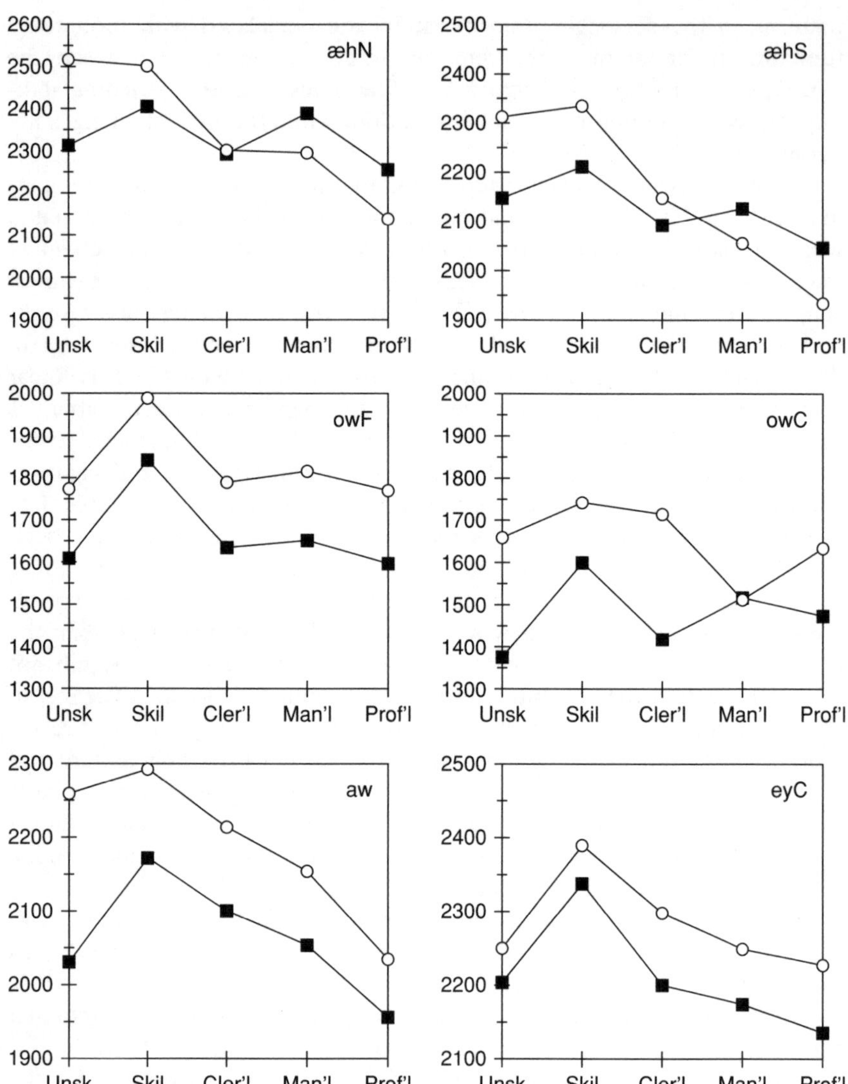


*Figure 9.2* Expected values of six sound changes in progress by gender for five occupational levels in the Philadelphia Neighborhood Study. Vertical axis shows expected F2 derived by adding the constant for each analysis to the occupational coefficient of table 9.1 and the female coefficient of table 8.5 to the female values. Females = open circles; males = solid squares. Occupational groups: Unsk = unskilled labor; Skil = skilled labor; Cler'l = clerical; Man'l = managerial; Prof'l = professional

occupational groups, with a steeper slope for females. For (æhN), the male pattern is almost flat, while women show a steep slope from unskilled down to the professional group.[2] This gender difference is clearly associated with the high level of social awareness of the (æh) variables described in chapter 6. (æhN) in particular is the most advanced and the most salient of the changes in progress.[3] Women show their expected linguistic conformity. If we project the history of (æh) backwards, and assume that at an earlier time it followed a curvilinear pattern, the present flat pattern in the working class must be the result of a retreat of the upper working class under the effect of its increasing stigmatization.

The third and fourth diagrams in figure 9.2 show the middle-range changes (owF) and (owC). The free allophone (owF) is further ahead than the checked one, the normal situation in the fronting of back vowels. In this case, the difference is small, from 100 to 200 Hz. The curvilinear pattern for (owF) is intact and neatly parallel for men and women. Table 9.1 shows that the peak for skilled workers is significant at the .01 level for men, but not for women. For the checked allophone (owC), the men again show a significant peak at the .01 level for skilled workers, while women display a general elevation for all working class speakers. Unlike the /æh/ allophones, neither of the /ow/ allophones shows a marked decline for the white-collar and professional groups. As chapter 6 demonstrated, the social evaluation of these fronting movements is much less marked than for the fronting and raising of tensed short **a**. The $r^2$ figures of table 9.1 indicate that these vowels are far less prominent in the sociolinguistic ecology of Philadelphia than the other variables, with only 10–20% of the variation among speakers accounted for by social factors.

The new and vigorous sound changes (aw) and (eyC) displayed the curvilinear pattern most clearly in figure 5.6. In the fifth diagram of figure 9.2, the profile for (aw) is curvilinear for men, but not for women, since the difference between "Unskilled" and "Skilled" for women is not significant. This situation supports Kroch's suggestion that both working class groups were similar at the outset, and that the curvilinear pattern is a secondary phenomenon, the result of a male retreat from a female-dominated change. However, the most recent change in this series, (eyC), does not show a flat working class effect for either men or women. The sixth diagram of figure 9.2 shows a close parallel of male and female social

[2] G. Sankoff points out (p.c.) that the relatively low position of the clerical group for women may in part be due to the fact that a considerable number of non-working women in the sample were classified by their husbands' occupations as skilled workers. If they had been active in the work force, it would probably have been as clerical workers, thus producing a more linear profile.

[3] Data from the *Atlas of North American English* shows that in almost all American dialects, short **a** before nasals is higher and more peripheral than other allophones, in some cases part of a continuum, as in Philadelphia, in other cases as a categorical difference.

class profiles, with the same steep slope upward from unskilled to skilled workers. For all five occupational groups, the coefficients are closely aligned. Table 9.1 shows that the peak of the skilled working group is a .05 effect for men, .01 for women. If (eyC) is the most recent of the changes presented here, it follows that the difference between men and women for unskilled workers in (owC) and (aw) is a secondary development. Kroch's interpretation that this represents a male retreat from a female-dominated change still stands. More specifically, it represents the refusal of men in the unskilled group to follow women as they approximate the limiting values reached by the female skilled workers.

Chapter 4 provided evidence that (eyC) is the most recent of the new and vigorous Philadelphia sound changes. Table 9.1 reinforces this conclusion. The advance of (eyC) shows a minimum amount of social differentiation: adjusted $r^2$ shows only 39% (for men) and 33% (for women) of the variation explained by age, occupation, and neighborhood factors, about two-thirds of the level reached by the analyses of (aw) and (æh). This relatively low involvement of social factors is characteristic of the earlier stages of change, when the major independent variables concern group membership rather than social status.

Though (eyC) may be the most recent change, both (aw) and (eyC) are ranked as "new and vigorous." They differ not so much in time of origin as in social sensitivity: there is ample evidence that (eyC) is at a lower level of social awareness than (aw).[4] Why should this be, if they both originated at about the same period? It should be borne in mind that (eyC) is new in two senses. First, because the raising and fronting of this vowel was not observed in earlier generations or in earlier descriptions. Secondly, because it represents a qualitative reversal of the "Southern Shift," in which the nucleus of this diphthong is lowered (chapter 6 of volume 1). The raising and fronting of /aw/, on the other hand, is a continuation of the process of fronting that led from an earlier [aʊ] to the original Philadelphia [æʊ]. It may also be associated with the raising and fronting of tense /æh/. Thus (aw) is a further development of an older process, while (eyC) is a new phenomenon entirely.

## 9.1 The case of (ay0)

Table 8.5 showed that one of the new and vigorous changes was exceptional in its relation to gender. While (aw) and (eyC) are strongly advanced

[4] This evidence was not advanced in chapter 6 because at the time that we constructed the subjective reaction test, we had no inkling that checked /ey/ was exhibiting this raising and fronting. The discovery of (eyC) was entirely the result of the quantitative analysis of the regression programs. To this day, we have no example of a public comment on the behavior of (eyC).

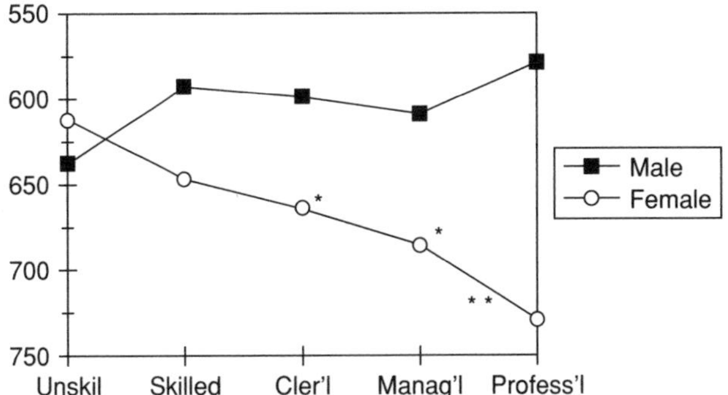


*Figure 9.3* Expected values for (ay0) by gender for five occupational levels in the Philadelphia Neighborhood Study. Vertical axis shows expected F1 derived by adding the constant for each analysis to the occupational coefficient (significance levels: * p < .05, ** p < .001)

for females, the reverse is true for (ay0), which showed a 36 Hz advantage for males. This figure is comparable to the 89 Hz advantage for females with (aw), since in our doubly-linear view of phonological space, F1 is weighted twice as heavily as F2 (and is perceptually more salient). Chapter 5 also found that (ay0) was exceptional in showing no clear social stratification. Separate analyses for men and women clarify this situation considerably.

Figure 9.3 is the gender-differentiated analysis of the social stratification of (ay0) that corresponds to the displays of figure 9.2 for the female-dominated changes. The pattern for men and women is quite different. Men operate at a higher level except for unskilled workers (the F1 axis is reversed so that the direction of change is upward as the vowel nucleus is centralized). There is a suggestion of a curvilinear pattern for men, except for the fact that the professional group shows an even higher value than the skilled working class. On the other hand, women show a strongly monotonic declining pattern, with significant and increasing declines for the middle class occupational groups.

The gender differential is strongly governed by occupation: it is non-existent for the unskilled workers, and increases steadily with higher occupational status until it reaches a maximum for the professional group. Analysis by age shows that the high value of (ay0) for professionals does not represent any recent change in progress. Figure 9.4 is a set of two scattergrams for females and males, plotting age against the height of /ay0/. A partial regression line is shown for each occupational group. The pattern for women is quite straightforward: for all groups except the managerial class, (ay0) is a monotonic function in apparent time; centralization increases as age declines. The slope is steeper for the clerical and professional groups, where the older professional women have the most open /ay0/ nuclei. The

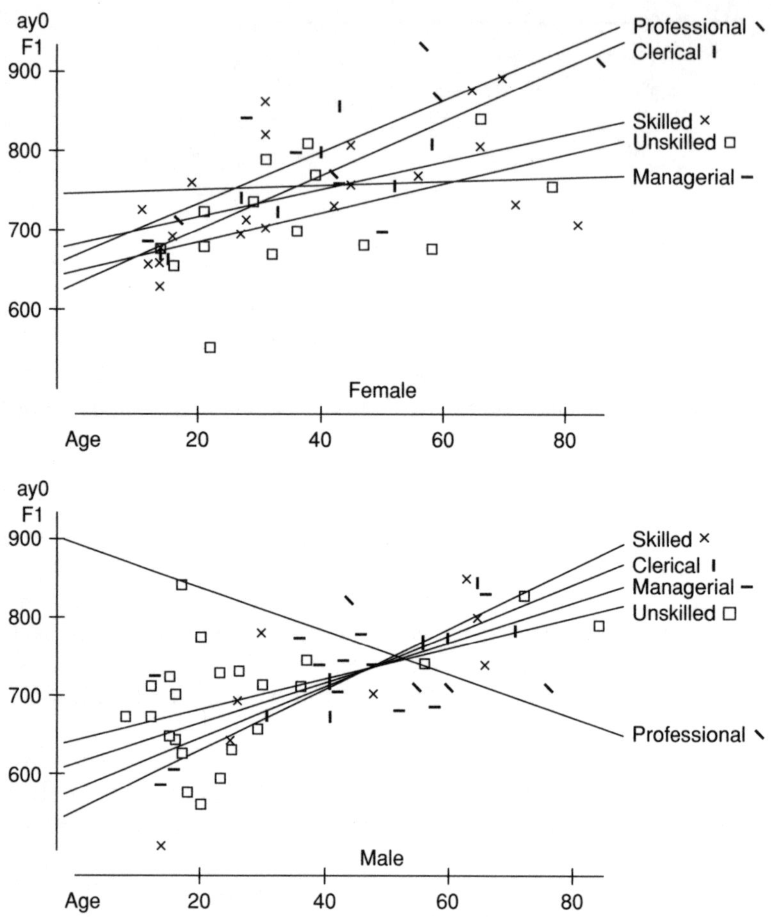


*Figure 9.4* Scattergrams of height of (ay0) by gender and occupation with partial regression lines

same is true for men with the striking exception of one group: the professional class. Here the partial regression line moves down instead of up, making it seem as if the change in progress is moving in the opposite direction. Closer inspection of the individual speakers shows that four older speakers, age 54, 55, 60, and 76, occupy a narrowly constricted intermediate range around 710 F1, and the direction of the line is determined by a single relatively low value of 821 for the 44-year-old speaker. Without more younger speakers, one cannot argue for a change in apparent time for the male professional class. The overall picture for men is the absence of any pattern of social stratification; for women, there is a higher rate of change in apparent time, and a consistent pattern of social stratification by occupation.

Chapter 5 noted that the development of (ay0) also involved a shift of the nucleus toward the back, registered by a lowering of F2. There is no significant gender difference in this backing process, with exactly the same advantage for speakers under 20 years old (–84 Hz F2 for women, –74 for men, both at $p < .02$).[5]

## 9.2 Developments over time by gender

The age coefficients of table 9.1 are the simplest way of indicating developments in apparent time. But multiple regression incorporates age as a linear function: that is, a constant rate of development over the entire age range of the population. There is no reason to believe that such linearity actually governs the development in apparent time. A more accurate view of development in time can be obtained by breaking the age continuum into decades, as in the third regression analyses of chapter 5. The diagrams of this section will show six divisions by age for each gender. The regression analyses from which they are drawn include also all significant occupational and neighborhood factors.

Figure 9.5 shows such decade-by-decade analyses by gender for the fronting of (aw). In addition to age by decade, the regression analysis also includes whatever contributions of other groups rise above the .05 level of significance.[6] The expected values for each group are projected by adding the age coefficient for that group to the constant term of the regression analysis. The upper series of open symbols shows the age progression for women, connected by solid lines. The dashed line is the product of a second regression analysis performed on the expected values for the six decades: a straight line drawn through those points. The slope of this line is 5.38, close to the value of 5.19 found when age was treated as a single quantitative independent variable in the second regression analysis of chapter 5 (table 5.4). The $r^2$ of .961 shows that the regression line superimposed on the decade-by-decade values accounts for 96% of the variation of those values from the mean for all ages. There is then, for women's use of (aw), very little difference between using age as a single quantitative variable (table 5.4) and the decade-by-decade analysis. The fronting of (aw) for women is an almost perfectly linear function of age. This result in combination with figure 9.2 is a quantitative re-statement of the curvilinear hypothesis: that a monotonic function of age is associated with a curvilinear function of social class.

[5] Only males show an effect of ethnicity: backing is strongly concentrated among Irish males (–73 Hz F2, $p < .02$). This rounded, backed, and raised nucleus in *pipe* and *fight* is one of the most distinctive features of the Philadelphia accent among young males.

[6] As shown in the figure caption, the curvilinear pattern is preserved but with a stronger effect for women, while the Wicket St. advantage appears only for men.

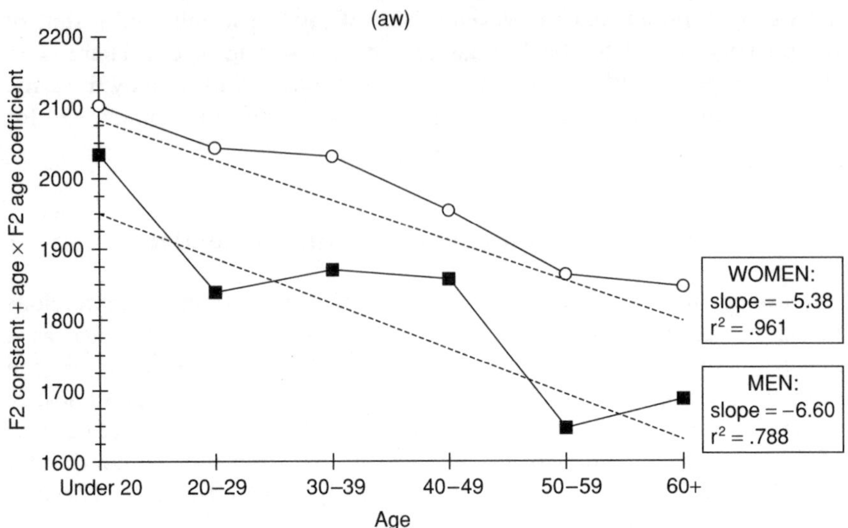


*Figure 9.5* Expected values by decade for the fronting of (aw) in the Philadelphia Neighborhood Study, with separate analyses by gender. Females: open circles; males: closed squares. Other factors: women: UWC 135 (p .03); UC –156 (p .05); men: UWC 93 (p .15); Wicket St. 222 (p .0003); Pitt St. 149 (p .04)

The lower solid line that connects the solid symbols shows the age progression for men by decade, with a comparable dashed regression line drawn through the six decades. Men also show an upward movement, with a slope that is even steeper: –6.60. But this progression is much less regular: the regression line accounts for only 79% of the variance. It is a step function rather than a straight line. The three steps identify three generations of speakers. The first generation, above 50 years old at the time of this study, is at the conservative level of 1650 Hz and furthest away from the level set by women. The second generation, 20 to 50 years old, is 200 Hz higher, around 1850 Hz. The third generation, below 20, has shifted another 200 Hz to the front, and is now not far from the level of the younger female speakers.

Many earlier accounts of the difference between men's and women's speech report that women are a generation ahead of men. Gauchat 1905 is explicit on this point. The generational effect appears clearly in Wolf and Jiménez' study of devoicing of /ž/ in Buenos Aires (figure 8.10). This is repeated here as Figure 8.10′ with dotted arrows indicating the relations of generations. Men 30 years old have a devoicing rate at the level of women 55 years old; the change has not affected either. Young men 15 years old have the same level as women 45 years old, both nearly 20% devoiced. Boys 12 years old show nearly 40% devoicing, about on the level of young women 30 years old. Thus the males show a level of devoicing

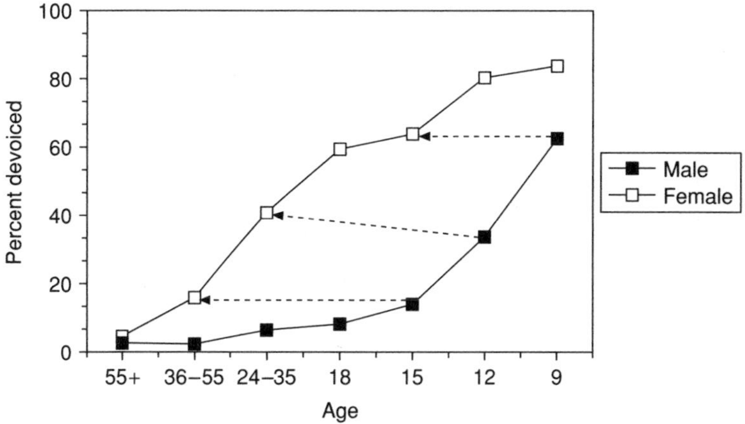


*Figure 8.10′* Devoicing of /ž/ in Buenos Aires by sex and age, with generational parallels indicated

close to that of the age group that their mothers belong to. The change among younger males accelerates, so that 9-year-old boys are at the level of 18-year-old girls.

The same generational pattern can be seen in Chae's study of the raising of (o) in Seoul (figure 8.11). Women increase their use of the variable sharply in the second generation, but men do not show a strong response until the third generation.

Returning to figure 9.5, it appears that the least fronted forms of (aw) are found in the speech of men in their 50s and 60s. F2 values between 1600 and 1700 correspond to a nucleus of /aw/ in low front or slightly back of front position. It follows that the current change began at that position, at [æ>ʊ], among women born at the turn of the century. As the nucleus of /aw/ rose along the front diagonal, it became progressively fronter and higher, while the glide target fell from [ʊ] to [o] to [ɔ]. Men do not participate in this change until Generation II: the (aw) fronting of men 20 to 49 years old is close to the (aw) of women in Generation I, in their 50s and 60s. The male Generation III, men under 20, is at exactly the level of the female Generation II, 20 to 39 years old.

A similar pattern appears in figure 9.6 for the other female-dominated new change, the fronting of (eyC). Again, women show a high degree of linearity in the decade-by-decade shift, with an $r^2$ that accounts for 84% of the variation, while men show a step-wise progression where a straight line through the decade values accounts for only 66%. The same generational divisions can be observed among men, though the values for the second generation are not as even as with (aw). In the previous section, it was noted that (aw) continues the long-term tendency for the fronting of the nucleus of M.E. uì, while (eyC) appears to be a retrograde movement,

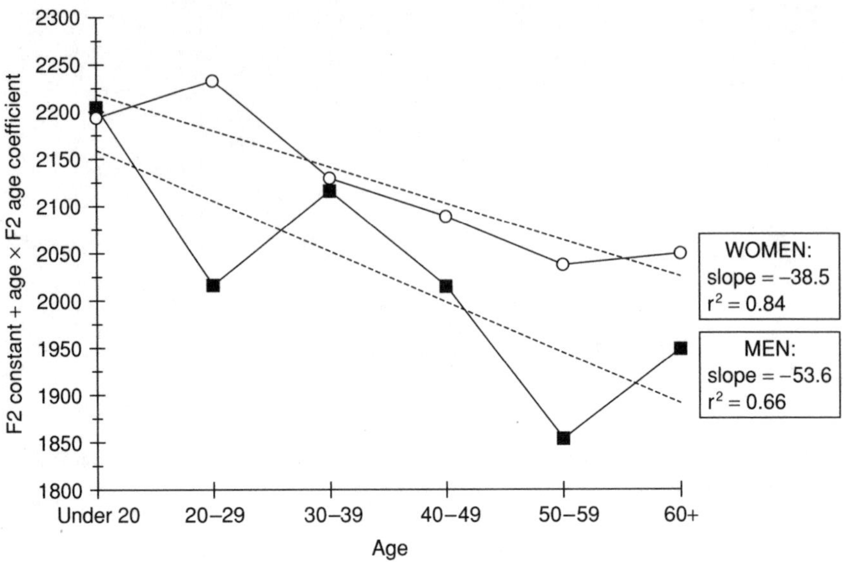


*Figure 9.6* Expected values by decade for the fronting of (eyC) in the Philadelphia Neighborhood Study, with separate analyses by gender. Females: open circles; males: closed squares. Other significant factors: Wicket St. male 183 ($p < .001$); skilled workers male 165 ($p < .01$), female 169 ($p < .01$)

reversing the long-standing participation of Philadelphia in the Southern-Shift lowering of the nucleus of /ey/. If that is the case, then the change may actually have started among women of Generation III, born in 1900–1920, and the low values for men would then represent the tendency to lower the nucleus that continues today in open syllables. In any case, the similarities between figures 9.5 and 9.6 carry forward the extensive parallels between these new and vigorous changes observed in the previous three chapters.

## 9.3 A gender-asymmetrical model of linguistic change

Figures 9.5 and 9.6 carry a clear message for the interpretation of the role of women as leaders of linguistic change from below. The effects of gender and occupation are independent for the new and vigorous changes in progress. For all occupational groups, men are a generation behind women: more specifically, men show levels of fronting similar to women of the previous generation. These patterns fit the observations of the gender differentiation of linguistic changes presented in chapter 8: that as Gauchat and Wolf and Jiménez found, women are at some stages a full generation ahead of men. The logical inference is difficult to avoid: men are at the level of linguistic change characteristic of their mothers because they acquired their first use of these variables from their mothers. Even more simply: the vernacular that we speak, the first language that we have mastered perfectly and use without doubt or hesitation – is our mother's vernacular. There will be later, postvernacular adjustments – these are in fact the central topic of chapter 12. But in learning language we must start somewhere, and there is no other place to start but with our mother's phones. Mothers of course are not the only source of first language phonetics: many children are raised by other female caregivers. (There is no community that I have been able to locate where the great majority of people do not learn their language from a female caretaker. But see note 6 of chapter 8.)

It is now well established that when mothers speak a language or dialect different from that of the speech community, children quickly learn to disregard that linguistic system and acquire before the age of 5 a local dialect that is phonetically matched to the local pattern. The principal data for this conclusion comes from the study of new communities (King of Prussia, Payne 1976, 1980; Milton Keynes, Kerswill and Williams 1994, Williams and Kerswill 1999).

The following section presents a model of the diffusion of linguistic change which attempts to account for the pairing of linear progressions for women with step-wise progressions for men in figures 9.5–9.6. It incorporates the insights of Kroch (1978), that males retreat from a female-dominated change; of Chambers (1995), that women are more active in the social evaluation of language than men; of Gordon and Heath (1998), that some phonetic movements are naturally favored by women and others by men; and of Sturtevant (1947) and Eckert (1999), that the diffusion of sound changes depends upon their association with one or the other of opposing social categories or reference groups.

Stage 0: Stability. Given the fact that each generation acquired its vernacular from female caregivers, phonetic systems will remain stable unless there is postvernacular modification. The last generation that is *not* involved in the change – generation zero – sets the ground level against which increments are measured.

Stage 1: Association of a variant with a reference group. Stability does not imply homogeneity. New variants arise as the result of dialect contact, or the mechanical consequences of previous changes (volume 1, chapter 20). The first stage in the diffusion of a sound change depends upon the more or less arbitrary association of such a variant with a particular reference group,[7] and its use to symbolize the cultural values of that group.

[7] Kroch 1978 argues that this association is in fact motivated: that working class speakers adopt "natural" changes and middle class speakers resist them. I have not been able to convince myself that the distinction between "natural" and "unnatural" changes is a clear or useful one, but the issues would carry us beyond the limits of this volume.

In Martha's Vineyard, this reference group was the eighth-generation Yankees; in the Detroit high schools, it was the Burnouts; in New York and Philadelphia it is the upper or middle working class.[8] This association occurs near the bottom of the S-shaped curve; the change begins to be accelerated within the reference group, and to a lesser extent, with those who interact most frequently with members of the group.

Stage 2: Gender specialization. The sound change becomes associated with one or the other gender. This association may not be entirely arbitrary; but if there is a phonetic basis for the female/male split as Heath and Gordon propose, the number of male- and female-dominated changes would have to be roughly equal. Otherwise, all vowel systems would in the long run be highly skewed in one direction or the other.[9]

Stage 3: Gender split. In the societies that have produced the data now available, males in the lower social classes show a consistent pattern of retreating from or resisting a female-dominated change (figures 8.10, 8.11, 9.5, and 9.6; see also figure 8.1 for stable variables). We see a level male pattern matched with a steadily ascending female pattern. For male-dominated changes, there is as yet no clear basis for predicting whether there will be a symmetrical female response, but the linear pattern of figure 9.4 indicates that women do not behave in the same way as men at this point.

Stage 4: First generation acceleration. When the children of the young women of Stage 2 enter the speech community, males show a sharp step upward in their use of the variable. Although the female children of that generation will also acquire the advanced phonetic base provided by their mothers, no discontinuity in the female linear pattern appears.[10]

Stage 5: Second generation acceleration. While females continue to accelerate in a linear fashion, the male children of the second generation of women to be affected by the change receive a second step-wise acceleration.

Stage 6: Third generation approximation. As changes near completion,[11] the difference between men and women becomes smaller. If the variable becomes a social marker or stereotype, a linear alignment with social class develops, along with the interaction between social class and gender

[8] See Merton 1957 for a fuller development of the concept of reference group.

[9] This follows inevitably from the long-term homeostasis of vowel systems; if there were a set of female-dominated changes, and this was larger than the male set, vowel systems would become highly skewed in the course of change.

[10] How such linear patterns are produced is a major topic of chapter 14, which develops a quantitative model of the *incrementation* of linguistic change.

[11] In one sense, phonetic changes are never complete, since their consequences reverberate throughout the system. But a particular phase of a change, like the raising of a vowel, or the change of frequency of a process, has a natural limit set by the nature of the vowel space and the limiting values of 0% or 100%. If such a process is active, it frequently shows a trajectory of four generations from initiation to near-completion, as in this model.

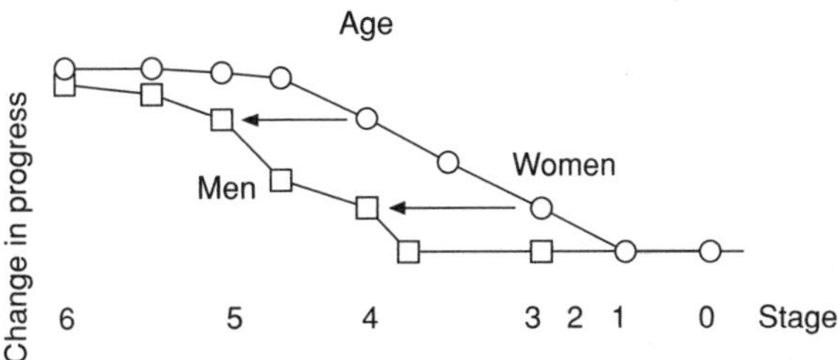


*Figure 9.7* A six-stage model of gender relations in linguistic change from below

observed in chapter 8. If the change is generally adopted in the community, gender differences will disappear.

Figure 9.7 is a schematic diagram of this six-stage model. The arrows are drawn from the female to the male side, indicating the direction of influence. The evidence presented above covers stages 3 through 5 of this model. The balance of this chapter will take up later stages of change from the Philadelphia study which will bear on stages 4–6, and look more closely at what happens when men are in the lead.

## 9.4 Nearly completed and middle-range changes in Philadelphia

Chapter 6 showed that the most salient of the nearly completed changes is (æhN), the allophone of /æ/ before nasals in *man*, *hand*, *Camden*, etc. Figure 9.8 shows separate male and female regression analyses by decade for this variable. As before, the data is drawn from a multivariate analysis that includes the five occupational levels of figure 9.2. The pattern of figure 9.8 differs sharply from the corresponding figures 9.5–9.6. The age slope for women is much shallower than for men: women appear to be nearing the top of the S-shaped curve of change, and the pattern by decade is *less* linear than for men. The regression line drawn through the female symbols accounts for only 35% of the variance, while the corresponding regression line for males shows a steeper slope (–3.67) and greater approximation to linearity (61% of the variation accounted for by the straight line). This is the opposite of the pattern for the new and vigorous changes.

The other significant factors listed in the figure caption indicate considerable difference between male and female responses to (æhN). Women show precipitous social stratification, while among men, only the upper class is significantly behind the others. This is the expected interaction of gender and occupational group for this nearly completed change, an interaction that was moderate for the new and vigorous change (aw) and nonexistent for (eyC).

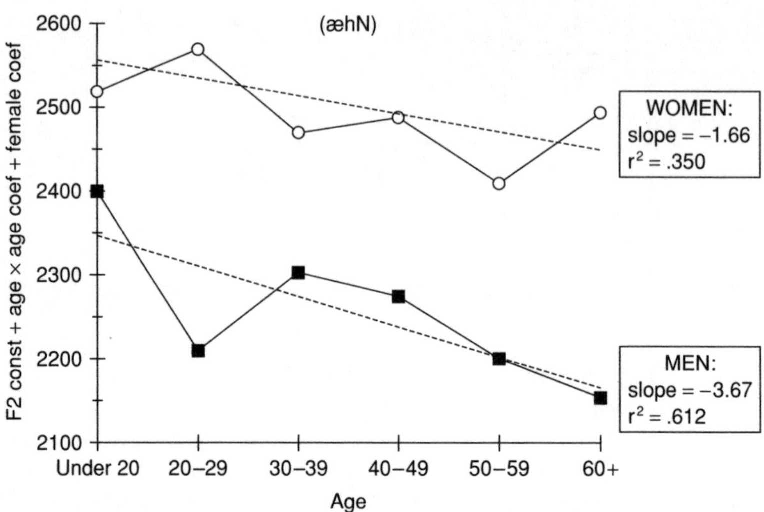


*Figure 9.8* Expected values by decade for the fronting of (æhN) in the Philadelphia Neighborhood Study, with separate analyses by gender. Females: open circles; males: closed squares. Other significant factors: Wicket St. male 131 ($p < .02$); Italian2 female 121 ($p < .05$); clerical female −213 ($p < .01$); managerial female −235 ($p < .01$); professional male −153 ($p < .05$), female −390 ($p < .0001$)

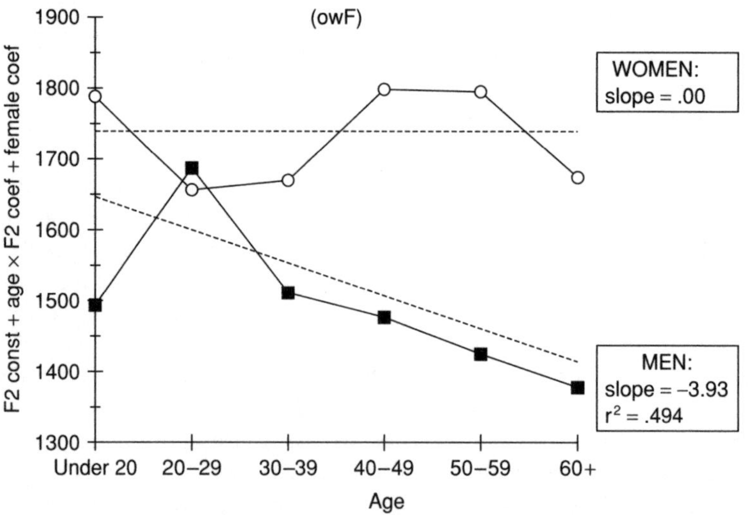


*Figure 9.9* Expected values by decade for the fronting of (owF) in the Philadelphia Neighborhood Study, with separate analyses by gender. Females: open circles; males: closed squares. Other significant factors: Italian2 female −221 ($p < .001$), male −265 ($p < .001$); Clark St. female −168 ($p < .01$)

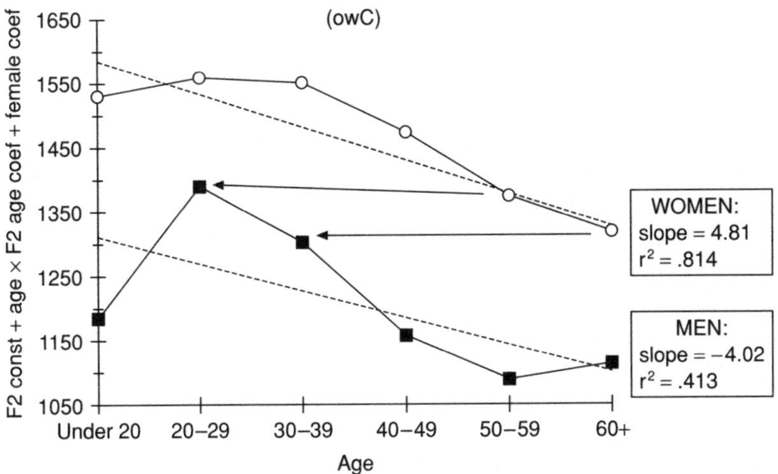


*Figure 9.10* Expected values by decade for the fronting of (owC) in the Philadelphia Neighborhood Study, with separate analyses by gender. Females: open circles; males: closed squares. Other significant factors: Wicket St. female 263 ($p < .001$), male 188 ($p < .01$)

Figures 9.9 and 9.10 show the development in apparent time of the mid-range changes, the fronting of free and checked /ow/. Though free (owF) has been rated as a "mid-range change," it may well be nearing its limiting value and be more appropriately classed with (æhN) and (uwF). There is no clear age differentiation of women, who oscillate about a value of 1730 Hz. For men, there is a fairly regular increase of value across age levels, converging with the level of the women in the young adult age group. Except for the sharp decline for the youngest male group, this corresponds closely to the model of late stages where the group that is farther behind begins to accelerate (Labov 1981). Like (æhN), this pattern is closest to stages 4–5–6 of the gender model in figure 9.7. The decline of the under-20 group is an additional factor that must be weighed seriously: there are 16 males under 20 distributed throughout the occupational groups.[12] The significance of this peak will be examined more closely in chapter 14, where it will become apparent that monotonic age functions are in fact impossible, and that every change must show a decline among younger speakers to some extent.

The development of (owC) over age groups by gender is shown in figure 9.10. This is a less advanced variable, located in the central portion

[12] The decline in the fronting of (ow) among the youngest speakers is not general, but confined to the working class groups. The curvilinear occupational pattern, shared by men and women in figure 9.2, is also general across age ranges: it holds for all but the 40–49 and 60+ age groups.

of the asymmetrical model (stages 2 to 5). Both men and women show a regular progression from older to younger age groups with a peak among the 20–29 age group. In this section of the model, the progression of women is more linear than that of men, with an adjusted $r^2$ for the regression line that is twice as high as that for men. The upward step for males brings the 30–39 year old men to the level of the 60+ women, and the 20–29 year olds to the level of the 50–59 year old women.

The absence of significant age constraints for (uwF) in chapter 5, social constraints in chapter 7, and gender coefficients in chapter 8 indicated that this variable may have reached its limiting value and should not be included among changes in progress. Figure 9.11 shows that this is a half-truth. The same general pattern appears as in the more active changes, with a gradual upward trend and men well behind women with a steeper slope. None of the values given here for women depart significantly from the reference group, speakers over 60, but all values for men except the 50–59 age group are significant, most below the .01 level. It is now evident that (uwF) is to be ranked among completed changes for women, but among mid-range changes for men. The arrow shows that men in their 20s are at the same level as women in their 50s, the same 30-year generation span that appeared in figure 9.10. Figure 9.11 must represent the second upward male step in the asymmetrical model. The first upward step would have affected men who are now in their 40s; we are missing the figures for their mothers, who would be 70-year-old women.

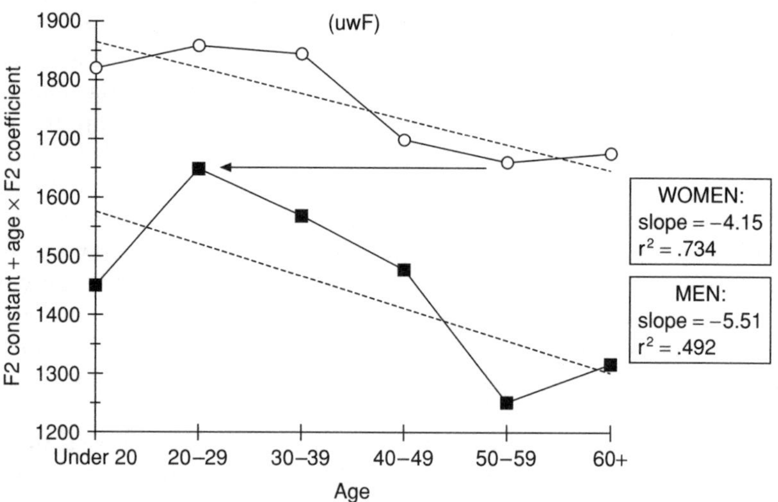


*Figure 9.11* Expected values by decade for the fronting of (uwF) in the Philadelphia Neighborhood Study, with separate analyses by gender. Females: open circles; males: closed squares. Other significant factors: Clark St. female −231 ($p < .02$); Wicket St. male 275 ($p < .001$); Pitt St. male 264 ($p < .02$)

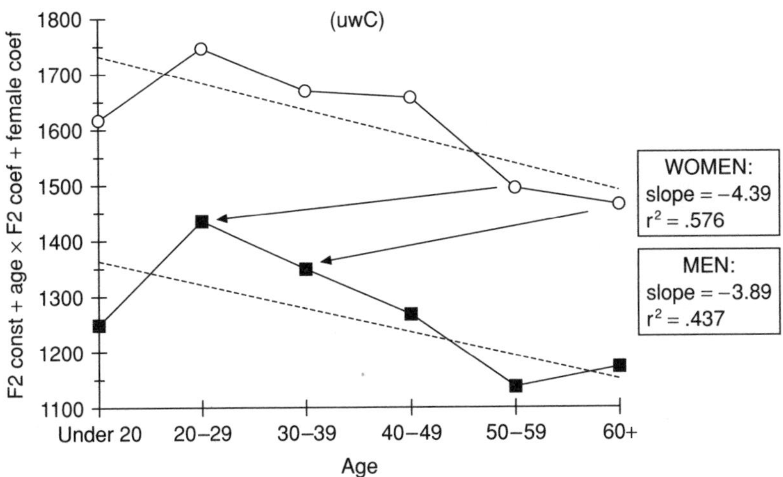


*Figure 9.12* Expected values by decade for the fronting of (uwC) in the Philadelphia Neighborhood Study, with separate analyses by gender. Females: open circles; males: closed squares. Other significant factors: Italian2 female –246 ($p < .05$); Wicket St. male 275 ($p < .01$)

Figure 9.12 shows the corresponding pattern by decade for the less advanced variable, (uwC). Men and women show a strikingly similar age distribution, and both show a decline with the youngest age group. The difference in adjusted $r^2$ for women and men is smaller than in other cases, and the step-like progression of males less marked. The 30-year generation lines extend from women in their 50s and 60s to men in their 20s and 30s. They are not flat, but descend from 75 to 100 Hz, departing somewhat from the model of figure 9.7.

## *Occupational stratification*

In the decade-by-decade analysis of the (uw) variables, there are no significant coefficients for women's occupational classes. But for men the situation is quite different. (uwF) and (uwC) show the pattern of figure 9.13, where all but one of the points are significantly different from the reference group, the unskilled workers. The two regression lines show a parallel slope upward from lower to higher status speakers. The fronting of (uw) thus has a different social interpretation in Philadelphia from the fronting of (ow), (æh), (aw), and (eyC). Since the fronting of (uw) is older than the fronting of (ow), this social stratification may be a later development, the result of a differential reaction to a female-dominated change. But except for the group under 20, this cannot be considered a "retreat," since all occupational groups show a general fronting across decades from the 60s

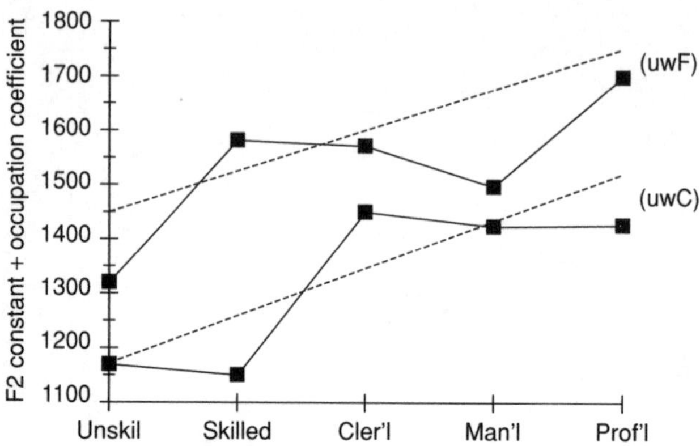


*Figure 9.13* Occupational stratification of the fronting of (uw) variables for men

to the 20s. The logic of the asymmetrical gender model will force male speakers to advance as long as women do so, though more slowly. It is not impossible that males will show a retrograde movement from that level, from their early childhood to their late teens.

This review of the nearly completed and middle-range changes in Philadelphia has added some further support to the asymmetric gender model of figure 9.7, establishing a distance between generations of 25 to 30 years. There are a number of distortions of the basic model, however, which are due to the development of social evaluation, to some extent an arbitrary and unpredictable factor. This social evaluation further increases the gender asymmetry. The gender that is further behind, in this case the males, has a greater development of social stratification than the gender which is ahead. This gender/social stratification may be curvilinear at first, as in the case of (ow), then roughly linear, as in the case of (uw).

## 9.5 The punctuating events

The study of these mid-range changes has reinforced the inference drawn from the examination of new and vigorous changes. Women are well in advance of men in almost all sub-groups. In all cases, women display a relatively steady advance, decade by decade, while men show a saccadic movement which appears to correspond to generational stages in the sound changes involved. Such generational waves point to punctuating events in the wider society; in most cases, these events are the large-scale population movements and consequent social changes associated with major wars. Since the breaks in the continuum are much clearer in the male figures than the female, we can identify the generational effects in the preceding figures as the first sharp increase in the male mean values:

| Decade of first sharp increase | |
|---|---|
| (aw) | 40–49 |
| (eyC) | 40–49 |
| (owF) | 20–29 |
| (owC) | 30–39 |
| (uwC) | 40–49 |
| (uwF) | 40–49 |

The (ow) variables differ from the others, so the picture is not conclusive. But the consensus of (aw), (eyC), (uwC), and (uwF) is that the first sharp increase in Philadelphia sound changes took place among males 40–49 years old.[13] This does not mean that these speakers were the first initiators of the sound changes of the 1970s; on the contrary, we interpret this sharp increase on the part of males to indicate that they were matching the vowel qualities of their mothers, who were 60–69 years old, and were born in the years 1913–22. The punctuating event that triggered the succession of generational changes portrayed here is most likely to have been World War I. The males over 50 we recorded in the 1970s therefore reflect the phonetic patterns of their mothers, born before the turn of the century.

## 9.6 The male-dominated variable: (ay0)

In table 8.5, eleven of the Philadelphia vowels involved in change showed sex coefficients favoring female speakers, and three favored males. One of these three is the almost completed change (ohr), another was an incipient change (ʌ), and the third is one of the three new and vigorous changes, (ay0), the centralization of the nucleus of /ay/ before voiceless finals. The analysis of this variable is a critical test case for the gender asymmetric model. If the step-like progression of males in female-dominated changes is the product of a generational adjustment of males to the levels of their mothers' vernacular, as argued above, such a step-like progression should be missing in a male-dominated change. Nor would we expect to find the situations reversed, with males showing a linear progression and females a step-like progression, since female children would not normally re-adjust their vernacular to their father's level.

Before considering the decade-by-decade growth of (ay0), another aspect of its gender asymmetry must be dealt with. Chapter 5 found a marked contrast in social stratification between (ay0) and the female-dominated variables: there was no significant differentiation of socioeconomic levels for (ay0). Separate analyses by gender show that the situation is quite

[13] We must assume that the sharp break in the nearly completed change (æhN) dates to a period earlier than the others.

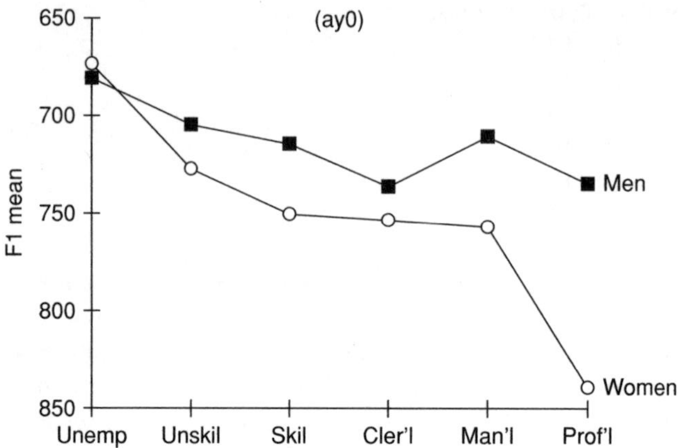


*Figure 9.14* Mean values of F1 for (ay0) by occupation and gender, for the 112 speakers of the Philadelphia Neighborhood Study

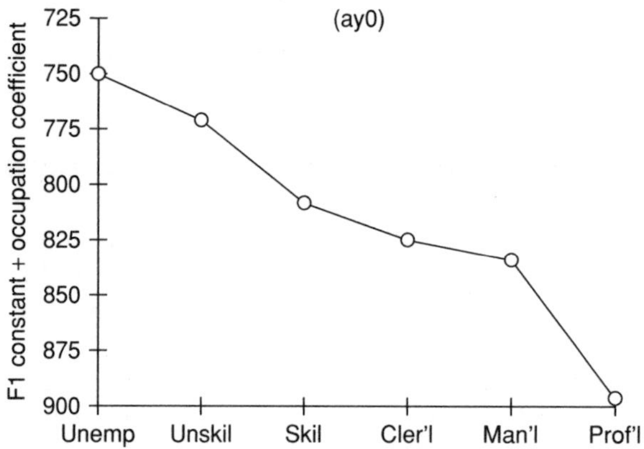


*Figure 9.15* Occupational stratification of (ay0) for women in a multiple regression analysis including age by decade and significant neighborhood and ethnic groups

different for men and women. Consider the simple display of figure 9.14, plotting the means for men and women for each occupational class. The lowest values of F1, indicating the most centralization, are found for the lowest social class – the group of unemployed – and here there is no difference between men and women. The mean F1 values rise slightly for the next three occupational classes, with moderate differences between the sexes. For the two highest occupational groups, the difference between men and women increases, and for the professional class, it is very large indeed. Multivariate analyses, taking age groups by decade into account as well as occupation, provide a more regular picture. There is no significant stratification by occupation (or SEC) in the separate analysis for men. But

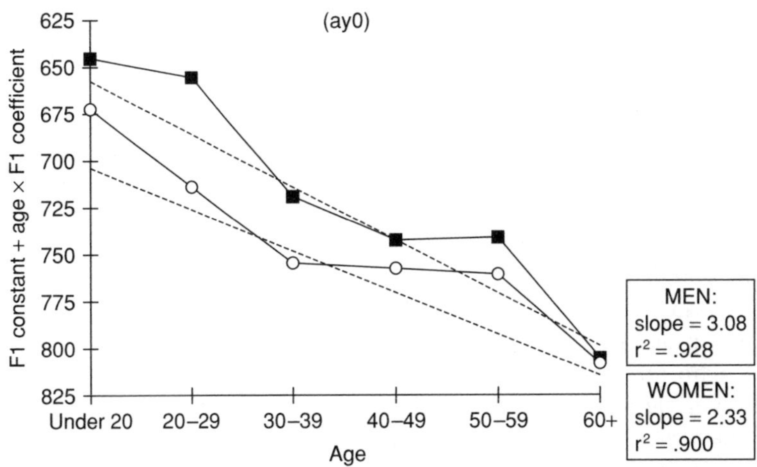


*Figure 9.16* Expected values by decade for the centralization of (ay0) before voiceless consonants in the Philadelphia Neighborhood Study, with separate analyses by gender. Females: open circles; males: closed squares. Other significant factors: Wicket St. male −58 ($p < .02$); Pitt St. female 51 ($p < .05$)

figure 9.15, the multivariate analysis for women only, shows a clear and regular differentiation by occupation for women. The lower the occupational class, the lower the mean F1 value, and the more centralized the vowel nucleus.[14] (ay0) is the opposite of the (uw) variables in that social stratification is found among women, but not among men. The link that joins both cases is that the social stratification is a property of the group that is behind in the development of the sound change. The significance of this reversal for (ay0) is not immediately apparent, but it will become increasingly important as we follow the behavior of the women who are the leaders of linguistic change in chapters 10–12. In any case, we can now proceed with the conviction that (ay0) is not immune from the same social processes that affect the other members of the vowel system.

Figure 9.16 shows the development of (ay0) by decade for the two genders in a form comparable to figures 9.5–9.6, 9.8–9.12 for the female-dominated changes. In this figure, the male and female distributions by decade are quite similar. Both show a progression that comes close to fitting a straight line, with similar slopes; the difference in $r^2$ is too slight to be considered. But the slopes of the two progressions are different: 3.08 for

[14] The treatment of occupational classes for (ay0) differs in one respect from the treatment in other analyses of this chapter. The residual category is in this case the professional class, rather than the unskilled workers. An idiosyncratic property of the male nonsignificant occupational values leads the program to reverse the normal relation of the constants when the usual procedure is followed. The value for the professional class in figure 9.15 is therefore the value of the regression constant.

men as against 2.33 for women. Beginning with speakers over 60, where there is no gender difference at all, the two lines gradually diverge in apparent time.[15] The (ay0) values for speakers who were 50–59 in 1975, born about 1925, indicate the very beginning of this centralization. Their expected value of 740 Hz is not far from the value for the low allophones of /ay/-final and before voiced segments. It follows that the centralization of /ay/ before voiceless obstruents is newer than (aw) which, according to the previous section, must have started its current trajectory shortly after World War I.

A second wave of increased sexual differentiation begins with the 30–39 age group among men. This conforms with the statement of Tucker in 1944, who remarked that the marked difference between /ay/ allophones before voiceless consonants and elsewhere in his own dialect did not exist in Philadelphia, where the two allophones were identical. The first significant centralization occurs for men around 35 years old in 1975, who would have been born after Tucker made his observations; the only centralization that Tucker could have heard was a moderate lowering to 730 Hz F1, used by boys who were then 10 to 20 years old. Assuming phonological stability, figure 9.16 indicates that women remained at this low level of centralization until about 1955.

The account of (ay0) given so far traces the mechanism of change as it diffuses throughout the social system, differentiating the population along the dimensions of gender and occupational class. Centralization began among men; it is not clear if it began in a particular group. No matter what slice of the age range among males we take in the present corpus, no significant differentiation by social factors appears. No internal development of the Philadelphia vowel systems suggests a structural motivation that triggered this change after World War II. Since this type of centralization is not specific to Philadelphia, but is found throughout Eastern Pennsylvania as well as many other sections of the country, (ay0) may well have entered the Philadelphia community from outside as the product of increased mobility during the war, like the change in the status of (r) in other Eastern seaboard cities.

If the male-initiated centralization of (ay0) did not begin in the lower class, we still have to account for the female pattern of social stratification, where the lowest social group has the most extreme values. A provisional answer is that the use of a male-dominated sound change is most acceptable to women in the lower or middle working class, among unskilled workers or unemployed, but that as one rises in the social spectrum, the use of centralized (and backed) values of (ay0) is felt to be less and less appropriate for women. Male recession from a female-dominated change is then

[15] The actual distance between the absolute values for men and women can vary considerably in an analysis of this kind, especially when nonsignificant factors are retained for comparability.

asymmetrically matched by a female recession from a male-dominated change. Both show a monotonic relationship with occupational classes, but in the opposite directions. For a female-dominated change, male distancing is inversely related to status; for a male-dominated change, female distancing is directly related to status.

The idea of a "retreat" of males or females from the advanced form of the other sex may not capture what is happening here. A retreat implies a retrograde movement across generations, where the process of linguistic change is reversed. In fact, we are more likely to find a slower rate of advance. Consider for example the professional women who are the furthest behind in the centralization of (ay0). Only five women are involved, but they show a regular progression in the direction of the change:

| *Age* | *No.* | *Mean* |
|---|---|---|
| <20 | 1 | 712 |
| 30–39 | 1 | 771 |
| 40–49 | 2 | 899 |
| 50–59 | 1 | 912 |

This suggests that the working class women are following behind the male leaders more actively than the women from the higher social classes. We are dealing more with the positive pull of the male model than a reaction against it. The converse would apply to men's reaction to those female-dominated changes which show a linear social stratification in the other direction, where higher socioeconomic groups are more strongly attracted to the incoming forms than the lower groups.

## 9.7 Conclusion

This review of gender differentiation has provided two distinct perspectives on the mechanism of change. On the one hand, the study of gender differences has advanced our understanding of the social location of the leaders of linguistic change. On the other, the comparison of male and female social class patterns has clarified our understanding of the role of gender in linguistic change.

### *The mechanism of diffusion across age groups*

There are two kinds of gender asymmetry in the data. One appears to be basic to the mechanism of change. Almost all the sound changes in progress studied here and elsewhere involve gender differentiation. Given the fact that women are the primary transmitters of language, it follows inevitably that the trajectories of change for men and women will not be the same.

The gender-asymmetric model will affect all social classes in the same way, though its output will be modified by changes that take place in speakers' vernaculars in the pre-adolescent and adolescent years.

### *Interaction of gender with social class*

In the earliest stages of linguistic change, the effects of sex and the effects of social class show a considerable degree of independence. The comparison of occupational and sex patterns in the Philadelphia Neighborhood Study shows parallel and independent effects for (eyC) and (owC), and somewhat different but still independent patterns for (owF) and (owC). In these four cases, age distributions indicate linguistic change advancing at a rapid rate, and in all four cases, a significant curvilinear pattern appears independent of gender differentiation. For these initial stages of change, there is no indication of the monotonic social stratification that is characteristic of late stages, nor of the hypercorrect pattern of the lower middle or clerical groups.

The life history of sound changes shows a changing social configuration as the level of social awareness rises. The minimal degree of social sensitivity is found for the fronting of (eyC), where there is no sign of interaction of gender and socioeconomic class. The fronting of (aw) occurs at a somewhat higher level of social awareness and shows the first signs of interaction of sex and social class, with a leveling of the difference between working class groups for women. A later stage appears for the (uw) and (ay0) variables, where the more advanced gender shows no clear social stratification but the less advanced gender does. The nearly completed (æh) variables have the maximum degree of social awareness in Philadelphia, and show no sign of a curvilinear pattern. For (æh), the relative position of the sexes is reversed: women in advance of men for the working classes, men in advance of women for the middle class occupational groups. The interaction of sex and social class reaches its most extreme form in such sociolinguistic stereotypes, where the stigmatized or prestige form is recognized and discussed in the speech community, and women of different social classes behave in predictably different ways.

As social awareness of a given change in progress develops, the tendency of women to conform to conservative norms is exaggerated for the second highest status group (in North America and Western Europe, the lower middle class; in occupational terms, clerks, primary school teachers, small shopkeepers). There can be no doubt that the social category of gender is part and parcel of the class system in these societies, and that women's behavior is related to their social status. In chapter 8, it was suggested that this hypercorrect pattern may be characterized as a greater investment by women in the social advancement of the family and accumulation of symbolic capital. In the chapters to follow, other interpretations will proceed from a close examination of the social networks in which women are involved and the life trajectories of the female leaders of linguistic change.

### *The role of women or the role of men?*

In the discussion of sex differences, much of the emphasis has been on the special behavior of women. The issue is sometimes raised as to whether one should focus on the behavior of men rather than women. Among the Australian adolescents studied by Eisikovits (figure 8.2), males seem to be the initiators of gender differentiation, reversing the normal direction of accommodation. But in all the other cases reviewed here, it is women who are the active agents of gender differentiation. As the innovators of most linguistic changes, they spontaneously create the differences between themselves and men. In adopting new prestige features more rapidly than men, and in reacting more sharply against the use of stigmatized forms, women are again the chief agents of differentiation, responding more rapidly than men to changes in the social status of linguistic variables. Men follow behind with a lesser degree of investment in the social values of linguistic variation.[16]

### *Change before gender differentiation?*

The earliest gender specialization identified in the gender-asymmetrical model of figure 9.7 is seen as operating upon some pre-existing variation. To the extent that we can recognize with Gordon and Heath a biologically based gender preference for certain types of sound changes, gender as a social category simply ratifies a differentiation that has already taken place. But since chapter 8 showed that such preferences are not binding, and often reversed, we must see gender specialization as a social process that can operate with any type of phonetic material. Eckert 1988 shows the female advantage developing in later stages of the Northern Cities Shift, where early stages were sensitive to other, gender-neutral factors: social categories based on orientation to adult norms. In the *ANAE* data (table 8.4), a male advantage remains only for the latest stage; if present trends continue, we might well expect it to shift to a female-led change.

### *The relation of gender differentiation to larger social structures*

Volume 1 of this work indicated that many aspects of chain shifting are regulated by the structure of the linguistic system. A central question for this volume is whether or not external social variables are intimately

[16] A clear illustration of this principle appears in Gal 1978. The shift from Hungarian to German was correlated with membership in non-peasant networks for both men and women to about the same degree (.78 and .74 respectively). But the correlation with age was much less for men than women (.69 and .93 respectively).

involved in the ordinary mechanism of linguistic change. Gender appears to be a critical variable for this problem. Since gender differentiation is almost always prominent in linguistic change, it would seem that social factors cannot be separated from the normal process of change and the evolution of language. In the early stages of change – at the lowest levels of social awareness – gender operates as an independent and powerful factor. It follows that the forces active in qualitatively new changes include social factors, and that any effort to account for the initiation of change by purely internal arguments will fail to a significant degree. A question to be pursued is the size of the social structures involved: the family, the peer group, the local speech community, or a larger region or the nation as a whole. The correlation of an early stage of a sound change with a local social category like Burnouts is challenging. Given the generality of the Northern Cities Shift throughout the vast area of the Inland North, we would expect to find such a correlation repeated in many cities, if we can identify the same social structures. Later chapters will suggest that the social position of the Burnouts, as described in detail by Eckert (1989a), is not unrelated to the mechanism of gender differentiation presented here. As Eckert's work shows, the "Burnout" and "Jock" categories are age-specific transformations of the more general social class categories used to describe the adult Philadelphia and New York City populations.

To the extent that gender differentiation is closely linked with social class differentiation, it may also be linked to the large-scale dislocations that set the initiating conditions for change, rather than the mechanism of response to those conditions. Evidence in this chapter has pointed to World War I as such a dislocating event for several of the Philadelphia sound changes, and World War II for (ay0). Such grand punctuating events make sense out of the erratic progression of sound changes in time, but we are far from understanding how they are linked to the development of the Philadelphia sound changes or the Northern Cities Shift.

### *The immediate social context of gender differentiation*

The gender-asymmetric model accounts for the step-wise advance of men, but it takes as a given the linear progression in women's use of a linguistic change. No insight has been provided so far into the mechanism behind this steady upward movement or the driving force behind it. The following four chapters will search for such a mechanism, and with it, a glimpse of factors that have some legitimate claim to be the causes of linguistic change. The first step will be to pursue the social relationships in which the female leaders of change are involved. This will allow us to focus on them not as anonymous members of social categories, but as clearly identified individuals whose personal histories will illuminate the central questions of this volume.

# Part C

## *The Leaders of Linguistic Change*

# 10

# *Social Networks*

The studies described so far have located the leaders of linguistic change from below as members of the more prosperous, upwardly mobile sections of the local community, for the most part women. To this end, a wide variety of data have been mobilized: the age, gender, occupation, education, social mobility, house value, house upkeep, ethnicity, foreign language background, and generational status of the speakers. These are the types of demographic data that are extracted from a survey of individuals similar to the New York City study, where contact with each subject begins and ends with a single interview. Though these data are rich and reliable, they cannot carry us much further in the search for the leaders of linguistic change.

The Philadelphia Neighborhood Study anticipated that the assignment of individuals to social categories would not be sufficient to address the causes and social mechanism of linguistic change. The methods of the Neighborhood Study as outlined in chapter 2 included not one but a series of interviews, along with participation in social gatherings, the collection of social histories, and a second series of systematic inquiries into social network relations. This chapter will present the results of this systematic inquiry, and the chapters to follow will draw more heavily upon the knowledge base from repeated interviews and ethnographic observations. But first it will be useful to consider the range of other results that have been gotten through the study of social networks, and some of the issues of sociolinguistic method and theory that have been raised in this connection.

## 10.1 The sociolinguistic use of social networks

The history and practice of the linguistic study of social networks is well reviewed in three recent sources: L. Milroy 1980, J. Milroy 1990, and Chambers 1995. All three treatments take a balanced approach to network studies, viewing them as one of several means of gathering information that would help to understand linguistic behavior. However, a number of papers have appeared since the Milroys' studies in Belfast which assume or explicitly assert that the multiplexity or density of social networks would replace other measures of social structure, in particular the measurement of social class through occupation, education, or indices of consumption. The study of social networks is presented as a higher form of social analysis than the study of social class and more suitable for sociolinguistic analysis.[1] Thus Le Page and Tabouret-Keller write:

> Networks are a means of defining social units with which to correlate kinds of linguistic behavior. They are a more satisfactory alternative to . . . social or economic or other groups. (1985:116)

There are clear advantages to the study of groups as opposed to isolated individuals. Studies of people in their social networks allow us to record them speaking with the people they usually speak to – friends, family, and work associates. Since most random samples of speech communities concentrate on individuals, one must reconstruct hypothetical networks that surround these individuals to interpret their behavior.

What would it mean to study a community of a million speakers by using social networks and only social networks? This problem is not clearly distinct from Bloomfield's thought experiment of recording the total network of speech interactions, a total record of each time one person speaks to another (1933:476). Such a massive data base might allow us to model the speech community through the mechanics of interaction alone with no reference to education, income, occupation, ethnicity, status, prestige or stigma, or other attitudes.[2] Such a mechanical approach is attractive in many ways: it is conceptually economical and it is based upon the act of speaking itself.

The best network studies must fall far short of this hypothetical goal. Most of them are devoted to one or two isolated groups of a dozen speakers or so. It is no easier to understand the sociolinguistic behavior of such an isolated small group than it is to understand the speech of an isolated individual. The social significance of the speaker's use of linguistic variables, across different topics, channels, tasks, addressees, and social

[1] Some of the work that strongly promotes the analysis of social networks takes a strong position on both of these issues. Boissevain 1974 asserts that the understanding of human behavior requires us to start with individuals "acting as self-interested entrepreneurs." At the same time, he argues that the structural-functional view of Merton and others contributes nothing at all to that understanding, and that it is a misguided conspiracy to repress the obvious truth of his own views.

[2] As noted in chapter 1, such a data base was approximated by an analysis of average daily traffic flow on the highways of the Eastern United States. It did succeed in predicting the location of major dialect boundaries, except for the boundary of the New York City dialect which was a striking exception. The confinement of that dialect to the immediate environs of the metropolis is undoubtedly the result of negative attitudes toward that city's dialect (Labov 1966a, chapter 14).

contexts, is a derivative of variation in the wider community (Bell 1984, Preston 1989). Unless a representative sample of that wider community is available, interpretations of the individual or the small group are largely a matter of guesswork.

What, then, is the solution? How can we combine the insights from the study of small groups with the knowledge gained from a representative sample of the speech community? Random samples of groups are out of the question, for there is no way to enumerate all of the intersecting social groups in a community. One can, however, create a judgment sample of groups that represent main neighborhoods, ethnic groups, and social classes in the community. Such an effective judgment sample of local networks requires prior studies of relative power, income, employment, house values – from a national census if available, or from local surveys if necessary. Chapter 2 presented the effort of the Philadelphia Neighborhood Study to achieve such a sample. When such a judgment sample agrees with a random sample, such as the Philadelphia Telephone Survey, we can have considerable confidence in the results, especially when the numbers are large enough to permit multivariate analysis. More generally, the linguistic significance of social network data is maximal when:

1 Previous studies have identified the major linguistic variables of the wider community and traced their patterns of stylistic and social variation. Social class, age, gender, and ethnicity will continue to explain the greatest part of the variance, as this chapter will show.
2 All members of the group share the same social history in terms of residence and dialect contact. When they do not, the effect of these differences in social history must be accounted for by wider studies of the type indicated in (1).

Many network studies have focused on situations where the small group is an exponent of a nonstandard dialect, receding under the impact of the regional standard that surrounds it. The expected result is that members of networks with greater density and multiplexity will maintain their local dialects more vigorously than others. Speakers with more connections to other groups (weak ties) will show more influence of the more mobile surrounding society in their speech (Milroy 1980:196).[3]

The search for the leaders of linguistic change has focused on neighborhoods with a different relation to the surrounding community. Within these local networks are the leading exponents of new and vigorous changes which spread outward to influence in varying degrees the speech of several

[3] This is in fact consistent with the results of studies of the social networks of speakers of African American Vernacular English in Harlem (Labov 1972b) and Philadelphia (Labov and Harris 1986).

million people. The linguistic changes in progress ultimately affect everyone in the wider speech community, including those at the peak of the socioeconomic hierarchy, reluctantly but inevitably carried along by the force of the linguistic tide. The effort to locate the leaders of linguistic change will draw upon everything we can gather about the local social relations in the most advanced neighborhoods, but it is not immediately clear how these local relations will affect the dramatic expansion of the sound changes.

Any perspective on social network research must be profoundly modified by the recent publication of Eckert's full report on her research in the suburban Detroit high school, "Belten High" (1999). Much of the explanation of the current findings is to be found in Eckert's work, based on ethnographic observation, interviewing, and measurement of sound change among adolescents. Whereas the Philadelphia study draws upon participant observation for interpretation, the quantitative correlations are carried out on interview responses alone. Eckert's observations of clothing, spatial location, smoking, and cruising patterns are reduced to quantitative form and tightly tied to her measurements of sound change. The following four chapters will move steadily toward the location of the leaders of linguistic change, but ultimately they will draw upon Eckert's findings on adolescent behavior to explain what is found in the adult community.

Whatever explanations and accounts emerge from the study of social networks must be related to other social measures. Will social network scores replace the effect of social class, occupation, neighborhood, ethnicity, or will they add further to the information that these broader categories have given? A clear answer to this question will come from a multivariate analysis that looks simultaneously at both types of data. Unfortunately, most studies of social networks are limited in the numbers of their subjects,[4] and even the univariate statistics on the influence of network position often fail to reach significance.

This chapter will address these questions by adding social network data to the view of the Philadelphia changes in progress that has been obtained by the study of age, gender, social class, neighborhood, and ethnicity in chapters 5–9. First, however, it may be helpful to use multivariate analysis to probe further into earlier studies of social networks. We can profitably build upon the re-analysis of the Belfast data on neighborhood, age, and gender first presented in chapter 7.

[4] The Belfast study was limited to 46 speakers (Milroy 1980:202–3). The study in South Harlem was based on 19 members of the Jets and 36 members of the Cobra networks (Labov 1972b). The analysis of the Philadelphia networks to follow will be based on 39 speakers. Two exceptional studies that involved larger numbers are Bortoni-Ricardo 1985, who studied 118 speakers, and Eckert's study of Belten High School, which focuses on 69 speakers against the background of a much larger social network (Eckert 1999:fig. 8.1).

## 10.2 Social networks in Belfast

In her summary of the Belfast study, L. Milroy (1980) states that "the main orientation of this book has been towards questions not of linguistic change, but of linguistic stability" (p. 185). She addresses the question that has troubled sociolinguists from the outset: how is the structure of stable sociolinguistic variation maintained? Milroy argues that the existence of dense, multiplex networks in local working class communities provides the evidence that covert norms maintain the stability of linguistic forms that are overtly stigmatized by the dominant society.

The Appendix to Milroy 1980 gives data on network scores, in addition to the data on generation, gender, and neighborhood that was used in chapter 7. The classification of the 46 speakers by their social networks employs a scale ranging from 0 to 5, derived from the number of five conditions satisfied. These included one measure of density (membership in a high-density, territorially based cluster) and four measures of multiplexity (kinship in the neighborhood, workmates from the neighborhood, workmates of the same sex from the neighborhood, and leisure time spent with these workmates) (L. Milroy 1980:141–2).

Table 10.1 adds these network scores to the regression analyses of table 7.1. It is evident that network scores add information, rather than replace other correlations. The outlined boxes indicate the cases where there is a change in the effects found in table 7.1 (mostly effects of male gender), but these are minor differences. Shaded boxes indicate reduction of the effect; the open box shows an increase. The picture remains essentially the

*Table 10.1* Regression coefficients for nine Belfast variables by gender, age, neighborhood, and network scores. Significance: **bold**, $p < .001$; underlined, $p < .01$; plain, $p < .05$; *italic*, $p < .10$. Open boxed areas = increase in value compared to table 7.1; shaded areas = decrease

| | *(th)* | *(a)* | *(e$^1$)* | *(e$^2$)* | *(ʌ$^1$)* | *(ʌ$^2$)* | *(ai)* | *(i)* | *(o)* |
|---|---|---|---|---|---|---|---|---|---|
| Means | 56.16 | 2.53 | 81.6 | 64.5 | 42.7 | 29.32 | 2.28 | 2.02 | 90.3 |
| Std dev. | 30.01 | 0.53 | 23.7 | 21.7 | 20.7 | 23.92 | 0.35 | 0.34 | 16.4 |
| Male | **28** | 0.43 | **27** | 19.0 | | | | | |
| Younger | | | | | | | | 0.27 | 13.8 |
| Younger men | | | | | | 20.74 | | | |
| Older men | | | | | 16.0 | −16.1 | | | |
| Younger women | | | | | | *−14.2* | | | |
| Hammer | | | | | | | 0.25 | 0.28 | 12.3 |
| Network scores | 6.45 | **0.16** | | *3.2* | *3.5* | | 0.07 | | |
| $r^2$ increase (%) | 10 | 19 | | 3 | 5 | | 9 | | |

*Table 10.2* Regression coefficients for nine Belfast variables by age and neighborhood and network scores, in separate analyses by gender. Significance: **bold**, p < .001; <u>underlined</u>, p < .01; plain, p < .05; *italic*, p < .10

| | *(th)* | *(a)* | *(e¹)* | *(e²)* | *(ʌ¹)* | *(ʌ²)* | *(ai)* | *(i)* | *(o)* |
|---|---|---|---|---|---|---|---|---|---|
| *Male [n = 23]* | | | | | | | | | |
| Means | 73.7 | 2.82 | 95.11 | 68.2 | 50.0 | 35.0 | 2.30 | 2.04 | 91.8 |
| Std dev. | 26.1 | 0.41 | 9.2 | 23.0 | 21.9 | 24.0 | 0.33 | 0.35 | 11.7 |
| Younger | | <u>−0.43</u> | *−7.34* | | | **36.4** | 0.27 | <u>0.34</u> | <u>13.8</u> |
| Ballymacarett | | <u>0.55</u> | | | | | | | |
| Hammer | | | | | | | | | |
| Clonard | | | | | | | | <u>−3.6</u> | |
| Network scores | | | 3.26 | | *3.36* | | | | |
| *Female [n = 23]* | | | | | | | | | |
| Means | 40.1 | 2.23 | 81.6 | 64.5 | 34.7 | 29.32 | 2.26 | 1.99 | 88.8 |
| Std dev. | 24.0 | 0.47 | 23.7 | 21.7 | 16.3 | 23.92 | 0.38 | 0.33 | 20.2 |
| Younger | | | | | | | | | |
| Ballymacarett | | | −26 | | | | | | |
| Hammer | | | | | | | <u>0.47</u> | | |
| Clonard | | | | | | *17.3* | | | **−30** |
| Network scores | 6.64 | <u>0.23</u> | | | | | *0.07* | | <u>6.23</u> |

same: (th), (a), ($e^1$), and ($e^2$) are male-dominated variables, (ai), (i), and (o) are strongest in the Hammer neighborhood, and (i) and (o) show change in apparent time.

What does the multivariate analysis of network scores add to our understanding of the sociolinguistic patterns of Belfast? They generally match the findings reported in L. Milroy 1980, but in a format that allows comparison with other community studies. The network effects are strongest for the two male-dominated variables (th) and (a), the most overtly recognized stereotypes of working class Belfast speech. Correlations below the usual level of significance appear for $e^2$ and $ʌ^1$, but not for $e^1$ or $ʌ^2$. A .05 network effect appears as an effect on (ai), but this cannot be weighed too heavily when we are examining 72 (9 × 8) possibilities. No network effects appear for the two variables (i) and (o), the only ones that show signs of change in progress in apparent time.

These results fit well with Milroy's exposition of the role of dense, multiplex networks as conservative factors, insulating local communities from the negative evaluation of their speech patterns by socially dominant norms. As Milroy points out, they also fit the results of network studies among minority groups such as the study of the South Harlem adolescents (Labov 1972b). But to the extent that (o) and (i) represent change in progress, no influence of social networks is coupled with such changes.

The age/gender interactions previously located in the Belfast data are consonant with Milroy's emphasis on the high degree of interaction between gender and network scores. It is therefore appropriate to carry out a separate regression analysis for each gender, as we did in chapter 9. Table 10.2 shows that the differences in the means of men and women correspond closely to the gender coefficients of table 10.1. Significant age coefficients appear only in the male section. The negative figures for (a) and ($e^1$) indicate that young men are moving away from the local norms, while the positive figures for the four variables on the right indicate that young men are advancing the local norms. Of the four significant network coefficients (not counting $p < .10$), three are on the female side. Of these, one appears for a variable with a positive development in apparent time – 6.23 for (o). However, it is the men who show a change in apparent time, and women whose use is correlated with network scores. It is also somewhat unexpected that for the stereotypical, male-dominated variables (a) and (th), the network effect appears only among women, and not among men as we might expect.

Though there are some regularities in this picture, they are not easy to interpret. The clear neighborhood effects of tables 7.1 and 10.1 have disappeared, particularly the fact that the Hammer led in the two changes in apparent time. Instead, there is a scattering of neighborhood effects. Considering only effects at the .01 level, each of the three neighborhoods emerges as leading significantly in only one of the 18 possible cases. This contrasts sharply with the consistent advantage of Wicket St. in Philadelphia.

*Table 10.3* Regression coefficients for nine Belfast variables by age and gender and network scores, in separate analyses by neighborhood. Significance: **bold**, p < .001; underlined, p < .01; plain, p < .05

| | *(th)* | *(a)* | *(e¹)* | *(e²)* | *(ʌ¹)* | *(ʌ²)* | *(ai)* | *(i)* | *(o)* |
|---|---|---|---|---|---|---|---|---|---|
| *Ballymacarett [n = 14]* | | | | | | | | | |
| Younger | | | | | | | | | **19** |
| Male | 37.4 | | | | | | | | |
| Network scores | | 0.24 | | | | | 0.16 | | |
| *Clonard [n = 15]* | | | | | | | | | |
| Younger | | –0.48 | | | | | | | |
| Male | | 0.43 | | | | | | | 19.7 |
| Network scores | | 0.29 | | | | | | | |
| *Hammer [n = 17]* | | | | | | | | | |
| Younger | | | | | –23.5 | | | | –5.68 |
| Male | | | | | | | | | |
| Network scores | | | | | 9.5 | | | | 2.91 |

*Table 10.4* Mean network scores by gender in Belfast

| | *Mean* | *Std dev.* |
|---|---|---|
| Women | 2.09 | 1.59 |
| Men | 2.91 | 1.44 |

Another approach to an understanding of the Belfast data is to do separate regression analyses by neighborhood (table 10.3). With these smaller units, effects at the .05 level must be accepted. Network scores are correlated with sound change in 2 of 9 possibilities for Ballymacarett, 1 for Clonard, and 2 for Hammer. Milroy's figure 6.1, designed to show that network influences (th) in Ballymacarett but not in the other neighborhoods, corresponds here to a large gender effect of 37.4 percentage points, and no significant network effect.[5] On the other hand, table 10.3 does restore the view of the Hammer as a leading neighborhood for at least one of the linguistic changes taking place.

Gender and network scores: the Milroys report that network scores are higher among men than among women. This has been widely cited and related to the explanation of the diffusion of linguistic change (Downes 1998). However, table 10.4 shows that this difference falls far short of

[5] Milroy observes quite accurately that in Ballymacarett, sex and network effects are highly correlated (p. 159). But it is also true that network scores do not add significantly to the prediction of the linguistic behavior of these 14 speakers.

significance: it is only about one half of the standard deviations. Moreover, table 10.2 shows that there is more correlation between network scores and linguistic variables for women than for men. There is only one figure for men at a significance level of $p < .05$, and three for women. Whether or not men have greater density and/or multiplexity in their social relations than women, this fact does not appear to be related to linguistic behavior. Most importantly for the present investigation, women show the only correlation of network scores with change in apparent time. As we will see below, the effect of social networks on linguistic variation is almost entirely a female phenomenon in Philadelphia.

Table 10.2 illustrates Milroy's statement that in the long run, detailed quantitative analysis demonstrates "the very great complexity of various sources of influence on a speaker's language" (p. 165) and that the results of the analysis indicate merely that "particular 'bits' of the language are particularly significant . . . to different subgroups in the population" (p. 163). While table 10.1 supports Milroy's central theme that network scores add to our understanding of sociolinguistic structure, and "are of great importance in predicting language use" (p. 160), table 10.2 confirms her further statement that "network patterns of the sexes, age groups and areas are very different." Milroy's breakdown by neighborhood finds that networks function consistently only in Ballymacarett, and in other neighborhoods there is "little significant correlation between language use and network structure" (p. 159).

Three characteristics of the Belfast data may be obscuring the important insights of the investigators and limit how far they can be generalized to the North American situation. These all proceed from the historical location of the study in Belfast at the height of the troubles, where a tremendous amount was accomplished in the face of extraordinary difficulties. First is sample size. The total of 46 speakers is evidently not enough to yield a clear view of the intersection of age, gender, neighborhood, and network, given the extensive interaction among these variables. The major effects are not robust enough to persist when the configuration of regression variables changes. Second is the limitation to working class Belfast neighborhoods without a view of the larger sociolinguistic structure. Third is the fundamental characteristic of European speech communities noted above. As in so many other reports from European countries, we do not find the sweeping changes from below that introduce new patterns and relations like the Northern Cities Shift or the Philadelphia sound changes. The strongest effects are the retreat (or more recently, expansion) of well-known, overtly stigmatized variables (Holmquist 1988, Hinskens 1992, Williams and Kerswill 1999). In Belfast, the major effect of a dense social network, as Milroy finds it, is to act as a brake on linguistic change. The question remains open as to what role networks will play when linguistic change is in its prime, when the vernacular is vigorously advancing, and when the standard dialect of the dominant social classes follows behind the others in reluctant disarray. That is the question that the Philadelphia data is designed to address.

## 10.3 Social networks in Philadelphia

Chapter 5 reported some of the experimental data from the second series of interviews in the Philadelphia Neighborhood Study. The main purpose of these interviews was to obtain systematic data on the social interactions of each person on the block and in the wider neighborhood. This would not have been as effectively carried out in the first interview. The "second" interview was in many cases a third, fourth, or even tenth recording made by the field workers Anne Bower, Deborah Schiffrin, and Arvilla Payne. By the time they sat down to ask questions about interaction on the block, the neighborhood people were free to mention by name a wide range of people who were common acquaintances.

A second interview that Anne Bower recorded with Agnes ("Ag") D. of Pitt St. illustrates the density and multiplexity of block relations. Ag's work at the local school intersects with her relations with her neighbors. She uses the example of one unpleasant neighbor – an isolate without normal social skills – as a way of underlining her main position, that her most important friendship network is outside of the local block.

The following narrative was triggered by a discussion of unpleasant people in the neighborhood by one of Ag's best friends, Betty I.

> Yeh, I don't know if you can understand. Y'know, this is a fr'instance. Now this is just happening right now, so that's why I'll use this fr'instance. OK? There's a woman who lives across the street – I won't mention any names, but she'll [Betty] know immediately who I'm speaking of. Uh – the woman obviously – has really had a hard life. She's married to a man much younger than herself, but nobody really cares for her because she's the type of woman that – uh – is very outspoken and a lot of people just don't care for her . . . she's more or less *crude*, y'know.
>
> Now she works at the school, and a lot of people don't want to be – uh – bothered with her. Now there was this dinner they had – a retirement dinner they had for the principal, right? Now *nobody* – there's other people on the street that *also* work at the school – they didn' wanna be involved with this woman. A'right now. I feel sorry for her. So, I automatically said, "Yes, I'll go with you." When we reached the place, y'know, the Hilton, I was supposed to sit at the table with the teachers, and with Anna Mae. And . . . she s's to me, she s's to me, "you're gonna sit right at *my* table." So I immediately just off the top of my head, I s's, "Well, no, I'm supposed to sit . . ." But then I looked over at

her and I seen her sitting by herself, and I just couldn't let her sit there by herself, right.

Now the same woman w'n I wasn't here – now this has happened twice. My daughter got her hair cut – now this sounds ridiculous to you but it bothers me – she says – uh – she says to my daughter, "You look like a boy with your hair cut." Now why insult my kid and I have – she'll tell you about my kids. To me they're special 'cause I'm their mother, but my kids *are* good kids and they done *very well* in school. Right, a lot of other kids . . . But they're ready to tear me apart because of my kids, y'know. But that's why I don't bother with anybody around here, I'd rather not – but that's the way they are. Now she wouldn't *dare* say this to my daughter if I was sitting right there . . . This is just recent. Last night is the second time she says to my daughter, "Gee, you look like a boy with your new hair cut."

To me, that is the lowest, that is being *so* ignorant . . .

Anne responded sympathetically with the rhetorical question, "How can an adult be so *ignorant?*"

### *The communication indices*

In the later phases of the Philadelphia study, the research group turned to the problem of finding comparative measures of social interaction that might help account for the patterns of diffusion of linguistic change that are documented in chapters 5–9. The problem was not learning more about the people we had been dealing with. After three years of intimate association with the central figures in each neighborhood, journals and tapes were filled with neighborhood gossip; we had no shortage of information on how our speakers interacted with each other. The chapters to follow will draw upon that extensive knowledge base. But the knowledge gained from participant observation is not easily matched with the movement of vowels across phonological space for an entire community. No matter how well we may get to know a particular sponsor or household, we cannot hope to know everyone equally well. First interviews are comparable, but in the course of further social interaction, we get to know people to different degrees. We knew more about Kate Corcoran of Wicket St. than we knew about her daughter Barbara, and we knew more about Barbara than we knew about three of her friends who sat in on one group recording. The problem is to extract from our knowledge of the community a set of precise and comparable indices of social interaction that will not be biased by the history of our participation. The communication interviews and the communication index were designed to provide such a data base.

The term *communication index* reflects the focus on verbal interaction as the product of social relations. The communication indices are not dissimilar from the criteria used to construct the Belfast multiplexity scores, which involve the number of kin and workmates in the neighborhood, and they define the sets of social relations that are often referred to as social networks.

The communication interviews were designed and written by the team of field workers Bower, Schiffrin, and Payne, after reviewing the methods and results presented in Bott 1955, Granovetter 1973, and others. The questions raised and the topics discussed in the interview produced a map of the relative intensities of local interaction as the product of a person's membership in local communication networks. The chief focus was on two aspects of interaction that might relate to participation in the Philadelphia sound changes. First was the density of interaction within the block. This clearly provides a measure of the opportunities to influence the speech of others on the block or be influenced by them. The second is the relative proportion of the person's social network that is geographically centered on the block and in the wider neighborhood. The block, as noted above, is defined as an I-beam shape: the houses facing each other along a residential block together with those houses on the near side of the intersecting streets that define the block. The *neighborhood* is a larger unit whose limits are subject to variable social definition by residents.[6]

Communication interviews were completed with 61 subjects. Four indices were constructed from an examination of the data.

C1 is a measure of density of block interaction through estimates of the number of neighbors the subject dealt with in everyday life. The questions asked how many people on the block the person would *say hello to*, *have coffee with*, *visit with*, *invite to a party*, *go out with*, or *confide in*. The subject selected one of five possible responses, coded as:

| | *rank* |
|---|---|
| everyone on the block | 4 |
| 6–10 people | 3 |
| 3–5 people | 2 |
| 1–2 people | 1 |
| no one | 0 |

The mean of the C1 codes was rounded to an integer value.

C2 is also a measure of density of interaction, but involved potential rather than actual contact. Speakers were asked to name the people on the block that they would *visit with*, *go out with*, *telephone*, *confide in*, *ask for medical advice*, *invite to a party*, *ask to take charge of a problem*. They were also asked to name their *best friend*, *close friends*, and whoever had the *nicest*

[6] One of ten questions used by Edwards 1992, a network study of the African American community in Detroit, was agreement with the statement, "Most of my friends live in this neighborhood."

*house on the block*. The C2 measure is the number of categories in which the person named someone on the block.

C3 and C4 are measures of localization of friendship patterns, derived from questions on where the individual's friends lived. The measure was the percentage of named friends who lived in the neighborhood (for C3) or the block (for C4). These were coded as follows:

| | |
|---|---|
| 81–100% | 1 |
| 61–80% | 2 |
| 41–60% | 3 |
| 21–40% | 4 |
| 0–20% | 5 |

This numbering system actually redefines C3/4 as the percentage of friends who live *off* the block or *out of* the neighborhood, for reasons that will become clear below.

Thirty-eight of the 61 communication interviews were with speakers whose vowel systems were analyzed to form the data base of the previous chapters. Though this number is considerably reduced from the total of 112, and is smaller than the Belfast sample, it is concentrated in the intact neighborhoods examined in chapter 7, and includes most of the members of the central networks in those neighborhoods. This chapter will examine the relation of the communication indices to the advancement of the vowel changes in Philadelphia.

Before correlating the four communication indices with the linguistic data, it will be helpful to see what their internal relations are. Table 10.5 is a correlation matrix of the four indices. It shows that C1 is quite independent of C2, but is negatively correlated with C3 and C4. C2 does not appear to have any close connection with any of the others. The highest correlation is between C3 and C4, which is quite natural considering that they differ only as to whether the block or the neighborhood is concerned. The negative correlation of C1 with C3 and C4 also seems natural, when we consider that the higher C1, the higher the density of interaction, and the lower C4, the higher the proportion of friends found on the block.

*Table 10.5* Pearson product-moment correlations of the four communication indices (n = 38)

| | *C1* | *C2* | *C3* | *C4* |
|---|---|---|---|---|
| C1 | 1.000 | | | |
| C2 | −0.042 | 1.000 | | |
| C3 | −0.202 | 0.101 | 1.000 | |
| C4 | −0.286 | 0.022 | 0.465 | 1.000 |

*Table 10.6* Pearson product-moment correlations of the four communication indices with the fronting of (aw) and (eyC) (n = 36)

| | *C1* | *C2* | *C3* | *C4* | *(eyC)* | *(aw)* |
|---|---|---|---|---|---|---|
| (eyC2) | −0.038 | 0.071 | −0.044 | **0.432** | 1.000 | |
| (aw2) | **0.156** | 0.122 | 0.046 | **0.249** | 0.729 | 1.000 |

Table 10.6 adds (aw) and (eyC) to this correlation matrix. The highest correlation in this table – .729 – appears between the second formants of (eyC) and (aw); as chapter 4 showed, they are tightly related in the Philadelphia vowel system. Of the four communication indices, C4 shows the strongest correlation with the linguistic variables. Despite the significant correlation of .465 between C3 and C4, C3 has almost no relation at all to the vowel changes. The same situation repeats throughout the vowel system, no matter what form of analysis is used, and C3 will therefore be excluded from the analyses to follow. Repeated comparisons of C1 and C2 also lead to the conclusion that C1 is more highly correlated with the linguistic variables than C2.

The positive correlation of C1 with (aw) is in the expected direction, but the stronger positive correlations of C4 were unexpected. We originally thought that a high proportion of local friends would mark a leader of sound change, but the opposite turned out to be the case for (aw) and for almost all other vowels. The higher the proportion of a person's friends live *off* the block, the more likely that person is to use advanced forms of the Philadelphia sound changes.

The correlations of table 10.6 do not tell us whether these relations will persist when gender, age, and social class are taken into account. In fact, the implications of table 10.5 persist throughout the work to follow. Multivariate analyses confirmed that in every case, C1 provides a stronger correlation with vowel changes than C2. The subjects' estimation of the number of people they reacted with on the block provided a more consistent view of their relations than the more miscellaneous and less quantitative criteria of C2. Multivariate analyses also confirm the stronger effect of C4 as against C3. The quantitative analysis of the social network dimension will proceed upon the conclusion that C1 is to be preferred to C2 and C4 to C3.

Since C1 and C4 both correlate with the vowel shifts, stronger correlations should be obtained by combining the two into a single index, C5. In fact, it appears that individually, C1 and C4 vary considerably in their influence, but combined they regularly produce a significant and positive effect. The range of C1 is from 4 to 21, while the range of C4 is from 1 to

5. In order to give equal weight of the two factors, a combined index C5 is calculated as (C1/4) + C4. Positive correlations and significant regression coefficients are found between C5 and (æhN), (æhS), (aw), (eyC), and (owF).

The group of 38 subjects will not be considered as a whole, however. The analysis to follow will accept the guidance of earlier findings on the effect of gender. Chapters 8 and 9 showed that the development of the sound changes and the current level reached were quite different for men and women. Table 10.2 showed that most of the significant network scores were found for women. Not only did women show more significant network correlations than men, but network scores were correlated with changes in progress only for women. It would therefore be wise to separate the 17 men from the 21 women in the communication study.

Differences between men and women in the mean values of the communication indices favor women slightly in all cases, but they do not even approach significance. On the other hand, differences in the correlation of communication indices with linguistic changes are absolute. The results with men are simple and quite clear. The communication index C5 shows no significant effects for any variable. All significant effects of network scores are found with women.

In dealing with the effects of network scores, we must be alert to the question as to whether they explain or replace the results that locate the leaders of change in the larger social structure. More than a few have followed Le Page and Tabouret-Keller's argument, cited above, that social network analysis is "a more satisfactory alternative" to the study of linguistic distributions in larger social or economic groupings. This is an idea that must be taken seriously, since if it were true it would greatly simplify the studies of language in its social context. In testing this possibility, we must bear in mind that the strong effects of socioeconomic class, neighborhood, and gender may be severely attenuated in shifting down from the 112 speakers of the neighborhood study to the 21 women for whom we have both communication patterns and acoustic analysis. Such a drastic reduction might prevent any effect from emerging as significant.

The first step is therefore to repeat the earlier multiple regression analysis with this reduced sample, using the independent variables that were found significant in chapter 9.[7]

Table 10.7 displays the significant regression coefficients for age by decade, social class, neighborhood, and ethnicity for this reduced group. Surprisingly enough, all of the major effects are preserved, many in a stronger form than in the full study. There are no upper class speakers in

[7] For a measure of social class, the analyses of this chapter will use the combined SEC index, which is slightly stronger than the effect of occupation alone.

*Table 10.7* Significant regression coefficients for 21 female speakers in the Philadelphia Neighborhood Study. Significance: **bold**, p < .001; underlined, p < .01; plain, p < .05; *italic*, p < .10

| | *(æhN)* | *(æhS)* | *(aw)* | *(eyC)* | *(owC)* | *(owF)* | *(uwC)* | *(uwF)* |
|---|---|---|---|---|---|---|---|---|
| <20 years | 202 | **217** | 332 | 262 | 193 | 205 | | 313 |
| 20–29 years | | | 243 | 163 | 262 | −170 | 342 | |
| 30–39 years | 110 | **238** | 182 | | | | | |
| Upper working class | 186 | **244** | 197 | 152 | | | | |
| Lower middle class | *−127* | | | | 160 | | 307 | *163* |
| Wicket St. | | | | | 200 | 157 | | |
| Italian | | | | | −176 | **−390** | **−457** | **−461** |
| $r^2$ (adj) | 54 | 62 | 51 | 48 | 76 | 73 | 61 | 54 |

the communication study, and very few upper middle class speakers in the subset. However, we find:

- The age pattern by decade is reproduced, with speakers under 20 years showing a strong advantage except for (uwC), and some fluctuation between the young adults 20–29 and 30–39.
- The curvilinear pattern is intact for the new and vigorous changes (aw) and (eyC) and reappearing for the nearly completed changes (æhN) and (æhS). The lower middle class advantage is stable for the checked middle-range changes, but has all but disappeared for the free vowels.
- The advantage of the Wicket St. neighborhood is not reproduced, except for the /ow/ variables.
- The negative effect of Italian ethnicity (primary or secondary) on the fronting of /ow/ and /uw/ is maintained and considerably strengthened.

Given these stable results, we can add the C5 communication index to these regression analyses to discover if it can in fact replace them. The results are shown in table 10.8. There is indeed a moderately strong and significant effect of C5 for all the variables but two – (uwC) and (uwF). The effect of C5 is strongest for the vowel with the highest degree of social awareness, (æhN), but only marginal for its partner (æhS). For (aw), (eyC), and (owF) the C5 coefficients are steady and well below the .05 level of significance.

It is a remarkable fact that in table 10.8 there is very little change in the other sociolinguistic factors; the effect of C5 is almost entirely additive. No factors previously found significant are lost when C5 is added to the regression analysis. Table 10.9 provides an exact comparison of tables 10.7 and 10.8, showing for each cell the percent change in the coefficient. Most changes are small; the maximum change is a 35% increase in the effect of the lower middle class on (owF). On the whole, the effect of the addition of C5 on the other factors in the analysis is neutral. The next to last line shows the average changes in the other factors; the average of these figures is –.07. Most important is the percent of variation explained as shown by the adjusted $r^2$. In table 10.8 this figure rises to values as high as 81%, higher than any figure shown so far in this volume. Table 10.9 shows the percent changes in this statistic. For all but (uwC) the figures are sizeable and positive.

The conclusion is that the effect of social networks on the Philadelphia vowel changes is substantial, extensive, and stable, considerably more powerful for these 21 speakers than for the 16 women of the Belfast study. Social network factors do not replace the effect of age, social class, neighborhood, or ethnicity. The social network effects are not the largest, but they add essential information to the description of the leaders of linguistic change. Furthermore, they suggest that the leading position of women in linguistic

*Table 10.8* Addition of the C5 communication index to the significant regression coefficients for 21 female speakers in the Philadelphia Neighborhood Study. Significance: **bold**, p < .001; underlined, p < .01; plain, p < .05; *italic*, p < .10

| | *(æhN)* | *(æhS)* | *(aw)* | *(eyC)* | *(owC)* | *(owF)* | *(uwC)* | *(uwF)* |
|---|---|---|---|---|---|---|---|---|
| C5 communication index | **52** | *32* | 48 | 46 | *36* | 57 | | |
| <20 years | 209 | **214** | **327** | 229 | 212 | **236** | | 342 |
| 20–29 years | | | 209 | | 231 | −216 | 386 | |
| 30–39 years | 119 | **251** | 201 | | | | | |
| Upper working class | 164 | **217** | 165 | *127* | | | | |
| Lower middle class | | | | | 191 | 137 | 268 | 222 |
| Wicket St. | | | | | 176 | 121 | | |
| Italian | | | | | −239 | **−524** | −375 | **−568** |
| $r^2$ (adj) | 73 | 68 | 61 | 51 | 80 | 81 | 60 | 57 |

*Table 10.9* Percent change in significant coefficients with addition of C5 communication index

| | *(æhN)* | *(æhS)* | *(aw)* | *(eyC)* | *(owC)* | *(owF)* | *(uwC)* | *(uwF)* |
|---|---|---|---|---|---|---|---|---|
| <20 years | 3 | −1 | −2 | −14 | 9 | 13 | | 8 |
| 20–29 years | | | −16 | | −13 | 21 | 11 | |
| 30–39 years | 8 | 5 | 9 | | | | | |
| Upper working class | −13 | −12 | −19 | −20 | | | | |
| Lower middle class | | | | | 16 | 35 | −15 | 27 |
| Wicket St. | | | | | −14 | −31 | | |
| Italian | | | | | 26 | 26 | −22 | 19 |
| Average change | −1 | −3 | −7 | −17 | 5 | 13 | −8 | 18 |
| $r^2$ (adj) | 26 | 9 | 16 | 6 | 5 | 10 | −2 | 5 |

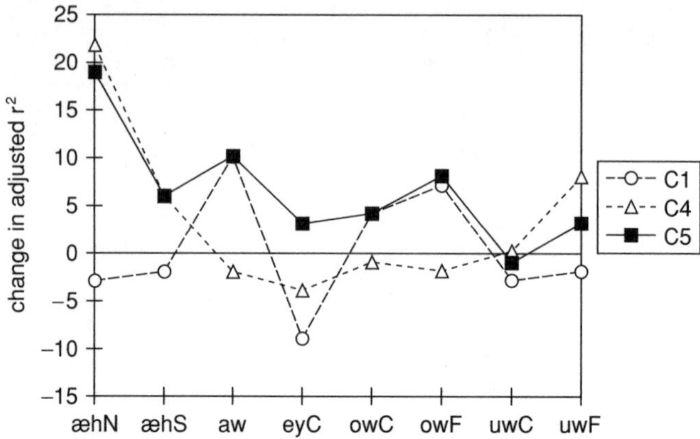


*Figure 10.1* Contribution of C1, C4, and C5 to amount of variation explained in the regression analysis of Philadelphia vowels for women

change reflects a style of social interaction that is different from that used by men.[8]

## *The social significance of the combined communication index*

The remarkable results obtained with the combined C5 index are not self-explanatory. We did not predict that the leaders of linguistic change would have the highest proportion of friends off the local block, as we predicted the curvilinear pattern. What, then, does the combination of C1 and C4 signify in terms of social mechanisms?

One way of analyzing the contribution of C1 and C4 is to examine the amount they contribute to the statistical explanation of the variation inherent in the vowel shifts. Figure 10.1 is a graphic presentation of the difference in adjusted $r^2$ when C1, C4, and C5 are added separately to the analysis reported in table 10.8. Table 10.9 showed that for all but (uwC), there is an addition of at least 5% to the total amount of variance explained by the combined index C5. Figure 10.1 shows that for the two nearly completed changes (æhN) and (æhS), all of this contribution comes from C4, the percentage of friends living off the block. For (aw), (owC), and (owF), it

[8] There is a bias in the construction of the communication indices that may have exaggerated the specialization of network effects for women. Several of the questions were framed for the communication index C1 in a form more suggestive of women's social activities than men's. While men are as likely as women to *say hello* to someone, *go out with* someone, or *invite* someone *to a party*, women are more likely than men to *have coffee with* someone, *visit with* someone, or *confide in* someone. The field workers and analysts who constructed these questions were women, and were thinking more of women's activities than of men's. In future studies, that bias might be eliminated by shifting the male questionnaire to substitute *have a drink with* for *have coffee with*, *tell our troubles to* someone for *confide in* someone, etc. However, the other component of C5, the C4 index, shows no such bias.

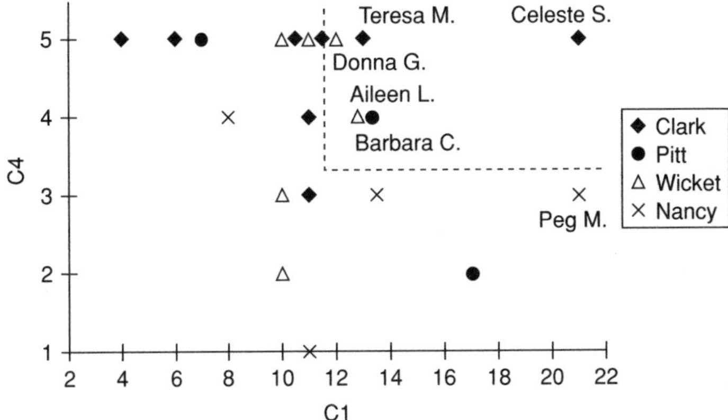


*Figure 10.2* Location of the 21 female speakers of the communication study on the field defined by C1 (density of interaction within the block) and C4 (proportion of friends living off the block)

is the reverse: C4 contributes little by itself, and almost all of the effect seems to stem from C1, the density of interaction within the block. The case of (eyC) is not at all clear. Here neither index contributes anything to the analysis, but combined, they produce a coefficient of 45, significant at the .05 level. On the whole, the two indices combine in a synergistic manner: whatever position in social networks tends to favor the advancement of sound changes is the result of joint location along the dimensions of C1 and C4.

It should not be surprising that the (uw) variables are exceptional in showing no significant effect of the communication indices. In chapter 9, it was found that women showed only slight age stratification for these variables, and no social stratification at all.

It may be helpful at this point to examine a plot of C1 against C4 to see where individual speakers are located (figure 10.2). The vertical axis is C4, running from 1 (0–20% of friends living off the block) to 5 (80–100%). The horizontal axis is C1, the speakers' estimates of how many people they interact with in six social events. Four neighborhoods are represented here: the South Philadelphia neighborhoods Clark and Pitt St. are shown by solid symbols; the North Philadelphia neighborhood of Wicket St. is shown by open triangles; and the middle class Nancy Drive by x's. The area of special interest here is the upper right quadrant, marked off by dashed lines, which contains the speakers who are high in both dimensions. Contrary to preliminary expectations, Nancy Drive has at least one resident, Peg M., who shows as dense a pattern of interaction as anyone in the working class neighborhoods; but no Nancy Drive residents are in the upper right quadrant because most of their friends are located on the same block (this is true of the men as well). In newly formed King of Prussia, most neighborhood

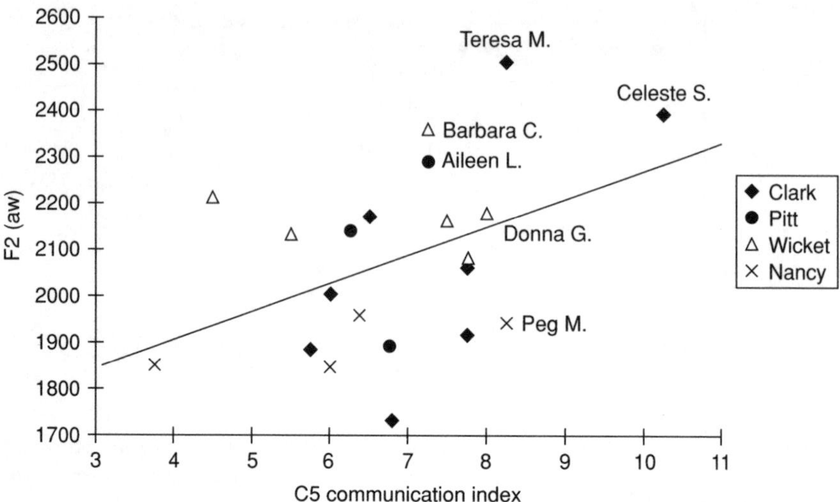


*Figure 10.3* Scatterplot of F2 of (aw) by index C5 for 21 female subjects of the communication study by neighborhood, with regression line and leading speakers identified

friendships are relatively recent products of juxtaposition on the block, and these networks have not had time to expand to a wider geographic area. The speakers located in the upper right quadrant include two residents of Clark St., Celeste S. (45) and Teresa M. (14); two residents of Wicket St., Donna G. (21) and Barb C. (16); and one from Pitt St., Aileen L. (27). The persons who show the combination of high C1 and high C4 therefore cover a wide range of working class neighborhoods, ages, and social classes. This is of course a necessary condition for the independence of social class and social network effects that produce the additive effects of tables 10.7–8.

The next step is to locate the same 21 female speakers on new scatterplots with the unified communication index C5 on the horizontal axis, and the vowel shifts as the dependent variables on the vertical axis. Figure 10.3 shows this relationship for the new and vigorous change (aw). The regression line shows a positive relationship between the two variables. Their correlation coefficient is .438, with a regression coefficient of 62 that is significant at the .05 level.[9] The same five speakers we identified in the upper right quadrant of figure 10.2 appear here as leading exponents of the fronting of (aw). Four of them, Teresa M., Celeste S., Barb C., and Aileen L., have the highest values of (aw), considerably above the regression line. This means that C5 alone does not predict the actual degree of fronting: this is true only for Donna G., whose value falls very close to the regression line. For the four other speakers, there must be other factors

[9] This regression figure pertains only to the female subjects of figure 10.4.

that are responsible for the high values of (aw) F2. Similarly, Peg M. from Nancy Drive is considerably below the regression line: her high value of C5 is not correlated with a correspondingly high degree of fronting of (aw). Consultation with table 10.8 tells us that among other factors involved here is socioeconomic class. A regression analysis of (aw2) for women with age, SEC and neighborhood included as independent variables shows that the upper middle class women have an expected level of 301 Hz behind the bench mark of the lower working class. Peg M. is in fact 295 Hz below the level of Aileen L.

The same picture emerges from the plot of (eyC) against C5. Figure 10.4 locates the high runners for C5 and shows that they have the same relative positions. The regression coefficient for C5 on (eyC) is similar: 57, at the .05 level, and the correlation coefficient between C5 and (eyC) is .462. Here it is evident that Teresa M. and Barb C. are much higher above the regression line than Celeste S. is. The main additional factor is obviously their age. Table 10.8 shows that speakers under 20 show an advantage of about 229 Hz for the F2 of (eyC), which accounts for a good part of the relative advance of Teresa M. over Celeste S.

The fact that the high runners for C5 are equally leaders in (aw) and (eyC), and that the means for the individual speakers fall into place in a consistent way, confirms the importance of C5 in the mechanism of linguistic change and diffusion, beyond the simple coefficients of table 10.8. But what about those with low C5 values? Do low values of C5 predict lower values of (aw2) and (eyC2)? The general regression lines on figures 10.3

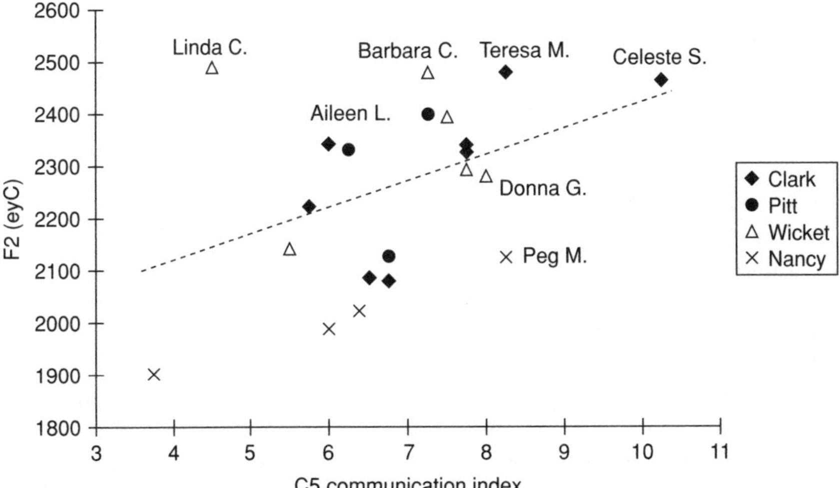


*Figure 10.4* Scatterplot of F2 of (eyC) by index C5 for 21 female subjects of the communication study by neighborhood, with regression line and leading speakers identified

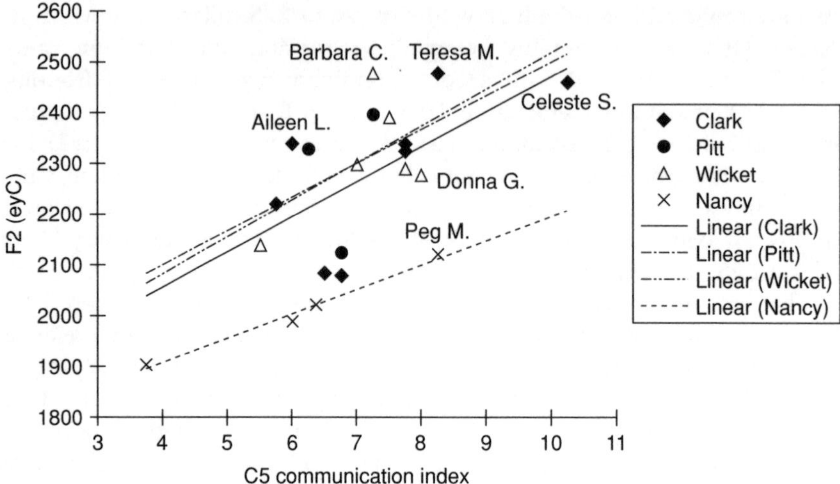


*Figure 10.5* Scatterplot of F2 of (eyC) by index C5 for 21 female subjects of the communication study by neighborhood, with partial regression lines for neighborhoods (Linda C. removed)

and 10.4 argue yes, but this is essentially a restatement of the regression coefficient of table 10.8. If C5 is an important predictor of linguistic change, then it should operate with equal force on subsets of the communication subjects. If the effect of C5 on the fronting of (eyC) is a noisy one, or actually the product of chance fluctuation (which is the case for one out of 20 effects at the .05 level), it will not be reproduced for such small sub-groups (Clark 8, Pitt 3, Wicket 6, Nancy 4). Three of the four regression slopes are similar, but one is not: Wicket St. fails to show the same positive correlation between C5 and (eyC). A closer examination of the six Wicket St. speakers shows that this is the result of a single exceptional speaker, Linda C., who has a low C5 of 4.5 but a high (eyC) score of 2489. If she is removed from the analysis, the lines for the three working class neighborhoods coincide almost perfectly, as shown in figure 10.5, and the middle class Nancy Drive runs roughly parallel at a lower level.

Given the general parallelism, the high C5 value of Peg M. on Nancy Drive can be considered relevant to her use of (eyC). In fact it has the same effect on her use of (eyC) as the high values of Celeste S. and Teresa M. have on theirs. The regression line for Nancy Drive is an excellent fit: it runs right through the four x symbols. C5 thus accounts for almost all the variance in the fronting of (eyC) by the women from Nancy Drive.

Throughout the discussion thus far, there have been many indications that (eyC) is the youngest of the new and vigorous changes, and lies close to the point where a sound change in progress first begins to develop a significant social distribution. The comparative regularity and simplicity of figure 10.5 testifies to the absence of the secondary reactions produced by later social factors, though the aberrant case of Linda C. indicates that the alignment of social factors is not perfectly regular.

The overall statement of table 10.8 is that the progress of (eyC) among women is predicted by three social factors: age, social class, and C5. To say that age influences the change is redundant as apparent time as used here is simply a way of tracing the fact of change. To understand change is then not only to discover how the C5 index relates to linguistic behavior, but also to see how social class position is related to the communication indices. The first question will be the topic of the rest of this chapter; the second will be a concern of the ones to follow.

### *Sociometric indications of centrality and its relation to the communication indices*

The technique for investigating local neighborhoods used in the Philadelphia project begins with entrance into the neighborhood, initiation of first contacts, location of one or several sponsors, and the exploration of the social network (Labov 1984).[10] In the working class neighborhoods, the initial contacts were made by the field worker on the street. It is a characteristic of Philadelphia row houses that people make themselves freely available for interaction outside their houses, usually on the three limestone front steps that lead down from the front door. Initial contacts are often people of some importance and prominence on the block; or they may be a first step toward locating the central figures of the block or neighborhood.[11]

These central figures are well known to community residents and are easily identified by them. Sometimes they are *block captains*, people who assume responsibility for mobilizing voters, collecting funds, and other local political tasks. They may also be heads of local organizations: veterans' groups, fraternal organizations, or social clubs. But most importantly, they are the centers of informal networks. Their houses are the sites of frequent comings and goings of family, neighbors, and friends, and they are at the center of telephone networks. Bower's entrance into the Clark Street network was facilitated by the fact that an afternoon coffee klatsch met regularly at the home of her chief sponsor, Celeste S.

The relationship between the C5 index and the diffusion of sound change can be seen most clearly by superimposing this information on sociometric diagrams of the main Clark St. network derived from answers

[10] These techniques are also the basis of the course Linguistics 560 taught at Penn from 1973 to the present, methods used in a much larger body of sociolinguistic work, and more fully reported in Labov and Sankoff (to appear).

[11] In the middle class King of Prussia area, different methods were used to locate initial contacts, usually through institutions like churches.

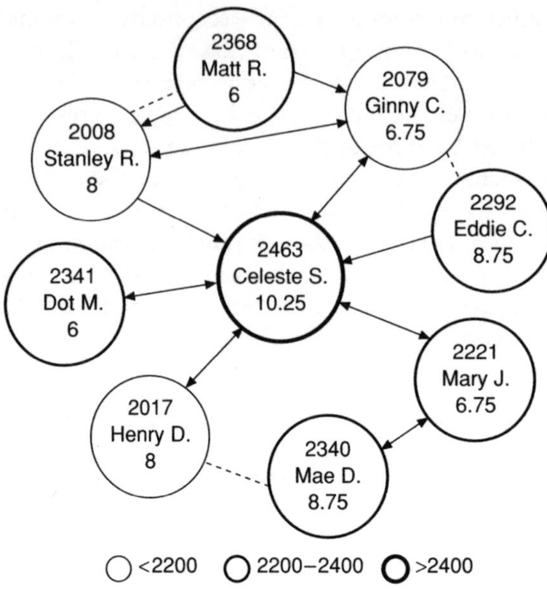


*Figure 10.6* Sociometric diagram of symmetric and asymmetric mentions in the communication interviews in the Clark St. neighborhood. Dashed lines = family connections. Upper figure = (eyC2) in Hz; lower figure = C5 communication index

to the question, "Where do your friends live?" Celeste's immediate social network is displayed in figure 10.6. Symmetric mentions are shown by double-headed arrows, where each person names the other. Asymmetric mentions, where one person names the other but is not named, are shown by lighter, single-headed arrows. The double-headed arrow between Stanley R. and Ginny C. means that each mentioned the other; the single arrow from Matt R. to his brother Stanley shows that Matt mentioned Stanley but Stanley did not mention Matt. The dashed lines are kinship relations: Matt and Stanley R. are brothers; Ginny C. and Eddie C. are brother and sister; Mae D. and Henry D. are wife and husband. Within each circle are three pieces of information. The top line shows the normalized mean for the second formant of (eyC), which as we have just seen is most consistently correlated with C5 for all neighborhoods. The middle line is the speaker's name, and the bottom line is the C5 index.

Figure 10.6 displays the centrality of Celeste's position in this Clark St. neighborhood network. In sociometric terminology, Celeste is a *star*: someone who unites several sub-groups through symmetric linkings, and is automatically mentioned by everyone. As the top line in her circle shows, her (eyC2) rating is the highest in the network. The third line shows that her C5 index is also the highest. We can then add the property of *centrality* to the characterization of the leaders of linguistic change. Celeste's central position indicates that people look to her as a point of reference, and are likely to be influenced by her actions, behavior, and opinions. If the Philadelphia sound changes were stable, or retreating, like most European variables, we could end the analysis with the proposition that dense networks like these tend to reinforce, stabilize, and resist the decay of local forms. But the opposite is happening, not only in Philadelphia but throughout North America. In networks like Clark Street, (eyC) and (aw) are steadily advancing. How is the sociometric centrality of a leader of sound change connected with the process of ongoing change?

Given the structure of figure 10.6, it seems likely that Celeste's high level of (eyC) and other sound changes would spread outward and gradually raise the level of use by others. Local social networks of this kind allow leading figures to exert linguistic influence on others, and so by the principle of local density, create local peaks in the profile of the sound change. But this does not address the question as to how Celeste S. came to have a higher (eyC) level than the others in the first place, a question that will occupy us for the next three chapters.

An initial question is how it comes about that C5 is correlated with centrality. C5 is a composite of C1, a measure of local density of interaction, and C4, a measure of independence from the immediate local environment. The centrality of Celeste S. in this network cannot have anything to do with C1, which is a measure of the density of interaction on the *block*. None of the other people in figure 10.6 live on Celeste's immediate block, which is actually Clark St. itself. Her C4 rating is 5 (80–100% of friends living off the block); in fact, all of the friends she mentioned in response to this question of where her friends lived were located off the block. At the same time, Celeste's C1 index was 21, the highest in the survey (matched only by Peg M.); far from ignoring her neighbors on Clark St., she claims to say hello to, have coffee with, invite to parties, go out with, and confide in everyone on the block. Only for the question about "visiting" did she reduce this number to 1–2. As we will see in the next chapter, this is not a great exaggeration.[12]

Celeste's high ranking on C5 is characteristic of the leaders of sound change in Philadelphia, and should help to decipher the social significance of this index. The key to understanding C5 is the nature of C4, the proportion of friends off the block. The distribution of C4 values is skewed toward high responses, with almost half at the maximum level of 5:

[12] There is a certain circularity in the central position of Celeste S., since she was the source of introductions to most of the other individuals in figure 10.6. When the communication interviews took place, everyone had known Anne Bower for some time, and many had met her with many other local people. Still, if they remembered that Celeste was the one who referred Anne to them, they would be more likely to mention her name. Though this may exaggerate Celeste's position, the situation shown in figure 10.6 cannot be entirely an artifact of the original introductions.

| *Rank* | *n* | |
|---|---|---|
| 1 | 4 | 0–20% |
| 2 | 3 | 21–40% |
| 3 | 8 | 41–60% |
| 4 | 5 | 61–80% |
| 5 | 18 | 81–100% |

A regression analysis of C4 on SEC shows a surprising relationship: a coefficient of –.23 at the $p < .01$ level. This means that the higher the social class, the lower the number of friends named off the block. In other words, middle class people in this sample of 38 are *more* likely than working class people to have their most intimate friends on the same block. On the other hand, C1 has a strongly positive relation to SEC: .59, indicating that on the whole, the middle class subjects interact more frequently with people on their block than working class people do.[13]

These figures should not lead us to believe that there is more communication among neighbors in the suburbs than the city. Field work in Philadelphia over 30 years has firmly established that the total amount of social interaction in the working class Philadelphia row house neighborhoods is much greater than in the suburbs like King of Prussia. The large number of family and friendship connections in the working class areas creates a rich and complex texture of human intercourse that is greatly reduced in the more sparsely settled lawn-and-garden ecology of Nancy Drive. The explanation for this unexpected result lies in the contrast between *block* and *neighborhood*. The people at the low end of the C4 index are limited in their everyday interactions to their immediate geographical neighbors, and do not participate in the web of kin and friends that inevitably spreads across blocks within the neighborhood and ultimately across neighborhoods. A low value on C4 – indicating a high proportion of friends on the block – therefore indicates limitations in the person's network structure.

The indices developed so far will not account for all of the detail in figure 10.6. There is nothing to explain the fact that Matt R. has a C5 index lower than his brother Stanley, but a much higher (eyC) value. As we have seen, network scores are not highly correlated with linguistic development for men. The position of (eyC) for Mae D. with a C5 of 8.75 and for Mary J. with a C5 of 6.75 is about what we would expect in comparison to Celeste S. Not only is the sociometric structure centered about Celeste, but the statistical predictions made by the regression analysis also fit her demographic profile. Table 10.10 is an analysis of the residuals for the (eyC) analysis: the amount of unexplained variation. Column A shows the raw residuals: that is, the amount in Hz that the mean value of (eyC)

[13] We have to bear in mind that there are actually fewer people on the blocks of Nancy Drive than on Wicket St., so that "everyone," coded as 4, refers to a smaller number.

*Table 10.10* (eyC) residuals for the Clark St. network in the regression analyses of table 10.8. Column A = raw residuals; column B = externally studentized residuals

| | *A* | *B* |
|---|---|---|
| Celeste S. | 3 | 0.03 |
| Mary J. | −33 | −0.31 |
| Henry D. | −44 | −0.26 |
| Stanley R. | −53 | −0.31 |
| Dot M. | 75 | 0.70 |
| Ginny C. | −94 | −0.77 |
| Mae D. | 121 | 1.04 |
| Eddie C. | 230 | 1.43 |
| Matt R. | 306 | 2.03 |

deviates from the prediction made by the significant coefficients. Column B is a measure of deviance that is standardized by variance of the residuals. The nine members of the Clark St. network are listed in increasing order of absolute magnitude of Column A. The fact that Celeste is at the top of the list shows that her use of (eyC) is close to what would be predicted by her age, socioeconomic status, and C5 index.

The neighborhood structure of Wicket St. is somewhat more complex than that of the Clark St. neighborhood. As figure 2.3 in chapter 2 showed, there are two distinct social patterns on the same block, the Kendell (K.) network and the Corcoran (C.) network. The sociometric diagram of figure 10.7 shows two stars, Kate C. and Meg K., each surrounded by those who name them. There is a connection here between the two stars, who name each other, and also a connection through Linda R., who mentions both. Otherwise, the two groups are quite distinct, though they live quite close together. Unlike the situation on Clark St., most of the people shown here actually live on Wicket St. itself, and in that sense the Wicket St. networks are more local.

What is most striking about the two networks is that the central figures in each have different relations to the process of linguistic change. Meg K. has a relatively low level of advancement of (eyC), and most of those in her immediate group have higher values. Kate C. has moderately high value, but it is in her immediate family that the change is advanced the furthest. Her daughter Barbara C. and particularly her son, Rick C., are leading exponents of the fronting of (eyC).[14] The C5 indices match this development in general. Kate C. is two full points higher than Meg K., and her son has the highest value in this neighborhood. Kate C.'s network is at the

[14] And other Philadelphia variables as well, as chapter 12 will show.

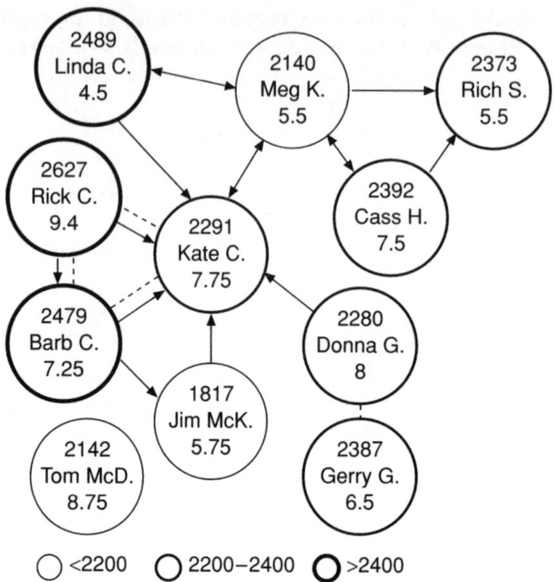


*Figure 10.7* Sociometric diagram of symmetric and asymmetric mentions in the communication interviews in the Wicket St. neighborhood. Dashed lines = family connections. Upper figure = (eyC2) in Hz; lower figure = C5 communication index

center of the (eyC) sound shift, but Meg K.'s is not. The opposition between Kate C. and Meg K. is of great importance for our understanding of the mechanism of sound change, and this will be explored in chapter 12.

So far, the examination of the embedding of sound change in networks has focused on the new and vigorous changes, and particularly the most recent, the raising of (eyC). With the exception of (ay0), all of the Philadelphia sound changes reflect a common social pattern. This can be disengaged most easily by a principal components analysis. This approach is particularly useful when linguistic variables form a coherent cluster of related movements, which is the case with the vowel system. While the regression analyses take as their input a wealth of pre-coded social information, a principal components analysis only accepts the linguistic data. If its output can be shown to converge with the results of the regression analyses in this chapter, it will provide strong confirmation of both sets of results (Poplack 1981, Horvath 1985, and Sankoff 1988). Such a convergence is possible only when the abstract dimensions that emerge from the principal components analysis are easily interpretable as linguistic or social dimensions.[15]

[15] In this respect, principal component analysis is similar to the multi-dimensional scaling used in volume 1, chapter 17. There the results of the analysis proved to be readily interpretable in phonetic terms.

A principal components analysis was carried out on eight vowel variables: (æhN), (æhS), (eyC), (aw), (owC), (owF), (uwC), (uwF). The first two Eigen Values accounted for 48% and 26% of the variance; none of the others were responsible for more than 6%. These first two vectors can then be used to create a series of X and Y values in which each speaker is located, according to the value of the eight variables. Figure 10.8 shows the result, with the two dimensions labeled *U1* and *U2*. Three neighborhood networks are displayed: Clark St., Wicket St., and Nancy Drive. All three are clearly grouped: Clark St. on the right, and Nancy Drive and Wicket St. on the left.

The U1 dimension, which accounts for 48% of the variance, is the one of greatest interest to the study of change. It clearly reflects the process of change. The most conservative figures are at the top, with positive U1 values, and the most advanced speakers at the bottom. To a certain extent, this dimension reflects the ages of the speakers, but within any one generation, there are sizeable differences. On the Clark St. side, we see the familiar figures, Teresa M. and Celeste S. Celeste's good friend Dot M., who is 72 years old, is as far down the diagram as she is.

The leading position of Wicket St. in the development of the Philadelphia sound system is clearly shown in the general shift downward of the Wicket St. tokens. The most conservative speaker from Wicket St., Jim McK., is at the top of the diagram, and Tom McD., who is 65, is much further advanced in the process of change. The conservative leader of the Kendell network, Meg K., is almost as low on the U1 dimension as Celeste S.[16] The advanced speakers from Wicket St. are the lowest on U1: Kate C.'s two children, Barbara and Rick C.

The second dimension, U2, operates to separate neighborhoods. From all that we have learned so far, it seems likely that the isolation of the Clark St. group on the right is associated with the great difference between them and others in the fronting of the back vowels. This left–right opposition corresponds to the treatment of the fronting of /uw/ and /ow/, where Clark St. is from 300 to 600 Hz behind the others. Chapter 7 showed that this is primarily an effect of Italian ethnicity, but here it appears as a neighborhood effect. When a principal components analysis is run with only the front vowels, the left–right opposition tends to disappear.

The middle class neighborhood of Nancy Drive is indicated by x's, and is clearly segregated at mid left of the diagram. The one speaker who stood out from the rest on figures 10.4 and 10.5, Peg M., is also located on the left. However, Peg M. is in the far upper left corner. In spite of her leading position with the new and vigorous changes, the principal components algorithm separates her from the other middle class speakers in a distinctive way.

[16] Because data on /uwC/ was missing from Meg K.'s vowel analysis, her position was extrapolated from a principal component analysis of six vowels.

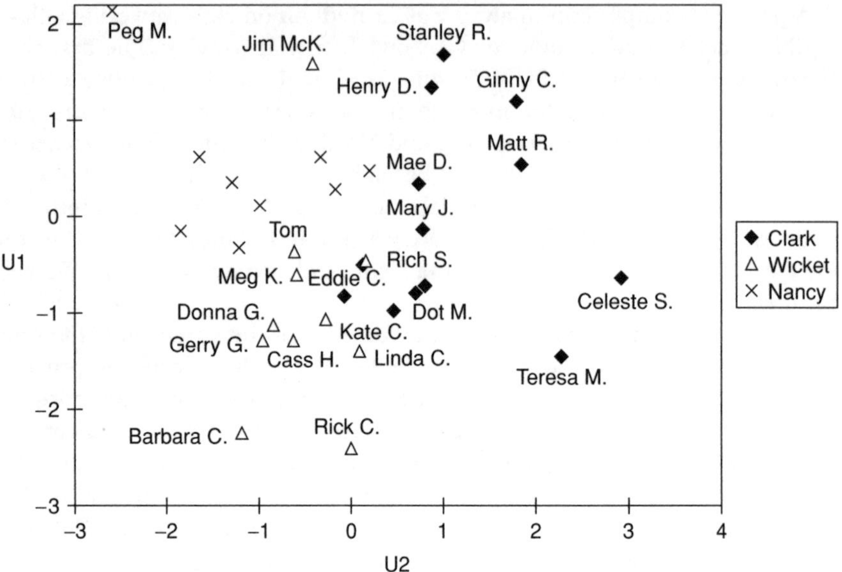


*Figure 10.8* Principal components analysis of speakers from the Philadelphia Neighborhood Study (n = 112) on the basis of the normalized means of (æhN), (æhS), (eyC), (aw), (owC), (owF), (uwC), and (uwF) (the 36 speakers displayed are those with communication indices and reliable means for all 8 vowels)

Figure 10.8 confirms in considerable detail the social network relationships brought out in figures 10.6–10.7, showing that they are not a property of one or two vowels. The diagram shows the linguistic crystallization of social structure in several senses: the clustering of neighborhoods, the association of families, and the isolation of the leaders of change: Celeste S., Teresa M., Rick C., and Barbara C. These individuals will be the central focus of the chapters to follow.

## 10.4 The two-step flow of influence

This chapter has established that the leaders of linguistic change are people at the center of their social networks, who other people frequently refer to, with a wider range of social connections than others. This description comes very close to the description of the "opinion leaders" that emerged from studies of the diffusion of cultural traits, opinions, and practices in the 1940s and 1950s. The first of these studies was *The People's Choice* (Lazarsfeld et al. 1949), a study of voting behavior in Erie County, Ohio. Though it was originally designed to study how mass media influenced voting decisions, its major finding was that mass media have less influence than was previously supposed. *The People's Choice* reported that voting patterns were more likely to show the results of personal influence than influence of the mass media. Following this result, other studies undertook the work of charting the impact and the flow of personal influence in social interaction. A smaller study in Rovere, NJ, directed by Merton (1949), distinguished two types of influentials in a way that is quite relevant to our current interests. Merton identified *cosmopolitan* influentials as mobile individuals who do not feel rooted to any local community, and are highly selective in their pattern of local contacts; they exert influence through their prestige, authority, and their knowledge base. *Local* influentials are committed to their community and do not even consider leaving it; they are concerned with knowing as many people as possible and developing frequent contacts; their influence rests on "an elaborate network of personal relationships," and is exerted through a sympathetic understanding of the local situation. The image that we have developed of the leaders of linguistic change is much closer to the local influential than the cosmopolitan.

The work of greatest interest for our understanding of linguistic change is reported in *Personal Influence* (Katz and Lazarsfeld 1955, hereafter K&L). This project was formed to investigate a hypothesis that was first formulated in the Erie County study: "the two-step flow of communication." K&L propose that most of the population is not influenced directly by the mass media. Instead, ideas flow from the mass media to opinion leaders and from them to the less active sections of the population (p. 32). The study began with interviews with 800 women in Decatur, Illinois. Evidence of acts of influence was obtained by asking the women to remember occasions where they were influenced by someone else in four arenas of daily decision making: marketing, fashions, public affairs, and movie-going. In most reports of change of mind, no personal contact came to mind (59%). But in 260 cases of opinion change, an individual act of influence was remembered. A second interview, with a questionnaire specifically directed to acts of influence, generated 1549 accounts of a person influencing others or being influenced. The interviewers did not accept these subjective accounts until they were confirmed; they sought out the other person mentioned, and in 634 cases succeeded in interviewing them. In two-thirds of the cases, the event was confirmed; it was denied in only 10%; and was not recalled in the remaining quarter (p. 154).

A woman was designated as an "opinion leader" if (1) she told the interviewers in both interviews that she had recently been asked for advice in a specific area, or (2) reported this in one interview and said that she was more likely than her friends to be asked for advice in that area. Of the four topics of investigation, fashion leadership offers the closest parallel to linguistic change. Fashion is different from the other areas in that leadership declines with each step in the life cycle: 48% of the young unmarried girls are fashion leaders, 31% of small family wives, 18% of large family

*Table 10.11* The flow of fashion influence among status levels outside the family

| *Her fashion leader's status* | *Influencees' status* | | | |
|---|---|---|---|---|
| | *Low* | *Middle* | *High* | *Total* |
| Low | 5 | 7 | 3 | 15 |
| Middle | **17** | **47** | 11 | 75 |
| High | 2 | 13 | **17** | 32 |
| Total | 24 | 67 | 31 | 122 |

Source: Katz and Lazarsfeld 1955, table 31

wives, and 14% of matrons with grown children. K&L also show that *interest* in fashion is an independent factor favoring fashion leadership. The effect of high and low interest in fashion is maintained for each stage in the life cycle (p. 252). The relation of the life cycle to language change will be a major topic of chapter 14.[17]

The social status of opinion leaders was determined by two objective indices: education and rent. If education and rent were both higher than the median, the person was rated high; if both were lower, the rating was low; all others were of middle status. Table 10.11 shows the flow of fashion influence within and across these status groups. The diagonal, representing influence within a status group, accounts for only 69 of the 122 acts of fashion influence. In 32 cases influence was exerted by a higher status person on a lower status person; in 21 cases, it was the reverse. Most importantly, it appears that women of middle status exerted the greatest influence, 61% of the total number of cases. Most acts of communication occur within the same status group or with adjacent groups: only five of the acts of influence represent contacts between high and low status women.

K&L developed an index of gregariousness, based on answers to the question, "How many people are there with whom you are friendly and talk with fairly often, who are not and never have been your neighbor?" This is a close parallel to the C4 index of the Philadelphia study, which measured the proportion of friends living off the block. They were also asked, "What organizations, clubs, or discussion groups do you belong to?" The median number of friends mentioned was seven; if a person

[17] Not all of the traits that define opinion leaders are relevant to language change, at least not change from below. Katz and Lazarsfeld were concerned with the rate at which fashion leadership is exported to other groups, but their export index would be difficult to apply to language. It depends on the level of interest, or "saliency" of fashion. If a group develops more fashion leadership than the interest of its own group would sustain, this provides a measure of the rate of export. Such a measure might certainly apply to the diffusion of vocabulary, but requires a higher degree of consciousness than the linguistic system provides.

*Table 10.12* Percent of fashion leadership by status and gregariousness

| | *Status (%)* | | |
|---|---|---|---|
| *Gregariousness Score* | *High* | *Middle* | *Low* |
| High | 22 | **36** | 24 |
| Medium | 31 | 24 | 17 |
| Low | 21 | 17 | **11** |

Source: Katz and Lazarsfeld 1955, table 32

was higher than the mean, and belonged to one or more clubs, they were rated high in gregariousness; if they were below the mean and belonged to no clubs, they were rated low; all others were rated medium. Status and gregariousness were related: the higher the status, the higher the proportion of people "high" in gregariousness; the lower the status, the higher the proportion of people "low" in gregariousness.

On the whole, gregariousness was correlated with fashion leadership: those with high gregariousness included 29% leaders; medium gregariousness 23%; and low, only 15%. When gregariousness is broken down by status in table 10.12, that relationship is found only in the middle status group. The overall view that comes from table 10.11 is also modified: preeminence of middle status people in fashion leadership is confined to those with high gregariousness. The fashion leaders are concentrated among middle status, gregarious women.

The K&L classification of high, middle, and low status is based on a much simpler approach than that used in the Philadelphia Neighborhood Study. "Middle status" can be translated into "upper working class or lower middle class," or perhaps, "centrally located social group." This is the socioeconomic grouping that appeared consistently throughout the Philadelphia Neighborhood Study. The common pattern is the exclusion of lower and higher class groups that do not participate fully in the social processes involved. The relation between fashion leaders and leaders of linguistic change is perhaps clearest in the trenchant statement of K&L that sums up their findings:

> Fashion leaders are concentrated among young women, and among young women of high gregariousness. Status level plays some part, too, in giving women a head start for leadership in this area, but it is not a major factor. There is some indication that fashion influence travels down the status ladder to a modest extent and there is very slight evidence for an upward flow between age groups. The overall picture in the case of fashion is women influencing other women very much like themselves, with particularly heavy traffic within the group of younger, gregarious women who do not belong to the lowest status level. (p. 331)

To sum up the parallels between the leaders of linguistic change and fashion leaders:

1 The leaders are women; men play no significant role.[18]
2 The highest concentration of leaders is in the groups centrally located in the socioeconomic hierarchy; that is, leadership forms a curvilinear pattern.
3 The leaders are people with intimate contacts throughout their local groups, who influence first people most like themselves.
4 The leaders are people who are not limited to their local networks, but have intimate friends in the wider neighborhood.
5 These wider contacts include people of different social statuses, so that influence spreads downward and upward from the central group.

These extensive and surprising parallels between leadership in fashion and in linguistic change indicate a common mechanism of diffusion of cultural traits. But one cannot avoid the question, is the diffusion of changes in fashion a good model for the diffusion of language change? At this point, a more general consideration of the nature of fashion is in order, and a review of the work done on fashion leadership since the Decatur study.[19]

## 10.5 A general view of fashion and fashion leaders

It is only natural for scholars to regard fashion as a superficial and trivial topic, and it is not surprising that one of the basic papers on the topic begins with the statement, "This paper is an invitation to sociologists to take seriously the topic of fashion" (Blumer 1969). In everyday life we use the term to refer to superficial variations in the visible, outer integument of the self: variations in clothes, make-up, and hair arrangement. Many academics lean to the view that such variations make very little difference to the essential processes of acquiring and transmitting information, producing goods, and improving the quality of life. Yet Blumer argues that "fashion should be recognized as a central mechanism in forming social order . . . it needs to be lifted out of the area of the bizarre, the irrational, and the inconsequential" (p. 290). Furthermore, he aligns himself with the argument of Bell 1949 that "in sociological studies fashion plays the role which has been allotted to *Drosophila* . . . in the science of genetics,"

[18] The initial targets of the Decatur study were women, but Katz and Lazarsfeld had ample opportunity to inquire into the role of men in influencing women. In the area of fashion it was negligible, but in public affairs, quite the other way around.
[19] In the account of the literature on fashion to follow, I have drawn heavily on the review provided by Weimann (1982, ch. 8), a former student of Elihu Katz.

that is, it provides a rich body of data on rapid and visible mutations. This thought increases the appeal of fashion as a visible correlate of the rapid linguistic changes that have swept over North America in the second half of the twentieth century.

Sociological discussions of fashion inevitably begin with Simmel's 1904 paper on the topic. Simmel pointed out the paradoxes associated with fashion, particularly that its role as a stabilizing process leads to uniformity while the emphasis on individual variation leads to rapid and continual change.

> Thus fashion represents nothing more than one of the many forms of life by the aid of which we seek to combine in uniform spheres of activity the tendency towards social equalization with the desire for individual differentiation and change. (pp. 542–3)

Rather than argue for fashion as a universal, Simmel saw fashion as a form of class differentiation in a relatively open class society. To draw further upon the parallel between language change and fashion change, it may be necessary to modify the uniformitarian principle, and consider that mechanisms of change may not be the same in other periods of history and other forms of society.

It is natural that Simmel, writing at the turn of the century, saw fashion change as initiated by the upper class, primarily as the imitation of each class by the next lower class. This was the explicit position of Gabriel Tarde, whose laws of imitation were reviewed in chapter 1. For Tarde (1873), fashion is "a continuous waterfall of imitation." If modern work on fashion leaders has not modified this view of fashion as change from above, the implications of this work for the explanation of linguistic change from below will be limited.

Like linguists, sociologists are prone to explain social behavior by inferring a series of covert attitudes for which the main evidence is the behavior itself. Anspach in *The Why of Fashion* (1967) argues that "the initiating spark is the social need of people to be like others and yet to be distinct from others" (pp. 5–6). A theory that embraces the need to be like others and the need to be distinct from others is capable of explaining any combination of events.

Just as linguists may see language change as a change of fashion, many scholars outside of linguistics see fashion as a form of communication, applying "symbolic interaction theory" or "semiotic analysis" (Lurie 1981, Stone 1962, Eco 1979, Simon-Miller 1985). Although much of this discussion is general and discursive, many empirical studies have confirmed the fundamental insight of Katz and Lazarsfeld 1955. It is well established that decisions about fashion were more commonly influenced by personal contacts than by the mass media. At the same time, they have added further complications to the two-step flow of influence model, particularly in distinguishing various types of leadership.

Shrank and Gilmore 1973 supplied a questionnaire on clothing choices to 145 American college women. The analysis distinguished two types of leadership: *innovativeness* and *opinion leadership*, and correlated these traits with scales derived from other questions: attitudes toward conformity, interest in clothing, social insecurity, and socioeconomic level. The correlations showed significant differences in correlations of innovativeness and opinion leadership on all but one of their scales. This has led to extensive work on whether the innovators are in fact those who influence others, or on the other hand, whether fashion leaders merely approve and convey innovations to their group. The answers to this question are far from conclusive: if the two types exist, there is clearly a great deal of overlap between them (Baumgarten 1975). Nevertheless, the importance of the issue is clear (see J. Milroy 1992:148). As far as the Philadelphia sound changes or the Northern Cities Shift are concerned, there is no useful way that we can isolate *innovators*: that is, locate the people who used a given linguistic form for the first time. However, we can think of an innovator as someone who introduces a form used by one group to another group (as J. Milroy points out, an agent similar to Boissevain's *broker* (1974)). In the sociometric diagrams of this chapter, such a broker would appear as a marginal person with high communication scores. In figure 10.7, Linda R. might be such a person, connecting two sub-networks. No such person is found in figure 10.6 for Clark Street. Celeste appears there as both leader and innovator.[20]

As research on fashion leaders developed, it moved in directions that appear to be less and less comparable to linguistic inquiries and less useful for explaining linguistic change. Recent studies are largely questionnaires administered to classes of college students, a far cry from the representative sampling and interviewing of the Decatur study, with no independent confirmation of acts of influence. Instead, people who were self-rated as fashion leaders are rated for such complex and subtle traits as "fashion venturesomeness," "cognitive style," "general self-confidence," "relative self-confidence," or "cognitive clarity."

Even if research on opinion leadership had remained closer to the ground, it would be important to bear in mind the deep-seated difference between fashion and language. Decisions on fashion are conscious decisions, or close to consciousness; linguistic change from below is entirely hidden from leaders as well as followers, at least in the early stages represented by (eyC) and (aw). Even when people become aware of change in its late stages, as with (æhN), efforts to control behavior have limited success.

[20] Unless, of course, she was strongly influenced by some other persons earlier in her career who are not available in our study (see chapter 11).

The structural controls on linguistic change developed in volume 1 do not seem to exist for fashion. There is nothing in fashion comparable to the principle that mergers cannot be reversed by linguistic means (volume 1, chapter 12), or the way in which misunderstanding controls the drift of vowel targets (volume 1, chapter 20). Nevertheless, variation in fashion and language share many properties in addition to the five characteristics of the leaders of change given in the preceding section.

The features of language involved in the linguistic changes we have been tracing are the audible equivalent of the visual effects of fashion. The presentation of the self is very much dependent on the content of what is said, but there are many cognitively equivalent ways of saying the same thing, in grammar, lexical choice, and phonetic realization. Both fashion and language can change rapidly, at comparable speeds, depending on the feature involved. Like linguistic changes, changes in fashion are sporadic: some features are stable for centuries, like the tradition of men wearing trousers, or older women putting their hair up, others change from year to year, like favored colors in makeup, hem length, or hair styles. As in language, people are aware of only a small number of the decisions they make in regard to fashion, primarily the features that change, and rarely are conscious of the persistent features of their culture, the unchanging aspect of fashion. Unlike language, fashion changes rarely continue in the same direction over long periods of time, since they do not appear to be constrained by such powerful physical or cognitive factors. However, if one looks at the amount of the body covered by bathing costumes, one can see a long-term reduction that has persisted over at least two centuries.

On the whole the resemblances between changes in fashion and changes in language are enough to make us believe that the mechanism of diffusion shares many common properties. None of the other three areas of influence studied by Katz and Lazarsfeld – marketing, public affairs, or movie-going – yield such close parallels.

## 10.6 Who leads the leaders?

One of the greatest differences between research on fashion leadership and on linguistic change is the interest in mass media. Both the funding and the rationale for much of the research on personal influence lay in testing the efficacy of advertising. Research on the question of how leaders are influenced therefore focused on the mass media. However, a certain amount of recent research raises the same question about the influence on leaders that the Decatur study raised about the people they led.

A number of studies show that opinion leaders are influenced by interpersonal sources as well as mass media (Andersen and Garrison 1976, Heath and Bekker 1986). In a South African study, Heath and Bekker found that black opinion leaders were more active in interpersonal communication than others. In Australia, a study of time diaries showed that time spent in exchanging opinions was correlated most highly with influence on the opinions of others, rather than time spent watching television or listening to the radio (March and Tebbutt 1979).

Given the fact that leaders spent a great deal of time exchanging opinions with others, it is an open question as to whether they are influenced more by their contacts with other leaders like themselves, or with marginal individuals who play the role of brokers or innovators. Wright and Cantor 1967 and Robinson 1976 argue for horizontal flow between opinion leaders. Weimann 1982 is a study of an Israeli Kibbutz which found that opinion leaders, centrally located in their social networks, often rely on marginally located individuals to import information. He found that the central members of the network were characterized by a high rate of strong to weak ties (about two-thirds), while marginals had mostly weak ties (72%). Weimann concluded that the marginals served as communicative bridges through their weak ties.

The leaders of linguistic change who have emerged from the Philadelphia study show an unusual combination of centrality with a high frequency of social interaction outside of their immediate locality. It is not possible to identify these wider connections with the "weak ties" of opinion leadership, since there is no evidence that the social obligations and commitments are weaker than those that operate within the block. Chapter 12 will provide a view of how these local connections operate in everyday life. The position of the leaders of linguistic change in social networks can be summarized as a form of *expanded centrality*. Leaders of linguistic change are centrally located in social networks which are expanded beyond their immediate locality.

The two chapters that follow will reinforce this characterization, which is not inconsistent with the findings of L. Milroy on the importance of weak ties. Weak ties may not only serve as pipelines for the influence of the regional standard, but also as the channels through which the mounting tide of linguistic change engulfs an entire city. But if this is so, the question remains as to why the model provided by the marginal member is copied by the central figure of a network. It would seem more likely that one central member would influence another.

The data on hand does not resolve this issue. Our view of social networks is limited to the networks themselves, and does not rise to the larger view that we would need of connections between social networks. The immediate perspective shows us the central members of the group in the interaction with their immediate friends, but not the broader interactions that unify the speech community. We have some knowledge of where these interactions take place in Philadelphia: at political meetings, at organizational meetings for the Mummer's Day Parade, at veterans' organizations, meetings of the

Patrolman's Benevolent Association. Yet no systematic recordings have been made or studied that will show us what happens when speakers of different neighborhoods interact. Some insight into this question may be found in chapter 12, which will carry us into the daily life of the leaders of sound change. But first we must apply what has been learned about social networks to the as yet unresolved gender paradox: that women are conformists for one type of language variable, and nonconformists for another.

# 11

# *Resolving the Gender Paradox*

The leaders of linguistic change have been located as women (chapter 8) who are members of the upper working class or skilled work force (chapter 5), with a dense network of local ties and a broad range of connections outside the local neighborhood (chapter 10). Chapter 9 argued that the leading position of women in linguistic change may be related to the asymmetry of gender in first language transmission. It was also found that the relation of women to language change is closely correlated with their position in social networks, but this is not the case for men (chapter 10). So far, we have not confronted directly the fact that linguistic change from below represents a challenge to the established norms of society, and that the leaders of change are behaving in a way that is inconsistent with the female conformity that was such a prominent feature of chapter 8. This chapter will confront this issue directly, and present a resolution to the apparent paradox which has not been introduced before.

## 11.1 The conformity paradox

One of the most thorough and deeply considered treatments of gender differences in language is Wolfram and Schilling-Estes 1998. They find an "apparent contradiction":

> Women appear to be more conservative than men, in that they use more standard variants . . . At the same time, women appear to be more progressive than men, because they adopt new variants more quickly. (p. 187)

As a first step in resolving this opposition, they cite Labov 1990 in associating the first tendency with stable variation and almost completed changes, the second with newer changes. However, it seems to me that the problem remains of why the same persons are sometimes "conservative" and sometimes "progressive." This appears more clearly if we replace these terms with "conforming" and "nonconforming." The contradictory pattern of behavior remains:

| *In* | *women are more* | |
|---|---|---|
| Stable sociolinguistic variables | conservative | conforming |
| Change from above | progressive | conforming |
| Change from below | progressive | nonconforming |

The *Gender Paradox* might be re-stated as a *Conformity Paradox,* best stated with the converse of conformity, *deviation.*

*Women deviate less than men from linguistic norms when the deviations are overtly proscribed, but more than men when the deviations are not proscribed.*

One might brush this aside as no different from the common observation that people will break rules of conduct when they think they can get away with it. But such a facile treatment would be false to the real situation. Women (and most men) take linguistic norms seriously, and are deeply perturbed when they discover that they have deviated from them. In raising and tensing /æ/ to [iə], backing /e/ to [^], or fronting /ow/ to [ɛɔ], women are deviating more than men from the norms of established pronunciation, and when such deviations rise to public awareness, they are roundly condemned by the users themselves. Once they are aware of it, speakers of the language often find their own behavior paradoxical.

The gender paradox raises issues that are quite distinct from the problem of chapter 8 – why women conform more than men to established linguistic norms. Here we are concerned with explaining why women of the same age and same social background adhere to prescriptive norms in one case, and deviate from them in another.

## 11.2 The strategy of this chapter: combining stable variables with changes in progress

This chapter will use the data from stable sociolinguistic variables to characterize each individual's degree of conformity to the dominant sociolinguistic norms, and data from the same person's position in changes in progress to define their degree of deviation from their parents' or grandparents' norms. The combination of these two data sets will throw light on the conformity paradox.

### *Three stable sociolinguistic variables*

Chapter 3 presented the history and current status of three stable sociolinguistic variables in Philadelphia. The three variables show speakers' orientations toward overt sociolinguistic norms in different ways. For (ing), the alternation of velar and apical nasals in unstressed syllables, the informal form was strongly dominant in most interviews, and there is less social stratification than in other studies. The measure of negative concord, (neg), shows a sharp division between the working class and middle class speakers, in their use of nonstandard forms. Though (neg) will play a role in this analysis, it does not discriminate among individuals as sharply as a more gradient variable. The ideal variable for our purpose is (dh), the index for the use of fricative, affricate, or dental for /ð/, which ranges from 0 up to 200 (in this data set from 0 to 185).

Figure 11.1 presents histograms for each of the stable sociolinguistic variables in casual speech.[1] The solid portion of the bar shows the numbers of men in each category; the open portions, the numbers of women. Several important properties of (dh) emerge from this display. First, there is a strong gender differentiation, with females concentrated at lower values, males at higher values. Secondly, there is an indication of a bimodal distribution, with one mode at 70, the other at twice this value, 140. This upper mode includes women with values as high as those of the highest men. For conciseness, I will refer to this variable henceforth as (dha).

## *Re-analyzing changes in progress*

The Philadelphia Neighborhood Study gathered data on the stable sociolinguistic variables from 183 subjects. This did not include all of the 112 speakers studied in chapters 5–9: the 15 members of the upper class interviewed by Kroch were not included, and 11 others are missing. We then have data on both sets of variables for 86 speakers. The first step is therefore to be sure that these 86 speakers preserve the essential sociolinguistic patterns that have been presented for the entire set.

Table 11.1 presents the significant regression coefficients for five Philadelphia vowel changes in progress for the 86 speakers with both data sets. For comparability with chapter 9, separate analyses are done for males and females and occupation is used as the measure of socioeconomic class. The main features of table 9.1 are reproduced.

- Age coefficients appear for all variables, though they do not reach the .05 level of significance for women in the case of (eyC) and (owF). The largest coefficients are found with (aw) and (eyC) for women. Men and women are identical for (eyC).
- The curvilinear pattern is reproduced consistently for men in all five variables in the form of a significant advantage for the skilled working class. For women this pattern appears only with the most recent change, (eyC).

[1] Casual or careful speech might be chosen for any of the investigations of this chapter, but the picture that emerges for casual speech (Style A) gives a wider range of nonstandard forms and reveals the operation of the social forces involved more clearly.

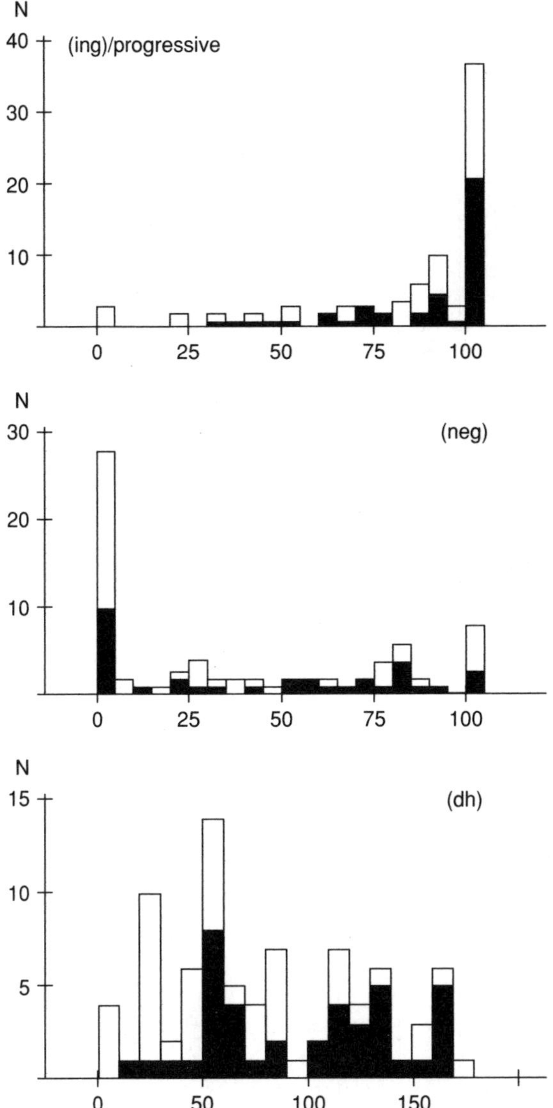


*Figure 11.1* Distribution of values for three stable sociolinguistic variables in Style A (casual speech) in the Philadelphia Neighborhood Study (solid bars, men; open bars, women)

- Women but not men show a strong linear social stratification for (æhN), and a similar but weaker pattern for (aw).
- Wicket Street is in a leading position for the first four sound changes for men; for women, this is true only for (owC).

*Table 11.1* Regression analysis of five sound changes for 86 subjects of the Philadelphia Neighborhood Study with acoustic and sociolinguistic analysis: age and significant occupational, neighborhood, and ethnic coefficients. Significance: **bold**, p < .001; <u>underlined</u>, p < .01; plain, p < .05; *italic*, p < .10

| | *(æhN)* | | *(aw)* | | *(eyC)* | | *(owC)* | | *(owF)* | |
|---|---|---|---|---|---|---|---|---|---|---|
| | *M* | *F* | *M* | *F* | *M* | *F* | *M* | *F* | *M* | *F* |
| Constant | 2337 | 2490 | 2035 | 2247 | 2257 | 2265 | 1307 | 1616 | 1622 | 1960 |
| Age | **−3.30** | −0.53 | **−6.12** | **−4.73** | **−4.70** | *−2.50* | −2.55 | <u>−3.81</u> | −2.48 | *−7.55* |
| Skilled | 137 | | 162 | | 155 | 140 | 219 | | 181 | |
| Clerical | | −196 | | | | | | | | |
| Managerial | | −230 | | *−166* | | | <u>239</u> | | | |
| Professional | | **−368** | | <u>−374</u> | | | | | | |
| Wicket St. | **162** | | <u>202</u> | | 148 | | 190 | <u>204</u> | | |
| Pitt St. | **207** | | *166* | | | | | | | |
| Italian | | | | | | | | *−111* | −241 | −379 |

*Table 11.2* Major social factors in the regression analysis of (dh) comparing SEC index and occupation. Effect = Coefficient × mean

| *Variable* | *Coefficient* | *Effect* | *p* |
|---|---|---|---|
| (a) | | | |
| SEC | –7.98 | 63.36 | ≤0.0001 |
| Female | –34.13 | –17.06 | –0.0005 |
| $r^2$ (adj) | 36.4% | | |
| (b) | | | |
| Occupation | –17.44 | –50.75 | ≤0.0001 |
| Female | –32.78 | –16.34 | 0.0014 |
| $r^2$ (adj) | 29.0% | | |

This data set displays the diffusion of linguistic change throughout the city of Philadelphia. In the earliest stages of change there is little difference in the social distribution of men and women. But as the changes progress, the social class distributions for men and women change, with working class men and middle class women falling behind.

### *Occupation or SEC?*

Chapters 8 and 9 used occupation as a measure of socioeconomic class, since it was more sensitive to gender differences. Chapter 3 showed that (dh) had a monotonic social distribution no matter what indices were used, but SEC turned out to have a greater effect and more explanatory value than any of the individual indices (table 3.7). Table 11.2 compares the two measures of the social distribution of (dha) for the 86 subjects of the combined analysis. The effect of SEC is stronger than that of occupation, and the adjusted $r^2$ is higher. The SEC index will therefore be used in the analyses to follow.

## 11.3 Correlations between stable sociolinguistic variables and changes in progress

The simplest way to see the interrelationships of stable sociolinguistic variables and changes in progress is to assemble a correlation matrix, using the Pearson product-moment correlation. Table 11.3 shows such a matrix, with nine changes in progress involving raising of the second formant and two sociolinguistic variables, (dh) and (neg), in two styles. The highest correlations, shown in bold, are found as expected within the two separate sets. For vowels, in the upper left corner, the highest correlations are among

*Table 11.3* Pearson product-moment correlations of Philadelphia sound changes (second formants) and stable sociolinguistic variables (b = careful speech, a = casual speech)

| | *(æhN)* | *(æhD)* | *(æhS)* | *(eyC)* | *(aw)* | *(owC)* | *(owF)* | *(uwC)* | *(uwF)* | *(dhb)* | *(dha)* | *(negb)* | *(nega)* |
|---|---|---|---|---|---|---|---|---|---|---|---|---|---|
| (æhN) | 1 | | | | | | | | | | | | |
| (æhD) | **0.807** | **1** | | | | | | | | | | | |
| (æhS) | **0.833** | **0.836** | **1** | | | | | | | | | | |
| (eyC) | **0.668** | **0.624** | **0.64** | **1** | | | | | | | | | |
| (aw) | **0.724** | **0.734** | **0.704** | **0.663** | 1 | | | | | | | | |
| (owC) | 0.182 | 0.127 | 0.118 | 0.234 | 0.328 | 1 | | | | | | | |
| (owF) | 0.095 | 0.184 | 0.133 | 0.109 | 0.228 | 0.293 | 1 | | | | | | |
| (uwC) | −0.08 | −0.08 | −0.11 | −0.13 | 0.048 | **0.482** | 0.005 | 1 | | | | | |
| (uwF) | −0 | −0.01 | −0.15 | 0.005 | 0.081 | 0.22 | 0.065 | 0.139 | 1 | | | | |
| (dhb) | 0.23 | 0.389 | 0.31 | 0.176 | 0.205 | −0.32 | 0.012 | −0.14 | −0.14 | 1 | | | |
| (dha) | 0.284 | **0.505** | 0.388 | 0.241 | 0.261 | −0.25 | 0.113 | −0.19 | −0.18 | **0.823** | **1** | | |
| (negb) | 0.312 | 0.354 | 0.383 | 0.204 | 0.221 | −0.17 | −0.01 | −0.13 | −0.11 | **0.603** | **0.557** | **1** | |
| (nega) | 0.286 | 0.382 | 0.365 | 0.187 | 0.145 | −0.06 | 0.076 | −0.11 | −0.04 | **0.531** | **0.59** | **0.696** | 1 |

the three allophones of /æh/ – above .800. Slightly lower, from .600 to .700, are the correlations among /aw/, /eyC/, and the /æh/ allophones. No such correlation is found between the allophones of /ow/ and /uw/: they are quite distinct from each other. The only moderately high correlation in this area is the value of .293 for /owF/ and /owC/. In the fronting of back vowels, the strongest connection is shown between /uwC/ and /owC/, at .482. The highest correlation among the sociolinguistic variables, the bold box at lower right, is .823 for the two styles of (dh); the others are in the .500 to .600 range.

Large areas of table 11.3 have very low values, close to zero. There are no sizeable correlations between the fronting of the back vowels /owC/ and /uwC/ and anything else: neither the fronting of /æh/, /eyC/, and /aw/, nor the sociolinguistic variables. But there is one area of moderate correlation between sociolinguistic variables and changes in progress, in the boxed area in the lower left corner of the table (dha) is strongly correlated with (æhD), and most of the correlations between the sociolinguistic variables and the /æh/ variables are well above .300. To the right of this is the set of correlations between the four sociolinguistic variables and the new and vigorous changes /eyC/ and /aw/. These numbers are small, but all positive. This is somewhat unexpected; these new and vigorous changes do not carry a strong social load, though table 11.1 showed that /aw/ has developed social stratification among women. But /eyC/, which shows no signs of being a social marker, has a positive correlation with all four sociolinguistic variables.

Comparing the four sociolinguistic variables, it appears that (dha) has the highest correlations with all five vowel changes. This supports the decision to concentrate on (dha) in the analyses to follow.

## 11.4 The relation of (dha) to linguistic changes for women of different social classes

The clearest view of the relation of (dha) to the linguistic changes in progress can be obtained with a scatterplot. Since the main focus is on the behavior of women, the female half of the population will be examined separately. Let us also divide the social hierarchy into two parts, those with SEC from 0 to 6 (middle working class) and those with SEC 7 to 14 (upper working class and middle class). Figure 11.2 is the distribution of the two new and vigorous changes, (eyC) and (aw), for the lower section, SEC 0 to 6. It is immediately evident that there is no relation here. For (aw), the regression line is flat (coefficient 0.18), with r .06. For (eyC), the slope is .054, well below any level of significance, with r = .18. The same situation repeats for the (æh) variables.

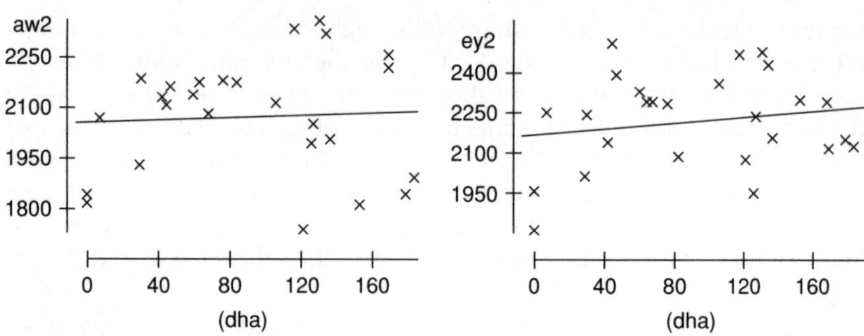


*Figure 11.2* Scatterplot of second formants of (aw) and (eyC) against (dha) for women of middle working class (SEC < 7)

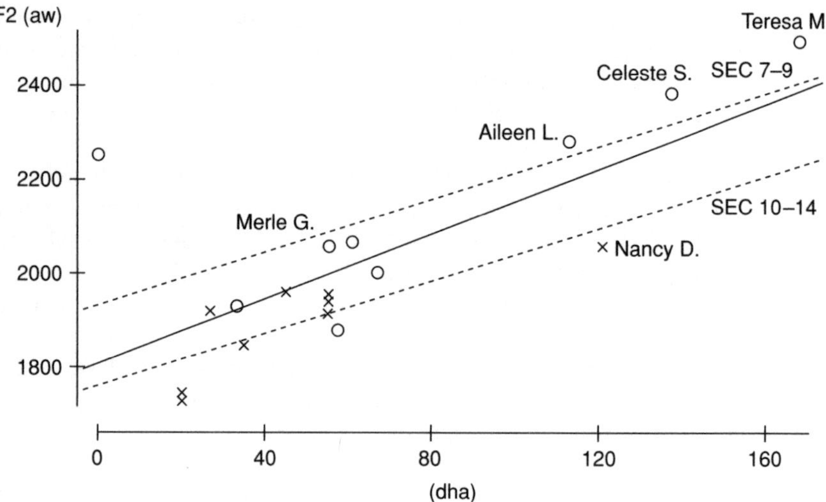


*Figure 11.3* Scatterplot of (aw) against (dha) for women with SEC 7 to 14. Circles = upper working class, SEC 7–9; X's = middle class, SEC 10–14

A different picture emerges from figure 11.3, the corresponding scatterplot of (aw) against (dha) for the 17 women in the upper half of the socioeconomic scale. That upper half is further subdivided: the upper working class (SEC 7–9) is distinguished from the lower middle class and upper middle class (SEC 10–14). A strong and positive relation between (dha) and (aw) emerges: the more a person uses the nonstandard forms of the interdental fricatives, the more advanced the vowel change. The regression coefficient is 3.53, with $p < .001$. While the general correlation between (dha) and (aw) was only .261, for this subset the correlation is .742. This correlation and regression slope is maximized when the SEC division is made between SEC 6 and 7; any other division shows a weaker relationship for the upper half.

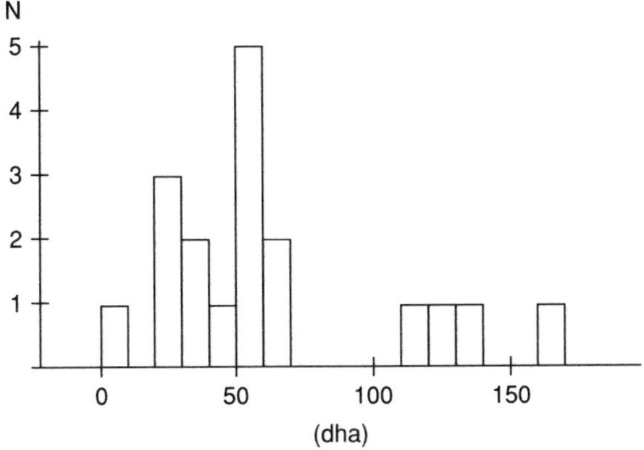


*Figure 11.4* Distribution of (dha) values for women with SEC 7 to 14

This tight correlation was unexpected. To this point in the LCV study, no relationship had been established between the advanced forms of the new sound changes and nonstandard speech. In formulating the gender paradox, both were called deviations from established norms, but nonstandard (dh) is most strongly associated with lower working class speakers who do not use the most advanced forms of (aw).[2]

Given this tight relationship, it is not surprising to see in figure 11.3 the leaders of linguistic change in the same relative position that they had in figure 10.5. Teresa M. and Celeste S. are well in advance of the others on both dimensions, (aw) and (dha).[3]

The (dha) pattern for this population shows the striking bimodal distribution of figure 11.4. Most of the speakers have a (dha) value below 70, while 4 speakers show values above 110. Among these four are two of the leaders of linguistic change. To appreciate the nature of this bimodality, one must recognize a certain divide in the use of (dh) in regard to "standard" vs. "nonstandard." The affricate is recognized as less cultivated than the fricative, but it is only the interdental stop that is clearly nonstandard. One can have a (dh) index of 40, 50, or 60 without using any stops, but it is not possible to have an index greater than 100 without them. Therefore the four female speakers above 100 have to be heard to some degree as "nonstandard," while the speakers below 70 need not be heard that way at all.

Together, figures 11.3 and 11.4 resolve the conformity paradox for (aw). As it was formulated, the paradox assumed that women behaved

[2] It is true that there is no significant difference in the use of (aw) between the female middle working class and the upper working class.

[3] Barbara C. and Rick C. do not appear here as the Wicket St. network has a lower socioeconomic status.

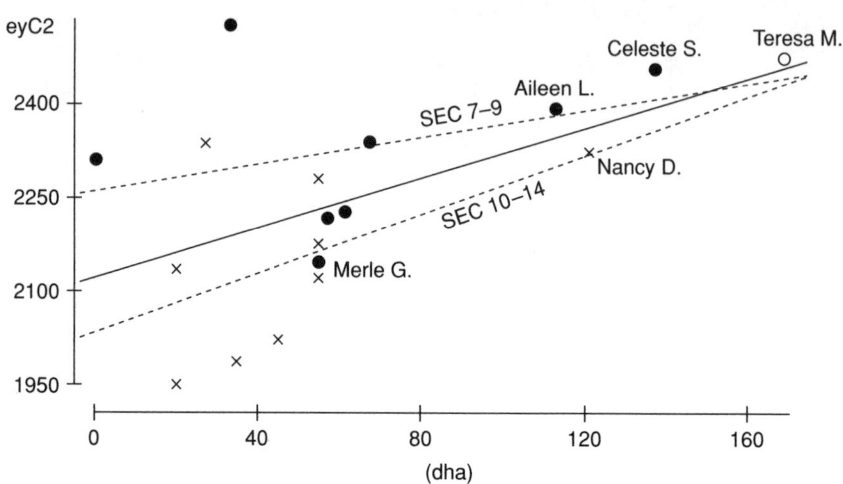


*Figure 11.5* Scatterplot of (eyC2) against (dha) for women with SEC 7 to 14. Circles = upper working class, SEC 7–9; X's = middle class, SEC 10–14

in an inconsistent way, treating new sound changes differently from old ones and stable variables. This was an error. The women who deviate from established norms of (aw) also deviate from the established norms of (dha), and those who conform to the older norms of (aw) also conform to the standard norms of (dha). Two different sets of women are involved. Or to put it another way, the leaders of linguistic change differ consistently from the rest of the population.

The discovery of this split within the female population takes us one further step in the search for the leaders of linguistic change. Given the bimodal distribution of figure 11.4, we may ask from a linguistic point of view, what is it that identifies this group as a unit? The partial regression line 10–14 is parallel to the 7–9 line. It has appeared in many other ways that the two centrally located groups are not sharply distinguished from each other. On the other hand, the upper working class is quite distinct from the middle working class, as shown by a comparison of figures 11.3 and 11.2. In the following chapter, the dynamics of this relationship between middle and upper working class will begin to emerge.

Figure 11.5 is the parallel display for the second formant of the other new and vigorous change, (eyC). The horizontal position of each speaker is the same as in figure 11.3, since the abscissa remains (dha), and Teresa M. and Celeste S. remain the speakers with the highest values. With the exception of one speaker (Linda C.), Teresa M. and Celeste S. are the most advanced users of (eyC). For the upper working class SEC 7–9, the slope of the relationship is more gradual; the leaders of linguistic change are not as far ahead of the general population as with (aw).

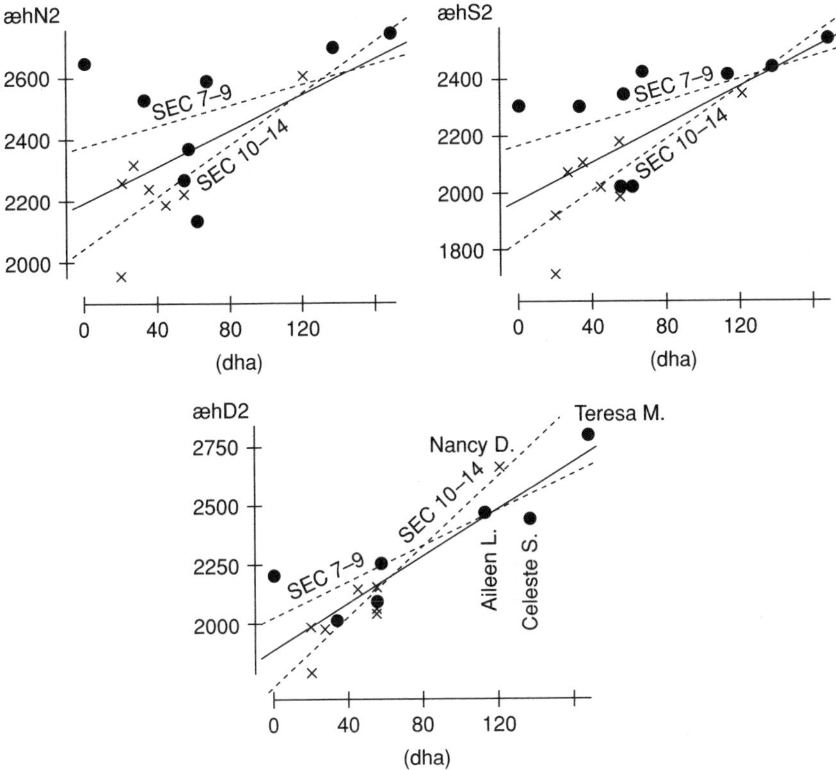


*Figure 11.6* Scatterplots of (æhN2), (æhS2), and (æhD2) against (dha) for women with SEC 7 to 14. Circles = upper working class, SEC 7–9; X's = middle class, SEC 10–14

Similar patterns are found for (æhS) and (æhN) in figure 11.6. The regression lines again slope upward, but the shallower slope of the upper working class line indicates that the high users of (dha) are leading in the linguistic change by a smaller amount. The fact that the slope for the upper working class is less than that for the middle class speakers is a reflection of the fact that these forms are less highly stigmatized for the upper working class, and less similar to (dha) in this respect. The third allophone of /æ/, (æhD), displays a steeper slope, with the four leaders of linguistic change well ahead of the rest of the population in both (dha) and (æhD) value.

The progression of slopes shows a relationship between the degree of advancement of change and the correlation with (dha). Table 11.4 shows this relationship, in r-correlations, in the overall regression coefficients, the t-ratios of the regression relationship, and their probabilities. Figure 11.7 shows graphically the rise and fall of the correlations in the progression from the most recent change to new and vigorous changes and then to nearly

*Table 11.4* Regression coefficients for (dha) on five linguistic changes in progress for female speakers with SEC 7–14

| | *r* | *Coefficient* | *t-ratio* | *p* |
|---|---|---|---|---|
| (eyC) | 0.702 | 2.85 | 2.54 | 0.035 |
| (aw) | 0.742 | 3.54 | 4.43 | 0.0004 |
| (æhD) | 0.885 | 5.04 | 6.84 | <0.00001 |
| (æhS) | 0.671 | 3.32 | 3.50 | 0.003 |
| (æhN) | 0.580 | 3.00 | 2.76 | 0.015 |

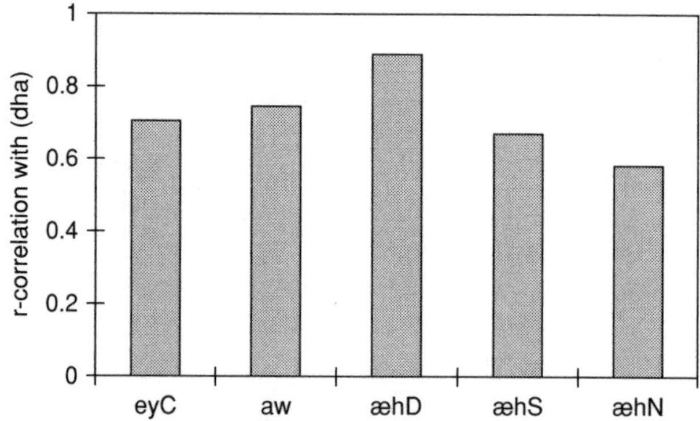


*Figure 11.7* Correlations of (dha) with five linguistic changes in progress for female speakers with SEC 7 to 14

completed changes.[4] This progression resembles the curvilinear distribution of figure 9.1b, in which gender differentiation rises and falls with age coefficients. One would think that gender differentiation and identification with (dh) would increase steadily over time if the variable rises to social awareness, which (æhN) has done to a certain extent (chapter 6). Yet this is not the case. Instead, it appears that a linguistic change in Philadelphia passes through a stage in which its sociolinguistic significance rises to a maximum, and then declines. The peak is located at the point of inflection of the S-shaped curve, where the age coefficient – the slope that indicates the rate of change – is at a maximum. (See volume 1, p. 65.)

One might expect to find the middle-range variables (ow) and (uw) located somewhere in this continuum. However, their sociolinguistic dynamic seems to be of an altogether different kind. No significant correlation with (dha)

[4] The (æhD) allophone of /æ/ has been shown at a number of points to behave more like a new and vigorous change than a nearly completed change. This shows up first in the overall age coefficient in table 5.3. Because the data on (æhD) is sparser, depending on the three words *mad, bad, glad*, it is not always included in the discussions of the new and vigorous changes.

is found for women in the SEC 7–14 range for (owC), (owF), (uwC), or (uwF). We would not of course expect to see such a relationship for the male-dominated change (ay0), and none appears: the overall regression line is flat.

## 11.5 Combined male and female analysis

The male side of this correlation between (dha) and linguistic change in progress has not yet been considered. Chapter 9 found a variety of different relations between men and women in age and social stratification, depending on the stage of development of the change involved. For the lower half of the social spectrum, SEC 0–6, no significant correlations appear between (dha) and linguistic changes in progress. However, the picture for men is not exactly the same as for women. There is a consistent tendency for the second formants of all five front vowels to be correlated positively with (dha). Though for each vowel, the regression coefficients fall short of the .05 level, the combined probability of all five vowels favoring this correlation to the extent they do is less than .02.[5] Figure 11.8 shows the characteristic pattern for this series: in this case for (aw). At upper right, the symbol for Rick C. is isolated from the others, with the highest value of (aw) and a value of (dha) close to the highest. In the principal components display of figure 10.8, Rick C. was displayed as the most advanced speaker in the Wicket Street neighborhood.

The overall distribution of (dha) for the lower half of the SEC range is similar to that for the upper half, but with a symmetric reversal of the

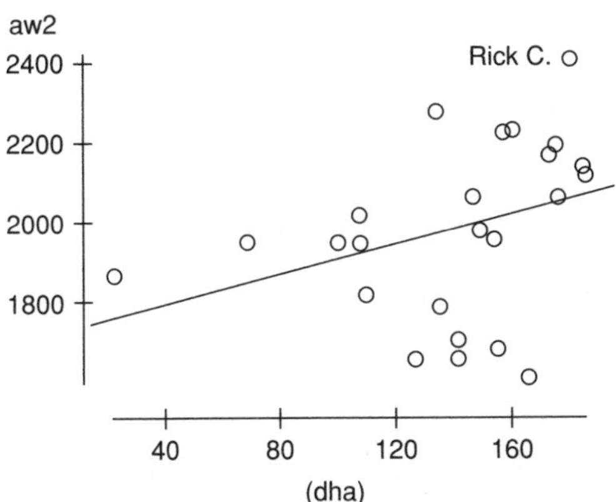


*Figure 11.8* Scatterplot of (dha) against second formant of (aw) for males with SEC < 7

[5] Since chi-square for the series of five is $-2 \times \text{sum}(\log(p_i))$.

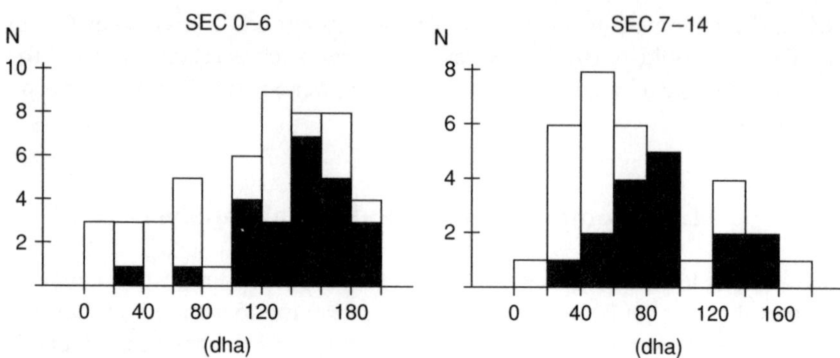


*Figure 11.9* Distribution of (dha) for the upper and lower half of the SEC range (solid bars = men; open bars = women)

major concentrations (figure 11.9). Both show bimodal distributions, with a division around the value of (dha) = 100. For the lower SEC group, the major concentration is in the high values of (dha), greater than 100, with all but two men in this region. The minority with values of (dha) less than 100 includes half of the women in this SEC range. The right-hand diagram shows the corresponding distribution for the upper working class and middle class, but here the majority concentration is in the lower half of (dha) values. In this majority peak, the female speakers are strongly shifted toward the lower end. But in the smaller minority of those with values of (dha) > 100, there are equal numbers of men and women (4).

For the men in the upper half of the SEC range, the relationship between (dha) and the linguistic changes in progress is almost exactly the same as for the women in that range. Again, there are significant coefficients for (aw), (æhD), and (æhS), and weaker effects for (eyC) and (æhN). Even more striking is the parallel rise and fall of r-correlations, shown in figure 11.10. The decline of this correlation with nearly completed changes is precisely the same for men as for women, even though men and women behave differently for many of these changes in progress.

The similarity of the male and female patterns for the upper SEC range appears more concretely in the combined scatterplot of figure 11.11. Here the slopes of the regression lines are almost perfectly parallel. Each gender is divided into an upper working class and middle class distribution. The major difference between men and women is that women are concentrated in the higher ranges of (aw), while men are shifted downward and to the right, with lower values of (aw) and higher values of (dha).

As firm as this relationship is for the front vowels, it does not hold for any of the linguistic changes that originate among back vowels: /ay0/, /uw/, or /ow/. Nevertheless, it may be instructive to look at the pattern produced when all vowels and stable sociolinguistic variables of the correlation

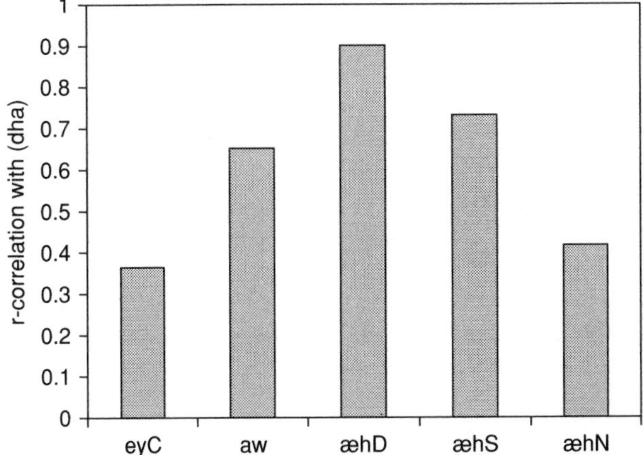


*Figure 11.10* Correlations of (dha) with five linguistic changes in progress for male speakers with SEC 7 to 14

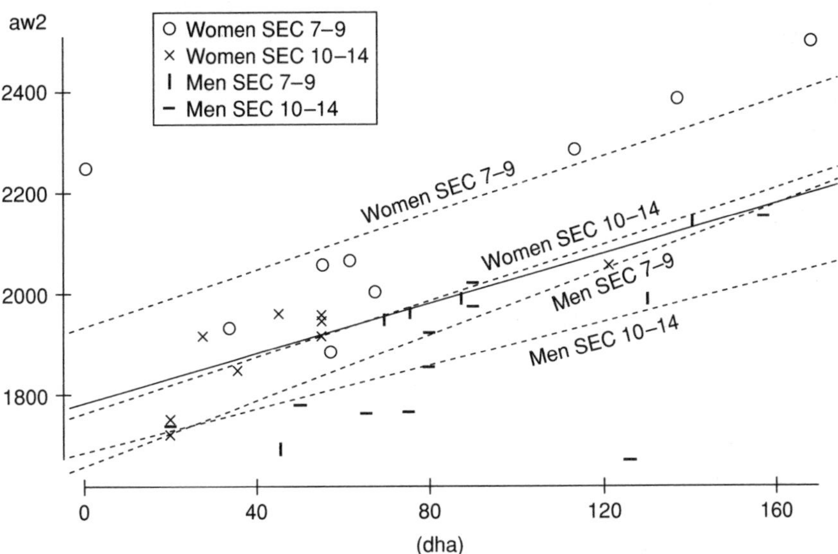


*Figure 11.11* Combined scatterplot of (dha) against (aw) for men and women of the upper SEC range, 7 to 14

matrix table 11.3 are taken into account. Figure 11.12 is based on a principal components analysis of 13 measurements for each speaker. Only 56 of the 86 speakers are shown, since values in one style or the other tend to be missing for some. Separate three-dimensional plots are displayed for each gender, though the analysis is based on the combined set. The first

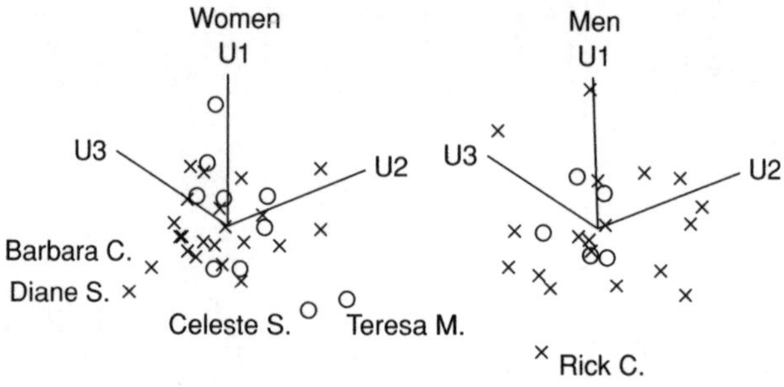

*Figure 11.12* Plots by gender of the first three principal components based on the data for the 13 variables of table 11.3 for 56 speakers

principal component, U1, accounts for 36.7% of the variance; the second, U2, for 25.5%; and U3 for only 11%. It is clear that U1 is aligned along the axis of linguistic change. The leaders of linguistic change have the most negative values of U1, and the oldest and most conservative speakers, the highest positive values. Thus the familiar names of Celeste S., Teresa M., Barbara C., and Rick C. emerge at the bottom of the diagram. High values on the U2 dimension are associated with the South Philadelphia, Italian-dominated neighborhoods. Low values on U2 and positive values on U3 are associated with Wicket St. and the North Philadelphia neighborhoods. Since these two neighborhoods differ in the fronting of the back vowels, the addition of this third dimension reflects the inclusion of (uw) and (ow) in the analysis.

## 11.6 Incremental and saccadic leaders

The leaders of linguistic change who were identified in this and the last chapter are seen to have two different linguistic relationships to their friends and neighbors. Rick C., Barbara C., and Diane S. are members of the Wicket St. community. Chapter 7 showed that it is the most advanced as a neighborhood for all of the sound changes. As users of the Philadelphia vowel system, Wicket St. speakers are in the mainstream of linguistic change, one step ahead of their peers, and perhaps two steps ahead of their parents. Their use of the stable sociolinguistic variables is characteristic of their immediate community. They may be called *incremental leaders*.

In the more upwardly mobile sections of the Philadelphia speech community, we find leaders of linguistic change who have a different linguistic relation to their friends and neighbors. They stand out in sharp contrast to others in their sociolinguistic behavior. Their use of the Philadelphia sound changes is more than a step beyond their peers, and surpasses the level of other neighborhoods more advanced than their own. For them, this way of

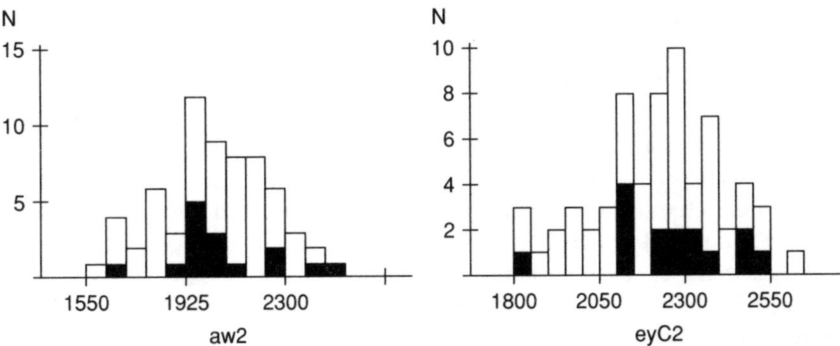


*Figure 11.13* Distribution of second formant (aw) and (eyC) values for working class speakers (SEC 0–9). Solid bars: upper working class, SEC 7–9. Saccadic leaders at right of each diagram

speaking is not a mode of conformity, but an expression of nonconformity, which matches their rejection of the dominant norms for the stable sociolinguistic variables. In this sense, they may be called *saccadic* leaders. Though they are not entirely responsible for the curvilinear pattern, in which the upper working class leads the entire community, they contribute strongly to this effect.[6] Figure 11.13 is a pair of histograms in which the upper working class speakers are shown as solid bars against the rest of the working class population (SEC 0–9). For (aw), the upper working class shows one very conservative speaker, 10 in the center, and four at the upper end. As a whole, the saccadic leaders have higher values than the incremental leaders. But from a phonetic point of view, they are not qualitatively different, neither in their use of linguistic changes in progress nor in their use of stable sociolinguistic variables. What distinguishes the saccadic leaders from others is their social and linguistic context. In the upper working class neighborhood, they contrast with their neighbors in two respects: their advanced use of the phonetic variables and their nonstandard use of sociolinguistic variables.

From the 112 speakers of the Philadelphia Neighborhood Study, we have isolated a half dozen leaders of linguistic change, incremental and saccadic. We have resolved the gender paradox, at least as far as Philadelphia is concerned. Yet there remain more than a few unanswered questions. More and more of the mechanism of change is exposed, but the motivating force behind it remains in the background.

[6] If we were to eliminate Celeste S., Teresa M., and Aileen L. from the final analysis of the second formant of (aw) presented in table 7.4, the coefficient of the upper working class would drop from 147 (p = .0002) to 108 (p = .013); for the second formant of (eyC), it would drop from 99 (p = .03) to 86 (p = .07).

In some way that is not yet delineated, the saccadic leaders appear to be agents of further advance of the sound changes, but do not affect the stable sociolinguistic variables. How does this come about? And why are the saccadic leaders so different from their neighbors? Chapter 9 showed that women advance sound changes in almost linear increments across age units smaller than generations. What causes this steady advance?

The next chapter will attack these questions by a different route. It will present a detailed portrait of the leaders of linguistic change who will, for the most part, speak for themselves. They will not be talking about language, but about social interaction: how they resolved conflicts with their families, neighbors, and employers, and got themselves to their present stage of life. We will then be in a much better position to attack the problem of the motivating forces behind linguistic change.

# 12

# *Portraits of the Leaders*

The studies of social networks in chapter 10 identified two members of the Clark Street network as leaders of linguistic change: Celeste S. and Teresa M., and two children of a Wicket Street family: Rick C. and Barbara C. These speakers showed high values of the new and vigorous linguistic changes relative to their peers by age and social status, and high values of the communicative index C5: that is, a high degree of interaction within the block *and* a high proportion of wider contacts off the block. Chapter 11 isolated the same leaders of the Clark Street network on the basis of their advanced forms of sound changes combined with high values of the stable sociolinguistic variable (dh) in casual speech. Granted that we know who these leaders are, and where they are located in the social structure, several questions follow:

1 How do they exert linguistic influence on their neighbors?
2 Where and when did they acquire the advanced forms that they use?

These are essentially questions about personal influence, and the Katz and Lazarsfeld (1955) findings on the two-step flow of influence, with its associated concepts of interest and gregariousness, must guide our thinking on the first question. On the second question, the K & L model has less to offer, since it deals with information that flows from the mass media. Linguistic changes from below are reflected in the mass media only faintly, and long after they are absorbed by the general population. To find out how influence is transmitted *to* the leaders, there is no point in asking what newspapers they read or what television shows they watch. To observe the flow of linguistic influence, we will want to observe their interaction in everyday life, with their peers, with their parents, and their children.

Inquiries into the mechanism of personal influence will add to our understanding of the forces behind linguistic change. By locating the leaders of change in the more prestigious ranks of local society we have undercut the traditional explanations of change as the result of isolation, ignorance, and laziness. Their central position in sociometric patterns indicates that they have a strong influence on their friends and acquaintances. Their high proportion of connections outside the local block suggests the routes by which information flows across neighborhoods. But we have as yet no suggestion as to why the influence which the leaders receive or generate is not a conservative one, or why these speakers were quicker than others to adopt more advanced forms of linguistic changes in progress. Some part of the answer will come from the field workers' observations of the leaders' behavior, their general reputation in the community, and the stories about them told by others. The greater part will come from the narratives that they tell themselves, in the many recordings made of these central figures in the course of the neighborhood study. We will want to pay particular attention to their accounts of how they dealt with friends and family in their adolescent years. Given the persistence and stability of phonological patterns after adolescence, it is likely that the adult patterns are not far from the levels of their high school years. Though the LCV records do not document the formation of adolescent social categories and alliances with the detail that Eckert (1999) gives us in her study of the Detroit area, we can use her findings to interpret the data obtained from our own interviews and interactions.

## 12.1 Celeste S.

Early in her study of the Clark St. neighborhood, Anne Bower located Celeste S. as a central person on the Clark St. block. Anne was first introduced to Celeste by the secretary of the local parish, Mae D., who was Celeste's best friend. Anne became a regular at the weekly coffee klatsch held at Celeste's house, and through Celeste she was gradually introduced to many members of the Clark St. neighborhood's principal networks. She recorded many personal interviews with Celeste, often with several others present and interacting. When Anne had gained Celeste's confidence to a high degree, she made a notable series of recordings which amounted to Celeste's history of the entire block, proceeding systematically from one house to another without skipping a number. Some of the key narratives were drawn from this session, but others, dealing with Celeste's early years, come from the first few interviews. All in all, the LCV archives show 8 recorded interviews from 1974 to 1991, including 17 tapes with Celeste and her family, a total of 18 hours of speech.

Figure 10.6 showed that Celeste has a C5 index of 10.25, composed of a C1 index of 21, and a C4 index of 5. These summary figures were designed to register the comparative position of each speaker in a network of social and communicative practices. The rich sources of data on Celeste S. will tell us a great deal about this particular leader of change in progress, but also yield a sense of how well the communication indices operate to capture social reality, at least for the upper end of the scale. Let us begin with the accounts which give some idea of Celeste's status and position on the block during the period of LCV.

### *The death of the mean old lady*

When a resident of a Philadelphia neighborhood dies, it is a common practice for someone to take up a collection from all the neighbors, to pay for a wreath, flowers at the funeral, or to defray the expenses of the funeral. On her block, Celeste was usually the one to assume this responsibility. In the course of the house-by-house discussion of the block with Anne Bower, Celeste told this story about a mean old lady on the street who departed quite far from the Clark Street norms of neighborly behavior. Anne's questions or remarks are in parentheses; all names are pseudonyms.

> (How do you know when somebody's died on the street?) They put a crepe on the door [laughs]. You should see the lady that died up the street. That was one neighbor that I couldn't stand. (Who was that?) Well where Bill Marinetti and Gloria lives, well her name was Joan, we used to call her Joan the witch. (Uh huh.) Because she used to work on 9th Street [the open air Italian market]. Her people owned a store on 9th Street. And she used to work on 9th Street. (Yeah.)
>
> And uh – she used to clean at night. And she used to wash the windas. And if you passed her windas, she used to call everybody a son of a bitch. She was just a – mean old lady. And if kids would sit on her steps she would throw water on them and stuff like . . . was just a cantankerous old lady. She wasn't old, though. She was only 52 when she died.

At this point, it becomes clear that Celeste could make mistakes, and had no hesitation about owning up to them.

> So one day, the undertaker, Leonetti comes around, he puts a crepe on her door. "Oh," I said, "Listen, you have the wrong house. What's the matter with you, puttin' a crepe on that door. That lady's a single lady. She goes to work every day."
>
> He said, "Well I'm sure, it's the name, Joan –" he said – I forgot what her last name was now. So I made him take the crepe off the door and go away [laughs]. So . . . about a few hours later, he said, "You know you're crazy. This lady's dead!"

The story now presents a clear view of what it means *not* to be neighborly on Clark Street.

> There, she had fell off a chair, and she had ruptured her spleen. And she walked to her nephew's house, with a ruptured spleen, and she died in the hospital the next day. She wouldn't call a neighbor or anything, you know, to help her. She was that kind of a person, 'cause – *any* neighbor on the street would have got the rescue squad for her, would have gone to the hospital with her. But no. And that – and she died.

> And guess who made the collection on the street? Me [laughs]. But I didn't go to her wake, 'cause I didn't like her.

Following Anne Bower's lead, let us look more closely at the kind of social negotiations and maneuverings that were required on such an occasion. In her response to Anne's inquiry, Celeste clarifies the situation by playing out the role in full.

> (What do you mean, "made the collection?") Well you'd go to each house, and you'd tell them that, you know, one of your neighbors died, and – (OK. Knock on the door. Here I am. "Oh, hello Celeste . . .")
>
> "Oh, hi, Ann. Well you know Joan died down the street. (I didn't know that.) Yeah, it's a sin. Well how much do you wanna give, Ann? 'Cause we're – what do you wanna do? Do you wanna make a flower, or do you wanna give a Mass card? What – tell me what. And we'll get everybody together and we'll see now – the majority rules, you know."

It's not clear that everybody actually got together to make the final decision. What seems to be happening is that Celeste manages to get people to agree in advance to whatever she believes the majority decision will be.

> And ah – they'll say, you'll say, "I don't care. Wherever you wanna put the money, if you wanna put it in a Mass card, or flowers, you wanna give it to the family, it's up to you."
>
> So usually you get a dollar from each house, usually a dollar, you get a dollar and a half, two dollars. You put the money together. So now maybe the family's a poor family. So you hand them the money. (There's no poor family on this street.) No, so usually they get flowers and Mass cards [laughs].

In answer to the question of who decides and who volunteers, Celeste provides a flexible blue-print.

> (OK. But somebody decides they're gonna go do it, right?) Mhm. (So who decides? Does somebody volunteer?) Well it's either your next door neighbor, or like if you know them, you get together and you knock on the door, "You wanna make the collection? I'll go with you. You get a pencil and paper –"
>
> (But you didn't like this lady.) Well, nobody else wanted to do it. And you couldn't let her die without flowers, or – she needed a Mass card, she really did.

Although this old lady rejected the neighborhood's rules for proper behavior, the neighborhood resolutely refused to exclude her from *its* way of paying proper respect.

> (So you got her flowers . . . ) *And* a Mass card. You know she's the only one that collected the most? (Did everybody feel guilty?) Yeah. I collected sixty-two dollars. (Did you really?) I got her a spray of flowers, and I got her a perpetual

Mass card. (What's a perpetual Mass card?) Well that'll last forever. They'll pray for her soul forever. [Laughs] She needed it.

### *How the angel did not go up*

From her various accounts of dealings with other residents of the block, it became evident that Celeste was not the kind of political figure whose success is due to their skill in saying what everyone wants to hear. Celeste was more than forthright in saying what she thought, and in asserting her rights whenever they were infringed on. At one point, Anne was inquiring about families on the block that had engaged in long-standing feuds, or had had words with each other. She remembered Celeste once telling her about how she had chased a neighbor with a butcher's knife, and finally got her to tell the full story. This began with another intricate social ritual – collecting of money to pay for lights to be strung up across the street at Christmas time.

> [Breath] See we had collected, you know, for the lights. So one of the neighbors down the street, she died, too. (A lot of people die on this block . . . ) Uh – her son – they wanted an extra set o' lights. So I said, "Let me go to the place that I got them," 'cause I only got them for three dollars a string. (Mhm.)
>
> So then, everybody got involved. It was Mary Coletti and I who did all the collecting and everything, everything was fine. And all of a sudden everybody gets involved and they made a mess. [Breath]
>
> So uh – this lady says, uh, this uh – Margaret Bono – "Oh, my son'll make them. He's an electrician." So he makes them and he charges all the neighbors twenty dollars a set. And there I paid three dollars. So I called her a crook. And I called her son a crook. I said – so, they were really mad at me.

Calling someone a crook on Clark Street is a strong move. It was certain to lead to a breach of social relations, reciprocal insults, and the suspension of the state of talk between the parties.[1] Celeste had determined to enter into no social relationship in which Margaret Bono was involved. A crisis arose in regard to a plastic angel, that Celeste was originally in charge of, but was now being stored at Margaret's house.

> So then when it was time for us to hang up the angel, on our – I made our lights go across the street. I called John [Santorini], I said, "You wanna string the lights up?"
>
> He says, "Yeah."
>
> So I had an angel see, that we used to hang on the middle of the street, near my house. So eh, Margaret has the angel in her house, so she calls down the street to John, and she says, "Oh John! Would you mind hanging this angel up while you're putting the string of lights up?"
>
> And I said [rough voice], "I don't want the angel."

[1] Cf. Bower 1984.

At this point the interchange escalated in a way that required Celeste to use all of her personal force.

> So Margaret said, "I'm not talking to you," she said, "Celeste S., I'm talking to John Santorini."
>
> So I says, "I don't care who you're talkin' to. That angel has to hang part on my property, and I don't want that goddamn angel."
>
> So she says, "Well John, you do what you wanna do."
>
> So John was afraid to say, "Yah, I'll put the angel up," 'cause he knows what woulda happen.
>
> So uh – she comes down walkin' with the angel. So I says, "Listen, you want the angel?" She says, "Yeah." I said, "Well you stand and hold it for Christmas. 'Cause there's no angel gonna be put on my property." So she got the angel and she put it on my pavement, and I got the angel and I threw it after her.

Margaret then committed a further violation of community norms. She made the dispute public by involving Celeste's husband Jim. This was particularly aggravating because Jim was sick and had stayed home to rest.

> So then she starts, she walks down to her house, stands on her doorstep, and she – my Jimmy's home that day, he was sick. And it was the first day my niece came to visit me, Gina. She had the little baby in the coach.[2]
>
> And she says, "Now Jim I wanna tell you about your wife!" And she went on a long string. And what a gossiper. [Well, after they hear this tape, they'll say that lady *is* a gossiper!] Eh – and she s – she called us all crooks, and you don't know what your wife is, and bla-bla-bla.
>
> And I said, "Margaret, you better shut up. Margaret, you better shut up. You better not bother my Jimmy."
>
> And she didn't shut up. I ran for the butcher knife and I ran after her. Then she ran in the house. Then she didn't come out any more [laughs]. She said I was crazy!
>
> But the angel did not go up.

It seems clear that the solid majority of the neighborhood was aligned with Celeste. From further accounts, this incident provoked even more anti-social behavior from Margaret. On holidays, she mailed anonymous cards to Celeste and others with insulting messages – not as anonymous as they could be, since they were in her handwriting and mailed from her place of work. The end result was social isolation, and finally, removal.

> Oh, but that lady moved. She moved, she couldn't live on this block. Nobody wanted her. *All* the neighbors were against her. (So she moved because of that? What happened?) She couldn't take it anymore. 'Cause everybody would avoid

[2] The Philadelphia term for "baby carriage" is *baby coach.*

her. (Her husband was as strange as she was?) Well her husband used to pick fights too. (Oh he did?) They were both kooks. So they moved to Upper Darby, that's where they belong.

### *The case of the procrastinating priest*

The following account was reported to me by Anne Bower from a conversation that was not recorded. At this time, for one reason or another, Celeste's position on the block had suffered a definite decline. Then she happened to hear (probably from her friend Mae D. at the local church) about a local boy in the service whose mother was dying of cancer. He had applied for leave to visit his mother, but nothing had happened – it was up to the parish priest to write a letter endorsing the application. Celeste walked into the church vestry, past her friend Mae, who was secretary, and proceeded into the back room where the priest was finishing his lunch. "You son of a gun," she said, "You don't have time to write a letter for a dying woman!" He jumped up and said, "Celeste, I was just going to write it." In telling the story she said, "I usually call him a bald-headed bastard, but I wasn't going to do it right then."

As we understood it, Celeste's standing in the neighborhood rose considerably after this incident.

These accounts show a woman full of wit and energy, quick to speak her mind and correct injustice, clearly a point of reference for everyone else on the block. She might well have influenced others to imitate her style of speaking, including her sound pattern – to the extent that adults do modify their original phonology. Though we have only indirect evidence on this point, let us assume that Celeste's (aw) and (eyC) levels were set in her adolescent years at roughly the levels shown, and that they may have risen only slightly since then. Celeste was in her middle 40s at the time of LCV. What can be said about her formative years, which were located some 40 years before, in the late 1930s and early 1940s? Fortunately, the many accounts Celeste has given us are rich in the narratives of personal experience that show how she dealt with others in her early years.

At first glance, the adolescent Celeste would seem to have been a very poor candidate to lead in any kind of change, linguistic or otherwise. She was raised in a traditional Italian family, where her every movement was closely monitored. From a linguistic viewpoint, her family was thoroughly Americanized. Her father was a shoemaker who was brought to the United States as a baby, and always considered himself an American citizen; only her grandmother spoke Sicilian. But from a cultural viewpoint, her situation was governed by the most conservative old world norms.

For the outside world, her father cut a dashing figure.

> . . . a very handsome man, about five nine and a half. Blond hair. They called him "Whitey." He was a great dancer, he liked to dance, and when he was in the mood, he'd joke. Always wore a white shirt, and a tie . . . and very nice shoes. My father made all my shoes.

But at home her father was a hard man to deal with.

> He was a crab. You weren't allowed to talk while you were eating. As soon as he walked in the door the food hadda be on the table, and it hadda be hot. My mother hadda be there. My mother could never be – out (when he came home). Never. There would be murder. And we sat down, and we ate. And you couldn't laugh, and you couldn't talk, until dinner was over. (Then what?) Go in the parlor and listen to the radio, the news. We hadda sit in the parlor and listen to the news with him. . . . My mother never sat down, she was always serving.

In such a household, girls were under the strictest control. They were in no position to follow the latest trends or display any independence.

> The girls were always so frightened, and backward. If we'd get company in the house . . . like friends of ours, the children weren't allowed to listen, if they had cake they weren't allowed to have it, until they left. You didn't have an opinion, you couldn't voice an opinion . . . You didn't know anything.

There was plenty of conflict at home; at times it was unbearable. Celeste's father was no one to be trifled with. When her boss held her at work an hour later than usual, her father accused her publicly of being a whore. Things got worse and worse, but there was no simple out.

> Well I'll never forget. I was 16, I packed my bags, I s's "I'm leaving. I am go – " 'Cause my mother and father was arguing. I don't know what they were fighting about. And it really is – there was always arguments and fights. 'Cause my father was such a grouse. And my mother was easy to get along with . . .
>
> I said "I'm leaving home." And that's what he said to me. You know, he didn't say, "Get out."
>
> "You go upstairs. Unpack that bag," he said, "or you'll never get out of this house alive."
>
> I went back upstairs . . .

Let us now see how Celeste dealt with this tense and highly controlled situation. This was the time of World War II, when Philadelphia was the seat of a great naval base; service men were everywhere. Celeste was fully conscious of the distinction between "good girls" and "bad girls." She was clearly the first kind, but it is evident that she had plenty of contact with the second.

> They'd dress the part . . . make-up. They'd dye their hair. I went to school with quite a few of them, you know, they would dye their hair, and I'd say "Ohhh!

You dyed your hair!" Always dark, real black, and always high pompadors on their head and eye make-up. Years ago, we never used eye make-up. That was sump'm . . . theatrical. But they did . . . eye things on . . . and all that stuff. That's all I'd have to come in the house.

Though Celeste operated within her own rules for good behavior, they were very far from the rules that her father would accept. The following is a vivid account of how Celeste managed her social relations.

My mother used to say – I used to go to the movies and she used to send a couple of boys up the street to watch who I used to be in the movies with. (Did she really?) Oh yeah.

But we were in cahoots, the boys and I. That's the only way you could get out – like we'd date. I would date. And like . . . my father would say, "Where you goin'?" "Well daddy now look! George's gonna take me –" George down the street. And daddy thought, "Oh boy, she's safe with Georgie." So Georgie would go *his* way, and I would go *my* way. And then we would meet, see, at a certain time. I'd say, "Please! Please, Georgie don't do that to me! You better be there!" He'd say, "Don't worry –" 'cause his father was just as bad as my father. We would meet, and we'd come home like two nice little kids.

But I used to go dance at the canteen. (The canteen?) Yeh, they had a canteen that was all service men. And you couldn't get in if you didn't have a date. And it'd have to be a service man – to take you in. But once you got in you could leave this guy, you know, and dance with everybody else. And that's what we used to do, stand in the corner. And wait for the fellas, and I'd say to one of the sailors, "Are you going in there?" And he'd say "Yeah," and I'd say "Would you take me in?" "Sure!" And they would take you – and nothing *bad* would happen in there. They really ran – the Salvation Army ran a beautiful thing. There was only coffee and doughnuts, there was no drinking, and soda, music. All night you'd *dance, dance, dance.* It was super![3]

In spite of the strictest controls, Celeste was able to manage her father; she managed Georgie; she managed the sailors. In fact, she developed a system.

You know down at the Navy Yard they used to give parties on the ships, and if you know any of the fellas on the ships, then you could go – to their parties. I forgot what they used to call them. And I had a book, with every phone number of every ship that pulled in port. . . . They were nice kids. They were all nice boys . . . they were all sports minded. My dates were all basketball games, football games . . . and movies . . . the corner ice cream parlor. I don't remember ever getting into any kind of situations . . . like . . .

Celeste didn't always succeed in getting what she wanted, but she never failed to speak up for her point of view. We have many stories that show

[3] The phonetic forms used in *bad* and *dance* are among the most extreme that we have recorded from Celeste or anyone else.

that when she was in her teens, Celeste reacted to injustice with the same fierce determination that she showed as an adult.

> I worked in Franklin Cedars Department Store. (What were you doing?) I started out as a salesgirl and got demoted to the stockroom [laughs]. (How old were you?) Oh, fourteen. It was during the war. And they needed all the help they can get. And the old sales ladies, there, you know . . .
>
> They had a sale that I'll never forget one day. And I made a hundred and sixteen dollars and they took it away from me and they gave it this old sales lady, 'cause I was called a contingent in the store. And I was so mad, and I hollered and screamed and yelled . . . and they demoted me to the stockroom.

The only clear way out of the tense situation at home was marriage. There is no reason to think that Celeste would marry anyone who came along. On the contrary, her account of how she met her husband shows her active character more than anything else. This story was recorded in a session with her friend Mae, who like Anne was hearing it for the first time.

> How did I meet him? I went to a dance, and uh, I saw this boy, he was in uniform. It was – right after the war had stopped. And I looked at him – and I was with a girl friend, and I said, "Now see that boy in the corner over there? I'm gonna marry him." I didn't even know him. (Did you have a feeling?) I guess. I guess I had a feeling. So it was a Sadie Hawkins night. Now Sadie Hawkins you asked the guys to dance. And I said, "This is great tonight! Boy, he's cute." So my girl friend's going, "You're crazy!" I said, "No, I'm not crazy. I'm gonna marry him, Phil." And uh, I went up to him and I asked him to dance. And he asked me for my phone number. Years ago they used to have matches, that all the service men carried, "Easy to pick up." VD? You know they all carried them in their pockets, so that's where I put my name – and you know Mae, he still has that. He still has it. Yeah.

The next step in the affair took a certain amount of management.

> . . . And see at that time my husband was in Walter Reed General Hospital from the Second World War, see, so he was on leave. And I didn't know it. I thought he was stationed here in Philly. So I didn't hear from him for about a month. But I used to see his boy friend, and I says, "Whatever happened to that – fella, you know, that uh –" He said, "I don't – when he comes, I'm gonna have him call you." And I had a date, it was on a Saturday, with a fella that used to play football for Southern, and uh – I was supposed to go up to a game with him out in Nor – uh – Mount – uh – not Mount Airy, they used to play up in the coal regions, our first – Allentown! And I was all set to go.
>
> And I get this call, from Jim, so I called him back and I said, "Oh I sprained my ankle and I just can't go." And oh God – what an excuse! So I went with Jimmy. And uh – oh, after the first date, we went steady.

Jim turned out to be everything that Celeste hoped for. He was a skilled worker (a draftsman), and a good provider. Moreover, he was always kind and considerate. But in marrying him, Celeste stepped outside of the expected bounds. He came from a different neighborhood. And he was Irish.

> He was so cute . . . he was adorable. Really cute, really good looking boy. And oh boy, I flipped over him. (From around here?) No, he was from 22nd St. And when his mother heard he was goin' with an Italian girl I think she had a stroke.

Celeste solved all of these problems, and wound up as a highly respected figure on one of the most prosperous blocks in South Philadelphia. She might have gone in a different direction. It is clear that she knew the bad kids, the burnouts of the time, and learned from them, but never lost sight of her own interests.

## 12.2 Teresa M.

The picture of Celeste, then, is not simply of a person with prestige, but someone who acts to change the world when she does not like what she sees. Let us now consider Teresa M., the 14-year-old who was the other Clark St. outlier in the charts of chapters 10–11. What sort of a person is she?

Though Teresa is still too young to give us the rich account of social life that we obtained from Celeste, it is clear that she is another strong character. She dominates her immediate circle of friends. She quit Catholic school when she was 9 because she couldn't put up with the way that the nuns smacked the kids around, and went to public school. She ran away from home several times because her mother hits her. And she is by no means a model girl:

> Mother said I don't care how much you drink, as long as it's in the house. She won't let me have no more than three cans, 'cause I'm a girl and I'm only fourteen.

Her picture of the New Year's party shows that she can escape this constraint:

> We were racin' for the beer, cold water sprayin' all over the place. Christmas and New Year, I woke up drunk, I was so drunk from the night before. It was really dynamite though. I dig on the bed drunk because you just lay down like you're floatin' and you go right to sleep.

At the same time, Teresa is a thoughtful girl with her eye on the main chance. She has a firm intention of going to Temple University and becoming a lawyer.

> It's not so much as being in front of people. I'll be accomplishing something to myself. I'll do something good. And I'll always have money to help people out.

She has clear and moderate views on women's lib, on prejudice, and on how to raise kids:

> I'm always gonna be open with my kids. You know tell 'em, you wanna smoke pot, go ahead, but I'm tellin' 'em, it's bad for you. I would rather you not do it.

There are clear parallels between Celeste as an adult and a teen, and Teresa at 14. Like Celeste, Teresa has escaped the domination of her family. She aligns herself with the burnout crowd, but only goes so far. She keeps the boys under control, aims to stay decent until she's married, and always has her eye on the future.

Thus leaders of linguistic change in our Philadelphia study can be oriented within the polar oppositions that Eckert (1999) has established in her studies of sound changes in the high school social categories. In Eckert's terms, they are in-betweens, who align themselves with the burnouts in resistance to what they see as the senseless regulations of adult authorities. But they do not follow the burnout path beyond that. Their fundamental nonconformity is subordinated to their clear view of what it takes to be successful in our society. This is the orientation that eventually places them at the peak of the curvilinear pattern. In that position, they are influential. But they retain their fundamental pattern of nonconformity and reaction to injustice, and much of their standing in the community is due to their ability to create social change.

## 12.3 The Corcorans

Figure 2.3 showed that the Wicket St. block included several distinct social networks on Wicket St., one revolving about the Kendell family, the other centered on the Corcoran family (who, so far, we have indicated with the initial C.). Figure 10.7 showed that the two central figures of these interrelated networks are Meg Kendell and Kate Corcoran. As we have seen, Wicket St. is relatively poor compared to Clark St., and the houses have a uniformly low value, so there is little room for differentiation in the SEC index. In many ways, the Corcorans and Kendells are similar: basically Irish, middle working class. The occupational ranking of both families is "3" on the scale of 1 to 6 (chapter 2). Since Kate Corcoran left school after the 10th grade, and Meg Kendell graduated high school, the overall SEC ratings are 6 for Meg Kendell and 5 for Kate Corcoran.

However, their detailed life histories show deeper differences. Meg's husband had a steady job, but she went back to work at an office job

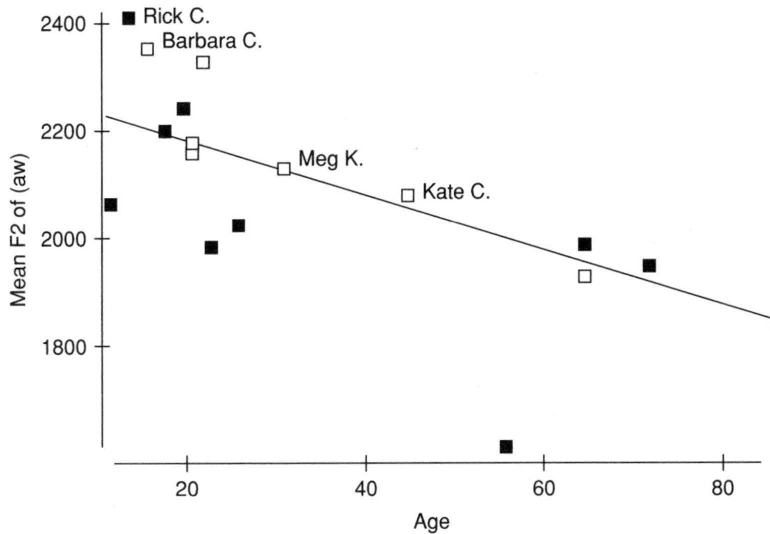


*Figure 12.1* Age vs. fronting of (aw) for Wicket Street. Open squares = women; solid squares = men

at the time that the study began, and after a year or so had moved up to office manager. One of the reasons that Kate's first marriage had foundered was because her husband could not support her. She went on welfare for two years when the children were young, then went back to work as a waitress. Her second marriage had also run into trouble at that time, mostly because of conflicts with her husband's older stepchildren, but they moved out and the situation stabilized.

Meg is a proper person. Her house is well kept up, she speaks carefully, and she looks down on others who don't maintain the same standard. Kate is less concerned (and less able) to keep up appearances. She is forthright and can be rough spoken, especially about people on the block who "think their shit don't stink." Meg and Kate are quite sharply differentiated in their social orientation, though they share the same upward aspiration for their children. Meg's style of life is akin to that of the lower middle class. Although one branch of Kate's family descends from the "First Families of Virginia," she retains a lower working class style of living and speaking.

This portrait of the leaders of change will not be concerned primarily with Meg and Kate. Figure 12.1 is a plot of the fronting of (aw) against age for the Wicket Street speakers; both Meg and Kate are located close to the regression line that establishes the normal relation of age to (aw). In other words, their use of the variable is typical or appropriate for their ages. Two outliers in this display are the two youngest children of Kate, Rick (13) and Barbara (16), and it is their life style that will be our main focus. First, it will be helpful to get a closer look at Kate's life, for Rick and Barbara are the products of a family tradition centered around strong and independent women who freely speak their minds.

Several years after Kate was first married, her husband got a job in his home town of Detroit, and the family moved there. He lost that job, and after three months, Kate decided that she had had enough.

> So I said to 'im, "I'm gonna call my mother." And you know, to me, "You're gonna what?" I said, "I'm gonna call my mother." I come down off the step and there was like a phone booth at the corner (Mm) of the house. Oh I had change and I called my mother. And I said to her, "I wanna come home." She s'd, "And then you come home." (That's what mothers are for.) So, she said to me, "Yeh. Bring the baby." She said, "He wants to come with ya, fine. If he don't, tell him, 'Well, I'm goin'." (Mhm) She said, "And that's – the way you do it."

Money was not the main problem here. Kate was alienated by the isolating style of the Detroit apartment complexes, and longed for the intense community life of Philadelphia's row houses.

> I said, "Well Mom," I said, "he's not makin' any effort to get a job or anything, and after all," I said, "*I* can't go over to his mother and ast her for a quart of milk." Now she knew – she lived like across the street and around the corner from us. (Mm) Right. She never even so much as come over and ast if my baby needed a quart of milk. (Mm) And to me – this how – this wasn't how my family was – if my kids needed a quart of milk, they woulda made sure that I had a quart o' milk for them. You know?

Kate's way of dealing with her mother-in-law is typical of her straight-from-the-shoulder way of dealing with any dispute.

> So – I said "I can't take it," and I said, "and her and I," I s'd, "we just aren't gonna get along." And I said, "and there's no sense in kidding myself." (Mm) I said, "I tried," I said, "It didn't work out." I wound up tellin' her to get out of my house, well out of my home which was, the apartment that we lived in, and I said, "and eh – I guess she'll nev –" I said, "As far as I'm concerned," and I said, "if she never talks to me, it'd be too soon," you know. (Mm)

Kate refuses the dignity of the term "home" to the Detroit apartment house she was living in. She then put the issue to her husband in exactly the terms that her mother had laid out, and once again showed that she was in control of the situation.

> So he said, "All right," he said, "I'll go." He said, "But how I'm gonna get the money?" I said, "Don't worry about the money." But I used to have a habit, when I'd go to the store, if I'd break a dollar bill, and I'd have ninety-nine – if I'd only spend a penny out of it, and I had 99 cents change, I used to take it and

> throw it in the drawer. (That's a good idea.) And like – I went up – the stairs, and I counted out the money, that I had – throwed in the drawer. And, to begin with, I was always used to having money. (Yeh.) You know I mean like, I made good money when I was a waitress. (Right.)

Now let us turn to Kate's 16-year-old daughter, Barbara, growing up in Philadelphia. Her family situation was far from ideal; she did not get along with her stepfather, Kate's second husband, and there was plenty of conflict with her mother. But Barbara seems to be a well-adjusted person who has a strong inclination to upward mobility. This is coupled with a conscious rejection of the dominant racist ideology of working class Kensington.

While most of the young people in her neighborhood went to Catholic school, Barbara followed a different route in public school, since the family did not have enough money to pay the relatively low tuition of Catholic school. In school she made friends with blacks as well as whites, and developed attitudes directly contrary to those of most young people on the block.

> I went to Stetson. I got used to it [being with black people]. And I hadda work with 'em and tutor 'em with 'em and all. And I think you know, you *have* to work with 'em and do stuff with 'em, you know, and you have to live with them the rest of your life . . .

She joined the Neighborhood Youth Corps. There she developed an interest in physical therapy, and has decided to make that her life career. She plans to go to Temple, the largest city university, to get a degree in physical therapy. Her main orientation is toward helping people: she likes people, she says.

Yet Barbara was raised in a neighborhood where open conflict was as prominent as cooperation. There was also no shortage of conflict on the block, where her mother was a formidable force.

> The fire plug, it's right across the street from my house . . . and one of the kids down the other block, y'know . . . The girl across the street has the wrench, and they wou'n' turn it on, so they got their monkey wrenches . . . and they turned it on. They put it all the way up to the curb, and sprayed, it all come in the windows. My older brother was ready to hit him. And he's only twelve, and my brother's eighteen. His mother come up. His mother's a real giant, she's got muscles on her, y'know and my mother's real small, and she was gonna hit her. And there was a big fight all summer . . .

Kate put a great deal of effort into trying to get Barbara to behave like the more respectable people on the block; not only to clean her room, but to keep out of street fights. Tough as she was, Kate did not want

Barbara to follow in her footsteps. However, Barbara was not a stay-at-home; she was well into the center of community life. For a girl, that often meant defending herself against the predatory tactics of other girls. Early in her first interview, Anne Bower asked Barbara, "What would make you annoyed?"

> [Laughs] That question really came up, 'cause I was going with some kid, Jimmy Kromusch, and the 27th of this month woulda been 10 months . . . it came to, I think May, he asked me last January, and Gina started her stuff, and [laughs] I really got mad. (What was she doin'?) You know she'd just go 'round with him whenever I wasn't around, she'd make a pass at 'im. Till I found out. And then I went after her. You know, me bein' a girl, my mom says, "Don't fight!" (And did you?) Yes I did. I really did. Oh, I bet her so bad.[4] I says, "Don't touch 'im!" I says, " 'cuz I'm warnin' ya." (Did you really hit her?) Yeah. Fist fight . . . I'm not sayin' that I'm really good, you know . . .

Like all good fighters, Barbara disclaims her expertise. But she was frequently called on to use her skills when girls (or boys) violated the norms of acceptable behavior. In this case, Anne's inquiry into the norms for a fair fight produced this extraordinary account.

> Last year I got in a fight . . . wit' this girl. She's built like a Mack truck. She scraped my face – she had nails. She's lucky I di'nt. She scraped my face all like this. I have a li'l scar here. She punched me in the jaw, y'know. I almost had t'get stitches, y'know. It was really bad.

The fight was triggered by a serious violation of local etiquette. Perhaps the most defiant challenge, in Philadelphia as in so many other cities, is for one girl to call another a whore.

> . . . she called me a whore. And I got back at her I says, "I'm not –" I says, "You got nerve." I says, "You just gave up two kids." (Yeah.) Yeah, she had two abortions. And . . . during this year she had – she – was pregnant. And I think she had the baby in June. And she gave it up. I s's, "You got a nerve calling anybody a whore." And – that's the fight you know.

In this fight, the odds were more heavily weighted against Barbara than usual. But she did reasonably well.

> And she pulled my hair. I pulled her back. She got me down on the ground. So she's pulling my hair, scratching my face. I'm went kickin'. (Where do you kick so it really hurts . . . ) I kicked her everywhere. Y'know, she was right over top of me. I went there, and there, and there [laughs]. Everyplace, y'know.

[4] The nonstandard preterit form of *beat* in North Philadelphia is regularly *bet*.

When a fight lasts any length of time, neighbors tend to gather, and kin give the support that's needed.

> And the worst thing about it, her mom would stand on the step and say, "Come on, Sheryl, let's go. Come on, Sheryl, let's go."

But in Barbara's case, family support wasn't as solid. Her brother consistently took sides against her in conflicts with her mother, and distracted her rather than encouraged her.

> And my brother was standin' there. He knows, I pick a fight, my mother's not supposed to know about it. You know, she don't believe in girl fightin' . . . now. He say, "I'm tellin' Mom." "SHUT YOUR DAMN MOUTH!" I would holler, y'know. And . . . she'd start cursin' at me.

The last sentence is part of a violent argument between Barbara, Sheryl, and Sheryl's mother. At that moment, Kate appeared on the scene.

> And I turn around I says, "Well you call me an f—in whore." An' the next thing my mother's right behind me. And her mother says, "What did she call you?" And I said it *straight out.* (Yep.) My mother behind me an' all. I liked to died, because before that I said an f—in whore, yeah?

There follows an extraordinary metalinguistic exchange.

> And then she s's, what she says is, "Oh an F-H." An' then "I mean, an F-W" I goes.[5]

Barbara, with her mother present, is uncertain what she should do. But Kate had no doubt:

> I says, "Mom, I didn' say that before, you know." So she goes, "Get finished with the fight." She says, "And if you don't beat her, I'll beat you up."

In Kensington, some norms of behavior are strictly ordered. Though Kate believes that girls should not fight, this insult is unacceptable.

Barbara's final evaluation of the situation revolves about the basic norms that govern a fair fight in Kensington:

> I got some good out of her, and she got some good out of me. But I was scarred, y'know. And . . . I'm still scraped up and all. (Jeez. Well did you wreak damage on her?) Oh yeah. (How did she look when you were finished?) She didn't look so hot. But I was taught up, y'know, if you're gonna have a fight, do it fair with the fist.

[5] Barbara and Kate disagree on the spelling of *whore*. Note that "f—in" is pronounced [ɛfɪn].

Barbara does not lose sight of her mother's insistence on proper behavior. But her whole family is firmly oriented toward the basic imperative to defend yourself against insult, injury, and injustice.

> (Did you fight a lot when you were a little girl?) I, I really don't think I – [breath] I know one time, my aunt was sayin', Y'know, I go back t'see – y'know, I talk to her an all a lot. She'd say, "There's a girl around here, she's – married now, she's sixteen, she's got a li'l baby," she s's, "when youse were little, youse used to fight like crazy. She used to beat you so simple it wasn't funny. And one day I got so mad at youse fightin', I said, 'You go out there or else I'll beat you'." [hh] I went out an' I beated h – y'know? And my mother says – my aunt goes, "Now 'kay, now, you finally did it."

It does not seem likely that Barbara's switch between "mother" and "aunt" is accidental here. Her aunt gave her the kind of support that she wished her mother had given her – support that her mother finally did give in exactly the same words.

The three leaders of linguistic change who we have examined so far – Celeste S., Teresa M., and Barbara Corcoran – are not drawn from the same mold. Celeste grew up in a traditional, conservative Italian household where the main constraint was against free communication with boys. In Teresa's time, the issue was drinking and drugs. In Barbara's household, the main arguments revolved around fighting. The theme that unites the three is the determination to escape from unreasonable adult controls, and to maintain their status in the fierce competition of the everyday world. At the same time, they were not limited by or submerged in the world view of their peers. They all follow a path of upward mobility and self-interest that insulates them from a surrounding adolescent ideology that is entirely governed by its rejection of adult norms.[6]

## 12.4 Rick Corcoran

In the search for leaders of linguistic change in Philadelphia neighborhoods (figure 12.1), one younger male stood out: Barbara's younger brother Rick. He showed extremely advanced values of (aw), (eyC), and other variables as well. Interviews with Rick span a period of two and a half years, from $13\frac{1}{2}$ to 16 years of age. Throughout he showed himself to be a tough little kid who could take care of himself on the streets and knew what he wanted out of life. Rick was indeed little: at 13 he was 4 foot $11\frac{1}{2}$ inches. He hoped that he would never grow taller, because he wanted to be a jockey. There was some hope for this: his father, who owned a couple of

[6] The "burnout" ideology described in detail in Eckert 1986, 1999.

horses and trained them, was only 5′6″. His mother Kate was 5 foot even. Every morning Rick left his row house in North Philadelphia for the race track at Liberty Bell, where he cleaned the stalls, walked the horses, watered and fed them. If it was a warm day, he gave them a bath before they ate. He exercised the horses too, and riding them around the track was hard work: it seemed to him sometimes that his arms would be pulled out of their sockets.

In this extract, Rick is reminiscing about his role as the leader of the little guys when he was 8 or 9. Much of their action was in rehearsal for confrontations that were about to take place, but somehow did not.

> If you want to be in our gang you used to have to do all kinds o' stuff. Like I used to have like a little gang . . . The way our gang was, right? We used to have big guys, an' little guys. And I was in charge of the little guys. Y'know. I had them so good. We had one fight. We coulda had one fight. The kids come up the street y'know lookin' for trouble, right? All of us little guys on the cars, top o' trucks, under the trucks right? . . . hidin' behind the cars an' all. If those kids woulda came up, an' started any trouble, all we hadda do was jump out . . . behin' 'em, walk up, nice an' quiet, and jump up on the backs, an' grab 'em, start chokin' 'em like 'at or sump'm, or else pull their hair, twist their arm in the back, like you try to break it, an' the big guys come up, boom boom boom!

When Anne Bower asked Rick why he was chosen by the big guys to be the leader of the little guys, he guessed that it was maybe because he was so small. Rick was conscious of his position as a short kid, but he never apologized for it.

> Y'know . . . how small I am now. Right? An' everybody thinks a small guy is really weak. Right. But they don't know how a small guy can always take care of himself better than a big guy can.

It's a common observation that boys who grew up as the biggest in their age group are much less involved in fighting than little kids, who have to prove their ability over and over again. This was the case with Rick.

> See how I am, I bet up a kid named Jimmy Bending, right? and he towers over me. Right? And I bet him up. 'Cause he thought he was real big, pickin' on me, y'know, he was always pickin' on the little kids. So I showed him one day. Showed him three times. First time I gave him a bloody nose, second time he gave me one. And then the third time we had a fight, me and him really went at it. Nobody got nuttin' but – we really got a few punches goin'. Y'know. Nobody could break us up.

As so often happens in North Philadelphia, grown-ups are very much involved in kids' fights. Though the adults believe that kids have to stand up and defend themselves, they often intervene on their behalf when things are not going well. And as we have seen before, Kate Corcoran was never far from the scene.

> Then the kid's father came out, right? grabbed 'im – grabbed my arm, and mom says uh, "You'd better – get your hands off him" right? And the guy lived next door. Not Jerry, but the guy used to live there before? . . . His tire iron was out there, layin' by the side of the car. 'Cause he was fixin' his tire. And he's watchin' me and him go at it. And this guy Mr. Bennet come over to me. He was bombed! And he grabbed me, yeh. And mom says, "Git your dirty hands offa him!"

What follows is not an actual event, but rather what must have been Kate's account to Rick of what would have happened if the kid's father had not obeyed her command.

> So my mom, she's probably ready to – if he hadda touched me again, my mom was gonna – was gonna bend down, pick up the tire iron, and boom! right across the head . . .

Tough as he was, Rick had a strong sense of when violence was called for and when it was not.

> . . . or else you jus' say, "Take it to the street." That's a dirty way of sayin' it because . . . If you're the one that's always lookin' for the fight, you know you're always gonna lose. The person – if you wanna jus' show him, that . . . you're not supposed to be pickin' on me, why don't you go pickin' on somebody else your own size, right?

And though he came out on top most of the time,[7] he showed an unexpected sensitivity to emotions, his own and others'.

> Then he said – he went home cryin'. Then when I got in the house I started to cry. Because, after a good fight, y'know, it does hafta get out . . . after a *good* fight. But I am grown up more than I was a couple o' years ago. Before I always usta cry when I had a fight. Now I don't. 'Cause I always feel sorry for him . . . when I bet him up.

All of the charts show that Rick and Barbara are together on the advancing edge of Philadelphia sound changes. As children of Kate Corcoran, they carry on the family ability to defy neighborhood norms of proper and polite behavior. Like his sister, Rick is committed to the opposing set of norms which center about the need for self-defense, resistance to injustice,

[7] These are of course Rick's own accounts. But they were not contradicted by his friend John S., who participated with Rick in joint interviews for all the data cited here.

and a commitment to whatever violence is needed to achieve those ends. And like his sister, Rick is already committed to an upward path that might well earn enough money to move him out of the lower working class environment of Wicket Street.

However, Rick is the first male we have encountered among the leaders of linguistic change. The fact that he is very short – and might have a shorter vocal tract – might have something to do with the difference between him and other boys. There always remains some suspicion that our method of normalization does not fully compensate for differences in vocal tract length. But Rick has a fairly deep voice for someone his age, with an F0 considerably lower than that of his best friend John S., which suggests that he has neither abnormally short vocal cords or vocal tract.

The leaders of linguistic change on Wicket St. are not different in their social orientation and trajectories from the leaders on Clark St. Chapter 11 showed that they are also similar in their close association of (dha) and linguistic changes in progress. Where they differ is in their relation to their immediate surroundings. Celeste stands out from her neighbors in her cultural style and leadership. Kate, and to a certain extent her children, fits in. However, Kate's children seem to share the upward orientation that may bring them closer to Celeste's position as they grow up.

## 12.5 Individuals as regression variables

The series of quantitative analyses in chapters 5–9 progressively narrowed the search for the leaders of linguistic change until we could characterize them with some precision as women of the upper working class and several speakers from the Kensington area. Chapters 10 and 11 further refined this characterization by pointing to women with a particular type of network configuration and a long history of social and linguistic nonconformity. But this was at the cost of eliminating two-thirds of the original population for whom we did not have full data on communication networks.

The proposal of these last two chapters is that Celeste S., Teresa M., and the Corcorans are effectively different from the rest of the population by social traits other than their age, gender, ethnicity, and neighborhood. It follows that we should be able to explain more of the residual variance in the full sample by adding these individuals as dummy variables to the regression: e.g. the variable "Celeste S." will be given the value 1 if the speaker is Celeste S., otherwise it will carry the value 0. Table 12.1 shows the result of adding these individuals to the regression analyses of chapter 7 for six sound changes. All but the last involve fronting by an increase of F2: the nearly completed stigmatized (æhN), the new and vigorous changes (aw) and (eyC), the middle-range changes (owC) and (owF). The last column shows values for (ay0), the centralization of /ay/ before voiceless consonants. To facilitate the comparison of (ay0) values to the others, they are multiplied by –2.[8] Where the effect of individual leaders is significant, the adjusted $r^2$ rises about 8%. Once again, it will be essential to re-examine the main effects of gender, class, and neighborhood to be sure that the additions are additions and not substitutions for what has gone before. A comparison of table 12.1 with the tables of chapter 7 will show that there is little change in the values of the original regression variables. The findings of table 12.1 can be summed up as follows:

*Gender*: The predominance of women in all the sound changes but the last is maintained across the board, with a maximum effect for the new and vigorous changes.

*SEC*: For the stigmatized (æhN), the expected linear social stratification is maintained, with lower middle class, upper middle class, and upper class using progressively less fronted forms – and differentiating this variable from all others. The curvilinear pattern is maintained for the new and vigorous variables, with the upper working class significantly ahead. A similar effect appears for the lower middle class for free /ow/.

*Age*: The stability of (æhN) resembles the stable sociolinguistic variables studied in chapter 3, with an adolescent peak and a flat adult pattern. The new and vigorous changes (aw), (eyC), (ay0) show the strongest age stratification.

*Neighborhood*: Wicket St. is ahead, across the board.

*Ethnicity*: Speakers with primary Italian ethnicity are significantly behind in the fronting of /ow/.[9]

*Individual leaders of change*: The additions of the two South Philadelphia leaders of change make large and significant contributions to the analysis of the fronting of (æhN) and (aw). In fact, these coefficients are larger than any of the group coefficients. Even though a single individual is involved, the result is significant at the .05 level. The value for (eyC) for Celeste is also larger than any others, but the significance level is only .14. We would not expect to find such an effect for the fronting of /ow/, since this is very much behind in the Italian neighborhoods of South Philadelphia. For (uw) and (ow), the addition of the Corcorans, Rick and Barbara, has a very large and significant effect, considerably greater than any other coefficients.

The last column of table 12.1 answers the question raised about Rick Corcoran. Are his high values for F2 the result of inadequate normalization of a short vocal tract, which might lead his formant values to resemble

[8] Since in all displays and charts, 100 Hz on the vertical axis for F1 corresponds to 200 Hz on the horizontal axis for F2, and the direction of change for (ay0) is a lowering of the value of F1.

[9] This applies to the /uw/ variables as well, which are not shown here. There is a significant negative effect of secondary German ethnicity on the fronting of /aw/, but this is difficult to interpret.

*Table 12.1* Regression coefficients for 112 speakers from the Neighborhood Study by gender, SEC, age, neighborhood, ethnicity, and individual leaders of linguistic change

| | (æhN) | (aw) | (eyC) | (owC) | (owF) | −2 × (ay0) |
|---|---|---|---|---|---|---|
| Female | 56* | 110*** | 98*** | 77* | 85** | −80*** |
| UWC | | 96** | 99* | | | |
| LMC | −75† | | | | 126** | |
| UMC | −124** | | | | | |
| UC | −243*** | | | | | |
| Under 20 | 71* | 299*** | 202*** | | | 254*** |
| 20–29 | | 165*** | 130** | 186*** | 118** | 218*** |
| 30–39 | | 181*** | 110** | 152*** | | 120** |
| 40–49 | | 169*** | | | | 96* |
| 50–59 | | | | | | 94* |
| Wicket St. | 113** | 206*** | 170*** | 110* | 55 | 68* |
| Pitt St. | 131** | 140*** | | | | |
| Clark St. | 73† | | 100* | | | |
| Nancy Dr. | | | | 146** | | |
| So. Phila | | | | | | 166** |
| Italian | | | | −83* | −138** | |
| Celeste S. | 295* | 342* | 240 | | | |
| Teresa M. | 271† | 326* | | | | |
| Barbara C. | | | | 370* | 404* | |
| Rick C. | | 237† | 301† | 419* | 329* | 242* |
| $r^2$ (adj) | 0.53 | 0.65 | 0.41 | 0.35 | 0.37 | 0.47 |

*** p < .001, ** p < .01, * p < .05, † p < .10

those of women rather than men? This is not the case. Rick is also a strong leader in the male-dominated centralization of (ay0), where none of the females show significant coefficients. Inadequate normalization would diminish this effect by yielding larger values of F1 for Rick C. The fact that Rick C. is a leader of linguistic change across the board reinforces our confidence in the normalization algorithm which is an essential part of the analytical procedure.

Table 12.1 demonstrates that the leading position of these four individuals is not an artifact of a reduced data set: it applies to the full sample of 112 speakers as a whole. It seems likely that the features of the leaders of linguistic change sketched in the last two chapters are the same features that are responsible for their leading position in the larger community that we have sampled.

## 12.6 The leaders of palatalization in Cairo Arabic

The portraits of the leaders that emerge from our studies of Philadelphia are consonant with the view that stems from the LES study, and from exploratory work in cities throughout the United States and Britain. When a change from below is detected or suspected in a city, it has been found that the most advanced speakers can regularly be located among young women, 20 to 30 years old, from ethnic groups that arrived two to three generations before, upwardly mobile, and with the social characteristics described in the last two chapters. In chapter 8, it was shown that women are the leaders of the Northern Cities Shift across a vast area of the continent involving hundreds of cities. However, the more detailed portrait of the leaders of change that has emerged from this chapter is not so easily confirmed. Information comparable to this chapter is not to be found in the studies of the backing of (el) in Norwich (Trudgill 1974b), the lenition of (ch) in Panama City (Cedergren 1973), the aspiration of (r) in Belo Horizonte (Oliveira 1983), the fronting of (aw) in Vancouver (Chambers and Hardwick 1985), the raising of (o) in Seoul (Chae 1995), or in the vowel shifts of Belfast (Milroy and Milroy 1978), which have been so rich in reports of communication networks. It is therefore of special interest to encounter a detailed description of the leaders of change in Haeri's (1996) account of palatalization in Cairo Arabic.

Chapter 5 presented the curvilinear social pattern characteristic of this process (figure 5.17) and chapter 8 showed that women are far ahead of men (figure 8.12). The role of gender in this process is also underlined by the interaction between sex of the interviewer and sex of the subject. Haeri interviewed 60 speakers herself, and had a male assistant interview 25. Women from the lower middle and middle middle classes increased their use of strong palatalization by 50 to 100% in talking to a male interviewer.

Haeri presents considerable detail from the life histories of the four women who are the leaders of this change in progress, with 50% or more strong palatalization. Her sketches of their characters and social situation are of the greatest importance for our inquiry:

> The first speaker, Omm Hossein, is a burly 45-year-old woman who is divorced, has six children, and never went to school. She is the breadwinner, indeed the head of her large household which has her own children and their children. Although she has grown sons and daughters, most of them are dependent on her income and on her general management both within and outside of their household. She is a maid/cook/caretaker in the home of some American residents of Cairo. In a two-hour interview with Omm Hossein, she told me many personal stories. At least three of them had to do with arguments which had ended up in physical fights.
>
> The second speaker, Manal, is 30 years old, is married and has five children. She has a high school diploma and has worked at many different jobs. From what

she told me of her life, she has consistently challenged her husband, her parents, her brothers and her community on the restrictions they have wanted to place on her life-style; and has taken them to task when they've exhibited double standards regarding the proper behavior of men and women. Most of the time, her husband is not around and she is the one who takes care of the needs of her children, their education, and their upbringing.

Nahid is a very lively and energetic 25-year-old accountant who works in a small company. She has a high school diploma from a public school. Although there are pressures on her to get married, she prefers to first establish her economic independence. She says that she is closer to her mother because she finds it impossible to have a discussion with her father, who usually tries to impose his views on her. (pp. 98–9)

Haeri concludes, "If I were to look for a set of adjectives common to these speakers, I would say they have strong characters, are independent, and in general have 'tough' personalities." This portrait of the leaders of change is a remarkable parallel to the descriptions of the leaders of linguistic change in Philadelphia. Like the Philadelphia women, the Cairo leaders of linguistic change refuse to conform to the conventions of proper behavior when it does not suit their interests; they denounce those conventions when they recognize them as unjust; and they take on the major responsibilities for maintaining their families' position.

## 12.7 The leaders of linguistic change

To sum up the findings so far on the leaders of linguistic change, we find that they are women who have achieved a respected social and economic position in the local networks. As adolescents, they aligned themselves with the social groups and symbols that resisted adult authority, particularly when it was perceived as unfairly or unjustly administered, without deviating from their upwardly mobile path within the local social structure.

How does this portrait of the leaders of linguistic change further the search for the causes of linguistic change? This chapter has presented a view of people taking deliberate and conscious actions that identify their social position and define their relations with the community. Their linguistic choices cannot be described as actions in the same sense. The level or rate of use of a stochastic variable is at the level of consciousness comparable to walking and breathing. There is no evidence that attitudes, ideologies, and opinions that people express in so many words will bear directly upon linguistic changes from below. These attitudes may influence who a person talks to and how often they talk, and so affect the flow of linguistic influence and the diffusion of sound changes within and across local social networks. From this point of view, the use of local Philadelphia speech forms is the product of speakers' social trajectories, and we can best explain the leaders' linguistic performances by the history of their social contacts in their formative years.

The exchange of linguistic tokens and influence is not entirely symmetrical. It is very likely that the leaders of linguistic change will exert more influence than they receive. And no matter how economical we are in our interpretations, we cannot avoid the inference that proceeds from the correlation of (dha) and the linguistic changes in progress. Advanced linguistic forms are deviations from the pre-existing norms, and no one can doubt that high (dha) values are widely accepted to be such deviations. The history of our leaders of linguistic change is a history of nonconformity, and their sociolinguistic position is a display of nonconformity.

We now begin to see the channels by which linguistic changes flow across local networks, across neighborhoods, to affect virtually every citizen of a great metropolis. The wellsprings of linguistic change in Philadelphia are the middle working class neighborhoods in the Irish-dominated areas of Kensington. Kensington is not only the oldest settled working class area, but the white neighborhood that most directly defies the middle class sanctions against violence, profanity, and hard drinking. As the census figures of chapter 2 showed, it is not the most favored site for upward social mobility. But throughout the middle decades of the twentieth century, the linguistic influence of Kensington has been carried outward to other working class neighborhoods. The vectors were people who coupled a nonconformist ideology with the ability to look after their own best interests, and carried the linguistic influence of Kensington into what we have called the upper working class. These are the influentials with wider contacts who are, in all likelihood, responsible for the geographic homogeneity of the Philadelphia speech community. This chapter has shown Celeste S. as the prototypical influential. At what point this outward current of sound change in progress intersected with her early history is hard to say. It seems very likely that she acquired her advanced form of the Philadelphia system in her high school years from people who were not as upwardly mobile as she was. In any case, our view of the city in the 1970s finds her established among the most vigorous exponents of the Philadelphia linguistic system in one of the most prosperous areas of South Philadelphia.

This chapter has also drawn a detailed portrait of the Kensington matrix from which the Philadelphia sound changes appear to have originated. In Kensington, as in South Philadelphia, the local leaders are people who have been taught how to defend themselves, and learned that lesson. But Celeste was tough in a different way. She did not hesitate to use violence when it was called for. But her primary weapons were linguistic: negotiation, persuasion, and denunciation, all enlisted under a profound intolerance for cupidity, hypocrisy, and injustice. These are the qualities that make a great leader of linguistic change.

So far, so good. We have begun to understand the social mechanism that projects the saccadic leaders like Celeste and Teresa in every generation. But behind these advanced speakers there is also a steady succession of incremental leaders, in Pitt St. and Clark St., as well as Wicket St. The linear advance of sound change among women indicates a series of intervening influentials in each neighborhood, not one in every decade, but perhaps one in every year. What are the links that bind this series of incremental leaders into a seamless succession of speakers, one more advanced than the next? The next chapter will attack this question by confronting the largest and most mysterious problem of all, the problem of transmission.

# Part D

## *Transmission, Incrementation, and Continuation*

# 13

# *Transmission*

This volume began by reviewing a number of traditional questions about language change that have not yet received satisfactory answers. Efforts to explain linguistic change have been baffled by the sporadic character of its actuation, its abrupt termination, and its continued renewal. Following Meillet's (1921) insight that a correlation with the specifics of social change and social structure would be needed to account for these unpredictable events, we followed the strategy of searching for the location of the leaders of linguistic change in the social fabric. That search has been reasonably successful, and we can say with some assurance that the diffusion of systematic linguistic change in large cities is promoted by women who combine upward mobility with a consistent rejection of the constraining norms of polite society. The next step in the exploration of the principles of language change is to confront a problem that has not been entered into the agenda of historical linguistics until now.

## 13.1 The transmission problem

Chapter 9 introduced the observation that we all speak our mother's vernacular. Granted the many complexities superposed upon this base by later language learning, we necessarily begin with the phonetics, phonology, morphology, and syntax that we acquired from our first caretaker, normally female. The general condition for linguistic change can then be stated in a very simple way: *children must learn to talk differently from their mothers*. Let us refer to this process as *vernacular re-organization*. When and how vernacular re-organization takes place is the first aspect of the transmission problem. The age limitation on this process – the closing off of the critical period – is a recognized research problem that has received much attention from students of second language learning, though work on the acquisition of second dialects is the most relevant to our inquiry into vernacular re-organization. This chapter will consider some recent work on the structural limitations of this process and the social matrix in which it takes place. But the transmission problem has a further aspect that goes beyond any current research. The linguistic changes examined in this volume are not confined to a single generation; they extend across three, four, or more generations of speakers. This is true of most of the changes in the historical record. The general condition for such changes can be re-stated as follows:

*Children must learn to talk differently from their mothers, and these differences must be in the same direction in each succeeding generation.*

How is this possible? This is the core of the *transmission problem*. On the face of it, it is more difficult than any considered so far.[1] To the best of my knowledge, the problem in this form has not been discussed or even recognized in the literature of historical linguistics: yet to understand how any long-range change is possible, we have to have some idea of how such transmission takes place.

To approach the transmission problem, this chapter will first review the simpler cases of stable situations and nondirectional changes, then proceed to attack the larger problem as stated above. In addition to the data considered so far, the discussion will draw from three important sources of information on vernacular re-organization: the work of Payne and of Roberts in Philadelphia, of Kerswill and Williams in Milton Keynes, and of Eckert in the suburbs of Detroit.

The transmission problem is the obverse of the problem of acquisition. Those who stress the innate character of the acquisition process tend to focus upon the activity of the child. From this perspective, the parental generation plays a passive role, providing only the minimal stimulus for the active acquisition of the child. This follows from established observations that parents rarely provide negative information on language structure, and that differences in the style of parent–child interaction are not accompanied by radical differences in the rate of acquisition (Morgan and Travis 1989). The transmission problem also deals with the active role of the learner, but equal attention must be given to the detailed template provided by older members of the speech community, at home, on the street, and in the school.

Age is a crucial variable here. Vernacular re-organization must take place in the window of opportunity between first learning and the effective stabilization of the linguistic system. When that stabilization takes place – the end range of the critical period – has not been fixed in current research. The two most important studies on the problem of second dialect acquisition deal with in-migrant families of young adults and their children. Payne (1980) and Kerswill and Williams (to appear) show that parents acquire

[1] The problem has been considered in its macro-aspect, the mysterious problem of long-term *drift*, that is, the tendency of languages to evolve in the same direction over millennia (Sapir 1921).

very little of the local dialect while children acquire it almost completely. But the generation gap in their data yields no information on ages 18 to 30. For the moment, we will focus on vernacular re-organization among children 3 to 17 years old, and return to reconsider the upper limit.

The chapter will begin with a consideration of what seems to be a simpler problem: the acquisition of stable sociolinguistic variables. This turns out to be more difficult than it appears at first glance. We will then consider the acquisition of directional change, beginning with the earliest stages of acquisition, and proceeding through successive age ranges to the adults who represent the end result of the processes involved.

## 13.2 The transmission of stable sociolinguistic variables

In the simplest possible case of transmission, the child's pattern is a reproduction of the parents' invariant pattern. Here the "problem" of transmission seems to be a transparent one. Parents need only continue to speak the language as they learned it, and children will acquire it with whatever acquisition device they possess. That is not to bypass the well-known problem as to how children acquire the complex rule systems of adults, but simply to say that no special problem of transmission is involved.

The situation is not so simple in the case of a stable variable, like (ing) – the English alternation of unstressed /in/ and /iŋ/ – which shows regular social and stylistic stratification in all parts of the English speaking world (chapter 3). It is a random variable: no one can predict with certainty whether an adult will use /in/ and /iŋ/ in any one case. How would we expect children to interpret this lack of consistency, and how is this variation transmitted to them?

When children hear alternations in vocabulary, they normally reinterpret one or the other variant. For example, New York City in 1963 had two words for a round, toroid-shaped pastry: the local word *cruller* (from Dutch *kroeller*) and the national word *doughnut*. The young adult generation had already resolved this by shifting the local word to designate a long twisted pastry. In Philadelphia, the local word *newsy* is in variation with the national word *nosy*, both meaning "curious about someone else's private business." Many speakers attempt to resolve this by saying that *newsy* is a term of reproach, while *nosy* is not.

Children do not reinterpret sociolinguistic variables in this way. Instead, they match their parents' variation. In recent years, a series of investigations have explored the question of the age at which children first show the variable patterns characteristic of the adult speech community (Guy and Boyd 1990, Labov 1989b, Roberts 1993). The most extensive, dealing with the youngest children, is Roberts' study of the acquisition of variable patterns by white children 3 to 5 years old in South Philadelphia (1993). She obtained as much data from these young children as others normally obtain from adults, using a series of elicitation techniques especially adapted to this age group.

In the case of consonant cluster simplification, Roberts confirmed for her 3- to 5-year-olds the results found for 7- and 8-year-olds. These language learners matched their parents' probabilities for the phonological environment affecting this process, and for the grammatical constraint of monomorphemic vs. past tense clusters. They did not match their parents' level of simplification for derivational forms *left*, *kept*, *sold*, etc., which they treated like monomorphemic forms. The clear inference is that the probabilities that are matched are not attached to surface objects like specific verbs, but to abstract categories like *inflectional suffix* or *past tense*. Children only match their parents' probabilities of simplification when they match their grammatical analyses.

## *The transmission of (ing)*

In the Lower East Side of New York City, it was found that speakers did not develop the full range of sociolinguistic competence until late adolescence, depending on social class, though some signs of it appeared at a much younger age (Labov 1964). Among the earliest signs of sociolinguistic competence, and the easiest to measure, is style shifting in production, and a number of reviews have appeared recently which emphasize such style shifting in the pre-adolescent years (Romaine 1984, Chambers 1995). The case of (ing) is particularly interesting for the study of early acquisition because it involves the transmission of both grammatical and stylistic constraints. Figures 3.4 and 3.8 showed the grammatical factors that condition (ing) for the Philadelphia Neighborhood Study: the frequency of the /in/ form increases regularly in the series adjective, noun, gerundive, gerund, participle, progressive, future. The same constraint shows up in almost every area of the English speaking world (Houston 1985).[2] The variable (ing) also shows a regular pattern of stylistic and social variation that is summed up for the Philadelphia Neighborhood Study in figure 13.1.

Roberts (1993) found that children below 5 years old match the adult grammatical constraints on (ing), and in addition, show the basic stylistic constraint in which /in/ is favored in less formal speech.

How is this pattern transmitted? Chapter 3 presented the evidence that (ing) is not a recent development, but rather a transformation of a stable tradition that originated with the grammatical choice between the Old

[2] Except the US Southern States, where the /in/ form is close to 100% in spontaneous speech.

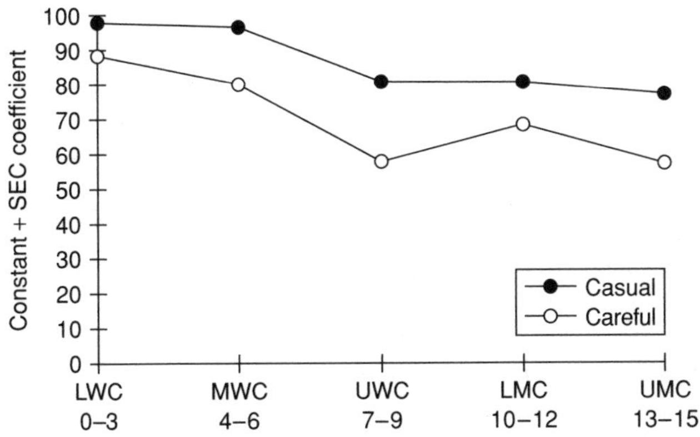


*Figure 13.1* Expected values of (ing) by social class and style for the Philadelphia Neighborhood Study (n = 178), from regression analysis using age, gender, neighborhood, and ethnic categories

English verbal noun in *-inge* and participle in *-inde*. A discrete opposition between verbal noun and participle was replaced by a stochastic weighting of the variants /in/ and /iŋ/ in any unstressed syllable. Despite the conversion of the spelling system to a consistent *-ing* notation, the alternation has continued for over a millennium (Houston 1985). Since the primary constraint opposing verbal /in/ to nominal /iŋ/ is not transmitted through the written language or in schools, it must have been the result of vernacular transmission during the entire period. Aside from the geographic differentiation, in which /in/ was favored in Scotland and the North, and /iŋ/ in Southern England,[3] we do not know much about the status of the alternation during most of this period. Within the past couple of centuries, the social and stylistic constraints of chapter 3 have become clearly established, operating in a similar way throughout the English speaking world. How are these social and stylistic weightings on the (ing) variable transmitted across generations?

The transmission of variation across generations involves the process of probability matching that was identified in volume 1, chapter 20 as an integral part of the mechanism of chain shifting. Probability matching is perhaps the most general form of transmission of information. It is shown in the rapid calculations of animals in foraging behavior (Gallistel 1990) as well as the acquisition of local styles and dialects by human beings. But for children to reproduce the adult system, it is not enough for them to recognize the existence of two alternants and their per cent distribution. The child must identify the categories and sub-categories that constrain

[3] See Map 18.1 of Houston 1991 or figure 1 in Labov 1995 for the more exact geographic pattern.

the adult language and derive similar probabilities for each. The case of (ing) is critical because there is no synchronic link between the /in/ and /iŋ/ variants and the categories that determine the choice between them. There is no phonetic conditioning of the choice between apical and velar nasals, no stress pattern that would intervene between the grammatical categories and the employment of /in/ or /iŋ/, nor any principle of reduction, economy, or least effort that would operate here to favor one or the other variant.[4] Instead, a series of historical accidents led to the assignments of /in/ to the pole of informality and to the verbal side of a noun–verb continuum, and these assignments have been reliably transmitted across many generations of language learners.

The classes *noun*, *gerund*, *participle*, *adjective*, *verb* are salient categories required for the learning of morphology and syntax, and it is not surprising that they are available for the learning of (ing) variation. The basis for the children's acquisition of the adult pattern of stylistic variation is more elusive.

The stylistic categories used by Roberts for children's speech productions involve a simple binary division between narrative (casual speech) as against all others (careful speech). This is a useful simplification of the 8-fold style categories used for adults (Labov to appear). But it does not seem likely that the children had identified narrative as the contextual category most relevant to style. Instead, it seems more probable that they abstract a continuous stylistic dimension from a variety of speech contexts. Bell (1984) and Preston (1989) have proposed that stylistic stratification is derived from social stratification. Yet for children of this age, it is not likely that the distinction between less formal and more formal speech stems from an association with the way people of different social classes speak; their experience is focused on the home and pre-school play context. It seems most likely that the children associate the formal end of the speech continuum, and /iŋ/, with the style used in disciplinary and didactic situations, when the child is in trouble and/or is being instructed. It also seems likely that the other end of the continuum, the least formal type of speech, occurs in intimate and friendly situations, where social distance between adult and child is reduced, when everything is going well as far as the child is concerned. Children 3 to 5 years old pay close attention to this dimension, since it indicates to them if they are being placed in the category of "good" or "bad" children and will be rewarded or punished for what they have done. I would therefore suggest that the formal/informal dimension is not a vague abstraction for children, but a useful scale of reference that is called upon many times during the day as the child responds to adults, deals with older kids, and tries to keep out of trouble.

[4] While it is true that apical inflections are favored generally in Indo-European, in Caribbean Creoles, Austronesian, and other language families we find the velar nasal the default category.

The general proposal is that the use of a sociolinguistic variable is learned by association of variants with one or the other pole of an organizing principle of social life. The rule is: the more formal the speech, the higher the probability of /iŋ/, the less formal, the higher the probability of /in/. How this dimension is identified, and how this association is acquired, will be considered more carefully in the following section dealing with change in progress.

## 13.3 The transmission of change

There are more than a few puzzling and anomalous aspects to the concept of "transmission of change." Yet in the simplest cases, there seems to be no problem at all in understanding what happens. Some changes in the language may be called "elementary:" they consist of a simple step, which is not apt to be repeated or form part of an overall pattern. The introduction of new elements of the general vocabulary is prototypical; they are rapidly acquired by all members of the speech community, at whatever age. This is seen most clearly when adults enter a new community. Though they never acquire the local phonological system, they rapidly acquire the general local vocabulary. Payne 1976 shows that active local Philadelphia terms like *hoagie*, "a long sandwich with meat and cheese," are known to adults born out-of-state as well as their children. When a new term enters the community, it is simply transmitted to children along with the rest of the vocabulary.

### *Directional change*

The changes that have the most profound effect and represent the main stream of linguistic evolution are not isolated shifts of single elements, but movements of one or more elements in a continuous direction. The archetype of such directional change is the chain shifting of segments which rotate in the same direction for several generations. Such chain shifts are often renewed in a second and third cycle, many generations later. The first and second German consonant shifts are the best-known example in the consonant domain. In vowel systems, the prototype is the English Great Vowel Shift, followed today by the Southern Shift in Southern England, the Southern United States, Australia, and New Zealand. In these repeated scenarios, the same general principles of chain shifting produce different outcomes, since they operate on different initial configurations.

Systematic sound changes in many language families, from Indo-European to Sino-Tibetan, have acted steadily over many generations to reduce the amount of information at the end of words: neutralizing final consonants and ultimately deleting them, reducing final vowels to schwa, deleting schwa, and so on, with profound effect on the grammars and word structure of the languages involved. In Germanic and the Romance languages, neutralization of place of articulation in final consonants led to an extreme simplification of the inflectional system. As changes progress, what was a sound change independent of grammar is transformed into a trend toward the steady reduction of inflectional morphology, independent of sound change. In some cases, the reduction of segmental information has led to the replacement of segmental distinctions by tone systems. In most cases, sound changes have led to a steady erosion of the inflectional system, sometimes with a resulting change of language typology to an isolating system, with compensating alterations in syntax. Sound changes are often the driving force behind grammatical change. Both sound change and grammatical changes move in a steady trajectory over many generations.

Though many scholars have pondered these facts, and organized them into wide-ranging theoretical schemata, it is remarkable that our field has not yet addressed the question of how such directional changes are transmitted.

### *Proposals for change at first acquisition*

Scholars who are primarily engaged in the search for invariance rather than the study of variation have given thought to the problem of how the process of acquisition may lead to language change. Halle (1962) suggested that children effect change in the linguistic system by re-organizing the data provided by their parents' systems into a simpler set of rules. This involves a two-step mechanism: (1) in the course of their adult life, parents make additions to their grammars that are not fully integrated into the system, since in later life they no longer have the capacity to re-organize their grammar into an optimal system; and (2) when children learn the language with their more systematic language acquisition device, they create a new set of simpler and more efficient schemata, with slightly different output (cf. Lightfoot 1997).

This is an ingenious and plausible suggestion, and it would be interesting to know if studies of change in progress can locate a concrete example. A rapid re-organization of the rules is found in the rapid progress of mergers, particularly when the distinction between long and short open /o/ collapses (Herold 1990). In chapter 11 of volume 1, figures 11.5a and b contrasted the /o/ and /oh/ systems of a father and his son, showing a total collapse of the distinction in one generation. In a single step, the son abandoned a distinction that (as Herold suggests) the father maintained but may no longer have found useful in distinguishing words. It is hard to see other types of sound changes as simplifications of this sort. Chain shifts and most lenitions seem to be initiated as complications in the rule or constraint system. They are noted first in those environments that most favor the change, leading to allophonic conditioning that complicates the rule system, and it is only later, when the change is almost completed, that the rule is simplified. Thus if rule simplification is more likely than rule complication, it is the least likely thing that happens first, and the most likely thing that happens last.[5] In the history of languages, changes that complicate rules are evenly interspersed with changes that simplify rules.

A second suggestion put forward by those engaged in the search for invariance is that change can take place without any transmission at all. Bickerton (1981) argues that when pidgin languages acquire native speakers, the children who are the first native generation of Creole speakers ignore completely the language structures used by their parents, and re-create the grammar by means of their innate "bioprogram." The explorations to follow will allow us to examine this possibility more closely.

Both of these suggestions modify the principle that a child's first language is modeled on the mother's vernacular. There is no reason to think that the first formed grammar is identical to the input from the mother, so there surely is room for the mechanisms suggested by Halle, Lightfoot, and Bickerton. If it could be shown how such mechanisms would produce directional change across generations, these arguments would be even more persuasive. Though Bickerton's main proposal is based on the formation of new Creoles, it might also be supported by any observations of children who disregard their parents' vernacular because it is radically different from that of the majority. Close studies of first language acquisition by children whose caretakers are not native speakers should then show no trace of a vernacular with non-native features.

## *The relationship between children and parents*

Whenever families move into a new speech community, it is a commonplace observation that the children adopt the local vernacular rather than that of their parents. The analysis of language development in the midst of language change will therefore begin with those cases in which the parents' vernacular is the most disfavored, to see how much of it survives in children's speech patterns.

### DISCONTINUITY AND CONTINUITY IN A NEW CREOLE FORMATION

The most likely place to look for discontinuities in early acquisition is in the formation of new Creoles, where parental influence is traditionally regarded as minimal. Figure 13.2 shows a variable where children who are

[5] An observation originally made by W. S.-Y. Wang. This view of phonological change is supported by the development of the tensing of broad **a** and its continuation in the USA (volume 1, ch. 18). However, it runs counter to the Constant Constraints effect established for syntax by Kroch (1989), an issue that has not yet been decisively resolved.

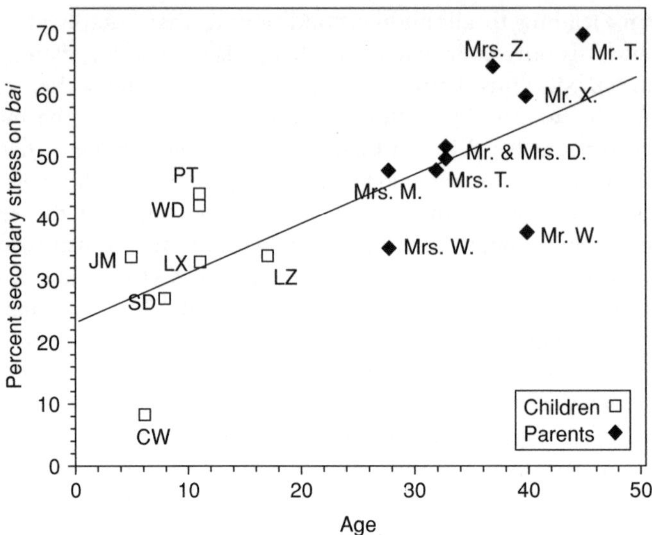


*Figure 13.2* Reduction of stress on the future marker *bai* in Tok Pisin for adults and children (from Sankoff and Laberge 1973 [1980])

new native speakers of Tok Pisin move beyond their parents. This is the morphophonemic reduction of the future *bai*, from an earlier *baimbai*, the first element in the Tok Pisin verb phrase structure (Sankoff and Laberge 1973). In the adult pidgin, this receives secondary stress half of the time, as in /em bai i go/ "he will go;" among children, only 30% of the time. On the other hand, children show a thoroughly reduced *bai* 10% of the time, as in /em b-i go/, while this occurs with adults in only 1% of the tokens. Figure 13.2 locates seven children and nine adults in this development. The horizontal axis is age; the vertical axis is the per cent secondary stress on *bai*. The children, shown as hollow squares, are grouped together with no percentage higher than 47%. The adults show a steady progression upward with age, up to 70%. There is a significant regression line to show the effect of age on the adults' use of *bai*, with an $r^2$ of 40, accounting for 40% of the adult variance. The flat regression line for children explains only 3% of the variance. Thus children's use of *bai* seems to be a stable system, quite removed from the adult model.

These results then seem consistent with the idea that children can completely disregard or remake the linguistic system that they acquired from their parents. To look more closely into the situation, we can take advantage of the fact that the child and adult samples were not independent of each other. The sample included seven sets of parents and children. Sankoff recently re-examined figure 13.2, and drew lines connecting each child with his or her parent or parents (figure 13.3). Almost all lines are parallel.

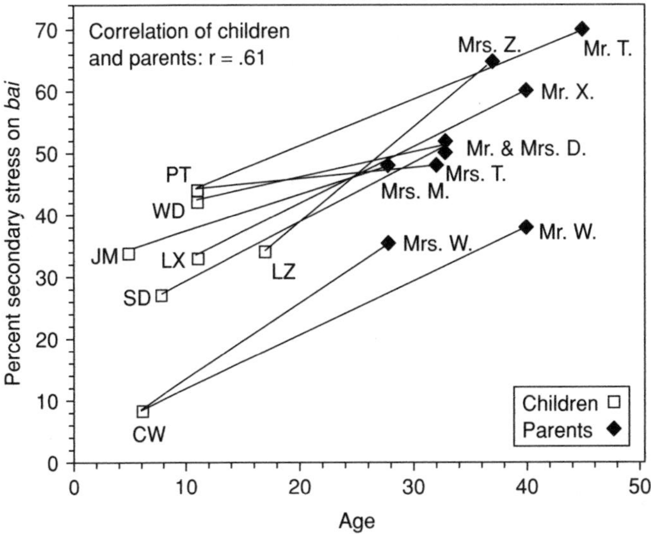


*Figure 13.3* Correlation of children and parents in the reduction of stress on the future marker *bai* in Tok Pisin

The children with the highest use of secondary stress on *bai* are the children of parents with the highest use, and those with the lowest use are the children of the lowest users. The highest child on the left, PT, has two parents in the sample: the only case of mother and father with different stress patterns. His use of *bai* is close to that of his mother, but compared to other children it is typical of what would be projected from the influence of his father. The general relation of parents to children can be assessed by a simple r-correlation. As shown in the upper left of figure 13.3, the correlation is reasonably large and positive, .61, and significant at the .02 level. These new native speakers of Tok Pisin are not linguistic orphans, remote from the influence of their parents. They have moved to a new system, but each child reflects the level that they started from when they first acquired the use of BAI from their caretakers. Their system is a regular projection from the language of their parents.

## *The acquisition of sociolinguistic norms in the new community of Milton Keynes*

Kerswill and Williams' research in Milton Keynes was designed to trace vernacular re-organization in a new community, composed of in-migrants from many different areas of England (Williams and Kerswill 1999, Kerswill and Williams to appear). Milton Keynes did not exist in 1971, but grew to 123,000 in 1981 and 176,000 in 1991. Three-quarters of its residents came

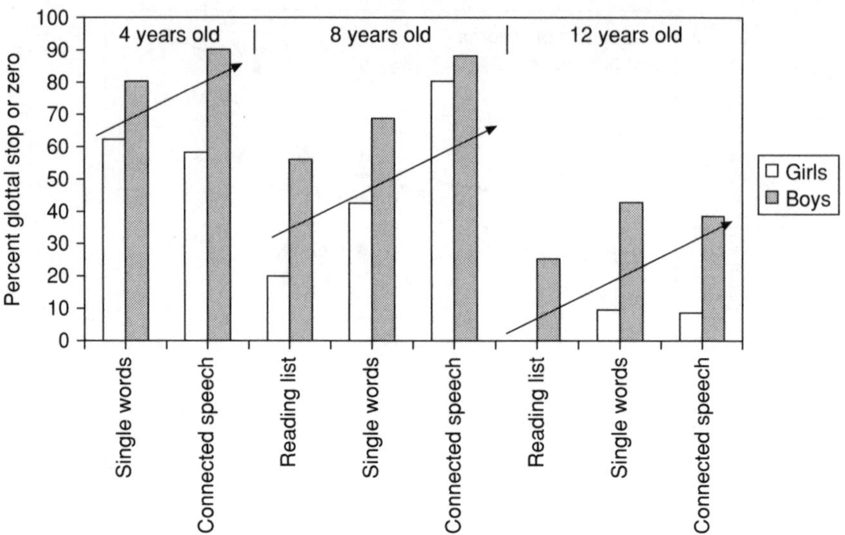


*Figure 13.4* Percent glottal stop or zero for intervocalic /t/ in Milton Keynes by age and style (from Kerswill and Williams 1994, table 6)

from southeastern England: 35% from London, 32% from other southern counties, but only 3% from the immediate sub-region within 15 minutes' drive. This project was elegantly and carefully designed to record the phonology of 8 boys and 8 girls in each of three age levels: 4, 8, and 12 years old, together with the caretakers of each, a total of 96 speakers. The new Milton Keynes dialect that arose was a distinct entity: it combined some features of London and the home counties with some remnants of the local dialect.

The Milton Keynes developments share several features in common with the stable community of South Philadelphia. Comparable to the acquisition of stable sociolinguistic variables in Philadelphia is the acquisition of style shifting with the glottalization of intervocalic /t/ in *bottle, butterfly, battery, button, knitting, little,* etc. This is a feature of the London dialect which is spreading into nearby cities like Reading and Milton Keynes. Figure 13.4 shows a steady decline of use with age. Among 12-year-olds, the level of glottalization is quite low, and it is almost absent among girls. Both male and female 8-year-olds show a regular style shift, using more glottal stops as they move from reading style to connected speech. Among the 4-year-olds, the effect is weaker: only the boys shift style. As in South Philadelphia, the recognition of stylistic constraints develops between ages 3 and 8.

#### RELATION OF CHILDREN TO CARETAKERS

In Milton Keynes, children learn a new dialect. But the break between children and parents is far from absolute. The wide range of pronunciations of the (ow) variable provides a good opportunity to compare the two

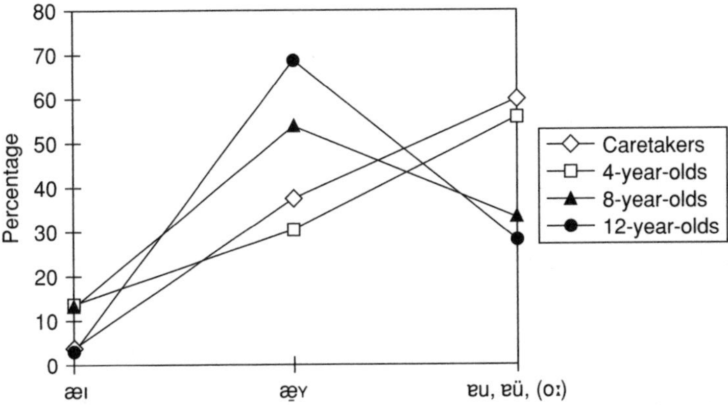


*Figure 13.5* Development of local phonetic forms for (ow) in Milton Keynes by age (from Kerswill and Williams 1994)

generations. Figure 13.5 shows the development of local phonetic forms for (ow), comparing the use of children 4, 8, and 12 years old with their female caretakers. The most conservative forms are on the right, with back upglides and centralized nuclei (and including a few monopthongs for families who came from the North). On the left is the current London form [æɪ] with a low front unrounded nucleus and a completely unrounded front glide. The (ow) forms in the center show the developing Milton Keynes consensus, with a slightly less fronted nucleus and a front rounded glide. It is immediately apparent that the 4-year-olds' and the caretakers' values are quite close: they both show about 30% of the local variant and around 60% of the conservative variants. It follows that the 4-year-olds have acquired their dialect forms from their caretakers and are not yet registering any strong linguistic influence from the local speech community. The 8-year-olds show a striking departure from this pattern, with over 50% of the local norm, and the 12-year-olds even more so, with 70% of the Milton Keynes form. The break between parental and peer group influence is clearly located between the ages of 4 and 8.

## 13.4 Directional language change among Philadelphia children

One of the most remarkable examples of directional transmission at an early age is found in the lexical diffusion of the tensing of short **a** in South Philadelphia. Philadelphia short **a** is tensed categorically only in closed syllables. The 1970s studies showed a low level of tensing in open syllables before /n/ and /l/, with lexical diffusion favoring one word in particular, *planet*. In addition to her studies of the acquisition of stable sociolinguistic

*Table 13.1* Differentiation of *planet* and *Janet* for children and adults in South Philadelphia

| | *Adults 18–80, 1974–7* | | *Children 3–5, 1990* | |
|---|---|---|---|---|
| | *n* | % | *n* | % |
| All NV | 256 | 0.04 | 250 | 57 |
| *planet* | 17 | 18 | 134 | 93 |
| *Janet* | 3 | 0 | 41 | 37 |
| *hammer* | 3 | 0 | 28 | 4 |

Source: table 1, Roberts and Labov 1995

variables, Roberts (Roberts and Labov 1995) examined the acquisition of the short **a** tensing pattern. To elicit pronunciation of words that do not occur often in spontaneous speech, she used a picture-naming game, and introduced the word *planet* with a drawing that all adults would name "planet" without hesitation. On first viewing, the children regularly called it "a ball;" Roberts corrected them by saying, "No, it's a planet," and in later repetitions of the game most of the children used that word. In Roberts' pronunciation, *Janet* is tense and *planet* is relatively lax. Despite the fact that they seemed to have learned the word from her, the children's overall pattern was quite different from hers, with a much higher frequency of tensing for *planet*. Table 13.1 shows her results for the children as against the adults recorded between 1974 and 1977.

In the children's speech, the overall level of tensing before intervocalic /n/ has risen from .04% to 57%. Furthermore, *planet* has risen from 18% to 93%; the proper name *Janet* also shows tensing at a level of 37%.[6] Thus the children have adopted the adults' arbitrary selection of *planet* as a word to be tensed and developed the change further.

Table 13.1 is a clear and immediate case of directional transmission. How can one account for these children's ability to follow the path of change? They have increased the degree of tensing for a word they hardly knew. One answer might be that their knowledge was greater than it appeared to be in the picture-naming game.[7] But in order to sense the direction of

[6] The contrast of *hammer* and *camera* vs. *Janet* and *planet* is motivated by their phonetic form: the following dark syllable /ər/ has been shown to affect the vowel productions of the first syllable. But there is no reason to expect more tensing in *Janet* than in *planet*: we expect the reverse. Yet *planet* is tensed more than twice as often as *Janet*.

[7] One girl, Janell, was recorded at a third session re-playing the picture-naming game. When she saw a card with a planet on it, she said, "Ball." Julie said, "No, you remember that we call that a *planet*." Janell said, "Oh, *planet*. E.T. lives on a planet."

*Table 13.2* Differentiation of *planet* and *Janet* by younger and older children in South Philadelphia

| | Children 3;2–3;10 | | Children 3;11–4;11 | |
|---|---|---|---|---|
| | *n* | % | *n* | % |
| All NV | 132 | 52 | 130 | 60 |
| *planet* | 60 | 90 | 74 | 96 |
| *Janet* | 29 | 65 | 14 | 10 |
| *hammer* | 14 | 7 | 14 | 0 |

Source: table 2, Roberts and Labov 1995

change within the Philadelphia system, they would have to have observed and noted their parents' pronunciation of the word several times, and also observed a series of pronunciations of someone younger than their parents. It seems that accurate inferences about the direction of change can be made on the basis of a very small amount of data.

Table 13.2 shows that this development does depend upon increasing experience. Roberts divided the children into two groups, younger (3;2 to 3;10) and older (3;11 to 4;11). For the older group, tensing of *planet* has advanced even further and is close to 100%, while the tensing of *Janet* has receded to 10%, and *hammer*, *camera*, etc. remain minimal. Thus children as young as 4 years old are capable of absorbing the direction of change in the community norms, and advancing further in the direction indicated by this vector. It seems probable that they have acquired this information from parents, older siblings, and other slightly older children in the local community. This particular variable does not involve the kind of social factors involved in the stylistic patterning of (ing). The lexical distribution of short **a** words carries no detectable social loading. It is not noticed overtly by community members, is never the topic of social comment, and shows no style shifting. The children's inference on direction of change must be drawn from age distributions alone.

### *Transmission among pre-adolescents in King of Prussia*

In most stable communities, the linguistic influence of peers and parents largely coincide. We can best observe their separate influences by locating sites for observation where the influence of parents is clearly distinct from that of the surrounding community. This was the case in Payne's study (1976, 1980) of the acquisition of the Philadelphia dialect in King of Prussia, a new community where half of the parents came from Philadelphia, and half from out of state.[8] In the course of the LCV project, Payne studied the progress of 34 out-of-state children in their acquisition of six Philadelphia phonetic variables. These are phonetic outputs governed by simple conditions, like the fronting of /ow/ and /uw/ to [ɛ˃o] and [ɪu] except before liquids. She found that most of the children acquired these patterns within one or two years of residence in Philadelphia. Children who came to King of Prussia before the age of 9 showed more learning of local phonetic rules than those who came afterward, but there were a good range of individual differences. To assess the factors responsible for these differences, Payne recorded for each child the age of arrival in Philadelphia, the number of years under Philadelphia influence, and the number of years under the influence of other dialects. To register social influences, she entered into the matrix the number of peers mentioned by a child in the interview, the number of times the child was mentioned by others, and the number of times that siblings and parents were named. The dependent variable in the study was the number of Philadelphia phonetic variables that were used at a given criterion of consistency, compared to the number by which their parents' dialect differed from the Philadelphia dialect.

Payne reported that the major social variable was age of arrival in the Philadelphia community. While she had expected that the child's place in the local peer group would affect the acquisition of phonetic features, she found no such effect. This result has been regarded as confirming other reports of the importance of the critical age in language learning, and evidence for the primacy of cognitive over social factors in the acquisition of dialect forms. However, a multiple regression re-analysis of Payne's data yields a different result. The most significant independent variable was the number of times that the speaker was mentioned by peers – which is the most sensitive index of the density of the speaker's social network. No significant effect of age, age of arrival, or years spent in Philadelphia appears in any re-configuration of the regression analysis. Figure 13.6 is a scattergram of 29 out-of-state children studied by Payne; the horizontal axis is the number of mentions, the vertical axis is the proportion of Philadelphia sound changes learned. At upper right are four speakers with 100% success and the maximum number of mentions, from 13 to 16. At lower left are six children with no variables learned, and a low number of mentions. The regression equation has a sharp and significant slope. Figure 13.6 does not indicate any strong tendency among the more socially isolated children: some acquire the Philadelphia sound changes and some do not. But all those with more than ten mentions sound like Philadelphians.

[8] The out-of-state parents came from high prestige areas of New York, New England, and the Midwest. The LCV study was designed to give every advantage to parental influence, to assess the relative influence of family and peers on the acquisition of language. King of Prussia was a recently created suburb where half of the residents were Philadelphians, and the other families from out of state had relatively higher prestige jobs than the Philadelphians.

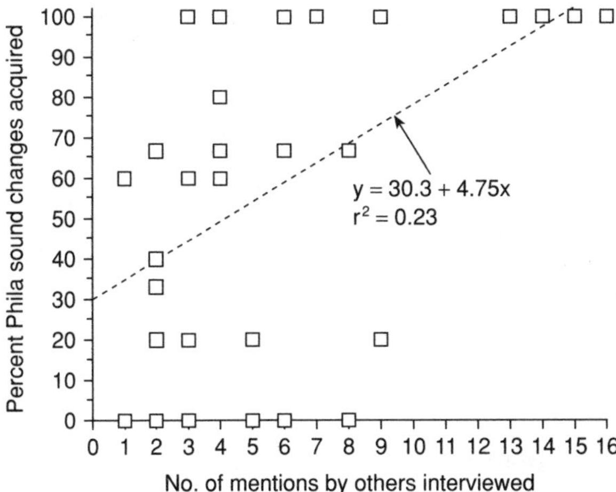


*Figure 13.6* Acquisition of Philadelphia sound changes by number of mentions by others interviewed

*Table 13.3* Factors influencing the acquisition of Philadelphia sound changes by out-of-state children

| | *Coefficient* | $p <$ |
|---|---|---|
| Mentions by peers | 0.033 | 0.030 |
| Mentions of siblings | 0.145 | 0.004 |
| Relative success in acquiring the short **a** pattern | 0.397 | 0.008 |

Table 13.3 shows the significant results of the multiple regression analysis where the dependent variable is the proportion of Philadelphia phonetic variables acquired. The coefficient for number of mentions by peers is .033. The range of mentions is from 0 to 16, so the maximum difference is 16 × .033, or .5, that is, half of the possible learning range. The second social effect, mentions of siblings, is about the same size, since the range is 0 to 4. The third effect seems to reflect general learning capacity. It is the *relative* success in acquiring the short **a** pattern. Payne's well-known finding is that the out-of-state children did not succeed in learning this complex distribution, but their relative success can be dichotomized into "fair" and "poor." This factor contributes significantly to the variance. But age of arrival and number of years spent in Philadelphia had no significant effect.

These out-of-state children are not leaders of linguistic change; they are simply trying to hit the local target. But similar findings are reported by Kerswill and Williams for the Milton Keynes study of a moving target.

They give a qualitative summary of the relation of peer group structure to the advancement of (ow). "All the high scorers . . . are very well integrated into a (mainly school-centered) group of friends; they are sociable and are often cited as friends by other children" (Kerswill and Williams 1994). While the high scorers all have a common property, there is no one feature that unites the low scorers who are distanced from their peers: "either the child has a reserved personality, perhaps coupled with poor relationships at home; or, for reasons to do with the family's beliefs, the child is not exposed to the mainstream of popular culture, and becomes an outsider." This collection of traits forms a close parallel to the description of the lames of South Harlem (Labov 1972c).

## 13.5 Transmission among adolescents in Detroit

The most systematic data on the linguistic forces that operate among adolescents is provided by Eckert in her study of "Belten High" in "Neartown," a suburb of Detroit (1999). She completed a close study of social networks that was cited in chapter 10, involving several hundred students, through long-term observation in the hallways, courtyards, and environs of the school, personal interviews, and auxiliary studies in a community closer to Detroit, "Urban City." Her analysis of the social structure of the high school is published separately as *Jocks and Burnouts* (1989a). It shows these two polar groups as exemplifying the organizing values by which all students classify themselves. Most high schools in the USA are dominated by a group of students who are strongly invested in middle class values, are oriented to college, and in general seek to achieve their goals by conforming to the normative institutions established by adults. These are the Jocks. The other group – known as the Burnouts, Jells, etc. – takes the opposite tack of resistance to adult authority. Burnouts seek to achieve their goals by escaping from adult control, and rely upon local connections and local resources. It is within this intricate social structure that Eckert traces the progress of linguistic change.

As a metropolis of the Inland North, Detroit is fully engaged in the Northern Cities Shift [NCS]. Despite the fact that the city itself is dominated by a large African American population which does not participate in this sound change, the *Atlas of North American English* shows that the remaining whites and the surrounding suburbs are leading exponents of the NCS. Eckert studied the stages of the NCS through impressionistic ratings of the progress of each element.[9] Each variable was categorized in

[9] Eckert herself discovered the link which completes the circular character of the Northern Cities Shift, the backing of /ʌ/, which is particularly strong in the Detroit area, but had not been noted before by other investigators.

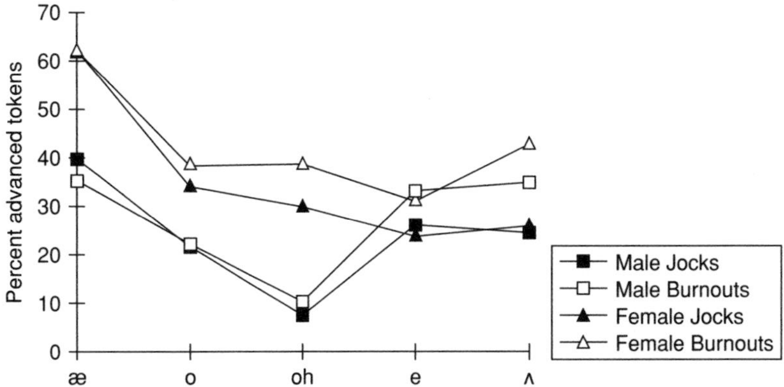


*Figure 13.7* Relations of gender and social class in the development of the Northern Cities Shift in Belten High (from Eckert 1989b)

four or five levels; these were then reduced to a single dichotomy, whether the vowel showed an advanced form or not, and the resultant discrete data submitted to a logistic regression analysis.

Eckert's correlations of linguistic and social factors have been published and widely discussed (1986, 1988, 1989b, 1999). Two social oppositions are correlated most strongly with the development of linguistic change: female vs. male and jocks vs. burnouts. Adherence to the jock or burnout ideology is largely predicted by the class status of the students' families. But there is enough social re-organization in the high school that the progress of the linguistic change is linked significantly to the jock/burnout categories, but not to parents' social class. The jock/burnout dimension is best seen as the high school realization of social class, so that the two social dimensions of figure 13.7 are most comparable to gender and social class in the Philadelphia neighborhoods. Eckert's most striking overall result, shown in figure 13.7, is that in the course of the Northern Cities Shift class stratification gives way to gender differentiation. The most recent stages in the shift – the backing of /e/ and /ʌ/ – are led by the burnouts and show no significant gender effect. The older, more developed stages – the raising of /æ/, fronting of /o/, and lowering of /oh/ – show the females well ahead (and for females, only, burnouts in advance of jocks (1996)).

Figure 13.7 might be taken as counter-evidence to the asymmetric gender model of chapter 9, which indicates that female-dominated changes were led by females from the very beginning. But further data from Eckert and McConnell-Ginet 1992 shows that the leaders of linguistic change in Belten High are indeed female from the outset. Table 13.4 gives Varbrul weights for the backing of /ʌ/ and also divides the female burnouts into the archetypical female burnouts – the burned-out burnouts – and the main group. Here the leaders of linguistic change are once again seen to be female.

*Table 13.4* Varbrul weights for the backing of /ʌ/ in Belten High, for social categories and gender

| | |
|---|---|
| Male jocks | 0.32 |
| Female jocks | 0.42 |
| Male burnouts | 0.54 |
| Main female burnouts | 0.47 |
| Burned-out female burnouts | 0.93 |

Source: Eckert and McConnell-Ginet 1992, table 19.3

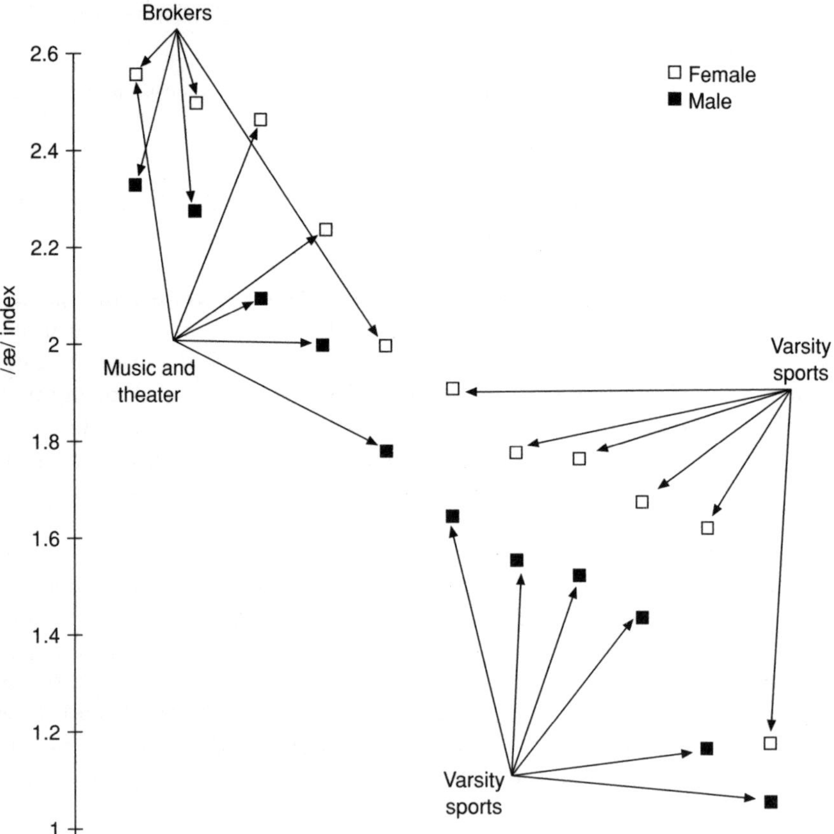


*Figure 13.8* Distribution of /æ/ values for 22 jocks in Belten High, by gender and main social activity

The relation between sound change and social activity is displayed at the other end of the social spectrum in figure 13.8; the data is derived from an unpublished paper of Eckert's. The values for the oldest and most advanced change in the NCS, the raising and fronting of /æ/, are shown for 22 male and female jocks. (The vertical axis is the (æ) index value, and the horizontal axis simply displays each individual in a separate column.) The major differentiation is by social activity, not gender. The most advanced speakers are four *brokers* – people who transmit information between jocks, burnouts, and other groups. Next are those engaged in music and theatre, a legitimate adult-sponsored jock activity. The lowest values of (æ) are used by the varsity athletes. For all three activities, it is evident that females are ahead of males, yet the major differentiation is not by gender but by social activity. High school girls engaged in varsity athletics show lower forms of (æ) than male brokers or theater people, and one girl athlete has one of the lowest scores of all.

What is particularly significant for the study of language change is the correlation between the local linguistic market place and the advancement of change. The highest values are shown by brokers, whose status is almost entirely defined by verbal activity, in gossip and negotiation. Almost as prominent is the role of language for the theater and music people. But the status of varsity athletes is in no way involved with the use of language; on the contrary, they stereotypically avoid verbosity.

Today, the raising of (æ) has spread to be a general characteristic of the Belten community; it is certainly not a symbol of working class or non-conformist youth. If the history of (æ) is comparable to the history of (ʌ), we have to project an earlier stage of the variable when it was introduced and led by the working class contingent, just as the backing of (ʌ) is today. How did the transition from one status to the other take place? Our best indication comes from a consideration of the behavior of the majority group at Belten High, the in-betweens.

In Eckert's account, the majority of the Belten population are not defined or do not define themselves as jocks or burnouts. They were commonly referred to as *in-betweens*, sharing characteristics with jocks on the one hand, and with burnouts on the other. They are not bound to avoid or conform to behaviors that are required or forbidden for jocks and burnouts. Eckert quotes one in-between who dislikes the jock/burnout split and suffers from it:

> And I was never a jock and I was never a burnout. I hung around with most, you know, or like there was the jocks and the burnouts who'd sit and give each other dirty looks in the halls, you know . . . And I just thought that was dumb as could be, you know. So I associated with everybody. . . . And so that kind of made me feel like a slight outcast you know. Somebody left in between the realms, you know.

For those variables that are led by burnouts, the in-betweens as a whole score slightly lower than the jocks.[10] But the in-betweens can be differentiated by their participation in characteristic burnout activities: smoking in the school courtyard, which jocks categorically avoid, and the activity of cruising the highways and parks close to Detroit. For the more recent stages of the Northern Cities Shift and for the raising of (ay0), these activities are

[10] Except for the raising of (ay0), where they fall in between jocks and burnouts.

better predictors of linguistic participation than the jock/burnout polarity. This effect appears most strongly in the backing of (e), where in-betweens who use the courtyard have much higher scores than those who do not; in-between boys who cruise are much closer to burnouts than in-betweens who do not.

Eckert's data shows us how the cascade model of the NCS – diffusion from the largest cities to the next largest cities, and so on down – looks from the standpoint of a white suburban population. The leading exponents of the most recent stages of the NCS are those with the strongest connections to Detroit, the burnouts. As the shift progresses, it develops a gender dichotomy; girls, and particularly burnout girls, are the most advanced in the three oldest stages. But in Neartown, as in all other communities in the Inland North, this pattern spreads gradually to encompass the whole community. Neartown does not develop a class dialect that separates working class from middle class, but instead shows a continuum. In the adult community, the most advanced users of the NCS are no longer to be found among the lower and middle working class speakers who were burnouts in their high school days. Fasold's analysis of Detroit in the 1960s, given in figure 8.14, showed that women led in the first two stages of the NCS, as they do in Eckert's data. Furthermore, women showed a clear curvilinear pattern, with the lower middle class in advance of the working class and the upper middle class. The Belten High data prefigures this generalization of sound change across the entire speech community. It does not predict the future path of burnout girls, who are now leading in the raising and fronting of (ʌ). If the Detroit suburbs should follow the path of the Philadelphia community, as outlined in the last five chapters, we would expect that the burnout girls would fall behind as they grew older. The adult leaders of linguistic change are most likely to be drawn from the in-betweens who have guarded the connections and social resources that would lead to upward social mobility.

Conversely, we can project the Philadelphia situation back to the high school context of the 1950s. As far as the data carries us, the adult leaders of linguistic change in Philadelphia appear to have been in-betweens in their high school years. While they had connections with the groups who were committed to the rejection of adult norms, they were themselves not committed to this program. They maintained an upwardly mobile path that separated them from lower and middle working class orientation in later years.

## *Principles of linguistic change: five steps in the transmission of urban linguistic change*

The principles of linguistic change that are the main topic of this volume concern the way in which change interacts with and is motivated by features of the social system. These principles do not form a series of distinct findings that can be labeled separately, as with the principles of volume 1. The central theoretical construction is a view of language socialization: the successive stages of the child's interpretation of linguistic variation. The transmission of linguistic change is inevitably tied to these successive interpretations and re-interpretations. The data presented so far supports the following *Principles of Transmission*:

1 Children begin their language development with the pattern transmitted to them by their female caretakers, and any further changes are built on or added to that pattern.
2 Linguistic variation is transmitted to children as stylistic differentiation on the formal/informal dimension, rather than as social stratification. Formal speech variants are associated by children with instruction and punishment, informal speech with intimacy and fun.
3 At some stage of socialization, dependent on class status, children learn that variants favored in informal speech are associated with lower social status in the wider community.
4 Linguistic changes from below develop first in spontaneous speech at the most informal level. They are unconsciously associated with non-conformity to sociolinguistic norms, and advanced most by youth who resist conformity to adult institutional practices.
5 Linguistic changes are further promoted in the larger community by speakers who have earlier in life adopted symbols of nonconformity without taking other actions that lessen their socioeconomic mobility.

One might call these Principles of *Urban* Transmission because the social patterns described are typical of the social stratification of large cities and the operation of the socioeconomic hierarchy. Most linguistic changes do spread from large cities. In those changes that spread from rural and small town areas (Bailey, Wikle, and Sand 1991), step (4) might take a somewhat different form. The norms that are recognized and resisted by rural speakers are the "polite" behavior associated with urban patterns. Here the polarity of rural/urban comes into play instead of the social class dimension.

The same reservations must be made in regard to more remote societies and more remote periods of history. The mechanism of stages 1–5 is based on a high degree of social mobility. In those societies where class stratification takes different forms from the more continuous, finely graded system of modern western societies, we must be ready to modify the uniformitarian principle in favor of a more historically specific account of the mechanism of change.

## *Sound changes in adult use: the Carol Meyers recording*

The discussion of the transmission problem so far has carried us through adolescence and the high school years. The situation is less clear when we turn to adults. No studies of speech communities have given us a close view of linguistic correlates of the transition from high school to job or college, and the establishment of households by young adults in their 20s. Our next clear view of sociolinguistic behavior is of adults in their 30s and 40s, who may have lost much of their ability to modify their linguistic system as a whole. Yet their linguistic behavior is far from rigid. They exhibit dramatic patterns of style shifting in the different sub-sections of a sociolinguistic interview, and a close study of this variation may give us a clue to the mechanism of the changes taking place in the community. Since interviews give us only a rough sample of the style shifting that takes place in everyday life, we need to record our subjects in the full range of social interaction with family, friends, and colleagues on the job.

The best view we have of the adult pattern of style shifting is from chapter 4 of Hindle's (1980) study of the speech of Carol Meyers, a Philadelphian who was recorded by Payne during the course of an entire day, in a broad spectrum of social activities. The excellent sound quality of this series of recordings[11] and the variety of social interactions make them a unique source for the study of style shifting in spontaneous speech. In the morning, Carol Meyers was recorded at a travel agency where she worked; we hear her dealing with customers, talking to airline agents, interacting with her fellow workers, and in joking interchanges with her boss. In the afternoon, she went to the track and a doctor's office, where recording was not possible. In the evening, she was recorded at home at dinner time with her husband Robert and Payne, who lived at the house. The home recording has extended silences, and very little overlap among speakers. As Hindle characterizes the scene, "There seems to be little invested in the management of self presentation; the three participants are on familiar and well-defined ground" (p. 105). The next night was the meeting time for a regular evening bridge game, and Carol Meyers was recorded in lively and intimate exchanges with four members of the group.[12]

> The talk during the three hours of the bridge game reflects the deep involvement of peers in their personal interactions. There is much tension and excitement palpable throughout; and though there is little noticeable hostility, it is clear that the women are delicately arranging their relations with each other within the group.

[11] The recordings were made with a Nagra IV-S stereo recorder, and Sennheiser 405 cardioid microphones. The microphones were placed on Meyers' desk at work, on the dinner table, and on the bridge table.

[12] She was close friends with two of them (one a fellow worker at the travel agency) and less intimate with the two others. There is some conversation during the play of the game, but the liveliest interactions were recorded between hands, and before the game actually started.

The conversations range from procedures and actions for playing bridge, to movies, tax assessment, and dirty jokes. (Hindle 1980:108)

Carol Meyers was not a part of the Philadelphia Neighborhood Study, but she matched the leaders of linguistic change closely in her social and linguistic patterns. She was about the age and social position of Celeste S. She lived in Cherry Hill, a nearby New Jersey suburb that is an integral part of the Philadelphia speech community. Her husband is a high school industrial arts teacher. When the study of Philadelphia began, she had just begun work at a travel agency; by the end of the study, she had become manager of a branch office. Like Celeste, she was at the center of many social circles. It was not an accident that the bridge game met at her house. Her personal style was outgoing and effusive; she never hesitated to make jokes at the expense of those in authority. At one point, the boss of her agency came in late after calling in sick. He explained that he had thrown up in his car "dry," Carol interrupted, "Of course not! You wouldn't throw up wet in that new car!" Her linguistic patterns place her in the forefront of advancing changes. But the Hindle study goes beyond mean values; we can see when Carol Meyers was in the forefront of change, and when she was not.

Hindle carried out an acoustic analysis of all of Meyers' recorded speech.[13] In an effort to isolate the factors that controlled variation in her speech, he carried out a wide range of multiple regression analyses. The strongest and most significant effects were found to be the major social contexts: the Office, Home, and the Bridge Game. Figure 13.9 shows Hindle's main results.[14] For each vowel, there are three symbols: triangles represent the mean values of the vowels for the Bridge Game, the circles for the Office, and squares for the dinner at Home. The formant values of most vowels shifted significantly during the bridge game, when Carol Meyers was interacting in the liveliest fashion with her close friends. For (æhN), (æhS), (eyC), and (aw) the triangle representing the bridge game is significantly fronter and higher than the others. No marked style shift appears for the (ow) and (uw) variables. In high back position, (ohr) also shows a shift for the Game context in the direction of change.[15] (ahr), a completed change, shows the same pattern. The low vowels show a consistent downward shift for the Game context. In the case of (æ) this is in the direction of an incipient change for the community; for (ay0), a male-dominated feature, it is in the opposite direction from the direction of community change, and similarly for /ʌ/.

[13] A complete chart of the measurements of 500 short **a** vowels is given as figure 1-2 of Labov 1989a.

[14] Data for the (æh) variables is added to Hindle's table 4.4, and the Game value for (iyC) is expanded to its correct value.

[15] Note that this is a male-dominated change.

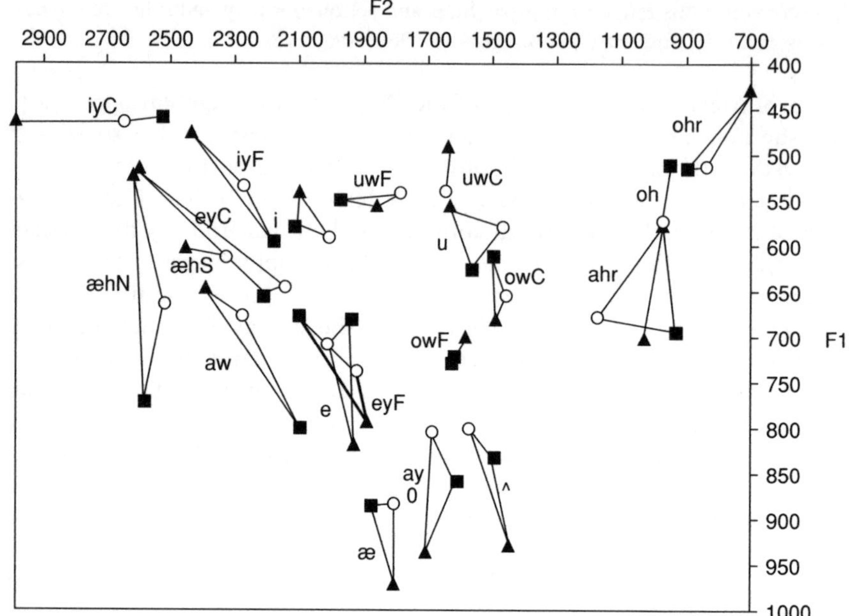


*Figure 13.9* Mean formant values for Carol Meyers in three contexts: Office (open circles), Home (solid squares), and Bridge Game (solid triangles)

In addition to these major contextual settings, Hindle identified a set of discourse category of *keys*: *businesslike*, *serious*, *light*, *excited*, *complaint*, and *residual*. The largest category is *businesslike*, which involves the transaction of the business specific to each context: travel information in the Office, passing the salt at Dinner, bridge play at the Game. The most significant correlation for this context is with the raising of F1 in (ay0), the male-dominated change in Philadelphia. The opposite effect is found with *complaint*, where significant correlation is found with (æh) and (aw), both female-dominated changes. Hindle cites Carol's remarks to her fellow travel agent Dot at the office as an example of such a complaint:

> And I have four couples want to go on a cruise and they only have off from the 20th to the 29th. . . . Oh these people that make up their minds to go somewhere one week before, I could kill them!

The category of *complaint* is crucial for an inquiry into the social forces behind sound change: here affect and emphasis are combined with a socially loaded activity. The regression coefficient for F1 of (aw) for Complaint is −82 Hz: that is, one must expect the nucleus to raise 82 Hz further in the direction of the sound change than the mean for all other keys ($p < .05$). Table 13.5 gives a more detailed view of F2 of (æh). Here the effect is in

*Table 13.5* F2 values for individual (æh) tokens in Complaint vs. other keys in the Carol Meyers recordings

| | *Complaint* | | *Residual* | |
|---|---|---|---|---|
| | *word* | *F2* | *word* | *F2* |
| *(æhS)* | | | | |
| | last | 2544 | last | 2406 |
| | last | 2734 | laugh | 2139 |
| | last | 2351 | laugh | 2460 |
| | half | 2773 | ask | 2192 |
| | | | pass | 2468 |
| | | | pass | 2682 |
| Mean | | 2601 | | 2391 |
| Std dev. | | 194 | | 199 |
| *(æhN)* | | | | |
| | jam | 2679 | can't | 2593 |
| | jam | 2437 | can't | 2375 |
| | Anne's | 2529 | stamp | 2417 |
| | | | stamp | 2355 |
| | | | man | 2657 |
| | | | chance | 2575 |
| Mean | | 2548 | | 2495 |
| Std dev. | | 122 | | 128 |

Source: Hindle 1980, table 4.7

the fronting dimension: F2 increases with complaints. Though the numbers are too small to reach statistical significance, they suggest that strong social affect is associated with advanced forms of the variable.

There are two possible interpretations of figure 13.9 and the correlations with discourse key. The first is that these are *phonological* shifts, based on and derived from the social stratification of these variables in the community. As usual, the same variables are involved in social stratification and style shifting (chapter 3). This fact is reflected in figure 13.10, which relates Carol Meyers' vowel shifting to the general view of change in apparent time provided by figure 4.8. For each of 14 vowels, the circle shows the mean values for the community as a whole, the tail of the arrow shows the expected values for speakers who are 25 years older than the mean, and the head of the arrow shows the expected values for speakers who are 25 years younger than the mean. The three values for Carol Meyers' use of (aw) are superimposed at lower left. The direction of Meyers' style shifting from Home to Office to Game is parallel to the direction of change in the

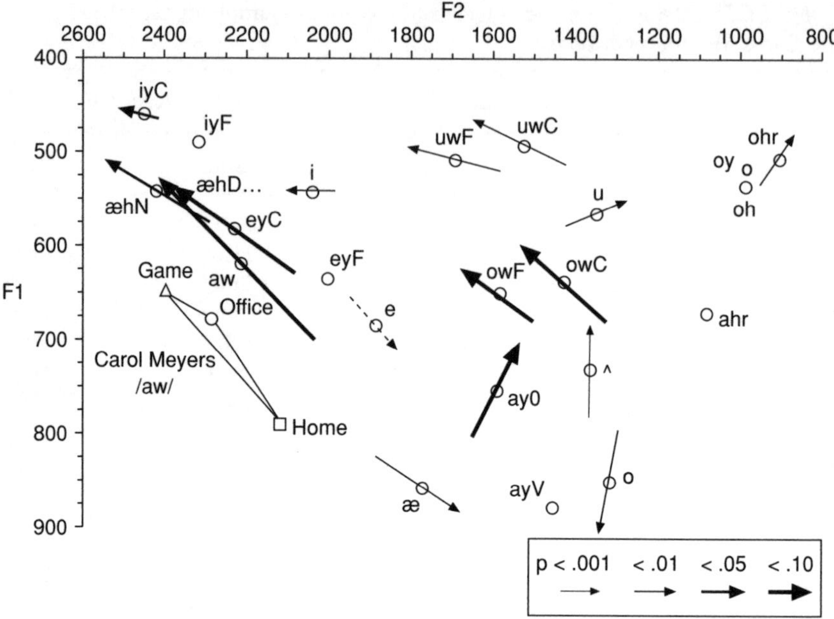


*Figure 13.10* Superposition of Carol Meyers' values for (aw) on the movement of Philadelphia vowels in apparent time (= figure 4.8). Circles: mean values for 112 speakers in the Neighborhood Study. Vectors connect values for groups 25 years older and younger than the mean

speech community. In dealing with her close friends, Meyers shifts her vowel system toward more advanced forms of the Philadelphia sound changes that are led by women. In general, the axes of style shifting for Carol Meyers are parallel to the axes of linguistic change.[16]

For the male-dominated centralization of /ay/ before voiceless consonants, Carol Meyers follows the community pattern in businesslike contexts, but moves in the opposite direction in interaction with her female friends in the Bridge game. Her shifts in social interaction can be said to mirror the sexual differentiation of the variables in the community.

A second interpretation of figure 13.9 is *phonetic*: Carol Meyers' style shifting may simply be an overall phonetic shift, not related to the specific sound changes of Philadelphia. If that is so, then her behavior is dictated by a universal iconic relationship between expressivity and articulatory

[16] The main exception is the case of (æhN), where the Office mean drops down vertically, with a much higher F2 than the normal route of change. We can recognize here the sign of stylistic correction in Office style. As chapter 6 showed, (æhN) is the most highly stigmatized of the Philadelphia variables, and this type of correction, more common in New York than in Philadelphia, typically retains the tense, front position for the corrected vowel while correcting its height.

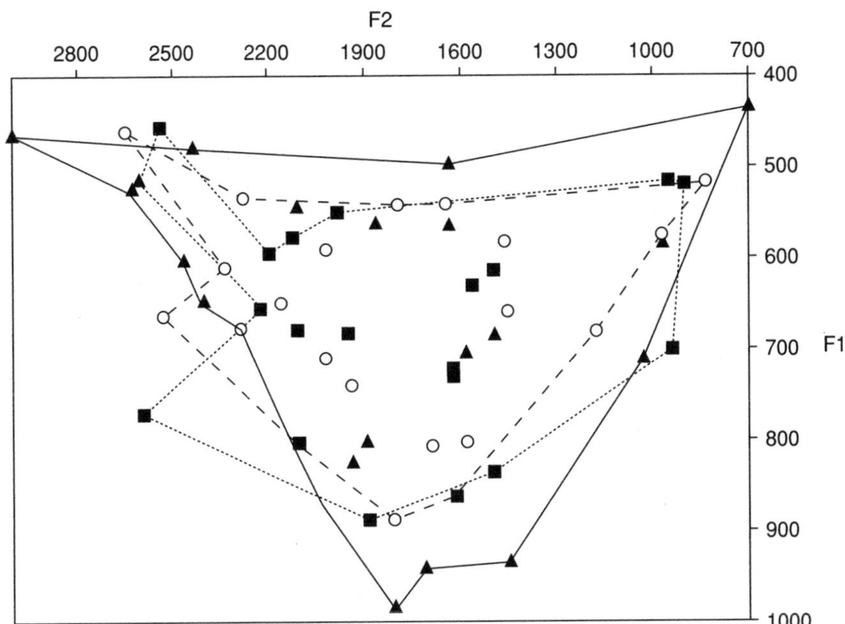


*Figure 13.11* The outer envelope of Carol Meyers' contextual styles, based on figure 13.9. Solid line = Game; dashed line = Home; dotted line = Office

gesture. Figure 13.11 displays the overall vowel space occupied by the three contextual styles: the solid line connects the outermost Game means; the dashed line the Home means; and the dotted line the Office means. It can be seen that the Game context expands phonological space to include the other contexts, except for a few tokens in mid position. In the high front, high back, and low areas, the Game context extends beyond the other two; there is no consistent pattern differentiating Office and Home. It is possible then to read Carol Meyers' style shifting in the Game context as the natural reflex of a more expressive stance, in which lip spreading, jaw opening, and lip rounding are all exaggerated to produce the effects of figure 13.11. What evidence is there that figure 13.9 is a more specific adaptation to the Philadelphia system, that is, phonological shifting?

The phonetic hypothesis must be able to predict mechanically which vowels move downward in the Game context, and which move upward. (aw), (eyF), and (e) are actually at about the same height, but they show the reverse direction of style shifting. For (aw), the Game context follows the direction of ongoing change; for (eyF), the Game context opens further, as it presumably did in earlier versions of the Philadelphia dialect; and for (e), it follows an incipient direction of change, which appears now to be more fully realized (chapter 15). There is a shift in the Game context to high peripheral position in front and back, but little corresponding shift for the centralizing variables (uwF), (uwC), (owF), (owC). It is true that they do not shift strongly frontward, but only for (uwC) does the Game context move at all toward the outer periphery of the vowel system. This would follow from the phonological account, since upward movement is not a socially motivated direction for these vowels: if anything, the vowels are shifting downward.

Though the phonetic account of style shifting cannot easily be set aside, the most consistent account of Carol Meyers' style shifting favors the phonological interpretation. We will proceed then on the assumption that the style shifting exhibited by Carol Meyers articulates the social processes of Philadelphia sound change. Armed with the insight that women talking to women in an informal style shift toward forms used by younger adults, an observer could infer the direction of language change.[17]

It is not impossible that young children learn the dimensions of style shifting from observation of their parents' behavior, as we did from figure 13.9. But it seems more likely that the strongest influence on children is generated by other children one or two years older than they are, and that Carol Meyers' behavior reflects style shifting that she learned in her adolescent, formative years.

Such an inference is supported by the fact that adults have only limited ability to change their behavior when a new pattern arrives on the scene. This is seen most clearly in the consequences of the replacement after World War II of the traditional prestige dialect in New York City by an r-pronouncing variety (Labov 1966a). The variable (r) registers a change from above, in which almost all New Yorkers pronounce postvocalic /r/ with a consonantal [r], and more frequently in more formal styles. It was shown in figure 4.3 of volume 1 that the stratification of (r) in 1962 was replicated in 1986, with a surprisingly small increase in the overall use of [r] – 12% in 24 years. For most New Yorkers, consonantal [r] remained a superposed feature, acquired in their adult years. In the Lower East Side interviews, they showed very little success when they tried to read a passage with the explicit instruction to pronounce every **r** as a consonant.

It follows that the systematic shifting exhibited by Carol Meyers in figures 13.9–13.10 is the inheritance of her formative years and not the result of a process of continuing change over the past 20 years. Let us accept it as established that the more advanced forms of the linguistic changes in progress are used by women in intimate and excited conversation with their peers – other women. Let us also accept the fact that adolescent girls, whose systems are more malleable than Carol Meyers', are the lead-

[17] The same inference could not be drawn by a sophisticated observer from the use of adolescent forms since, as we have seen, an adolescent spike is characteristic of stable sociolinguistic variables (chapter 3).

ing recipients of the transmission of change. In South Philadelphia schools, or at Belten High, a girl at age 12 will observe the advanced forms used by girls at age 16, and may advance her own use by copying them. This is transmission in the simplest sense of transmitting forms, but it does not yet account for the regular and linear increment that we observed among young women in chapter 9. We have yet to confront the problem of incrementation, which is the topic of the next chapter.

# 14

# *Incrementation*

The last chapter made considerable progress in establishing the social site of the transmission of linguistic change. The next issue to confront is the mechanism by which changes advance in a step-by-step fashion – that is, the *incrementation problem.* Throughout this exploration of the social factors in linguistic change, a crucial issue has been pushed to the outskirts of the discussion, and it remains as a gap in the mechanism of transmission sketched above. The problem is seen in its clearest form in the prototypical new and vigorous linguistic change where women are a generation in advance of men. That model showed a near-linear, decade-by-decade advance of women which remains unaccounted for. How and why does this incrementation take place?

## 14.1 Stabilization

Chapter 4 of volume 1 reviewed four real-time studies of linguistic change in progress that helped to interpret apparent-time distributions. Age stratification at present may represent age-grading which repeats in every generation: all speakers shift their level of the variable as they grow older. Or age stratification may represent generational change, in which speakers maintain a constant level after an initial period of acquisition and socialization. If speakers are indeed labile, and the whole community changes together, the real-time study will find that the apparent-time study understated the degree of change that was taking place.

None of these real-time studies provided clear evidence on whether older speakers had maintained a stable system, though they indicated some degree of real-time change and some indication of age-grading. Cedergren's re-study of the lenition of (ch) in Panama City (1973, 1984) found that the change had advanced about 10% for those 40 to 70 years old. But matching age groups over the 13-year interval, one could see evidence for communal change, since speakers in that age range had advanced beyond their 1973 level. Chapter 4 of volume 1 concluded that there was enough evidence of communal change to suspect that apparent-time studies had under-estimated the rate of change.

A recent study of the Swedish town Eskilstuna by Nordberg and his colleagues re-examined the community after 29 years (Nordberg 1975, Nordberg and Sundgren 1998). Their trend study included a panel of 13 speakers from 1967 who were re-interviewed in 1996. One clear case of change in progress was reported, the leveling of the local definite plural neuter suffix *-ena* in favor of standard *-en*. Here the panel members who were under 45 years old in 1967 showed about as much increase as the community as a whole, though those 50 and over were unchanged. Nordberg and Sundgren conclude that dialects have stabilized after the age of 50. This agrees with the evidence cited in chapter 4 on the stability of older Philadelphia speakers (Labov and Auger 1998). The lability of speakers 30–50 may be characteristic of changes from above as opposed to changes from below, or of morphology as opposed to phonology, but it underlines the fact that the assumption of stability for young adults, built into the models that follow, may have to be revised.

The models of sound change developed below set the age of phonological stabilization at 17.[1] This is not a substantive statement, but a simplification that will permit us to follow the consequences of other assumptions in a manageable space.

## 14.2 A model of linear sound change

Given the fact that girls as well as boys start at the level of their mothers' vowel system, it must be that girls increase their use of the linguistic change in progress by re-organizing the vernacular they first acquired. The simplest assumption is that this increment is a continuous one from the period when children first emerge from the linguistic domination of their parents (4–5) to the time when their linguistic system stabilizes (17–20, or perhaps beyond). The discussion to follow will center on the construction of a linear model of incrementation for this time period. The model will be simplified by setting two constants. A generation will be fixed at 28 years. The age of relative stabilization (or "critical age") will be set at 17 to keep the shape of the model within bounds. The same results will follow from any other age of stabilization.

Figure 14.1 diagrams the expected value of the change for a single speaker, year by year. We will assume that she is female, and is participating

[1] Seventeen is the age at which the declining ability to acquire native syntactic intuitions hits bottom in Johnson and Newport's experiments (1989). Some of the evidence from Payne's study of King of Prussia (chapter 13) suggests that 8 or 9 may be a more critical age for the acquisition of abstract phonological rules. For some variables, young adults continue to advance in their late teens and early 20s, and in the Nordberg and Sundgren study reported above, into their 30s and 40s.

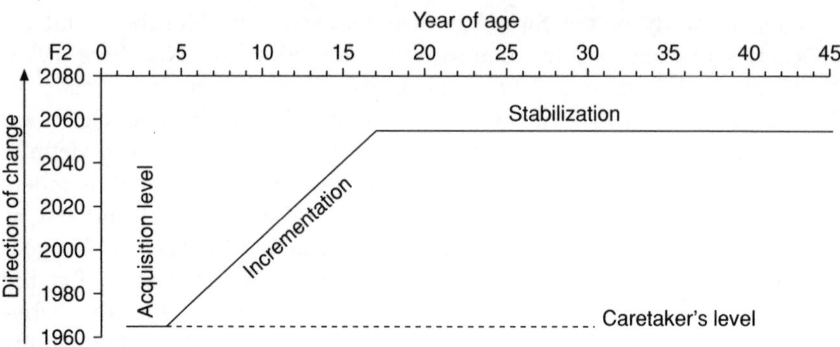


*Figure 14.1* A linear model of incrementation for a single female speaker from 1 to 45 years of age

in a female-dominated change. The level of the variable is set at first acquisition from 1 to 3 years of age, at the level of the 30-year-old caretaker, at the arbitrary level 0 in this model. The second formant increases from age 4 over the next 13 years. At the age of 17, the incrementation stops, and the phonological system stabilizes.

As the simplest possibility, assume that this model holds for everyone: that when change is initiated, all female speakers show the same rate of incrementation during their formative years. Let us further assume that this is a simple mechanical process and set parameters arbitrarily as follows. Children preserve the system of their caretakers until the age of 4, and undergo the influence of the change to a stabilization age of 17. The change will be measured in arbitrary units beginning with 0 and advancing in the speech of each individual by 1 unit per year. A generation is set at 25 years: that is, the mean age of mothers when first giving birth is 25.

Figure 14.2 shows the consequences for the speech community of such a uniform incrementation of a change that began in 1900. The vertical axis represents units and the horizontal axis shows age of speakers. The first year tracked (with solid circles) at the bottom of figure 14.2 is 1925. At this time, the speech of the caretakers is still at the base level 0. The 5-year-olds who have just emerged from that level have advanced in one year to unit 1, while the 9-year-olds have moved to 5. The 17-year-olds are at 13, the stable level reached and maintained by all speakers aged 17 to 25 (i.e., those born 1900 to 1908). Speakers born before 1900 are not affected by the change and remain at the base line 0.

Given such uniform incrementation, the 1925 pattern will be repeated without change until 1929. But 1930 will introduce a new phenomenon. For the first time, 5-year-olds whose mothers were affected by the change

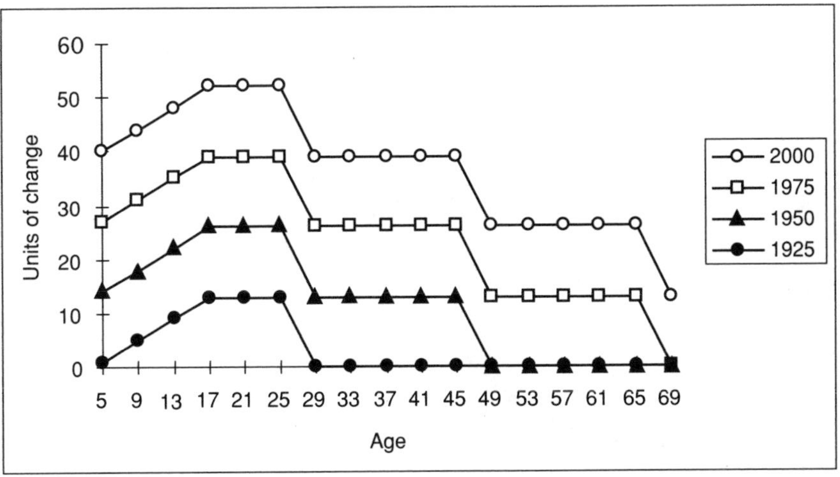


*Figure 14.2* Age profiles of a linguistic change in progress with uniform incrementation of the change

will enter the wider speech community. These are the children whose mothers were born in 1900. As they have acquired the phonetic forms of their mothers (or other female caretakers), they will begin with a base level of 13 and at the age of 5 reach 14.

The black triangles in figure 14.2 track the situation reached in 1950. At this point the school-age population will follow an upward trajectory from 14 to 26, and stabilize at that level to age 29. Speakers who are 29 to 45 years old will have continued the level of stabilization 13 that they achieved, and only those 49 years and older will preserve the base level 0 of those who were never affected by the change.

The step-wise pattern of 1950 is repeated in 1975 and 2000. The discontinuities represented in the discrete levels are generational effects, created by the waves of innovation introduced by children whose mothers are at a discretely higher level of change than the generation that preceded them. This is not the linear pattern that was found for women in chapters 9 and 11, but resembles the pattern of men, which was interpreted as the results of the generational influence of female caretakers.

In place of a uniform increment, we can substitute a more plausible model of linguistic change in progress. Many convergent findings indicate that linguistic change follows a logistic progression (Bailey 1973:77; Weinreich, Labov, and Herzog 1968; Kroch 1989; volume 1, pp. 65–7), in which change starts out slowly, reaches a maximum rate at mid-course, and slows down again asymptotically at the end. The logistic expression (1) generates such a distribution:

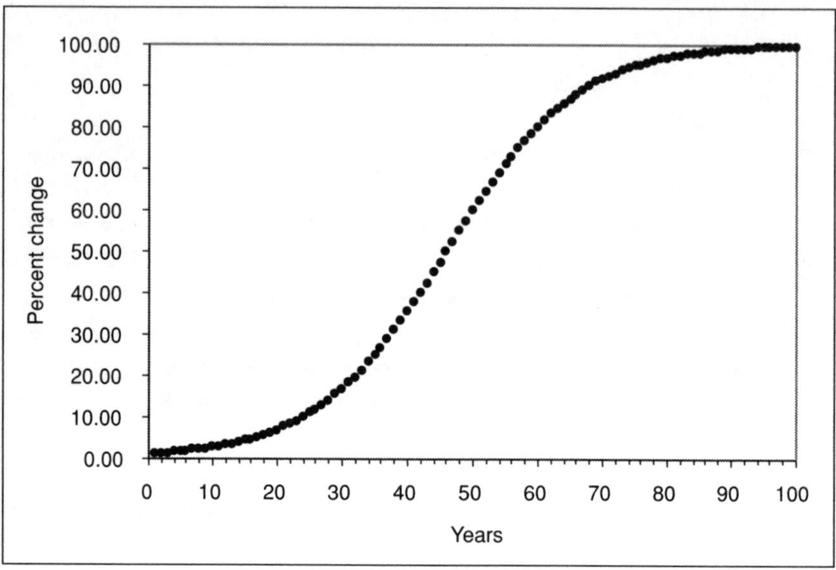


*Figure 14.3* 100-year progress of a change with logistic incrementation

(1) $I = K_1/(1 + K_2/N_0 \times e^{-rt})$

Here $K_1$ is the maximum possible change in one year, $K_2$ the limits of the sound change, $N_0$ is the initial year, *r* is the rate of change, and *t* is time in years. Setting $K_1$ and $K_2$ at 100 with $N_0$ as year 1, and *r* as 0, generates figure 14.3, showing the progress of the change from 0 to 100, year by year. Figure 14.4 plots for each year the increment over the preceding year. These increments are very small at the outset, and rise to a maximum midway in the change before declining in a symmetrical manner. The following development of logistic incrementation will use the numerical values underlying these figures, given in full in table 14.1.

Figure 14.5 tracks the progress of a linguistic change which follows such a logistic progression, beginning in 1900 and extending over the 20th century. The horizontal axis is the age of the speaker, calculated at 4-year intervals, and the vertical axis is the abstract scale that shows the progress of the change from a minimum of 0 to a maximum of 100. The bottom line, marked with solid circles, is the profile for the year 1925. The value for a given point is calculated by summing the increments for each year in which the speaker was subject to the change in progress. Children 9 years old, for example, will have participated in the change from age 5 to 9, from 1921 to 1925. They have reached the level of 3.98, which is the sum of the increments in the third column of table 14.1 for years 21 through 25. The maximum level of 7.64 is attained by 17-year-olds, who have

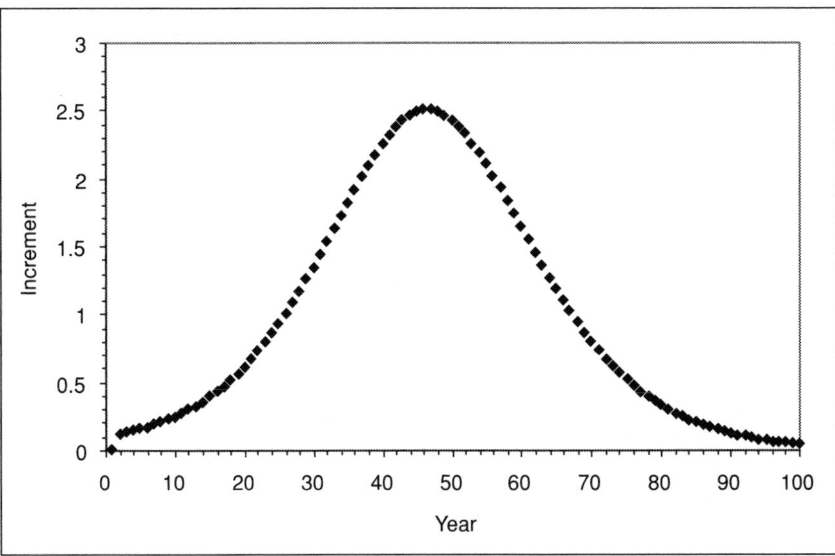


*Figure 14.4* Rise and fall of rate of incrementation of a logistic curve

participated in the change for 13 years, from 1913 to 1925. Though the change is (hypothetically) stabilized at age 17, those who are now 21 years old have a lower value than the 17-year-olds, since they participated in the change at an earlier period, from 1909 to 1921. The sum of the increments of table 14.1 for years 9 to 21 is only 5.37. The 1925 curve then declines further to the level of 0 for 29 years and beyond, since by hypothesis the change only affected those who entered the wider speech community after 1900.

The calculations for 1950 are more complex, since they must add the increment of the child to the level attained by the child's mother. A girl 5 years old in 1950 was born in 1945. Her mother, who is now 30 years old (given the hypothetical 25-year generation), was born in 1920; she participated fully in the change from 1925 to 1937. The sum of the increments in table 14.1 for years 25 to 37 is the maximum level reached by the mother: 18.87. To this we add the increment for the one year, 1950, when the 5-year-old participated in the change (2.43), to yield 21.30.

The curve for 1950 rises steeply, since this is the point in the logistic curve where the slope reaches the maximum, and then declines symmetrically for the first four values. The right-hand branch of this curve corresponds to the adult pattern that approximates linearity in the Philadelphia sound changes in figure 9.5. The curve of figure 14.5 does not maintain the same slope but flattens toward the lower end. It is, however, closer to a straight line than the step-wise pattern of figure 14.2. A straight line drawn through

*Table 14.1* Logistic table of 1-year increments over a century

| *Year* | *Level* | *Increment* | *Year* | *Level* | *Increment* | *Year* | *Level* | *Increment* | *Year* | *Level* | *Increment* |
|---|---|---|---|---|---|---|---|---|---|---|---|
| 1 | 1.09 | 0.00 | 26 | 11.87 | 1.01 | 51 | 62.12 | 2.38 | 76 | 95.23 | 0.47 |
| 2 | 1.21 | 0.11 | 27 | 12.95 | 1.09 | 52 | 64.45 | 2.32 | 77 | 95.67 | 0.43 |
| 3 | 1.33 | 0.13 | 28 | 14.12 | 1.17 | 53 | 66.70 | 2.26 | 78 | 96.06 | 0.40 |
| 4 | 1.47 | 0.14 | 29 | 15.38 | 1.26 | 54 | 68.89 | 2.18 | 79 | 96.43 | 0.36 |
| 5 | 1.62 | 0.15 | 30 | 16.73 | 1.35 | 55 | 70.99 | 2.10 | 80 | 96.75 | 0.33 |
| 6 | 1.79 | 0.17 | 31 | 18.17 | 1.44 | 56 | 73.00 | 2.02 | 81 | 97.05 | 0.30 |
| 7 | 1.97 | 0.18 | 32 | 19.70 | 1.53 | 57 | 74.93 | 1.92 | 82 | 97.33 | 0.27 |
| 8 | 2.18 | 0.20 | 33 | 21.33 | 1.63 | 58 | 76.76 | 1.83 | 83 | 97.58 | 0.25 |
| 9 | 2.40 | 0.22 | 34 | 23.06 | 1.73 | 59 | 78.50 | 1.74 | 84 | 97.80 | 0.23 |
| 10 | 2.65 | 0.25 | 35 | 24.88 | 1.82 | 60 | 80.14 | 1.64 | 85 | 98.01 | 0.21 |
| 11 | 2.92 | 0.27 | 36 | 26.79 | 1.92 | 61 | 81.68 | 1.54 | 86 | 98.19 | 0.19 |
| 12 | 3.21 | 0.30 | 37 | 28.80 | 2.01 | 62 | 83.13 | 1.45 | 87 | 98.36 | 0.17 |
| 13 | 3.54 | 0.33 | 38 | 30.89 | 2.09 | 63 | 84.49 | 1.36 | 88 | 98.52 | 0.15 |
| 14 | 3.90 | 0.36 | 39 | 33.07 | 2.17 | 64 | 85.75 | 1.27 | 89 | 98.65 | 0.14 |
| 15 | 4.29 | 0.39 | 40 | 35.32 | 2.25 | 65 | 86.93 | 1.18 | 90 | 98.78 | 0.13 |
| 16 | 4.72 | 0.43 | 41 | 37.63 | 2.32 | 66 | 88.03 | 1.09 | 91 | 98.90 | 0.11 |
| 17 | 5.19 | 0.47 | 42 | 40.01 | 2.37 | 67 | 89.04 | 1.01 | 92 | 99.00 | 0.10 |
| 18 | 5.70 | 0.51 | 43 | 42.43 | 2.42 | 68 | 89.98 | 0.94 | 93 | 99.09 | 0.09 |
| 19 | 6.27 | 0.56 | 44 | 44.89 | 2.46 | 69 | 90.84 | 0.87 | 94 | 99.18 | 0.09 |
| 20 | 6.88 | 0.61 | 45 | 47.37 | 2.48 | 70 | 91.64 | 0.80 | 95 | 99.26 | 0.08 |
| 21 | 7.55 | 0.67 | 46 | 49.87 | 2.50 | 71 | 92.38 | 0.73 | 96 | 99.33 | 0.07 |
| 22 | 8.28 | 0.73 | 47 | 52.37 | 2.50 | 72 | 93.05 | 0.67 | 97 | 99.39 | 0.06 |
| 23 | 9.07 | 0.79 | 48 | 54.86 | 2.49 | 73 | 93.67 | 0.62 | 98 | 99.45 | 0.06 |
| 24 | 9.93 | 0.86 | 49 | 57.32 | 2.46 | 74 | 94.24 | 0.57 | 99 | 99.50 | 0.05 |
| 25 | 10.86 | 0.93 | 50 | 59.74 | 2.43 | 75 | 94.76 | 0.52 | 100 | 99.55 | 0.05 |

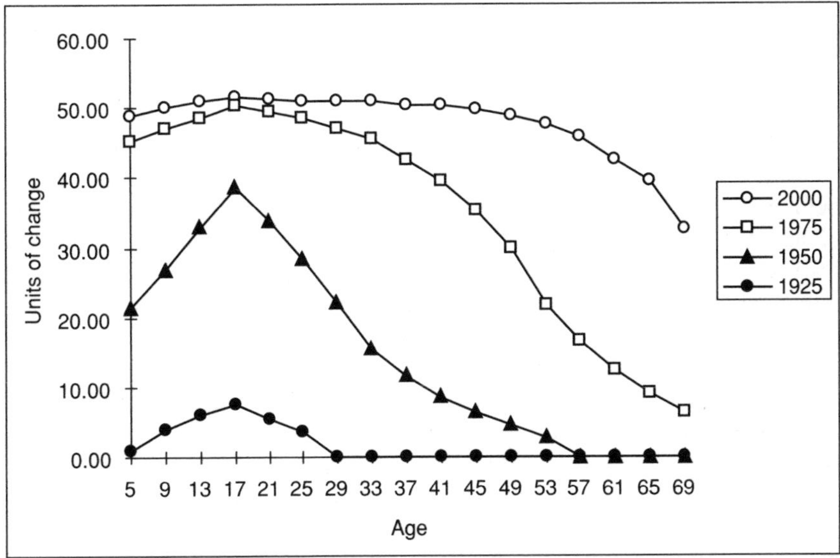


*Figure 14.5* Age profiles for females of a linguistic change in progress with logistic incrementation of the change

the eleven points from age 17 to 57 shows a good fit: $r^2$ is .953, close to the value of .961 found for the (aw) age pattern of female speakers in figure 9.5. A parallel calculation for the step-wise progression of figure 14.2 yields an $r^2$ of .84, not far from the slope of .79 for men in figure 9.5.

A central point of interest in these calculations is the transition from speakers whose mothers were affected by the change to those whose mothers were not. Consider first the 29-year-olds in 1950. Their mothers, then 54 years old, were born in 1896, and went to school in 1900 when the change had just begun. But the mothers of the 33-year-olds in 1950 were not involved in the change. They were then 58 years old, were born in 1892, and began school in 1896, four years before the change had begun. In figure 14.5 there is no sharp discontinuity in the curve between 29- and 33-year-olds, but rather a shift to a shallower slope.

The calculations for 1975 and 2000 require parallel calculations that take into account the cumulative contributions of each generation, considering that mothers at each generation raise the entering level of their children to the maximum level attained in their formative years. The maximum value for 17-year-olds in 1975, for example, is the sum of their grandmothers' increments from 1913 to 1925, their mothers' increments from 1938 to 1950, and their own participation in the change from 1963 to 1975. As the change advances to completion, age differences become minimal, so that in 2000 the curve rises to a maximum at 17 years and declines, but departs very little from a straight line.

The question remains as to whether the logistic incrementation fully accounts for the linear advance among adult women, or whether this is the result of further smoothing. The real-time studies reviewed in chapter 4 of volume 1 all indicate some further movement of adult speakers which demands modification of our initial assumptions that those over 17 years of age no longer participate in the advancement of change. Whatever further modifications are necessary, it appears that the logistic relation of rate of change to time – or a similar S-shaped function – is a reasonable first approximation to the incrementation problem.

The modeling of sound change in progress by logistic incrementation has broader implications. The logistic function has been used most prominently in population genetics to model the competition between species or varieties, with one gradually replacing the other. So far, we have been looking at the raising of (æ) or the fronting of (uw) as a gradual movement in a continuous phonetic substratum, and it is very likely that it begins in this way. But if the change from below develops social evaluation, the social perception of this process is more likely to be a polar opposition between "advanced" forms and normal forms. Eckert's study of the Northern Cities Shift in Detroit (chapter 13) followed this logic in converting an n-ary series of impressionistic levels into a binary opposition of advanced vs. non-advanced, and submitted this to the Varbrul logistic regression with good results. The implications of the logistic model for the mechanism of change will be developed further in the exploration of the mechanism of change in chapters 15 and 16.

## *The peak in apparent time*

The focus so far has been on how to account for the linear pattern of the adult female speakers. There are other features of the shape of the curves generated here. One of the most striking is the existence of the peak near the age of stabilization.

A peak in apparent time was not expected in early work on change in progress. It was assumed that the apparent-time reflection of a vigorous change would continue in the same direction as the age group became younger and younger. This pattern was reflected in the backing of (el) in Norwich (Trudgill 1974b), and seemed to be characteristic of the New York City and Panama City changes that formed the basis for the curvilinear hypothesis as presented in chapter 1. That formulation states that *a monotonic distribution in age groups is associated with a curvilinear pattern in the socioeconomic hierarchy*. But for a number of linguistic changes, a drop-off in index values was reported for speakers under 20, and this led to

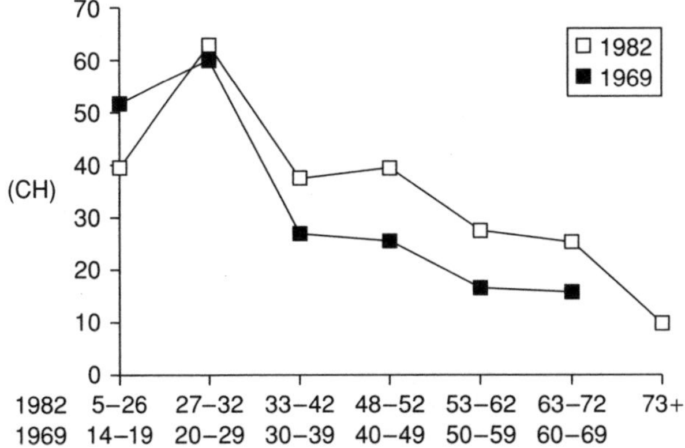


*Figure 14.6* Real-time re-study of the lenition of (ch) in Panama City by Cedergren (1973, 1984)

speculation that the changes may in fact have reached their limit and were receding. This was the case in Ash's study of the vocalization of (l) in Philadelphia (1982a), which peaked with speakers in their 20s. Chapter 4 of volume 1 reviewed the real-time studies of Panama City by Cedergren (figure 4.8, reproduced here as figure 14.6). No explanation of the fall-off in lenition for the youngest group was given; we now see that this is a general requirement of change in progress.

A peak in apparent time did not appear in the uniform incrementation model of figure 14.2. However, the logistic incrementation of figure 14.5 must show such a peak because the experience of each yearly cohort carries it further than the speakers a year older. The existence of the peak in empirical studies then provides further confirmation that this model conforms to the actual situation.

The results of chapter 9 did not show the population profile in enough detail to check the existence of such a peak. To do so, we need to break down the female population into smaller age groups. Since 17 is the crucial age, we would want to create several groups below 17. The data from the Philadelphia Neighborhood Study allows us to create the following age categories:[2]

| *Age* | *No. of speakers* |
|---|---|
| Under 13 | 6 |
| 13–16 | 17 |
| 17–29 | 22 |

[2] Though 17 was picked as the critical age for stabilization, the set of four 17-year-olds in the PNS data was not as representative of the culminating sound changes as the 16-year-olds. I have therefore included the 17-year-olds with the older group of young adults.

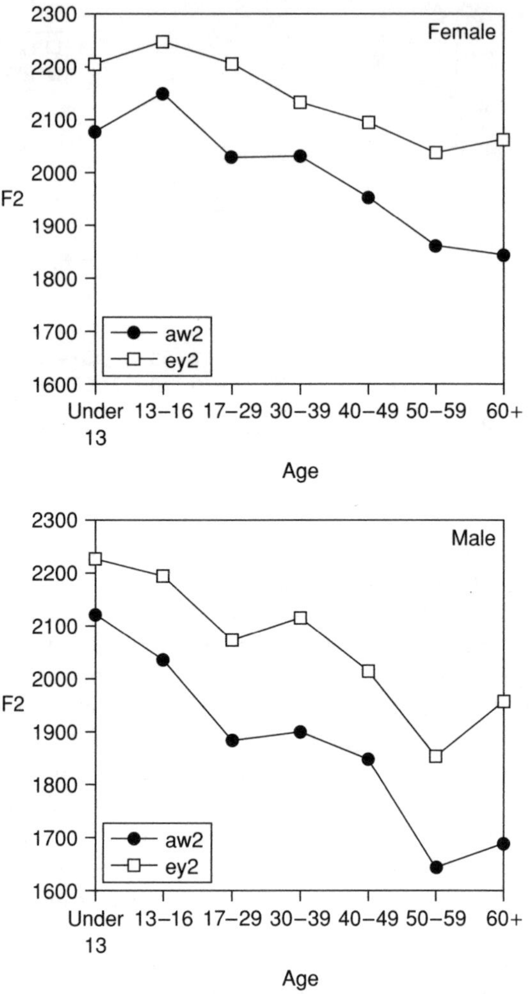


*Figure 14.7* Expected values for (aw2) and (eyC2), calculated by adding constants to age regression coefficients for female and male subjects with younger age groups subdivided

Figure 14.7 displays the expected values for the two new and vigorous changes (aw) and (eyC), using these modified age categories. They are expanded forms of figures 9.5 and 9.6, re-arranged to group the female distributions above, and the male distributions below. All significant occupation and neighborhood categories are retained in these analyses.[3] The familiar

[3] The curvilinear pattern is retained in all analyses, with positive values for the skilled occupational group (aw2 female 83, male 117; eyC2 female 173, male 179). Wicket St. was significantly ahead for males only (aw2 170, eyC2 179).

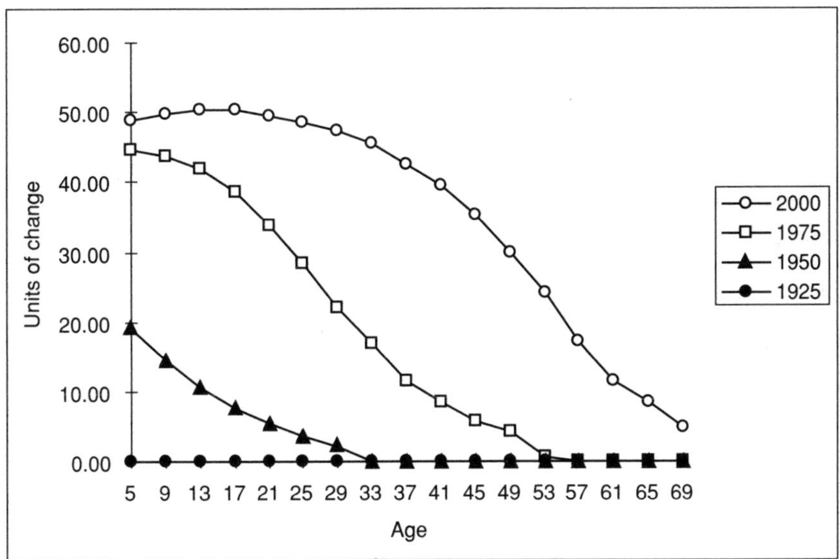


*Figure 14.8* Age profile for males of a linguistic change in progress with logistic incrementation of the change

linear pattern for females appears up to 13–16 years, with a peak at the 13–16 age group. Below this is the corresponding pattern for males, with the step-like pattern culminating in an upward movement to the youngest group. The empirical data thus shows the peak that was predicted by the model designed to show an increment over time for women in a linguistic change led by women. The fact that men show the reverse pattern fits the prediction made by the gender-asymmetric model: that their participation in the change is due to the increment inherited from their female caretaker, not from the incrementation process of figure 14.5.

The model for change in the male population that corresponds to figure 14.5 will have no incrementation component for the individual. The value for each age group for each generation will be calculated entirely from the experience of the speaker's mother (and by inheritance, grandmother and great-grandmother). Figure 14.8 shows the result for males in the hypothetical change extending from 1900 to 2000. For the year 1925, there is no change evident, since none of the speakers have mothers who had participated in the change. For the year 1950, there is a steeply descending pattern which is entirely the product of the mother's initial contribution. No peak is shown in 1975, but in 2000, the figure shows the same slight peak that appeared for women in figure 14.5.

The logistic incrementation model therefore reflects the major difference between the patterns of linguistic change of men and women observed in

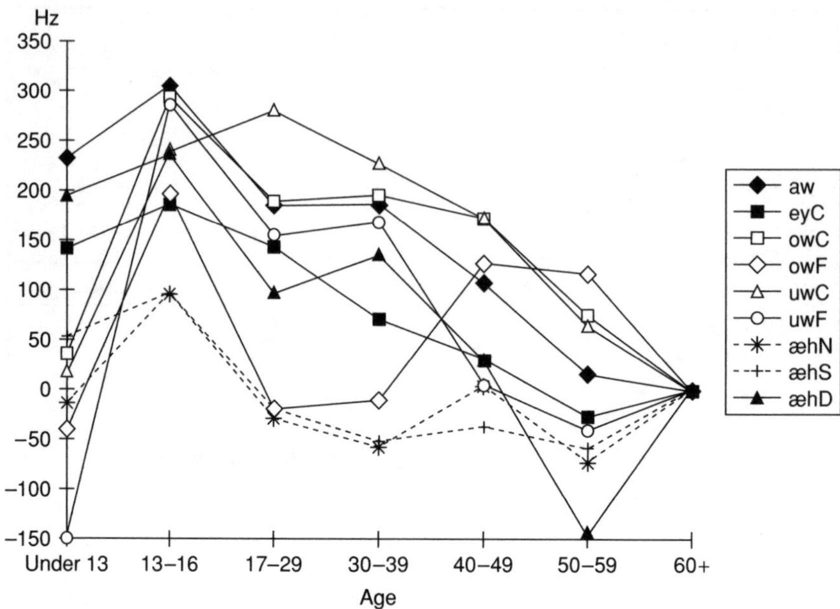


*Figure 14.9* Age coefficients for female speakers in nine linguistic changes in progress led by women in Philadelphia

figure 14.7. However, the male step-wise pattern of figures 9.5 and 9.6 does not emerge as clearly from these calculations. Fitting a straight line to the 1975 curve, we have an $r^2$ of .93. Though this is lower than that for women, it is considerably higher than that found in the speech community. The logistic incrementation model does not fully account for this difference between adult men and women in this respect.

The female increments from under 13 to 13–16 in figure 14.7 are not in themselves significant. If we take under 13 as the residual group in the regression, the probability that the elevation of the 13–16 group is due to chance is .4907 for (aw) and .6837 for (eyC). However, there are nine distinct linguistic changes in progress in Philadelphia where women are in the lead, and the incrementation model developed here should apply to all of them if it is valid. Figure 14.9 shows the age coefficients for all nine of these variables plotted in a single display. Since they all involve the raising of the second formant, they are on a roughly comparable scale, ranging from −150 to 350 Hz. Every one of these variables shows a peak in apparent time; for (uwC), this is in the 17–29 age group; for all the others it is in the 13–16 age group. This is strong confirmation of the logistically varying incremental model of figure 14.2. There are several ways to calculate the significance of this

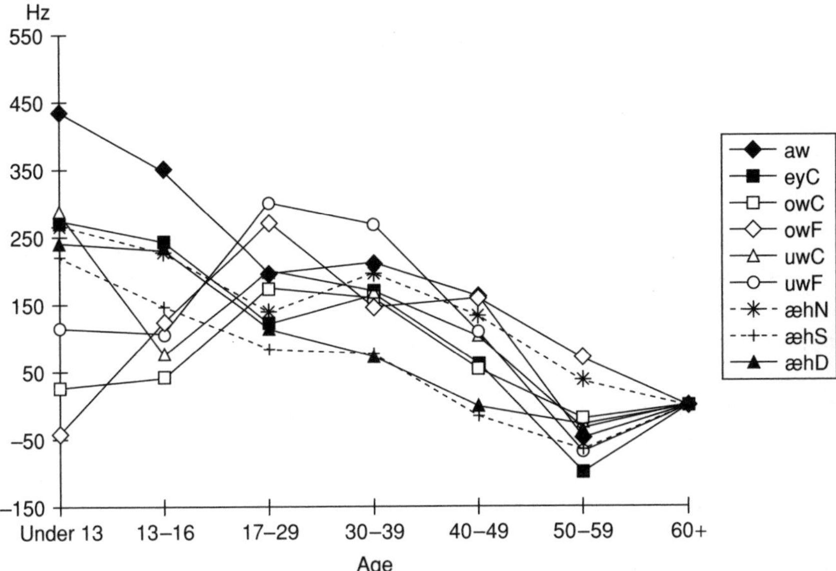


*Figure 14.10* Age coefficients for male speakers in nine linguistic changes in progress led by women in Philadelphia

result. Simply considering the series as a binary choice: a peak present or absent, the probability of getting all nine with a peak is $1/2^9$, or .0019. A more accurate assessment uses the sum of the logarithms of the probabilities derived from the t-test of the regression coefficients. Twice the negative of this sum is the chi-squared value of the series, 29.23; with eight degrees of freedom, the probability of such a result being due to chance is .0003.

In figure 14.9, the three new and vigorous changes are shown with solid figures and heavy lines: the similarity of the three patterns is evident. The middle-range changes, shown with lighter solid lines and empty symbols, are less regular in the adult distribution, but are remarkably uniform in the steep slope of the shift upward from the under 13 group to the 13–16 group. The nearly completed changes are shown as dashed lines with crosses; their overall age slopes and upward shifts are quite small.

When the same method is applied to the male speakers in the Philadelphia Neighborhood Study, the results are much less regular (figure 14.10). The new and vigorous changes (aw), (eyC), and (æhD) are again quite parallel and show a rising pattern to the youngest age group with no adolescent peak. The same is true for the nearly completed changes (æhN) and (æhS). However, the middle-range changes generally show a peak in the 17–29 year old group. It is therefore possible that these middle-range changes are receding before they reach completion. The very sharp decline with the under 13 group for women in figure 14.9 and the peak for males at 17–29 both point in this direction.

## *A restatement of the curvilinear hypothesis*

It is now clear that linguistic change in progress follows a curvilinear pattern in both the social and age dimensions. The original distinction between stable variables and change from below no longer holds. The curvilinear hypothesis of chapter 1 is best restated in terms of the adult population:

Stable sociolinguistic variables combine a flat age distribution for adults with a monotonic social class stratification; changes in progress combine a monotonic distribution in adult age groups with a curvilinear pattern in the socioeconomic hierarchy.

This restatement has the advantage of describing the age pattern for stable sociolinguistic variables in a way consistent with the findings of chapter 3, and excluding the characteristic adolescent spike for stigmatized variables.

## *Accounting for male-dominated changes*

The male-dominated variable that contrasts with the nine female-dominated changes is (ay0). Figure 14.11 shows the expected male and female values, calculated by adding the coefficients for each age group to the regression constant, and adding to this the gender coefficient (36 Hz for females). The centralization of the nucleus progresses upwards from the base level of the over-60 group, as we have seen before, with males in the lead. In this case, males show a peak at 13–16 and females show a continued upward climb.

It is not a simple matter to adapt the incremental model to a male-dominated change. If we make the converse assumptions of the female model – that men have a logistically varying year-by-year increment, but women do not, the women would remain at a permanent floor of zero. Without any input from their mothers, men would follow a pattern roughly similar to figure 14.5, but at a considerably slower rate, while women would not participate in the change at all. Yet this is not what happens: women do not abstain from the centralization of /ay0/, but follow closely behind men as a whole.

There are several ways in which women may follow the change of (ay0) at a lower level. They may have a slower rate of change. Or they

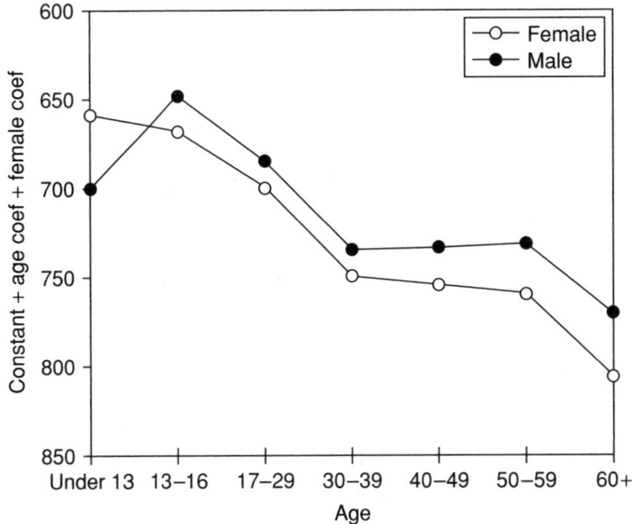


*Figure 14.11* Expected values for (ay0) calculated from regression constant, age coefficients, and gender coefficient, by age and gender

may have a lower limit on the amount of change in any given year (the $K_1$ variable in the logistic formula). Or they may begin to imitate the male change at a later age, at 13, 14, or 15. The difficulty here is that this chapter has been representing the speech community as if all men and women were behaving in the same way, while chapters 5–12 demonstrated the opposite. The tendencies modeled in figure 14.2 seem to be largely independent of the forces that operate to distinguish Celeste S.'s advanced use of (aw) and (eyC) from Mae D.'s conservative stance. But this is not so for (ay0). Figures 9.14 and 9.15 showed a steep social cline in the use of (ay0) by social class. While there is an enormous difference between the use of (ay0) by men and women among professionals, there is no difference at all among unskilled workers. In this respect, (ay0) is the opposite of (eyC), where gender and class effects are independent.[4] Efforts to model (ay0) for the population as a whole are not likely to be rewarding at this point, as a single case with no decisive means of accounting for how women enter into the development of the variable.

[4] The middle-range changes are intermediate in the degree of independence of gender and class, and the nearly completed changes show considerable interaction. An increase of social awareness of the changes accompanies this interaction. But (ay0) is far from a social stereotype, and overt social stigmatization contributes nothing to the gender differences that we see here.

## *Beginnings and endings*

The account put forward in the previous section applies most forcefully to young speakers whose mothers have been affected by the changes in progress. Not only do their mothers give them an advanced base, but they also model the patterns of style shifting in the direction of the change. But what about the first generation, whose mothers are at the base line? Change in the first generation must move slowly because it is motivated primarily by mechanical factors: the re-adjustment of asymmetric systems produced by probability matching by the next generation. The model of figure 14.4 shows that change during that first generation is indeed slow, so slow that it might not have been detected as significant by instrumental analyses. That is the case for several changes noted by the Philadelphia Neighborhood Study in the mid-1970s: the lowering of /e/ and /æ/, and the backing of /ʌ/ were described as incipient changes (possible, but not proved by significant age coefficients). Acceleration logically begins when the incipient change is attached to or is associated with a particular style or social group: a social category like *burnout* or a neighborhood like *Kensington*. This association is an arbitrary, almost accidental event. It is likely that most incipient changes will never be so associated, and never make much further progress. If the change becomes associated with the male gender, whatever acceleration does occur will be damped by mechanical factors. In the second generation, children will obtain their first input from relatively conservative female caretakers, and will begin their linguistic trajectories at a less advanced rather than more advanced position. The majority of such male-dominated incipient changes may disappear without trace. Those that do survive are mostly associated with female speakers of an upwardly mobile class, and follow the linear portion of the logistic curve by the logic outlined above.

We know that eventually, most changes reach the top portion of an S-shaped curve, and then decelerate, approaching a limit asymptotically. There is nothing about the curve that demands this. In population biology, the deceleration occurs in the growth of a population when it approaches the carrying capacity of the environment. No such limit exists in linguistic structure. However, there are natural limits to certain phonetic changes which approach the outer envelope of phonetic possibilities. When the nucleus of /æ/ reaches high front position, it cannot go much further in that direction. Sound change can turn it in another direction, as in a shift of syllabicity which would convert it to a rising diphthong. Another type of limiting factor is confusion and merger with another phoneme. When the nucleus of /ow/ reaches a front, non-peripheral target, [E$^{>}$U], it may have reached such a limit, since the corresponding peripheral nucleus, [E$^{<}$U], is identified with /aw/. We cannot take such structural limits as absolute, given the fact that mergers are so frequent. Yet the same mechanical force that initiates change will act to limit it in such a situation.

## *The forces driving change*

The problem of incrementation seems to have received some promising answers as far as female-dominated changes are concerned. A combination of mechanical factors (step-wise incrementation from caretakers) and socially driven factors (the logistic incrementation) produces a near-linear decline with age for adults and a less linear increase with age for children. We are now in a position to make some educated guesses on the nature of the force that drives the system forward.

Despite the fact that the community system advances over time, a girl who enters this system must quickly perceive that girls older than she is use more advanced forms of changing linguistic variables. In adopting these more advanced forms, the speaker is following the normal path of taking the behavior of older children as a model. Following the incrementation pattern, she eventually surpasses their level. This can occur only when they have become linguistic adults, with a stabilized phonology, while she is still advancing. The crucial question is to explain why the incrementation advances up the S-shaped curve.

Volume 1 put forward a mechanical account of the motivating force behind chain shifts (pp. 586–7). For any given phoneme with an asymmetrical pattern of neighbors, there is a slightly higher probability of outliers being misunderstood if they overlap the margin of security of a near neighbor than if they extend in a direction where there is no neighbor. As the child matches her probability distribution with the observed productions of caretakers and older children, the loss of outliers in one direction will automatically shift her means in the opposite direction. Thus there is a systematic tendency for vowels to shift in the direction of a hole in the pattern. Though this explains the predominance of pull chains, it does not explain two facts: (1) not all holes in patterns are filled; not all chain shifts are activated at all times, and (2) push chains do occur (as when, for example, the backing of /e/ precedes the backing of /ʌ/ in the Northern Cities Shift). There must be a social force that activates the shift and drives the increment.

In chapter 13, it was observed that linguistic forms become associated with polarities such as formal/informal, older/younger, higher/lower, local/outsider, jock/burnout. In most cases, the majority of speakers will be identified as in-betweens for any given polarity, and shift their behavior as their orientation toward the polar targets changes. It seems likely that what is perceived is not a specific target in terms of frequency or formant

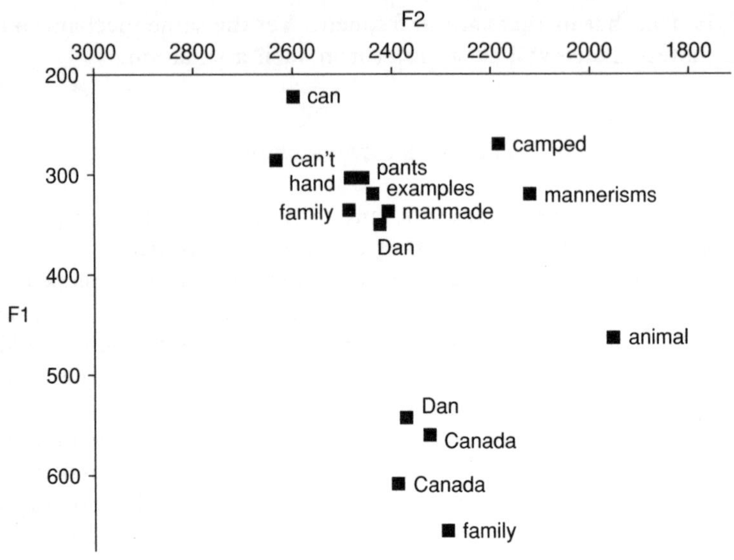


*Figure 14.12* Distribution of /æ/ before nasal consonants for Jeannette S., 56, Rochester, NY, Telsur 359

level, but a dimension or direction of shifting. Here the role of the outliers takes on considerable importance. Most distributions of vowel changes in progress do not show symmetric distributions around the mean. A few pronunciations are skewed from the rest in the direction of the change, and as a result the median is always more conservative than the mean. The mean itself does not exhibit the full impact of the change in progress as well as these outliers, which are emphatic, fully stressed tokens whose advanced position is not fully attributable to their phonetic environments. Figure 14.12 shows an extreme example in the speech of one of the most advanced exponents of the Northern Cities Shift, Jeannette S. from Rochester. Only short /æ/ vowels before nasal consonants are shown. A conservative group of tokens, with mostly open syllables, is focused around F1, F2 values of 600, 2300. A cluster of more advanced tokens with closed syllables is concentrated at 325, 2500, and one outlier to these outliers, the word *can*, is at 224, 2600. Though the initial velar and following nasal contribute to this advanced position, it is the strenuous articulation of this one token that leads to its extreme raising and fronting, emblematic of the movement of /æ/ from [æ] to [iːə].

It seems likely that outliers play an important role in establishing the polarity of sociolinguistic dimensions – perhaps more important in their social impact than the mean. This is not due entirely to their advanced position, but also to the social and stylistic setting in which they are used, prefigured in the acquisition of stylistic polarity by small children discussed earlier in chapter 13. The following chapter will pursue the role of outliers in an overall view of the development of sound changes in North America. Before turning to this large-scale study, we will want to consider the role of outliers and style shifting in everyday life. Our best evidence for the way in which stylistic variation relates to sound change is drawn from the study of adults, long after they have stabilized their system.

# 15

# *Continuation*

The transmission problem, as it was formulated in chapter 13, seemed truly formidable. With the help of quantitative modeling of the Philadelphia data base, some progress has been made toward an understanding of the social trajectories of the leaders of linguistic change, and how change is transmitted across generations and across neighborhoods. There remains, as always, the actuation problem. Why here and now? The beginnings of change are as mysterious as ever. Why *not* here and *not* now? Endings are equally difficult to understand. The obverse of the actuation problem is *continuation*. If change has already begun and is not coming to an end, it is continuing. What is the force that was missing a hundred years ago, that fuels the engine of the Northern Cities Shift today and keeps it moving? Since ongoing changes are the main focus of this work, it seems reasonable to attack the actuation problem through its counterpart, the continuation problem.

## 15.1 Continued change in the Philadelphia dialect

One question must be present in the mind of the reader who has followed the discussion so far. What is happening in Philadelphia today? Most of the data that has been analyzed here was gathered in the 1970s, over twenty years ago. Are the nearly completed changes finished? Do middle-range changes continue? Are the new and vigorous changes progressing further? Have the incipient changes been in fact realized? Surely the changes over the past twenty years would have something to tell us about the mechanism of change.

Chapter 4 of volume 1 reviewed various types of real-time studies and their results. Re-interviews of the same individual (panel studies) have not been as useful as drawing new samples (trend studies). The Linguistics Laboratory at the University of Pennsylvania has projected a second investigation of Philadelphia that would replicate the methods of the Philadelphia Neighborhood Study, but it must await the completion of the *Atlas of North American English*. In the meantime we can draw upon a number of sources to gain some insight into the present state of the city dialect, including the *Atlas* interviews.

## *The short a distribution*

Volume 1 laid out some of the issues concerning the complex and irregular split of historical short **a** into tense and lax forms. Chapter 18 concluded that this was a lexically conditioned rule, on the basis of Kiparsky's argument that changes in the rule over time had a rule-governed character. Current developments have justified that position.

In the 1970s, the active areas of change in the short **a** distribution were to be found before intervocalic /l/ and /n/. Chapter 13 of this volume summarized some of the recent developments in South Philadelphia, where children 3 to 5 years old have advanced the frequency of tensing in the favored word *planet*, and generally moved forward in the pattern of lexical diffusion (Roberts and Labov 1995). Banuazizi and Lipson studied tensing before /l/ in Port Richmond, a relatively conservative neighborhood in the working class areas of North Philadelphia (1998). They found that tensing before intervocalic and syllable-final /l/ has reached almost categorical status. The general hypothesis is that this addition of tensing environments is connected with the vocalization of /l/, though the issue is not entirely clear. In any case, the expansion of the tensing rule continues, as it has done since the broad **a** was first established before nasal clusters (chapter 18, volume 1).

## *Phonetic developments*

Our best information on the current vowel system comes from the *Atlas of North American English*, generated by the Telsur project at the Linguistics Laboratory at the University of Pennsylvania. Given the extraordinary range of vowel realizations that we have seen in the Philadelphia Neighborhood Study, it might seem impossible to describe the vowel system of a major city by drawing two telephone users at random, or six from a great metropolis. The uniformity and consistency of the regional dialects in the *Atlas* maps are the result of several factors:

- The upper working class and the lower middle class form the majority of the Euro-American population of North American cities.
- Telsur selects only local people born and raised in the city in question.[1] This further concentrates the pool of eligible people in the social classes of interest, since mobility is greatest in the upper middle class.
- The Telsur sample requires at least one woman between the ages of 20 and 40.

[1] "Born" is not quite accurate. People who came to the city before the age of 5 are admitted to the sample, on the basis of evidence such as that provided by Payne's work in King of Prussia (1976).

It goes without saying that some Telsur speakers will not represent the advancing wave of change, for all the reasons that have been documented in this volume. On the other hand, the Telsur sample in every large city includes speakers who are as advanced as any who have been encountered before, in Chicago, Detroit, Buffalo, Birmingham, or Knoxville. Given all that we know about Philadelphia, the results for that city will provide a test of the Telsur method as well as the methods of the LCV project.

### *The vowel systems of Telsur speakers*

Telsur subject #587 is Rosanne V., a 30-year-old woman who has all the social characteristics of a leader of linguistic change. She was interviewed in 1997 by Carol Orr. Her father was a welder, her mother a checker in the supermarket. She herself is now a registered nurse, and she is moving to the upper working class/lower middle class suburb of Upper Darby, adjoining the city to the northwest. Her vowel system would have been recognized as advanced if she had been recorded in 1977. Let us examine the system qualitatively to see if it has developed any new features or levels that were not found at that time.

Figure 15.1 displays the front upgliding vowels of Rosanne V., including two new and vigorous changes, (eyC) and (ay0). As far as (ay0) is concerned, Rosanne V. has the characteristic distinction of centralized /ay/ before voiceless consonants and a low nucleus elsewhere, somewhat fronted as is often the case with women. If Rosanne is typical of the 1990s, the

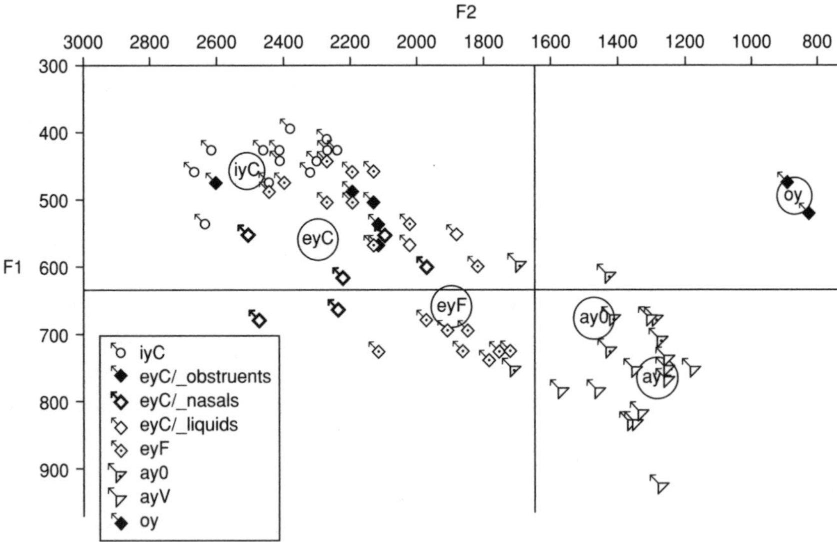


*Figure 15.1* Front upgliding vowels of Rosanne V., 30, Philadelphia, Telsur 587

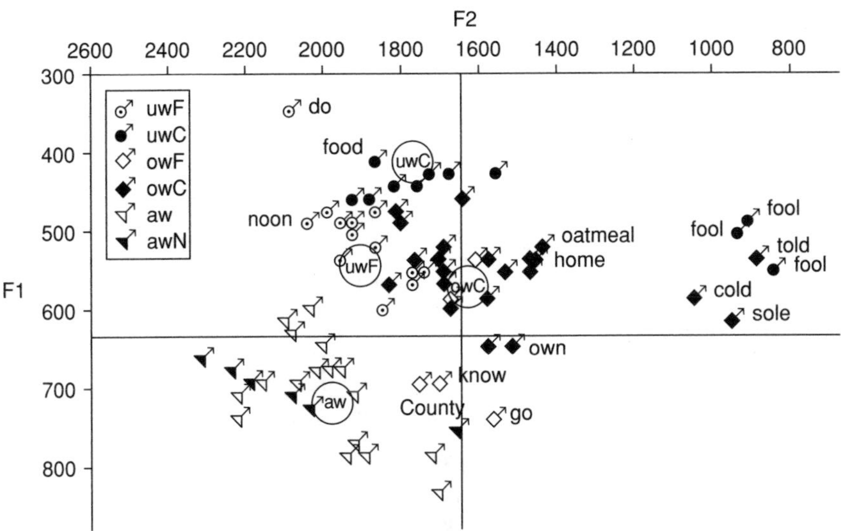


*Figure 15.2* Back upgliding vowels of Rosanne V., 30, Philadelphia

gap between males and females shown in figures 9.14–9.15 seems to have shrunk. In the front, (eyC) overlaps /iyC/, in a manner characteristic of advanced speakers. The /eyC/ tokens are subdivided according to the following segment, in a pattern that has not been observed before. All of the raised tokens are before obstruents (solid symbols). Tokens of /ey/ before nasals are much lower, in mid position, and considerably fronted (bold empty symbols). Throughout the *Atlas* records, one can observe a general Northern tendency to lower front vowels before nasals, but this splitting of (eyC) into two clear allophones redefines the variable. The raising is now a feature of /ey/ before obstruents, while /ey/ before resonants is at the level of /eyF/.[2] It remains to be seen how general is this redefinition in the Philadelphia community.

Figure 15.2 displays the back upgliding vowels, including the mid-range changes (uw) and (ow) as well as the new and vigorous change (aw). The (aw) pattern is not extreme, with nuclei located mostly below the midline. Vowels before nasals are not clearly distinguished from others. On the other hand, (uw) and (ow) show a pattern distinct from that found in the 1970s in Philadelphia. It is not unusual to find /iw/ and /uwF/ front of center, though here they are not as far front as in many Southern dialects. Checked /uw/ and /ow/ are brought forward to fully central position, a configuration characteristic of the South Midland. The gap between the

[2] Here raising is being tracked along the front diagonal. If we continue the analysis of second formant values alone, then nasals are roughly at a level with the obstruents, and vowels before /l/ are further back, as usual. However, the overlap with /iyC/ involves both formants.

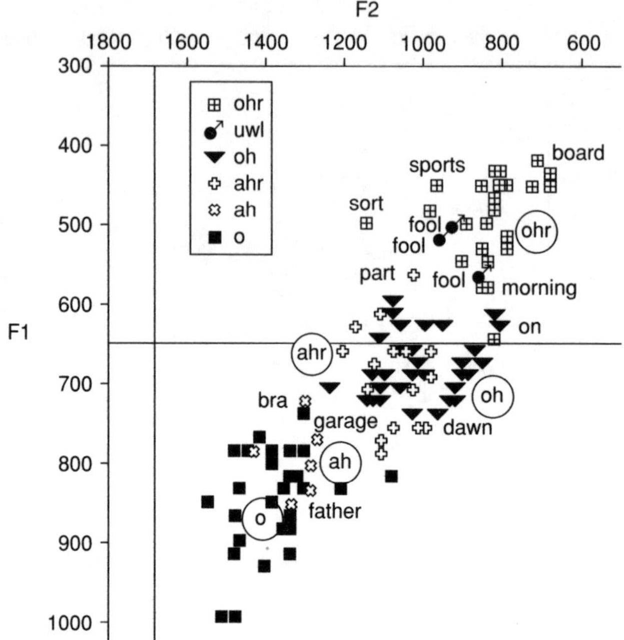


*Figure 15.3* Back vowels before /r/ of Rosanne V., Philadelphia

fronted vowels and those before /l/ is about 500 Hz; in the Philadelphia systems of the 1970s, this space is filled with the checked allophones.

In Rosanne V.'s speech, there is no longer the clear differentiation of checked and free /ow/ that predominated in the 1970s. The slower allophone appears to have caught up with the faster one in F2 terms. For both /ey/ and /ow/, the difference between checked and free is largely a matter of height.

Philadelphia is undergoing the well-known chain shift of back vowels before /r/:

/ahr/ → /ohr/ → /uhr/

The first stage of this process was completed in the 1970s; the advance of /ahr/ to a low back vowel was then a constant for all Philadelphia speakers. The raising of /ohr/ to /uhr/ was a nearly completed change at that time,[3] but some speakers did not show /ohr/ in fully high position, and there was a small age coefficient. In figure 15.3, /ohr/ is solidly established in high back position. Though no tokens of /uhr/ are available here, most /ohr/ tokens are well above the level of /uw/ before /l/, which defines high back position.

[3] As in all other Midland cities, Philadelphia had an absolute merger of /owr/ and /ohr/, so that "/ohr/" here represents both word classes.

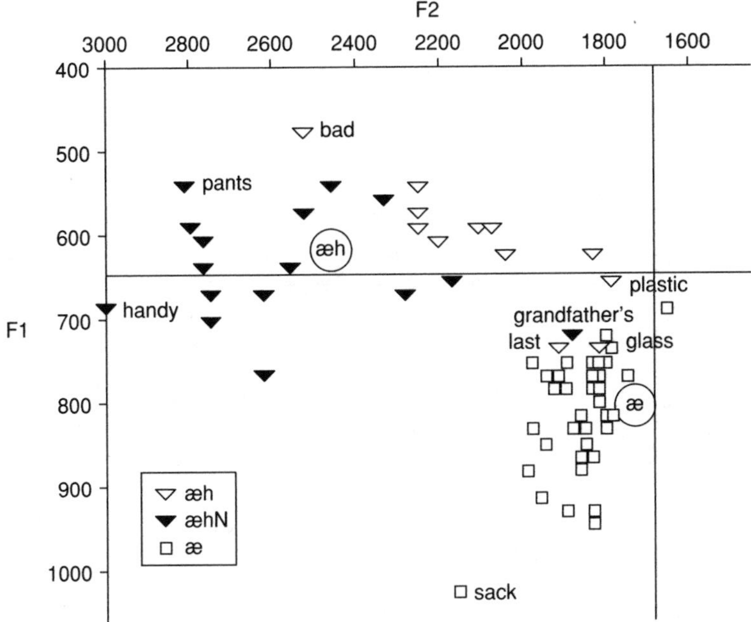


*Figure 15.4* Short **a** distribution of Rosanne V., Philadelphia

It is also evident that the nucleus of /ahr/ is identified with the nucleus of /oh/, while /ah/ in *father*, *bra*, *garage*, is identified with /o/.

The short **a** pattern of Rosanne V. shows no striking innovations. The separation between tense /æh/ and lax /æ/ shown in figure 15.4 is quite clean. Just as in the system of Carol Meyers, several tense vowels with strongly disfavoring segmental environment abut on the lax /æ/ group: *grandfather*, *last*, and *glass*. If these fell in the lax category, they would be in its lower right region. The word *plastic*, which was variable in the 1970s, is here in the tense category, with the lowered and backed position appropriate to an initial obstruent cluster and a following syllable. Among the tense vowels, one can remark that the separation of the vowels before nasals and others is more complete than we are used to seeing in the 1970s.

Among the linguistic changes in progress in Philadelphia in the 1970s, several were rated "incipient." Their age coefficients were not significant, and there were no signs of them in earlier reports, but they indicated coordinated movements in a direction that was logically tied to developments within the system. The lowering of the short front vowels, /i/, /e/, and /æ/, is a pattern now known as the *Canadian shift* (Clarke et al. 1995) from its strong realization among young speakers in Canada. For reasons that are still not clear, Philadelphia has partially resigned from the South and joined itself to northern patterns.

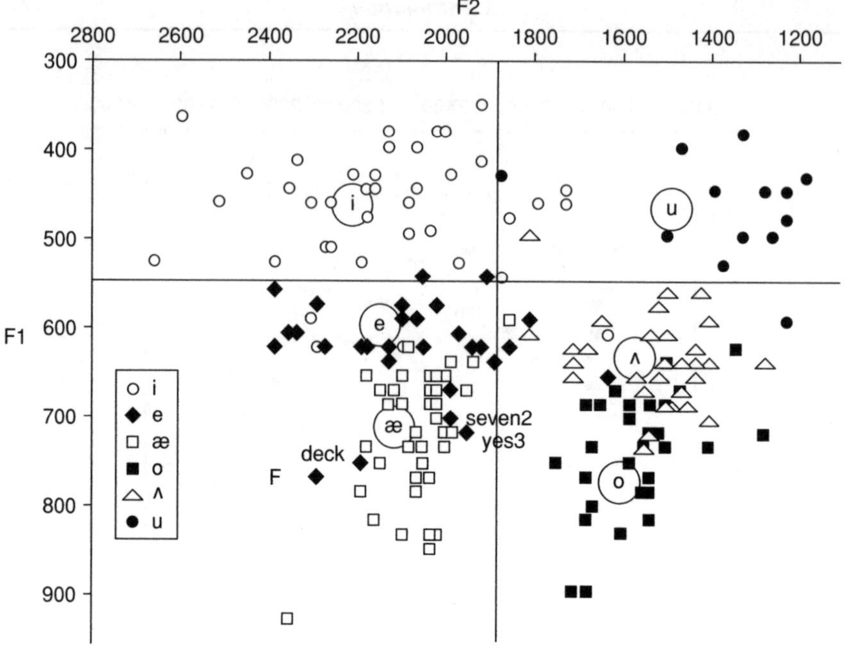


*Figure 15.5* Short vowels of Rosanne V., Philadelphia

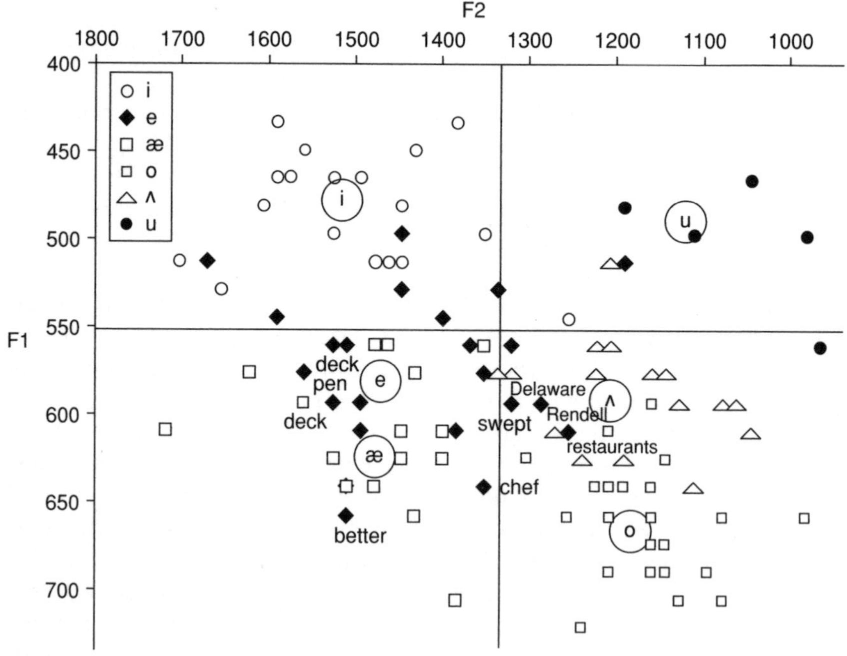


*Figure 15.6* Short vowels of Jackson O., 28, Philadelphia

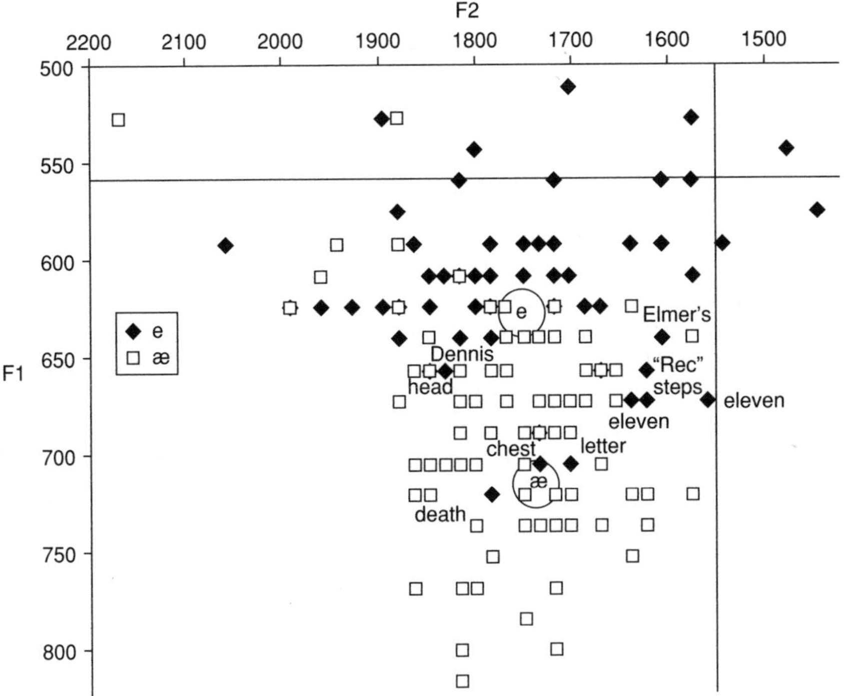


*Figure 15.7* Lowering of /e/ in the vowel system of Chris G., 22, Philadelphia

The strongest of these incipient changes is the lowering of /e/, as may be seen in figure 4.8. The study of natural misunderstandings in Philadelphia in the 1980s and 1990s has gathered a number of examples of the lowering of /e/ leading to confusion with /æ/, as in *laughed* for *left*. Explicit evidence appears in figure 15.5, a detailed display of the short vowels of Rosanne V. The majority of the /e/ tokens are in lower mid position, but four are clearly shifted into low position: *F*, *deck*, *seven*, and *yes*. The same development is seen in an even more striking fashion in another Telsur subject from Philadelphia, Jackson O. Figure 15.6 shows the short vowel system of this speaker. The mean position of the three front vowels clearly shows that /e/ has descended and overlapped considerably with /æ/. Four tokens of /e/ appear in low position, in the midst of the /æ/ pattern: *better*, *chef*, two of *pen*, and two of *deck* – the same word that appears in this position in figure 15.5. (The other low tokens of /e/ are strongly centralized in accordance with their phonetic environment.)

Perhaps the most detailed and careful study of any Philadelphia speaker was carried out recently on the vowel system of a young man, Chris G., from North Philadelphia, who works in Penn's buildings and grounds department. Figure 15.7 plots the distributions of /e/ and /æ/ at twice the scale of the other diagrams in this chapter. The lowering of /e/ into the /æ/ area is evidenced in simple monosyllables: *head, chest, death, steps, Rec,* as well as polysyllables: *eleven, letter, Elmer's.* This downward movement of /e/ matches the strongest lowering tendencies recorded for /e/ in Chicago (Labov, Yaeger, and Steiner 1972, figure 23). There is every reason to believe that the incipient lowering of /e/ in the regression equations of the 1970s has matured into a new and vigorous change in the 1990s, though we do not yet have enough speakers to be sure.

Chris G. showed a second feature that may or may not prove to be general in the future of the Philadelphia dialect. Tensed short **a** before nasals, (æhN), seems to have reached the limits of raising and fronting for many speakers of the 1970s. These nuclei are upper mid, rather than high, in Chris G.'s system. Quite a few of them have lost the inglide, and so become homonymous with /eyC/. In Chris's speech, *tan* clearly rhymes with *stain.*

A complete re-study of Philadelphia speech is needed if we were to determine just which of the sound changes studied in this volume have continued to develop, and which have not. However, some strong lines of continuation have been indicated:

1 Lexical diffusion in the short **a** class has continued: words with short **a** in open syllables before /n/ and /l/ have been added to the tense category.
2 The raising of /ohr/ has moved closer to completion, with consequent merger with /uwr/.
3 The middle-range fronting of checked /uwC/ and /owC/ has moved forward to fully central position, decreasing or eliminating the distance between checked and free vowels.
4 The incipient lowering of /e/ has become a fully realized change in progress.

### *The role of outliers in the Philadelphia sound changes*

Chapter 14 advanced the idea that outliers play a major role in the development of sound change: that they are the main objects of socially motivated projection. Figure 15.2 shows the prominence of a single token of *do* in the fronting of (uwF) by Rosanne V., as well as the leading position of *know* and *go* in the lowering and fronting of (owF). Though the raising of (æh) is almost complete in Philadelphia, *bad* and *pants* emerge as outliers in figure 15.4. A single token of *sack* holds the same position at the other end of the distribution, suggesting that the incipient lowering of (æ) has become a reality. But it is in the early stages of change that the role of outliers is truly prominent, and the lowering of (e) in Philadelphia illustrates this process. In figure 15.5, *deck* and the letter *F* are lowered well into the /æ/ range, with no obvious phonetic motivation. In figure 15.6, the *better* and *chef* of Jackson O. are well below the mean for /æ/. In figure

15.7, *death* and *chest* are well separated from the main body of the /e/ distribution. There is nothing in the phonetic environment of these nuclei that leads to higher F1 values; as fully stressed monosyllables, they seem to point toward a target that has only recently been realized in the Philadelphia speech community. These examples call for a systematic study of the role of outliers in linguistic change, the topic of the following section.

## 15.2 The incrementation of sound change in North America

The Philadelphia community has served as a useful platform for this inquiry into the causes of change since it includes many different stages in the life history of change. To trace the role of outliers with greater precision, we need to see the same variable as incipient, new and vigorous, middle-range, and nearly completed. The data created by the Telsur project for the *Atlas of North American English* will serve this purpose if we can locate a set of changes that are moving in the same direction across the entire continent. Changes like the Northern Cities Shift or the Southern Shift, that move different dialects in opposite directions, will not do for this purpose. The raising and tensing of /æ/ was once quite general throughout the USA, but is showing clear evidence of reversal in several regions. The most promising sound changes for this purpose are the fronting of /uw/ and /ow/; this process is general throughout North America and shows minimal evidence of movement in a contrary direction.

To study the fronting of these vowels on a large scale, this section will draw upon the data base of 110,000 measurements of the vowel systems of 361 subjects of the Telsur project. For each individual system, the data is more plentiful and more accurate than that provided for the Philadelphia Neighborhood Study, since techniques of measurement and knowledge of sound change have both advanced considerably in the interim.[4] The 361 vowel systems have been plotted, normalized, and analyzed by the Plotnik program. The normalized data is then extracted, combining data for any set of vowels or allophones for all 361 speakers into a single file of three thousand to ten thousand tokens. In this file, each token is accompanied by demographic information extracted from the Telsur files, including the gender and age of the speaker, the population of the speech community, and the dialect region as determined by the geographic analysis of the *Atlas*. The resultant data set then yields a number of critical statistics for the fronting of F2 in each dialect: means,

[4] The value of this data is largely due to the skill and phonetic understanding of Charles Boberg, who did the great majority of the measurements for the Telsur project in the years 1994–8. Maciej Baranowski contributed significantly to this data base in the two following years.

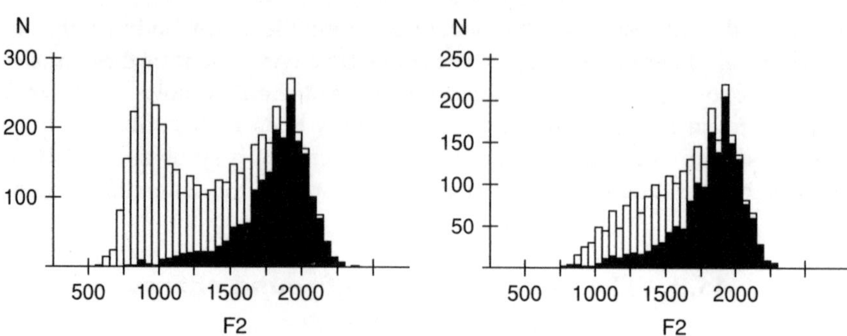


*Figure 15.8* Left: Bimodal distribution of all /uw/ in North America (solid columns: coronal onsets). Right: Distribution of /uw/ excluding vowels before /l/ (solid columns: coronal onsets)

standard deviations, skewness, range, maxima and minima. Finally, the formant data for each vowel is submitted to regression analysis to determine the effect of age, gender, population size, and other social variables on the degree of fronting, as well as a wide variety of internal, phonetic constraints. The Telsur sample provides considerable age variation, since at least one speaker from the 20–40 age range and the 40–60 age range was interviewed in every community. The Telsur sample was not stratified by social class, but there is sufficient variation to show significant effects of occupation and education.

In this process, /uw/ is divided into two distinct allophones. The nuclei of syllables with coronal onsets (*two*, *do*, *noon*, *shoes*, etc.) are fronted to a far greater extent than the complementary set with non-coronal onsets (in *roof*, *boots*, *coop*, *coo*, etc.). Figure 15.8 (left) displays the striking bimodal character of the distribution of /uw/ as a whole. The coronal onset allophones occupy the great bulk of the higher mode, and the non-coronal onsets the lower mode. The bimodal character of this distribution is due to allophones before /l/, which do not participate in the fronting process (except for a moderate shift in some Southern dialects). Figure 15.8 (right) is a histogram of /uw/ with vowels before /l/ excluded. There is now a single mode in front position at 1900 Hz, but the striking differentiation of coronal and non-coronal allophones remains clear.[5]

The question then remains as to whether this global fronting of /uw/ and /ow/ follows the same social pattern as the new and vigorous changes

[5] To this point, /uw/ and /ow/ have been presented as divided into checked and free variables, (uwC) and (owC) vs. (uwF) and (owF). In Philadelphia, this distinction is quite powerful, but it does not prove to have equal weight for these two vowels for most other dialects. For the majority of dialects, the coronal/non-coronal distinction is the predominant factor for /uw/, and slightly outweighs free vs. checked for /ow/.

*Table 15.1* Regression analysis of F2 of 2619 (uw) tokens not before /l/

| | *Coefficient* | *Prob. for t* |
|---|---|---|
| Constant | 1557 | ≤0.0001 |
| Phonetic factors | | |
| Coronal onset | 357 | ≤0.0001 |
| Final | 70 | ≤0.0001 |
| Social factors | | |
| Age | −3.6 | ≤0.0001 |
| Southern region | 112 | ≤0.0001 |
| Northern region | −233 | ≤0.0001 |
| Women, occ > 40 | 44 | ≤0.0001 |
| Men, occ < 30 | 77 | 0.0022 |

in Philadelphia that have been at the central focus of this work. Chapter 8 demonstrated that the leading position of women in new sound changes was not limited to Philadelphia but was also characteristic of the great changes sweeping across the Inland North. The results of our close examination of Philadelphia will be further strengthened if there are indications of similar forces operating in sound changes that affect all of North America. It is not likely that these global events will exactly match the configuration of local phenomena like the Philadelphia treatment of (aw) or (eyC). One must also bear in mind that the social correlations for (ow) were moderate and for (uw), almost non-existent.

A total of 5005 measured tokens of /uw/ are available for analysis in the Telsur data. Setting aside the sizeable number of vowels collected before /l/, table 15.1 displays the results of a regression analysis of 2619 tokens of /uw/.

The largest single factor in this table is coronal onset, which shows a 357 Hz advantage in F2 over non-coronal onsets. (This sub-class of /uw/ will be referred to henceforth as /Tuw/, as opposed to /Kuw/ for the same vowel with non-coronal onsets.) Absolute final position contributes a moderate increment: words like *too*, *do* are significantly in advance of words like *noon* and *toot*. Among the social factors, there appears a powerful overall trend in apparent time, fronting increasing with decreasing age. This factor is of the same order of magnitude as the new and vigorous changes in Philadelphia: speakers who are 50 years different in age will show 175 Hz difference in their raising of F2. The next two factors in table 15.1 refer to large regional groupings of North American dialects that will be displayed in detail below: it is evident that the South is considerably ahead, and the North considerably behind in the fronting process. Finally, the table indicates a significant interaction of gender and social class. The occupational scale used here is much more detailed than that of the Philadelphia study. It is an application of the NORC 100-point scale of occupational prestige originally developed by Duncan (1961) and updated by Nakao and Treas (1990, 1992). Women whose occupational rating is higher than 40 favor the fronting of (uw) by a moderate amount, but with a t-test probability as low as any other factor. In addition there is an unexpected positive factor for men with low occupational ratings, which turns out ultimately to be specific to the Northern region. It indicates an interaction between gender, social class, and geography that goes beyond the scope of this presentation. On the whole, table 15.1 indicates that the fronting of /uw/ is a variable (uw) with sociolinguistic conditioning similar to but not identical with the Philadelphia sound changes.

While the separation of /uw/ and /ow/ before /l/ is a qualitative phenomenon, the distinctions among American dialects in the fronting of both vowels are quantitative. Nevertheless, they provide the simplest and most systematic way of organizing the major dialect groups of North America. Figure 15.9 plots (Tuw) and (Tow) – the mean second formants of /uw/ and /ow/ after coronal onsets for all North American dialects.[6] The dialects are those identified by the *Atlas of North American English*, largely on the basis of qualitative features.[7] The relative degree of fronting of the two vowels establishes three major dialect clusters which are also well defined geographically.

In figure 15.9, two local urban dialects define the two extreme positions.[8] At lower right is Providence, with back positions of both (Tuw) and (Tow) – 1338 and 1081 respectively. At upper left is Charleston, with the maximum fronting of both vowels, at 1990 for (Tuw) and 1739 for (Tow). In the middle right part of the diagram is a group of four Northern dialects that show moderate fronting of (Tuw) but relatively little for (Tow): in increasing order of (Tow), the North Central States (1172), the Inland North (1202), Northern New England including the Maritime Provinces (1264), and Southern New England (1296).

At the top of figure 15.9 is a series of dialects that all show strong fronting of (Tuw) but with a wide range for (Tow). Canada is at upper right; the 1144 value for (Tow) is not much higher than that of Providence. The Western region is considerably more advanced, with (Tow) of 1306.

[6] Since /uw/ with coronal onsets is quite distinct from the non-coronal group, a comparison of /uw/ and /ow/ should use only vowels after coronal onsets for both, even though the distinction between coronal and non-coronal is not as sharp for /ow/ as it is for /uw/.

[7] The Inland North is defined by the front–back alignment of /e/ and /o/, and the reversal of relative height and fronting of /e/ and /ey/; the Mid-Atlantic States are defined by the existence of a lexical split of the short **a** class; the South is defined by monophthongization of /ay/ finally and before obstruents.

[8] All values of the (Tuw) and (Tow) variables in the following discussion are mean values of the second formant in Hz.

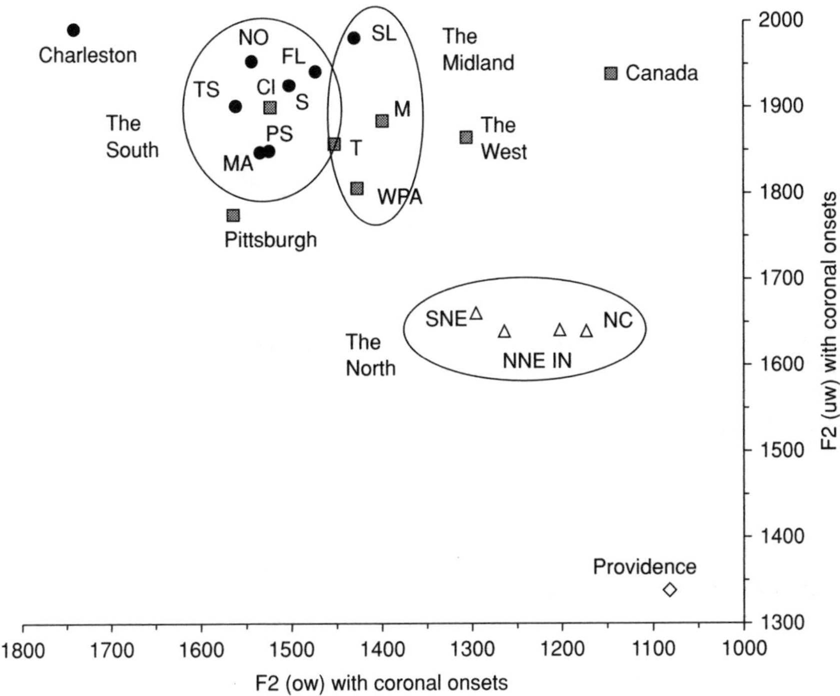


*Figure 15.9* Fronting of /uw/ and /ow/ after coronal onsets for all North American dialects. The North: SNE: Southern New England; NNE: Northern New England and the Maritime Provinces; IN: Inland North; NC: North Central. The Midland: SL: St Louis; CI: Cincinnati; WPA: Western Pennsylvania; T: Transitional; M: the balance of the Midland. The South: NO: New Orleans; FL: Florida; PS: Piedmont South; TS: Texas South; MA: Mid-Atlantic; S: balance of the South

Still further to the left are a group of Midland dialects: St Louis, Western Pennsylvania (not including Pittsburgh), and the main body of Midland dialects marked "M." For the Midland, fronting of (Tow) is distinctly less than for the large group of Southern dialects, where values center around 1500. Cincinnati, the Midland dialect which most closely adjoins the South, is located in the middle of the Southern group. Pittsburgh is unique in showing a relatively high degree of fronting of (Tow) compared to (Tuw) – 1564 vs. 1774. A set of dialects marked "T" for "Transitional" is located exactly on the border between the Midland and the South. These transitional dialects are exactly those that fall geographically in such an area.

Figure 15.9 shows that the fronting of (Tow) follows behind the fronting of (Tuw) for all communities, but that North American dialects fall into a small number of discrete types in the relative advancement of these two sound changes.

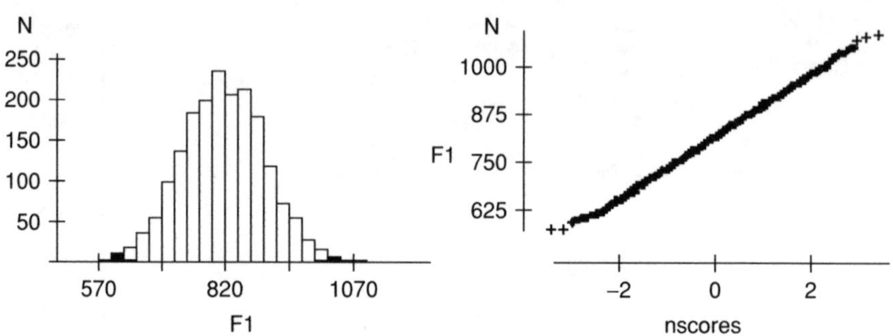


*Figure 15.10* Normal distribution for F1 of (o) in the Midland dialect region. Left: Histogram of 1912 tokens. Mean: 816 Hz. Median: 816 Hz. Std deviation: 82 Hz. Skewness: 0.045. Kurtosis: −0.08. Solid columns: outliers (> 2.5 std dev. from the mean). Right: Normal probability plot for the same data

## *Skewing*

For a vowel that is not involved in change in progress the distribution of formant values approximates the normal curve, as shown for the normalized first formant of /o/ in the Midland region in figure 5.10. The left-hand side is a histogram showing the symmetrical bell-shaped curve. In such symmetrical distributions, the median is equivalent to the mean. When data fits the normal distribution closely, the normal probability plot is a straight line, as shown on the right-hand side of figure 15.10.

Two measures of fit to the normal distribution are *skewness* and *kurtosis*. Kurtosis is a measure of the relative steepness or shallowness of the curve; in figure 15.10 it approximates zero. It will not play a role in the discussion to follow. The parameter that will be most important in tracing the path and mechanism of sound change is *skewness*, a measure of the left–right symmetry of the tails of the distribution. It is defined in terms of the second and third moments around the mean.

2nd moment: $$m_2 = \frac{1}{n}\sum x_i^2 - \bar{x}^2$$

3rd moment: $$m_3 = \frac{1}{n}\sum x_i^3 - \frac{3}{n}\bar{x}\sum x_i^2 + 2\bar{x}^3$$

Skewness: $$\gamma_1 = \frac{m_3}{m_2^{3/2}}$$

Positive values of skewness are associated with a larger tail to the right, with an excess of higher values. Negative skewness indicates the opposite: a larger tail to the left, with an excess of lower values.

Positive or negative skewing is not equivalent to the presence of outliers. Skewing is a quantitative concept, while *outlier* is essentially qualitative. In

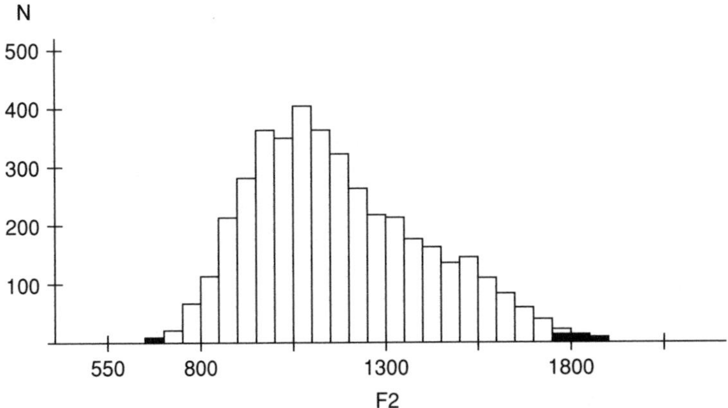


*Figure 15.11* Distribution of (Kow) tokens for all dialects combined. Mean: 1175 Hz. Median: 1135 Hz. Skewness: 0.533. n = 4231. Solid columns indicate outliers

figure 15.10, outliers are defined as tokens in the highest and lowest 1% of the distribution, which places them more than 2.5 standard deviations from the mean. Their distribution can be seen to be symmetrical in figure 15.10. In fact there are exactly 19 high outliers and 19 low outliers. Outliers can also be identified by a discontinuity between them and the main distribution, which increases their salience for the observer. Such outliers often represent errors in measurement. In the Telsur data, outliers are routinely checked by comparing auditory impressions with other nearby vowel tokens. There are no clear discontinuities in figure 15.10; seven clear errors have been removed by this process.

The investigation of fronting will maintain the coronal vs. non-coronal onset distinction for /ow/ as well as /uw/, though it does not divide /ow/ as sharply as it does /uw/. Four variables are therefore involved in this process: (Tuw), (Kuw), (Tow), and (Kow), where "T" indicates coronal onset and "K" indicates non-coronal onset. The least advanced process is the fronting of (Kow). Figure 15.11 is a histogram of (owC) values, with solid columns again indicating outliers beyond 2.5 standard deviations. There is clearly skewing to the right. The mean is considerably higher than the median, and the skewness index is .533. There are 42 high outliers but only 11 low outliers.

Such positive skewing is characteristic of much of the data to be examined, and it will be important to follow its implications for our inquiry into the forces operating in linguistic change. Four different factors may account for the excess of outliers in one direction or the other:

1 Physiological limitations. When the articulation of a phoneme is close to the physiological (and acoustic) limits of possible vowel production,

there will be fewer outliers in the direction of those limits and more in the other direction on any given dimension.

2 Phonetic limitations. When the duration of a vowel nucleus is limited due to reduced stress, or the presence of complex codas or following syllables, the realization of the vowel falls short of the target. Such vowels are frequently found in a more centralized position while the target for fully stressed monosyllables is closer to the periphery. Since Telsur data includes only vowels with primary stress, the main effects to be noted here will be the segmental environment: the complexity of the coda and the number of following syllables (see table 18.1 of volume 1).
3 Structural asymmetry. When a phoneme has an asymmetrical set of neighbors, the functional economy of the vowel system favors more outliers in the direction where the nearest neighbor is more distant, according to the mechanism outlined in chapter 20 of volume 1:586–8.
4 Socially motivated projection. As suggested in the last chapter, certain outliers may be perceived as more representative of the main tendency of the variable than the modal values, and so increase in number.

In order to see which factors are responsible for skewing, and investigate the relation of skewness to linguistic change, it will be helpful to examine relative skewness for each regional dialect as it is involved in the fronting of /uw/ and /ow/. A series of scatterplots will display the relationships between the advancement of the change and skewing for all dialects of figure 15.9, with mean F2 on the horizontal axis and the skewness index on the vertical axis. The abscissa will be expanded to the minimum and maximum F2 values in the entire data set, so that the horizontal position of a dialect places it in the range of possible changes.

Figure 15.12 is a plot of F2 vs. skewing for (Kow). As in other diagrams to follow, there is a main distribution leading from upper right to lower left. The diagram yields a striking negative correlation between the advancement of the sound change and skewness: in this case, r = –.77. The majority of the dialects show positive skewing, starting with Northern dialects, clustered around .5; the seven more advanced dialects, Southern, Mid-Atlantic, and Pittsburgh (PI), show negative skewing. The relation of this vigorous progression to the mechanism of change will be the major topic of this section.

The F2 value is not the only indication of a relation between skewness and change. In these diagrams, bold labels represent dialects with significant negative regression coefficients for age, indicating increased fronting in apparent time. Italic symbols represent the reverse: positive age coefficients that indicate a movement to backer vowels with younger speakers. The most conservative dialect in figure 15.12, the North Central states, shows such

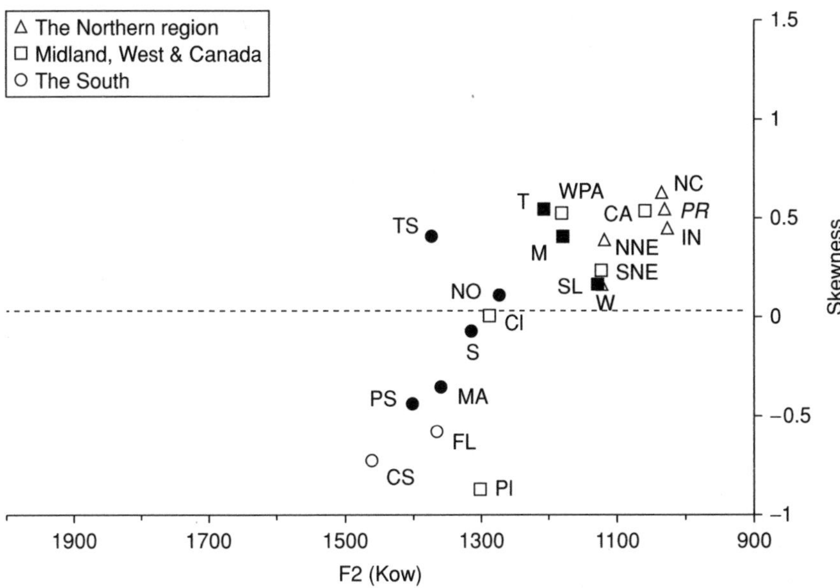


*Figure 15.12* The relation between skewing and fronting of (ow) after non-coronal onsets for 20 regional dialects. $r^2 = -.77$. Solid symbols: significant negative age coefficients. Italic labels: significant positive age coefficients

*Table 15.2* Number of speakers in each *ANAE* dialect

| *Dialect* | *Symbol* | *No. speakers* |
|---|---|---|
| Providence | PR | 3 |
| Northern N.E. | NNE | 17 |
| North Central | NC | 36 |
| Inland North | IN | 61 |
| Southern N.E. | SNE | 6 |
| Pittsburgh | PI | 3 |
| Western PA | WPA | 8 |
| Transitional | T | 13 |
| West | W | 45 |
| Canada | CA | 15 |
| Midland | M | 72 |
| Cincinnati | CI | 5 |
| St Louis | SL | 4 |
| Mid-Atlantic | MA | 12 |
| Texas South | TS | 8 |
| Piedmont South | PS | 17 |
| South | S | 27 |
| Florida | FL | 4 |
| New Orleans | NO | 2 |
| Charleston | CS | 3 |
| Total | | 361 |

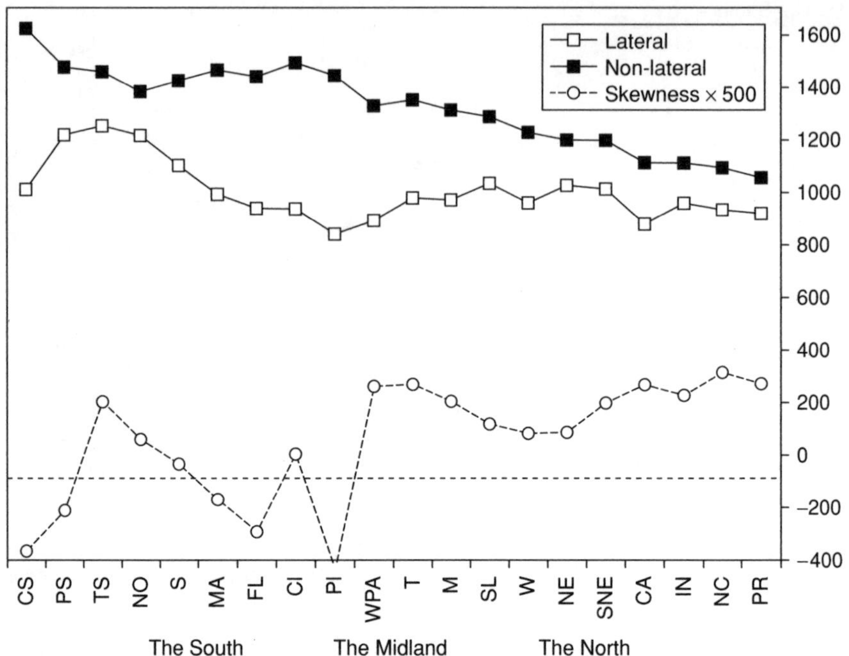


*Figure 15.13* The relation of (Kow) to /ow/ vowels before /l/, compared to skewness (× 500) for 20 North American dialects. Vertical axis represents mean F2 in Hz for (Kow)

a retrograde movement, but it is the only case. A belt of dialects show change in apparent time from Texas South and the West down to Charleston (CS). Only one of the advanced dialects does not: Pittsburgh.[9]

Among the factors that may influence the skewness of (Kow), the first – physiological limitations of the system – must be considered, since for most dialects (Kow) is close to the back periphery of phonological space. The position of this physiological limit is indicated by the allophone of (Kow) before /l/, which in all except the Southern dialects remains in fully backed position. In all of the calculations presented so far, /ow/ vowels before /l/ are excluded from (Tow) and (Kow). The allophones before /l/ will be referred to below as (owl).

Figure 15.13 shows the mean values of /ow/ vowels before /l/ compared to all others. For the five conservative Northern dialects and Canada, the two means are quite close, only about 100 Hz apart. Beginning with the West and the Midland, the value of non-lateral (Kow) rises steadily, while (owl) remains below 1000 Hz, and in fact show remarkably lower values

[9] Significance of age coefficients must be related to the size of the sample as well as the size of the effect; table 15.2 can be consulted in this respect.

*Table 15.3* Regression coefficients for (Kow) for 3062 vowels for all dialects

| *Variable* | *Coefficient* | *t-prob* |
|---|---|---|
| Constant | 1149 | ≤0.0001 |
| Age | −1.1 | 0.0001 |
| Following nasal | −48 | 0.0044 |
| Following voiced segment | 79 | ≤0.0001 |
| Following apical place | −61 | ≤0.0001 |
| Complex coda | 44 | 0.0048 |
| Simple monosyllables | 137 | ≤0.0001 |

for Pittsburgh and Western Pennsylvania while the main body of (Kow) vowels shows fronter values. The Southern dialects show somewhat higher values for (Kow), but (owl) rises sharply. For the most advanced Southern dialects – the Piedmont South and Texas South – the distance between the (Kow) and the (owl) is no greater than for the Northern dialects. For Charleston, this situation is sharply reversed, with maximum values for (Kow) and minimum for (owl). The maximum mean distance between (Kow) and (owl) is found in Western Pennsylvania, Pittsburgh, and Cincinnati, amounting to 500 Hz.

The dashed line in figure 15.13 shows the skewness for each dialect for (Kow) (multiplied by 500). Where skewness is most strongly positive, the (Kow) values are close to (owl), indicating that they are near the maximum limit for back vowels, and as distance increases, skewness declines. This is consistent with the simple mechanical factor that the direction of skewing is the product of distance from the periphery. There is simply more room for tokens to deviate from the mean in the upper tail than the lower tail.

Table 15.3 gives the results of a regression analysis of the factors that favor or disfavor the fronting of 3062 tokens of (Kow). The constant of 1149 Hz indicates a moderately back starting position. A significant age factor of −1.1 shows a moderate change in apparent time: an advance of 55 Hz for a speaker 15 years old over a speaker 65 years old. The effect of a following nasal is the reverse of that found for front vowels: it shifts a vowel 48 Hz toward the back periphery. Among these environmental effects, the largest is the 137 Hz advantage for simple monosyllables: an important factor to be borne in mind when we consider the mechanism of this sound change.

Figure 15.14 displays the pattern for (Kuw), the corresponding set of /uw/ vowels after non-coronals in *roof*, *boots*, *coo*, *move*, etc. The range of F2 values for this variable is approximately the same as for (Kow). All but four dialects show positive skewing, but the same linear pattern appears,

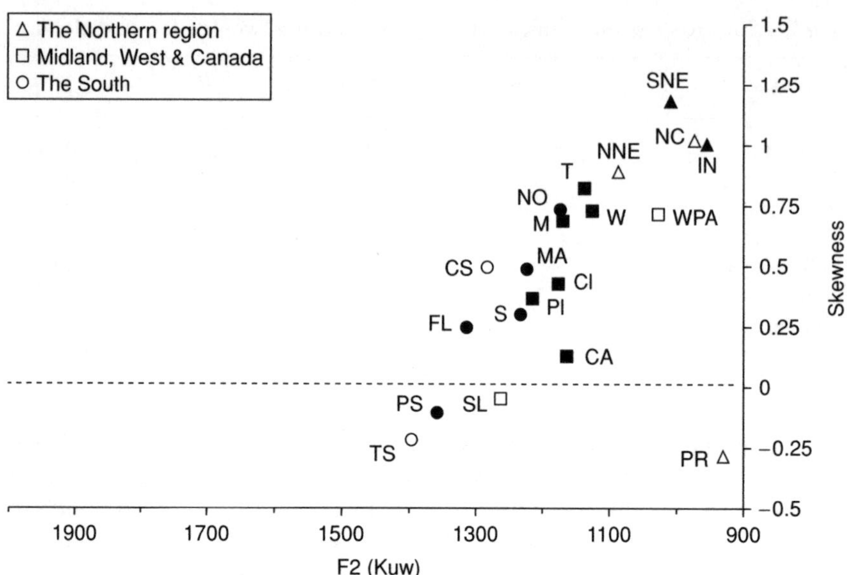


*Figure 15.14* The relationship of skewing to the advancement of (Kuw) for 20 North American dialects. Solid symbols: significant negative age coefficients

increasing F2 correlated with falling skewness (r = −.56).[10] The number of dialects that show significant age correlations is greater than with (Kow): 13 of the 20 dialects.

Figures 15.12–15.14 show that the positive tail develops in the early stages of fronting, as a few favoring forms lead the change with increasing F2. As the change progresses, there is an increasing development of the negative tail with lower F2. This follows naturally from the simple physical consequences of moving away from the periphery.

Figure 15.15a presents the relation between skewing and advancement of variable (Tow) in *no, know, toast,* etc. At first glance, the distribution of dialects appears to be altogether different from that of figures 15.12 and 15.14. There is no longer a linear relationship between the F2 of the variable and the decline of skewing. On the contrary, many dialects with advanced values of (Tow) are close to zero on the skewing axis. The picture becomes clearer if one notes that the Midland and Transitional dialects occupy a narrow vertical ellipse in the central portion of the diagram. If these are removed the picture is considerably clearer, as in figure 15.15b. The conservative dialects are grouped at upper right: Canada with the least

[10] The fact that the r-correlation is lower is entirely due to the one aberrant value for Providence. Without Providence, the Pearson r-correlation is −.88.

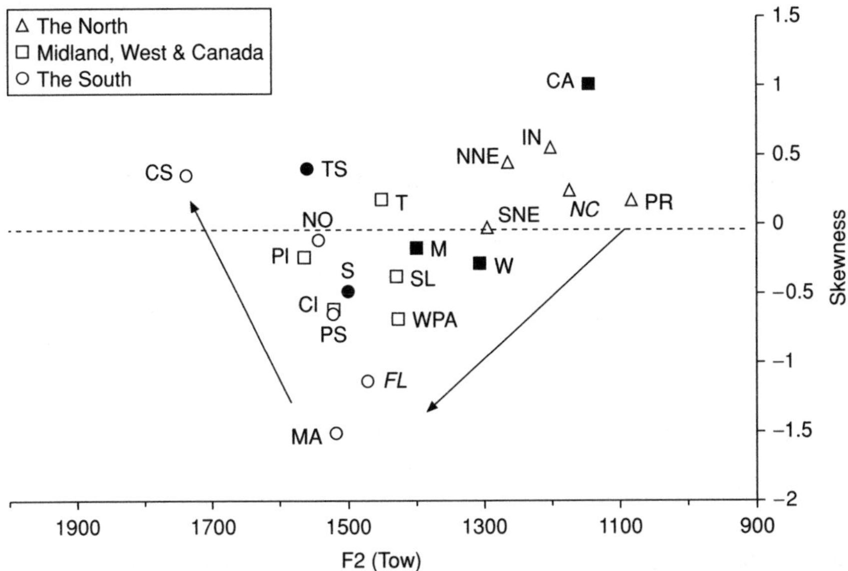


*Figure 15.15a* The relation between skewing and fronting of (Tow) for 20 regional dialects. Solid symbols: significant negative age coefficients. Italic labels: significant positive age coefficients

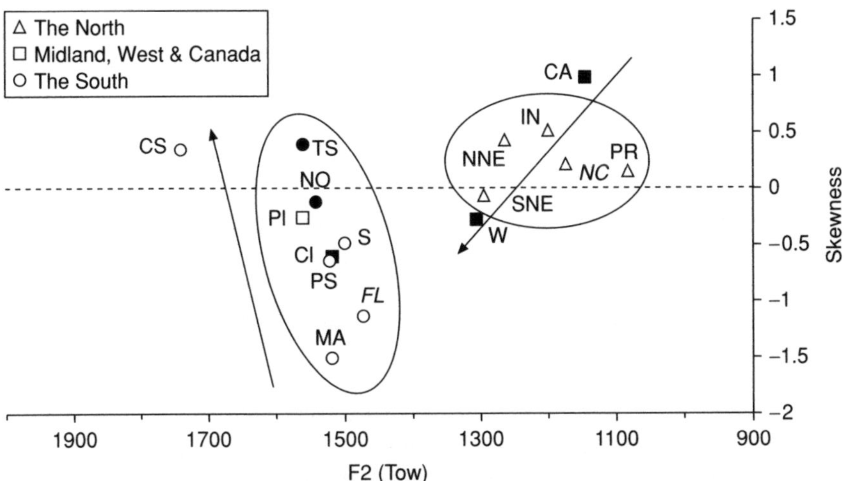


*Figure 15.15b* The relation between skewing and fronting of (Tow) with Midland and Transitional dialects removed

fronting and most positive skewness; then four of the Northern dialects, all with slightly less positive skewing, but with varying degrees of a moderate fronting; and SNE and the West, further along on the usual path of increased fronting and decreased skewness. The Southern dialects form a completely different pattern. A series that begins with the Mid-Atlantic and ends with Texas South follows a near-linear progression with a steady diminution in negative skewing until there is no significant skewing at all. The r-correlation of this line is positive: .66, and the slope of the line is .016; as F2 increases by 100 Hz, skewing increases by 1.6.

As in other diagrams, Charleston occupies an isolated position at upper left.

It is not difficult to interpret the new pattern shown by (Tow). It is considerably more advanced than (Kow) or (Kuw) and reveals the later stages of the fronting process. This pattern indicates a four-step process:

1 Fronting begins with a group of outliers which skew the distribution heavily in the direction of the change.
2 As the change proceeds, a larger and larger proportion of tokens is shifted in this direction until symmetry is restored.
3 As the change approaches some limiting value, the number of advanced outliers decreases, so that the less favored tokens form a tail skewed in the direction opposite to the change.
4 When the change is completed, the less advanced forms join the main body, producing once again a symmetrical normal distribution.

The pattern is analogous to the distribution of runners in a race: at the start, everyone is bunched together and one cannot distinguish the fast runners from the slow; in the middle of the race they are spread out according to their inherent speeds; at the end, they are gathered together just as they were at the beginning.

The final diagram in this series is the relationship of skewing to the fronting of the most advanced variable, (Tuw) in *do*, *two*, etc. The entire configuration is shifted well to the left in figure 15.16. Even the most conservative dialect, Providence, has (Tuw) at 1300 Hz, and a sizeable number of the Southern dialects have means above 1900 Hz, which is in the region of cardinal [ü].

The bifurcated configuration of figure 15.15 is here repeated with even greater clarity. The five conservative dialects are lined up to the right, and show a progression downwards towards the Transitional dialects, an r-correlation of –.87. The Midland, Canada, Western PA, and the Transitional dialects no longer occupy the center of the diagram: they have shifted to the extreme right, with high F2 values, and are aligned with the Southern dialects in a linear progression of decreasing negative skewing with increasing F2. Pearson's r is .68. The slope of this line is .0098: that is, for every

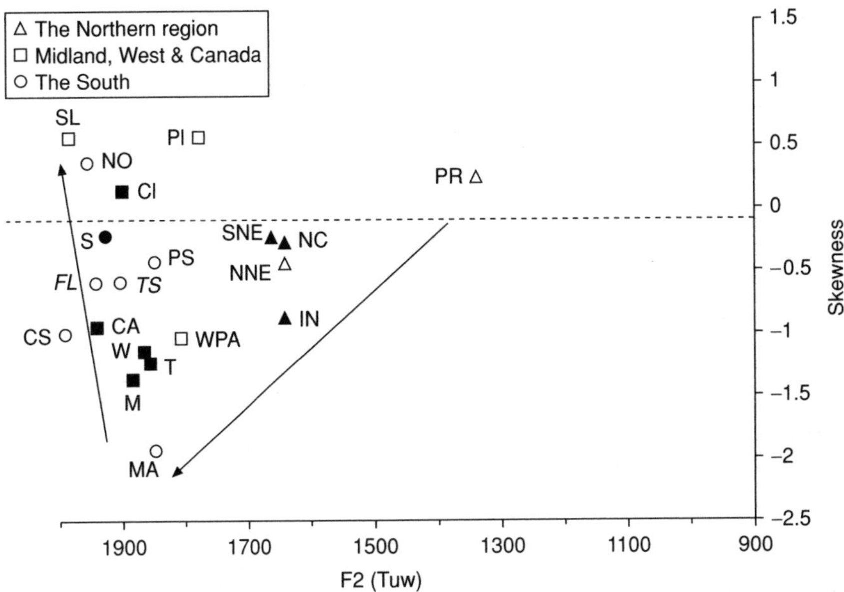


*Figure 15.16* The relationship of skewing to the advancement of (Tuw) in 20 North American dialects. Solid symbols: significant negative age coefficients

100 Hz that F2 increases, negative skewing declines by almost 1. The slope is similar to, but not quite as steep as with (Tow).

The bold symbols, indicating change in apparent time, are distributed quite differently from figures 15.12 and 15.14. Three of the four Northern dialects at upper right show significant age coefficients in the direction of the change. In the low central part of the diagram are grouped all those dialects that were intermediate in figure 15.15: the West, the Midland, Canada, and the Transitional dialects; they all show significant age coefficients. But further along, only two of the dialects in the right-hand progression show this pattern, the South and Cincinnati, and two show a reverse (positive) age effect. As a whole, the most advanced dialects are not progressing further in the change, but appear to have reached a limit.

## *Characterization of the outliers*

A crucial step in unraveling the mechanism of sound change is to determine the character of the tokens in the positive and negative tails of the distribution studied in the last section. So far, the regular progression of a sound change from positive to negative skewing and then to normal symmetry was seen to be a mechanical consequence of its relation to the periphery of phonological space and to other phonemes. Limitations on the extension of variants in one direction or another are responsible for such asymmetries, and these limitations are of two different kinds. When a phoneme is close to the periphery of phonological space, there are physical constraints on the production of sounds beyond a certain limit. When a phoneme is close to the margin of security of a neighboring phoneme, it is perceptual constraints that come into play. Following the scheme for the mechanism of chain shifting in chapter 20 of volume 1, it is argued that a closely neighboring phoneme forms a perceptual barrier to the extension of the variants of a given phoneme in that direction. Outliers that fall within the normal range of dispersion of a neighboring phoneme (say within two standard deviations) will have a distinctly higher probability of being misunderstood as a member of that phoneme than as a member of the intended target. As a result, such nuclei will not form part of the pool of tokens that the language learner uses to calculate the mean of the intended phoneme. This will have a conservative effect in preventing any further extension.

The initial positive skewing at the beginnings of change is thus the result of limitations on phoneme production in the direction of lower F2. In the case of (Tow) and (Tuw), the negative skewing in the later stages of change was not the result of this type of limitation – these phonemes do not approach the front periphery of the vowel system. Instead they approach the margins of security of other phonemes.

The mean value of F2 for (Tuw) in the South is 1920 Hz; the mean F2 of /i/ is very close, 1992 Hz, and the mean value for /iyF/ is not far away, 2177 Hz. Data from the study of Cross-Dialectal Comprehension bears more directly on the point. In Gating experiments, the highly fronted Birmingham tokens were consistently misunderstood by Northerners (and many Southerners) as /iy/. The (iw) word *knew* in the phrase *knew the guy* was frequently heard as /iy/ and interpreted as *need the guy* or *near the guy*. Of 96 Chicago judges, 50% heard *knew* as a front rounded /uw/ and 26% as /iy/. The vowel of the Kuw token *bouffed* was misunderstood in isolation most frequently as short /i/ (21%) or /iy/ (13%), and only 27% heard /uw/. Even among the Birmingham subjects themselves, only a minority (38%) heard /uw/ in isolated words: 17% heard /iy/ and 17% heard /i/. This suggests that Birmingham /Tuw/ has reached a structural limit; high outliers are very likely to be misunderstood as members of another category.

What kinds of /uw/ and /ow/ variants do we expect to find in the left-hand tail that defines positive skewing or in the right-hand tail that defines negative skewing? If a vowel has a stable peripheral target, it is expected that outliers towards the center of phonological space are nuclei of limited duration, in syllables with complex codas or polysyllabic structure. Their centralized position would be the result of the fact that there is insufficient time for the articulators to be displaced from rest position to targets at the periphery of the vowel system (Liljencrants and Lindblom 1972).

Such a pattern is characteristic of stable vowel targets that are located at the periphery of phonological space. Table 15.4 shows the effects of syllable

*Table 15.4* Effect of complex codas on a stable vowel: regression coefficients for F1 of /o/ (n = 9098)

| | *Coefficient* | *Prob. (t)* |
|---|---|---|
| Constant | 826 | |
| Complex coda | −13 | <0.00001 |
| Following syllables | −26 | <0.00001 |

*Table 15.5* Regression coefficients for F2 of /uw/. Vowels before /l/ are excluded (n = 3310)

| | *No. America* | | *North* | | *Midland* | | *South* | |
|---|---|---|---|---|---|---|---|---|
| | *Coeff.* | *p* | *Coeff.* | *p* | *Coeff.* | *p* | *Coeff.* | *p* |
| Age × 50 | −215 | <0.0001 | −275 | <0.0001 | −155 | | −186 | <0.0001 |
| Female | 32 | 0.0007 | | | 44 | <0.0001 | 59 | <0.0001 |
| Coronal onset | 334 | <0.0001 | 420 | <0.0001 | 361 | <0.0001 | 292 | <0.0001 |
| Final | 62 | 0.0001 | 82 | 0.007 | 94 | <0.0001 | | |
| Polysyllabic | −98 | 0.08 | | | | | | |
| Mean | 1653 | | 1482 | | 1709 | | 1771 | |
| $r^2$ | 0.37 | | 0.43 | | 0.55 | | 0.47 | |

and word structure on the F1 distribution of /o/ that was shown to be normally distributed in figure 15.10. If there are two following consonants rather than one, the expected value of F1 is shifted toward the center by 13 Hz. If there is in addition one or two following syllables, there is an additional and larger shift of 26 Hz.

Just the opposite situation is found for a change in progress in which the nucleus moves away from the periphery. Table 15.5 shows the regression coefficients for /uw/. Vowels before laterals are excluded, since they follow an entirely different pattern as will appear in the sequel. The table lists figures for the continent of North America as a whole, then for three major regional divisions.[11] The next to last row of the table shows the mean value of F2, which for all of North America is well beyond the general midpoint of the normalized vowel systems, 1550. The three regions show increasing means from North to Midland to South. Age coefficients, multiplied by 50, are shown in the first row. These are negative, significant, and sizeable for the continent and all regions, indicating continuing change in apparent

[11] The "Midland" here includes Canada, the West, St Louis, Western Pennsylvania, and Pittsburgh, following the pattern of figure 15.9. Cincinnati is included in the South.

*Table 15.6* Regression coefficients for F2 of /ow/. Vowels before /l/ are excluded (n = 3310)

| | *No. America* | | *North* | | *Midland* | | *South* | |
|---|---|---|---|---|---|---|---|---|
| | *Coeff.* | *p* | *Coeff.* | *p* | *Coeff.* | *p* | *Coeff.* | *p* |
| Age × 50 | −59 | <0.0001 | 36 | 0.006 | −68 | <0.0001 | −186 | <0.0001 |
| Female | 33 | 0.0007 | | | | | 77 | <0.0001 |
| Coronal onset | 120 | <0.0001 | 125 | <0.0001 | 149 | <0.0001 | 125 | <0.0001 |
| Final | 110 | <0.0001 | 110 | <0.0001 | 103 | <0.0001 | 75 | <0.0001 |
| Polysyllabic | −42 | <0.0001 | | | −53 | <0.0001 | −45 | 0.0008 |
| Mean | 1267 | | 1117 | | 1276 | | 1452 | |
| $r^2$ | 0.14 | | 0.24 | | 0.19 | | 0.22 | |

time. Females lead in this change generally by a moderate amount, and this is echoed in all regions except the North. The largest favoring factor is the presence of a coronal onset, as we have seen before. The crucial factor here is the fourth row, which indicates the effect of a word-final, free vowel as in *two*, *do*, etc. These tokens are shifted by 62 Hz in the direction of the change for North America as a whole. The effect is repeated for the North and the Midland, but disappears for the South. As figure 15.16 demonstrated, the Southern dialects that have approached the limit of this fronting process have symmetrical distributions.

Table 15.6 shows the comparable situation for the fronting of /ow/. As the last row shows, the internal factors account for a smaller percentage of the variance than for (uw), yet the information on the composition of the left and right tails of the distribution is even clearer. The mean values show a regular progression from the conservative Northern dialects, to the intermediate Midland region, and the advanced South. The age coefficients are smaller than those for /uw/, and not as uniform: the Northern region is not joined with the others in change in apparent time, nor does it show a female gender advantage. The third row shows a uniform effect of coronal onset, the largest of the internal factors, yet considerably smaller than that for /uw/.

The crucial data of table 15.6 appears in the fourth and fifth rows. Vowels in word-final position show a significant advantage of 75 to 110 Hz for the three regions. Furthermore, for all but the North, there is a regular and significant negative coefficient for polysyllabic words, where one or two syllables follow the stressed nucleus. The /ow/ data reinforces the inference from the /uw/ distributions that the outliers in the direction of change show a high concentration of fully stressed monosyllables, while the negative outliers concentrate words with complex codas and following syllables. It follows that in this process of /uw/ and /ow/ fronting, the target at which

*Table 15.7* Regression coefficients for F2 of /uw/ and /ow/ before /l/ for all of North America and by region (n = 2524)

| | *No. America* | | *North* | | *Midland* | | *South* | |
|---|---|---|---|---|---|---|---|---|
| | *Coeff.* | *p* | *Coeff.* | *p* | *Coeff.* | *p* | *Coeff.* | *p* |
| Age × 50 | 81 | <0.0001 | 56 | 0.0003 | 60 | <0.0001 | 72 | <0.0001 |
| Female | −56 | 0.0007 | −31 | 0.0004 | | | −102 | <0.0001 |
| Monosyllabic | −49 | <0.0001 | −77 | <0.0001 | −19 | 0.04 | −49 | 0.007 |
| Mean | 959 | | 905 | | 931 | | 1068 | |
| $r^2$ | 0.07 | | 0.11 | | 0.05 | | 0.11 | |

speakers aim is not the mean, but is shifted in the direction of the change. Furthermore, it is suggested that the extreme outliers in the direction of the change are not heard as aberrant tokens, but as exemplars and archetypes of the change in progress.

It also follows that for mid-back vowels that are not engaged in the change in progress, the opposite pattern should be found. Fully stressed monosyllables should predominate in the tail that is closer to the periphery and polysyllables should be more fully represented in the more centralized tail. The allophones of /uw/ and /ow/ before /l/ provide a further test of the conclusions drawn from tables 15.3 to 15.6. Here the prosodic factors are considerably simplified, since absolute final position does not exist, and the number of cases with complex codas is limited (primarily words ending in *–old*). The main prosodic opposition will then be monosyllables vs. polysyllables (*pole* vs. *Polish*).

Table 15.7 presents combined data for /uw/ and /ow/ before /l/, both for North America as a whole and for the major regional dialects.[12] The mean values show the progression expected from figure 15.9, with a distinct shift toward the front for Southern dialects. But for most dialects, the back vowels before /l/ are close to the periphery of phonological space. Since there is little change in progress here, and there is less phonetic differentiation, it is natural that $r^2$ will be quite low, since most of the variation is random perturbation around the mean and not the result of the phonetic or social factors considered here.

Table 15.7 shows the reversal of the relative position of monosyllables and polysyllables that we expected for an allophone located at the back periphery. Monosyllabic words show a sizeable and significant negative

[12] The dialect pattern of /uw/ vowels before /l/ matches closely the pattern shown for /owl/ in figure 15.13. There are differences in the distribution of the lexicon, with many more polysyllabic forms with /ow/, but the similarities in what follows are much greater than the differences.

coefficient −49. This holds for each of the regions, though the effect is somewhat smaller in the Midland. Thus the target of /owl/ and /uwl/ is located further back than the mean distribution, and polysyllables drift to the center, exactly the opposite of the main body of the /uw/ and /ow/ nuclei as they shift toward a more and more centralized target. It is also striking to see that the social factors are reversed. Instead of negative age coefficients, the pre-lateral allophones show positive figures, indicating that younger people are shifting these allophones further to the back. This holds for all regions equally. Finally, this pre-lateral shift agrees with the great majority of the sound changes that are studied here. The negative coefficients for Female indicate that women have lower F2 values for /uw/ and /ow/ before /l/. Furthermore, this difference between men and women is increasing for younger speakers.[13]

The net effect of these two contrary movements – the general advance of /uw/ and /ow/ and the increasing retraction of nuclei before /l/ – is to increase the phonetic differentiation of the two sets of nuclei. We have already seen that this distance is at a maximum in Western Pennsylvania (figure 15.13). This is also the region of maximal vocalization of syllable-final /l/ (Ash 1982a,b), a loss of the conditioning factor that leads to a phonologization of the allophonic difference, so that the fronting of /ow/ and /uw/ in this condition can be seen as increasing phonemic dispersion, maximizing the margins of security of the newly split phonemes. But it is also possible that the effect is a mechanical one, a maximal differentiation of a tense nucleus from a lax glide which is also seen before vocalized /r/. On the other hand, one cannot rule out the possibility that the increasing retraction of vowels before /l/ is driven by socially motivated projection, a negative evaluation of the fronting of pre-lateral /uw/ and /ow/.

Figure 15.13 also showed a group of dialects where the fronting of /ow/ before /l/ reached a maximum of 1250 Hz, only 200 Hz below the value for the main body of /ow/ for those dialects, and fronter than all /ow/ in conservative dialects. These dialects – Texas South and the Piedmont South – are those that have been identified as the most extreme exemplars of the Southern Shift: the monophthongization of /ay/, the reversal of the relative positions of /e/ and /ey/, and the reversal of /i/ and /iy/. If the fronting of /owl/ and /uwl/ is continuing in these dialects, parallel to the mainstream, then monosyllables should favor further advance, and polysyllables lag behind.

Table 15.8 shows the significant regression coefficients for these dialects as compared to all others. Women have more retracted vowels than men, as in all other dialects. But for these advanced dialects, there is no

[13] Separate regression analyses for men and women show the same retraction of monosyllabic forms and the same direction of change in apparent time; but the age coefficient for women (1.97) is about twice the size of the age coefficient for men (1.08).

*Table 15.8* Phonetic and social constraints on fronting of /ow/ and /uw/ before /l/ for the most advanced dialects (Piedmont South, Texas South, New Orleans) vs. all others

| | *Advanced dialects* | | *Others* | |
|---|---|---|---|---|
| | *Coeff.* | *p* | *Coeff.* | *p* |
| Age × 50 | 244 | <0.0001 | 39 | 0.0002 |
| Female | −42 | 0.011 | −57 | <0.0001 |
| Monosyllabic | — | | −46 | <0.0001 |
| Mean | 1482 | | 1292 | |

significant difference between monosyllables and polysyllables, indicating that there is some difference between these dialects and others in the question that is the main focus of this section: the role of outliers. The key to the situation may lie in the large difference in the age coefficients. The positive age coefficient for the advanced dialects is six times as large as that for all others combined. When the analysis is performed for men and women separately, the result is the same: no significant difference between monosyllables and polysyllables, and both with large positive age coefficients (women, 5.29; men, 4.19). No phonetic or phonological effect can be identified which would be responsible for this difference. It seems most likely that in these areas, extreme fronting of /uw/ and /ow/ before /l/ has taken on a negative social evaluation, and women are leading in the retreat from this most advanced position.

The proposition being examined in this section is that outliers are perceived as archetypes and models of the newer forms in linguistic change from below. It does not immediately apply to variables that are receding from their peak in response to negative social evaluation in a late stage of change. However, it seems likely that monosyllabic, fully stressed forms would be primary targets of social evaluation in any case. There seems to be a clear opposition between changes that center on fully stressed syllables, essentially forms of fortition, and changes that reduce, lenite, and erode segments. Stressed syllables should therefore lead in fortition, and unstressed polysyllables in lenition.

In fact, monosyllables do behave very differently from polysyllables in this situation. Table 15.9 shows the results for these advanced dialects when separate regression analyses are performed on these two classes of words, before /l/ and not before /l/. For vowels before /l/, age and gender effects are concentrated in the (stressed) monosyllables, and these effects disappear in polysyllables. The right half of the table shows that vowels not before /l/ behave in the opposite way. Age coefficients are negative,

*Table 15.9* Social constraints on fronting of /ow/ and /uw/ in the most advanced dialects by syllable structure for vowels before /l/ and not before /l/

| | *Before /l/* | | | *Not before /l/* | | | |
|---|---|---|---|---|---|---|---|
| | *Monosyllables (n = 177)* | | *Polysyllables (n = 62)* | *Monosyllables (n = 578)* | | *Polysyllables (n = 152)* | |
| | *Coeff.* | *p* | *Coeff.* | *Coeff.* | *p* | *Coeff.* | *p* |
| Age | 296 | <0.0001 | — | –132 | 0.0002 | –262 | <0.0001 |
| Female | –74 | 0.025 | — | 89 | <0.0001 | 78 | 0.005 |
| Mean | 1158 | | 1218 | 1607 | | 1490 | |

not positive, indicating that younger people use more advanced forms of /uw/ and /ow/. The gender coefficients show that women are in the lead in this advance. And the mean for monosyllables is more advanced than the mean for polysyllables.

Table 15.9 provides a striking demonstration that stressed monosyllables lead in the vowel changes that are sweeping across North America. This cannot be the result of simple articulatory or phonetic factors, since monosyllables lead in both directions: toward the periphery or away from it, depending on the nature of the change. It is not possible to explain the predominant role of monosyllables by functional arguments that depend upon maximal dispersion or the adjustment of margins of security. It follows, therefore, that it is the salient character of stressed monosyllables that is responsible for their leading position. This in turn reinforces the proposition that in the course of sound change, outliers carry more weight than more central members of the distribution, and that the perceived central tendency of /uw/ and /ow/ is shifted toward the outliers in the positive tails.

### *Implications of the saliency of monosyllabic targets*

This investigation of the fronting of /uw/ and /ow/ in North America as a whole has provided evidence for a *Target Principle* of linguistic change. In linguistic changes that hold constant or increase the amount of phonetic substance, the phonemic target for succeeding generations is not the general mean but is shifted (by some undetermined amount) toward the salient outliers in the direction of the change. In vowel shifts, these salient outliers are stressed monosyllables in which the nucleus has the maximum duration needed to reach that target.

This principle concerns structural factors, but it is not predicted by any structural argument concerning the communicative function of language. There is nothing about physical or structural limitations that brings stressed monosyllables to the advancing forefront of change as outliers. The relation of the salient outliers to the general mean is determined by the relation to the general mean of the target adopted by younger speakers. Given a particular change in progress, the general principles of chain shifting will predict that relation. However, the implementation of a change in that direction, and the development of a distinct target for the salient outliers, is a fact specific to the community in question, and is not predictable by structural factors.

This study of change on a large scale has also given strong support to the systematic alignment of gender with linguistic change, and makes it seem even less likely that these changes are motivated by purely internal considerations. Yet it is not at all evident what social motivations can operate upon linguistic changes as broadly based as the fronting of /uw/ and /ow/. There may be a mechanism by which local social practices can become generalized to affect an entire city, but it is not at all clear how they can account for changes that affect an entire continent.

The final chapter will define these unresolved questions more closely, examine the evidence for the social support for continuation, and try to clarify the meaning of "socially motivated projection."

# 16

# *Conclusion*

The first volume of this study made it clear that linguistic change in progress is heavily constrained by the physical environment in which it takes place, and by structural factors that limit the course of change. At the same time, it is argued that the forces that move and motivate change, and are responsible for incrementation and transmission across generations, are largely social in nature. This final chapter will look once more at how these factors interact, and try to define more closely the social process that I have called *socially motivated projection.*

## 16.1 The linguistic basis for continuation

Throughout this volume, it is assumed that the principles of linguistic change developed in the first volume of this work are actively constraining the direction, if not the rate, of change. The previous chapter listed factors that might affect the skewing of individual vowels, but did not focus on the underlying principles that operate on whole systems. In the Philadelphia dialect, the most immediate object of our study, these principles can be seen to operate in many ways.

- The principle that mergers expand at the expense of distinctions (chapter 11, volume 1) applies in Philadelphia to the merger of /ohr/ and /uhr/, and probably to the merger of /e/ and /ʌ/ before intervocalic /r/, though there is no clear evidence of change in progress here.
- The general principles of chain shifting (chapters 5–6, volume 1) are realized in the shift of the peripheral vowels before /r/, /ahr/ → /ohr/ → /uhr/. The fronting of /ow/ is chained to the fronting and raising of /aw/, so that these stand in relation to each other as mid front peripheral /aw/ and nonperipheral /aw/. However, the similar new and vigorous change represented by the raising of (eyC) responds to no such structural account.
- The principles of functional economy outlined by Martinet (1955) may be considered to apply to any situation where the movement of one phoneme is dictated by the configuration of neighboring phonemes.

> They apply to the raising of /æh/ to [eːə] and [iːə], given the absence of any substantial /eh/ and /ih/ phonemes, and to the fronting of /uw/ and /ow/. Chapter 15 produced evidence that /uw/ has reached a limiting position in the South, constrained by the type of structural factors that Moulton (1962) has elucidated for Swiss German.

To the extent that general linguistic principles apply, they form the favorable undercurrent, or perhaps prevailing wind, for changes now in progress. Given enough social motivation or contrary linguistic pressures, retrograde movements can be set in motion, just as a boat may tack into the wind. When all other conditions on change are balanced or neutralized, structural principles might in themselves be a sufficient basis for continuation. This seems particularly true for the expansion of mergers, where social pressures and social consciousness are minimal.

Perhaps the most striking example of continuation encountered so far in this discussion is the Northern Cities Shift. The series of changes that began in the middle of the twentieth century affect in a uniform way the vast area of the Inland North, stretching from Madison, Wisconsin to Syracuse, New York. Thirty-five million people follow the same principles of chain shifting, in an area of 81,000 square miles neatly delimited by settlement patterns that took shape a hundred years before the change began. No current communication pattern accounts for this uniformity, and in the absence of any other explanation, it seems necessary to attribute it to the unopposed operation of the structural principles of chain shifting.

General principles apply to terminations as well as continuations. Some are physical. In Philadelphia, the raising of (æh) to high front position may be approaching a physical limit, determined by the limiting movements of the supra-glottal tract and their acoustic consequences. Thus a vowel can be only so open or so closed.[1] When a sound change approaches this limit the further shift of its mean value must decelerate. Following the logic of the last chapter that outliers are important targets in the mechanism of change, a point is reached when outliers are no longer possible in the direction of the ongoing change. Other limits are structural. The gradual elimination of one of two competing forms automatically follows the asymptotic behavior of the upper section of the logistic curve. But it frequently happens that such a terminal point does not lead to the extinction of the change, but to its re-alignment. Monophthongs can become diphthongs, diphthongs can become monophthongs, vowels may be glottalized (chapter 9 of volume 1).

[1] Though such limits are not always so obvious. It is generally considered that the limits of a high vowel are set by the possibility of a resonant nucleus, but sound change in Stockholm (Kotsinas, p.c.) has led to the replacement of high tense cardinal [i] with a voiceless fricative, that is moving from 1 open to 0 open in the terminology of chapter 8, volume 1.

Principles of functional economy may dictate the termination of a change, as in the case of free (uwF).

### *Changes not accounted for*

Despite the many successes of structural and physical principles in accounting for change, many changes defy them. The new development in Philadelphia phonology that was most clearly documented in chapter 15 is the lowering of /e/. This is not a chain shift accompanied by correlated movements of /i/ and /æ/. The considerable overlap of /e/ and /æ/ runs contrary to the conservative pressures of a functional economy, and to the proposed mechanism of probability matching of chapter 20 of volume 1. It poses the same problem as any other case of a push chain, like the backing of /e/ against a stationary /ʌ/ in the Chicago version of the Northern Cities Shift (chapter 6, volume 1). We must infer that the lowering of (e) has received some other source of support beyond the relatively weak principle that short vowels are lowered more often than they are raised. In the absence of a structural explanation, this movement can only be attributed to a projection of social values onto the phonetic process. At this point the logic of volume 2 must replace the logic of volume 1. A search for the causes of a given change will be realized as a search for the leaders of that change. In a future inquiry, we might well begin the search for a projection of social values onto the lowering of /e/ by searching for the human exponents of that process. To justify any such research program, let us consider how successful the search has been for the leaders of linguistic changes of the 1970s.

## 16.2 The social location of the leaders of change

The central program of this volume has been the search for the social location of the leaders of linguistic change, as one approach to an understanding of the causes and motivations of change. The multiple regression analyses of the Philadelphia Neighborhood Study, reinforced by the Philadelphia telephone survey, confirmed the initial hypothesis of the curvilinear pattern. The restated version of the *Curvilinear Principle* that emerged in chapter 14 locates the leaders of change in the central section of the socioeconomic hierarchy. For the new and vigorous changes (aw, eyC) and the middle-range (owC), the age coefficients for the upper working class were significantly ahead of those for other working class and middle classes. This was seen with equal clarity in the major component of the socioeconomic index, occupation: skilled workers were significantly in advance of unskilled workers and the unemployed (chapter 5).

Studies of neighborhood in chapter 7 found that the oldest settled working class neighborhood, Kensington, was consistently ahead of other areas. This finding is not easily realized as a general principle – there are not enough comparable studies of class and neighborhood – but it sets up a certain tension between two descriptions of the leaders of change which was developed further in chapters 10–12. One set of leaders – the Kendell family of Wicket St. – are middle working class located firmly in the center of the geographic, cultural, and economic core of Kensington. They exemplify the full development of the cultural matrix in which the original Philadelphia dialect developed. The other set – headed by Celeste S. and Teresa M. of Clark St. – seemed at first sight to be prototypical South Philadelphians. But the closer view of chapters 11 and 12 showed that they – and Celeste in particular – are a special type of upwardly mobile South Philadelphians who are instruments of social as well as linguistic change.

Gender has been a crucial focus of this inquiry, and the principles governing the role of gender in linguistic change have carried us further toward our goal than any other. Any theory of the causes of change must deal with the general finding that in the good majority of linguistic changes, women are a full generation ahead of men, and show a near-linear, decade-by-decade increment. Men, on the other hand, showed a more step-wise incrementation by generations for female-dominated changes. A model based on the asymmetry of child-rearing fitted the Philadelphia data reasonably well. The step-wise male pattern was attributed to the simple fact that the starting point for every speaker is the linguistic level of the female caretaker who first transmitted language to him (chapter 9).

Chapter 10 further defined the leaders of linguistic change, selecting those women who have the highest degree of social interaction on their local blocks, and the greatest proportion of their friends and contacts outside the block. The most striking gender differentiation is found in the fact that positions in social networks are strongly correlated with women's linguistic behavior, but this is not true for men. Chapter 11 found that these leaders were not among those women who conformed closely to the norms of proper linguistic behavior when stable sociolinguistic variables were involved. On the contrary, they were equally nonconformist in their treatment of stigmatized variables (chapter 11). Studies of the individual leaders of change traced their life-long history of nonconformity (chapter 12). It was hypothesized that in their early career they adopted the linguistic symbols of nonconformity, and maintained them (or developed them further) in their upward path later in life. The parallel with the leaders in the development of palatalization in Cairo provided striking confirmation of this pattern. The leaders of linguistic change are therefore seen as those responsible for the diffusion of linguistic change throughout the urban speech community, and for the geographic uniformity of that community. Though it is not excluded that they continue to develop linguistic changes in young adulthood, and influence those around them, the hypothesis is that most linguistic influence is exerted in early and middle adolescence, before the system stabilizes. The adult behavior of the leaders of linguistic change is taken as a reflection and a consequence of their behavior in their formative years.

To sum up, the study of linguistic change in Philadelphia shows that the oldest working class neighborhoods are the geographic and cultural matrix in which the local dialect was formed and continues to advance. Upper working or lower middle class speakers with a wider range of social contacts carry these developments forward in a pattern that ultimately affects the entire speech community.

## 16.3 Transmission and incrementation

The transmission problem is viewed as a separate and critical issue for the theory of linguistic change: how children learn to talk differently from their parents, and in the same direction, over many generations (chapter 13). The empirical studies in Philadelphia, King of Prussia, Detroit, and Milton Keynes point to a re-organization of the vernacular in pre-adolescent and adolescent years. The early stages of change in particular show a close correlation with the individual's alignment on bi-polar social dimensions, with a male/female polarity developing shortly thereafter. Considerable attention was given to the development of an abstract model of transmission which would predict the steady, near-linear incrementation observed in girls and young women. A logistically varying incrementation which continues until stabilization in late adolescence generated a model of change in the community without clear generational breaks for women (chapter 14). It correctly predicted the presence of an adolescent peak among adult women and its absence among adult men, but it did not account for the generational breaks that persist for men. The forces that produce such steady incrementation are the causes of linguistic change that we have been searching for.

### *The role of outliers*

Studies of the same sound changes across many dialects showed a regular progression from positive to negative skewing as the changes progressed (chapter 15). In positively skewed dialects, the outliers are stressed and stressable monosyllables. It is hypothesized that these outliers carry the main load of social evaluation in the course of change. The evidence for this view includes (1) the study of an entire day's recording of Carol Meyers, in which vowels move in the direction of linguistic change when she is in close interaction with female friends; and (2) the positive skewing of variables in the early stages of change, with the most salient monosyllables at the high end of the distribution.

### *Socially motivated projection*

At various points the discussion of the mechanism of linguistic change has introduced the term "socially motivated projection" to indicate the assignment of social value to salient outliers in the direction of change. Such a projection is needed to account for the fact that in female-dominated changes young women consistently increase their use of a linguistic variable with each succeeding year, at a rate of increase greater than that of the next oldest cohort, while (in such a change) men do not. Socially motivated projection is conceived as the force behind the near-linear incrementation of change among women in the logistically varying model. To give such a notion content, it is necessary to specify what social values are assigned to the salient outliers. For this purpose, we must now turn to a larger view of the social basis of linguistic change.

## 16.4 The social basis of linguistic change

The starting point of a historical and evolutionary approach to language change is that one cannot account for change by any universal trait of human beings or of language (Meillet 1926:17). This principle has been restated many times in many ways, but taking a leaf from a frequently turned page in recent discussions of evolution, it can be encapsulated as the *Principle of Contingency*. Factors determining the course of linguistic change are drawn from a pattern of social behavior that is not linked in any predictable way to the linguistic outcome. A certain linkage between social dimensions and linguistic traits is established as the result of an arbitrary and accidental concatenation in history. If the tape were to be replayed, there is no reason to think that the outcome would be the same (Gould 1989:284–91). The social support for progressive incrementation must spring from a contingent event in the history of the speech community. The most likely place to look for such events is a change in the demographic composition of the community.

### *Changes in the composition of the speech community*

The doctrine of first effective settlement (Zelinsky 1992) limits the influence of new groups entering an established community, in asserting that the original group determines the cultural pattern for those to follow, even if these newcomers are many times the number of the original settlers. This is consistent with the fact that New York City, Philadelphia, Boston, and Chicago, cities largely composed of 19th-century immigrants from Europe, show only slight influences from the languages of these ethnic groups in the form of the local dialect.[2]

In any one generation, if the numbers of immigrants rise to a higher order of magnitude than the extant population, the doctrine may be overthrown, with qualitative changes in the general speech pattern.[3] This is what happened in the massive immigration of Slavic speakers into the coal-mining towns of Eastern Pennsylvania in the early 20th century, a clear and simple case of linguistic change – the merger of /o/ and /oh/ – motivated by population change (Herold 1997; chapter 11 of volume 1). Otherwise, the effect of these waves of immigration is more indirect, and they modify in subtle ways the course of the sound changes already in progress. Chapter 7 documented the influence of Italian ethnicity on the fronting of /uw/ and /ow/ in Philadelphia. As in so many other cases, our knowledge of cross-linguistic influence is not strong enough to explain why this particular group should fall behind other ethnic groups whose substrate languages do not differ from Italian in the relevant vowel configuration.[4] But here we are not so much concerned with substrate effects as with the possibility that the series of immigrations into Philadelphia described in chapter 2 is related to the motivating force for continued incrementation of the Philadelphia sound changes.

In Martha's Vineyard, it was found that the Portuguese and Indian groups did not participate in the centralization of (ay) and (aw) until they entered into the mainstream of the local economy and politics (Labov 1963).[5] When they did so, there was a re-orientation of the relations of (ay) and (aw), with much stronger centralization of (aw) than we find among the up-island Yankees. In New York City, the second generation of Jews and Italians did compete with established older groups in the local job and housing market, and were indistinguishable from the third generation in their use of the local dialect (chapter 7, Labov 1976). But there was also a marked difference between the two ethnic groups in which of two parallel sound changes was more advanced: the raising of (eh) or the raising of (oh) (Labov 1966a,b).

[2] This principle has been independently formulated at least twice in Creole studies, by Sankoff (1980) as the "first past the post" principle, and by Mufwene (1996) as the "founder effect."

[3] In the history of plantation colonization, the year in which the slave population outnumbered the slave owners in any given colony is referred to by Baker and Corne (1982) as "Event 1," the point from which the evolving Creole language began to diverge markedly from the language of the colonizers.

[4] Herold's many contributions to the theory of merger still fall short of accounting for why a Croatian, Polish, or Czech substrate should favor the merger in the low back vowels.

[5] In the case of the Portuguese, this was a matter of three generations; for the Indians, as many as eight.

Let us consider how the second generation of new immigrants might perceive a relevant social dimension associated with the linguistic change in progress, much as children 3 to 5 years old in Philadelphia perceived the dimension of formality/informality associated with (ing). The urban newcomers' major concern is the acquisition of local rights and privileges: jobs, housing, small business variances, the use of streets and other public places for local merchandising and recreation. Since the oldest settled groups showed the strongest development of the local variables (Hershberg 1981; chapter 7 above), it is not unreasonable for those variables to be associated with the polar oppositions local/nonlocal, privileged/nonprivileged. Given the principle that it is the salient outliers of a linguistic change in progress that are the targets of acquisition rather than the means or medians, reproduction of these outliers provides a reasonable mechanism of incrementation. Succeeding cohorts of second-generation members of the incoming groups will perceive not only the outliers of the established groups, but the outliers of members of their own group. As those numbers increase through continued in-migration, the exposure to group-internally accelerated forms will increase. The deceleration of the change will follow when the relative success of the entering group in gaining local privileges diminishes the strength of the association of advanced forms of the variable with local origin and privilege.

The mechanism proposed by Sturtevant (1947) differs from this scenario in that it involves the identification of the linguistic variable with a particular reference group, and the decision to adopt certain forms as a way of being associated with the traits of that group. This account of the process is elaborated by Le Page and Tabouret-Keller (1985).

> The individual creates his systems of verbal behavior so as to resemble those common to the group or groups with which he wishes from time to time to be identified, to the extent that
>
> (a) he is able to identify those groups
> (b) his motives are sufficiently clear-cut and powerful
> (c) his *opportunities* for learning are adequate
> (d) his *ability* to learn – that is, to change his habits where necessary – is unimpaired.

The authors develop this scheme to account for language variation in a creole-speaking society where the linguistic options are more discrete and socially visible than the changes discussed in this volume. We do not see Carol Meyers or Celeste S. as creating a system of verbal behavior so much as responding to ambient pressures to shift their habitual range of values of Philadelphia variables. The "clear-cut and powerful" motives of (b) do not exist in Philadelphia. If we play back recordings of the choices that speakers have actually made, they are embarrassed and apologize for speaking that way.

It does not seem likely that the linkage between linguistic and social structure involves the association of forms or frequencies with particular groups, and calculations of the consequences of adopting their speech forms. As always, it is good practice to consider first the simpler and more mechanical view that social structure affects linguistic output through changes in the frequency of interaction. The entrance of the Portuguese and Indians into the local social structure of Martha's Vineyard may be coextensive with the increase of their daily conversational interaction with the Yankees. The same machinery may apply to the interaction of urban villagers in the great cities. In the case of dialect boundaries, the great majority of locations are predictable by mechanical factors, but a few run counter to this tendency under the influence of powerful social affect.[6] The major problem with this simpler account arises in dealing with the special behavior of African Americans in the United States.

### *The exclusion of African Americans*

What has been said about the entrance of new groups into American society does not apply to the largest set of population changes that have ever taken place in the large Northern cities of the United States: the arrival of great numbers of African Americans from the rural South, along with the rapid growth of the Hispanic population.

So far, the sound changes sweeping across the United States have been portrayed as if they were general phenomena affecting to varying degrees all levels of the speech community. But this is not so. In Boston, New York, Philadelphia, Buffalo, Detroit, Cleveland, Chicago, San Francisco, and Los Angeles, the progress of the sound changes we have been studying stops short at the racial line. All speakers who are socially defined as white, mainstream, or Euro-American, are involved in the changes to one degree or another. There are leaders, and there are followers, but in the mainstream community it is almost impossible to find someone who stands completely apart. But for those children who are integral members of a sub-community that American society defines as "non-white" – Black, Hispanic, or native American – the result is quite different. No matter how frequently they are exposed to the local vernacular, the new patterns of regional sound change do not surface in their speech. On the deeper levels of syntax and semantics, the African American community is carried ever further away on a separate current of grammatical change, and a very sizeable fraction of the Hispanic speakers move with them. The situation of the growing Asian-American community is not yet clear, but present

[6] Studies of average daily traffic flow show that the locations of traditional American dialect boundaries are correlated with troughs in communication, with the exception of New York City (Labov 1974).

indications show that in Philadelphia, at least, second-generation speakers of English do not adopt features of the local dialect. Further research on different sectors of the Asian-American community should illuminate the significance of belonging to a "non-white" sector of American society.

That is not to say by any manner or means that all African Americans speak alike. The enormous range of speech forms within the African American community takes us from the relatively uniform African American Vernacular English of the inner cities [AAVE] to a Standard African American English which is distinguished from other standards only by a small set of phonological features. There are a large number of upper middle class African Americans whose speech is effectively identical with that of their white counterparts. There are not, however, a large number of African Americans whose speech would be identified with the local dialect used by whites. Such individuals exist, but they are rare, and almost always the result of an early upbringing removed from the inner city African American speech community.[7]

This is a unique fact about the United States; there is no parallel in any European country. In London, locally born members of Jamaican families use a dialect that is not clearly distinguishable from that of other working class Londoners.[8] The special situation of the United States is a consequence of the large and increasing residential segregation of African Americans in the Northern Cities (Labov and Harris 1986, Hershberg et al. 1981). Studies of the African American phonetic and grammatical systems in Philadelphia gave the first indication that black and white speech patterns were diverging rather than converging (Ash and Myhill 1986); since that time, stronger evidence has been accumulated by Bailey and his associates (Bailey 1993; Bailey and Maynor, 1987, 1989). The fact that the regional dialects used in the white community are developing in the pattern described in these volumes, and that blacks do not participate in this process in any large city, is a major factor in the steady and growing separation of black and white speech patterns.

Acoustic studies of the speech of black Philadelphians show that older members of the community are partially aligned with the Philadelphia system: they approximate the short **a** pattern and show a configuration of back vowels before /r/ that is not dissimilar. Younger African American speakers show increasing departure from the Philadelphia system, with

[7] The situation described here is typical of all of the Northern and Midland cities that have been studied so far. In Southern dialect areas the distance between African American and white vernaculars is not as great, but there is indication that it is increasing (Bailey 1993, Wolfram et al. 2000).

[8] In the 1980s, I recorded a series of Jamaican youth in Battersea Park, London. I returned the next day with a tape which had six extracts from their speech, and asked a series of white Londoners to identify their ethnic background. Two of the six were identified as white by the majority of listeners, and none of them were unhesitatingly identified as black.

central to back nuclei for /aw/,[9] fronting of /ay/, and extremely back nuclei for /uw/ and /ow/. Their general Northern black phonology also shows the stylistic monophthongization of /ay/, variable vocalization of (r), merger of /i/ and /e/ before nasals, and the systematic tensing of short /e/ before /d/. An experimental procedure which modified the nuclei of /aw/, /ow/, and /æh/ of black speakers by resynthesizing with higher second formants showed great sensitivity to this phonetic parameter (Graff, Labov, and Harris 1986). The simple fronting of the nucleus of /aw/ in *out* and *house* led to an extreme shift of ethnic identification from black to white, equal to the most extreme natural style shifting. When black, white, or Puerto Rican subjects heard the fronted form of /aw/, the great majority switched their identification of the ethnicity of the speaker from black to white. Thus the most conservative Philadelphia dialect, with low front [æo], is distinctively marked as "white" for the black population.

One can explain the nonparticipation of African Americans in the sound changes of this volume as the result of the same type of factor that may have operated among the Portuguese and Indians on Martha's Vineyard: the perception that their own use of local dialect forms will not lead to full membership in local society. It can also be accounted for as the result of decreasing frequency of face-to-face interaction with speakers of the mainstream local dialect during their formative years. The research in North Philadelphia cited above indicates that increases in such interaction lead to the partial acquisition of grammatical features of the local dialects, but not to participation in the new and vigorous sound changes in progress in the white community (Labov and Harris 1986).

The difficulty is that there are many possible explanations for the phonological divergence of AAVE. Do African Americans abstain from participation in the mainstream sound changes because they do not recognize the leaders of linguistic change as reference groups, because their own system is developing in an entirely different direction, because they are isolated from these changes in their formative years, or because they do not believe that adopting these changes will gain the local rights and privileges associated with them for white speakers, or some combination of the above? This topic must be reserved for another volume, because it is so specific to the social conditions of the United States, and because the rapid development and divergence of African American Vernacular English enters areas of linguistic analysis quite different from those dealt with here.

## *The social mobility of the leaders of change*

The changes in the composition of the speech community considered so far have been the result of new members entering from outside. But

[9] Except before and after nasals.

perhaps the most important changes in the community are internal: alterations in the relative social status of members. Such social mobility is not a constant or a universal. It is sensitive to any great disturbance in the conditions of a given society. Upward social mobility is minimized during depressions, and accelerated in more prosperous periods. In wartime, people get access to occupations that were previously barred to them – as in the case of women and blacks in the United States during World War II. And as we have seen, upward social mobility appears to be a primary characteristic of the leaders of linguistic change. This inquiry has established that leaders of linguistic change in urban society are able and energetic, nonconformist women who absorb and maintain lower class linguistic forms in their youth, and maintain them in their upwardly mobile trajectory in later years.[10] They are the main instruments of the diffusion of change throughout the urban area, since they have a wider range of contacts than others. Prominent among their friends and neighbors, their own speech patterns become a model for others to follow. Furthermore, their resistance to normative community pressures precludes any tendency to recede from the linguistic patterns established in their youth.

Social mobility has been related to language change on a large scale. The development of the doctrine of correctness in England has been related to the growth of an upwardly mobile merchant class whose early education did not match their newly achieved social positions.[11] The Great Vowel Shift may have been accelerated in London by such a merchant class, largely from the Southeast of England (Wyld 1936). High rates of social mobility are one of the primary characteristics of North American society, and it is possible that the more rapid development of linguistic change and divergence of North American dialects as compared with the relative stability of European dialects is connected with this fact.

Social mobility involves interactions among social classes that may be a crucial component of the linguistic changes we have been studying. Let us return for a moment to Kroch's (1978) position that the working class is the originating source of linguistic change, and that the middle class resists such change on ideological grounds.[12] This seemed to run counter to the observed findings that either the upper working class or the lower middle class were the most advanced in the process of change – the "centrally located" classes – and that there was no important break between middle class and working class as far as linguistic change was concerned. Kroch's view can be refined by the findings of chapter 11, which show that the

[10] How much they develop these linguistic variables further in early adulthood remains an open question.

[11] See chapter 8, n. 21.

[12] I set aside the discussion of "naturalness," which has many problems not crucial for the main issues discussed here.

upper working class and lower middle class are divided into a majority who are bound by commitment to established norms, and a minority who are not.

The mechanism of change that has been disengaged from the Philadelphia Neighborhood Study, and from Eckert's work in the Detroit area, is a different view of the operation of social class, and yet not very different from Kroch's. Although the most advanced speakers are to be found in the upwardly mobile groups, they build on and develop changes that originated in the lower working class. The basic concept is that linguistic change is a deviation from accepted norms: it is a type of nonconformity to the dominant patterns of society. This is not limited to those norms that are publicly endorsed in schools and churches. The mean values for (uw) and (ow) that are displayed in chapter 15 are well-established local norms. They may be criticized or condemned by speech teachers and university people, but they are firmly established normative patterns which replaced earlier norms. The question on the causes of linguistic change can then be restated: how and when do people begin to depart from those earlier norms and continue to do so?

The lower working class is the primary locus of nonconformity in urban communities.[13] A broad range of sociological literature focuses on their deviations from middle class norms, in their refusal to recognize prohibitions against smoking, drugs, cursing, and fighting. Lower working class people also deviate from broader public norms held by the majority of the working class, in many aspects: house upkeep, self-presentation, and religion. From the Philadelphia data, it appears that lower working class speakers are a prominent source of linguistic innovation in the early stages of change, but fall slightly behind as change gathers momentum and becomes characteristic of the community as a whole. The retreat of lower working class men from female-dominated change is just one aspect of this process. As we have seen, it is the sub-group of upwardly mobile youth – primarily women – who advance and generalize the change until it becomes the community norm in the broadest sense. This is the social underpinning of the large-scale development witnessed in figures 15.8–15.17.

## *The larger picture*

The major part of this volume has focused on the local development of sound changes in Philadelphia, with a sideways glance at many other cities – Belfast, Cairo, Detroit, Milton Keynes. Following the search for the leaders of linguistic change, the field of view was successfully narrowed

[13] One often thinks of middle class drop-outs, hippies, and artists as the main nonconformists, because they are most visible and the most innovative. However, the main resistance to the dominant norms of society is to be found in the lower working class, as argued here.

until it achieved the portraits of the individual leaders in chapter 12. Chapter 15 widened the field of view to embrace an entire continent. This yielded rich findings on the mechanism of change, but it has also opened the door to some of the most puzzling questions of large-scale change.

Figures 15.9–15.16 showed that the same sound changes are operating on a broad sweep across the entire North American continent. While the fronting of (uw) and (ow) form part of different configurations in various dialects, the mechanism and the conditioning factors are the same throughout. The Northern Cities Shift is an even more striking example of the uniformity of sound change, as noted at the beginning of this chapter. Throughout the South, common features of the Southern Shift appear in distant areas, from North Carolina to Texas: the monophthongization of /ay/, the tensing and raising of /i/, /e/, and /æ/, the lowering of the lax nuclei of /iy/ and /ey/, the raising and fronting of /ʌ/.

If the incrementation of these changes is driven by socially motivated projections, how can we explain the fact that they affect so many millions of people in widely separated cities who have no connection with each other?

## 16.5 Global polarities of socially motivated projection

The model proposed by Sturtevant for the social implementation of change involved the identification of particular reference groups, and this is the basis of the further elaboration by Le Page and Tabouret-Keller. This model is appropriate for the social situations they described: a discrete and conscious choice of creole systems by individuals whose social identity is in part determined by their physical characteristics. It also may apply to the racial opposition in the United States, where discrete changes in linguistic systems are associated with discrete group assignment, dictated by a binary theory of race. But within the mainstream, Euro-American communities of North America, there is no strong evidence for the association of ongoing linguistic change with particular, identifiable social groups. Instead, it seems likely that the social projection to salient outliers has to do with more abstract social dimensions or polarities.

Though language use is coupled in a first analysis with specific situations or speakers, it often becomes evident with further experience that the association is more general than this. On Martha's Vineyard, the centralization of (ay) and (aw) was correlated with specific groups – Yankees vs. Portuguese, Up-islanders vs. Down-islanders – but ultimately was understood as correlated with a more general dimension, local vs. nonlocal. Though this may seem to be a binary opposition, it operates on linguistic forms as a continuous dimension, as the variable moves steadily forward from one generation to the next (Labov 1965). Objectively speaking, this advance is correlated negatively with age. But it would be difficult to think of children wanting to adopt a younger and younger way of speaking. As the incremental model indicates, children imitate those one step older than they are. And imitation cannot lead to incrementation. At least until late adolescence, children do not overshoot the mark set by their elders. Yet by the time they reach the age of the children who were their models, they overmatch them in their use of the same linguistic variable. What is the mechanism that leads to this incrementation?

### *The nonconformity hypothesis*

Whether we are studying stable sociolinguistic variation or change in progress, the attitudes that emerge from the speech community almost always reinforce the prestige forms taught in schools and the older forms of the language. Chapter 6 showed that in Philadelphia, no significant difference could be found between the job and friendship scales for stable variables or changes in progress. Though investigators speak freely of "covert norms," the main evidence for their existence is simply the fact that nonstandard forms persist.[14] In this section, I would like to develop a hypothesis that is supported by the evidence of chapters 11 and 12. It deals with norms that are covert in some situations, but emerge more freely in others.

The second of the five steps in the mechanism of change put forward in chapter 13 is the early recognition of the formal/informal dimension. It was suggested that children drew the value of this opposition from specific situations when their parents were angry, didactic, relaxed, or intimate. The range of formal/informal also covers the range of socially acceptable behavior. In an appropriate informal situation, most adults tolerate the use of the /in/ variant, negative concord, and lenis stops for (dh), but react against them in more formal situations as inappropriate or even defiant of social norms.[15] The formal/informal polarity can be extended to include behaviors that are not considered acceptable at all and are transformed into a dimension of *conformity/nonconformity* (or more simply "*good*"/"*bad*").

[14] See, for example, the article of Ryan (1979) on "Why do low-prestige language varieties persist?" Despite her strong conviction that the answer to her question lies in the existence of covert norms, she reports that "the expected group differences, indicating stronger solidarity preferences for the nonstandard speech by Mexican Americans than Anglo Americans, were not observed. It may be that the formal setting (a group study conducted in a high school classroom) inhibited the Mexican Americans from revealing their true feelings of solidarity and identification with their ethnic speech."

[15] Important evidence for this point is drawn from Seligman, Tucker, and Lambert 1972. This is an elegant experiment that sorted out the comparative effects on teachers of a child's appearance, writing, drawing, and speech. The combinations of nonstandard (Québecois) speech with highly rated photographs, writing, and drawing produced the reaction that the child would be high on the "toughness" scale. We can interpret this finding as the teachers' perception of a disciplinary problem indicated by the deliberate defiance of social norms.

It is clearest in the use of curse words like *damn*, *shit*, *fuck*. Though their use rises in informal situations, they are not considered "informal." Children are taught the social taboo on these words early in life, and learn that their use is a form of nonconformity that will evoke penalties from adult caretakers. At some point, the use of advanced forms of ongoing sound changes acquires a position on the conformity/nonconformity dimension. The *Nonconformity Hypothesis* can be stated as:

*The first social stratification of language acquired by children is the reinterpretation of stylistic stratification on the formal/informal dimension as conforming vs. nonconforming speech.*

That dimension is more general than membership in named categories like *Jocks* and *Burnouts*, and is in fact a classifying feature of the behaviors that define membership in these groups. It does not seem that advanced forms of the Northern Cities Shift are associated with "membership" in a "group." Eckert's study of the *In-betweens* shows that speakers place themselves on a continuous dimension for which the actual terms *Jocks* and *Burnouts* are simply points of orientation. The dimension extends beyond these categories, as the existence of *Burned-out Burnouts* makes clear.

The generality of the conformity dimension may be linked to the generality of linguistic change across Philadelphia (the fronting of /aw/), across the Inland North (the Northern Cities Shift), across all of North America (the fronting of /uw/), or across the entire English speaking world (the new verb of quotation, *be like*).[16] The hypothesis that is put forward here is closely linked to Eckert's general hypothesis about the reigning opposition in the high schools of the United States. *Jocks and Burnouts* is based on work in a few high schools in the Detroit area. To the extent that this opposition applies to American society generally, we can expect some success in projecting a general account of the social factors driving the linguistic changes.

There are many different orienting labels that are used to define the dimension of nonconformity. The nonconformists can be "Jells," "rough," "tough," or simply "bad." But the general concept of conformity aligns this social dimension with linguistic innovation. At various times and places, the linguistic forms may well be aligned with other dimensions as well, which reinforce the forward movement: local/nonlocal, female/male, urban/rural, modern/old-fashioned. But the nonconformist/conformist polarity has a privileged position for congruence with the process of language change. It helps to explain its most general social characteristic. A great deal of evidence shows that whenever speakers become aware of a change in the

[16] For the international status of this development, see Tagliamonte and Hudson 1999.

mechanism of the language – the grammar or the sound system – they reject that change. In the course of interviewing many thousands of subjects, I and my colleagues have found older people who liked the social changes around them. They often admire the new cars, airplanes, computers, television sets, even the new music or new foods available at the supermarket. But no one has ever said, "I really like the way young people talk today, it's so much better than the way we talked when I was growing up."

My discussions of this issue inevitably produce smiles and laughter among linguists, but for others it is a serious and emotional issue. The most general and most deeply held belief about language is the *Golden Age Principle*:

*At some time in the past, language was in a state of perfection.*

It is understood that in such a state, every sound was correct and beautiful, and every word and expression was proper, accurate, and appropriate. Furthermore, the decline from that state has been regular and persistent, so that every change represents a falling away from the golden age, rather than a return to it. Every new sound will be heard as ugly, and every new expression will be heard as improper, inaccurate, and inappropriate. Given this principle it is obvious that language change must be interpreted as nonconformity to established norms, and that people will reject changes in the structure of language when they become aware of them.

Subtle and well-constructed experiments will be required to define more accurately the governing polarities of socially motivated projection. The central theme of this section is not to define the substance of the sociolinguistic parameters involved. It is to suggest that we are not dealing with anything as concrete as a reference group, but rather with abstract polarities which may take the same form in many widely separated speech communities. The socioeconomic hierarchy, reflected in occupation, education, income, or some combination of these, is such a polarity. In the mobile society of North America, there is no "membership" in the upper working class, and there are no "upper working class people" to be identified, admired, or stigmatized. There are indeed ethnic groups, and membership in the Italian or Jewish groups is a social fact. There are also recognized neighborhoods; residence at K&A or 6th & Wolfe is an established and particular fact about a given speaker. Facts like these are too particular and too concrete to be identified with the large-scale linguistic changes that sweep across Philadelphia or the Inland North. It is therefore no accident that neighborhood and ethnicity play such a marginal role in the characterization of linguistic change in chapter 7.

One might argue that chapters 8, 9, and 11 dealt with firmly established social groups where membership is clear and discretely established: men and women. There is all the more reason to listen carefully to those who would argue that gender does not affect language as such a dichotomous division, but rather as a set of socially negotiated behaviors that change over time (Eckert and McConnell-Ginet 1992). Men and women do behave differently in the course of linguistic change, but there is no clearly defined dialect that may be called "men's speech" or "women's speech."[17] Eckert's work in Detroit schools shows that what was characteristic of men at one stage may be characteristic of women at another. Thus as far as language is concerned, female/male is an abstract and continuous polarity. Our observations of the speech of Carol Meyers show just such a series of shifts on a continuous dimension rather than a switch from "men's" speech to "women's" speech.

The situation is quite different when it comes to the black/white dimension in American society. Here there is discrete group membership, and a well-defined vernacular for each group. And for this reason, the development of AAVE and the nonparticipation of black speakers in ongoing sound changes follows a different dynamic and different social principles from those considered in this chapter.

Finally, it may be observed that the very generality of these abstract polarities makes it possible to conceive of how linguistic change may be driven in the same directions across thousands of miles in many separate speech communities. As much as we have learned from the close study of Philadelphia, even more is to be expected from the examination of the extraordinary uniformity of the Northern Cities Shift throughout the Inland North, and the regional shifts of the South and Canada. The general principles of chain shifting outlined in volume 1 give us one clue to the uniformity of these great regional developments. If this volume has added anything to our understanding of linguistic change, there must also be an explanation for the uniformity of socially motivated projection throughout these vast areas. The nonconformity hypothesis is submitted as a first step in that direction.

The implications of the nonconformity hypothesis go beyond regional uniformity. There is also a consequence for the further understanding of the motivating force behind transmission across generations and the continued renewal of linguistic change. At many points the discussion has underlined the importance of change in the makeup of the speech community. But ongoing linguistic change is not confined to those areas that have received large-scale immigration from other regions. From another point of view, every community is continually receiving new members. The adolescents who enter into adult status have the same problem as any in-migrant from afar. In our society, all but a few are engaged in an uncertain struggle for secure jobs, housing, mates, and social status. The

[17] A good contrast with the modern urban situation is the well-known article of Mary Haas (1944) which describes such dialects in Koasati.

degree to which those entering members conform to established norms characterizes the strategy of their campaign to achieve these goods, as poorly defined as that campaign may be. The major conclusions of this volume can then be re-formulated as two principles of linguistic change.

1 The Nonconformity Principle: *Ongoing linguistic changes are emblematic of nonconformity to established social norms of appropriate behavior, and are generated in the social milieu that most consistently defies those norms.*

The Nonconformity Principle is conceived as an explanatory principle, directed at the motive force that leads to incrementation, transmission, and continuation. It is a logical conclusion from the consecutive investigations of chapters 9 through 12. These studies showed that the leaders of linguistic change are not simply members of the upper working class, not simply women, but women with a particular ability to confront established norms and the motivation to defy them. This principle must, however, be linked to the empirical findings of earlier chapters which led to the Curvilinear Principle: that the leaders of change are in the central, upwardly mobile groups. These chapters also established the principle that women are normally the leaders in change from below. How does the Nonconformity Principle relate to these earlier findings?

The fact that women are the leaders in most changes from below has been seen to follow inevitably from the asymmetry of language transmission. It is the nonconforming behavior of these women that makes them leaders of linguistic change, not their gender. But what is the connection between the Curvilinear Principle and the Nonconformity Principle? We know that many lower class people are nonconformists in their defiance of accepted social norms in the wider society. Yet they do not originate linguistic change.

The answer emerges from the close correlation between the position of the leaders of linguistic change and the opinion leaders in studies of personal influence (chapter 10). It is not any nonconformist who will lead the community in the incrementation of linguistic change. It is the nonconformist who is looked up to by her neighbors, considered to be a source of information and a model of good judgment. To make this connection, a second principle is needed.

2 The Constructive Nonconformity Principle: *Linguistic changes are generalized to the wider community by those who display the symbols of nonconformity in a larger pattern of upward social mobility.*

The Constructive Nonconformity Principle [CNP] links the Nonconformity Principle to the Curvilinear Principle. It follows from the broader observation that large metropolitan communities are geographically uniform, as a result of the fact that new linguistic norms spread rapidly across the city limits. The CNP appears to have a solid foundation in studies of new and vigorous linguistic changes, in studies of personal influence, and in the uniform base for orderly linguistic differentiation that is characteristic of the metropolis.

The CNP describes the behavior of adults at a stage when their phonological systems are relatively stable. The insights gained from Eckert's studies of the Northern Cities Shift in high schools concern adolescents. The changes in progress reported in chapter 8 do not all show a peak in the adolescent years, but the peak predicted in chapter 14 is most commonly found among speakers from 13 to 19/20 years old. Does the pattern described by the CNP relate to adolescents as well as young adults? Eckert has established that in the later stages of the Northern Cities Shift the major opposition is female/male (figure 13.7), and the leaders of the most advanced stage are females who show all the signs of upward social mobility (figure 13.8). At the same time, we must reserve the possibility that change continues to advance to a significant degree among young adults.

This extension of the Nonconformity Principle connects the several principles of linguistic change that have emerged in this volume to provide a reasonable scenario for the mechanism of linguistic change. The following stages represent the social trajectory of a linguistic change that takes on social evaluation; it does not apply to most mergers and other changes which run their course without taking on symbolic value of any kind. We begin with the instability that is the consequence of an asymmetry in linguistic structure.

1 For a given phoneme with mean P and asymmetrical neighbors, outliers in the direction of the farther neighbor N1 are heard as valid tokens more often than outliers in the direction of the nearer neighbor N2.
2 New language learners acquire a mean value P′ shifted in the direction of N1.
3 Steps (1) and (2) continue for succeeding generations irrespective of social evaluation, so that both P′ and N1-outliers are steadily shifted in the N1 direction.
4 Outliers in the N1 direction (N1-outliers) are heard as characteristic of younger speakers and emphatic, less monitored speech, deviant from the accepted norm of older speakers.
5 Younger nonconformist speakers consequently use a higher frequency of N1-outliers.
6 Female speakers increase their use of N1-outliers beyond that of men, so that these outliers are now heard as characteristic of female speech.
7 Male nonconformist speakers retreat from the use of N1-outliers.

8 Upwardly mobile female nonconforming speakers spread the use of N1-outliers and shifted P′ means to the limits of the speech community.
9 A pattern of social stratification of P develops with the highest values of the variable in communities with the highest concentration of upwardly mobile nonconforming speakers.
10 The use of N1-outliers rises to public awareness and irregular social correction begins.

Stage (8) is a restatement of the CNP. As such, it is the crucial link that has emerged from the search for the leaders of linguistic change, the central focus of this volume. Nonconformity here indicates deviation from the dominant norms of adult society, whatever they may be. The generality of nonconformism allows us to avoid fixing the generating center of change at any particular point in the socioeconomic hierarchy. In any society with a reasonable degree of social mobility, the CNP will tend to concentrate the leaders of linguistic change in a centrally located group – the upper working class or the lower middle class. In a society with little social mobility, they will remain in the lowest social class, and change will spread upward from that point (Oliveira 1983).

This outline of the social motivation of linguistic change is a model of change from below, originating within the linguistic and social system. It does not deal with influences that may stem from dialect contact or the substrate effects of other mother tongues. Nor does it take into account the consequences of the division of American speech communities into a white and non-white component. The nonconformist groups that are specified here are essentially white nonconformists. In some marginal sectors of intense and hostile conflict, white lower class speakers will show the influence of black speech patterns, but this is not the norm in the highly segregated cities of the urban North and West. It is possible that some of the motivating force behind the renewal of linguistic change among whites is a reaction against the pressure from non-white groups to claim their share of jobs, housing, and other local privileges (Labov 1980). This was an important element in the social motivation of sound change in the first study of this kind (Labov 1963). However, this cross-ethnic pressure has not been demonstrated for the larger segregated cities that are the focus of this volume, and more studies of the interface between black and white speech communities will be needed before it can be evaluated for the nation as a whole.

# Afterword

In this volume, I have tried to use every available resource of sociolinguistic research and analysis to illuminate long-standing problems of linguistic change. As the foreword stated, the two chief data bases for this inquiry are drawn from studies that are separated by a period of twenty years. The study of Philadelphia achieved a detailed and local description of the speakers of the language in their neighborhoods and social networks. At the outset, the major results were confirmed by a telephone survey that covered the entire city with input data that approximated less closely the speech of everyday life. Almost every chapter has expanded the implications of these findings by drawing data from a much larger survey of North America as a whole, again from a telephone survey of individuals. A wide variety of analytical methods has been brought to bear upon these materials. Multiple regression and principal component analyses have played a major role in extracting the underlying regularities that govern language change. The combination of these with extensive cross-tabulations and graphic displays was needed to display the full regularity of the relations involved. These tools were required in the step-by-step search for the leaders of linguistic change, as the familiar sociolinguistic dimensions of age, social class, gender, ethnicity, neighborhood, and social networks were explored more deeply. Once these individuals had been located, the fuller portrait of their characters and life histories in chapter 12 was essential in the search for a fuller understanding of the mechanism and motivation of linguistic change. Only with that understanding could we approach in a meaningful way the more general and abstract problems of transmission, incrementation, and continuation in the chapters that followed.

To the extent that the end results are useful, it is important for me to reiterate my indebtedness to my colleagues in these two major enterprises. In the study of linguistic change and variation in Philadelphia, I was joined by Anne Bower, Elizabeth Dayton, Gregory Guy, Don Hindle, Matt Lennig, Arvilla Payne, Shana Poplack, and Deborah Schiffrin. In the Telsur survey and the *Atlas of North American English*, my chief collaborators are Sherry Ash and Charles Boberg, with major contributions from Thomas Macieski, Carol Orr, David Bowie, Shawn Maeder, Christine Moisset, and Maciej Baranowski. These are not my only colleagues in this enterprise.

Throughout, I have drawn with pleasure and profit from the brilliant work of James and Lesley Milroy, Jack Chambers, Paul Kerswill, Peter Trudgill, and Penelope Eckert. In the course of writing this volume, I have come to realize that there is no simple way in which I can discharge my deep indebtedness to these colleagues or do justice to their contributions. I feel an equal sense of admiration for Celeste S., the leader of linguistic change who stands as archetype and exemplar throughout this work, and gratitude for the insights she and Anne Bower have given us in their joint inquiries into the workings of the Clark Street community. Yet those who have followed the history of sociolinguistic research from its inception some thirty-odd years ago, will appreciate the ways in which this work flows naturally from the perspective first put forward by Uriel Weinreich, whose name must stand opposite the title page in this volume as in the first.

# *References*

Abdel-Jawad, Hassan 1981. Phonological and social variation in Arabic in Amman. University of Pennsylvania dissertation.

Abdel-Jawad, Hassan R. 1987. Cross-dialectal variation in Arabic: competing prestigious forms. *Language in Society* 16: 359–67.

Alba, Orlando 1990. *Variacion Fonetica y Diversidad Social en el Espanol Dominicano de Santiago*. Santiago: Pontificia Universidad Catolica Madre Y Maestra.

Albo, Xavier 1970. Social constraints on Cochabamba Quecha. Cornell University dissertation: Latin American Studies Progam, Dissertation Series No. 19.

Alexander, John K. 1973. Poverty, fear and continuity: an analysis of the poor in late eighteenth-century Philadelphia. In Allen Davis and Mark Haller (eds), *The Peoples of Philadelphia: A History of Ethnic Groups and Lower-Class Life, 1790–1940*. Philadelphia: Temple University Press, pp. 13–36.

Andersen, Peter A., and John P. Garrison 1976. Media consumption and population characteristics of political opinion leaders. *Communication Quarterly* 26: 40–50.

Anisfeld, Elizabeth, and Wallace E. Lambert 1964. Evaluational reactions of bilingual and monolingual children to spoken languages. *Journal of Abnormal and Social Psychology* 69(1): 89–97.

Anshen, Frank 1969. Speech variation among Negroes in a small southern community. New York University dissertation.

Anspach, Karlyne 1967. *The Why of Fashion*. Ames: The Iowa State University Press.

Ash, Sharon 1982a. The vocalization of /l/ in Philadelphia. University of Pennsylvania dissertation.

Ash, Sharon 1982b. The vocalization of intervocalic /l/ in Philadelphia. *The SECOL Review* 6: 162–75.

Ash, Sharon, and John Myhill 1986. Linguistic correlates of inter-ethnic contact. In D. Sankoff (ed.), *Diversity and Diachrony*. Philadelphia: John Benjamins, pp. 33–44.

Babbitt, E. H. 1896. The English of the lower classes in New York City and vicinity. *Dialect Notes* 1: 457–64.

Bailey, Charles-James N. 1973. *Variation and Linguistic Theory*. Washington, D.C.: Center for Applied Linguistics.

Bailey, Guy 1993. A perspective on African-American English. In Dennis Preston (ed.), *American Dialect Research*. Philadelphia: Benjamins, pp. 287–318.

Bailey, Guy, and Natalie Maynor 1987. Decreolization? *Language in Society* 16: 449–73.

Bailey, Guy, and Natalie Maynor 1989. The divergence controversy. *American Speech* 64: 12–39.

Bailey, Guy, and Gary Ross 1992. The evolution of a vernacular. In M. Rissanen et al. (eds), *History of Englishes: New Methods and Interpretations in Historical Linguistics*. Berlin: Mouton de Gruyter, pp. 519–31.

Bailey, Guy, Tom Wikle, Jan Tillery, and Lori Sand 1991. The apparent time construct. *Language Variation and Change* 3: 241–64.

Baker, P., and C. Corne 1982. *Isle de France Creole: Affinities and Origins*. Ann Arbor: Karoma Press.

Bakir, Murthada 1986. Sex differences in the approximation to Standard Arabic: a case study. *Anthropological Linguistics* 28: 3–9.

Baltzell, E. Digby 1958. *Philadelphia Gentlemen: The Making of a National Upper Class*. New York: Free Press.

Banuazizi, Atissa, and Mimi Lipson 1998. The tensing of /æ/ before /l/: an anomalous case for short-a rules of white Philadelphia speech. In Claude Paradis (ed.), *Papers in Sociolinguistics: NWAVE-26 a l'Université Laval*. Quebec: Editions Nota Bene.

Bauer, Robert S. 1982. Lexical Diffusion in Hong Kong Cantonese: "Five" Leads the Way. Paper given at the 8th annual BLS meeting.

Baugh, John 1983. *Black Street Speech: Its History, Structure and Survival*. Austin: University of Texas Press.

Baumgarten, Steven A. 1975. The innovative communicator in the diffusion process. *Journal of Marketing Research* 12: 12–18.

Beckman, Mary E., Kenneth De Jong, Sun-Ah Jun, and Sook-Huang Lee 1992. The interaction of coarticulation and prosody in sound change. *Language and Speech* 35: 45–58.

Bell, Allan 1984. Language style as audience design. *Language in Society* 13: 145–204.

Bell, Quentin 1949. *On Human Finery*. New York: A. A. Wyn.

Bickerton, Derek 1981. *Roots of Language*. Ann Arbor: Karoma Press.

Binzen, Peter 1970. *Whitetown, USA*. New York: Random House.

Bloch, Bernard, and Trager, G. L. 1942. Outline of linguistic analysis. LSA Special Publication, 82 pp. Washington, D.C.: Linguistic Society of America.

Bloomfield, Leonard 1933. *Language*. New York: Henry Holt.

Blumer, Herbert 1969. Fashion: from class differentiation to collective selection. *Sociological Quarterly* 10: 275–91.

Boissevain, Jeremy 1974. *Friends of Friends: Networks, Manipulators, and Coalitions*. Oxford: Basil Blackwell.

Bortoni-Ricardo, Stella M. 1985. *The Urbanization of Rural Dialect Speakers: A Sociolinguistic Study in Brazil*. Cambridge: Cambridge University Press.

Bott, Elizabeth 1955. Urban families: conjugal roles and social networks. *Human Relations* VI(4): 345–84.

Bourdieu, Pierre 1980. The production of belief: contribution to an economy of symbolic goods. *Media, Culture and Society* 2: 261–93.

Bower, Anne 1984. The construction of stance in conflict narrative. University of Pennsylvania dissertation.

Bradley, David, and Maya Bradley 1979. *Melbourne Vowels*. Working Papers in Linguistics 5. University of Melbourne, Linguistics Section.

Braga, Maria Luisa 1982. A study of left dislocation and topicalization in Cape Verdean Creole. University of Pennsylvania dissertation.

Brouwer, Dede 1989. *Gender Variation in Dutch. A Sociolinguistic Study of Amsterdam Speech*. Dordrecht: Foris Publications. Topics in Sociolinguistics 8.

Burstein, Alan 1981. Immigrants and residential mobility: the Irish and Germans in Philadelphia. In Theodore Hershberg (ed.), *Philadelphia: Work, Space, Family and Group Experience in the Nineteenth Century*. New York: Oxford University Press, pp. 174–203.

Callary, R. E. 1975. Phonological change and the development of an urban dialect in Illinois. *Language in Society* 4: 155–70.

Cameron, Richard 1991. Pronominal and null subject variation in Spanish: constraints, dialects and functional compensation. University of Pennsylvania dissertation.

Carver, Craig M. 1987. *American Regional Dialects: A Word Geography*. Ann Arbor: University of Michigan Press.

Casper, Lynne M. 1997. My Daddy takes care of me: fathers as care providers. Census Current Population Reports: Household Economic Studies. Report P70-59.

Cedergren, Henrietta 1973. The interplay of social and linguistic factors in Panama. Unpublished Cornell University dissertation.

Cedergren, Henrietta 1984. Panama Revisited: Sound Change in Real Time. Paper given at NWAVE, Philadelphia, 1984.

Cedergren, Henrietta, and David Sankoff 1974. Variable rules: performance as a statistical reflection of competence. *Language* 50: 333–55.

Chae, Seo-Yong 1995. External constraints on sound change: the raising of /o/ in Seoul Korean. University of Pennsylvania dissertation.

Chambers, J. K. 1995. *Sociolinguistic Theory*. Oxford: Blackwell.

Chambers, J. K., and Margaret F. Hardwick 1985. Dialect homogeneity and incipient variation: changes in progress in Toronto and Vancouver. In J. Harris and R. Hawkins (eds), *Sheffield Working Papers in Language and Linguistics* 2. Sheffield: School of Modern Languages and Linguistics, University of Sheffield.

Chomsky, Noam 1964. *Comments for Project Literacy Meeting*. Project Literacy Reports No. 2. Ithaca: Cornell University.

Chomsky, Noam, and Morris Halle 1968. *The Sound Pattern of English*. New York: Harper & Row.

Christy, Craig 1983. *Uniformitarianism in Linguistics*. Philadelphia: John Benjamins.

Clark, Dennis 1973. The Philadelphia Irish: persistent presence. In Allen Davis and Mark Haller (eds), *The Peoples of Philadelphia: A History of Ethnic Groups and Lower-Class Life, 1790–1940*. Philadelphia: Temple University Press, pp. 135–54.

Clarke, Sandra 1987. Dialect mixing and linguistic variation in a non-overtly stratified society. In Keith M. Denning et al. (eds), *Variation in Language: NWAVE-XV at Stanford*. Stanford: Department of Linguistics, Stanford University, pp. 74–85.

Clarke, Sandra, Folrd Elms, and Amani Youssef 1995. The third dialect of English: some Canadian evidence. *Language Variation and Change* 7: 209–28.

Cloward, Richard A., and Lloyd E. Ohlin 1960. *Delinquency and Opportunity: A Theory of Delinquent Gangs*. Glencoe, IL: The Free Press.

Cofer, Thomas 1972. Linguistic variability in a Philadelphia speech community. University of Pennsylvania dissertation.

Cook, Stanley 1969. Language change and the emergence of an urban dialect in Utah. Unpublished University of Utah dissertation.

Cukor-Avila, Patricia 1995. The evolution of AAVE in a rural Texas community: an ethnolinguistic study. University of Michigan dissertation.

Danielsson, Bror 1948. *Studies on the Accentuation of Polysyllabic Latin, Greek, and Romance Loan-Words in English: with special reference to those ending in -able, -ate, -ator, -ible, -ic, -ical, and -ize*. Stockholm: Almqvist & Wiksells.

Darwin, Charles 1871. *The Descent of Man, and Selection in Relation to Sex*. 1st edn, 2 vols. London: John Murray.

Davis, Allen F., and Mark H. Haller 1973. *The Peoples of Philadelphia: A History of Ethnic Groups and Lower-Class Life, 1790–1940*. Philadelphia: Temple University Press.

Dayton, Elizabeth 1996. Grammatical categories of the verb in African American Vernacular English. University of Pennsylvania unpublished PhD dissertation.

De Camp, L. Sprague 1933. Transcription of "The North Wind" as spoken by a Philadelphian. *Le Maître Phonétique*.

Delattre, Pierre, Alvin M. Liberman, Franklin S. Cooper, and Louis J. Gerstman 1952. An experimental study of the acoustic determinants of vowel color: observations on one- and two-formant vowels synthesized from spectrographic patterns. *Word* 8: 195–210.

Di Paolo, Marianna 1988. Pronunciation and categorization in sound change. In K. Ferrara et al. (eds), *Linguistic Change and Contact*: NWAVE XVI. Austin: Dept of Linguistics, University of Texas, pp. 84–92.

Dobson, E. J. 1957. *English Pronunciation 1500–1700*. Vol. II: *Phonology*. Oxford: Oxford University Press.

Douglas-Cowie, Ellen 1978. Linguistic code-switching in a Northern Irish village: social interaction and social ambition. In P. Trudgill (ed.), *Sociolinguistic Patterns in British English*. London: Edward Arnold, pp. 37–51.

Downes, William 1998. *Language and Society*, 2nd edn. Cambridge: Cambridge University Press.

Dressler, Wolfgang, and Alexander Grosu 1972. Generative Phonologie und indogermanische Lautgeschichte: Eine kritische Wurdigung. *Indogermanische-Forschungen* 77: 19–72.

DuBois, W. E. B. 1967. *The Philadelphia Negro: A Social Study*. Philadelphia: Schocken Books.

Duncan, Otis D. 1961. A socioeconomic index for all occupations. In A. Reiss (ed.), *Occupations and Social Status*. New York: The Free Press, pp. 109–38.

Eckert, Penelope 1986. The roles of high school social structure in phonological change. Chicago Linguistic Society.

Eckert, Penelope 1988. Adolescent social structure and the spread of linguistic change. *Language in Society* 17: 183–208.

Eckert, Penelope 1989a. *Jocks and Burnouts: Social Categories and Identities in the High School*. New York: Teachers College Press.

Eckert, Penelope 1989b. The whole woman: sex and gender differences in variation. *Language Variation and Change* 1: 245–68.

Eckert, Penelope 1991. Social polarization and the choice of linguistic variants. In P. Eckert (ed.), *New Ways of Analyzing Sound Change*. New York: Academic Press.

Eckert, Penelope 1996. Age of a sociolinguistic variable. In Florian Coulmas (ed.), *Handbook of Sociolinguistics*. Oxford: Blackwell.

Eckert, Penelope 1999. *Linguistic Variation as Social Practice*. Oxford: Blackwell.

Eckert, Penelope, and Sally McConnell-Ginet 1992. Think practically and look locally: language and gender as community-based practice. *Annual Review of Anthropology* 21: 461–90.

Eco, Umberto 1979. *A Theory of Semiotics*. Bloomington: Indiana University Press.

Edwards, Walter F. 1992. Sociolinguistic behavior in a Detroit inner-city black neighborhood. *Language in Society* 21: 93–115.

Eisikovits, Edina 1981. Inner-Sydney English: an investigation of grammatical variation in adolescent speech. University of Sydney dissertation.

Fasold, Ralph 1969. A sociolinguistic study of the pronunciation of three vowels in Detroit speech. Mimeograph.

Feagin, Crawford 1979. *Variation and Change in Alabama English*. Washington, D.C.: Georgetown University Press.

Feldberg, Michael 1973. Urbanization as a cause of violence: Philadelphia as a test case. In Allen Davis and Mark Haller (eds), *The Peoples of Philadelphia: A History of Ethnic Groups and Lower-Class Life, 1790–1940*. Philadelphia: Temple University Press, pp. 53–70.

Ferguson, Charles A. 1975. "Short a" in Philadelphia English. In Estellie Smith (ed.), *Studies in Linguistics in Honor of George L. Trager*. The Hague: Mouton, pp. 259–74.

Fillmore, Charles J., Daniel Kempler, and William S-Y. Wang (eds) 1979. *Individual Differences in Language Ability and Language Behavior*. New York: Academic Press.

Fischer, John L. 1958. Social influences on the choice of a linguistic variant. *Word* 14: 47–56.

Frank, Yakira 1948. The speech of New York City. Unpublished University of Michigan dissertation.

Frazer, Timothy C. 1983. Sound change and social structure in a rural community. *Language in Society* 12: 313–28.

Frazer, Timothy 1987. Attitudes towards regional pronunciation. *Journal of English Linguistics* 20: 89–100.

Gal, Susan 1978. Peasant men can't get wives: linguistic change and sex roles in a bilingual community. *Language in Society* 7: 1–17.

Gal, Susan 1980. *Language Shift: Social Determinants of Linguistic Change in Bilingual Austria*. New York: Academic Press.

Gallistel, Randolph 1990. *The Organization of Learning*. Cambridge, MA: MIT Press.

Gambhir, Surendra 1981. The East Indian speech community in Guyana: a sociolinguistic study with special reference to Koine formation. University of Pennsylvania dissertation.

Gauchat, Louis 1905. L'unité phonétique dans le patois d'une commune. In *Aus Romanischen Sprachen und Literaturen: Festschrift Heinrich Mort*, pp. 175–232.

Gay, Thomas 1977. Effect of speaking rate on vowel formant movements. Haskins Laboratories Status Report on Speech Research 51–52: 101–17.

Gehl, Jan 1977. *Interface*. Melbourne: Department of Architecture and Building, Melbourne University.

Gerson, Stanley 1967. *Sound and Symbol in the Dialogue of the Works of Charles Dickens*. A survey of the divergencies from normally received spellings in the dialogue of Dickens' works, together with an investigation into Dickens' methods of conveying an impression of divergent sounds of speech. Stockholm: Almqvist & Wiksell.

Gerstman, Louis J. 1967. Classification of self-normalized vowels. Paper delivered to 1967 Conference on Speech Communication and Processing.

Gilbert, Dennis, and Joseph A. Kahl 1993. *The American Class Structure: A New Synthesis*. Belmont, CA: Wadsworth Publishing Co.

Gleason, H. A. 1961. *An Introduction to Descriptive Linguistics*, rev. edn. New York: Holt, Rinehart and Winston.

Gordon, Elizabeth 1997. Sex, speech and stereotypes: why women use prestige speech forms more than men. *Language in Society* 26: 1–14.

Gordon, Matthew, and Jeffrey Heath 1998. Sex, sound symbolism and sociolinguistics. *Current Anthropology* 39.

Gould, Stephen Jay 1989. *Wonderful Life*. New York: W. W. Norton.

Graff, David, William Labov, and Wendell A. Harris 1986. Testing listeners' reactions to phonological markers. In D. Sankoff (ed.), *Diversity and Diachrony*. Philadelphia: John Benjamins, pp. 45–58.

Granovetter, Mark 1973. The strength of weak ties. *American Journal of Sociology* 78: 1360–80.

Greenberg, Joseph H. 1959. Language and evolution. In *Evolution and Anthropology: A Centennial Appraisal*. Washington, D.C.: Anthropological Society of Washington.

Greenberg, Joseph 1969. Some methods of dynamic comparison in linguistics. In J. Puhvel (ed.), *Substance and Structure in Linguistics*. Berkeley: University of California Press, pp. 147–204.

Gregersen, Frans, and Inge Lise Pedersen (eds) 1991. *The Copenhagen Study in Urban Sociolinguistics. Parts I and II*. Copenhagen: C. A. Reitzels Forlag.

Gryner, Helena, and Alizira Tavares de Macedo 1981. La prononciation du *s* post-vocalique: deux processus de changement linguistique en portugais. In D. Sankoff and H. Cedergren (eds), *Variation Omnibus*. Alberta: Linguistic Research, pp. 135–40.

Guy, Gregory R. 1980. Variation in the group and the individual: the case of final stop deletion. In W. Labov (ed.), *Locating Language in Time and Space*. New York: Academic Press, pp. 1–36.

Guy, Gregory R., and Sally Boyd 1990. The development of a morphological class. *Language Variation and Change* 2: 1–18.

Guy, Gregory, B. Horvath, J. Vonwiller, E. Daisley, and I. Rogers 1986. An intonational change in progress in Australian English. *Language in Society* 15: 23–52.

Haas, Mary R. 1944. Men's and women's speech in Koasati. *Language* 20: 142–9. Reprinted in D. Hymes (ed.), *Language in Culture and Society*. New York: Harper & Row, 1964, pp. 228–33.

Habick, Timothy 1980. Sound change in Farmer City: a sociolinguistic study based on acoustic data. University of Illinois at Urbana-Champaign dissertation.

Haeri, Niloofar 1987. Male/female differences in speech: an alternative interpretation. In Keith M. Denning et al. (eds), *Variation in Language: NWAVE-XV at Stanford.* Stanford: Department of Linguistics, Stanford University, pp. 173–82.

Haeri, Niloofar 1996. *The Sociolinguistic Market of Cairo: Gender, Class and Education.* London: Kegan Paul International.

Halle, Morris 1962. Phonology in generative grammar. *Word* 18: 54–72.

Harris, John 1985. *Phonological Variation and Change: Studies in Hiberno-Irish.* Cambridge: Cambridge University Press.

Haudricourt, A. G., and A. G. Juilland 1949. *Essai pour une histoire structurale du phonétisme français.* Paris: C. Klincksieck.

Hazen, Kirk 2000. *Identity and Ethnicity in the Rural South: A Sociolinguistic View through Past and Present BE.* Publication of the American Dialect Society 83. Durham: Duke University Press.

Heath, M. R., and S. J. Bekker 1986. *Identification of Opinion Leaders in Public Affairs, Educational Matters, and Family Planning in the Township of Atteridgeville.* Pretoria: Human Sciences Research Council.

Henry, O. 1945. *The Best Short Stories of O. Henry.* Selected, and with an introduction, by Bennett A. Cerf and Van H. Cartnell. New York: The Modern Library.

Hermann, E. 1929. Lautveränderungen in der individualsprache einer Mundart. *Nachrichten der Gesellsch. der Wissenschaften zu Göttingen.* Phl.-his. Kll., 11, 195–214.

Herold, Ruth 1990. Mechanisms of merger: the implementation and distribution of the low back merger in Eastern Pennsylvania. University of Pennsylvania dissertation.

Herold, Ruth 1997. Solving the actuation problem: merger and immigration in eastern Pennsylvania. *Language Variation and Change* 9: 149–64.

Hershberg, Theodore (ed.) 1981. *Philadelphia: Work, Space, Family and Group Experience in the Nineteenth Century.* New York: Oxford University Press.

Hershberg, Theodore, et al. 1981. A tale of three cities: blacks, immigrants and opportunity in Philadelphia, 1850–1880, 1930, 1970. In T. Hershberg (ed.), *Philadelphia: Work, Space, Family and Group Experience in the Nineteenth Century.* New York: Oxford University Press, pp. 461–95.

Hibiya, Junko 1988. Social stratification of Tokyo Japanese. University of Pennsylvania dissertation.

Hindle, Donald 1974. Syntactic variation in Philadelphia: positive *anymore.* Pennsylvania Working Papers on Linguistic Change and Variation, No. 5. Philadelphia: Linguistics Laboratory, University of Pennsylvania.

Hindle, Donald 1978. Approaches to vowel normalization in the study of natural speech. In D. Sankoff (ed.), *Linguistic Variation: Models and Methods.* New York: Academic Press, pp. 161–72.

Hindle, Donald 1980. The social and structural conditioning of phonetic variation. University of Pennsylvania Ph.D. dissertation.

Hindle, Donald, and Ivan Sag 1973. Some more on *anymore.* In R. Fasold and R. Shuy (eds), *Analyzing Variation in Language.* Papers NWAVE II. Washington, D.C.: Georgetown University Press.

Hinskens, Frans Léon Marie Paul 1992. Dialect leveling in Limburg: structural and sociolinguistic aspects. Catholic University of Nijmegen dissertation.

Hock, Hans Heinrich 1986. *Principles of Historical Linguistics*. Berlin: Mouton de Gruyter.

Hockett, Charles 1958. *A Course in Modern Linguistics*. New York: Macmillan.

Hoekje, Barbara 1978. Make or Let? MS. Paper submitted to Linguistics 660, 1978.

Hollingshead, August, and Frederick Redlich 1958. *Social Class and Mental Illness*. New York: John Wiley.

Holmquist, Jonathan C. 1985. Social correlates of a linguistic variable: a study in a Spanish village. *Language in Society* 14: 191–203.

Holmquist, Jonathan 1987. Style choice in a bidialectal Spanish village. *International Journal of the Sociology of Language*: 21–30.

Holmquist, Jonathan 1988. *Language Loyalty and Linguistic Variation: A Study in Spanish Cantabria*. Dordrecht: Foris.

Hong, Yunsook 1991. *A Sociolinguistic Study of Seoul Korean*. Seoul: Research Center for Peace and Unification of Korea.

Horvath, Barbara 1985. *Variation in Australian English: The Sociolects of Sydney*. London: Cambridge University Press.

Horvath, B., and D. Sankoff 1987. Delimiting the Sydney speech community. *Language in Society* 16: 179–204.

Houston, Anne 1985. Continuity and change in English morphology: the variable (ING). Chapter 6: Establishing the continuity between past and present morphology, pp. 220–86. University of Pennsylvania Ph.D. dissertation.

Houston, Anne 1991. A grammatical continuum for (ING). In P. Trudgill and J. Chambers (eds), *Dialects of English: Studies in Grammatical Variation*. Singapore: Longman Singapore, pp. 241–57.

Hoyenga, Katherine B., and Kermit T. Hoyenga 1993. *Gender Related Differences: Origins and Outcomes*. Boston: Allyn & Bacon.

Hubbell, Allan F. 1962. *The Pronunciation of English in New York City. Consonants and Vowels*. New York: King's Crown Press, Columbia University.

Humboldt, Wilhelm von 1836. *Über die Kawisprache*. Part I, *Über die verschiedenheit des Menschlichen Sprachbaues und Ihren Einfluss auf die geisteige Entwickelung des Menschengeschlechts*. Berlin: Abhandlungen der Akademie der Wissenschaften zu Berlin.

Hymes, Dell 1961. Functions of speech: an evolutionary approach. In F. C. Gruber (ed.), *Anthropology and Education*. Philadelphia: University of Pennsylvania Press.

Jahangiri, Nader 1980. A sociolinguistic study of Persian in Teheran. London University dissertation.

Jain, Dhanesh K. 1973. Pronominal usage in Hindi: a sociolinguistic study. University of Pennsylvania dissertation.

Jakobson, Roman 1972. Principles of historical phonology. In A. R. Keiler (ed.), *A Reader in Historical and Comparative Linguistics*. New York: Holt, Rinehart and Winston, pp. 121–38.

Jespersen, Otto 1921. *Language: Its Nature, Development and Origin*. New York: W. W. Norton & Co. [1946].

Johnson, S. Jacqueline, and Elissa L. Newport 1989. Critical period efforts in second-language learning: the influence of maturational state on the acquisition of English as a second language. *Cognitive Psychology* 21: 60–99.

Kaisse, Ellen M. 1977. On the syntactic environment of a phonological rule. Papers from the Regional Meetings, Chicago Linguistic Society.

Katz, Elihu, and Paul Lazersfeld 1955. *Personal Influence*. Glencoe, IL: Free Press.

Kemp, William, and Malcah Yaeger-Dror 1991. Changing realizations of A in *(a)tion* in relation to the front A–back A opposition in Quebec French. In P. Eckert (ed.), *New Ways of Analyzing Sound Change*. New York: Academic Press.

Kenyon, John 1948. Cultural levels and functional varieties of English. *College English* 10: 31–6.

Kerswill, Paul 1993. Rural dialect speakers in an urban speech community: the role of dialect contact in defining a sociolinguistic concept. *International Journal of Applied Linguistics* 3(1): 33–56.

Kerswill, Paul, and Ann Williams 1994. A New Dialect in a New City: Children's and Adults' Speech in Milton Keynes. Final report to Economic and Social Research Council.

Kerswill, Paul and Ann Williams to appear. Creating a new town koine: children and language change in Milton Keynes. *Language in Society*.

Kimura, Doreen 1983. Sex differences in cerebral organizations for speech and praxic functions. *Canadian Journal of Psychology* 37: 19–35.

King, Robert 1969. *Historical Linguistics and Generative Grammar*. New York: Holt, Rinehart, and Winston.

King, Robert 1975. Integrating linguistic change. In K. H. Dahlstedt (ed.), *The Nordic Languages and Modern Linguistics*. Stockholm: Almqvist & Wiksell, pp. 47–69.

Kiparsky, Paul 1971. Historical linguistics. In W. Dingwall (ed.), *A Survey of Linguistic Science*. College Park: University of Maryland, pp. 577–649.

Kiparsky, Paul 1982. *Explanation in Phonology*. Dordrecht: Foris.

Knack, Rebecca 1991. Ethnic boundaries in linguistic variation. In P. Eckert (ed.), *New Ways of Analyzing Sound Change*. New York: Academic Press.

Kökeritz, Helge 1953. *Shakespeare's Pronunciation*. New Haven: Yale University Press.

Kroch, Anthony 1978. Toward a theory of social dialect variation. *Language in Society* 7: 17–36.

Kroch, Anthony 1989. Reflexes of grammar in patterns of language change. *Language Variation and Change* 1: 199–244.

Kroch, Anthony 1996. Dialect and style in the speech of upper class Philadelphia. In G. Guy, C. Feagin, D. Schiffrin, and J. Baugh (eds), *Towards a Social Science of Language*, vol. 1. Philadelphia: John Benjamins, pp. 23–46.

Kurath, Hans 1939. *Handbook of the Linguistic Geography of New England*. Providence, RI: American Council of Learned Societies.

Kurath, Hans 1949. *Word Geography of the Eastern United States*. Ann Arbor: University of Michigan Press.

Kurath, Hans, and Raven I. McDavid, Jr. 1961. *The Pronunciation of English in the Atlantic States*. Ann Arbor: University of Michigan Press.

Kurylowicz, Jerzy 1964. On the methods of internal reconstruction. In H. G. Lunt (ed.), *Proceedings of the Ninth International Congress of Linguistics*. The Hague: Mouton.

Labov, William 1963. The social motivation of a sound change. *Word* 19: 273–309. Revised as ch.1, pp. 1–42 in *Sociolinguistic Patterns*. Philadelphia: University of Pennsylvania Press, 1972.

Labov, William 1964. Stages in the acquisition of standard English. In R. Shuy (ed.), *Social Dialects and Language Learning*. Champaign, IL: National Council of Teachers of English, pp. 77–103. Reprinted in H. B. Allen and Gary Underwood (eds), *Readings in American Dialectology*. New York: Appleton-Century-Crofts, 1971, pp. 473–98.

Labov, William 1965. On the mechanism of linguistic change. *Georgetown Monographs on Language and Linguistics* 18: 91–114. Reprinted as ch. 7 in *Sociolinguistic Patterns*. Philadelphia: University of Pennsylvania Press, 1972.

Labov, William 1966a. *The Social Stratification of English in New York City*. Washington, D.C.: Center for Applied Linguistics.

Labov, William 1966b. The effect of social mobility on linguistic behavior. In S. Lieberson (ed.), *Explorations in Sociolinguistics*. Bloomington: Indiana University Press, pp. 186–203.

Labov, William 1972a. Negative attraction and negative concord in English grammar. *Language* 48: 773–818. Revised as ch. 4 of *Language in the Inner City* (1972), Philadelphia: University of Pennsylvania Press.

Labov, William 1972b. *Sociolinguistic Patterns*. Philadelphia: University of Pennsylvania Press.

Labov, William 1972c. The linguistic consequences of being a lame. *Language in Society* 2: 81–115. Reprinted in *Language in the Inner City* (1972), Philadelphia: University of Pennsylvania Press, pp. 255–97.

Labov, William 1972d. Where do grammars stop? In R. Shuy (ed.), *Georgetown Monograph on Languages and Linguistics* 25, pp. 43–88.

Labov, William 1974. Language change as a form of communication. In Albert Silverstein (ed.), *Human Communication*. Hillsdale, NJ: Erlbaum, pp. 221–56.

Labov, William 1976. The relative influence of family and peers on the learning of language. In R. Simone et al. (eds), *Aspetti Socioling. Dell' Italia Contemporanea*. Rome: Bulzoni.

Labov, William 1980. The social origins of sound change. In W. Labov (ed.), *Locating Language in Time and Space*. New York: Academic Press, pp. 251–66.

Labov, William 1981. What can be inferred about change in progress from synchronic descriptions? In D. Sankoff and H. Cedergren (eds), *Variation Omnibus* [NWAVE VIII]. Alberta: Linguistic Research, pp. 177–200.

Labov, William 1982. Building on empirical foundations. In W. Lehmann and Y. Malkiel (eds), *Perspectives on Historical Linguistics*. Amsterdam/Philadelphia: John Benjamins, pp. 17–92.

Labov, William 1984. Field methods of the Project on Linguistic Change and Variation. In J. Baugh and J. Sherzer (eds), *Language in Use*. Englewood Cliffs, NJ: Prentice-Hall, pp. 28–53.

Labov, William 1988. The judicial testing of linguistic theory. In D. Tannen (ed.), *Language in Context: Connecting Observation and Understanding*. Norwood, NJ: Ablex, pp. 159–82.

Labov, William 1989a. The child as linguistic historian. *Language Variation and Change* 1: 85–94.

Labov, William 1989b. The exact description of the speech community: short *a* in Philadelphia. In R. Fasold and D. Schiffrin (eds), *Language Change and Variation*. Washington, D.C.: Georgetown University Press, pp. 1–57.

Labov, William 1989c. The limitations of context. *Chicago Linguistic Society* 25, Part 2, pp. 171–200.

Labov, William 1990. The intersection of sex and social class in the course of linguistic change. *Language Variation and Change* 2: 205–54. Reprinted in J. Cheshire and P. Trudgill (eds), *The Sociolinguistics Reader*, vol. 2: *Gender and Discourse*. London: Arnold, 1998, pp. 7–52.

Labov, William 1992. On the adequacy of natural languages I: the development of tense. In J. Singler (ed.), *Pidgin and Creole Tense-Mood-Aspect Systems*. Philadelphia: John Benjamins, pp. 1–58.

Labov, William 1995. The two futures of linguistics. In Ik-Hwan Lee (ed.), *Linguistics in the Morning Calm 3: Selected Papers from SICOL-1992*. Seoul: Hanshin Publishing Co., 1995, pp. 113–48.

Labov, William, to appear. The anatomy of style. To appear in P. Eckert and J. Rickford.

Labov, William, and Sharon Ash 1997. Understanding Birmingham. In C. Bernstein, T. Nunnally, and R. Sabino (eds), *Language Variety in the South Revisited*. Tuscaloosa: University of Alabama Press, pp. 508–73.

Labov, William, Sharon Ash, and Charles Boberg in press. *Atlas of North American English*. Berlin: Mouton de Gruyter.

Labov, William, and Julie Auger 1998. The effect of normal aging on discourse: a sociolinguistic approach. In Hiram H. Brownell and Yves Joanette (eds), *Narrative Discourse in Neurologically Impaired and Normal Aging Adults*. San Diego, CA: Singular Publishing Group, pp. 115–34.

Labov, William, P. Cohen, C. Robins, and J. Lewis 1968. A study of the non-standard English of Negro and Puerto Rican Speakers in New York City. Cooperative Research Report 3288, vols I and II. Philadelphia: U.S. Regional Survey (Linguistics Laboratory, University of Pennsylvania).

Labov, William, and Wendell A. Harris 1986. De facto segregation of black and white vernaculars. In D. Sankoff (ed.), *Diversity and Diachrony*. Philadelphia: John Benjamins, pp. 1–24.

Labov, William, and Wendell Harris 1994. Addressing social issues through linguistic evidence. In J. Gibbons (ed.), *Language and the Law*. London and New York: Longman, pp. 265–305.

Labov, William, Mark Karan, and Corey Miller 1991. Near-mergers and the suspension of phonemic contrast. *Language Variation and Change* 3: 33–74.

Labov, William, and Gillian Sankoff, to appear. *The Study of the Speech Community*.

Labov, William, Malcah Yaeger, and Richard Steiner 1972. *A Quantitative Study of Sound Change in Progress*. Philadelphia: US Regional Survey.

Ladefoged, Peter 1957. Information conveyed by vowels. *Journal of The Acoustical Society of America* 29(1): 98–104.

Laferriere, Martha 1979. Ethnicity in phonological variation and change. *Language* 55: 603–17.

Lambert, Wallace 1967. A social psychology of bilingualism. In J. Macnamara (ed.), *Problems of Bilingualism*. *Journal of Social Issues* 23: 91–109.

Lavandera, Beatriz 1975. Linguistic structure and sociolinguistic conditioning in the use of verbal endings in 'SI' clauses. University of Pennsylvania Ph.D. dissertation.

Lazarsfeld, Paul F., Bernard Berelson, and Hazel Gaudet 1949. *The People's Choice.* New York: Columbia University Press.

Lebofsky, Dennis 1970. The lexicon of the Philadelphia metropolitan area. Princeton University dissertation.

Lefebvre, Anne 1991. *Le Français de la Région Lillioise.* Paris: Publications de la Sorbonne.

Lehmann, Winfred P. (ed.) 1967. *A Reader in Nineteenth-Century Historical Indo-European Linguistics.* Bloomington: Indiana University Press.

Lennig, Matthew 1978. Acoustic measurement of linguistic change: the modern Paris vowel system. University of Pennsylvania dissertation.

Lenski, Gerhard E. 1954. Status crystallization: a non-vertical dimension of social status. *American Sociological Review* 19: 405–13.

Leonard, Sterling A. 1929. *The Doctrine of Correctness in English Usage 1700–1800.* London.

Le Page, Robert B., and Andree Tabouret-Keller 1985. *Acts of Identity: Creole-based Approaches to Language and Ethnicity.* Cambridge: Cambridge University Press.

Levine, Lewis, and H. Crockett Jr 1966. Speech variation in a Piedmont community: postvocalic *r.* In S. Lieberson (ed.), *Explorations in Sociolinguistics. Sociological Inquiry* 36, No. 2.

Lightfoot, David 1997. Catastrophic change and learning theory. *Lingua* 100: 171–92.

Liljencrants, J., and Lindblom, B. 1972. Numerical simulation of vowel quality systems: the role of perceptual contrast. *Language* 48: 839–62.

Lin, Yen-Hwei 1988. Consonant variation in Taiwan Mandarin. In K. Ferrara et al. (eds), *Linguistic Change and Contact: NWAV-XVI.* Austin: Department of Linguistics, University of Texas, pp. 200–8.

López, Leticia 1983. A sociolinguistic analysis of /s/ variation in Honduran Spanish. University of Minnesota dissertation.

Lurie, Alison 1981. *The Language of Clothes.* New York: Random House.

Luthin, Herbert W. 1987. The story of California (ow): the coming-of-age of English in California. In Keith M. Denning et al. (eds), *Variation in Language: NWAV-XV at Stanford.* Stanford: Department of Linguistics, Stanford University, pp. 312–24.

Lyell, Sir Charles 1873. *The Geological Evidences of the Antiquity of Man*, 4th edn. London: John Murray (1st edn, 1863).

Macaulay, R. K. S. 1978. Variation and consistency in Glaswegian English. In P. Trudgill (ed.), *Sociolinguistic Patterns in British English.* London: Edward Arnold, pp. 132–43.

Maccoby, Eleanor E., and Carol N. Jacklin 1974. *The Psychology of Sex Differences.* Stanford: Stanford University Press.

Makhoul, J. 1975. Spectral linear prediction: properties and applications. *IEEE Transactions on Acoustics, Speech and Signal Processing*, ASSP-23, No. 3.

March, Robert M., and Margaret W. Tebbutt 1979. Housewife product communication activity patterns. *Journal of Social Psychology* 107: 63–9.

Martinet, André 1955. *Economie des changements phonétiques.* Berne: Francke.

McCafferty, Kevin 1998. Shared accents, divided speech community? Changes in Northern Ireland English. *Language Variation and Change* 10: 97–122.

Meillet, Antoine 1921. *Linguistique historique et linguistique générale.* Paris: La société linguistique de Paris.

Meillet, Antoine 1926. *Linguistique historique et linguistique générale,* 2nd edn. Paris: Librairie Ancienne Honoré Champion.

Merton, Robert K. 1949. Patterns of influence. In Paul F. Lazarsfeld and Frank N. Stanton (eds), *Communications Research.* New York: Harper and Brothers, pp. 180–219.

Merton, Robert K. 1957. *Social Theory and Social Structure.* Glencoe, IL: Free Press.

Milroy, J. 1990. *Linguistic Variation and Change.* Oxford and New York: Blackwell.

Milroy, James 1992. *Linguistic Variation and Change: On the Historical Sociolinguistics of English.* Oxford: Blackwell.

Milroy, James, and Lesley Milroy 1978. Belfast: change and variation in an urban vernacular. In P. Trudgill (ed.), *Sociolinguistic Patterns in British English.* London: Edward Arnold, pp. 19–36.

Milroy, Lesley 1980. *Language and Social Networks.* Oxford: Basil Blackwell.

Mock, Carol 1979. The social maturation of pronunciation: a family case study. *The Rural Learner* 1: 23–37. School of Education and Psychology, Southwest Missouri State University, Springfield, Missouri.

Modaressi, Yahya 1978. A sociolinguistic investigation of modern Persian. University of Kansas dissertation.

Moore, Samuel, S. Meech, and H. Whitehall 1935. *Middle English Dialect Characteristics and Dialect Boundaries.* University of Michigan Language and Literature Series.

Morales, Humberto Lopez 1986. Velarization of -/N/ in Puerto Rican Spanish. In D. Sankoff (ed.), *Diversity and Diachrony.* Philadelphia: John Benjamins, pp. 105–13.

Morgan, James L., and Lisa L. Travis 1989. Limits on negative information in language input. *Journal of Child Language* 16: 532–52.

Mougeon, Raymond, and Edouard Beniak 1987. The extralinguistic correlates of core lexical borrowing. In Keith M. Denning et al. (eds), *Variation in Language: NWAV-XV at Stanford.* Stanford: Department of Linguistics, Stanford University, pp. 337–47.

Mougeon, Raymond, Edouard Beniak, and André Valli 1988. VAIS, VAS, M'A in Canadian French: a sociohistorical study. In K. Ferrara et al. (eds), *Linguistic Change and Contact: NWAV-XVI.* Austin: Department of Linguistics, University of Texas, pp. 250–62.

Moulton, William G. 1962. Dialect geography and the concept of phonological space. *Word* 18: 23–32.

Mufwene, Salikoko 1996. The Founder Principle in creole genesis. *Diachronica* 13: 83–134.

Müller, Max 1861. Lectures on the Science of Language, Delivered at the Royal Institution of Great Britain in April, May and June, 1861. First Series. London: Longman, Green, Longman & Roberts.

Nakao, Keiko, and Judith Treas 1990. *Computing 1989 Occupational Prestige Scores.* GSS Methodological Report No. 69. Chicago: National Opinion Research Council.

Nakao, Keiko, and Judith Treas 1992. *The 1989 Socioeconomic Index of Occupations: Construction from the 1989 Occupational Prestige Scores*. GSS Methodological Report No. 74. Chicago: National Opinion Research Council.

Nearey, Terence 1977. Phonetic feature system for vowels. University of Connecticut dissertation.

Nicholas, J. Karl n.d. Study of a sound change in progress. Interdepartmental program in linguistics, University of North Carolina, Greensboro.

Nichols, P. C. 1976. Black women in the rural south: conservative and innovative. In B. Dubois and I. Crouch (eds), *Proceedings of Conference on the Sociology of the Languages of American Women*. San Antonio, TX: Trinity University.

Nordberg, Bengt 1975. Contemporary social variation as a stage in a long-term phonological change. In K.-H. Dahlstedt (ed.), *The Nordic Languages and Modern Linguistics*. Stockholm: Almqvist & Wiksell, pp. 587–608.

Nordberg, Bengt, and Eva Sundgren 1998. On observing real-time language change: a Swedish case study. FUMS Report No. 190. Uppsala: Enheten för Sociolingvistik, Institutionen för Nordiska Språk vid Uppsala Universitet.

Nordström, P.-E., and B. Lindblom 1975. A normalization procedure for vowel formant data. Paper 212 at the Eighth International Congress of Phonetic Sciences, Leeds.

Oliveira, Marco de 1983. Phonological variation in Brazilian Portuguese. Unpublished University of Pennsylvania dissertation.

Owens, Thompson W., and Paul M. Baker 1984. Linguistic insecurity in Winnipeg: validation of a Canadian Index of Insecurity. *Language in Society* 13: 337–50.

Paul, Hermann 1891. *Principien der Sprachgeschichte*, new and rev. edn. Translated from the 2nd edn of the original by H. A. Strong. London and New York: Longmans, Green.

Payne, Arvilla 1976. The acquisition of the phonological system of a second dialect. University of Pennsylvania dissertation.

Payne, Arvilla 1980. Factors controlling the acquisition of the Philadelphia dialect by out-of-state children. In W. Labov (ed.), *Locating Language in Time and Space*. New York: Academic Press, pp. 143–78.

Pederson, Lee A. 1965. *The Pronunciation of English in Metropolitan Chicago*. Publications of the American Dialect Society #44.

Peterson, Gordon E., and Harold L. Barney 1952. Control methods used in a study of the vowels. *Journal of the Acoustical Society of America* 24: 175–84.

Peterson, Peter G. 1985. *-ing* and *-in*: The Persistence of History? Paper given at ALS Annual Conference, Brisbane.

Poplack, Shana 1979. Function and process in a variable phonology. University of Pennsylvania dissertation.

Poplack, Shana 1980. The notion of the plural in Puerto Rican Spanish: competing constraints on /s/ deletion. In W. Labov (ed.), *Locating Language in Time and Space*. New York: Academic Press, pp. 55–68.

Poplack, Shana 1981. Mortal phonemes as plural morphemes. In D. Sankoff and H. Cedergren (eds), *Variation Omnibus*. Alberta: Linguistic Research, pp. 59–72.

Preston, Dennis 1989. Style, Status, Change: Three Sociolinguistic Axioms. Paper given at NWAVE XVII.

Preston, Dennis 1996. Where the worst English is spoken. In Edgar Schneider (ed.), *Focus on the USA*. Amsterdam: Benjamins.

Rand, David, and David Sankoff 1991. *Goldvarb 2.0*. Program and documentation. Montreal: Centre de recherches mathématiques, Université de Montréal.

Reiss, Albert J. 1965. *Occupations and Social Status*. With Otis Dudley Duncan and Paul K. Hatt. New York: Free Press.

Rickford, John 1979. Variation in a creole continuum. University of Pennsylvania dissertation.

Rickford, John R., Arnetha Ball, Renee Blake, Raina Jackson, and Nomi Martin 1991. Rappin on the copula coffin: theoretical and methodological issues in the analysis of copula variation in African-American Vernacular English. *Language Variation and Change* 3: 103–32.

Ringe, Donald A. 1992. On calculating the factor of chance in language comparison. *Transactions of the American Philosophical Society* 82: 1–110.

Roberts, Julie 1993. The acquisition of variable rules: *t,d* deletion and *-ing* production in preschool children. University of Pennsylvania dissertation.

Roberts, Julie, and William Labov 1995. Learning to talk Philadelphian: acquisition of short *a* by pre-school children. *Language Variation and Change* 7: 101–12.

Robinson, John P. 1976. Interpersonal influence in election campaigns: two step flow hypotheses. *Public Opinion Quarterly* 40: 304–19.

Romaine, Suzanne 1984. *The Language of Children and Adolescents: The Acquisition of Communicative Competence*. Oxford: Blackwell.

Ryan, Ellen Bouchard 1979. Why do low-prestige language varieties persist? In Howard Giles and Robert N. St Clair (eds), *Language and Social Psychology*. Baltimore: University Park Press, pp. 145–57.

Sallam, A. M. 1980. Phonological variation in Egyptian spoken Arabic: a study of the uvular and related plosive types. *Bulletin of the School of Oriental and African Studies* 43: 1.

Sankoff, David 1988. Sociolinguistics and syntactic variation. In F. Newmeyer (ed.), *Linguistics: The Cambridge Survey*. Cambridge: Cambridge University Press.

Sankoff, David, and William Labov 1979. On the uses of variable rules. *Language in Society* 8: 189–222.

Sankoff, David, and Gillian Sankoff 1973. Sample survey methods and computer-assisted analysis in the study of grammatical variation. In R. Darnell (ed.), *Canadian Languages in their Social Context*. Edmonton, Alberta: Linguistic Research, pp. 7–64.

Sankoff, Gillian 1980. *The Social Life of Language*. Philadelphia: University of Pennsylvania Press.

Sankoff, Gillian, and Suzanne Laberge 1973. On the acquisition of native speakers by a language. *Kivung* (1973): 32–47. Reprinted in Gillian Sankoff (1980), *The Social Life of Language*. Philadelphia: University of Pennsylvania Press, pp. 195–210.

Santorini, Beatrice 1989. The generalization of the verb-second constraint in the history of Yiddish. University of Pennsylvania dissertation.

Sapir, Edward 1921. *Language: An Introduction to the Study of Speech*. New York: Harcourt, Brace & Co.

Saussure, Ferdinand de 1949. *Cours de Linguistique Générale*, 4th edn. Paris: Payot.

Saussure, Ferdinand de 1959. *Course in General Linguistics*. Translated by Wade Baskin. New York: Philosophical Library.

Scherre, Maria Marta, and Anthony J. Naro 1992. The serial effect on internal and external variables. *Language Variation and Change* 4: 1–13.

Schiffrin, Deborah 1981. Tense variation in narrative. *Language* 57: 45–62.

Schilling-Estes, Natalie, and Walt Wolfram 1999. Alternative models of dialect death: Dissipation vs. concentration. *Language* 75: 486–521.

Schmidt, Richard 1986. Sociolinguistic variation in spoken Arabic in Egypt: a re-examination of the concept of diglossia. Brown University dissertation.

Seligman, C. R., G. R. Tucker, and W. E. Lambert 1972. The effects of speech style and other attributes on teachers' attitudes towards pupils. *Language in Society* 1: 131–42.

Sherman, Julia A. 1978. *Sex-related Cognitive Differences: An Essay on Theory and Evidence*. Springfield, IL: Charles C. Thomas.

Shopen, Tim, and Benji Wald 1982. The Use of (ing) in Australian English. MS.

Shrank, Holy L., and D. Lois Gilmore 1973. Correlates of fashion opinion leadership: implications for fashion process theory. *The Sociological Quarterly* 14: 534–43.

Shuy, Roger, Walt Wolfram, and William K. Riley 1967. *A Study of Social Dialects in Detroit*. Final Report, Project 6-1347. Washington, D.C.: Office of Education.

Silva, David James 1988. The sociolinguistic variance of low vowels in Azorean Portuguese. In K. Ferrara et al. (eds), *Linguistic Change and Contact: NWAV-XVI*. Austin: Department of Linguistics, University of Texas, pp. 336–44.

Silva-Corvalán, Carmen 1981. Extending the sociolinguistic variable to syntax: the case of pleonastic clitics in Spanish. In D. Sankoff and H. Cedergren (eds), *Variation Omnibus*. Alberta: Linguistic Research, pp. 335–42.

Silva-Corvalán, Carmen 1986. The social profile of a syntactico-semantic variable: three verb forms in Old Castile. In D. Sankoff (ed.), *Diversity and Diachrony*. Philadelphia: John Benjamins, pp. 279–92.

Simmel, Georg 1904. Fashion. *International Quarterly* 10: 130–55.

Simon-Miller, Francoise 1985. Commentary: signs and cycles in the fashion system. In Michael R. Solomon (ed.), *The Psychology of Fashion*. Lexington, MA: Lexington Books, pp. 71–81.

Stone, Gregory P. 1962. Appearances and the self. In Arnold R. Rose (ed.), *Human Behavior and Social Interaction*. Boston: Houghton Mifflin, pp. 86–118.

Sturtevant, Edgar 1947. *An Introduction to Linguistic Science*. New Haven: Yale University Press, ch. VIII, esp. pp. 81–4.

Swadesh, Morris 1971. *The Origin and Diversification of Language*, ed. Joel Sherzer. London: Routledge.

Tagliamonte, Sali, and Rachel Hudson 1999. Be like et al. beyond America: the quotative system in British and Canadian youth. *Journal of Sociolinguistics* 3: 147–72.

Tarallo, Fernando 1983. Relativization strategies in Brazilian Portuguese. Ch. 6: Relativization. University of Pennsylvania Ph.D. dissertation.

Tarde, Gabriel 1873. *Les Lois d'imitation*. English translation, New York: Henry Holt, 1903.

Taylor, Ann 1994. The change from SOV to SVO in Ancient Greek. *Language Variation and Change* 6: 1–37.

Thibault, Pierrette 1983. Equivalence et grammaticalisation. University of Montréal dissertation.

Thomason, Sarah, and Terrence Kaufman 1988. *Language Contact, Creolization, and Genetic Linguistics.* Berkeley: University of California Press.

Thornton, Simon, and Freda Brack (eds) 1977. The Interface between Public and Private Territories in Residential Areas: A study by students of Architecture at Melbourne University under the supervision of Jan Gehl. Melbourne: Department of Architecture and Building.

Toon, Thomas E. 1983. *The Politics of Early Old English Sound Change.* New York: Academic Press.

Trudgill, Peter 1972. Sex, covert prestige and linguistic change in urban British English. *Language in Society* 1: 179–95.

Trudgill, Peter 1974a. Linguistic change and diffusion: description and explanation in sociolinguistic dialect geography. *Language in Society* 3: 215–46. Reprinted as ch. 3 of *On Dialect: Social and Geographical Perspectives.* New York: New York University Press, 1984.

Trudgill, Peter 1974b. *The Social Differentiation of English in Norwich.* Cambridge: Cambridge University Press.

Trudgill, Peter 1986. *Dialects in Contact.* Oxford and New York: Blackwell.

Tucker, R. Whitney 1944. Notes on the Philadelphia dialect. *American Speech* 19: 39–42.

Underhill, Robert 1988. LIKE is, like, focus. *American Speech* 63: 234–46.

van Ostade, Ingrid Tieken Boon 1982. Double negation. *Neophilologue* 66: 278–85.

Varbero, Richard A. 1973. Philadelphia's South Italians in the 1920's. In Allen Davis and Mark Haller (eds), *The Peoples of Philadelphia: A History of Ethnic Groups and Lower-Class Life, 1790–1940.* Philadelphia: Temple University Press, pp. 255–76.

Veatch, Thomas 1992. Racial Barriers and Phonological Merger. Paper given at NWAVE XXI, Ann Arbor, October 1992.

von Raumer, Rudolph 1856. Linguistic-Historical Change and the Natural-Historical Definition of Sounds. *Zeitschrift für die Osterreichischen Gymnasien* V: 353–73. Translated by W. Lehmann. In W. Lehmann (ed.), *A Reader in Nineteenth Century Historical Indo-European Linguistics.* Indiana University Press, 1967, pp. 67–86.

Wakita, Hisashi 1975. Estimation of the vocal-tract length from acoustic data. Paper given to 87th meeting of the Acoustical Society of America, New York City.

Wald, Benji 1973. Variation in the system of tense markers of Mombasa Swahili. Columbia University dissertation.

Wald, Benji, and Timothy Shopen 1979. A Researcher's Guide to the Sociolinguistic Variable (ING). MS, ch. 6, pp. 1–53. Reprinted in Timothy Shopen and Joseph Williams (eds), *Style and Variables in English* (1981), Cambridge, MA: Winthrop Publishers.

Warner, Sam Bass Jr. 1968. *The Private City: Philadelphia in Three Periods of its Growth.* Philadelphia: University of Pennsylvania Press.

Warner, W. Lloyd 1960. *Social Class in America: A Manual of Procedure for the Measurement of Social Status.* New York: Harper.

Waterman, John T. 1963. *Perspectives in Linguistics*. Chicago: University of Chicago Press.

Weimann, Gabriel 1982. On the importance of marginality: one more step into the two-step flow of communication. *American Sociological Review* 47(6): 764–73.

Weinberg, Maria Fontanella de 1974. Un Aspecto Sociolinguistico del Espanol Bonaerense: la -S en Bahia Blanca. Bahia Blanca: Cuadernos de Linguisticca.

Weiner, E. Judith, and William Labov 1983. Constraints on the agentless passive. *Journal of Linguistics* 19: 29–58.

Weinreich, Uriel, William Labov, and Marvin Herzog 1968. Empirical foundations for a theory of language change. In W. Lehmann and Y. Malkiel (eds), *Directions for Historical Linguistics*. Austin: University of Texas Press, pp. 97–195.

Whitney, William Dwight 1868. *Language and the Study of Language*. New York: Charles Scribner & Co.

Whitney, William Dwight 1904. *Language and the Study of Language: Twelve Lectures on the Principles of Language Science*, 6th edn. New York: Charles Scribner & Co.

Williams, Ann, and Paul Kerswill 1999. Dialect levelling: continuity vs. change in Milton Keynes, Reading and Hull. In P. Foulkes and G. Docherty (eds), *Urban Voices*. London: Arnold.

Wolf, Clara, and Elena Jiménez 1979. A sound change in progress: devoicing of Buenos Aires /ž/. MS.

Wolfram, Walt 1969. *A Sociolinguistic Description of Detroit Negro Speech*. Arlington, VA: Center for Applied Linguistics.

Wolfram, Walt 1993. Ethical considerations in language awareness programs. *Issues in Applied Linguistics* 4: 225–55.

Wolfram, Walt, and Natalie Schilling-Estes 1998. *American English*. Oxford: Blackwell.

Wolfram, Walt, Erik Thomas, and Elaine Green 2000. The regional context of earlier African American speech: reconstructing the development of African American Vernacular English. *Language in Society* 29(3).

Woods, Howard 1979. A socio-dialectology survey of the English spoken in Ottawa: a study of sociological and stylistic variation in Canadian English. University of British Columbia dissertation.

Wright, Charles R., and Muriel Cantor 1967. The opinion seeker and avoider: steps beyond the opinion leader concept. *Pacific Sociological Review* 10: 33–43.

Wurman, Richard S., and Gallery, J. A. 1972. *Man-Made Philadelphia: A Guide to its Physical and Cultural Environment*. Cambridge, MA: MIT Press.

Wyld, Henry Cecil 1936. *A History of Modern Colloquial English*. London: Basil Blackwell.

Zelinsky, Wilbur 1992. *The Cultural Geography of the United States. A Revised Edition*. Englewood Cliffs, NJ: Prentice-Hall.

# Index

*Note*: Page numbers in *italics* refer to figures, tables and diagrams.